THE GREAT
WRITERS
LIBRARY

Tragedies

Front cover: Lear Weeping Over The Body of Cordelia (detail) by James Barry.
© Tate Gallery, London

 Published in 1988 for the Great Writers library by Marshall Cavendish Partworks Ltd, 58 Old Compton Street, London W1V 5PA. Printed and bound in Spain by Printer Industria Gráfica, Barcelona.
D.L.B. 32481-1988
This is a facsimile reproduction of an edition published in 1908 by J. M. Dent & Co., London.

ISBN 0-86307-7080

"... what a piece of work is a man! how noble in reason! how infinite in faculty! in form and moving how express and admirable! in action how like an angel! in apprehension how like god! the beauty of the world! the paragon of animals! And yet, to me, what is this quintessence of dust? man delights not me..."

HAMLET II, ii

Tragedies

WILLIAM
SHAKESPEARE

CONTENTS

L·D·F·

THE TRAGEDY OF ROMEO AND JULIET

DRAMATIS PERSONÆ

Escalus, *prince of Verona.*
Paris, *a young nobleman, kinsman to the prince.*
Montague, Capulet, } *heads of two houses at variance with each other.*
An old man, of the Capulet family.
Romeo, *son to Montague.*
Mercutio, *kinsman to the prince, and friend to Romeo.*
Benvolio, *nephew to Montague, and friend to Romeo.*
Tybalt, *nephew to Lady Capulet.*
Friar Laurence, *a Franciscan.*
Friar John, *of the same order.*
Balthasar, *servant to Romeo.*
Sampson, Gregory, } *servants to Capulet.*
Peter, *servant to Juliet's nurse.*
Abraham, *servant to Montague.*
An Apothecary.
Three Musicians.
Page to Paris; another Page: an Officer.

Lady Montague, *wife to Montague.*
Lady Capulet, *wife to Capulet.*
Juliet, *daughter to Capulet.*
Nurse to Juliet.

Citizens of Verona; kinsfolk of both houses; Maskers, Guards, Watchmen, and Attendants.
Chorus.
Scene: *Verona; Mantua.*

The Prologue

Enter Chorus.

Chor. Two households, both alike in dignity,
In fair Verona, where we lay our scene,
From ancient grudge break to new mutiny,
Where civil blood makes civil hands unclean.
From forth the fatal loins of these two foes
A pair of star-cross'd lovers take their life;
Whose misadventured piteous overthrows
Do with their death bury their parents' strife.
The fearful passage of their death-mark'd love,
And the continuance of their parents' rage,
Which, but their children's end, nought could remove,
Is now the two hours' traffic of our stage;
The which if you with patient ears attend,
What here shall miss, our toil shall strive to mend.

ACT I—Scene I

Verona. A public place.

Enter Sampson and Gregory, of the house of Capulet, with swords and bucklers.

Sam. Gregory, on my word, we 'll not carry coals.
Gre. No, for then we should be colliers.
Sam. I mean, an we be in choler, we 'll draw.
Gre. Ay, while you live, draw your neck out o' the collar.

Sam. I strike quickly, being moved.

Gre. But thou art not quickly moved to strike.

Sam. A dog of the house of Montague moves me.

Gre. To move is to stir, and to be valiant is to stand: therefore, if thou art moved, thou runn'st away.

Sam. A dog of that house shall move me to stand: I will take the wall of any man or maid of Montague's.

Gre. That shows thee a weak slave; for the weakest goes to the wall.

Sam. 'Tis true; and therefore women, being the weaker vessels, are ever thrust to the wall: therefore I will push Montague's men from the wall and thrust his maids to the wall.

Gre. The quarrel is between our masters and us their men.

Sam. 'Tis all one, I will show myself a tyrant: when I have fought with the men, I will be cruel with the maids; I will cut off their heads.

Gre. The heads of the maids?

Sam. Ay, the heads of the maids, or their maidenheads; take it in what sense thou wilt.

Gre. They must take it in sense that feel it.

Sam. Me they shall feel while I am able to stand: and 'tis known I am a pretty piece of flesh.

Gre. 'Tis well thou art not fish; if thou hadst, thou hadst been poor John. Draw thy tool; here comes two of the house of Montagues.

Enter Abraham and Balthasar.

Sam. My naked weapon is out: quarrel; I will back thee.

Gre. How! turn thy back and run?

Sam. Fear me not.

Gre. No, marry; I fear thee!

Sam. Let us take the law of our sides; let them begin.

Gre. I will frown as I pass by, and let them take it as they list.

Sam. Nay, as they dare. I will bite my thumb at them; which is a disgrace to them, if they bear it.

Abr. Do you bite your thumb at us, sir?

Sam. I do bite my thumb, sir.

Abr. Do you bite your thumb at us, sir?

Sam. [*Aside to Gre.*] Is the law of our side, if I say ay?

Gre. No.

Sam. No, sir, I do not bite my thumb at you, sir; but I bite my thumb, sir.

Gre. Do you quarrel, sir?

Abr. Quarrel, sir! no, sir.

Sam. But if you do, sir, I am for you: I serve as good a man as you.

Abr. No better.

Sam. Well, sir.

Enter Benvolio.

Gre. [*Aside to Sam.*] Say 'better': here comes one of my master's kinsmen.

Sam. Yes, better, sir.

Abr. You lie.

Sam. Draw, if you be men. Gregory, remember thy swashing blow. [*They fight.*

Ben. Part, fools! [*Beating down their weapons.*
Put up your swords; you know not what you do.

Enter Tybalt.

Tyb. What, art thou drawn among these heartless hinds?
Turn thee, Benvolio, look upon thy death.

Ben. I do but keep the peace: put up thy sword,
Or manage it to part these men with me.

Tyb. What, drawn, and talk of peace! I hate the word,
As I hate hell, all Montagues, and thee:
Have at thee, coward! [*They fight.*

Enter several of both houses, who join the fray; then enter Citizens and Peace-officers, with clubs.

First Off. Clubs, bills, and partisans! strike! beat them down!
Down with the Capulets! down with the Montagues!

Enter old Capulet in his gown, and Lady Capulet.

Cap. What noise is this? Give me my long sword, ho!

La. Cap. A crutch, a crutch! why call you for a sword?

Cap. My sword, I say! Old Montague is come,
And flourishes his blade in spite of me.

Enter old Montague and Lady Montague.

Mon. Thou villain Capulet!—Hold me not, let me go.

La. Mon. Thou shalt not stir one foot to seek a foe.

Enter Prince Escalus, with his train.

Prin. Rebellious subjects, enemies to peace,
Profaners of this neighbour-stained steel,
Will they not hear? What, ho! you men, you beasts,
That quench the fire of your pernicious rage
With purple fountains issuing from your veins,
On pain of torture, from those bloody hands
Throw your mistemper'd weapons to the ground,
And hear the sentence of your moved prince.
Three civil brawls, bred of an airy word,
By thee, old Capulet, and Montague,
Have thrice disturb'd the quiet of our streets,
And made Verona's ancient citizens
Cast by their grave beseeming ornaments,
To wield old partisans, in hands as old,
Canker'd with peace, to part your canker'd hate:
If ever you disturb our streets again,

Your lives shall pay the forfeit of the peace.
For this time, all the rest depart away:
You, Capulet, shall go along with me;
And, Montague, come you this afternoon,
To know our farther pleasure in this case,
To old Free-town, our common judgement-place.
Once more, on pain of death, all men depart.
[*Exeunt all but Montague, Lady Montague, and Benvolio.*

Mon. Who set this ancient quarrel new abroach?
Speak, nephew, were you by when it began?

Ben. Here were the servants of your adversary
And yours close fighting ere I did approach:
I drew to part them: in the instant came
The fiery Tybalt, with his sword prepared;
Which, as he breathed defiance to my ears,
He swung about his head, and cut the winds,
Who, nothing hurt withal, hiss'd him in scorn:
While we were interchanging thrusts and blows,
Come more and more, and fought on part and part,
Till the prince came, who parted either part.

La. Mon. O, where is Romeo? saw you him to-day?
Right glad I am he was not at this fray.

Ben. Madam, an hour before the worshipp'd sun
Peer'd forth the golden window of the east,
A troubled mind drave me to walk abroad;
Where, underneath the grove of sycamore
That westward rooteth from the city's side,
So early walking did I see your son:
Towards him I made; but he was ware of me,
And stole into the covert of the wood:
I, measuring his affections by my own,
Which then most sought where most might not be found,
Being one too many by my weary self,
Pursued my humour, not pursuing his,
And gladly shunn'd who gladly fled from me.

Mon. Many a morning hath he there been seen,
With tears augmenting the fresh morning's dew,
Adding to clouds more clouds with his deep sighs:
But all so soon as the all-cheering sun
Should in the farthest east begin to draw
The shady curtains from Aurora's bed,
Away from light steals home my heavy son,
And private in his chamber pens himself,
Shuts up his windows, locks fair daylight out,
And makes himself an artificial night:

Black and portentous must this humour prove,
Unless good counsel may the cause remove.
Ben. My noble uncle, do you know the cause?
Mon. I neither know it nor can learn of him.
Ben. Have you importuned him by any means?
Mon. Both by myself and many other friends:
But he, his own affections' counsellor,
Is to himself—I will not say how true—
But to himself so secret and so close,
So far from sounding and discovery,
As is the bud bit with an envious worm,
Ere he can spread his sweet leaves to the air,
Or dedicate his beauty to the sun.
Could we but learn from whence his sorrows grow,
We would as willingly give cure as know.

Enter Romeo.

Ben. See, where he comes: so please you step aside,
I 'll know his grievance, or be much denied.
Mon. I would thou wert so happy by thy stay,
To hear true shrift. Come, madam, let 's away.
[*Exeunt Montague and Lady.*
Ben. Good morrow, cousin.
Rom. Is the day so young?
Ben. But new struck nine.
Rom. Ay me! sad hours seem long.
Was that my father that went hence so fast?
Ben. It was. What sadness lengthens Romeo's hours?
Rom. Not having that which, having, makes them short.
Ben. In love?
Rom. Out—
Ben. Of love?
Rom. Out of her favour, where I am in love.
Ben. Alas, that love, so gentle in his view,
Should be so tyrannous and rough in proof!
Rom. Alas, that love, whose view is muffled still,
Should without eyes see pathways to his will!
Where shall we dine? O me! What fray was here?
Yet tell me not, for I have heard it all.
Here 's much to do with hate, but more with love:
Why, then, O brawling love! O loving hate!
O any thing, of nothing first create!
O heavy lightness! serious vanity!
Mis-shapen chaos of well-seeming forms!
Feather of lead, bright smoke, cold fire, sick health!
Still-waking sleep, that is not what it is!

This love feel I, that feel no love in this.
Dost thou not laugh?
Ben. No, coz, I rather weep.
Rom. Good heart, at what?
Ben. At thy good heart's oppression.
Rom. Why, such is love's transgression.
Griefs of mine own lie heavy in my breast;
Which thou wilt propagate, to have it prest
With more of thine: this love that thou hast shown
Doth add more grief to too much of mine own.
Love is a smoke raised with the fume of sighs;
Being purged, a fire sparkling in lovers' eyes;
Being vex'd, a sea nourish'd with lovers' tears:
What is it else? a madness most discreet,
A choking gall and a preserving sweet.
Farewell, my coz.
Ben. Soft! I will go along:
An if you leave me so, you do me wrong.
Rom. Tut, I have lost myself; I am not here;
This is not Romeo, he 's some other where.
Ben. Tell me in sadness, who is that you love?
Rom. What, shall I groan and tell thee?
Ben. Groan! why, no,
But sadly tell me who.
Rom. Bid a sick man in sadness make his will:
Ah, word ill urged to one that is so ill!
In sadness, cousin, I do love a woman.
Ben. I aim'd so near when I supposed you loved.
Rom. A right good mark-man! And she 's fair I love.
Ben. A right fair mark, fair coz, is soonest hit.
Rom. Well, in that hit you miss: she 'll not be hit
With Cupid's arrow; she hath Dian's wit,
And in strong proof of chastity well arm'd,
From love's weak childish bow she lives unharm'd.
She will not stay the siege of loving terms,
Nor bide the encounter of assailing eyes,
Nor ope her lap to saint-seducing gold:
O, she is rich in beauty, only poor
That, when she dies, with beauty dies her store.
Ben. Then she hath sworn that she will still live chaste?
Rom. She hath, and in that sparing makes huge waste;
For beauty, starved with her severity,
Cuts beauty off from all posterity.
She is too fair, too wise, wisely too fair,
To merit bliss by making me despair:

She hath forsworn to love; and in that vow
Do I live dead, that live to tell it now.
Ben. Be ruled by me, forget to think of her.
Rom. O, teach me how I should forget to think.
Ben. By giving liberty unto thine eyes;
Examine other beauties.
Rom. 'Tis the way
To call hers, exquisite, in question more:
These happy masks that kiss fair ladies' brows,
Being black, put us in mind they hide the fair;
He that is strucken blind cannot forget
The precious treasure of his eyesight lost:
Show me a mistress that is passing fair,
What doth her beauty serve but as a note
Where I may read who pass'd that passing fair?
Farewell: thou canst not teach me to forget.
Ben. I'll pay that doctrine, or else die in debt. [*Exeunt.*

Scene II

A street.

Enter Capulet, Paris, and Servant.

Cap. But Montague is bound as well as I,
In penalty alike; and 'tis not hard, I think,
For men so old as we to keep the peace.
Par. Of honourable reckoning are you both;
And pity 'tis you lived at odds so long.
But now, my lord, what say you to my suit?
Cap. But saying o'er what I have said before:
My child is yet a stranger in the world;
She hath not seen the change of fourteen years:
Let two more summers wither in their pride
Ere we may think her ripe to be a bride.
Par. Younger than she are happy mothers made.
Cap. And too soon marr'd are those so early made
The earth hath swallow'd all my hopes but she,
She is the hopeful lady of my earth:
But woo her, gentle Paris, get her heart;
My will to her consent is but a part;
An she agree, within her scope of choice
Lies my consent and fair according voice.
This night I hold an old accustom'd feast,
Whereto I have invited many a guest,
Such as I love; and you among the store,
One more, most welcome, makes my number more.
At my poor house look to behold this night

Earth-treading stars that make dark heaven light :
Such comfort as do lusty young men feel
When well-apparell'd April on the heel
Of limping winter treads, even such delight
Among fresh female buds shall you this night
Inherit at my house ; hear all, all see,
And like her most whose merit most shall be :
Which on more view, of many mine being one
May stand in number, though in reckoning none.
Come, go with me. Go, sirrah, trudge about
Through fair Verona ; find those persons out
Whose names are written there, and to them say,
My house and welcome on their pleasure stay.
[*Exeunt Capulet and Paris.*

Serv. Find them out whose names are written here ! It is written that the shoemaker should meddle with his yard and the tailor with his last, the fisher with his pencil and the painter with his nets ; but I am sent to find those persons whose names are here writ, and can never find what names the writing person hath here writ. I must to the learned. In good time.

Enter Benvolio and Romeo.

Ben. Tut, man, one fire burns out another's burning.
One pain is lessen'd by another's anguish ;
Turn giddy, and be holp by backward turning ;
One desperate grief cures with another's languish :
Take thou some new infection to thy eye,
And the rank poison of the old will die.

Rom. Your plantain-leaf is excellent for that.

Ben. For what, I pray thee ?

Rom. For your broken shin.

Ben. Why, Romeo, art thou mad ?

Rom. Not mad, but bound more than a madman is ;
Shut up in prison, kept without my food,
Whipt and tormented and— God-den, good fellow.

Serv. God gi' god-den. I pray, sir, can you read ?

Rom. Ay, mine own fortune in my misery.

Serv. Perhaps you have learned it without book : but, I pray, can you read anything you see ?

Rom. Ay, if I know the letters and the language.

Serv. Ye say honestly : rest you merry !

Rom. Stay, fellow ; I can read. [*Reads.*
'Signior Martino and his wife and daughters ; County Anselme and his beauteous sisters ; the lady widow of Vitruvio ; Signior Placentio and his lovely nieces ; Mercutio

and his brother Valentine; mine uncle Capulet, his wife, and daughters; my fair niece Rosaline; Livia; Signior Valentio and his cousin Tybalt; Lucio and the lively Helena.'
A fair assembly: whither should they come?

Serv. Up.

Rom. Whither?

Serv. To supper; to our house.

Rom. Whose house?

Serv. My master's.

Rom. Indeed, I should have ask'd you that before.

Serv. Now I 'll tell you without asking: my master is the great rich Capulet; and if you be not of the house of Montagues, I pray, come and crush a cup of wine. Rest you merry! [*Exit.*

Ben. At this same ancient feast of Capulet's
Sups the fair Rosaline whom thou so lovest,
With all the admired beauties of Verona:
Go thither, and with unattainted eye
Compare her face with some that I shall show,
And I will make thee think thy swan a crow.

Rom. When the devout religion of mine eye
Maintains such falsehood, then turn tears to fires;
And these, who, often drown'd, could never die,
Transparent heretics, be burnt for liars!
One fairer than my love! the all-seeing sun
Ne'er saw her match since first the world begun.

Ben. Tut, you saw her fair, none else being by,
Herself poised with herself in either eye:
But in that crystal scales let there be weigh'd
Your lady's love against some other maid,
That I will show you shining at this feast,
And she shall scant show well that now seems best.

Rom. I 'll go along, no such sight to be shown,
But to rejoice in splendour of mine own. [*Exeunt.*

Scene III

A room in Capulet's house.

Enter Lady Capulet and Nurse.

La. Cap. Nurse, where 's my daughter? call her forth to me.

Nurse. Now, by my maidenhead at twelve year old,
I bade her come. What, lamb! what, lady-bird!—
God forbid!—Where 's this girl? What, Juliet!

Enter Juliet.

Jul. How now! who calls?

Nurse. Your mother.

Jul. Madam, I am here. What is your will?

La. Cap. This is the matter. Nurse, give leave awhile,
We must talk in secret :—nurse, come back again;
I have remember'd me, thou 's hear our counsel.
Thou know'st my daughter 's of a pretty age.
Nurse. Faith, I can tell her age unto an hour.
La. Cap. She 's not fourteen.
Nurse. I 'll lay fourteen of my teeth,—
And yet, to my teen be it spoken, I have but four,—
She is not fourteen. How long is it now
To Lammas-tide?
La. Cap. A fortnight and odd days.
Nurse. Even or odd, of all days in the year,
Come Lammas-eve at night shall she be fourteen.
Susan and she—God rest all Christian souls!—
Were of an age: well, Susan is with God;
She was too good for me :—but, as I said,
On Lammas eve at night shall she be fourteen;
That shall she, marry; I remember it well.
'Tis since the earthquake now eleven years;
And she was wean'd,—I never shall forget it—
Of all the days of the year, upon that day:
For I had then laid wormwood to my dug,
Sitting in the sun under the dove-house wall;
My lord and you were then at Mantua :—
Nay, I do bear a brain :—but, as I said,
When it did taste the wormwood on the nipple
Of my dug, and felt it bitter, pretty fool,
To see it tetchy, and fall out with the dug!
Shake, quoth the dove-house: 'twas no need, I trow,
To bid me trudge.
And since that time it is eleven years;
For then she could stand high-lone; nay, by the rood,
She could have run and waddled all about;
For even the day before, she broke her brow:
And then my husband,—God be with his soul!
A' was a merry man—took up the child:
'Yea,' quoth he, 'dost thou fall upon thy face?
Thou wilt fall backward when thou hast more wit;
Wilt thou not, Jule?' and, by my holidame,
The pretty wretch left crying, and said 'Ay.'
To see now how a jest shall come about!
I warrant, an I should live a thousand years,
I never should forget it: 'Wilt thou not, Jule?' quoth he;
And, pretty fool, it stinted, and said 'Ay.'
La. Cap. Enough of this; I pray thee, hold thy peace.

Nurse. Yes, madam: yet I cannot choose but laugh
To think it should leave crying, and say 'Ay':
And yet, I warrant, it had upon its brow
A bump as big as a young cockerel's stone;
A perilous knock; and it cried bitterly:
'Yea,' quoth my husband, 'fall'st upon thy face?
Thou wilt fall backward when thou comest to age;
Wilt thou not, Jule?' it stinted, and said 'Ay.'
Jul. And stint thou too, I pray thee, nurse, say I.
Nurse. Peace, I have done. God mark thee to his grace!
Thou wast the prettiest babe that e'er I nursed:
An I might live to see thee married once,
I have my wish.
La. Cap. Marry, that 'marry' is the very theme
I came to talk of. Tell me, daughter Juliet,
How stands your disposition to be married?
Jul. It is an honour that I dream not of.
Nurse. An honour! were not I thine only nurse,
I would say thou hadst suck'd wisdom from thy teat.
La. Cap. Well, think of marriage now; younger than you
Here in Verona, ladies of esteem,
Are made already mothers. By my count,
I was your mother much upon these years
That you are now a maid. Thus then in brief;
The valiant Paris seeks you for his love.
Nurse. A man, young lady! lady, such a man
As all the world—why, he 's a man of wax.
La. Cap. Verona's summer hath not such a flower.
Nurse. Nay, he 's a flower; in faith, a very flower.
La. Cap. What say you? can you love the gentleman?
This night you shall behold him at our feast:
Read o'er the volume of young Paris' face,
And find delight writ there with beauty's pen;
Examine every married lineament,
And see how one another lends content;
And what obscured in this fair volume lies
Find written in the margent of his eyes.
This precious book of love, this unbound lover,
To beautify him, only lacks a cover:
The fish lives in the sea; and 'tis much pride
For fair without the fair within to hide:
That book in many's eyes doth share the glory,
That in gold clasps locks in the golden story:
So shall you share all that he doth possess,
By having him making yourself no less.

Nurse. No less! nay, bigger: women grow by men.
La. Cap. Speak briefly, can you like of Paris' love?
Jul. I'll look to like, if looking liking move:
But no more deep will I endart mine eye
Than your consent gives strength to make it fly.

Enter a Servingman.

Serv. Madam, the guests are come, supper served up, you called, my young lady asked for, the nurse cursed in the pantry, and every thing in extremity. I must hence to wait; I beseech you, follow straight.

La. Cap. We follow thee. [*Exit Servingman.*] Juliet, the county stays.

Nurse. Go, girl, seek happy nights to happy days. [*Exeunt.*

Scene IV

A street.

Enter Romeo, Mercutio, Benvolio, with five or six other Maskers, and Torch-bearers.

Rom. What, shall this speech be spoke for our excuse?
Or shall we on without apology?
Ben. The date is out of such prolixity:
We'll have no Cupid hoodwink'd with a scarf,
Bearing a Tartar's painted bow of lath,
Scaring the ladies like a crow-keeper;
Nor no without-book prologue, faintly spoke
After the prompter, for our entrance:
But, let them measure us by what they will,
We'll measure them a measure, and be gone.
Rom. Give me a torch: I am not for this ambling;
Being but heavy, I will bear the light.
Mer. Nay, gentle Romeo, we must have you dance.
Rom. Not I, believe me: you have dancing shoes
With nimble soles: I have a soul of lead
So stakes me to the ground, I cannot move.
Mer. You are a lover; borrow Cupid's wings,
And soar with them above a common bound.
Rom. I am too sore enpierced with his shaft
To soar with his light feathers, and so bound,
I cannot bound a pitch above dull woe:
Under love's heavy burthen do I sink.
Mer. And, to sink in it, should you burthen love;
Too great oppression for a tender thing.
Rom. Is love a tender thing? it is too rough,
Too rude, too boisterous, and it pricks like thorn.
Mer. If love be rough with you, be rough with love;

Prick love for pricking, and you beat love down.
Give me a case to put my visage in:
A visor for a visor! what care I
What curious eye doth quote deformities?
Here are the beetle-brows shall blush for me.

Ben. Come, knock and enter, and no sooner in
But every man betake him to his legs.

Rom. A torch for me: let wantons light of heart
Tickle the senseless rushes with their heels;
For I am proverb'd with a grandsire phrase;
I'll be a candle-holder, and look on.
The game was ne'er so fair, and I am done.

Mer. Tut, dun's the mouse, the constable's own word:
If thou art dun, we'll draw thee from the mire
Of this sir-reverence love, wherein thou stick'st
Up to the ears. Come, we burn daylight, ho.

Rom. Nay, that's not so.

Mer. I mean, sir, in delay
We waste our lights in vain, like lamps by day.
Take our good meaning, for our judgement sits
Five times in that ere once in our five wits.

Rom. And we mean well, in going to this mask;
But 'tis no wit to go.

Mer. Why, may one ask?

Rom. I dreamt a dream to-night.

Mer. And so did I.

Rom. Well, what was yours?

Mer. That dreamers often lie.

Rom. In bed asleep, while they do dream things true.

Mer. O, then, I see Queen Mab hath been with you.
She is the fairies' midwife, and she comes
In shape no bigger than an agate-stone
On the fore-finger of an alderman,
Drawn with a team of little atomies
Athwart men's noses as they lie asleep:
Her waggon-spokes made of long spinners' legs;
The cover, of the wings of grasshoppers;
Her traces, of the smallest spider's web;
Her collars, of the moonshine's watery beams;
Her whip, of cricket's bone; the lash, of film;
Her waggoner, a small grey-coated gnat,
Not half so big as a round little worm
Prick'd from the lazy finger of a maid:
Her chariot is an empty hazel-nut,
Made by the joiner squirrel or old grub,

Time out o' mind the fairies' coachmakers.
And in this state she gallops night by night
Through lovers' brains, and then they dream of love;
O'er courtiers' knees, that dream on court'sies straight;
O'er lawyers' fingers, who straight dream on fees;
O'er ladies' lips, who straight on kisses dream,
Which oft the angry Mab with blisters plagues,
Because their breaths with sweetmeats tainted are:
Sometime she gallops o'er a courtier's nose,
And then dreams he of smelling out a suit;
And sometime comes she with a tithe-pig's tail
Tickling a parson's nose as a' lies asleep,
Then dreams he of another benefice:
Sometime she driveth o'er a soldier's neck,
And then dreams he of cutting foreign throats,
Of breaches, ambuscadoes, Spanish blades,
Of healths five fathom deep; and then anon
Drums in his ear, at which he starts and wakes,
And being thus frighted swears a prayer or two,
And sleeps again. This is that very Mab
That plats the manes of horses in the night,
And bakes the elf-locks in foul sluttish hairs,
Which once untangled much misfortune bodes:
This is the hag, when maids lie on their backs,
That presses them and learns them first to bear,
Making them women of good carriage:
This is she—

Rom. Peace, peace, Mercutio, peace!
Thou talk'st of nothing.

Mer. True, I talk of dreams;
Which are the children of an idle brain,
Begot of nothing but vain fantasy,
Which is as thin of substance as the air,
And more inconstant than the wind, who wooes
Even now the frozen bosom of the north,
And, being anger'd, puffs away from thence,
Turning his face to the dew-dropping south.

Ben. This wind you talk of blows us from ourselves;
Supper is done, and we shall come too late.

Rom. I fear, too early: for my mind misgives
Some consequence, yet hanging in the stars,
Shall bitterly begin his fearful date
With this night's revels, and expire the term
Of a despised life closed in my breast,
By some vile forfeit of untimely death:

But He, that hath the steerage of my course,
Direct my sail! On, lusty gentlemen.

Ben. Strike, drum. [*Exeunt.*

Scene V

A hall in Capulet's house.

Musicians waiting. Enter Servingmen, with napkins.

First Serv. Where's Potpan, that he helps not to take away? he shift a trencher! he scrape a trencher!

Sec. Serv. When good manners shall lie all in one or two men's hands, and they unwashed too, 'tis a foul thing.

First Serv. Away with the joint-stools, remove the court-cupboard, look to the plate. Good thou, save me a piece of marchpane; and, as thou lovest me, let the porter let in Susan Grindstone and Nell. Antony, and Potpan!

Sec. Serv. Ay, boy, ready.

First Serv. You are looked for and called for, asked for and sought for, in the great chamber.

Third Serv. We cannot be here and there too. Cheerly, boys; be brisk a while, and the longer liver take all.

[*They retire behind.*

Enter Capulet, with Juliet and others of his house, meeting the Guests and Maskers.

Cap. Welcome, gentlemen! ladies that have their toes
Unplagued with corns will have a bout with you:
Ah ha, my mistresses! which of you all
Will now deny to dance? She that makes dainty,
She, I'll swear, hath corns; am I come near ye now?
Welcome, gentlemen! I have seen the day
That I have worn a visor, and could tell
A whispering tale in a fair lady's ear,
Such as would please: 'tis gone, 'tis gone, 'tis gone:
You are welcome, gentlemen! Come, musicians, play.
A hall, a hall! give room! and foot it, girls.

[*Music plays, and they dance.*

More light, you knaves; and turn the tables up,
And quench the fire, the room is grown too hot.
Ah, sirrah, this unlook'd-for sport comes well.
Nay, sit, nay, sit, good cousin Capulet;
For you and I are past our dancing days:
How long is 't now since last yourself and I
Were in a mask?

Sec. Cap. By 'r lady, thirty years.

Cap. What, man! 'tis not so much, 'tis not so much
'Tis since the nuptial of Lucentio,

Come Pentecost as quickly as it will,
Some five and twenty years; and then we mask'd.
Sec. Cap. 'Tis more, 'tis more: his son is elder, sir;
His son is thirty.
Cap. Will you tell me that?
His son was but a ward two years ago.
Rom. [*To a Servingman*] What lady's that, which doth enrich [the hand
Of yonder knight?
Serv. I know not, sir.
Rom. O, she doth teach the torches to burn bright!
It seems she hangs upon the cheek of night
Like a rich jewël in an Ethiop's ear;
Beauty too rich for use, for earth too dear!
So shows a snowy dove trooping with crows,
As yonder lady o'er her fellows shows.
The measure done, I'll watch her place of stand,
And, touching hers, make blessed my rude hand.
Did my heart love till now? forswear it, sight!
For I ne'er saw true beauty till this night.
Tyb. This, by his voice, should be a Montague.
Fetch me my rapier, boy. What dares the slave
Come hither, cover'd with an antic face,
To fleer and scorn at our solemnity?
Now, by the stock and honour of my kin,
To strike him dead I hold it not a sin.
Cap. Why, how now, kinsman! wherefore storm you so?
Tyb. Uncle, this is a Montague, our foe;
A villain, that is hither come in spite,
To scorn at our solemnity this night.
Cap. Young Romeo is it?
Tyb. 'Tis he, that villain Romeo.
Cap. Content thee, gentle coz, let him alone,
He bears him like a portly gentleman;
And, to say truth, Verona brags of him
To be a virtuous and well-govern'd youth:
I would not for the wealth of all this town
Here in my house do him disparagement:
Therefore be patient, take no note of him:
It is my will, the which if thou respect,
Show a fair presence and put off these frowns,
An ill-beseeming semblance for a feast.
Tyb. It fits, when such a villain is a guest:
I'll not endure him.
Cap. He shall be endured:
What, goodman boy! I say, he shall: go to;

Am I the master here, or you? go to.
You'll not endure him! God shall mend my soul,
You'll make a mutiny among my guests!
You will set cock-a-hoop! you'll be the man!

Tyb. Why, uncle, 'tis a shame.

Cap. Go to, go to;
You are a saucy boy: is't so, indeed?
This trick may chance to scathe you, I know what:
You must contrary me! marry, 'tis time.
Well said, my hearts! You are a princox; go:
Be quiet, or— More light, more light! For shame!
I'll make you quiet. What, cheerly, my hearts!

Tyb. Patience perforce with wilful choler meeting
Makes my flesh tremble in their different greeting.
I will withdraw: but this intrusion shall,
Now seeming sweet, convert to bitterest gall. [*Exit.*

Rom. [*To Juliet*] If I profane with my unworthiest hand
This holy shrine, the gentle fine is this,
My lips, two blushing pilgrims, ready stand
To smooth that rough touch with a tender kiss.

Jul. Good pilgrim, you do wrong your hand too much,
Which mannerly devotion shows in this;
For saints have hands that pilgrims' hands do touch,
And palm to palm is holy palmers' kiss.

Rom. Have not saints lips, and holy palmers too?

Jul. Ay, pilgrim, lips that they must use in prayer.

Rom. O, then, dear saint, let lips do what hands do;
They pray, grant thou, lest faith turn to despair.

Jul. Saints do not move, though grant for prayers' sake.

Rom. Then move not, while my prayer's effect I take.
Thus from my lips by thine my sin is purged. [*Kissing her.*

Jul. Then have my lips the sin that they have took.

Rom. Sin from my lips? O trespass sweetly urged!
Give me my sin again.

Jul. You kiss by the book.

Nurse. Madam, your mother craves a word with you.

Rom. What is her mother?

Nurse. Marry, bachelor,
Her mother is the lady of the house,
And a good lady, and a wise and virtuous:
I nursed her daughter, that you talk'd withal;
I tell you, he that can lay hold of her
Shall have the chinks.

Rom. Is she a Capulet?
O dear account! my life is my foe's debt.

Ben. Away, be gone; the sport is at the best.
Rom. Ay, so I fear; the more is my unrest.
Cap. Nay, gentlemen, prepare not to be gone;
We have a trifling foolish banquet towards.
Is it e'en so? why, then, I thank you all;
I thank you, honest gentlemen; good night.
More torches here! Come on then, let 's to bed.
Ah, sirrah, by my fay, it waxes late:
I 'll to my rest. [*Exeunt all but Juliet and Nurse.*
Jul. Come hither, nurse. What is yond gentleman?
Nurse. The son and heir of old Tiberio.
Jul. What 's he that now is going out of door?
Nurse. Marry, that, I think, be young Petruchio.
Jul. What 's he that follows there, that would not dance?
Nurse. I know not.
Jul. Go ask his name. If he be married,
My grave is like to be my wedding bed.
Nurse. His name is Romeo, and a Montague,
The only son of your great enemy.
Jul. My only love sprung from my only hate!
Too early seen unknown, and known too late!
Prodigious birth of love it is to me,
That I must love a loathed enemy.
Nurse. What 's this? what 's this?
Jul. A rhyme I learn'd even now
Of one I danced withal. [*One calls within* 'Juliet.'
Nurse. Anon, anon!
Come, let 's away; the strangers all are gone. [*Exeunt.*

ACT II—Prologue

Enter Chorus.

Chor. Now old desire doth in his death-bed lie,
And young affection gapes to be his heir;
That fair for which love groan'd for and would die,
With tender Juliet match'd, is now not fair.
Now Romeo is beloved and loves again,
Alike bewitched by the charm of looks,
But to his foe supposed he must complain,
And she steal love's sweet bait from fearful hooks:
Being held a foe, he may not have access
To breathe such vows as lovers use to swear;
And she as much in love, her means much less
To meet her new beloved any where:
But passion lends them power, time means, to meet,
Tempering extremities with extreme sweet. [*Exit.*

Scene I

A lane by the wall of Capulet's orchard.

Enter Romeo, alone.

Rom. Can I go forward when my heart is here?
Turn back, dull earth, and find thy centre out.
[*He climbs the wall, and leaps down within it.*

Enter Benvolio with Mercutio.

Ben. Romeo! my cousin Romeo!
Mer. He is wise;
And, on my life, hath stol'n him home to bed.
Ben. He ran this way, and leap'd this orchard wall:
Call, good Mercutio.
Mer. Nay, I'll conjure too.
Romeo! humours! madman! passion! lover!
Appear thou in the likeness of a sigh:
Speak but one rhyme, and I am satisfied;
Cry but 'ay me!' pronounce but 'love' and 'dove;
Speak to my gossip Venus one fair word,
One nick-name for her purblind son and heir,
Young Adam Cupid, he that shot so trim
When King Cophetua loved the beggar-maid!
He heareth not, he stirreth not, he moveth not;
The ape is dead, and I must conjure him.
I conjure thee by Rosalind's bright eyes,
By her high forehead and her scarlet lip,
By her fine foot, straight leg and quivering thigh,
And the demesnes that there adjacent lie,
That in thy likeness thou appear to us!
Ben. An if he hear thee, thou wilt anger him.
Mer. This cannot anger him: 'twould anger him
To raise a spirit in his mistress' circle
Of some strange nature, letting it there stand
Till she had laid it and conjured it down;
That were some spite: my invocation
Is fair and honest, and in his mistress' name
I conjure only but to raise up him.
Ben. Come, he hath hid himself among these trees,
To be consorted with the humorous night:
Blind is his love, and best befits the dark.
Mer. If love be blind, love cannot hit the mark.
Now will he sit under a medlar-tree,
And wish his mistress were that kind of fruit
As maids call medlars when they laugh alone.
O, Romeo, that she were, O, that she were

An open et cetera, thou a poperin pear!
Romeo, good night: I 'll to my truckle-bed;
This field-bed is too cold for me to sleep:
Come, shall we go?

Ben. Go then, for 'tis in vain
To seek him here that means not to be found. [*Exeunt.*

Scene II

Capulet's orchard.

Enter Romeo.

Rom. He jests at scars that never felt a wound.
[*Juliet appears above at a window.*
But, soft! what light through yonder window breaks?
It is the east, and Juliet is the sun!
Arise, fair sun, and kill the envious moon,
Who is already sick and pale with grief,
That thou her maid are far more fair than she:
Be not her maid, since she is envious;
Her vestal livery is but sick and green,
And none but fools do wear it; cast it off.
It is my lady; O, it is my love!
O, that she knew she were!
She speaks, yet she says nothing: what of that?
Her eye discourses, I will answer it.
I am too bold, 'tis not to me she speaks:
Two of the fairest stars in all the heaven,
Having some business, do intreat her eyes
To twinkle in their spheres till they return.
What if her eyes were there, they in her head?
The brightness of her cheek would shame those stars,
As daylight doth a lamp; her eyes in heaven
Would through the airy region stream so bright
That birds would sing and think it were not night.
See, how she leans her cheek upon her hand!
O, that I were a glove upon that hand,
That I might touch that cheek!

Jul. Ay me!

Rom. She speaks:
O, speak again, bright angel! for thou art
As glorious to this night, being o'er my head,
As is a winged messenger of heaven
Unto the white-upturned wondering eyes
Of mortals that fall back to gaze on him,
When he bestrides the lazy-pacing clouds
And sails upon the bosom of the air.

Jul. O Romeo, Romeo! wherefore art thou Romeo?
Deny thy father and refuse thy name;
Or, if thou wilt not, be but sworn my love,
And I 'll no longer be a Capulet.
Rom. [*Aside*] Shall I hear more, or shall I speak at this?
Jul. 'Tis but thy name that is my enemy;
Thou art thyself, though not a Montague.
What 's Montague? it is nor hand, nor foot,
Nor arm, nor face, nor any other part
Belonging to a man. O, be some other name!
What 's in a name? that which we call a rose
By any other name would smell as sweet;
So Romeo would, were he not Romeo call'd,
Retain that dear perfection which he owes
Without that title. Romeo, doff thy name,
And for thy name, which is no part of thee,
Take all myself.
Rom. I take thee at thy word:
Call me but love, and I 'll be new baptized;
Henceforth I never will be Romeo.
Jul. What man art thou, that, thus bescreen'd in night,
So stumblest on my counsel?
Rom. By a name
I know not how to tell thee who I am:
My name, dear saint, is hateful to myself,
Because it is an enemy to thee;
Had I it written, I would tear the word.
Jul. My ears have yet not drunk a hundred words
Of thy tongue's uttering, yet I know the sound:
Art thou not Romeo, and a Montague?
Rom. Neither, fair maid, if either thee dislike.
Jul. How camest thou hither, tell me, and wherefore?
The orchard walls are high and hard to climb,
And the place death, considering who thou art,
If any of my kinsmen find thee here.
Rom. With love's light wings did I o'er-perch these walls,
For stony limits cannot hold love out:
And what love can do, that dares love attempt;
Therefore thy kinsmen are no let to me.
Jul. If they do see thee, they will murder thee.
Rom. Alack, there lies more peril in thine eye
Than twenty of their swords: look thou but sweet,
And I am proof against their enmity.
Jul. I would not for the world they saw thee here.
Rom. I have night's cloak to hide me from their eyes;

And but thou love me, let them find me here:
My life were better ended by their hate,
Than death prorogued, wanting of thy love.
Jul. By whose direction found'st thou out this place?
Rom. By love, that first did prompt me to inquire;
He lent me counsel, and I lent him eyes.
I am no pilot; yet, wert thou as far
As that vast shore wash'd with the farthest sea,
I would adventure for such merchandise.
Jul. Thou know'st the mask of night is on my face,
Else would a maiden blush bepaint my cheek
For that which thou hast heard me speak to-night.
Fain would I dwell on form, fain, fain deny
What I have spoke: but farewell compliment!
Dost thou love me? I know thou wilt say 'Ay,'
And I will take thy word: yet, if thou swear'st,
Thou mayst prove false: at lovers' perjuries,
They say, Jove laughs. O gentle Romeo,
If thou dost love, pronounce it faithfully:
Or if thou think'st I am too quickly won,
I'll frown and be perverse and say thee nay,
So thou wilt woo; but else, not for the world.
In truth, fair Montague, I am too fond;
And therefore thou mayst think my 'haviour light:
But trust me, gentleman, I'll prove more true
Than those that have more cunning to be strange.
I should have been more strange, I must confess,
But that thou overheard'st, ere I was ware,
My true love's passion: therefore pardon me,
And not impute this yielding to light love,
Which the dark night hath so discovered.
Rom. Lady, by yonder blessed moon I swear,
That tips with silver all these fruit-tree tops,—
Jul. O, swear not by the moon, th' inconstant moon,
That monthly changes in her circled orb,
Lest that thy love prove likewise variable.
Rom. What shall I swear by?
Jul. Do not swear at all;
Or, if thou wilt, swear by thy gracious self,
Which is the god of my idolatry,
And I'll believe thee.
Rom. If my heart's dear love—
Jul. Well, do not swear: although I joy in thee,
I have no joy of this contract to-night:
It is too rash, too unadvised, too sudden,

Too like the lightning, which doth cease to be
Ere one can say 'It lightens.' Sweet, good night!
This bud of love, by summer's ripening breath,
May prove a beauteous flower when next we meet.
Good night, good night! as sweet repose and rest
Come to thy heart as that within my breast!

Rom. O, wilt thou leave me so unsatisfied?

Jul. What satisfaction canst thou have to-night?

Rom. The exchange of thy love's faithful vow for mine.

Jul. I gave thee mine before thou didst request it:
And yet I would it were to give again.

Rom. Wouldst thou withdraw it? for what purpose, love?

Jul. But to be frank, and give it thee again.
And yet I wish but for the thing I have:
My bounty is as boundless as the sea,
My love as deep; the more I give to thee,
The more I have, for both are infinite.
I hear some noise within; dear love, adieu!
[*Nurse calls within.*
Anon, good nurse! Sweet Montague, be true.
Stay but a little, I will come again. [*Exit.*

Rom. O blessed, blessed night! I am afeard,
Being in night, all this is but a dream,
Too flattering-sweet to be substantial.

Re-enter Juliet, above.

Jul. Three words, dear Romeo, and good night indeed.
If that thy bent of love be honourable,
Thy purpose marriage, send me word to-morrow,
By one that I'll procure to come to thee,
Where and what time thou wilt perform the rite,
And all my fortunes at thy foot I'll lay,
And follow thee my lord throughout the world.

Nurse. [*Within*] Madam!

Jul. I come, anon.—But if thou mean'st not well,
I do beseech thee—

Nurse. [*Within*] Madam!

Jul. By and by, I come:—
To cease thy suit, and leave me to my grief:
To-morrow will I send.

Rom. So thrive my soul,—

Jul. A thousand times good night! [*Exit*

Rom. A thousand times the worse, to want thy light.
Love goes toward love, as schoolboys from their books,
But love from love, toward school with heavy looks.
[*Retiring slowly.*

Re-enter Juliet, above.

Jul. Hist! Romeo, hist!—O, for a falconer's voice,
To lure this tassel-gentle back again!
Bondage is hoarse, and may not speak aloud;
Else would I tear the cave where Echo lies,
And make her airy tongue more hoarse than mine,
With repetition of my Romeo's name.
Romeo!

Rom. It is my soul that calls upon my name:
How silver-sweet sound lovers' tongues by night,
Like softest music to attending ears!

Jul. Romeo!

Rom. My dear?

Jul. At what o'clock to-morrow
Shall I send to thee?

Rom. At the hour of nine.

Jul. I will not fail: 'tis twenty years till then.
I have forgot why I did call thee back.

Rom. Let me stand here till thou remember it.

Jul. I shall forget, to have thee still stand there,
Remembering how I love thy company.

Rom. And I'll still stay, to have thee still forget,
Forgetting any other home but this.

Jul. 'Tis almost morning; I would have thee gone:
And yet no farther than a wanton's bird,
Who lets it hop a little from her hand,
Like a poor prisoner in his twisted gyves,
And with a silk thread plucks it back again,
So loving-jealous of his liberty.

Rom. I would I were thy bird.

Jul. Sweet, so would I:
Yet I should kill thee with much cherishing.
Good night, good night! parting is such sweet sorrow
That I shall say good night till it be morrow. [*Exit.*

Rom. Sleep dwell upon thine eyes, peace in thy breast!
Would I were sleep and peace, so sweet to rest!
Hence will I to my ghostly father's cell,
His help to crave, and my dear hap to tell. [*Exit.*

Scene III

Friar Laurence's cell.

Enter Friar Laurence, with a basket.

Fri. L. The grey-eyed morn smiles on the frowning night,
Chequering the eastern clouds with streaks of light;
And flecked darkness like a drunkard reels

From forth day's path and Titan's fiery wheels:
Now, ere the sun advance his burning eye,
The day to cheer and night's dank dew to dry,
I must up-fill this osier cage of ours
With baleful weeds and precious-juiced flowers.
The earth that 's nature's mother is her tomb;
What is her burying grave, that is her womb:
And from her womb children of divers kind
We sucking on her natural bosom find,
Many for many virtues excellent,
None but for some, and yet all different.
O, mickle is the powerful grace that lies
In herbs, plants, stones, and their true qualities:
For nought so vile that on the earth doth live,
But to the earth some special good doth give;
Nor aught so good, but, strain'd from that fair use,
Revolts from true birth, stumbling on abuse:
Virtue itself turns vice, being misapplied,
And vice sometime 's by action dignified.
Within the infant rind of this small flower
Poison hath residence, and medicine power:
For this, being smelt, with that part cheers each part,
Being tasted, slays all senses with the heart.
Two such opposed kings encamp them still
In man as well as herbs, grace and rude will;
And where the worser is predominant,
Full soon the canker death eats up that plant.

Enter Romeo.

Rom. Good morrow, father.
Fri. L. Benedicite!
What early tongue so sweet saluteth me?
Young son, it argues a distemper'd head
So soon to bid good morrow to thy bed:
Care keeps his watch in every old man's eye,
And where care lodges, sleep will never lie;
But where unbruised youth with unstuff'd brain
Doth couch his limbs, there golden sleep doth reign:
Therefore thy earliness doth me assure
Thou art up-roused by some distemperature;
Or if not so, then here I hit it right,
Our Romeo hath not been in bed to-night.
Rom. That last is true; the sweeter rest was mine.
Fri. L. God pardon sin! wast thou with Rosaline?
Rom. With Rosaline, my ghostly father? no;
I have forgot that name and that name's woe.

Fri. L. That 's my good son: but where hast thou been then?
Rom. I'll tell thee ere thou ask it me again.
I have been feasting with mine enemy;
Where on a sudden one hath wounded me,
That 's by me wounded: both our remedies
Within thy help and holy physic lies:
I bear no hatred, blessed man, for, lo,
My intercession likewise steads my foe.
Fri. L. Be plain, good son, and homely in thy drift;
Riddling confession finds but riddling shrift.
Rom. Then plainly know my heart's dear love is set
On the fair daughter of rich Capulet:
As mine on hers, so hers is set on mine;
And all combined, save what thou must combine
By holy marriage: when, and where, and how,
We met, we woo'd and made exchange of vow,
I 'll tell thee as we pass; but this I pray,
That thou consent to marry us to-day.
Fri. L. Holy Saint Francis, what a change is here!
Is Rosaline, that thou didst love so dear,
So soon forsaken? young men's love then lies
Not truly in their hearts, but in their eyes.
Jesu Maria, what a deal of brine
Hath wash'd thy sallow cheeks for Rosaline!
How much salt water thrown away in waste,
To season love, that of it doth not taste!
The sun not yet thy sighs from heaven clears,
Thy old groans ring yet in mine ancient ears;
Lo, here upon thy cheek the stain doth sit
Of an old tear that is not wash'd off yet:
If e'er thou wast thyself and these woes thine,
Thou and these woes were all for Rosaline:
And art thou changed? pronounce this sentence then:
Women may fall when there 's no strength in men.
Rom. Thou chid'st me oft for loving Rosaline.
Fri. L. For doting, not for loving, pupil mine.
Rom. And bad'st me bury love.
Fri. L. Not in a grave,
To lay one in, another out to have.
Rom. I pray thee, chide not: she whom I love now
Doth grace for grace and love for love allow;
The other did not so.
Fri. L. O, she knew well
Thy love did read by rote and could not spell.
But come, young waverer, come, go with me,

In one respect I 'll thy assistant be;
For this alliance may so happy prove,
To turn your households' rancour to pure love.

Rom. O, let us hence; I stand on sudden haste.

Fri. L. Wisely and slow: they stumble that run fast. [*Exeunt.*

Scene IV

A street.

Enter Benvolio and Mercutio.

Mer. Where the devil should this Romeo be?
Came he not home to-night?

Ben. Not to his father's; I spoke with his man.

Mer. Ah, that same pale hard-hearted wench, that Rosaline,
Torments him so that he will sure run mad.

Ben. Tybalt, the kinsman to old Capulet,
Hath sent a letter to his father's house.

Mer. A challenge, on my life.

Ben. Romeo will answer it.

Mer. Any man that can write may answer a letter.

Ben. Nay, he will answer the letter's master, how he dares, being dared.

Mer. Alas, poor Romeo, he is already dead! stabbed with a white wench's black eye; shot thorough the ear with a love-song; the very pin of his heart cleft with the blind bow-boy's butt-shaft: and is he a man to encounter Tybalt?

Ben. Why, what is Tybalt?

Mer. More than prince of cats, I can tell you. O, he 's the courageous captain of compliments. He fights as you sing prick-song, keeps time, distance and proportion; rests me his minim rest, one, two, and the third in your bosom: the very butcher of a silk button, a duellist, a duellist; a gentleman of the very first house, of the first and second cause: ah, the immortal passado! the punto reverso! the hai!

Ben. The what?

Mer. The pox of such antic, lisping, affecting fantasticoes; these new tuners of accents! 'By Jesu, a very good blade! a very tall man! a very good whore!' Why, is not this a lamentable thing, grandsire, that we should be thus afflicted with these strange flies, these fashion-mongers, these perdona-mi's, who stand so much on the new form that they cannot sit at ease on the old bench? O, their bones, their bones!

Enter Romeo.

Ben. Here comes Romeo, here comes Romeo.

Mer. Without his roe, like a dried herring: O flesh, flesh, how art thou fishified! Now is he for the numbers that Petrarch flowed in: Laura to his lady was but a kitchen-wench; marry, she had a better love to be-rhyme her; Dido, a dowdy; Cleopatra, a gipsy; Helen and Hero, hildings and harlots; Thisbe, a grey eye or so, but not to the purpose. Signior Romeo, bon jour! there's a French salutation to your French slop. You gave us the counterfeit fairly last night.

Rom. Good morrow to you both. What counterfeit did I give you?

Mer. The slip, sir, the slip; can you not conceive?

Rom. Pardon, good Mercutio, my business was great; and in such a case as mine a man may strain courtesy.

Mer. That's as much as to say, Such a case as yours constrains a man to bow in the hams

Rom. Meaning, to court'sy.

Mer. Thou hast most kindly hit it.

Rom. A most courteous exposition.

Mer. Nay, I am the very pink of courtesy.

Rom. Pink for flower.

Mer. Right.

Rom. Why, then is my pump well flowered.

Mer. Well said: follow me this jest now, till thou hast worn out thy pump, that, when the single sole of it is worn, the jest may remain, after the wearing, solely singular.

Rom. O single-soled jest, solely singular for the singleness!

Mer. Come between us, good Benvolio; my wits faint.

Rom. Switch and spurs, switch and spurs; or I'll cry a match.

Mer. Nay, if thy wits run the wild-goose chase, I have done; for thou hast more of the wild-goose in one of thy wits than, I am sure, I have in my whole five: was I with you there for the goose?

Rom. Thou wast never with me for anything when thou wast not there for the goose.

Mer. I will bite thee by the ear for that jest.

Rom. Nay, good goose, bite not.

Mer. Thy wit is a very bitter sweeting; it is a most sharp sauce.

Rom. And is it not well served in to a sweet goose?

Mer. O, here's a wit of cheveril, that stretches from an inch narrow to an ell broad!

Rom. I stretch it out for that word 'broad;' which added to the goose, proves thee far and wide a broad goose.

Mer. Why, is not this better now than groaning for love? now art thou sociable, now art thou Romeo; now art thou what thou art, by art as well as by nature: for this drivelling love is like a great natural, that runs lolling up and down to hide his bauble in a hole.

Ben. Stop there, stop there.

Mer. Thou desirest me to stop in my tale against the hair.

Ben. Thou wouldst else have made thy tale large.

Mer. O, thou art deceived; I would have made it short: for I was come to the whole depth of my tale, and meant indeed to occupy the argument no longer.

Rom. Here 's goodly gear!

Enter Nurse and Peter.

Mer. A sail, a sail!

Ben. Two, two; a shirt and a smock.

Nurse. Peter!

Peter. Anon?

Nurse. My fan, Peter.

Mer. Good Peter, to hide her face; for her fan 's the fairer of the two.

Nurse. God ye good morrow, gentlemen.

Mer. God ye good den, fair gentlewoman.

Nurse. Is it good den?

Mer. 'Tis no less, I tell you; for the bawdy hand of the dial is now upon the prick of noon.

Nurse. Out upon you! what a man are you!

Rom. One, gentlewoman, that God hath made himself to mar.

Nurse. By my troth, it is well said; 'for himself to mar,' quoth a'? Gentlemen, can any of you tell me where I may find the young Romeo?

Rom. I can tell you; but young Romeo will be older when you have found him than he was when you sought him: I am the youngest of that name, for fault of a worse.

Nurse. You say well.

Mer. Yea, is the worst well? very well took, i' faith; wisely, wisely.

Nurse. If you be he, sir, I desire some confidence with you.

Ben. She will indite him to some supper.

Mer. A bawd, a bawd, a bawd! So ho!

Rom. What hast thou found?

Mer. No hare, sir; unless a hare, sir, in a lenten pie, that is something stale and hoar ere it be spent. [*Sings.*

An old hare hoar,
And an old hare hoar,
Is very good meat in lent:
But a hare that is hoar,
Is too much for a score,
When it hoars ere it be spent.

Romeo, will you come to your father's? we'll to dinner thither.

Rom. I will follow you.

Mer. Farewell, ancient lady; farewell [*Singing*] 'lady, lady, lady.'

[*Exeunt Mercutio and Benvolio.*

Nurse. Marry, farewell! I pray you, sir, what saucy merchant was this, that was so full of his ropery?

Rom. A gentleman, nurse, that loves to hear himself talk, and will speak more in a minute than he will stand to in a month.

Nurse. An a' speak any thing against me, I 'll take him down, an a' were lustier than he is, and twenty such Jacks; and if I cannot, I 'll find those that shall. Scurvy knave! I am none of his flirt-gills; I am none of his skains-mates. [*Turning to Peter*] And thou must stand by too, and suffer every knave to use me at his pleasure?

Peter, I saw no man use you at his pleasure; if I had, my weapon should quickly have been out, I warrant you: I dare draw as soon as another man, if I see occasion in a good quarrel and the law on my side.

Nurse. Now, afore God, I am so vexed that every part about me quivers. Scurvy knave! Pray you, sir, a word: and as I told you, my young lady bade me inquire you out; what she bade me say, I will keep to myself: but first let me tell ye, if ye should lead her into a fool's paradise, as they say, it were a very gross kind of behaviour, as they say: for the gentlewoman is young, and therefore, if you should deal double with her, truly it were an ill thing to be offered to any gentlewoman, and very weak dealing.

Rom. Nurse, commend me to thy lady and mistress. I protest unto thee—

Nurse. Good heart, and, 'i faith, I will tell her as much: Lord, Lord, she will be a joyful woman.

Rom. What wilt thou tell her, nurse? thou dost not mark me.

Nurse. I will tell her, sir, that you do protest; which, as I take it, is a gentlemanlike offer.

Rom. Bid her devise
Some means to come to shrift this afternoon;
And there she shall at Friar Laurence' cell
Be shrived and married. Here is for thy pains.

Nurse. No, truly, sir; not a penny.

Rom. Go to; I say you shall.

Nurse. This afternoon, sir? well, she shall be there.

Rom. And stay, good nurse, behind the abbey-wall:
Within this hour my man shall be with thee,
And bring thee cords like a tackled stair;
Which to the high top-gallant of my joy
Must be my convoy in the secret night.
Farewell; be trusty, and I 'll quit thy pains:
Farewell; commend me to thy mistress.

Nurse. Now God in heaven bless thee! Hark you, sir.

Rom. What say'st thou, my dear nurse?

Nurse. Is your man secret? Did you ne'er hear say,

Two may keep counsel, putting one away?

Rom. I warrant thee, my man 's as true as steel.

Nurse. Well, sir; my mistress is the sweetest lady—Lord, Lord! when 'twas a little prating thing—O, there is a nobleman in town, one Paris, that would fain lay knife aboard; but she, good soul, had as lieve see a toad, a very toad, as see him. I anger her sometimes, and tell her that Paris is the properer man; but, I 'll warrant you, when I say so, she looks as pale as any clout in the versal world. Doth not rosemary and Romeo begin both with a letter?

Rom. Ay, nurse; what of that? both with an R.

Nurse. Ah, mocker! that 's the dog's name; R is for the—No; I know it begins with some other letter—and she hath the prettiest sententious of it, of you and rosemary, that it would do you good to hear it.

Rom. Commend me to thy lady.

Nurse. Ay, a thousand times. [*Exit Romeo.*] Peter!

Pet. Anon?

Nurse. Peter, take my fan, and go before, and apace. [*Exeunt.*

Scene V

Capulet's orchard.

Enter Juliet.

Jul. The clock struck nine when I did send the nurse;
In half an hour she promised to return.
Perchance she cannot meet him: that 's not so.
O, she is lame! love's heralds should be thoughts,
Which ten times faster glide than the sun's beams,
Driving back shadows over louring hills:
Therefore do nimble-pinion'd doves draw love,
And therefore hath the wind-swift Cupid wings.
Now is the sun upon the highmost hill
Of this day's journey, and from nine till twelve
Is three long hours; yet she is not come.
Had she affections and warm youthful blood,
She would be as swift in motion as a ball;
My words would bandy her to my sweet love,
And his to me:
But old folks, many feign as they were dead;
Unwieldly, slow, heavy and pale as lead.

Enter Nurse, with Peter.

O God, she comes! O honey nurse, what news?
Hast thou met with him? Send thy man away.

Nurse. Peter, stay at the gate. [*Exit Peter.*

Jul. Now, good sweet nurse,— O Lord, why look'st thou sad?
Though news be sad, yet tell them merrily;
If good, thou shamest the music of sweet news
By playing it to me with so sour a face.

Nurse. I am a-weary; give me leave awhile.
Fie, how my bones ache! what a jaunce have I had!

Jul. I would thou hadst my bones and I thy news:
Nay, come, I pray thee, speak; good, good nurse, speak.

Nurse. Jesu, what haste? can you not stay a while?
Do you not see that I am out of breath?

Jul. How art thou out of breath, when thou hast breath
To say to me that thou art out of breath?
The excuse that thou dost make in this delay
Is longer than the tale thou dost excuse.
Is thy news good, or bad? answer to that;
Say either, and I 'll stay the circumstance:
Let me be satisfied, is 't good or bad?

Nurse. Well, you have made a simple choice; you know not how to choose a man: Romeo! no, not he; though his face be better than any man's, yet his leg excels all men's; and for a hand, and a foot, and a body, though they be not to be talked on, yet they are past compare: he is not the flower of courtesy, but, I 'll warrant him, as gentle as a lamb. Go thy ways, wench; serve God. What, have you dined at home?

Jul. No, no: but all this did I know before.
What says he of our marriage? what of that?

Nurse. Lord, how my head aches! what a head have I!
It beats as it would fall in twenty pieces.
My back o' t' other side,—ah, my back, my back!
Beshrew your heart for sending me about,
To catch my death with jauncing up and down!

Jul. I' faith, I am sorry that thou art not well.
Sweet, sweet, sweet nurse, tell me, what says my love?

Nurse. Your love says, like an honest gentleman, and a courteous, and a kind, and a handsome, and, I warrant, a virtuous,—
Where is your mother?

Jul. Where is my mother! why, she is within;
Where should she be? How oddly thou repliest!
'Your love says, like an honest gentleman,
Where is your mother?'

Nurse. O God's lady dear!
Are you so hot? marry, come up, I trow;
Is this the poultice for my aching bones?
Henceforward do your messages yourself.

Jul. Here 's such a coil! come, what says Romeo?

Nurse. Have you got leave to go to shrift to-day?
Jul. I have.
Nurse. Then hie you hence to Friar Laurence' cell;
There stays a husband to make you a wife:
Now comes the wanton blood up in your cheeks,
They 'll be in scarlet straight at any news.
Hie you to church; I must another way,
To fetch a ladder, by the which your love
Must climb a bird's nest soon when it is dark
I am the drudge, and toil in your delight;
But you shall bear the burthen soon at night.
Go; I 'll to dinner; hie you to the cell.
Jul. Hie to high fortune! Honest nurse, farewell. [*Exeunt.*

Scene VI

Friar Laurence's cell.

Enter Friar Laurence and Romeo.

Fri. L. So smile the heavens upon this holy act
That after hours with sorrow chide us not!
Rom. Amen, amen! but come what sorrow can,
It cannot countervail the exchange of joy
That one short minute gives me in her sight:
Do thou but close our hands with holy words,
Then love devouring death do what he dare,
It is enough I may but call her mine.
Fri. L. These violent delights have violent ends,
And in their triumph die; like fire and powder
Which as they kiss consume: the sweetest honey
Is loathsome in his own deliciousness,
And in the taste confounds the appetite:
Therefore, love moderately; long love doth so;
Too swift arrives as tardy as too slow.

Enter Juliet.

Here comes the lady. O, so light a foot
Will ne'er wear out the everlasting flint.
A lover may bestride the gossamer
That idles in the wanton summer air,
And yet not fall; so light is vanity.
Jul. Good even to my ghostly confessor.
Fri. L. Romeo shall thank thee, daughter, for us both.
Jul. As much to him, else is his thanks too much.
Rom. Ah, Juliet, if the measure of thy joy
Be heap'd like mine, and that thy skill be more
To blazon it, then sweeten with thy breath
This neighbour air, and let rich music's tongue

Unfold the imagined happiness that both
Receive in either by this dear encounter.

Jul. Conceit, more rich in matter than in words,
Brags of his substance, not of ornament:
They are but beggars that can count their worth;
But my true love is grown to such excess,
I cannot sum up sum of half my wealth.

Fri. L. Come, come with me, and we will make short work;
For, by your leaves, you shall not stay alone
Till holy church incorporate two in one. [*Exeunt.*

ACT III—SCENE I

A public place.

Enter Mercutio, Benvolio, Page, and Servants.

Ben. I pray thee, good Mercutio, let 's retire:
The day is hot, the Capulets abroad,
And, if we meet, we shall not 'scape a brawl;
For now these hot days is the mad blood stirring.

Mer. Thou art like one of those fellows that when he enters the confines of a tavern claps me his sword upon the table, and says 'God send me no need of thee!' and by the operation of the second cup draws it on the drawer, when indeed there is no need.

Ben. Am I like such a fellow?

Mer. Come, come, thou art as hot a Jack in thy mood as any in Italy, and as soon moved to be moody, and as soon moody to be moved.

Ben. And what to?

Mer. Nay, an there were two such, we should have none shortly, for one would kill the other. Thou! why, thou wilt quarrel with a man that hath a hair more, or a hair less, in his beard than thou hast: thou wilt quarrel with a man for cracking nuts, having no other reason but because thou hast hazel eyes; what eye, but such an eye, would spy out such a quarrel? thy head is as full of quarrels as an egg is full of meat, and yet thy head hath been beaten as addle as an egg for quarrelling: thou hast quarrelled with a man for coughing in the street, because he hath wakened thy dog that hath lain asleep in the sun: didst thou not fall out with a tailor for wearing his new doublet before Easter? with another, for tying his new shoes with old riband? and yet thou wilt tutor me from quarrelling!

Ben. An I were so apt to quarrel as thou art, any man should buy the fee-simple of my life for an hour and a quarter.

Mer. The fee-simple! O simple!

Enter Tybalt and others.

Ben. By my head, here comes the Capulets.

Mer. By my heel, I care not.

Tyb. Follow me close, for I will speak to them.
Gentlemen, good den: a word with one of you.

Mer. And but one word with one of us? couple it with something; make it a word and a blow.

Tyb. You shall find me apt enough to that, sir, an you will give me occasion.

Mer. Could you not take some occasion without giving?

Tyb. Mercutio, thou consort'st with Romeo,—

Mer. Consort! what, dost thou make us minstrels? an thou make minstrels of us, look to hear nothing but discords: here's my fiddlestick; here's that shall make you dance. 'Zounds, consort!

Ben. We talk here in the public haunt of men:
Either withdraw into some private place,
Or reason coldly of your grievances,
Or else depart; here all eyes gaze on us.

Mer. Men's eyes were made to look, and let them gaze;
I will not budge for no man's pleasure, I.

Enter Romeo.

Tyb. Well, peace be with you, sir: here comes my man.

Mer. But I'll be hang'd, sir, if he wear your livery:
Marry, go before to field, he'll be your follower;
Your worship in that sense may call him man.

Tyb. Romeo, the love I bear thee can afford
No better term than this,—thou art a villain.

Rom. Tybalt, the reason that I have to love thee
Doth much excuse the appertaining rage
To such a greeting: villain am I none;
Therefore farewell; I see thou know'st me not.

Tyb. Boy, this shall not excuse the injuries
That thou hast done me; therefore turn and draw.

Rom. I do protest, I never injured thee,
But love thee better than thou canst devise
Till thou shalt know the reason of my love:
And so, good Capulet,—which name I tender
As dearly as mine own,—be satisfied.

Mer. O calm, dishonourable, vile submission!
Alla stoccata carries it away. [*Draws.*
Tybalt, you rat-catcher, will you walk?

Tyb. What wouldst thou have with me?

Mer. Good king of cats, nothing but one of your nine lives, that I mean to make bold withal, and, as you shall use me hereafter, dry-beat the rest of the eight. Will you pluck your sword out of his pilcher by the ears? make haste, lest mine be about your ears ere it be out.

Tyb. I am for you. [*Drawing.*

Rom. Gentle Mercutio, put thy rapier up.

Mer. Come, sir, your passado. [*They fight.*

Rom. Draw, Benvolio; beat down their weapons.
Gentlemen, for shame, forbear this outrage!
Tybalt, Mercutio, the prince expressly hath
Forbid this bandying in Verona streets:
Hold, Tybalt! good Mercutio!

[*Tybalt under Romeo's arm stabs Mercutio and flies with his followers.*

Mer. I am hurt;
A plague o' both your houses! I am sped:
Is he gone, and hath nothing?

Ben. What, art thou hurt?

Mer. Ay, ay, a scratch, a scratch; marry, 'tis enough.
Where is my page? Go, villain, fetch a surgeon. [*Exit Page.*

Rom. Courage, man; the hurt cannot be much.

Mer. No, 'tis not so deep as a well, nor so wide as a church-door; but 'tis enough, 'twill serve: ask for me to-morrow, and you shall find me a grave man. I am peppered, I warrant, for this world. A plague o' both your houses! 'Zounds, a dog, a rat, a mouse, a cat, to scratch a man to death! a braggart, a rogue, a villain, that fights by the book of arithmetic! Why the devil came you between us? I was hurt under your arm.

Rom. I thought all for the best.

Mer. Help me into some house, Benvolio,
Or I shall faint. A plague o' both your houses!
They have made worms' meat of me: I have it,
And soundly too: your houses!

[*Exeunt Mercutio and Benvolio.*

Rom. This gentleman, the prince's near ally,
My very friend, hath got this mortal hurt
In my behalf; my reputation stain'd
With Tybalt's slander,—Tybalt, that an hour
Hath been my kinsman: O sweet Juliet,
Thy beauty hath made me effeminate,
And in my temper soften'd valour's steel!

Re-enter Benvolio.

Ben. O Romeo, Romeo, brave Mercutio's dead!
That gallant spirit hath aspired the clouds,

Which too untimely here did scorn the earth.
Rom. This day's black fate on more days doth depend;
This but begins the woe others must end.

Re-enter Tybalt.

Ben. Here comes the furious Tybalt back again
Rom. Alive, in triumph! and Mercutio slain
Away to heaven, respective lenity,
And fire-eyed fury be my conduct now!
Now, Tybalt, take the 'villain' back again
That late thou gavest me; for Mercutio's soul
Is but a little way above our heads,
Staying for thine to keep him company:
Either thou, or I, or both, must go with him.
Tyb. Thou, wretched boy, that didst consort him here,
Shalt with him hence.
Rom. This shall determine that.
[*They fight; Tybalt falls.*
Ben. Romeo, away, be gone!
The citizens are up, and Tybalt slain:
Stand not amazed: the prince will doom thee death
If thou art taken: hence, be gone, away!
Rom. O, I am fortune's fool!
Ben. Why dost thou stay? [*Exit Romeo.*

Enter Citizens, &c.

First Cit. Which way ran he that kill'd Mercutio?
Tybalt, that murderer, which way ran he?
Ben. There lies that Tybalt.
First Cit. Up, sir, go with me;
I charge thee in the prince's name, obey.

Enter Prince, attended; Montague, Capulet, their Wives, and others.

Prin. Where are the vile beginners of this fray?
Ben. O noble prince, I can discover all
The unlucky manage of this fatal brawl:
There lies the man, slain by young Romeo,
That slew thy kinsman, brave Mercutio.
La. Cap. Tybalt, my cousin! O my brother's child!
O prince! O cousin! husband! O, the blood is spilt
Of my dear kinsman! Prince, as thou art true,
For blood of ours, shed blood of Montague.
O cousin, cousin!
Prin. Benvolio, who began this bloody fray?
Ben. Tybalt, here slain, whom Romeo's hand did slay;
Romeo that spoke him fair, bid him bethink

How nice the quarrel was, and urged withal
Your high displeasure: all this uttered
With gentle breath, calm look, knees humbly bow'd,
Could not take truce with the unruly spleen
Of Tybalt deaf to peace, but that he tilts
With piercing steel at bold Mercutio's breast;
Who, all as hot, turns deadly point to point,
And, with a martial scorn, with one hand beats
Cold death aside, and with the other sends
It back to Tybalt, whose dexterity
Retorts it: Romeo he cries aloud,
'Hold, friends! friends, part!' and, swifter than his tongue,
His agile arm beats down their fatal points,
And 'twixt them rushes; underneath whose arm
An envious thrust from Tybalt hit the life
Of stout Mercutio, and then Tybalt fled:
But by and by comes back to Romeo,
Who had but newly entertain'd revenge,
And to 't they go like lightning: for, ere I
Could draw to part them, was stout Tybalt slain;
And, as he fell, did Romeo turn and fly;
This is the truth, or let Benvolio die.

La. Cap. He is a kinsman to the Montague,
Affection makes him false, he speaks not true:
Some twenty of them fought in this black strife,
And all those twenty could but kill one life.
I beg for justice, which thou, prince, must give;
Romeo slew Tybalt, Romeo must not live.

Prin. Romeo slew him, he slew Mercutio;
Who now the price of his dear blood doth owe?

Mon. Not Romeo, prince, he was Mercutio's friend;
His fault concludes but what the law should end,
The life of Tybalt.

Prin. And for that offence
Immediately we do exile him hence:
I have an interest in your hate's proceeding,
My blood for your rude brawls doth lie a-bleeding;
But I'll amerce you with so strong a fine,
That you shall all repent the loss of mine:
I will be deaf to pleading and excuses;
Nor tears nor prayers shall purchase out abuses:
Therefore use none: let Romeo hence in haste,
Else, when he's found, that hour is his last.
Bear hence this body, and attend our will:
Mercy but murders, pardoning those that kill. [*Exeunt.*

Scene II

Capulet's orchard.

Enter Juliet.

Jul. Gallop apace, you fiery-footed steeds,
Towards Phœbus' lodging: such a waggoner
As Phaethon would whip you to the west,
And bring in cloudy night immediately.
Spread thy close curtain, love-performing night,
That runaways' eyes may wink, and Romeo
Leap to these arms, untalk'd of and unseen.
Lovers can see to do their amorous rites
By their own beauties; or, if love be blind,
It best agrees with night. Come, civil night,
Thou sober-suited matron, all in black,
And learn me how to lose a winning match,
Play'd for a pair of stainless maidenhoods:
Hood my unmann'd blood bating in my cheeks
With thy black mantle, till strange love grown bold
Think true love acted simple modesty.
Come, night, come, Romeo, come, thou day in night;
For thou wilt lie upon the wings of night
Whiter than new snow on a raven's back.
Come, gentle night, come, loving, black-brow'd night,
Give me my Romeo; and, when he shall die,
Take him and cut him out in little stars,
And he will make the face of heaven so fine,
That all the world will be in love with night,
And pay no worship to the garish sun.
O, I have bought the mansion of a love,
But not possess'd it, and, though I am sold,
Not yet enjoy'd; so tedious is this day
As is the night before some festival
To an impatient child that hath new robes
And may not wear them. O, here comes my nurse,
And she brings news, and every tongue that speaks
But Romeo's name speaks heavenly eloquence.

Enter Nurse, with cords.

Now, nurse, what news? What hast thou there? the cords
That Romeo bid thee fetch?

Nurse. Ay, ay, the cords.

[*Throws them down.*

Jul. Ay me! what news? why dost thou wring thy hands?

Nurse. Ah, well-a-day! he 's dead, he 's dead, he 's dead.
We are undone, lady, we are undone.

Alack the day! he 's gone, he 's kill'd, he 's dead.
Jul. Can heaven be so envious?
Nurse. Romeo can,
Though heaven cannot. O Romeo, Romeo!
Who ever would have thought it? Romeo!
Jul. What devil art thou that dost torment me thus?
This torture should be roar'd in dismal hell.
Hath Romeo slain himself? say thou but 'I,'
And that bare vowel 'I' shall poison more
Than the death-darting eye of cockatrice:
I am not I, if there be such an I,
Or those eyes shut, that make thee answer 'I.'
If he be slain, say 'I;' or if not, no:
Brief sounds determine of my weal or woe.
Nurse. I saw the wound, I saw it with mine eyes—
God save the mark!—here on his manly breast:
A piteous corse, a bloody piteous corse;
Pale, pale as ashes, all bedaub'd in blood,
All in gore blood: I swounded at the sight.
Jul. O, break, my heart! poor bankrupt, break at once!
To prison, eyes, ne'er look on liberty!
Vile earth, to earth resign, end motion here,
And thou and Romeo press one heavy bier!
Nurse. O Tybalt, Tybalt, the best friend I had!
O courteous Tybalt! honest gentleman!
That ever I should live to see thee dead!
Jul. What storm is this that blows so contrary?
Is Romeo slaughter'd, and is Tybalt dead?
My dear-loved cousin, and my dearer lord?
Then, dreadful trumpet, sound the general doom!
For who is living, if those two are gone?
Nurse. Tybalt is gone, and Romeo banished;
Romeo that kill'd him, he is banished.
Jul. O God! did Romeo's hand shed Tybalt's blood?
Nurse. It did, it did; alas the day, it did!
Jul. O serpent heart, hid with a flowering face!
Did ever dragon keep so fair a cave?
Beautiful tyrant! fiend angelical!
Dove-feather'd raven! wolvish-ravening lamb!
Despised substance of divinest show!
Just opposite to what thou justly seem'st,
A damned saint, an honourable villain!
O nature, what hadst thou to do in hell,
When thou didst bower the spirit of a fiend
In mortal paradise of such sweet flesh?

Was ever book containing such vile matter
So fairly bound? O, that deceit should dwell
In such a gorgeous palace!

Nurse. There 's no trust,
No faith, no honesty in men; all perjured,
All forsworn, all naught, all dissemblers.
Ah, where 's my man? give me some aqua vitæ:
These griefs, these woes, these sorrows make me old.
Shame come to Romeo!

Jul. Blister'd be thy tongue
For such a wish! he was not born to shame:
Upon his brow shame is ashamed to sit;
For 'tis a throne where honour may be crown'd
Sole monarch of the universal earth.
O, what a beast was I to chide at him!

Nurse. Will you speak well of him that kill'd your cousin?

Jul. Shall I speak ill of him that is my husband?
Ah, poor my lord, what tongue shall smooth thy name,
When I, thy three-hours' wife, have mangled it?
But wherefore, villain, didst thou kill my cousin?
That villain cousin would have kill'd my husband:
Back, foolish tears, back to your native spring;
Your tributary drops belong to woe,
Which you mistaking offer up to joy.
My husband lives, that Tybalt would have slain;
And Tybalt's dead, that would have slain my husband:
All this is comfort; wherefore weep I then?
Some word there was, worser than Tybalt's death,
That murder'd me: I would forget it fain;
But, O, it presses to my memory,
Like damned guilty deeds to sinners' minds:
'Tybalt is dead, and Romeo banished;'
That 'banished,' that one word 'banished,'
Hath slain ten thousand Tybalts. Tybalt's death
Was woe enough, if it had ended there:
Or, if sour woe delights in fellowship,
And needly will be rank'd with other griefs,
Why follow'd not, when she said 'Tybalt 's dead,'
Thy father, or thy mother, nay, or both,
Which modern lamentation might have moved?
But with a rear-ward following Tybalt's death,
'Romeo is banished:' to speak that word,
Is father, mother, Tybalt, Romeo, Juliet,
All slain, all dead. 'Romeo is banished.'
There is no end, no limit, measure, bound,

In that word 's death ; no words can that woe sound.
Where is my father, and my mother, nurse?

Nurse. Weeping and wailing over Tybalt's corse:
Will you go to them? I will bring you thither.

Jul. Wash they his wounds with tears: mine shall be spent,
When theirs are dry, for Romeo's banishment.
Take up those cords: poor ropes, you are beguiled,
Both you and I; for Romeo is exiled:
He made you for a highway to my bed;
But I, a maid, die maiden-widowed.
Come, cords; come, nurse; I 'll to my wedding-bed;
And death, not Romeo, take my maidenhead!

Nurse. Hie to your chamber: I 'll find Romeo
To comfort you: I wot well where he is.
Hark ye, your Romeo will be here at night:
I 'll to him; he is hid at Laurence' cell.

Jul. O, find him! give this ring to my true knight,
And bid him come to take his last farewell. [*Exeunt.*

Scene III

Friar Laurence's cell.

Enter Friar Laurence.

Fri. L. Romeo, come forth; come forth, thou fearful man:
Affliction is enamour'd of thy parts,
And thou art wedded to calamity.

Enter Romeo.

Rom. Father, what news? what is the prince's doom?
What sorrow craves acquaintance at my hand,
That I yet know not?

Fri. L. Too familiar
Is my dear son with such sour company:
I bring thee tidings of the prince's doom.

Rom. What less than dooms-day is the prince's doom?

Fri. L. A gentler judgement vanish'd from his lips,
Not body's death, but body's banishment.

Rom. Ha, banishment! be merciful, say 'death;'
For exile hath more terror in his look,
Much more than death: do not say 'banishment.'

Fri. L. Here from Verona art thou banished:
Be patient, for the world is broad and wide.

Rom. There is no world without Verona walls,
But purgatory, torture, hell itself.
Hence banished is banish'd from the world,
And world's exile is death: then 'banished'
Is death mis-term'd: calling death 'banished'

Thou cut'st my head off with a golden axe,
And smilest upon the stroke that murders me.
Fri. L. O deadly sin! O rude unthankfulness!
Thy fault our law calls death; but the kind prince,
Taking thy part, hath rush'd aside the law,
And turn'd that black word death to banishment:
This is dear mercy, and thou seest it not.
Rom. 'Tis torture, and not mercy: heaven is here,
Where Juliet lives; and every cat and dog
And little mouse, every unworthy thing,
Live here in heaven and may look on her,
But Romeo may not: more validity,
More honourable state, more courtship lives
In carrion-flies than Romeo: they may seize
On the white wonder of dear Juliet's hand,
And steal immortal blessing from her lips;
Who, even in pure and vestal modesty,
Still blush, as thinking their own kisses sin;
But Romeo may not; he is banished:
This may flies do, but I from this must fly:
They are free men, but I am banished:
And say'st thou yet, that exile is not death?
Hadst thou no poison mix'd, no sharp-ground knife,
No sudden mean of death, though ne'er so mean,
But 'banished' to kill me?—'Banished'?
O friar, the damned use that word in hell;
Howling attends it: how hast thou the heart,
Being a divine, a ghostly confessor,
A sin-absolver, and my friend profess'd,
To mangle me with that word 'banished'?
Fri. L. Thou fond mad man, hear me but speak a word.
Rom. O, thou wilt speak again of banishment.
Fri. L. I'll give thee armour to keep off that word;
Adversity's sweet milk, philosophy,
To comfort thee, though thou art banished.
Rom. Yet 'banish'd'? Hang up philosophy!
Unless philosophy can make a Juliet,
Displant a town, reverse a prince's doom,
It helps not, it prevails not: talk no more.
Fri. L. O, then I see that madmen have no ears.
Rom. How should they, when that wise men have no eyes?
Fri. L. Let me dispute with thee of thy estate.
Rom. Thou canst not speak of that thou dost not feel:
Wert thou as young as I, Juliet thy love,
An hour but married, Tybalt murdered,

Doting like me, and like me banished,
Then mightst thou speak, then mightst thou tear thy hair,
And fall upon the ground, as I do now,
Taking the measure of an unmade grave. [*Knocking within.*

Fri. L. Arise; one knocks; good Romeo, hide thyself.

Rom. Not I; unless the breath of heart-sick groans
Mist-like infold me from the search of eyes. [*Knocking.*

Fri. L. Hark, how they knock! Who 's there? Romeo, arise;
Thou wilt be taken.—Stay awhile!—Stand up; [*Knocking.*
Run to my study.—By and by!—God's will,
What simpleness is this!—I come, I come! [*Knocking.*
Who knocks so hard? whence come you? what 's your will?

Nurse. [*Within*] Let me come in, and you shall know my errand;
I come from Lady Juliet.

Fri. L. Welcome, then.

Enter Nurse.

Nurse. O holy friar, O, tell me, holy friar,
Where is my lady's lord, where 's Romeo?

Fri. L. There on the ground, with his own tears made drunk.

Nurse. O, he is even in my mistress' case,
Just in her case!

Fri. L. O woeful sympathy!
Piteous predicament!

Nurse. Even so lies she,
Blubbering and weeping, weeping and blubbering.
Stand up, stand up; stand, an you be a man:
For Juliet's sake, for her sake, rise and stand;
Why should you fall into so deep an O?

Rom. Nurse!

Nurse. Ah sir! ah sir! Well, death 's the end of all.

Rom. Spakest thou of Juliet? how is it with her?
Doth she not think me an old murderer,
Now I have stain'd the childhood of her joy
With blood removed but little from her own?
Where is she? and how doth she? and what says
My conceal'd lady to our cancell'd love?

Nurse. O, she says nothing, sir, but weeps and weeps;
And now falls on her bed; and then starts up,
And Tybalt calls; and then on Romeo cries,
And then down falls again.

Rom. As if that name,
Shot from the deadly level of a gun,
Did murder her, as that name's cursed hand
Murder'd her kinsman. O, tell me, friar, tell me,
In what vile part of this anatomy

Doth my name lodge? tell me, that I may sack
The hateful mansion. [*Drawing his sword.*

Fri. L. Hold thy desperate hand:
Art thou a man? thy form cries out thou art:
Thy tears are womanish; thy wild acts denote
The unreasonable fury of a beast:
Unseemly woman in a seeming man!
Or ill-beseeming beast in seeming both!
Thou hast amazed me: by my holy order,
I thought thy disposition better temper'd.
Hast thou slain Tybalt? wilt thou slay thyself?
And slay thy lady that in thy life lives,
By doing damned hate upon thyself?
Why rail'st thou on thy birth, the heaven and earth?
Since birth and heaven and earth, all three do meet
In thee at once, which thou at once wouldst lose.
Fie, fie, thou shamest thy shape, thy love, thy wit;
Which, like a usurer, abound'st in all,
And usest none in that true use indeed
Which should bedeck thy shape, thy love, thy wit:
Thy noble shape is but a form of wax,
Digressing from the valour of a man;
Thy dear love sworn, but hollow perjury,
Killing that love which thou hast vow'd to cherish;
Thy wit, that ornament to shape and love,
Mis-shapen in the conduct of them both,
Like powder in a skilless soldier's flask,
Is set a-fire by thine own ignorance,
And thou dismember'd with thine own defence.
What, rouse thee, man! thy Juliet is alive,
For whose dear sake thou wast but lately dead;
There art thou happy: Tybalt would kill thee,
But thou slew'st Tybalt; there art thou happy too:
The law, that threaten'd death, becomes thy friend,
And turns it to exile; there art thou happy:
A pack of blessings lights upon thy back;
Happiness courts thee in her best array;
But, like a misbehaved and sullen wench,
Thou pout'st upon thy fortune and thy love:
Take heed, take heed, for such die miserable.
Go, get thee to thy love, as was decreed,
Ascend her chamber, hence and comfort her:
But look thou stay not till the watch be set,
For then thou canst not pass to Mantua;
Where thou shalt live till we can find a time

To blaze your marriage, reconcile your friends,
Beg pardon of the prince, and call thee back
With twenty hundred thousand times more joy
Than thou went'st forth in lamentation.
Go before, nurse: commend me to thy lady,
And bid her hasten all the house to bed,
Which heavy sorrow makes them apt unto:
Romeo is coming.

Nurse. O Lord, I could have stay'd here all the night
To hear good counsel: O, what learning is!
My lord, I 'll tell my lady you will come.

Rom. Do so, and bid my sweet prepare to chide.

Nurse. Here, sir, a ring she bid me give you, sir:
Hie you, make haste, for it grows very late. [*Exit*

Rom. How well my comfort is revived by this!

Fri. Go hence; good night; and here stands all your state:
Either be gone before the watch be set,
Or by the break of day disguised from hence:
Sojourn in Mantua; I 'll find out your man,
And he shall signify from time to time
Every good hap to you that chances here:
Give me thy hand; 'tis late: farewell; good night.

Rom. But that a joy past joy calls out on me,
It were a grief, so brief to part with thee:
Farewell. [*Exeunt.*

Scene IV

A room in Capulet's house.

Enter Capulet, Lady Capulet, and Paris.

Cap. Things have fall'n out, sir, so unluckily,
That we have had no time to move our daughter.
Look you, she loved her kinsman Tybalt dearly,
And so did I. Well, we were born to die.
'Tis very late; she 'll not come down to-night:
I promise you, but for your company,
I would have been a-bed an hour ago.

Par. These times of woe afford no time to woo.
Madam, good night: commend me to your daughter.

La. Cap. I will, and know her mind early to-morrow;
To-night she's mew'd up to her heaviness.

Cap. Sir Paris, I will make a desperate tender
Of my child's love: I think she will be ruled
In all respects by me; nay more, I doubt it not.
Wife, go you to her ere you go to bed;
Acquaint her here of my son Paris' love;

And bid her, mark you me, on Wednesday next—
But, soft ! what day is this ?
Par. Monday, my lord.
Cap. Monday ! ha, ha ! Well, Wednesday is too soon ;
O' Thursday let it be : o' Thursday, tell her,
She shall be married to this noble earl.
Will you be ready ? do you like this haste ?
We 'll keep no great ado ; a friend or two ;
For, hark you, Tybalt being slain so late,
It may be thought we held him carelessly,
Being our kinsman, if we revel much :
Therefore we 'll have some half-a-dozen friends,
And there an end. But what say you to Thursday ?
Par. My lord, I would that Thursday were to-morrow.
Cap. Well, get you gone : o' Thursday be it then.
Go you to Juliet ere you go to bed,
Prepare her, wife, against this wedding-day.
Farewell, my lord. Light to my chamber, ho !
Afore me, it is so very very late,
That we may call it early by and by :
Good night. [*Exeunt.*

Scene V

Capulet's orchard.

Enter Romeo and Juliet, above, at the Window.

Jul. Wilt thou be gone ? It is not yet near day :
It was the nightingale, and not the lark,
That pierced the fearful hollow of thine ear ;
Nightly she sings on yond pomegranate-tree :
Believe me, love, it was the nightingale.
Rom. It was the lark, the herald of the morn,
No nightingale : look, love, what envious streaks
Do lace the severing clouds in yonder east :
Night's candles are burnt out, and jocund day
Stands tiptoe on the misty mountain tops :
I must be gone and live, or stay and die.
Jul. Yond light is not day-light, I know it, I :
It is some meteor that the sun exhales,
To be to thee this night a torch-bearer,
And light thee on thy way to Mantua :
Therefore stay yet ; thou need'st not to be gone.
Rom. Let me be ta'en, let me be put to death ;
I am content, so thou wilt have it so.
I 'll say yon grey is not the morning's eye,
'Tis but the pale reflex of Cynthia's brow ;

Nor that is not the lark, whose notes do beat
The vaulty heaven so high above our heads
I have more care to stay than will to go:
Come, death, and welcome! Juliet wills it so.
How is 't, my soul? let 's talk: it is not day.

Jul. It is, it is: hie hence, be gone, away!
It is the lark that sings so out of tune,
Straining harsh discords and unpleasing sharps.
Some say the lark makes sweet division;
This doth not so, for she divideth us:
Some say the lark and loathed toad change eyes;
O, now I would they had changed voices too!
Since arm from arm that voice doth us affray,
Hunting thee hence with hunts-up to the day.
O, now be gone; more light and light it grows.

Rom. More light and light: more dark and dark our woes!

Enter Nurse, to the chamber.

Nurse. Madam!

Jul. Nurse?

Nurse. Your lady mother is coming to your chamber:
The day is broke; be wary, look about. [*Exit.*

Jul. Then, window, let day in, and let life out.

Rom. Farewell, farewell! one kiss, and I 'll descend. [*Descends.*

Jul. Art thou gone so? my lord, my love, my friend!
I must hear from thee every day in the hour,
For in a minute there are many days:
O, by this count I shall be much in years
Ere I again behold my Romeo!

Rom. Farewell!
I will omit no opportunity
That may convey my greetings, love, to thee.

Jul. O, think'st thou we shall ever meet again?

Rom. I doubt it not; and all these woes shall serve
For sweet discourses in our time to come.

Jul. O God! I have an ill-divining soul.
Methinks I see thee, now thou art below,
As one dead in the bottom of a tomb:
Either my eyesight fails or thou look'st pale.

Rom. And trust me, love, in my eye so do you:
Dry sorrow drinks our blood. Adieu, adieu! [*Exit.*

Jul. O fortune, fortune! all men call thee fickle:
If thou art fickle, what dost thou with him
That is renown'd for faith? Be fickle, fortune;
For then, I hope, thou wilt not keep him long,
But send him back.

La. Cap. [*Within*] Ho, daughter! are you up?
Jul. Who is 't that calls? it is my lady mother!
Is she not down so late, or up so early?
What unaccustom'd cause procures her hither?

Enter Lady Capulet.

La. Cap. Why, how now, Juliet!
Jul. Madam, I am not well.
La. Cap. Evermore weeping for your cousin's death?
What, wilt thou wash him from his grave with tears?
An if thou couldst, thou couldst not make him live;
Therefore have done: some grief shows much of love,
But much of grief shows still some want of wit.
Jul. Yet let me weep for such a feeling loss.
La. Cap. So shall you feel the loss, but not the friend
Which you weep for.
Jul. Feeling so the loss,
I cannot choose but ever weep the friend.
La. Cap. Well, girl, thou weep'st not so much for his death
As that the villain lives which slaughter'd him.
Jul. What villain, madam?
La. Cap. That same villain, Romeo.
Jul. [*Aside*] Villain and he be many miles asunder.
God pardon him! I do, with all my heart;
And yet no man like he doth grieve my heart.
La. Cap. That is because the traitor murderer lives.
Jul. Ay, madam, from the reach of these my hands:
Would none but I might venge my cousin's death!
La. Cap. We will have vengeance for it, fear thou not:
Then weep no more. I'll send to one in Mantua,
Where that same banish'd runagate doth live,
Shall give him such an unaccustom'd dram
That he shall soon keep Tybalt company:
And then, I hope, thou wilt be satisfied.
Jul. Indeed, I never shall be satisfied
With Romeo, till I behold him—dead—
Is my poor heart so for a kinsman vex'd.
Madam, if you could find out but a man
To bear a poison, I would temper it,
That Romeo should, upon receipt thereof,
Soon sleep in quiet. O, how my heart abhors
To hear him named, and cannot come to him,
To wreak the love I bore my cousin
Upon his body that hath slaughter'd him!
La. Cap. Find thou the means, and I'll find such a man.
But now I'll tell thee joyful tidings, girl.

Jul. And joy comes well in such a needy time:
What are they, I beseech your ladyship?
La. Cap. Well, well, thou hast a careful father, child:
One who, to put thee from thy heaviness,
Hath sorted out a sudden day of joy,
That thou expect'st not, nor I look'd not for.
Jul. Madam, in happy time, what day is that?
La. Cap. Marry, my child, early next Thursday morn,
The gallant, young, and noble gentleman,
The County Paris, at Saint Peter's Church,
Shall happily make thee there a joyful bride.
Jul. Now, by Saint Peter's Church, and Peter too,
He shall not make me there a joyful bride.
I wonder at this haste; that I must wed
Ere he that should be husband comes to woo.
I pray you, tell my lord and father, madam,
I will not marry yet; and, when I do, I swear,
It shall be Romeo, whom you know I hate,
Rather than Paris. These are news indeed!
La. Cap. Here comes your father; tell him so yourself,
And see how he will take it at your hands.

Enter Capulet and Nurse.

Cap. When the sun sets, the air doth drizzle dew;
But for the sunset of my brother's son
It rains downright.
How now! a conduit, girl? what, still in tears?
Evermore showering? In one little body
Thou counterfeit'st a bark, a sea, a wind:
For still thy eyes, which I may call the sea,
Do ebb and flow with tears; the bark thy body is,
Sailing in this salt flood; the winds, thy sighs;
Who raging with thy tears, and they with them,
Without a sudden calm will overset
Thy tempest-tossed body. How now, wife!
Have you deliver'd to her our decree?
La. Cap. Ay, sir; but she will none, she gives you thanks.
I would the fool were married to her grave!
Cap. Soft! take me with you, take me with you, wife.
How! will she none? doth she not give us thanks?
Is she not proud? doth she not count her blest,
Unworthy as she is, that we have wrought
So worthy a gentleman to be her bridegroom?
Jul. Not proud, you have, but thankful that you have:
Proud can I never be of what I hate;
But thankful even for hate that is meant love.

Cap. How, how! how, how! chop-logic! What is this?
'Proud,' and 'I thank you,' and 'I thank you not;'
And yet 'not proud:' mistress minion, you,
Thank me no thankings, nor proud me no prouds,
But fettle your fine joints 'gainst Thursday next,
To go with Paris to Saint Peter's Church,
Or I will drag thee on a hurdle thither.
Out, you green-sickness carrion! out, you baggage!
You tallow-face!

La. Cap. Fie, fie! what, are you mad?

Jul. Good father, I beseech you on my knees,
Hear me with patience but to speak a word.

Cap. Hang thee, young baggage! disobedient wretch!
I tell thee what: get thee to church o' Thursday,
Or never after look me in the face:
Speak not, reply not, do not answer me;
My fingers itch. Wife, we scarce thought us blest
That God had lent us but this only child;
But now I see this one is one too much,
And that we have a curse in having her:
Out on her, hilding!

Nurse. God in heaven bless her!
You are to blame, my lord, to rate her so.

Cap. And why, my lady wisdom? hold your tongue,
Good prudence; smatter with your gossips, go.

Nurse. I speak no treason.

Cap. O, God ye god-den.

Nurse. May not one speak?

Cap. Peace, you mumbling fool!
Utter your gravity o'er a gossip's bowl;
For here we need it not.

La. Cap. You are too hot.

Cap. God's bread! it makes me mad:
Day, night, hour, tide, time, work, play,
Alone, in company, still my care hath been
To have her match'd: and having now provided
A gentleman of noble parentage,
Of fair demesnes, youthful, and nobly train'd,
Stuff'd, as they say, with honourable parts,
Proportion'd as one's thought would wish a man;
And then to have a wretched puling fool,
A whining mammet, in her fortune's tender,
To answer 'I 'll not wed; I cannot love,
I am too young; I pray you, pardon me.'
But, an you will not wed, I 'll pardon you:

Graze where you will, you shall not house with me:
Look to 't, think on 't, I do not use to jest.
Thursday is near; lay hand on heart, advise:
An you be mine, I 'll give you to my friend;
An you be not, hang, beg, starve, die in the streets,
For, by my soul, I 'll ne'er acknowledge thee,
Nor what is mine shall never do thee good:
Trust to 't, bethink you; I 'll not be forsworn. [*Exit.*

Jul. Is there no pity sitting in the clouds,
That sees into the bottom of my grief?
O, sweet my mother, cast me not away!
Delay this marriage for a month, a week;
Or, if you do not, make the bridal bed
In that dim monument where Tybalt lies.

La. Cap. Talk not to me, for I 'll not speak a word:
Do as thou wilt, for I have done with thee. [*Exit.*

Jul. O God!—O nurse, how shall this be prevented?
My husband is on earth, my faith in heaven:
How shall that faith return again to earth,
Unless that husband send it me from heaven
By leaving earth? comfort me, counsel me.
Alack, alack, that heaven should practise stratagems
Upon so soft a subject as myself!
What say'st thou? hast thou not a word of joy?
Some comfort, nurse.

Nurse. Faith, here it is.
Romeo is banish'd, and all the world to nothing,
That he dares ne'er come back to challenge you;
Or, if he do, it needs must be by stealth.
Then, since the case so stands as now it doth,
I think it best you married with the county.
O, he 's a lovely gentleman!
Romeo 's a dishclout to him: an eagle, madam,
Hath not so green, so quick, so fair an eye
As Paris hath. Beshrew my very heart,
I think you are happy in this second match,
For it excels your first: or if it did not,
Your first is dead, or 'twere as good he were
As living here and you no use of him.

Jul. Speakest thou from thy heart?

Nurse. And from my soul too;
Else beshrew them both.

Jul. Amen!

Nurse. What?

Jul. Well, thou hast comforted me marvellous much.

Go in, and tell my lady I am gone,
Having displeased my father, to Laurence' cell,
To make confession and to be absolved.
Nurse. Marry, I will, and this is wisely done. [*Exit.*
Jul. Ancient damnation! O most wicked fiend!
Is it more sin to wish me thus forsworn,
Or to dispraise my lord with that same tongue
Which she hath praised him with above compare
So many thousand times? Go, counsellor!
Thou and my bosom henceforth shall be twain.
I 'll to the friar, to know his remedy:
If all else fail, myself have power to die. [*Exit.*

ACT IV—Scene I

Friar Laurence's cell.

Enter Friar Laurence and Paris.

Fri. L. On Thursday, sir? the time is very short.
Par. My father Capulet will have it so;
And I am nothing slow to slack his haste.
Fri. L. You say you do not know the lady's mind:
Uneven is the course; I like it not.
Par. Immoderately she weeps for Tybalt's death,
And therefore have I little talk'd of love,
For Venus smiles not in a house of tears.
Now, sir, her father counts it dangerous
That she doth give her sorrow so much sway,
And in his wisdom hastes our marriage,
To stop the inundation of her tears,
Which, too much minded by herself alone,
May be put from her by society:
Now do you know the reason of this haste.
Fri. L. [*Aside*] I would I knew not why it should be slow'd.
Look, sir, here comes the lady toward my cell.

Enter Juliet.

Par. Happily met, my lady and my wife!
Jul. That may be, sir, when I may be a wife.
Par. That may be must be, love, on Thursday next.
Jul. What must be shall be.
Fri. L. That 's a certain text.
Par. Come you to make confession to this father?
Jul. To answer that, I should confess to you.
Par. Do not deny to him that you love me.
Jul. I will confess to you that I love him.
Par. So will ye, I am sure, that you love me.

Jul. If I do so, it will be of more price,
Being spoke behind your back, than to your face.
Par. Poor soul, thy face is much abused with tears.
Jul. The tears have got small victory by that;
For it was bad enough before their spite.
Par. Thou wrong'st it more than tears with that report.
Jul. That is no slander, sir, which is a truth,
And what I spake, I spake it to my face.
Par. Thy face is mine, and thou hast slander'd it.
Jul. It may be so, for it is not mine own.
Are you at leisure, holy father, now;
Or shall I come to you at evening mass?
Fri. L. My leisure serves me, pensive daughter, now.
My lord, we must entreat the time alone.
Par. God shield I should disturb devotion!
Juliet, on Thursday early will I rouse ye:
Till then, adieu, and keep this holy kiss. [*Exit.*
Jul. O, shut the door, and when thou hast done so,
Come weep with me; past hope, past cure, past help!
Fri. L. Ah, Juliet, I already know thy grief;
It strains me past the compass of my wits:
I hear thou must, and nothing may prorogue it,
On Thursday next be married to this county.
Jul. Tell me not, friar, that thou hear'st of this,
Unless thou tell me how I may prevent it:
If in thy wisdom thou canst give no help,
Do thou but call my resolution wise,
And with this knife I'll help it presently.
God join'd my heart and Romeo's, thou our hands;
And ere this hand, by thee to Romeo's seal'd,
Shall be the label to another deed,
Or my true heart with treacherous revolt
Turn to another, this shall slay them both:
Therefore, out of thy long-experienced time,
Give me some present counsel; or, behold,
'Twixt my extremes and me this bloody knife
Shall play the umpire, arbitrating that
Which the commission of thy years and art
Could to no issue of true honour bring.
Be not so long to speak; I long to die,
If what thou speak'st speak not of remedy.
Fri. L. Hold, daughter: I do spy a kind of hope,
Which craves as desperate an execution
As that is desperate which we would prevent.
If, rather than to marry County Paris,

Thou hast the strength of will to slay thyself,
Then is it likely thou wilt undertake
A thing like death to chide away this shame,
That copest with death himself to 'scape from it;
And, if thou darest, I 'll give thee remedy.

Jul. O, bid me leap, rather than marry Paris,
From off the battlements of yonder tower;
Or walk in thievish ways; or bid me lurk
Where serpents are; chain me with roaring bears;
Or shut me nightly in a charnel-house,
O'er-cover'd quite with dead men's rattling bones,
With reeky shanks and yellow chapless skulls;
Or bid me go into a new-made grave,
And hide me with a dead man in his shroud;
Things that to hear them told, have made me tremble;
And I will do it without fear or doubt,
To live an unstain'd wife to my sweet love.

Fri. L. Hold, then; go home, be merry, give consent
To marry Paris: Wednesday is to-morrow;
To-morrow night look that thou lie alone,
Let not thy nurse lie with thee in thy chamber:
Take thou this vial, being then in bed,
And this distill'd liquor drink thou off:
When presently through all thy veins shall run
A cold and drowsy humour; for no pulse
Shall keep his native progress; but surcease:
No warmth, no breath, shall testify thou livest;
The roses in thy lips and cheeks shall fade
To paly ashes; thy eyes' windows fall,
Like death, when he shuts up the day of life;
Each part, deprived of supple government,
Shall, stiff and stark and cold, appear like death:
And in this borrow'd likeness of shrunk death
Thou shalt continue two and forty hours,
And then awake as from a pleasant sleep.
Now, when the bridegroom in the morning comes
To rouse thee from thy bed, there art thou dead:
Then, as the manner of our country is,
In thy best robes uncover'd on the bier
Thou shalt be borne to that same ancient vault
Where all the kindred of the Capulets lie.
In the mean time, against thou shalt awake,
Shall Romeo by my letters know our drift;
And hither shall he come: and he and I
Will watch thy waking, and that very night

Shall Romeo bear thee hence to Mantua.
And this shall free thee from this present shame,
If no inconstant toy nor womanish fear
Abate thy valour in the acting it.

Jul. Give me, give me! O, tell not me of fear!

Fri. L. Hold; get you gone, be strong and prosperous
In this resolve; I'll send a friar with speed
To Mantua, with my letters to thy lord.

Jul. Love give me strength! and strength shall help afford.
Farewell, dear father! [*Exeunt.*

Scene II

Hall in Capulet's house.

Enter Capulet, Lady Capulet, Nurse, and two Servingmen.

Cap. So many guests invite as here are writ.
[*Exit First Servant.*
Sirrah, go hire me twenty cunning cooks.

Sec. Serv. You shall have none ill, sir, for I'll try if they can lick their fingers.

Cap. How canst thou try them so?

Sec. Serv. Marry, sir, 'tis an ill cook that cannot lick his own fingers: therefore he that cannot lick his fingers goes not with me.

Cap. Go, be gone. [*Exit Sec. Servant.*
We shall be much unfurnish'd for this time.
What, is my daughter gone to Friar Laurence?

Nurse. Ay, forsooth.

Cap. Well, he may chance to do some good on her:
A peevish self-will'd harlotry it is.

Enter Juliet.

Nurse. See where she comes from shrift with merry look.

Cap. How now, my headstrong! where have you been [gadding?

Jul. Where I have learn'd me to repent the sin
Of disobedient opposition
To you and your behests, and am enjoin'd
By holy Laurence to fall prostrate here,
To beg your pardon! pardon, I beseech you!
Henceforward I am ever ruled by you.

Cap. Send for the county; go tell him of this:
I'll have this knot knit up to-morrow morning.

Jul. I met the youthful lord at Laurence' cell,
And gave him what becomed love I might,
Not stepping o'er the bounds of modesty.

Cap. Why, I am glad on 't; this is well: stand up:
This is as 't should be. Let me see the county;
Ay, marry, go, I say, and fetch him hither.
Now, afore God, this reverend holy friar,
All our whole city is much bound to him.

Jul. Nurse, will you go with me into my closet,
To help me sort such needful ornaments
As you think fit to furnish me to-morrow?

La. Cap. No, not till Thursday; there is time enough.

Cap. Go, nurse, go with her: we 'll to church to-morrow.
[*Exeunt Juliet and Nurse.*

La. Cap. We shall be short in our provision:
'Tis now near night.

Cap. Tush, I will stir about,
And all things shall be well, I warrant thee, wife:
Go thou to Juliet, help to deck up her;
I 'll not to bed to-night; let me alone;
I 'll play the housewife for this once. What, ho!
They are all forth: well, I will walk myself
To County Paris, to prepare him up
Against to-morrow: my heart is wondrous light,
Since this same wayward girl is so reclaim'd. [*Exeunt.*

Scene III

Juliet's Chamber.

Enter Juliet and Nurse.

Jul. Ay, those attires are best: but, gentle nurse,
I pray thee, leave me to myself to-night;
For I have need of many orisons
To move the heavens to smile upon my state,
Which, well thou know'st, is cross and full of sin.

Enter Lady Capulet.

La. Cap. What, are you busy, ho? need you my help?

Jul. No, madam; we have cull'd such necessaries
As are behoveful for our state to-morrow:
So please you, let me now be left alone,
And let the nurse this night sit up with you,
For I am sure you have your hands full all
In this so sudden business.

La. Cap. Good night!
Get thee to bed and rest, for thou hast need.
[*Exeunt Lady Capulet and Nurse.*

Jul. Farewell! God knows when we shall meet again.
I have a faint cold fear thrills through my veins,

That almost freezes up the heat of life:
I 'll call them back again to comfort me.
Nurse!—What should she do here?
My dismal scene I needs must act alone.
Come, vial.
What if this mixture do not work at all?
Shall I be married then to-morrow morning?
No, no: this shall forbid it. Lie thou there.
[*Laying down a dagger.*
What if it be a poison, which the friar
Subtly hath minister'd to have me dead,
Lest in this marriage he should be dishonour'd,
Because he married me before to Romeo?
I fear it is: and yet, methinks, it should not,
For he hath still been tried a holy man.
How if, when I am laid into the tomb,
I wake before the time that Romeo
Come to redeem me? there 's a fearful point.
Shall I not then be stifled in the vault,
To whose foul mouth no healthsome air breathes in,
And there die strangled ere my Romeo comes?
Or, if I live, is it not very like,
The horrible conceit of death and night,
Together with the terror of the place,
As in a vault, an ancient receptacle,
Where for this many hundred years the bones
Of all my buried ancestors are pack'd;
Where bloody Tybalt, yet but green in earth,
Lies festering in his shroud; where, as they say,
At some hours in the night spirits resort;
Alack, alack, is it not like that I
So early waking, what with loathsome smells
And shrieks like mandrakes' torn out of the earth,
That living mortals hearing them run mad:
O, if I wake, shall I not be distraught,
Environed with all these hideous fears?
And madly play with my forefathers' joints?
And pluck the mangled Tybalt from his shroud?
And, in this rage, with some great kinsman's bone,
As with a club, dash out my desperate brains?
O, look! methinks I see my cousin 's ghost
Seeking out Romeo, that did spit his body
Upon a rapier's point: stay, Tybalt, stay!
Romeo, I come! this do I drink to thee.
[*She falls upon her bed, within the curtains.*

Scene IV

Hall in Capulet's house.

Enter Lady Capulet and Nurse.

La. Cap. Hold, take these keys, and fetch more spices, nurse.
Nurse. They call for dates and quinces in the pastry.

Enter Capulet.

Cap. Come, stir, stir, stir! the second cock hath crow'd,
The curfew-bell hath rung, 'tis three o'clock:
Look to the baked meats, good Angelica:
Spare not for cost.
Nurse. Go, you cot-quean, go,
Get you to bed; faith, you 'll be sick to-morrow
For this night's watching.
Cap. No, not a whit: what! I have watch'd ere now
All night for lesser cause, and ne'er been sick.
La. Cap. Ay, you have been a mouse-hunt in your time;
But I will watch you from such watching now.
[*Exeunt Lady Capulet and Nurse.*
Cap. A jealous-hood, a jealous-hood!

Enter three or four Servingmen, with spits, and logs, and baskets.

Now, fellow,
What 's there?
First Serv. Things for the cook, sir, but I know not what.
Cap. Make haste, make haste. [*Exit First Serv.*] Sirrah, fetch drier logs:
Call Peter, he will show thee where they are.
Sec. Serv. I have a head, sir, that will find out logs,
And never trouble Peter for the matter.
Cap. Mass, and well said; a merry whoreson, ha!
Thou shalt be logger-head. [*Exit Sec. Serv.*] Good faith, 'tis day:
The county will be here with music straight,
For so he said he would. [*Music within.*] I hear him near.
Nurse! Wife! What, ho! What, nurse, I say!

Re-enter Nurse.

Go waken Juliet, go and trim her up;
I 'll go and chat with Paris: hie, make haste,
Make haste: the bridegroom he is come already:
Make haste, I say. [*Exeunt.*

Scene V

Juliet's chamber.

Enter Nurse.

Nurse. Mistress! what, mistress! Juliet! fast, I warrant her, she

Why, lamb! why, lady! fie, you slug-a-bed!
Why, love, I say! madam! sweet-heart! why, bride!
What, not a word? you take your pennyworths now;
Sleep for a week; for the next night, I warrant,
The County Paris hath set up his rest
That you shall rest but little. God forgive me,
Marry, and amen, how sound is she asleep!
I needs must wake her. Madam, madam, madam!
Ay, let the county take you in your bed;
He 'll fright you up, i' faith. Will it not be?
[*Undraws the curtains.*
What, dress'd! and in your clothes! and down again!
I must needs wake you. Lady! lady! lady!
Alas, alas! Help, help! my lady 's dead!
O, well-a-day, that ever I was born!
Some aqua-vitæ, ho! My lord! my lady!

Enter Lady Capulet.

La. Cap. What noise is here?
Nurse. O lamentable day!
La. Cap. What is the matter?
Nurse. Look, look! O heavy day!
La. Cap. O me, O me! My child, my only life,
Revive, look up, or I will die with thee.
Help! help! call help.

Enter Capulet.

Cap. For shame, bring Juliet forth; her lord is come.
Nurse. She 's dead, deceased, she 's dead; alack the day!
La. Cap. Alack the day, she 's dead, she 's dead, she 's dead!
Cap. Ha! let me see her. Out, alas! she 's cold;
Her blood is settled and her joints are stiff;
Life and these lips have long been separated.
Death lies on her like an untimely frost
Upon the sweetest flower of all the field.
Nurse. O lamentable day!
La. Cap. O woeful time!
Cap. Death, that hath ta'en her hence to make me wail,
Ties up my tongue and will not let me speak.

Enter Friar Laurence and Paris, with Musicians.

Fri. L. Come, is the bride ready to go to church?
Cap. Ready to go, but never to return.
O son, the night before thy wedding-day
Hath death lain with thy wife: see, there she lies,
Flower as she was, deflowered by him.
Death is my son-in-law, death is my heir;
My daughter he hath wedded: I will die,

And leave him all; life, living, all is Death's.
Par. Have I thought long to see this morning's face,
And doth it give me such a sight as this?
La. Cap. Accurst, unhappy, wretched, hateful day!
Most miserable hour that e'er time saw
In lasting labour of his pilgrimage!
But one, poor one, one poor and loving child,
But one thing to rejoice and solace in,
And cruel death hath catch'd it from my sight!
Nurse. O woe! O woeful, woeful, woeful day!
Most lamentable day, most woeful day,
That ever, ever, I did yet behold!
O day! O day! O day! O hateful day!
Never was seen so black a day as this:
O woeful day, O woeful day!
Par. Beguiled, divorced, wronged, spited, slain!
Most detestable death, by thee beguiled,
By cruel cruel thee quite overthrown!
O love! O life! not life, but love in death!
Cap. Despised, distressed, hated, martyr'd, kill'd!
Uncomfortable time, why camest thou now
To murder, murder our solemnity?
O child! O child! my soul, and not my child!
Dead art thou! Alack, my child is dead;
And with my child my joys are buried!
Fri. L. Peace, ho, for shame! confusion's cure lives not
In these confusions. Heaven and yourself
Had part in this fair maid; now heaven hath all,
And all the better is it for the maid:
Your part in her you could not keep from death;
But heaven keeps his part in eternal life.
The most you sought was her promotion,
For 'twas your heaven she should be advanced:
And weep ye now, seeing she is advanced
Above the clouds, as high as heaven itself?
O, in this love, you love your child so ill,
That you run mad, seeing that she is well:
She 's not well married that lives married long,
But she 's best married that dies married young.
Dry up your tears, and stick your rosemary
On this fair corse, and, as the custom is,
In all her best array bear her to church:
For though fond nature bids us all lament,
Yet nature's tears are reason's merriment.
Cap. All things that we ordained festival,

Turn from their office to black funeral:
Our instruments to melancholy bells;
Our wedding cheer to a sad burial feast;
Our solemn hymns to sullen dirges change;
Our bridal flowers serve for a buried corse,
And all things change them to the contrary.

Fri. L. Sir, go you in; and, madam, go with him;
And go, Sir Paris; every one prepare
To follow this fair corse unto her grave:
The heavens do lour upon you for some ill;
Move them no more by crossing their high will.

[*Exeunt Capulet, Lady Capulet, Paris, and Friar.*

First Mus. Faith, we may put up our pipes, and be gone.

Nurse. Honest good fellows, ah, put up, put up;
For, well you know, this is a pitiful case. [*Exit.*

First Mus. Ay, by my troth, the case may be amended.

Enter Peter.

Pet. Musicians, O, musicians, 'Heart's ease, Heart's ease:' O, an you will have me live, play 'Heart's ease.'

First Mus. Why 'Heart's ease?'

Pet. O, musicians, because my heart itself plays 'My heart is full of woe:' O, play me some merry dump, to comfort me.

First Mus. Not a dump we; 'tis no time to play now.

Pet. You will not then?

First Mus. No.

Pet. I will then give it you soundly.

First Mus. What will you give us?

Pet. No money, on my faith, but the gleek; I will give you the minstrel.

First Mus. Then will I give you the serving-creature.

Pet. Then will I lay the serving-creature's dagger on your pate. I will carry no crotchets; I 'll re you, I 'll fa you; do you note me?

First Mus. An you re us and fa us, you note us.

Sec. Mus. Pray you, put up your dagger, and put out your wit.

Pet. Then have at you with my wit! I will dry-beat you with an iron wit, and put up my iron dagger. Answer me like men:

'When griping grief the heart doth wound
And doleful dumps the mind oppress,
Then music with her silver sound'—

why 'silver sound'? why 'music with her silver sound'?—What say you, Simon Catling?

First Mus. Marry, sir, because silver hath a sweet sound.

Pet. Pretty! What say you, Hugh Rebeck?

Sec. Mus. I say, 'silver sound,' because musicians sound for silver.

Pet. Pretty too! What say you, James Soundpost?

Third Mus. Faith, I know not what to say.

Pet. O, I cry you mercy; you are the singer: I will say for you. It is 'music with her silver sound,' because musicians have no gold for sounding:

'Then music with her silver sound
With speedy help doth lend redress.' [*Exit.*

First Mus. What a pestilent knave is this same!

Sec. Mus. Hang him, Jack! Come, we'll in here; tarry for the mourners, and stay dinner. [*Exeunt.*

ACT V—Scene I

Mantua. A street.

Enter Romeo.

Rom. If I may trust the flattering truth of sleep,
My dreams presage some joyful news at hand:
My bosom's lord sits lightly in his throne,
And all this day an unaccustom'd spirit
Lifts me above the ground with cheerful thoughts.
I dreamt my lady came and found me dead—
Strange dream, that gives a dead man leave to think!—
And breathed such life with kisses in my lips,
That I revived and was an emperor.
Ah me! how sweet is love itself possess'd,
When but love's shadows are so rich in joy!

Enter Balthasar, booted.

News from Verona! How now, Balthasar!
Dost thou not bring me letters from the friar?
How doth my lady? Is my father well?
How fares my Juliet? that I ask again;
For nothing can be ill, if she be well.

Bal. Then she is well, and nothing can be ill:
Her body sleeps in Capels' monument,
And her immortal part with angels lives.
I saw her laid low in her kindred's vault,
And presently took post to tell it you:
O, pardon me for bringing these ill news,
Since you did leave it for my office, sir.

Rom. Is it e'en so? then I defy you, stars!
Thou know'st my lodging: get me ink and paper,
And hire post-horses; I will hence to-night.

Bal. I do beseech you, sir, have patience:
Your looks are pale and wild, and do import
Some misadventure.

Rom. Tush, thou art deceived:
Leave me, and do the thing I bid thee do.
Hast thou no letters to me from the friar?
Bal. No, my good lord.
Rom. No matter: get thee gone,
And hire those horses; I 'll be with thee straight.
[*Exit Balthasar.*
Well, Juliet, I will lie with thee to-night.
Let 's see for means:—O mischief, thou art swift
To enter in the thoughts of desperate men!
I do remember an apothecary,
And hereabouts a' dwells, which late I noted
In tatter'd weeds, with overwhelming brows,
Culling of simples; meagre were his looks;
Sharp misery had worn him to the bones:
And in his needy shop a tortoise hung,
An alligator stuff'd and other skins
Of ill-shaped fishes; and about his shelves
A beggarly account of empty boxes,
Green earthen pots, bladders and musty seeds,
Remnants of packthread and old cakes of roses,
Were thinly scatter'd, to make up a show.
Noting this penury, to myself I said,
An if a man did need a poison now,
Whose sale is present death in Mantua,
Here lives a caitiff wretch would sell it him.
O, this same thought did but forerun my need,
And this same needy man must sell it me.
As I remember, this should be the house:
Being holiday, the beggar's shop is shut.
What, ho! apothecary!

Enter Apothecary.

Ap. Who calls so loud?
Rom. Come hither, man. I see that thou art poor;
Hold, there is forty ducats: let me have
A dram of poison; such soon-speeding gear
As will disperse itself through all the veins,
That the life-weary taker may fall dead,
And that the trunk may be discharged of breath
As violently as hasty powder fired
Doth hurry from the fatal cannon's womb.
Ap. Such mortal drugs I have; but Mantua's law
Is death to any he that utters them.
Rom. Art thou so bare and full of wretchedness,
And fear'st to die? famine is in thy cheeks,

Need and oppression starveth in thy eyes,
Contempt and beggary hangs upon thy back,
The world is not thy friend, nor the world's law:
The world affords no law to make thee rich;
Then be not poor, but break it, and take this.
Ap. My poverty, but not my will, consents.
Rom. I pay thy poverty and not thy will.
Ap. Put this in any liquid thing you will,
And drink it off; and, if you had the strength
Of twenty men, it would dispatch you straight.
Rom. There is thy gold, worse poison to men's souls,
Doing more murder in this loathsome world,
Than these poor compounds that thou mayst not sell:
I sell thee poison, thou hast sold me none.
Farewell: buy food, and get thyself in flesh.
Come, cordial and not poison, go with me
To Juliet's grave: for there must I use thee. [*Exeunt.*

Scene II

Friar Laurence's cell.

Enter Friar John.

Fri. J. Holy Franciscan friar! brother, ho!

Enter Friar Laurence.

Fri. L. This same should be the voice of Friar John.
Welcome from Mantua: what says Romeo?
Or, if his mind be writ, give me his letter.
Fri. J. Going to find a bare-foot brother out,
One of our order, to associate me,
Here in this city visiting the sick,
And finding him, the searchers of the town,
Suspecting that we both were in a house
Where the infectious pestilence did reign,
Seal'd up the doors and would not let us forth;
So that my speed to Mantua there was stay'd.
Fri. L. Who bare my letter then to Romeo?
Fri. J. I could not send it,—here it is again,—
Nor get a messenger to bring it thee,
So fearful were they of infection.
Fri. L. Unhappy fortune! by my brotherhood,
The letter was not nice, but full of charge
Of dear import, and the neglecting it
May do much danger. Friar John, go hence;
Get me an iron crow and bring it straight
Unto my cell.
Fri. J. Brother, I'll go and bring it thee. [*Exit.*

Fri. L. Now must I to the monument alone;
Within this three hours will fair Juliet wake:
She will beshrew me much that Romeo
Hath had no notice of these accidents;
But I will write again to Mantua,
And keep her at my cell till Romeo come:
Poor living corse, closed in a dead man's tomb! [*Exit.*

Scene III

A churchyard; in it a monument belonging to the Capulets.

Enter Paris and his Page, bearing flowers and a torch.

Par. Give me thy torch, boy: hence, and stand aloof:
Yet put it out, for I would not be seen.
Under yond yew-trees lay thee all along,
Holding thine ear close to the hollow ground;
So shall no foot upon the churchyard tread,
Being loose, unfirm, with digging up of graves,
But thou shalt hear it: whistle then to me,
As signal that thou hear'st something approach.
Give me those flowers. Do as I bid thee, go.

Page. [*Aside*] I am almost afraid to stand alone
Here in the churchyard; yet I will adventure. [*Retires.*

Par. Sweet flower, with flowers thy bridal bed I strew,—
O woe! thy canopy is dust and stones;—
Which with sweet water nightly I will dew,
Or, wanting that, with tears distill'd by moans:
The obsequies that I for thee will keep
Nightly shall be to strew thy grave and weep.
[*The Page whistles.*
The boy gives warning something doth approach.
What cursed foot wanders this way to-night,
To cross my obsequies and true love's rite?
What, with a torch! Muffle me, night, a while. [*Retires.*

Enter Romeo and Balthasar, with a torch, mattock, &c.

Rom. Give me that mattock and the wrenching iron.
Hold, take this letter; early in the morning
See thou deliver it to my lord and father.
Give me the light: upon thy life, I charge thee,
Whate'er thou hear'st or seest, stand all aloof,
And do not interrupt me in my course.
Why I descend into this bed of death
Is partly to behold my lady's face,
But chiefly to take thence from her dead finger
A precious ring, a ring that I must use
In dear employment: therefore hence, be gone:

But if thou, jealous, dost return to pry
In what I farther shall intend to do,
By heaven, I will tear thee joint by joint
And strew this hungry churchyard with thy limbs:
The time and my intents are savage-wild,
More fierce and more inexorable by far
Than empty tigers or the roaring sea.

Bal. I will be gone, sir, and not trouble you.

Rom. So shalt thou show me friendship. Take thou that:
Live, and be prosperous: and farewell, good fellow.

Bal. [*Aside*] For all this same, I'll hide me hereabout:
His looks I fear, and his intents I doubt. [*Retires.*

Rom. Thou detestable maw, thou womb of death,
Gorged with the dearest morsel of the earth,
Thus I enforce thy rotten jaws to open,
And in despite I'll cram thee with more food.
[*Opens the tomb.*

Par. This is that banish'd haughty Montague
That murder'd my love's cousin, with which grief,
It is supposed, the fair creature died,
And here is come to do some villanous shame
To the dead bodies: I will apprehend him. [*Comes forward.*
Stop thy unhallow'd toil, vile Montague!
Can vengeance be pursued further than death?
Condemned villain, I do apprehend thee:
Obey, and go with me; for thou must die.

Rom. I must indeed, and therefore came I hither.
Good gentle youth, tempt not a desperate man;
Fly hence and leave me: think upon these gone;
Let them affright thee. I beseech thee, youth,
Put not another sin upon my head,
By urging me to fury: O, be gone!
By heaven, I love thee better than myself,
For I come hither arm'd against myself:
Stay not, be gone: live, and hereafter say,
A madman's mercy bid thee run away.

Par. I do defy thy conjurations
And apprehend thee for a felon here.

Rom. Wilt thou provoke me? then have at thee, boy!
[*They fight.*

Page. O Lord, they fight! I will go call the watch. [*Exit.*

Par. O, I am slain! [*Falls.*] If thou be merciful,
Open the tomb, lay me with Juliet. [*Dies.*

Rom. In faith, I will. Let me peruse this face:
Mercutio's kinsman, noble County Paris!

What said my man, when my betossed soul
Did not attend him as we rode? I think
He told me Paris should have married Juliet:
Said he not so? or did I dream it so?
Or am I mad, hearing him talk of Juliet,
To think it was so? O, give me thy hand,
One writ with me in sour misfortune's book!
I 'll bury thee in a triumphant grave;
A grave? O, no, a lantern, slaughter'd youth;
For here lies Juliet, and her beauty makes
This vault a feasting presence full of light.
Death, lie thou there, by a dead man interr'd.
[*Laying Paris in the monument*
How oft when men are at the point of death
Have they been merry! which their keepers call
A lightning before death: O, how may I
Call this a lightning? O my love! my wife!
Death, that hath suck'd the honey of thy breath,
Hath had no power yet upon thy beauty:
Thou art not conquer'd; beauty's ensign yet
Is crimson in thy lips and in thy cheeks,
And death's pale flag is not advanced there.
Tybalt, liest thou there in thy bloody sheet?
O, what more favour can I do to thee
Than with that hand that cut thy youth in twain
To sunder his that was thine enemy?
Forgive me, cousin! Ah, dear Juliet,
Why art thou yet so fair? shall I believe
That unsubstantial death is amorous,
And that the lean abhorred monster keeps
Thee here in dark to be his paramour?
For fear of that, I still will stay with thee,
And never from this palace of dim night
Depart again: here, here will I remain
With worms that are thy chamber-maids; O, here
Will I set up my everlasting rest,
And shake the yoke of inauspicious stars
From this world-wearied flesh. Eyes, look your last!
Arms, take your last embrace! and, lips, O you
The doors of breath, seal with a righteous kiss
A dateless bargain to engrossing death!
Come, bitter conduct, come, unsavoury guide!
Thou desperate pilot, now at once run on
The dashing rocks thy sea-sick weary bark.
Here's to my love! [*Drinks.*] O true apothecary!

Thy drugs are quick. Thus with a kiss I die. [*Dies.*
Enter, at the other end of the churchyard, Friar Laurence, with a lantern, crow, and spade.

Fri. L. Saint Francis be my speed! how oft to-night
Have my old feet stumbled at graves! Who 's there?
Bal. Here 's one, a friend, and one that knows you well.
Fri. L. Bliss be upon you! Tell me, good my friend,
What torch is yond that vainly lends his light
To grubs and eyeless skulls? as I discern,
It burneth in the Capels' monument.
Bal It doth so, holy sir; and there 's my master,
One that you love.
Fri. L. Who is it?
Bal. Romeo.
Fri. L. How long hath he been there?
Bal. Full half an hour.
Fri. L. Go with me to the vault.
Bal. I dare not, sir:
My master knows not but I am gone hence;
And fearfully did menace me with death,
If I did stay to look on his intents.
Fri. L. Stay, then! I'll go alone: fear comes upon me;
O, much I fear some ill unlucky thing.
Bal. As I did sleep under this yew-tree here,
I dreamt my master and another fought,
And that my master slew him.
Fri. L. Romeo! [*Advances.*
Alack, alack, what blood is this, which stains
The stony entrance of this sepulchre?
What mean these masterless and gory swords
To lie discolour'd by this place of peace? [*Enters the tomb.*
Romeo! O, pale! Who else? what, Paris too?
And steep'd in blood? Ah, what an unkind hour
Is guilty of this lamentable chance!
The lady stirs. [*Juliet wakes.*
Jul. O comfortable friar! where is my lord?
I do remember well where I should be,
And there I am: where is my Romeo? [*Noise within.*
Fri. L. I hear some noise. Lady, come from that nest
Of death, contagion and unnatural sleep:
A greater power than we can contradict
Hath thwarted our intents: come, come away:
Thy husband in thy bosom there lies dead;
And Paris too: come, I'll dispose of thee
Among a sisterhood of holy nuns:

Stay not to question, for the watch is coming;
Come, go, good Juliet; I dare no longer stay.
Jul. Go, get thee hence, for I will not away. [*Exit Fri. L.*
What 's here? a cup, closed in my true love's hand?
Poison, I see, hath been his timeless end:
O churl! drunk all, and left no friendly drop
To help me after? I will kiss thy lips;
Haply some poison yet doth hang on them,
To make me die with a restorative. [*Kisses him.*
Thy lips are warm.
First Watch. [*Within*] Lead, boy: which way?
Jul. Yea, noise? then I'll be brief. O happy dagger!
[*Snatching Romeo's dagger.*
This is thy sheath [*Stabs herself*]; there rust, and let me die.
[*Falls on Romeo's body, and dies.*

Enter Watch, with the Page of Paris.

Page. This is the place; there, where the torch doth burn.
First Watch. The ground is bloody; search about the church-
Go, some of you, whoe'er you find attach. [yard:
Pitiful sight! here lies the county slain;
And Juliet bleeding, warm, and newly dead,
Who here hath lain this two days buried.
Go, tell the prince: run to the Capulets:
Raise up the Montagues: some others search:
We see the ground whereon these woes do lie;
But the true ground of all these piteous woes
We cannot without circumstance descry.

Re-enter some of the Watch, with Balthasar.

Sec. Watch. Here 's Romeo's man; we found him in the churchyard.
First Watch. Hold him in safety, till the prince come hither.

Re-enter Friar Laurence, and another Watchman.

Third Watch. Here is a friar, that trembles, sighs and weeps:
We took this mattock and this spade from him,
As he was coming from this churchyard's side.
First Watch. A great suspicion: stay the friar too.

Enter the Prince and Attendants.

Prince. What misadventure is so early up,
That calls our person from our morning rest?

Enter Capulet, Lady Capulet, and others.

Cap. What should it be that they so shriek abroad?
La. Cap. The people in the street cry Romeo,
Some Juliet, and some Paris, and all run
With open outcry toward our monument.
Prince. What fear is this which startles in our ears?

First Watch. Sovereign, here lies the County Paris slain;
And Romeo dead; and Juliet, dead before,
Warm and new kill'd.
Prince. Search, seek, and know how this foul murder comes.
First Watch. Here is a friar, and slaughter'd Romeo's man,
With instruments upon them fit to open
These dead men's tombs.
Cap. O heavens! O wife, look how our daughter bleeds!
This dagger hath mista'en, for, lo, his house
Is empty on the back of Montague,
And it mis-sheathed in my daughter's bosom!
La. Cap. O me! this sight of death is as a bell
That warns my old age to a sepulchre.

Enter Montague and others.

Prince. Come, Montague; for thou art early up,
To see thy son and heir more early down.
Mon. Alas, my liege, my wife is dead to-night;
Grief of my son's exile hath stopp'd her breath:
What further woe conspires against mine age?
Prince. Look, and thou shalt see.
Mon. O thou untaught! what manners is in this,
To press before thy father to a grave?
Prince. Seal up the mouth of outrage for a while,
Till we can clear these ambiguities,
And know their spring, their head, their true descent;
And then will I be general of your woes,
And lead you even to death: meantime forbear,
And let mischance be slave to patience.
Bring forth the parties of suspicion.
Fri. L. I am the greatest, able to do least,
Yet most suspected, as the time and place
Doth make against me, of this direful murder;
And here I stand, both to impeach and purge
Myself condemned and myself excused.
Prince. Then say at once what thou dost know in this.
Fri. L. I will be brief, for my short date of breath
Is not so long as is a tedious tale.
Romeo, there dead, was husband to that Juliet;
And she, there dead, that Romeo's faithful wife:
I married them; and their stol'n marriage-day
Was Tybalt's dooms-day, whose untimely death
Banish'd the new-made bridegroom from this city;
For whom, and not for Tybalt, Juliet pined.
You, to remove that siege of grief from her,
Betroth'd and would have married her perforce

To County Paris: then comes she to me,
And with wild looks bid me devise some means
To rid her from this second marriage,
Or in my cell there would she kill herself.
Then gave I her, so tutor'd by my art,
A sleeping potion; which so took effect
As I intended, for it wrought on her
The form of death: meantime I writ to Romeo,
That he should hither come as this dire night,
To help to take her from her borrow'd grave,
Being the time the potion's force should cease.
But he which bore my letter, Friar John,
Was stay'd by accident, and yesternight
Return'd my letter back. Then all alone
At the prefixed hour of her waking
Came I to take her from her kindred's vault,
Meaning to keep her closely at my cell
Till I conveniently could send to Romeo:
But when I came, some minute ere the time
Of her awaking, here untimely lay
The noble Paris and true Romeo dead.
She wakes, and I entreated her come forth,
And bear this work of heaven with patience:
But then a noise did scare me from the tomb,
And she too desperate would not go with me,
But, as it seems, did violence on herself.
All this I know; and to the marriage
Her nurse is privy: and, if aught in this
Miscarried by my fault, let my old life
Be sacrificed some hour before his time
Unto the rigour of severest law.

Prince. We still have known thee for a holy man.
Where 's Romeo's man? what can he say in this?

Bal. I brought my master news of Juliet's death,
And then in post he came from Mantua
To this same place, to this same monument.
This letter he early bid me give his father,
And threaten'd me with death, going in the vault,
If I departed not and left him there.

Prince. Give me the letter; I will look on it.
Where is the county's page, that raised the watch?
Sirrah, what made your master in this place?

Page. He came with flowers to strew his lady's grave;
And bid me stand aloof, and so I did:
Anon comes one with light to ope the tomb;

And by and by my master drew on him;
And then I ran away to call the watch.

Prince. This letter doth make good the friar's words,
Their course of love, the tidings of her death:
And here he writes that he did buy a poison
Of a poor 'pothecary, and therewithal
Came to this vault to die and lie with Juliet.
Where be these enemies? Capulet! Montague!
See, what a scourge is laid upon your hate,
That heaven finds means to kill your joys with love!
And I, for winking at your discords too,
Have lost a brace of kinsmen: all are punish'd.

Cap. O brother Montague, give me thy hand:
This is my daughter's jointure, for no more
Can I demand.

Mon. But I can give thee more:
For I will raise her statue in pure gold;
That whiles Verona by that name is known,
There shall no figure at such rate be set
As that of true and faithful Juliet.

Cap. As rich shall Romeo's by his lady's lie;
Poor sacrifices of our enmity!

Prince. A glooming peace this morning with it brings;
The sun for sorrow will not show his head:
Go hence, to have more talk of these sad things;
Some shall be pardon'd and some punished:
For never was a story of more woe
Than this of Juliet and her Romeo. [*Exeunt.*

THE TRAGEDY OF CORIOLANUS

DRAMATIS PERSONÆ

CAIUS MARCIUS, afterwards CAIUS MARCIUS CORIOLANUS.
TITUS LARTIUS, } generals against the
COMINIUS, } Volscians.
MENENIUS AGRIPPA, friend to Coriolanus.
SICINIUS VELUTUS, } tribunes of the
JUNIUS BRUTUS, } people.
YOUNG MARCIUS, son of Coriolanus.
A Roman Herald.
TULLUS AUFIDIUS, general of the Volscians.
Lieutenant to Aufidius.
Conspirators with Aufidius.
A Citizen of Antium.
Two Volscian Guards.

VOLUMNIA, mother to Coriolanus.
VIRGILIA, wife to Coriolanus.
VALERIA, friend to Virgilia.
Gentlewoman attending on Virgilia.

Roman and Volscian Senators, Patricians, Ædiles, Lictors, Soldiers, Citizens, Messengers, Servants to Aufidius, and other Attendants.

SCENE: *Rome and the neighbourhood; Corioli and the neighbourhood; Antium.*

ACT I—SCENE I

Rome. A street.

Enter a company of mutinous Citizens, with staves, clubs, and other weapons.

First Cit. Before we proceed any further, hear me speak.
All. Speak, speak.
First Cit. You are all resolved rather to die than to famish?
All. Resolved, resolved.
First Cit. First, you know Caius Marcius is chief enemy to the people.
All. We know 't, we know 't.
First Cit. Let us kill him, and we'll have corn at our own price. Is 't a verdict?
All. No more talking on 't; let it be done: away, away!
Sec. Cit. One word, good citizens.
First Cit. We are accounted poor citizens; the patricians, good. What authority surfeits on would relieve us: if they would yield us but the superfluity while it were wholesome, we might guess they relieved us humanely; but they think we are too dear: the leanness that afflicts us, the object of our misery, is as an inventory to particularize their abundance; our sufferance is a gain to them. Let us revenge this with our pikes, ere we become rakes: for the gods know I speak this in hunger for bread, not in thirst for revenge.
Sec. Cit. Would you proceed especially against Caius Marcius?
All. Against him first: he 's a very dog to the commonalty.
Sec. Cit. Consider you what services he has done for his country?
First Cit. Very well; and could be content to give him good report for 't, but that he pays himself with being proud.
Sec. Cit. Nay, but speak not maliciously.

First Cit. I say unto you, what he hath done famously, he did it to that end: though soft-conscienced men can be content to say it was for his country, he did it to please his mother and to be partly proud; which he is, even to the altitude of his virtue.

Sec. Cit. What he cannot help in his nature, you account a vice in him. You must in no way say he is covetous.

First Cit. If I must not, I need not be barren of accusations; he hath faults, with surplus, to tire in repetition. [*Shouts within.*] What shouts are these? The other side o' the city is risen: why stay we prating here? to the Capitol!

All. Come, come.

First Cit. Soft! who comes here?

Enter Menenius Agrippa.

Sec. Cit. Worthy Menenius Agrippa; one that hath always loved the people.

First Cit. He's one honest enough: would all the rest were so!

Men. What work's, my countrymen, in hand? where go you
With bats and clubs? the matter? speak, I pray you.

First Cit. Our business is not unknown to the senate; they have had inkling, this fortnight, what we intend to do, which now we'll show 'em in deeds. They say poor suitors have strong breaths: they shall know we have strong arms too.

Men. Why, masters, my good friends, mine honest neighbours,
Will you undo yourselves?

First Cit. We cannot, sir, we are undone already.

Men. I tell you, friends, most charitable care
Have the patricians of you. For your wants,
Your suffering in this dearth, you may as well
Strike at the heaven with your staves as lift them
Against the Roman state; whose course will on
The way it takes, cracking ten thousand curbs
Of more strong link asunder than can ever
Appear in your impediment. For the dearth,
The gods, not the patricians, make it, and
Your knees to them, not arms, must help. Alack,
You are transported by calamity
Thither where more attends you, and you slander
The helms o' the state, who care for you like fathers,
When you curse them as enemies.

First Cit. Care for us! True, indeed! They ne'er cared for us yet: suffer us to famish, and their store-houses crammed with grain; make edicts for usury, to support usurers; repeal daily any wholesome act established against the rich, and provide more piercing statutes daily, to chain up and restrain the poor. If the wars eat us not up, they will; and there 's all the love they bear us.

Men. Either you must
Confess yourselves wondrous malicious,
Or be accused of folly. I shall tell you
A pretty tale: it may be you have heard it;
But, since it serves my purpose, I will venture
To stale 't a little more.

First Cit. Well, I 'll hear it, sir: yet you must not think to fob off our disgrace with a tale: but, an 't please you, deliver.

Men. There was a time when all the body's members
Rebell'd against the belly; thus accused it:
That only like a gulf it did remain
I' the midst o' the body, idle and unactive,
Still cupboarding the viand, never bearing
Like labour with the rest; where the other instruments
Did see and hear, devise, instruct, walk, feel,
And, mutually participate, did minister
Unto the appetite and affection common
Of the whole body. The belly answer'd—

First Cit. Well, sir, what answer made the belly?

Men. Sir, I shall tell you. With a kind of smile,
Which ne'er came from the lungs, but even thus—
For, look you, I may make the belly smile
As well as speak—it tauntingly replied
To the discontented members, the mutinous parts
That envied his receipt; even so most fitly
As you malign our senators for that
They are not such as you.

First Cit. Your belly's answer? What!
The kingly-crowned head, the vigilant eye,
The counsellor heart, the arm our soldier,
Our steed the leg, the tongue our trumpeter,
With other muniments and petty helps
In this our fabric, if that they—

Men. What then?
'Fore me, this fellow speaks! what then? what then?

First Cit. Should by the cormorant belly be restrain'd,
Who is the sink o' the body,—

Men. Well, what then?

First Cit. The former agents, if they did complain,
What could the belly answer?

Men. I will tell you;
If you 'll bestow a small—of what you have little—
Patience awhile, you 'st hear the belly's answer.

First Cit. You 're long about it.
Men. Note me this, good friend;
Your most grave belly was deliberate,
Not rash like his accusers, and thus answer'd:
'True is it, my incorporate friends,' quoth he,
'That I receive the general food at first,
Which you do live upon; and fit it is,
Because I am the store-house and the shop
Of the whole body: but, if you do remember,
I send it through the rivers of your blood,
Even to the court, the heart, to the seat o' the brain;
And, through the cranks and offices of man,
The strongest nerves and small inferior veins
From me receive that natural competency
Whereby they live: and though that all at once,
You, my good friends,'—this says the belly, mark me—
First Cit. Ay, sir; well well.
Men. 'Though all at once cannot
See what I do deliver out to each,
Yet I can make my audit up, that all
From me do back receive the flour of all,
And leave me but the bran.' What say you to 't?
First Cit. It was an answer: how apply you this?
Men. The senators of Rome are this good belly,
And you the mutinous members: for examine
Their counsels and their cares, digest things rightly
Touching the weal o' the common, you shall find
No public benefit which you receive
But it proceeds or comes from them to you
And no way from yourselves. What do you think,
You, the great toe of this assembly?
First Cit. I the great toe! why the great toe?
Men. For that, being one o' the lowest, basest, poorest,
Of this most wise rebellion, thou go'st foremost:
Thou rascal, that art worst in blood to run,
Lead'st first to win some vantage.
But make you ready your stiff bats and clubs:
Rome and her rats are at the point of battle;
The one side must have bale.

Enter Caius Marcius.

Hail, noble Marcius!
Mar. Thanks. What 's the matter, you dissentious rogues,
That, rubbing the poor itch of your opinion,
Make yourselves scabs?
First Cit. We have ever your good word.

Mar. He that will give good words to thee will flatter
Beneath abhorring. What would you have, you curs,
That like nor peace nor war? the one affrights you,
The other makes you proud. He that trusts to you,
Where he should find you lions, finds you hares,
Where foxes, geese: you are no surer, no,
Than is the coal of fire upon the ice,
Or hailstone in the sun. Your virtue is
To make him worthy whose offence subdues him
And curse that justice did it. Who deserves greatness
Deserves your hate; and your affections are
A sick man's appetite, who desires most that
Which would increase his evil. He that depends
Upon your favours swims with fins of lead
And hews down oaks with rushes. Hang ye! Trust ye?
With every minute you do change a mind,
And call him noble that was now your hate,
Him vile that was your garland. What 's the matter,
That in these several places of the city
You cry against the noble senate, who,
Under the gods, keep you in awe, which else
Would feed on one another? What 's their seeking?
Men. For corn at their own rates; whereof, they say,
The city is well stored.
Mar. Hang 'em! They say!
They 'll sit by the fire, and presume to know
What 's done i' the Capitol; who 's like to rise,
Who thrives and who declines; side factions and give out
Conjectural marriages; making parties strong,
And feebling such as stand not in their liking
Below their cobbled shoes. They say there 's grain enough!
Would the nobility lay aside their ruth,
And let me use my sword, I 'ld make a quarry
With thousands of these quarter'd slaves, as high
As I could pick my lance.
Men. Nay, these are almost thoroughly persuaded;
For though abundantly they lack discretion,
Yet are they passing cowardly. But, I beseech you,
What says the other troop?
Mar. They are dissolved: hang 'em!
They said they were an-hungry; sigh'd forth proverbs,
That hunger broke stone walls, that dogs must eat,
That meat was made for mouths, that the gods sent not
Corn for the rich men only: with these shreds
They vented their complainings; which being answer'd,

And a petition granted them, a strange one—
To break the heart of generosity
And make bold power look pale—they threw their caps
As they would hang them on the horns o' the moon,
Shouting their emulation.

Men. What is granted them?

Mar. Five tribunes to defend their vulgar wisdoms,
Of their own choice: one 's Junius Brutus,
Sicinius Velutus, and I know not—'Sdeath!
The rabble should have first unroof'd the city,
Ere so prevail'd with me: it will in time
Win upon power and throw forth greater themes
For insurrection's arguing.

Men. This is strange.

Mar. Go get you home, you fragments!

Enter a Messenger, hastily.

Mess. Where 's Caius Marcius?

Mar. Here: what's the matter?

Mess. The news is, sir, the Volsces are in arms.

Mar. I am glad on 't: then we shall ha' means to vent
Our musty superfluity. See, our best elders.

Enter Cominius, Titus Lartius, and other Senators; Junius Brutus and Sicinius Velutus.

First Sen. Marcius, 'tis true that you have lately told us;
The Volsces are in arms.

Mar. They have a leader,
Tullus Aufidius, that will put you to 't.
I sin in envying his nobility;
And were I any thing but what I am,
I would wish me only he.

Com. You have fought together?

Mar. Were half to half the world by the ears, and he
Upon my party, I 'ld revolt, to make
Only my wars with him: he is a lion
That I am proud to hunt.

First Sen. Then, worthy Marcius,
Attend upon Cominius to these wars.

Com. It is your former promise.

Mar. Sir, it is;
And I am constant. Titus Lartius, thou
Shalt see me once more strike at Tullus' face.
What, art thou stiff? stand'st out?

Tit. No, Caius Marcius;
I 'll lean upon one crutch, and fight with t' other,
Ere stay behind this business.

Men. O, true-bred!
First Sen. Your company to the Capitol; where, I know,
Our greatest friends attend us.
Tit. [*To Com.*] Lead you on.
[*To Mar.*] Follow Cominius; we must follow you;
Right worthy you priority.
Com. Noble Marcius!
First Sen. [*To the Citizens*] Hence to your homes; be gone!
Mar. Nay, let them follow:
The Volsces have much corn; take these rats thither
To gnaw their garners. Worshipful mutiners,
Your valour puts well forth: pray, follow.
[*Citizens steal away. Exeunt all but Sicinius and Brutus.*
Sic. Was ever man so proud as is this Marcius?
Bru. He has no equal.
Sic. When we were chosen tribunes for the people,—
Bru. Mark'd you his lip and eyes?
Sic. Nay, but his taunts.
Bru. Being moved, he will not spare to gird the gods.
Sic. Bemock the modest moon.
Bru. The present wars devour him! he is grown
Too proud to be so valiant.
Sic. Such a nature,
Tickled with good success, disdains the shadow
Which he treads on at noon: but I do wonder
His insolence can brook to be commanded
Under Cominius.
Bru, Fame, at the which he aims.
In whom already he 's well graced, cannot
Better be held, nor more attain'd, than by
A place below the first: for what miscarries
Shall be the general's fault, though he perform
To the utmost of a man; and giddy censure
Will then cry out of Marcius 'O, if he
Had borne the business!'
Sic. Besides, if things go well,
Opinion, that so sticks on Marcius, shall
Of his demerits rob Cominius.
Bru. Come:
Half all Cominius' honours are to Marcius,
Though Marcius earn'd them not; and all his faults
To Marcius shall be honours, though indeed
In aught he merit not.
Sic. Let 's hence, and hear
How the dispatch is made; and in what fashion,

More than his singularity, he goes
Upon this present action.

Bru. Let 's along. [*Exeunt.*

Scene II

Corioli. The Senate-house.

Enter Tullus Aufidius, with Senators of Corioli.

First Sen. So, your opinion is, Aufidius,
That they of Rome are enter'd in our counsels,
And know how we proceed.

Auf. Is it not yours?
What ever have been thought on in this state,
That could be brought to bodily act ere Rome
Had circumvention? 'Tis not four days gone
Since I heard thence: these are the words: I think
I have the letter here: yes, here it is:
[*Reads*] 'They have press'd a power, but it is not known
Whether for east or west: the dearth is great;
The people mutinous: and it is rumour'd,
Cominius, Marcius your old enemy,
Who is of Rome worse hated than of you,
And Titus Lartius, a most valiant Roman,
These three lead on this preparation
Whither 'tis bent: most likely 'tis for you:
Consider of it.'

First Sen. Our army 's in the field:
We never yet made doubt but Rome was ready
To answer us.

Auf. Nor did you think it folly
To keep your great pretences veil'd till when
They needs must show themselves; which in the hatching,
It seem'd, appear'd to Rome. By the discovery
We shall be shorten'd in our aim, which was
To take in many towns ere almost Rome
Should know we were afoot.

Sec. Sen. Noble Aufidius,
Take your commission; hie you to your bands:
Let us alone to guard Corioli:
If they set down before 's, for the remove
Bring up your army; but, I think, you 'll find
They 've not prepared for us.

Auf. O, doubt not that;
I speak from certainties. Nay, more,
Some parcels of their power are forth already,
And only hitherward. I leave your honours.

If we and Caius Marcius chance to meet,
'Tis sworn between us, we shall ever strike
Till one can do no more.

All. The gods assist you!

Auf. And keep your honours safe!

First Sen. Farewell.

Sec. Sen. Farewell.

All. Farewell. [*Exeunt.*

Scene III

Rome. A room in Marcius' house.

Enter Volumnia and Virgilia: they set them down on two low stools and sew.

Vol. I pray you, daughter, sing, or express yourself in a more comfortable sort: if my son were my husband, I should freelier rejoice in that absence wherein he won honour than in the embracements of his bed where he would show most love. When yet he was but tender-bodied, and the only son of my womb; when youth with comeliness plucked all gaze his way; when, for a day of kings' entreaties, a mother should not sell him an hour from her beholding; I, considering how honour would become such a person; that it was no better than picture-like to hang by the wall, if renown made it not stir, was pleased to let him seek danger where he was like to find fame. To a cruel war I sent him; from whence he returned, his brows bound with oak. I tell thee, daughter, I sprang not more in joy at first hearing he was a man-child than now in first seeing he had proved himself a man.

Vir. But had he died in the business, madam: how then?

Vol. Then his good report should have been my son; I therein would have found issue. Here me profess sincerely: had I a dozen sons, each in my love alike, and none less dear than thine and my good Marcius, I had rather had eleven die nobly for their country than one voluptuously surfeit out of action.

Enter a Gentlewoman.

Gent. Madam, the Lady Valeria is come to visit you.

Vir. Beseech you, give me leave to retire myself.

Vol. Indeed, you shall not.
Methinks I hear hither your husband's drum;
See him pluck Aufidius down by the hair;
As children from a bear, the Volsces shunning him:
Methinks I see him stamp thus, and call thus:
'Come on, you cowards! you were got in fear,
Though you were born in Rome:' his bloody brow

With his mail'd hand then wiping, forth he goes,
Like to a harvest-man that 's task'd to mow
Or all, or lose his hire.

Vir. His bloody brow! O Jupiter, no blood!

Vol. Away, you fool! it more becomes a man
Than gilt his trophy: the breasts of Hecuba,
When she did suckle Hector, look'd not lovelier
Than Hector's forehead when it spit forth blood
At Grecian sword, contemning. Tell Valeria
We are fit to bid her welcome. [*Exit Gent.*

Vir. Heavens bless my lord from fell Aufidius!

Vol. He 'll beat Aufidius' head below his knee,
And tread upon his neck.

Enter Valeria, with an Usher and Gentlewoman.

Val. My ladies both, good day to you.

Vol. Sweet madam.

Vir. I am glad to see your ladyship.

Val. How do you both? you are manifest housekeepers. What are you sewing here? A fine spot, in good faith. How does your little son?

Vir. I thank your ladyship; well, good madam.

Vol. He had rather see the swords and hear a drum than look upon his schoolmaster.

Val. O' my word, the father's son: I 'll swear, 'tis a very pretty boy. O' my troth, I looked upon him o' Wednesday half an hour together; has such a confirmed countenance. I saw him run after a gilded butterfly; and when he caught it, he let it go again; and after it again; and over and over he comes, and up again; catched it again: or whether his fall enraged him, or how 'twas, he did so set his teeth, and tear it; O, I warrant, how he mammocked it!

Vol. One on 's father's moods.

Val. Indeed, la, 'tis a noble child.

Vir. A crack, madam.

Val. Come, lay aside your stitchery; I must have you play the idle huswife with me this afternoon.

Vir. No, good madam; I will not out of doors.

Val. Not out of doors!

Vol. She shall, she shall.

Vir. Indeed, no, by your patience; I 'll not over the threshold till my lord return from the wars.

Val. Fie, you confine yourself most unreasonably: come, you must go visit the good lady that lies in.

Vir. I will wish her speedy strength, and visit her with my prayers; but I cannot go thither.

Vol. Why, I pray you?

Vir. 'Tis not to save labour, nor that I want love.

Val. You would be another Penelope: yet, they say, all the yarn she spun in Ulysses' absence did but fill Ithaca full of moths. Come; I would your cambric were sensible as your finger, that you might leave pricking it for pity. Come, you shall go with us.

Vir. No, good madam, pardon me; indeed, I will not forth.

Val. In truth, la, go with me, and I 'll tell you excellent news of your husband.

Vir. O, good madam, there can be none yet.

Val. Verily, I do not jest with you; there came news from him last night.

Vir. Indeed, madam?

Val. In earnest, it 's true; I heard a senator speak it. Thus it is: the Volsces have an army forth; against whom Cominius the general is gone, with one part of our Roman power: your lord and Titus Lartius are set down before their city Corioli; they nothing doubt prevailing, and to make it brief wars. This is true, on mine honour; and so, I pray, go with us.

Vir. Give me excuse, good madam; I will obey you in every thing hereafter.

Vol. Let her alone, lady; as she is now, she will but disease our better mirth.

Val. In troth, I think she would. Fare you well, then. Come, good sweet lady. Prithee, Virgilia, turn thy solemnness out o' door, and go along with us.

Vir. No, at a word, madam; indeed, I must not. I wish you much mirth.

Val. Well then, farewell. [*Exeunt.*

Scene IV

Before Corioli.

Enter, with drum and colours, Marcius, Titus Lartius, Captains and Soldiers. To them a Messenger.

Mar. Yonder comes news: a wager they have met.

Lart. My horse to yours, no.

Mar. 'Tis done.

Lart. Agreed.

Mar. Say, has our general met the enemy?

Mess. They lie in view; but have not spoke as yet.

Lart. So, the good horse is mine.

Mar. I 'll buy him of you.

Lart. No, I'll nor sell nor give him: lend you him I will

For half a hundred years. Summon the town.
Mar. How far off lie these armies?
Mess. Within this mile and half.
Mar. Then shall we hear their 'larum, and they ours.
Now, Mars, I prithee, make us quick in work,
That we with smoking swords may march from hence,
To help our fielded friends! Come, blow thy blast.
They sound a parley. Enter two Senators with others, on the walls.
Tullus Aufidius, is he within your walls?
First Sen. No, nor a man that fears you less than he,
That 's lesser than a little. Hark, our drums [*Drum afar off.*
Are bringing forth our youth! we 'll break our walls,
Rather than they shall pound us up: our gates,
Which yet seem shut, we have but pinn'd with rushes;
They 'll open of themselves. Hark you, far off!
[*Alarum far off.*
There is Aufidius; list, what work he makes
Amongst your cloven army.
Mar. O, they are at it!
Lart. Their noise be our instruction. Ladders, ho!

Enter the army of the Volsces.

Mar. They fear us not, but issue forth their city.
Now put your shields before your hearts, and fight
With hearts more proof than shields. Advance, brave Titus:
They do disdain us much beyond our thoughts,
Which makes me sweat with wrath. Come on, my fellows:
He that retires, I 'll take him for a Volsce,
And he shall feel mine edge.

Alarum. The Romans are beat back to their trenches.
Re-enter Marcius, cursing.

Mar. All the contagion of the south light on you,
You shames of Rome! you herd of— Boils and plagues
Plaster you o'er; that you may be abhorr'd
Farther than seen, and one infect another
Against the wind a mile! You souls of geese,
That bear the shapes of men, how have you run
From slaves that apes would beat! Pluto and hell!
All hurt behind; backs red, and faces pale
With flight and agued fear! Mend, and charge home,
Or, by the fires of heaven, I 'll leave the foe,
And make my wars on you; look to 't: come on;
If you 'll stand fast, we 'll beat them to their wives,
As they us to our trenches followed.
Another alarum. The Volsces fly, and Marcius follows them to the gates.

So, now the gates are ope : now prove good seconds :
'Tis for the followers fortune widens them,
Not for the fliers: mark me, and do the like. [*Enters the gates.*

First Sol. Fool-hardiness ; not I.

Sec. Sol. Nor I. [*Marcius is shut in.*

First Sol. See, they have shut him in.

All. To the pot, I warrant him.

[*Alarum continues.*

Re-enter Titus Lartius.

Lart. What is become of Marcius ?

All. Slain, sir, doubtless.

First Sol. Following the fliers at the very heels,
With them he enters ; who, upon the sudden,
Clapp'd to their gates : he is himself alone,
To answer all the city.

Lart. O noble fellow !
Who sensibly outdares his senseless sword,
And, when it bows, stands up ! Thou art left, Marcius :
A carbuncle entire, as big as thou art,
Were not so rich a jewel. Thou wast a soldier
Even to Cato's wish, not fierce and terrible
Only in strokes ; but, with thy grim looks and
The thunder-like percussion of thy sounds,
Thou madest thine enemies shake, as if the world
Were feverous and did tremble.

Re-enter Marcius, bleeding, assaulted by the enemy.

First Sol. Look, sir.

Lart. O, 'tis Marcius !
Let 's fetch him off, or make remain alike.

[*They fight, and all enter the city.*

Scene V

Within Corioli. A street.

Enter certain Romans, with spoils.

First Rom. This will I carry to Rome.

Sec. Rom. And I this.

Third Rom. A murrain on 't ! I took this for silver.

[*Alarum continues still afar off*

Enter Marcius and Titus Lartius with a trumpet.

Mar. See here these movers that do prize their hours
At a crack'd drachma ! Cushions, leaden spoons,
Irons of a doit, doublets that hangmen would
Bury with those that wore them, these base slaves,
Ere yet the fight be done, pack up : down with them !
And hark, what noise the general makes ! To him !

There is the man of my soul's hate, Aufidius,
Piercing our Romans: then, valiant Titus, take
Convenient numbers to make good the city;
Whilst I, with those that have the spirit, will haste
To help Cominius.

Lart. Worthy sir, thou bleed'st;
Thy exercise hath been too violent
For a second course of fight.

Mar. Sir, praise me not;
My work hath yet not warm'd me: fare you well:
The blood I drop is rather physical
Than dangerous to me: to Aufidius thus
I will appear, and fight.

Lart. Now the fair goddess, Fortune,
Fall deep in love with thee; and her great charms
Misguide thy opposers' swords! Bold gentleman,
Prosperity be thy page!

Mar. Thy friend no less
Than those she placeth highest! So farewell.

Lart. Thou worthiest Marcius! [*Exit Marcius.*
Go sound thy trumpet in the market-place;
Call thither all the officers o' the town,
Where they shall know our mind. Away! [*Exeunt.*

Scene VI

Near the camp of Cominius.

Enter Cominius, as it were in retire, with Soldiers.

Com. Breathe you, my friends: well fought; we are come off
Like Romans, neither foolish in our stands,
Nor cowardly in retire: believe me, sirs,
We shall be charged again. Whiles we have struck,
By interims and conveying gusts we have heard
The charges of our friends. Ye Roman gods,
Lead their successes as we wish our own,
That both our powers, with smiling fronts encountering,
May give you thankful sacrifice!

Enter a Messenger.

Thy news?

Mess. The citizens of Corioli have issued,
And given to Lartius and to Marcius battle:
I saw our party to their trenches driven,
And then I came away.

Com. Though thou speak'st truth,
Methinks thou speak'st not well. How long is 't since?

Mess. Above an hour, my lord.

Com. 'Tis not a mile; briefly we heard their drums:
How couldst thou in a mile confound an hour,
And bring thy news so late?
Mess. Spies of the Volsces
Held me in chase, that I was forced to wheel
Three or four miles about; else had I, sir,
Half an hour since brought my report.

Enter Marcius.

Com. Who's yonder,
That does appear as he were flay'd? O gods!
He has the stamp of Marcius; and I have
Before-time seen him thus.
Mar. Come I too late?
Com. The shepherd knows not thunder from a tabor
More than I know the sound of Marcius' tongue
From every meaner man.
Mar. Come I too late?
Com. Ay, if you come not in the blood of others,
But mantled in your own.
Mar. O, let me clip ye
In arms as sound as when I woo'd; in heart
As merry as when our nuptial day was done,
And tapers burn'd to bedward!
Com. Flower of warriors,
How is 't with Titus Lartius?
Mar. As with a man busied about decrees:
Condemning some to death, and some to exile;
Ransoming him or pitying, threatening the other;
Holding Corioli in the name of Rome,
Even like a fawning greyhound in the leash,
To let him slip at will.
Com. Where is that slave
Which told me they had beat you to your trenches?
Where is he? call him hither.
Mar. Let him alone;
He did inform the truth: but for our gentlemen,
The common file—a plague! tribunes for them!—
The mouse ne'er shunn'd the cat as they did budge
From rascals worse than they.
Com. But how prevail'd you?
Mar. Will the time serve to tell? I do not think.
Where is the enemy? are you lords o' the field?
If not, why cease you till you are so?
Com. Marcius,
We have at disadvantage fought, and did

Retire to win our purpose.
Mar. How lies their battle? know you on which side
They have placed their men of trust?
Com. As I guess, Marcius,
Their bands i' the vaward are the Antiates,
Of their best trust; o'er them Aufidius,
Their very heart of hope.
Mar. I do beseech you,
By all the battles wherein we have fought,
By the blood we have shed together, by the vows
We have made to endure friends, that you directly
Set me against Aufidius and his Antiates;
And that you not delay the present, but,
Filling the air with swords advanced and darts,
We prove this very hour.
Com. Though I could wish
You were conducted to a gentle bath,
And balms applied to you, yet dare I never
Deny your asking: take your choice of those
That best can aid your action.
Mar. Those are they
That most are willing. If any such be here—
As it were sin to doubt—that love this painting
Wherein you see me smear'd; if any fear
Lesser his person than an ill report;
If any think brave death outweighs bad life,
And that his country's dearer than himself;
Let him alone, or so many so minded,
Wave thus, to express his disposition,
And follow Marcius.
[*They all shout, and wave their swords; take him up in their arms, and cast up their caps.*
O, me alone! make you a sword of me?
If these shows be not outward, which of you
But is four Volsces? none of you but is
Able to bear against the great Aufidius
A shield as hard as his. A certain number,
Though thanks to all, must I select from all: the rest
Shall bear the business in some other fight,
As cause will be obey'd. Please you to march;
And four shall quickly draw out my command,
Which men are best inclined.
Com. March on, my fellows:
Make good this ostentation, and you shall
Divide in all with us. [*Exeunt.*

Scene VII

The gates of Corioli.

Titus Lartius, having set a guard upon Corioli, going with drum and trumpet toward Cominius and Caius Marcius, enters with a Lieutenant, other Soldiers, and a Scout.

Lart. So, let the ports be guarded: keep your duties,
As I have set them down. If I do send, dispatch
Those centuries to our aid; the rest will serve
For a short holding; if we lose the field,
We cannot keep the town.
Lieu. Fear not our care, sir.
Lart. Hence, and shut your gates upon 's.
Our guider, come; to the Roman camp conduct us.
[*Exeunt.*

Scene VIII

A field of battle between the Roman and the Volscian camps.

Alarum as in battle. Enter, from opposite sides, Marcius and Aufidius.

Mar. I 'll fight with none but thee; for I do hate thee
Worse than a promise-breaker.
Auf. We hate alike:
Not Afric owns a serpent I abhor
More than thy fame and envy. Fix thy foot.
Mar. Let the first budger die the other's slave,
And the gods doom him after!
Auf. If I fly, Marcius,
Holloa me like a hare.
Mar. Within these three hours, Tullus,
Alone I fought in your Corioli walls,
And made what work I pleased: 'tis not my blood
Wherein thou seest me mask'd; for thy revenge
Wrench up thy power to the highest.
Auf. Wert thou the Hector
That was the whip of your bragg'd progeny.
Thou shouldst not 'scape me here.
[*They fight, and certain Volsces come in the aid of Aufidius. Marcius fights till they be driven in breathless.*
Officious, and not valiant, you have shamed me
In your condemned seconds. [*Exeunt.*

Scene IX

The Roman camp.

Flourish. Alarum. A retreat is sounded. Enter, from one side, Cominius with the Romans; from the other side, Marcius, with his arm in a scarf.

Com. If I should tell thee o'er this thy day's work,
Thou 'lt not believe thy deeds: but I 'll report it,
Where senators shall mingle tears with smiles;
Where great patricians shall attend, and shrug,
I' the end admire; where ladies shall be frighted,
And, gladly quaked, hear more; where the dull tribunes,
That, with the fusty plebeians, hate thine honours,
Shall say against their hearts 'We thank the gods
Our Rome hath such a soldier.'
Yet camest thou to a morsel of this feast,
Having fully dined before.

Enter Titus Lartius, with his power, from the pursuit.

Lart. O general,
Here is the steed, we the caparison:
Hadst thou beheld—

Mar. Pray now, no more: my mother,
Who has a charter to extol her blood,
When she does praise me grieves me. I have done
As you have done; that 's what I can: induced
As you have been; that 's for my country:
He that has but effected his good will
Hath overta'en mine act.

Com. You shall not be
The grave of your deserving; Rome must know
The value of her own: 'twere a concealment
Worse than a theft, no less than a traducement,
To hide your doings; and to silence that,
Which, to the spire and top of praises vouch'd,
Would seem but modest: therefore, I beseech you—
In sign of what you are, not to reward
What you have done—before our army hear me.

Mar. I have some wounds upon me, and they smart
To hear themselves remember'd.

Com. Should they not,
Well might they fester 'gainst ingratitude,
And tent themselves with death. Of all the horses,
Whereof we have ta'en good, and good store, of all
The treasure in this field achieved and city,
We render you the tenth; to be ta'en forth,
Before the common distribution, at

Your only choice.
Mar. I thank you, general;
But cannot make my heart consent to take
A bribe to pay my sword: I do refuse it,
And stand upon my common part with those
That have beheld the doing.
[*A long flourish. They all cry 'Marcius! Marcius!' cast up their caps and lances: Cominius and Lartius stand bare.*
Mar. May these same instruments, which you profane,
Never sound more! when drums and trumpets shall
I' the field prove flatterers, let courts and cities be
Made all of false-faced soothing!
When steel grows soft as the parasite's silk,
Let him be made a coverture for the wars!
No more, I say! For that I have not wash'd
My nose that bled, or foil'd some debile wretch,
Which without note here's many else have done,
You shout me forth
In acclamations hyperbolical;
As if I loved my little should be dieted
In praises sauced with lies.
Com. Too modest are you;
More cruel to your good report than grateful
To us that give you truly: by your patience,
If 'gainst yourself you be incensed, we'll put you,
Like one that means his proper harm, in manacles,
Then reason safely with you. Therefore, be it known,
As to us, to all the world, that Caius Marcius
Wears this war's garland: in token of the which,
My noble steed, known to the camp, I give him,
With all his trim belonging; and from this time,
For what he did before Corioli, call him,
With all the applause and clamour of the host,
CAIUS MARCIUS CORIOLANUS. Bear
The addition nobly ever!
[*Flourish. Trumpets sound, and drums.*
All. Caius Marcius Coriolanus!
Cor. I will go wash;
And when my face is fair, you shall perceive
Whether I blush, or no: howbeit, I thank you:
I mean to stride your steed; and at all times
To undercrest your good addition
To the fairness of my power.
Com. So, to our tent;
Where, ere we do repose us, we will write

To Rome of our success. You, Titus Lartius,
Must to Corioli back: send us to Rome
The best, with whom we may articulate
For their own good and ours.

Lart. I shall, my lord.

Cor. The gods begin to mock me. I, that now
Refused most princely gifts, am bound to beg
Of my lord general.

Com. Take 't; 'tis yours. What is 't?

Cor. I sometime lay here in Corioli
At a poor man's house; he used me kindly:
He cried to me; I saw him prisoner;
But then Aufidius was within my view,
And wrath o'erwhelm'd my pity: I request you
To give my poor host freedom.

Com. O, well begg'd!
Were he the butcher of my son, he should
Be free as is the wind. Deliver him, Titus.

Lart. Marcius, his name?

Cor. By Jupiter, forgot:
I am weary; yea, my memory is tired.
Have we no wine here?

Com. Go we to our tent:
The blood upon your visage dries; 'tis time
It should be look'd to: come. [*Exeunt.*

Scene X

The camp of the Volsces.

A flourish. Cornets. Enter Tullus Aufidius, bloody, with two or three Soldiers.

Auf. The town is ta'en!

First Sol. 'Twill be deliver'd back on good condition.

Auf. Condition!
I would I were a Roman; for I cannot,
Being a Volsce, be that I am. Condition!
What good condition can a treaty find
I' the part that is at mercy? Five times, Marcius,
I have fought with thee; so often hast thou beat me;
And wouldst do so, I think, should we encounter
As often as we eat. By the elements,
If e'er again I meet him beard to beard,
He 's mine, or I am his: mine emulation
Hath not that honour in 't it had; for where
I thought to crush him in an equal force,
True sword to sword, I 'll potch at him some way,

Or wrath or craft may get him.

First Sol. He 's the devil.

Auf. Bolder, though not so subtle. My valour 's poison'd
With only suffering stain by him; for him
Shall fly out of itself: nor sleep nor sanctuary,
Being naked, sick, nor fane nor Capitol,
The prayers of priests nor times of sacrifice,
Embarquements all of fury, shall lift up
Their rotten privilege and custom 'gainst
My hate to Marcius: where I find him, were it
At home, upon my brother's guard, even there,
Against the hospitable canon, would I
Wash my fierce hand in 's heart. Go you to the city;
Learn how 'tis held, and what they are that must
Be hostages for Rome.

First Sol. Will not you go?

Auf. I am attended at the cypress grove: I pray you—
'Tis south the city mills—bring me word thither
How the world goes, that to the pace of it
I may spur on my journey.

First Sol. I shall, sir. [*Exeunt.*

ACT II—SCENE I

Rome. A public place.

Enter Menenius, with the two Tribunes of the people, Sicinius and Brutus.

Men. The augurer tells me we shall have news to-night.

Bru. Good or bad?

Men. Not according to the prayer of the people, for they love [not Marcius.

Sic. Nature teaches beasts to know their friends.

Men. Pray you, who does the wolf love?

Sic. The lamb.

Men. Ay, to devour him; as the hungry plebeians would the noble Marcius.

Bru. He 's a lamb indeed, that baes like a bear.

Men. He 's a bear indeed, that lives like a lamb. You two are old men: tell me one thing that I shall ask you.

Both. Well, sir.

Men. In what enormity is Marcius poor in, that you two have not in abundance?

Bru. He 's poor in no one fault, but stored with all.

Sic. Especially in pride.

Bru. And topping all others in boasting.

Men. This is strange now: do you two know how you are

censured here in the city, I mean of us o' the right-hand file? do you?

Both. Why, how are we censured?

Men. Because you talk of pride now,—will you not be angry?

Both. Well, well, sir, well.

Men. Why, 'tis no great matter; for a very little thief of occasion will rob you of a great deal of patience: give your dispositions the reins, and be angry at your pleasures; at the least, if you take it as a pleasure to you in being so. You blame Marcius for being proud?

Bru. We do it not alone, sir.

Men. I know you can do very little alone; for your helps are many, or else your actions would grow wondrous single: your abilities are too infant-like for doing much alone. You talk of pride: O that you could turn your eyes toward the napes of your necks, and make but an interior survey of your good selves! O that you could!

Both. What then, sir?

Men. Why, then you should discover a brace of unmeriting, proud, violent, testy magistrates, alias fools, as any in Rome.

Sic. Menenius, you are known well enough too.

Men. I am known to be a humorous patrician, and one that loves a cup of hot wine with not a drop of allaying Tiber in't; said to be something imperfect in favouring the first complaint, hasty and tinder-like upon too trivial motion; one that converses more with the buttock of the night than with the forehead of the morning: what I think I utter, and spend my malice in my breath. Meeting two such wealsmen as you are,—I cannot call you Lycurguses—if the drink you give me touch my palate adversely, I make a crooked face at it. I can't say your worships have delivered the matter well, when I find the ass in compound with the major part of your syllables: and though I must be content to bear with those that say you are reverend grave men, yet they lie deadly that tell you you have good faces. If you see this in the map of my microcosm, follows it that I am known well enough too? what harm can your bisson conspectuities glean out of this character, if I be known well enough too?

Bru. Come, sir, come, we know you well enough.

Men. You know neither me, yourselves, nor any thing. You are ambitious for poor knaves' caps and legs: you wear out a good wholesome forenoon in hearing a cause between an orange-wife and a fosset-seller, and then rejourn the controversy of three-pence to a second day of audience. When you are hearing a matter between party and party, if you chance to be pinched with the colic, you make faces like mummers; set up the bloody flag against all patience; and, in roaring for a chamber-pot, dismiss the controversy bleeding, the more entangled by your hearing: all the peace you make in their cause is, calling both the parties knaves. You are a pair of strange ones.

Bru. Come, come, you are well understood to be a perfecter giber for the table than a necessary bencher in the Capitol.

Men. Our very priests must become mockers, if they shall encounter such ridiculous subjects as you are. When you speak best unto the purpose, it is not worth the wagging of your beards; and your beards deserve not so honourable a grave as to stuff a botcher's cushion, or to be entombed in an ass's pack-saddle. Yet you must be saying, Marcius is proud; who, in a cheap estimation, is worth all your predecessors since Deucalion; though peradventure some of the best of 'em were hereditary hangmen. God-den to your worships: more of your conversation would infect my brain, being the herdsmen of the beastly plebeians: I will be bold to take my leave of you. [*Brutus and Sicinius go aside.*

Enter Volumnia, Virgilia, and Valeria.

How now, my as fair as noble ladies,—and the moon, were she earthly, no nobler—whither do you follow your eyes so fast?
[the love of Juno, let's go.

Vol. Honourable Menenius, my boy Marcius approaches; for

Men. Ha! Marcius coming home? [approbation.

Vol. Ay, worthy Menenius; and with most prosperous

Men. Take my cap, Jupiter, and I thank thee. Hoo! Marcius
[coming home?

Vir. } *Val.* } Nay, 'tis true.

Vol. Look, here 's a letter from him: the state hath another, his wife another; and, I think, there 's one at home for you.

Men. I will make my very house reel to-night: a letter for me?

Vir. Yes, certain, there 's a letter for you; I saw 't.

Men. A letter for me! it gives me an estate of seven years' health; in which time I will make a lip at the physician: the most sovereign prescription in Galen is but empiricutic, and, to this preservative, of no better report than a horse-drench. Is he not wounded? he was wont to come home

Vir. O, no, no, no. [wounded.

Vol. O, he is wounded; I thank the gods for 't.

Men. So do I too, if it be not too much: brings a' victory in his pocket? the wounds become him.

Vol. On 's brows: Menenius, he comes the third time home with the oaken garland.

Men. Has he disciplined Aufidius soundly? [got off.

Vol. Titus Lartius writes, they fought together, but Aufidius

Men. And 'twas time for him too, I 'll warrant him that: an he had stayed by him, I would not have been so fidiused for all the chests in Corioli, and the gold that 's in them. Is the senate possessed of this?

Vol. Good ladies, let 's go. Yes, yes, yes; the senate has letters from the general, wherein he gives my son the whole name of the war: he hath in this action outdone his former deeds doubly.

Val. In troth, there 's wondrous things spoke of him.

Men. Wondrous! ay, I warrant you, and not without his true

Vir. The gods grant them true! [purchasing.

Vol. True! pow, wow.

Men. True! I 'll be sworn they are true. Where is he wounded? [*To the Tribunes*] God save your good worships! Marcius is coming home: he has more cause to be proud. Where is he wounded?

Vol. I' the shoulder and i' the left arm: there will be large cicatrices to show the people, when he shall stand for his place. He received in the repulse of Tarquin seven hurts i' the body.

Men. One i' the neck, and two i' the thigh; there 's nine that I know.

Vol. He had, before this last expedition, twenty five wounds upon him.

Men. Now it 's twenty seven: every gash was an enemy's grave. [*A shout and flourish.*] Hark! the trumpets.

Vol. These are the ushers of Marcius: before him he carries noise, and behind him he leaves tears:
Death, that dark spirit, in 's nervy arm doth lie;
Which, being advanced, declines, and then men die.

A sennet. Trumpets sound. Enter Cominius and Titus Lartius; between them, Coriolanus crowned with an oaken garland; with Captains and Soldiers, and a Herald.

Her. Know, Rome, that all alone Marcius did fight
Within Corioli gates: where he hath won,
With fame, a name to Caius Marcius; these
In honour follows Coriolanus.
Welcome to Rome, renowned Coriolanus! [*Flourish.*

All. Welcome to Rome, renowned Coriolanus!

Cor. No more of this, it does offend my heart;
Pray now, no more.

Com. Look, sir, your mother!

Cor. O,

You have, I know, petition'd all the gods
For my prosperity! [*Kneels.*
Vol. Nay, my good soldier, up;
My gentle Marcius, worthy Caius, and
By deed-achieving honour newly named,—
What is it?—Coriolanus must I call thee?—
But, O, thy wife!
Cor. My gracious silence, hail!
Wouldst thou have laugh'd had I come coffin'd home,
That weep'st to see me triumph? Ah, my dear,
Such eyes the widows in Corioli wear,
And mothers that lack sons.
Men. Now, the gods crown thee!
Cor. And live you yet? [*To Valeria*] O my sweet lady, pardon.
Vol. I know not where to turn: O, welcome home:
And welcome, general: and ye 're welcome all.
Men. A hundred thousand welcomes. I could weep,
And I could laugh; I am light and heavy. Welcome:
A curse begin at very root on 's heart,
That is not glad to see thee! You are three
That Rome should dote on: yet, by the faith of men,
We have some old crab-trees here at home that will not
Be grafted to your relish. Yet welcome, warriors:
We call a nettle but a nettle, and
The faults of fools but folly.
Com. Ever right.
Cor. Menenius, ever, ever.
Her. Give way there, and go on.
Cor. [*To Volumnia and Virgilia*] Your hand, and yours:
Ere in our own house I do shade my head,
The good patricians must be visited;
From whom I have received not only greetings,
But with them change of honours.
Vol. I have lived
To see inherited my very wishes
And the buildings of my fancy: only
There 's one thing wanting, which I doubt not but
Our Rome will cast upon thee.
Cor. Know, good mother,
I had rather be their servant in my way
Than sway with them in theirs.
Com. On, to the Capitol!
[*Flourish. Cornets. Exeunt in state, as before. Brutus and Sicinius come forward.*
Bru. All tongues speak of him, and the bleared sights

Are spectacled to see him: your prattling nurse
Into a rapture lets her baby cry
While she chats him: the kitchen malkin pins
Her richest lockram 'bout her reechy neck,
Clambering the walls to eye him: stalls, bulks, windows,
Are smother'd up, leads fill'd and ridges horsed
With variable complexions, all agreeing
In earnestness to see him: seld-shown flamens
Do press among the popular throngs, and puff
To win a vulgar station: our veil'd dames
Commit the war of white and damask in
Their nicely-gawded cheeks to the wanton spoil
Of Phœbus' burning kisses: such a pother,
As if that whatsoever god who leads him
Were slily crept into his human powers,
And gave him graceful posture.

Sic. On the sudden,
I warrant him consul.

Bru. Then our office may,
During his power, go sleep.

Sic. He cannot temperately transport his honours
From where he should begin and end, but will
Lose those he hath won.

Bru. In that there 's comfort.

Sic. Doubt not
The commoners, for whom we stand, but they
Upon their ancient malice will forget
With the least cause these his new honours; which
That he will give them make I as little question
As he is proud to do 't.

Bru. I heard him swear,
Were he to stand for consul, never would he
Appear i' the market-place, nor on him put
The napless vesture of humility,
Nor showing, as the manner is, his wounds
To the people, beg their stinking breaths.

Sic. 'Tis right.

Bru. It was his word: O, he would miss it rather
Than carry it but by the suit of the gentry to him,
And the desire of the nobles.

Sic. I wish no better
Than have him hold that purpose and to put it
In execution.

Bru. 'Tis most like he will.

Sic. It shall be to him then, as our good wills,

A sure destruction.

Bru. So it must fall out
To him or our authorities. For an end,
We must suggest the people in what hatred
He still hath held them; that to 's power he would
Have made them mules, silenced their pleaders and
Dispropertied their freedoms; holding them,
In human action and capacity,
Of no more soul nor fitness for the world
Than camels in the war, who have their provand
Only for bearing burthens, and sore blows
For sinking under them.

Sic. This, as you say, suggested
At some time when his soaring insolence
Shall touch the people—which time shall not want,
If he be put upon 't; and that 's as easy
As to set dogs on sheep—will be his fire
To kindle their dry stubble; and their blaze
Shall darken him for ever.

Enter a Messenger.

Bru. What 's the matter?

Mess. You are sent for to the Capitol. 'Tis thought
That Marcius shall be consul:
I have seen the dumb men throng to see him and
The blind to hear him speak: matrons flung gloves,
Ladies and maids their scarfs and handkerchers,
Upon him as he pass'd: the nobles bended,
As to Jove's statue, and the commons made
A shower and thunder with their caps and shouts:
I never saw the like.

Bru. Let 's to the Capitol,
And carry with us ears and eyes for the time,
But hearts for the event.

Sic. Have with you. [*Exeunt.*

Scene II

The same. The Capitol.

Enter two Officers, to lay cushions.

First Off. Come, come, they are almost here. How many stand for consulships?

Sec. Off. Three, they say: but 'tis thought of every one Coriolanus will carry it.

First Off. That 's a brave fellow; but he 's vengeance proud, and loves not the common people.

Sec. Off. Faith, there have been many great men that have

flattered the people, who ne'er loved them; and there be many that they have loved, they know not wherefore: so that, if they love they know not why, they hate upon no better a ground: therefore, for Coriolanus neither to care whether they love or hate him manifests the true knowledge he has in their disposition; and out of his noble carelessness lets them plainly see 't.

First Off. If he did not care whether he had their love or no, he waved indifferently 'twixt doing them neither good nor harm: but he seeks their hate with greater devotion than they can render it him, and leaves nothing undone that may fully discover him their opposite. Now, to seem to affect the malice and displeasure of the people is as bad as that which he dislikes, to flatter them for their love.

Sec. Off. He hath deserved worthily of his country: and his ascent is not by such easy degrees as those who, having been supple and courteous to the people, bonneted, without any further deed to have them at all into their estimation and report: but he hath so planted his honours in their eyes and his actions in their hearts, that for their tongues to be silent and not confess so much, were a kind of ingrateful injury; to report otherwise were a malice that, giving itself the lie, would pluck reproof and rebuke from every ear that heard it.

First Off. No more of him; he 's a worthy man: make way, they are coming.

A sennet. Enter, with Lictors before them, Cominius the Consul, Menenius, Coriolanus, Senators, Sicinius and Brutus. The Senators take their places; the Tribunes take their places by themselves. Coriolanus stands.

Men. Having determined of the Volsces and
To send for Titus Lartius, it remains,
As the main point of this our after-meeting,
To gratify his noble service that
Hath thus stood for his country: therefore, please you,
Most reverend and grave elders, to desire
The present consul, and last general
In our well-found successes, to report
A little of that worthy work perform'd
By Caius Marcius Coriolanus; whom
We met here, both to thank and to remember
With honours like himself.

First Sen. Speak, good Cominius:
Leave nothing out for length, and make us think
Rather our state 's defective for requital

Than we to stretch it out. [*To the Tribunes*] Masters o' the people,
We do request your kindest ears, and after,
Your loving motion toward the common body,
To yield what passes here.

Sic. We are convented
Upon a pleasing treaty, and have hearts
Inclinable to honour and advance
The theme of our assembly.

Bru. Which the rather
We shall be bless'd to do, if he remember
A kinder value of the people than
He hath hereto prized them at.

Men. That 's off, that 's off;
I would you rather had been silent. Please you
To hear Cominius speak?

Bru. Most willingly:
But yet my caution was more pertinent
Than the rebuke you give it.

Men. He loves your people;
But tie him not to be their bedfellow.
Worthy Cominius, speak. [*Coriolanus offers to go away.*] Nay, keep your place.

First Sen. Sit, Coriolanus; never shame to hear
What you have nobly done.

Cor. Your honours' pardon:
I had rather have my wounds to heal again,
Than hear say how I got them.

Bru. Sir, I hope
My words disbench'd you not.

Cor. No, sir: yet oft,
When blows have made me stay, I fled from words.
You sooth'd not, therefore hurt not: but your people,
I love them as they weigh.

Men. Pray now, sit down.

Cor. I had rather have one scratch my head i' the sun
When the alarum were struck than idly sit
To hear my nothings monster'd. [*Exit.*

Men. Masters of the people,
Your multiplying spawn how can he flatter—
That 's thousand to one good one—when you now see
He had rather venture all his limbs for honour
Than one on 's ears to hear it? Proceed, Cominius.

Com. I shall lack voice: the deeds of Coriolanus
Should not be utter'd feebly. It is held

That valour is the chiefest virtue and
Most dignifies the haver: if it be,
The man I speak of cannot in the world
Be singly counterpoised. At sixteen years,
When Tarquin made a head for Rome, he fought
Beyond the mark of others: our then dictator,
Whom with all praise I point at, saw him fight,
When with his Amazonian chin he drove
The bristled lips before him: he bestrid
An o'er-press'd Roman, and i' the consul's view
Slew three opposers: Tarquin's self he met,
And struck him on his knee: in that day's feats,
When he might act the woman in the scene,
He proved best man i' the field, and for his meed
Was brow-bound with the oak. His pupil age
Man-enter'd thus, he waxed like a sea;
And, in the brunt of seventeen battles since,
He lurch'd all swords of the garland. For this last,
Before and in Corioli, let me say,
I cannot speak him home: he stopp'd the fliers;
And by his rare example made the coward
Turn terror into sport: as weeds before
A vessel under sail, so men obey'd,
And fell below his stem: his sword, death's stamp,
Where it did mark, it took; from face to foot
He was a thing of blood, whose every motion
Was timed with dying cries: alone he enter'd
The mortal gate of the city, which he painted
With shunless destiny; aidless came off,
And with a sudden re-enforcement struck
Corioli like a planet: now all 's his:
When, by and by, the din of war gan pierce
His ready sense; then straight his doubled spirit
Re-quicken'd what in flesh was fatigate,
And to the battle came he; where he did
Run reeking o'er the lives of men, as if
'Twere a perpetual spoil: and till we call'd
Both field and city ours, he never stood
To ease his breast with panting.

Men. Worthy man!

First Sen. He cannot but with measure fit the honours
Which we devise him.

Com. Our spoils he kick'd at,
And look'd upon things precious, as they were
The common muck of the world: he covets less

Than misery itself would give; rewards
His deeds with doing them, and is content
To spend the time to end it.

Men. He's right noble:
Let him be call'd for.

First Sen. Call Coriolanus.

Off. He doth appear.

Re-enter Coriolanus.

Men. The senate, Coriolanus, are well pleased
To make thee consul.

Cor. I do owe them still
My life and services.

Men. It then remains
That you do speak to the people.

Cor. I do beseech you,
Let me o'erleap that custom, for I cannot
Put on the gown, stand naked, and entreat them,
For my wounds' sake, to give their suffrage: please you
That I may pass this doing.

Sic. Sir, the people
Must have their voices; neither will they bate
One jot of ceremony.

Men. Put them not to 't:
Pray you, go fit you to the custom, and
Take to you, as your predecessors have,
Your honour with your form.

Cor. It is a part
That I shall blush in acting, and might well
Be taken from the people.

Bru. Mark you that?

Cor. To brag unto them, thus I did, and thus;
Show them the unaching scars which I should hide,
As if I had received them for the hire
Of their breath only!

Men. Do not stand upon 't.
We recommend to you, tribunes of the people,
Our purpose to them: and to our noble consul
Wish we all joy and honour.

Senators. To Coriolanus come all joy and honour!

[*Flourish of cornets. Exeunt all but Sicinius and Brutus.*

Bru. You see how he intends to use the people.

Sic. May they perceive 's intent! He will require them,
As if he did contemn what he requested
Should be in them to give.

Bru. Come, we'll inform them

Of our proceedings here: on the market-place,
I know, they do attend us. [*Exeunt.*

Scene III

The same. The Forum.

Enter seven or eight Citizens.

First Cit. Once, if he do require our voices, we ought not to deny him.

Sec. Cit. We may, sir, if we will.

Third Cit. We have power in ourselves to do it, but it is a power that we have no power to do: for if he show us his wounds and tell us his deeds, we are to put our tongues into those wounds and speak for them; so, if he tell us his noble deeds, we must also tell him our noble acceptance of them. Ingratitude is monstrous: and for the multitude to be ingrateful, were to make a monster of the multitude; of the which we being members, should bring ourselves to be monstrous members.

First Cit. And to make us no better thought of, a little help will serve; for once we stood up about the corn, he himself stuck not to call us the many-headed multitude.

Third Cit. We have been called so of many; not that our heads are some brown, some black, some auburn, some bald, but that our wits are so diversely coloured: and truly I think, if all our wits were to issue out of one skull, they would fly east, west, north, south, and their consent of one direct way should be at once to all the points o' the compass.

Sec. Cit. Think you so? Which way do you judge my wit would fly?

Third Cit. Nay, your wit will not so soon out as another man's will; 'tis strongly wedged up in a blockhead; but if it were at liberty, 'twould, sure, southward.

Sec. Cit. Why that way?

Third Cit. To lose itself in a fog; where, being three parts melted away with rotten dews, the fourth would return for conscience sake, to help to get thee a wife.

Sec. Cit. You are never without your tricks: you may, you may.

Third Cit. Are you all resolved to give your voices? But that's no matter, the greater part carries it. I say, if he would incline to the people, there was never a worthier man.

Enter Coriolanus in a gown of humility, with Menenius.

Here he comes, and in the gown of humility: mark his behaviour. We are not to stay all together, but to come by him where he stands, by ones, by twos, and by threes. He's to make his requests by particulars; wherein every one of us has a single honour, in giving him our own voices with our own tongues: therefore follow me, and I 'll direct you how you shall go by him.

All. Content, content. [*Exeunt Citizens.*

Men. O sir, you are not right: have you not known
The worthiest men have done 't?

Cor. What must I say?—
'I pray, sir,'—Plague upon 't! I cannot bring
My tongue to such a pace. 'Look, sir, my wounds!
I got them in my country's service, when
Some certain of your brethren roar'd and ran
From the noise of our own drums.'

Men. O me, the gods!
You must not speak of that: you must desire them
To think upon you.

Cor. Think upon me! hang 'em!
I would they would forget me, like the virtues
Which our divines lose by 'em.

Men. You 'll mar all:
I 'll leave you: pray you, speak to 'em, I pray you,
In wholesome manner. [*Exit.*

Cor. Bid them wash their faces,
And keep their teeth clean. [*Re-enter two of the Citizens.*]
So, here comes a brace.

Re-enter a third Citizen.

You know the cause, sir, of my standing here.

Third Cit. We do, sir; tell us what hath brought you to 't.

Cor. Mine own desert.

Sec. Cit. Your own desert!

Cor. Ay, but not mine own desire.

Third Cit. How! not your own desire!

Cor. No, sir, 'twas never my desire yet to trouble the poor with begging.

Third Cit. You must think, if we give you any thing, we hope to gain by you.

Cor. Well then, I pray, your price o' the consulship?

First Cit. The price is, to ask it kindly.

Cor. Kindly! Sir, I pray, let me ha 't: I have wounds to show you, which shall be yours in private. Your good voice, sir; what say you?

Sec. Cit. You shall ha 't, worthy sir.

Cor. A match, sir. There 's in all two worthy voices begged. I have your alms: adieu.

Third Cit. But this is something odd.

Sec. Cit. An 'twere to give again,—but 'tis no matter.
[*Exeunt the three Citizens.*

Re-enter two other Citizens.

Cor. Pray you now, if it may stand with the tune of your voices that I may be consul, I have here the customary gown.

Fourth Cit. You have deserved nobly of your country, and you have not desired nobly.

Cor. Your enigma?

Fourth Cit. You have been a scourge to her enemies, you have been a rod to her friends; you have not indeed loved the common people.

Cor. You should account me the more virtuous, that I have not been common in my love. I will, sir, flatter my sworn brother, the people, to earn a dearer estimation of them; 'tis a condition they account gentle: and since the wisdom of their choice is rather to have my hat than my heart, I will practise the insinuating nod, and be off to them most counterfeitly; that is, sir, I will counterfeit the bewitchment of some popular man, and give it bountiful to the desirers. Therefore, beseech you, I may be consul.

Fifth Cit. We hope to find you our friend; and therefore give you our voices heartily.

Fourth Cit. You have received many wounds for your country.

Cor. I will not seal your knowledge with showing them. I will make much of your voices, and so trouble you no farther.

Both Cit. The gods give you joy, sir, heartily! [*Exeunt.*

Cor. Most sweet voices!
Better it is to die, better to starve,
Than crave the hire which first we do deserve.
Why in this woolvish toge should I stand here;
To beg of Hob and Dick that do appear,
Their needless vouches? Custom calls me to 't:
What custom wills, in all things should we do 't,
The dust on antique time would lie unswept,
And mountainous error be too highly heap'd
For truth to o'er-peer. Rather than fool it so,
Let the high office and the honour go
To one that would do thus. I am half through:
The one part suffer'd, the other will I do.

Re-enter three Citizens more.

Here come moe voices.
Your voices: for your voices I have fought;
Watch'd for your voices; for your voices bear
Of wounds two dozen odd; battles thrice six
I have seen, and heard of; for your voices have
Done many things, some less, some more: your voices:

Indeed, I would be consul.

Sixth Cit. He has done nobly, and cannot go without any honest man's voice.

Seventh Cit. Therefore let him be consul: the gods give him joy, and make him good friend to the people!

All. Amen, amen. God save thee, noble consul! [*Exeunt.*

Cor. Worthy voices!

Re-enter Menenius, with Brutus and Sicinius.

Men. You have stood your limitation; and the tribunes
Endue you with the people's voice: remains
That in the official marks invested you
Anon do meet the senate.

Cor. Is this done?

Sic. The custom of request you have discharged:
The people do admit you, and are summon'd
To meet anon upon your approbation.

Cor. Where? at the senate-house?

Sic. There, Coriolanus.

Cor. May I change these garments?

Sic. You may, sir.

Cor. That I'll straight do, and, knowing myself again,
Repair to the senate-house.

Men. I'll keep you company. Will you along?

Bru. We stay here for the people.

Sic. Fare you well.

[*Exeunt Coriolanus and Menenius.*

He has it now; and, by his looks, methinks
'Tis warm at 's heart.

Bru. With a proud heart he wore
His humble weeds. Will you dismiss the people?

Re-enter Citizens.

Sic. How now, my masters! have you chose this man?

First Cit. He has our voices, sir.

Bru. We pray the gods he may deserve your loves.

Sec. Cit. Amen, sir: to my poor unworthy notice,
He mock'd us when he begg'd our voices.

Third Cit. Certainly
He flouted us downright.

First Cit. No, 'tis his kind of speech; he did not mock us.

Sec. Cit. Not one amongst us, save yourself, but says
He used us scornfully: he should have show'd us
His marks of merit, wounds received for 's country.

Sic. Why, so he did, I am sure.

Citizens. No, no; no man saw 'em.

Third Cit. He said he had wounds which he could show in [private;

And with his hat, thus waving it in scorn,
'I would be consul,' says he: 'aged custom,
But by your voices, will not so permit me;
Your voices, therefore.' When we granted that,
Here was 'I thank you for your voices: thank you:
Your most sweet voices: now you have left your voices,
I have no further with you.' Was not this mockery?

Sic. Why, either were you ignorant to see 't,
Or, seeing it, of such childish friendliness
To yield your voices?

Bru. Could you not have told him,
As you were lesson'd, when he had no power,
But was a petty servant to the state,
He was your enemy; ever spake against
Your liberties and the charters that you bear
I' the body of the weal: and now, arriving
A place of potency and sway o' the state,
If he should still malignantly remain
Fast foe to the plebeii, your voices might
Be curses to yourselves? You should have said,
That as his worthy deeds did claim no less
Than what he stood for, so his gracious nature
Would think upon you for your voices, and
Translate his malice towards you into love,
Standing your friendly lord.

Sic. Thus to have said,
As you were fore-advised, had touch'd his spirit
And tried his inclination; from him pluck'd
Either his gracious promise, which you might,
As cause had call'd you up, have held him to;
Or else it would have gall'd his surly nature,
Which easily endures not article
Tying him to aught: so, putting him to rage,
You should have ta'en the advantage of his choler,
And pass'd him unelected.

Bru. Did you perceive
He did solicit you in free contempt
When he did need your loves; and do you think
That his contempt shall not be bruising to you
When he hath power to crush? Why, had your bodies
No heart among you? or had you tongues to cry
Against the rectorship of judgement?

Sic. Have you,
Ere now, denied the asker? and now again,
Of him that did not ask but mock, bestow

Your sued-for tongues?
Third Cit. He 's not confirm'd; we may deny him yet.
Sec. Cit. And will deny him:
I 'll have five hundred voices of that sound.
First Cit. I twice five hundred, and their friends to piece 'em.
Bru. Get you hence instantly, and tell those friends,
They have chose a consul that will from them take
Their liberties, make them of no more voice
Than dogs that are as often beat for barking,
As therefore kept to do so.
Sic. Let them assemble;
And, on a safer judgement, all revoke
Your ignorant election: enforce his pride
And his old hate unto you: besides, forget not
With what contempt he wore the humble weed,
How in his suit he scorn'd you: but your loves,
Thinking upon his services, took from you
The apprehension of his present portance,
Which most gibingly, ungravely, he did fashion
After the inveterate hate he bears you.
Bru. Lay
A fault on us, your tribunes; that we labour'd,
No impediment between, but that you must
Cast your election on him.
Sic. Say, you chose him
More after our commandment than as guided
By your own true affections; and that your minds,
Pre-occupied with what you rather must do
Than what you should, made you against the grain
To voice him consul: lay the fault on us.
Bru. Ay, spare us not. Say we read lectures to you,
How youngly he began to serve his country,
How long continued; and what stock he springs of,
The noble house o' the Marcians, from whence came
That Ancus Marcius, Numa's daughter's son,
Who, after great Hostilius, here was king;
Of the same house Publius and Quintus were,
That our best water brought by conduits hither;
And [Censorinus] nobly named so,
Twice being [by the people chosen] censor,
Was his great ancestor.
Sic. One thus descended,
That hath beside well in his person wrought
To be set high in place, we did commend
To your remembrances: but you have found,

Scaling his present bearing with his past,
That he 's your fixed enemy, and revoke
Your sudden approbation.

Bru. Say, you ne'er had done 't—
Harp on that still—but by our putting on:
And presently, when you have drawn your number,
Repair to the Capitol.

Citizens. We will so: almost all
Repent in their election. [*Exeunt Citizens.*

Bru. Let them go on;
This mutiny were better put in hazard,
Than stay, past doubt, for greater:
If, as his nature is, he fall in rage
With their refusal, both observe and answer
The vantage of his anger.

Sic. To the Capitol, come:
We will be there before the stream o' the people;
And this shall seem, as partly 'tis, their own,
Which we have goaded onward. [*Exeunt.*

ACT III—Scene I

Rome. A street.

Cornets. Enter Coriolanus, Menenius, all the Gentry, Cominius, Titus Lartius, and other Senators.

Cor. Tullus Aufidius then had made new head?

Lart. He had, my lord; and that it was which caused
Our swifter composition.

Cor. So then the Volsces stand but as at first;
Ready, when time shall prompt them, to make road
Upon 's again.

Com. They are worn, lord consul, so,
That we shall hardly in our ages see
Their banners wave again.

Cor. Saw you Aufidius?

Lart. On safe-guard he came to me; and did curse
Against the Volsces, for they had so vilely
Yielded the town: he is retired to Antium.

Cor. Spoke he of me?

Lart. He did, my lord.

Cor. How? what?

Lart. How often he had met you, sword to sword;
That of all things upon the earth he hated
Your person most; that he would pawn his fortunes
To hopeless restitution, so he might

Be call'd your vanquisher.
Cor. At Antium lives he?
Lart. At Antium.
Cor. I wish I had a cause to seek him there,
To oppose his hatred fully. Welcome home.

Enter Sicinius and Brutus.

Behold, these are the tribunes of the people,
The tongues o' the common mouth: I do despise them;
For they do prank them in authority,
Against all noble sufferance.
Sic. Pass no further.
Cor. Ha! what is that?
Bru. It will be dangerous to go on: no further.
Cor. What makes this change?
Men. The matter?
Com. Hath he not pass'd the noble and the common?
Bru. Cominius, no.
Cor. Have I had children's voices?
First Sen. Tribunes, give way; he shall to the market-place.
Bru. The people are incensed against him.
Sic. Stop,
Or all will fall in broil.
Cor. Are these your herd?
Must these have voices, that can yield them now,
And straight disclaim their tongues? What are your offices?
You being their mouths, why rule you not their teeth?
Have you not set them on?
Men. Be calm, be calm.
Cor. It is a purposed thing, and grows by plot,
To curb the will of the nobility:
Suffer 't, and live with such as cannot rule,
Nor ever will be ruled.
Bru. Call 't not a plot:
The people cry you mock'd them; and of late,
When corn was given them gratis, you repined,
Scandal'd the suppliants for the people, call'd them
Time-pleasers, flatterers, foes to nobleness.
Cor. Why, this was known before.
Bru. Not to them all.
Cor. Have you inform'd them sithence?
Bru. How! I inform them!
Com. You are like to do such business.
Bru. Not unlike,
Each way, to better yours.
Cor. Why then should I be consul? By yond clouds,

Let me deserve so ill as you, and make me
Your fellow tribune.

Sic. You show too much of that
For which the people stir: if you will pass
To where you are bound, you must inquire your way,
Which you are out of, with a gentler spirit;
Or never be so noble as a consul,
Nor yoke with him for tribune.

Men. Let 's be calm.

Com. The people are abused; set on. This paltering
Becomes not Rome; nor has Coriolanus
Deserved this so dishonour'd rub, laid falsely
I' the plain way of his merit.

Cor. Tell me of corn!
This was my speech, and I will speak 't again—

Men. Not now, not now.

First Sen. Not in this heat, sir, now.

Cor. Now, as I live, I will. My nobler friends,
I crave their pardons:
For the mutable, rank-scented many, let them
Regard me as I do not flatter, and
Therein behold themselves: I say again,
In soothing them, we nourish 'gainst our senate
The cockle of rebellion, insolence, sedition,
Which we ourselves have plough'd for, sow'd and scatter'd,
By mingling them with us, the honour'd number;
Who lack not virtue, no, nor power, but that
Which they have given to beggars.

Men. Well, no more.

First Sen. No more words, we beseech you.

Cor. How! no more!
As for my country I have shed my blood,
Not fearing outward force, so shall my lungs
Coin words till their decay against those measles,
Which we disdain should tetter us, yet sought
The very way to catch them.

Bru. You speak o' the people,
As if you were a god to punish, not
A man of their infirmity.

Sic. 'Twere well
We let the people know 't.

Men. What, what? his choler

Cor. Choler!
Were I as patient as the midnight sleep,
By Jove, 'twould be my mind!

Sic. It is a mind
That shall remain a poison where it is,
Not poison any further.
Cor. Shall remain
Hear you this Triton of the minnows? mark you
His absolute 'shall'?
Com. 'Twas from the canon.
Cor. 'Shall'!
O good, but most unwise patricians! why,
You grave but reckless senators, have you thus
Given Hydra here to choose an officer,
That with his peremptory 'shall,' being but
The horn and noise o' the monster's, wants not spirit
To say he'll turn your current in a ditch,
And make your channel his? If he have power,
Then vail your ignorance; if none, awake
Your dangerous lenity. If you are learn'd,
Be not as common fools; if you are not,
Let them have cushions by you. You are plebeians,
If they be senators: and they are no less,
When, both your voices blended, the great'st taste
Most palates theirs. They choose their magistrate;
And such a one as he, who puts his 'shall,'
His popular 'shall,' against a graver bench
Than ever frown'd in Greece. By Jove himself,
It makes the consuls base! and my soul aches
To know, when two authorities are up,
Neither supreme, how soon confusion
May enter 'twixt the gap of both and take
The one by the other.
Com. Well, on to the market-place.
Cor. Whoever gave that counsel, to give forth
The corn o' the storehouse gratis, as 'twas used
Sometime in Greece,—
Men. Well, well, no more of that.
Cor. Though there the people had more absolute power,
I say, they nourish'd disobedience, fed
The ruin of the state.
Bru. Why, shall the people give
One that speaks thus their voice?
Cor. I'll give my reasons,
More worthier than their voices. They know the corn
Was not our recompense, resting well assured
They ne'er did service for't: being press'd to the war,
Even when the navel of the state was touch'd,

They would not thread the gates. This kind of service
Did not deserve corn gratis: being i' the war,
Their mutinies and revolts, wherein they show'd
Most valour, spoke not for them: the accusation
Which they have often made against the senate,
All cause unborn, could never be the native
Of our so frank donation. Well, what then?
How shall this bosom multiplied digest
The senate's courtesy? Let deeds express
What's like to be their words: 'We did request it;
We are the greater poll, and in true fear
They gave us our demands.' Thus we debase
The nature of our seats, and make the rabble
Call our cares fears; which will in time
Break ope the locks o' the senate, and bring in
The crows to peck the eagles.

Men. Come, enough.

Bru. Enough, with over measure.

Cor. No, take more:
What may be sworn by, both divine and human,
Seal what I end withal! This double worship,
Where one part does disdain with cause, the other
Insult without all reason; where gentry, title, wisdom,
Cannot conclude but by the yea and no
Of general ignorance,—it must omit
Real necessities, and give way the while
To unstable slightness: purpose so barr'd, it follows,
Nothing is done to purpose. Therefore, beseech you,—
You that will be less fearful than discreet;
That love the fundamental part of state
More than you doubt the change on 't; that prefer
A noble life before a long, and wish
To jump a body with a dangerous physic
That's sure of death without it,—at once pluck out
The multitudinous tongue; let them not lick
The sweet which is their poison. Your dishonour
Mangles true judgement and bereaves the state
Of that integrity which should become 't;
Not having the power to do the good it would,
For the ill which doth control 't.

Bru. Has said enough.

Sic. Has spoken like a traitor, and shall answer
As traitors do.

Cor. Thou wretch, despite o'erwhelm thee!
What should the people do with these bald tribunes?

On whom depending, their obedience fails
To the greater bench: in a rebellion,
When what 's not meet, but what must be, was law,
Then were they chosen: in a better hour,
Let what is meet be said it must be meet,
And throw their power i' the dust.

Bru. Manifest treason!

Sic. This a consul? no.

Bru. The ædiles, ho!

Enter an Ædile.

Let him be apprehended.

Sic. Go, call the people: [*Exit Ædile.*] in whose name myself
Attach thee as a traitorous innovator,
A foe to the public weal: obey, I charge thee,
And follow to thine answer.

Cor. Hence, old goat!

Senators, &c. We 'll surety him.

Com. Aged sir, hands off.

Cor. Hence, rotten thing! or I shall shake thy bones
Out of thy garments.

Sic. Help, ye citizens!

Enter a rabble of Citizens, with the Ædiles.

Men. On both sides more respect.

Sic. Here's he that would take from you all your power.

Bru. Seize him, ædiles!

Citizens. Down with him! down with him!

Senators, &c. Weapons, weapons, weapons!

[*They all bustle about Coriolanus, crying,*
'Tribunes!' 'Patricians!' 'Citizens!' 'What, ho!'
'Sicinius!' 'Brutus!' 'Coriolanus!' 'Citizens!'
'Peace, peace, peace!' 'Stay! hold! peace!'

Men. What is about to be? I am out of breath.
Confusion 's near. I cannot speak. You, tribunes
To the people! Coriolanus, patience!
Speak, good Sicinius.

Sic. Hear me, people; peace!

Citizens. Let 's hear our tribune: peace!—Speak, speak, speak.

Sic. You are at point to lose your liberties:
Marcius would have all from you; Marcius,
Whom late you have named for consul.

Men. Fie, fie, fie!
This is the way to kindle, not to quench.

First Sen. To unbuild the city, and to lay all flat.

Sic. What is the city but the people?

Citizens. True,

The people are the city.
Bru. By the consent of all, we were establish'd
The people's magistrates.
Citizens. You so remain.
Men. And so are like to do.
Com. That is the way to lay the city flat,
To bring the roof to the foundation,
And bury all which yet distinctly ranges,
In heaps and piles of ruin.
Sic. This deserves death.
Bru. Or let us stand to our authority,
Or let us lose it. We do here pronounce,
Upon the part o' the people, in whose power
We were elected theirs, Marcius is worthy
Of present death.
Sic. Therefore lay hold of him;
Bear him to the rock Tarpeian, and from thence
Into destruction cast him.
Bru. Ædiles, seize him!
Citizens. Yield, Marcius, yield!
Men. Hear me one word;
Beseech you, tribunes, hear me but a word.
Ædiles. Peace, peace!
Men. [*To Brutus*] Be that you seem, truly your country's [friend,
And temperately proceed to what you would
Thus violently redress.
Bru. Sir, those cold ways,
That seem like prudent helps, are very poisonous
Where the disease is violent. Lay hands upon him,
And bear him to the rock.
Cor. No, I'll die here. [*Drawing his sword.*
There's some among you have beheld me fighting:
Come, try upon yourselves what you have seen me.
Men. Down with that sword! Tribunes, withdraw awhile.
Bru. Lay hands upon him.
Men. Help Marcius, help,
You that be noble; help him, young and old!
Citizens. Down with him, down with him!
[*In this mutiny, the Tribunes, the Ædiles, and the People, are beat in.*
Men. Go, get you to your house; be gone, away!
All will be naught else.
Sec. Sen. Get you gone.
Com. Stand fast;
We have as many friends as enemies.

Men. Shall it be put to that?
First Sen. The gods forbid!
I prithee, noble friend, home to thy house;
Leave us to cure this cause.
Men. For 'tis a sore upon us
You cannot tent yourself: be gone, beseech you.
Com. Come, sir, along with us.
Cor. I would they were barbarians—as they are,
Though in Rome litter'd—not Romans—as they are not,
Though calved i' the porch o' the Capitol,—
Men. Be gone:
Put not your worthy rage into your tongue:
One time will owe another.
Cor. On fair ground
I could beat forty of them.
Men. I could myself
Take up a brace o' the best of them: yea, the two tribunes.
Com. But now 'tis odds beyond arithmetic;
And manhood is call'd foolery, when it stands
Against a falling fabric. Will you hence
Before the tag return? whose rage doth rend
Like interrupted waters, and o'erbear
What they are used to bear.
Men. Pray you, be gone:
I'll try whether my old wit be in request
With those that have but little: this must be patch'd
With cloth of any colour.
Com. Nay, come away.
[*Exeunt Coriolanus, Cominius, and others.*
First Patrician. This man has marr'd his fortune.
Men. His nature is too noble for the world:
He would not flatter Neptune for his trident,
Or Jove for 's power to thunder. His heart 's his mouth:
What his breast forges, that his tongue must vent;
And, being angry, does forget that ever
He heard the name of death. [*A noise within.*
Here 's goodly work!
Sec. Pat. I would they were a-bed!
Men. I would they were in Tiber! What, the vengeance,
Could he not speak 'em fair?
Re-enter Brutus and Sicinius, with the rabble.
Sic. Where is this viper,
That would depopulate the city, and
Be every man himself?
Men. You worthy tribunes—

Sic. He shall be thrown down the Tarpeian rock
With rigorous hands: he hath resisted law,
And therefore law shall scorn him further trial
Than the severity of the public power,
Which he so sets at nought.
First Cit. He shall well know
The noble tribunes are the people's mouths,
And we their hands.
Citizens. He shall, sure on 't.
Men. Sir, sir,—
Sic. Peace!
Men. Do not cry havoc, where you should but hunt
With modest warrant.
Sic. Sir, how comes 't that you
Have holp to make this rescue?
Men. Hear me speak:
As I do know the consul's worthiness,
So can I name his faults,—
Sic. Consul! what consul?
Men. The consul Coriolanus.
Bru. He consul!
Citizens. No, no, no, no, no.
Men. If, by the tribunes' leave, and yours, good people,
I may be heard, I would crave a word or two;
The which shall turn you to no further harm
Than so much loss of time.
Sic. Speak briefly then;
For we are peremptory to dispatch
This viperous traitor: to eject him hence
Were but one danger, and to keep him here
Our certain death: therefore it is decreed
He dies to-night.
Men. Now the good gods forbid
That our renowned Rome, whose gratitude
Towards her deserved children is enroll'd
In Jove's own book, like an unnatural dam
Should now eat up her own!
Sic. He 's a disease that must be cut away.
Men. O, he 's a limb that has but a disease;
Mortal, to cut it off; to cure it, easy.
What has he done to Rome that 's worthy death?
Killing our enemies, the blood he hath lost—
Which, I dare vouch, is more than that he hath
By many an ounce—he dropp'd it for his country;
And what is left, to lose it by his country

Were to us all that do 't and suffer it
A brand to the end o' the world.

Sic. This is clean kam.

Bru. Merely awry: when he did love his country,
It honour'd him.

Men. The service of the foot
Being once gangrened, is not then respected
For what before it was.

Bru. We 'll hear no more.
Pursue him to his house, and pluck him thence;
Lest his infection, being of catching nature,
Spread further.

Men. One word more, one word.
This tiger-footed rage, when it shall find
The harm of unscann'd swiftness, will, too late,
Tie leaden pounds to 's heels. Proceed by process;
Lest parties, as he is beloved, break out,
And sack great Rome with Romans.

Bru. If it were so—

Sic. What do ye talk?
Have we not had a taste of his obedience?
Our ædiles smote? ourselves resisted? Come.

Men. Consider this: he has been bred i' the wars
Since he could draw a sword, and is ill school'd
In bolted language; meal and bran together
He throws without distinction. Give me leave,
I 'll go to him, and undertake to bring him
Where he shall answer, by a lawful form,
In peace, to his utmost peril.

First Sen. Noble tribunes,
It is the humane way: the other course
Will prove too bloody; and the end of it
Unknown to the beginning.

Sic. Noble Menenius,
Be you then as the people's officer.
Masters, lay down your weapons.

Bru. Go not home.

Sic. Meet on the market-place. We 'll attend you there:
Where, if you bring not Marcius, we 'll proceed
In our first way.

Men. I 'll bring him to you.
[*To the Senators*] Let me desire your company: he must come,
Or what is worst will follow.

First Sen. Pray you, let 's to him. [*Exeunt.*

Scene II

A room in Coriolanus's house.

Enter Coriolanus with Patricians.

Cor. Let them pull all about mine ears; present me
Death on the wheel, or at wild horses' heels;
Or pile ten hills on the Tarpeian rock,
That the precipitation might down stretch
Below the beam of sight; yet will I still
Be thus to them.

A Patrician. You do the nobler.

Cor. I muse my mother
Does not approve me further, who was wont
To call them woollen vassals, things created
To buy and sell with groats, to show bare heads
In congregations, to yawn, be still and wonder,
When one but of my ordinance stood up
To speak of peace or war.

Enter Volumnia.

I talk of you:
Why did you wish me milder? would you have me
False to my nature? Rather say, I play
The man I am.

Vol. O, sir, sir, sir,
I would have had you put your power well on,
Before you had worn it out.

Cor. Let go.

Vol. You might have been enough the man you are,
With striving less to be so: lesser had been
The thwartings of your dispositions, if
You had not show'd them how ye were disposed,
Ere they lack'd power to cross you.

Cor. Let them hang.

Vol. Ay, and burn too.

Enter Menenius with the Senators.

Men. Come, come, you have been too rough, something too [rough;
You must return and mend it.

First Sen. There's no remedy;
Unless, by not so doing, our good city
Cleave in the midst, and perish.

Vol. Pray, be counsell'd:
I have a heart as little apt as yours,
But yet a brain that leads my use of anger
To better vantage.

Men. Well said, noble woman!

Before he should thus stoop to the herd, but that
The violent fit o' the time craves it as physic
For the whole state, I would put mine armour on,
Which I can scarcely bear.

Cor. What must I do?

Men. Return to the tribunes.

Cor. Well, what then? what then?

Men. Repent what you have spoke.

Cor. For them! I cannot do it to the gods;
Must I then do 't to them?

Vol. You are too absolute;
Though therein you can never be too noble,
But when extremities speak. I have heard you say,
Honour and policy, like unsever'd friends,
I' the war do grow together: grant that, and tell me,
In peace what each of them by the other lose,
That they combine not there.

Cor. Tush, tush!

Men. A good demand.

Vol. If it be honour in your wars to seem
The same you are not, which, for your best ends,
You adopt your policy, how is it less or worse,
That it shall hold companionship in peace
With honour, as in war, since that to both
It stands in like request?

Cor. Why force you this?

Vol. Because that now it lies you on to speak
To the people; not by your own instruction,
Nor by the matter which your heart prompts you,
But with such words that are but roted in
Your tongue, though but bastards and syllables
Of no allowance to your bosom's truth.
Now, this no more dishonours you at all
Than to take in a town with gentle words,
Which else would put you to your fortune and
The hazard of much blood.
I would dissemble with my nature, where
My fortunes and my friends at stake required
I should do so in honour. I am in this,
Your wife, your son, these senators, the nobles;
And you will rather show our general louts
How you can frown than spend a fawn upon 'em,
For the inheritance of their loves and safeguard
Of what that want might ruin.

Men. Noble lady!

Come, go with us; speak fair: you may salve so,
Not what is dangerous present, but the loss
Of what is past.

Vol. I prithee now, my son,
Go to them, with this bonnet in thy hand;
And thus far having stretch'd it—here be with them—
Thy knee bussing the stones—for in such business
Action is eloquence, and the eyes of the ignorant
More learned than the ears—waving thy head,
Which often, thus, correcting thy stout heart,
Now humble as the ripest mulberry
That will not hold the handling: or say to them,
Thou art their soldier, and being bred in broils
Hast not the soft way which, thou dost confess,
Were fit for thee to use, as they to claim,
In asking their good loves; but thou wilt frame
Thyself, forsooth, hereafter theirs, so far
As thou hast power and person.

Men. This but done,
Even as she speaks, why, their hearts were yours;
For they have pardons, being ask'd, as free
As words to little purpose.

Vol. Prithee now,
Go, and be ruled: although I know thou hadst rather
Follow thine enemy in a fiery gulf
Than flatter him in a bower.

Enter Cominius.

Here is Cominius.

Com. I have been i' the market-place; and, sir, 'tis fit
You make strong party, or defend yourself
By calmness or by absence: all 's in anger.

Men. Only fair speech.

Com. I think 'twill serve, if he
Can thereto frame his spirit.

Vol. He must, and will.
Prithee now, say you will, and go about it.

Cor. Must I go show them my unbarb'd sconce? must I,
With my base tongue, give to my noble heart
A lie, that it must bear? Well, I will do 't:
Yet, were there but this single plot to lose,
This mould of Marcius, they to dust should grind it,
And throw 't against the wind. To the market-place!
You have put me now to such a part, which never
I shall discharge to the life.

Com. Come, come, we 'll prompt you.
Vol. I prithee now, sweet son, as thou hast said
My praises made thee first a soldier, so,
To havè my praise for this, perform a part
Thou hast not done before.
Cor. Well, I must do 't:
Away, my disposition, and possess me
Some harlot's spirit! my throat of war be turn'd,
Which quired with my drum, into a pipe
Small as an eunuch, or the virgin voice
That babies lulls asleep! the smiles of knaves
Tent in my cheeks, and schoolboys' tears take up
The glasses of my sight! a beggar's tongue
Make motion through my lips, and my arm'd knees,
Who bow'd but in my stirrup, bend like his
That hath received an alms! I will not do 't;
Lest I surcease to honour mine own truth,
And by my body's action teach my mind
A most inherent baseness.
Vol. At thy choice then:
To beg of thee, it is my more dishonour
Than thou of them. Come all to ruin: let
Thy mother rather feel thy pride than fear
Thy dangerous stoutness, for I mock at death
With as big heart as thou. Do as thou list.
Thy valiantness was mine, thou suck'dst it from me,
But owe thy pride thyself.
Cor. Pray, be content:
Mother, I am going to the market-place;
Chide me no more. I 'll mountebank their loves,
Cog their hearts from them, and come home beloved
Of all the trades in Rome. Look, I am going:
Commend me to my wife. I 'll return consul;
Or never trust to what my tongue can do
I' the way of flattery further.
Vol. Do your will. [*Exit.*
Com. Away! the tribunes do attend you: arm yourself
To answer mildly; for they are prepared
With accusations, as I hear, more strong
Than are upon you yet.
Cor. The word is 'mildly.' Pray you, let us go:
Let them accuse me by invention, I
Will answer in mine honour.
Men. Ay, but mildly.
Cor. Well, mildly be it then. Mildly! [*Exeunt.*

Scene III

The same. The Forum.

Enter Sicinius and Brutus.

Bru. In this point charge him home, that he affects
Tyrannical power: if he evade us there,
Enforce him with his envy to the people;
And that the spoil got on the Antiates
Was ne'er distributed.

Enter an Ædile.

What, will he come?
Æd. He's coming.
Bru. How accompanied?
Æd. With old Menenius and those senators
That always favour'd him.
Sic. Have you a catalogue
Of all the voices that we have procured,
Set down by the poll?
Æd. I have; 'tis ready.
Sic. Have you collected them by tribes?
Æd. I have.
Sic. Assemble presently the people hither:
And when they hear me say 'It shall be so
I' the right and strength o' the commons,' be it either
For death, for fine, or banishment, then let them,
If I say fine, cry 'Fine,' if death, cry 'Death,'
Insisting on the old prerogative
And power i' the truth o' the cause.
Æd. I shall inform them.
Bru. And when such time they have begun to cry,
Let them not cease, but with a din confused
Enforce the present execution
Of what we chance to sentence.
Æd. Very well.
Sic. Make them be strong, and ready for this hint,
When we shall hap to give 't them.
Bru. Go about it. [*Exit Ædile.*
Put him to choler straight: he hath been used
Ever to conquer and to have his worth
Of contradiction: being once chafed, he cannot
Be rein'd again to temperance; then he speaks
What's in his heart; and that is there which looks
With us to break his neck.
Sic. Well, here he comes.

Enter Coriolanus, Menenius, and Cominius, with Senators and Patricians.

Men. Calmly, I do beseech you.
Cor. Ay, as an ostler, that for the poorest piece
Will bear the knave by the volume. The honour'd gods
Keep Rome in safety, and the chairs of justice
Supplied with worthy men! plant love among 's!
Throng our large temples with the shows of peace,
And not our streets with war!
First Sen. Amen, amen.
Men. A noble wish.

Re-enter Ædile with Citizens.

Sic. Draw near, ye people.
Æd. List to your tribunes; audience: peace, I say!
Cor. First, hear me speak.
Both Tri. Well, say. Peace, ho!
Cor. Shall I be charged no further than this present?
Must all determine here?
Sic. I do demand,
If you submit you to the people's voices,
Allow their officers, and are content
To suffer lawful censure for such faults
As shall be proved upon you.
Cor. I am content.
Men. Lo, citizens, he says he is content:
The warlike service he has done, consider; think
Upon the wounds his body bears, which show
Like graves i' the holy churchyard.
Cor. Scratches with briers,
Scars to move laughter only.
Men. Consider further,
That when he speaks not like a citizen,
You find him like a soldier: do not take
His rougher accents for malicious sounds,
But, as I say, such as become a soldier
Rather than envy you.
Com. Well, well, no more.
Cor. What is the matter
That being pass'd for consul with full voice,
I am so dishonour'd that the very hour
You take it off again?
Sic. Answer to us.
Cor. Say, then: 'tis true, I ought so.
Sic. We charge you, that you have contrived to take

From Rome all season'd office, and to wind
Yourself into a power tyrannical;
For which you are a traitor to the people.

Cor. How! traitor!

Men. Nay, temperately; your promise.

Cor. The fires i' the lowest hell fold-in the people!
Call me their traitor! Thou injurious tribune!
Within thine eyes sat twenty thousand deaths,
In thy hands clutch'd as many millions, in
Thy lying tongue both numbers, I would say
'Thou liest' unto thee with a voice as free
As I do pray the gods.

Sic. Mark you this, people?

Citizens. To the rock, to the rock with him!

Sic. Peace!
We need not put new matter to his charge:
What you have seen him do and heard him speak,
Beating your officers, cursing yourselves,
Opposing laws with strokes, and here defying
Those whose great power must try him; even this,
So criminal and in such capital kind,
Deserves the extremest death.

Bru. But since he hath
Served well for Rome—

Cor. What do you prate of service?

Bru. I talk of that, that know it.

Cor. You?

Men. Is this the promise that you made your mother?

Com. Know, I pray you,—

Cor. I 'll know no further:
Let them pronounce the steep Tarpeian death,
Vagabond exile, flaying, pent to linger
But with a grain a day, I would not buy
Their mercy at the price of one fair word,
Nor check my courage for what they can give,
To have 't with saying 'Good morrow.'

Sic. For that he has,
As much as in him lies, from time to time
Envied against the people, seeking means
To pluck away their power, as now at last
Given hostile strokes, and that not in the presence
Of dreaded justice, but on the ministers
That do distribute it; in the name o' the people,
And in the power of us the tribunes, we,
Even from this instant, banish him our city,

In peril of precipitation
From off the rock Tarpeian, never more
To enter our Rome gates: i' the people's name,
I say it shall be so.

Citizens. It shall be so, it shall be so; let him away:
He 's banish'd, and it shall be so.

Com. Hear me, my masters, and my common friends,—

Sic. He 's sentenced; no more hearing.

Com. Let me speak:
I have been consul, and can show for Rome
Her enemies' marks upon me. I do love
My country's good with a respect more tender,
More holy and profound, than mine own life,
My dear wife's estimate, her womb's increase
And treasure of my loins; then if I would
Speak that—

Sic. We know your drift:—speak what?

Bru. There 's no more to be said, but he is banish'd,
As enemy to the people and his country:
It shall be so.

Citizens. It shall be so, it shall be so.

Cor. You common cry of curs! whose breath I hate
As reek o' the rotten fens, whose loves I prize
As the dead carcasses of unburied men
That do corrupt my air, I banish you;
And here remain with your uncertainty!
Let every feeble rumour shake your hearts!
Your enemies, with nodding of their plumes,
Fan you into despair! Have the power still
To banish your defenders; till at length
Your ignorance, which finds not till it feels,
Making not reservation of yourselves,
Still your own foes, deliver you as most
Abated captives to some nation
That won you without blows! Despising,
For you, the city, thus I turn my back:
There is a world elsewhere.

[*Exeunt Coriolanus, Cominius, Menenius, Senators and Patricians.*

Æd. The people's enemy is gone, is gone!

Citizens. Our enemy is banish'd! he is gone! Hoo! hoo!

[*They all shout, and throw up their caps.*

Sic. Go, see him out at gates, and follow him,
As he hath follow'd you, with all despite;
Give him deserved vexation. Let a guard

Attend us through the city.
Citizens. Come, come, let 's see him out at gates; come.
The gods preserve our noble tribunes! Come. [*Exeunt.*

ACT IV—Scene I

Rome. Before a gate of the city.

Enter Coriolanus, Volumnia, Virgilia, Menenius, Cominius, with the young Nobility of Rome.

Cor. Come, leave your tears; a brief farewell: the beast
With many heads butts me away. Nay, mother,
Where is your ancient courage? you were used
To say extremity was the trier of spirits;
That common chances common men could bear;
That when the sea was calm all boats alike
Show'd mastership in floating; fortune's blows,
When most struck home, being gentle wounded, craves
A noble cunning: you were used to load me
With precepts that would make invincible
The heart that conn'd them.
Vir. O heavens! O heavens!
Cor. Nay, I prithee, woman,—
Vol. Now the red pestilence strike all trades in Rome,
And occupations perish!
Cor. What, what, what!
I shall be loved when I am lack'd. Nay, mother,
Resume that spirit, when you were wont to say,
If you had been the wife of Hercules,
Six of his labours you 'ld have done, and saved
Your husband so much sweat. Cominius,
Droop not; adieu. Farewell, my wife, my mother.
I 'll do well yet. Thou old and true Menenius,
Thy tears are salter than a younger man's,
And venomous to thine eyes. My sometime general,
I have seen thee stern, and thou hast oft beheld
Heart-hardening spectacles; tell these sad women,
'Tis fond to wail inevitable strokes,
As 'tis to laugh at 'em. My mother, you wot well
My hazards still have been your solace: and
Believe 't not lightly—though I go alone,
Like to a lonely dragon, that his fen
Makes fear'd and talk'd of more than seen—your son
Will or exceed the common, or be caught
With cautelous baits and practice.
Vol. My first son,
Whither wilt thou go? Take good Cominius

With thee awhile: determine on some course,
More than a wild exposture to each chance
That starts i' the way before thee.

Cor. O the gods!

Com. I 'll follow thee a month, devise with thee
Where thou shalt rest, that thou mayst hear of us
And we of thee: so, if the time thrust forth
A cause for thy repeal, we shall not send
O'er the vast world to seek a single man,
And lose advantage, which doth ever cool
I' the absence of the needer.

Cor. Fare ye well:
Thou hast years upon thee; and thou art too full
Of the wars' surfeits, to go rove with one
That 's yet unbruised: bring me but out at gate.
Come, my sweet wife, my dearest mother, and
My friends of noble touch, when I am forth,
Bid me farewell, and smile. I pray you, come,
While I remain above the ground, you shall
Hear from me still, and never of me aught
But what is like me formerly.

Men. That 's worthily
As any ear can hear. Come, let 's not weep.
If I could shake off but one seven years
From these old arms and legs, by the good gods,
I 'ld with thee every foot.

Cor. Give me thy hand:
Come. [*Exeunt.*

Scene II

The same. A street near the gate.

Enter the two Tribunes, Sicinius and Brutus, with the Ædile.

Sic. Bid them all home; he 's gone, and we 'll no further.
The nobility are vex'd, whom we see have sided
In his behalf.

Bru. Now we have shown our power,
Let us seem humbler after it is done
Than when it was a-doing.

Sic. Bid them home:
Say their great enemy is gone, and they
Stand in their ancient strength.

Bru. Dismiss them home. [*Exit Ædile.*
Here comes his mother.

Enter Volumnia, Virgilia, and Menenius.

Sic. Let 's not meet her.

Bru. Why?
Sic. They say she 's mad.
Bru. They have ta'en note of us: keep on your way.
Vol. O, ye're well met: the hoarded plague o' the gods
Requite your love!
Men. Peace, peace; be not so loud.
Vol. If that I could for weeping, you should hear,—
Nay, and you shall hear some. [*To Brutus*] Will you be gone?
Vir. [*To Sicinius*] You shall stay too: I would I had the power
To say so to my husband.
Sic. Are you mankind?
Vol. Ay, fool; is that a shame? Note but this fool.
Was not a man my father? Hadst thou foxship
To banish him that struck more blows for Rome
Than thou hast spoken words?
Sic. O blessed heavens!
Vol. Moe noble blows than ever thou wise words;
And for Rome's good. I 'll tell thee what; yet go:
Nay, but thou shalt stay too: I would my son
Were in Arabia, and thy tribe before him,
His good sword in his hand.
Sic. What then?
Vir. What then!
He 'ld make an end of thy posterity.
Vol. Bastards and all.
Good man, the wounds that he does bear for Rome!
Men. Come, come, peace.
Sic. I would he had continued to his country
As he began, and not unknit himself
The noble knot he made.
Bru. I would he had.
Vol. 'I would he had!' 'Twas you incensed the rabble;
Cats, that can judge as fitly of his worth
As I can of those mysteries which heaven
Will not have earth to know.
Bru. Pray, let us go.
Vol. Now, pray, sir, get you gone:
You have done a brave deed. Ere you go, hear this:
As far as doth the Capitol exceed
The meanest house in Rome, so far my son—
This lady's husband here, this, do ye see?—
Whom you have banish'd, does exceed you all.
Bru. Well, well, we 'll leave you.
Sic. Why stay we to be baited
With one that wants her wits?

Vol. Take my prayers with you. [*Exeunt Tribunes.*
I would the gods had nothing else to do
But to confirm my curses! Could I meet 'em
But once a-day, it would unclog my heart
Of what lies heavy to 't.

Men. You have told them home;
And, by my troth, you have cause. You 'll sup with me?

Vol. Anger 's my meat; I sup upon myself,
And so shall starve with feeding. Come, let 's go:
Leave this faint puling, and lament as I do,
In anger, Juno-like. Come, come, come.
[*Exeunt Vol. and Vir.*

Men. Fie, fie, fie! [*Exit.*

Scene III

A highway between Rome and Antium.

Enter a Roman and a Volsce, meeting.

Rom. I know you well, sir, and you know me: your name, I think, is Adrian.

Vols. It is so, sir: truly, I have forgot you.

Rom. I am a Roman; and my services are, as you are, against 'em: know you me yet?

Vols. Nicanor? no.

Rom. The same, sir.

Vols. You had more beard when I last saw you, but your favour is well appeared by your tongue. What 's the news in Rome? I have a note from the Volscian state, to find you out there: you have well saved me a day's journey.

Rom. There hath been in Rome strange insurrections; the people against the senators, patricians and nobles.

Vols. Hath been! is it ended then? Our state thinks not so: they are in a most warlike preparation, and hope to come upon them in the heat of their division.

Rom. The main blaze of it is past, but a small thing would make it flame again: for the nobles receive so to heart the banishment of that worthy Coriolanus, that they are in a ripe aptness to take all power from the people, and to pluck from them their tribunes for ever. This lies glowing, I can tell you, and is almost mature for the violent breaking out.

Vols. Coriolanus banished!

Rom. Banished, sir.

Vols. You will be welcome with this intelligence, Nicanor.

Rom. The day serves well for them now. I have heard it said, the fittest time to corrupt a man's wife is when she 's fallen out with her husband. Your noble Tullus Aufidius will appear well in these wars, his great opposer, Coriolanus, being now in no request of his country.

Vols. He cannot choose. I am most fortunate, thus accidentally to encounter you: you have ended my business, and I will merrily accompany you home.

Rom. I shall, between this and supper, tell you most strange things from Rome; all tending to the good of their adversaries. Have you an army ready, say you?

Vols. A most royal one; the centurions and their charges, distinctly billeted, already in the entertainment, and to be on foot at an hour's warning.

Rom. I am joyful to hear of their readiness, and am the man, I think, that shall set them in present action. So, sir, heartily well met, and most glad of your company.

Vols. You take my part from me, sir; I have the most cause to be glad of yours.

Rom. Well, let us go together. [*Exeunt.*

Scene IV

Antium. Before Aufidius's house.

Enter Coriolanus in mean apparel, disguised and muffled.

Cor. A goodly city is this Antium. City,
'Tis I that made thy widows: many an heir
Of these fair edifices 'fore my wars
Have I heard groan and drop: then know me not;
Lest that thy wives with spits, and boys with stones,
In puny battle slay me.

Enter a Citizen.

Save you, sir.

Cit. And you.

Cor. Direct me, if it be your will,
Where great Aufidius lies: is he in Antium?

Cit. He is, and feasts the nobles of the state
At his house this night.

Cor. Which is his house, beseech you?

Cit. This, here, before you.

Cor. Thank you, sir: farewell. [*Exit Citizen.*
O world, thy slippery turns! Friends now fast sworn,
Whose double bosoms seem to wear one heart,
Whose hours, whose bed, whose meal and exercise
Are still together, who twin, as 'twere, in love
Unseparable, shall within this hour,
On a dissension of a doit, break out
To bitterest enmity: so, fellest foes,
Whose passions and whose plots have broke their sleep

To take the one the other, by some chance,
Some trick not worth an egg, shall grow dear friends
And interjoin their issues. So with me:
My birth-place hate I, and my love 's upon
This enemy town. I 'll enter: if he slay me,
He does fair justice; if he give me way,
I 'll do his country service. [*Exit.*

Scene V

The same. A hall in Aufidius's house.

Music within. Enter a Servingman.

First Serv. Wine, wine, wine!—What service is here! I think our fellows are asleep. [*Exit.*

Enter another Servingman.

Sec. Serv. Where 's Cotus? my master calls for him. Cotus! [*Exit.*

Enter Coriolanus.

Cor. A goodly house: the feast smells well; but I
Appear not like a guest.

Re-enter the first Servingman.

First Serv. What would you have, friend? whence are you?
Here 's no place for you: pray, go to the door. [*Exit.*

Cor. I have deserved no better entertainment,
In being Coriolanus.

Re-enter second Servingman.

Sec. Serv. Whence are you, sir? Has the porter his eyes in his head, that he gives entrance to such companions? Pray, get you out.

Cor. Away!

Sec. Serv. 'Away!' get you away.

Cor. Now thou 'rt troublesome.

Sec. Serv. Are you so brave? I 'll have you talked with anon.

Enter a third Servingman. The first meets him.

Third Serv. What fellow 's this?

First Serv. A strange one as ever I looked on: I cannot get him out o' the house: prithee, call my master to him. [*Retires.*

Third Serv. What have you to do here, fellow? Pray you, avoid the house.

Cor. Let me but stand; I will not hurt your hearth.

Third Serv. What are you?

Cor. A gentleman.

Third Serv. A marvellous poor one.

Cor. True, so I am.

Third Serv. Pray you, poor gentleman, take up some other station; here's no place for you; pray you, avoid: come.

Cor. Follow your function, go, and batten on cold bits.
[*Pushes him away from him.*

Third Serv. What, you will not? Prithee, tell my master what a strange guest he has here.

Sec. Serv. And I shall. [*Exit.*

Third Serv. Where dwell'st thou?

Cor. Under the canopy.

Third Serv. Under the canopy!

Cor. Ay.

Third Serv. Where 's that?

Cor. I' the city of kites and crows.

Third Serv. I' the city of kites and crows! What an ass it is! Then thou dwell'st with daws too?

Cor. No, I serve not thy master.

Third Serv. How, sir! do you meddle with my master?

Cor. Ay; 'tis an honester service than to meddle with thy mistress:
Thou pratest, and pratest; serve with thy trencher, hence!
[*Beats him away. Exit third Servingman.*

Enter Aufidius with the second Servingman.

Auf. Where is this fellow?

Sec. Serv. Here, sir: I 'ld have beaten him like a dog, but for disturbing the lords within. [*Retires.*

Auf. Whence comest thou? what wouldst thou? thy name?
Why speak'st not? speak, man: what 's thy name?

Cor. [*Unmuffling*] If, Tullus,
Not yet thou knowest me, and, seeing me, dost not
Think me for the man I am, necessity
Commands me name myself.

Auf. What is thy name?

Cor. A name unmusical to the Volscians' ears,
And harsh in sound to thine.

Auf. Say, what 's thy name?
Thou hast a grim appearance, and thy face
Bears a command in 't; though thy tackle 's torn,
Thou show'st a noble vessel: what 's thy name?

Cor. Prepare thy brow to frown:—know'st thou me yet?

Auf. I know thee not:—thy name?

Cor. My name is Caius Marcius, who hath done
To thee particularly, and to all the Volsces,
Great hurt and mischief; thereto witness may
My surname, Coriolanus: the painful service,
The extreme dangers, and the drops of blood
Shed for my thankless country, are requited
But with that surname; a good memory,
And witness of the malice and displeasure

Which thou shouldst bear me: only that name remains:
The cruelty and envy of the people,
Permitted by our dastard nobles, who
Have all forsook me, hath devour'd the rest;
And suffer'd me by the voice of slaves to be
Hoop'd out of Rome. Now, this extremity
Hath brought me to thy hearth: not out of hope—
Mistake me not—to save my life, for if
I had fear'd death, of all the men i' the world
I would have 'voided thee; but in mere spite,
To be full quit of those my banishers,
Stand I before thee here. Then if thou hast
A heart of wreak in thee, thou wilt revenge
Thine own particular wrongs, and stop those maims
Of shame seen through thy country, speed thee straight,
And make my misery serve thy turn: so use it
That my revengeful services may prove
As benefits to thee: for I will fight
Against my canker'd country with the spleen
Of all the under fiends. But if so be
Thou darest not this and that to prove more fortunes
Thou 'rt tired, then, in a word, I also am
Longer to live most weary, and present
My throat to thee and to thy ancient malice;
Which not to cut would show thee but a fool,
Since I have ever follow'd thee with hate,
Drawn tuns of blood out of thy country's breast,
And cannot live but to thy shame, unless
It be to do thee service.

Auf. O Marcius, Marcius!
Each word thou hast spoke hath weeded from my heart
A root of ancient envy. If Jupiter
Should from yond cloud speak divine things,
And say 'Tis true,' I 'ld not believe them more
Than thee, all noble Marcius. Let me twine
Mine arms about that body, where against
My grained ash an hundred times hath broke,
And scarr'd the moon with splinters: here I clip
The anvil of my sword, and do contest
As hotly and as nobly with thy love
As ever in ambitious strength I did
Contend against thy valour. Know thou first,
I loved the maid I married; never man
Sigh'd truer breath; but that I see thee here,
Thou noble thing! more dances my rapt heart

Than when I first my wedded mistress saw
Bestride my threshold. Why, thou Mars! I tell thee,
We have a power on foot; and I had purpose
Once more to hew thy target from thy brawn,
Or lose mine arm for 't: thou hast beat me out
Twelve several times, and I have nightly since
Dreamt of encounters 'twixt thyself and me;
We have been down together in my sleep,
Unbuckling helms, fisting each other's throat;
And waked half dead with nothing. Worthy Marcius,
Had we no quarrel else to Rome but that
Thou art thence banish'd, we would muster all
From twelve to seventy, and pouring war
Into the bowels of ungrateful Rome,
Like a bold flood o'er-beat. O, come, go in,
And take our friendly senators by the hands,
Who now are here, taking their leaves of me,
Who am prepared against your territories,
Though not for Rome itself.

Cor. You bless me, gods!

Auf. Therefore, most absolute sir, if thou wilt have
The leading of thine own revenges, take
The one half of my commission, and set down—
As best thou art experienced, since thou know'st
Thy country's strength and weakness—thine own ways;
Whether to knock against the gates of Rome,
Or rudely visit them in parts remote,
To fright them, ere destroy. But come in:
Let me commend thee first to those that shall
Say yea to thy desires. A thousand welcomes!
And more a friend than e'er an enemy;
Yet, Marcius, that was much. Your hand: most welcome.

[*Exeunt Coriolanus and Aufidius. The two Servingmen come forward.*

First Serv. Here's a strange alteration!

Sec. Serv. By my hand, I had thought to have strucken him with a cudgel; and yet my mind gave me his clothes made a false report of him.

First Serv. What an arm he has! he turned me about with his finger and his thumb, as one would set up a top.

Sec. Serv. Nay, I knew by his face that there was something in him: he had, sir, a kind of face, methought,—I cannot tell how to term it.

First Serv. He had so; looking as it were— Would I were hanged, but I thought there was more in him than I could think.

Sec. Serv. So did I, I 'll be sworn: he is simply the rarest man i' the world.

First Serv. I think he is: but a greater soldier than he, you

Sec. Serv. Who? my master? [wot one.

First Serv. Nay, it 's no matter for that.

Sec. Serv. Worth six on him. [greater soldier.

First Serv. Nay, not so neither: but I take him to be the

Sec. Serv. Faith, look you, one cannot tell how to say that: for the defence of a town, our general is excellent.

First Serv. Ay, and for an assault too.

Re-enter third Servingman.

Third Serv. O slaves, I can tell you news; news, you rascals!

First and Sec. Serv. What, what, what? let 's partake.

Third Serv. I would not be a Roman, of all nations; I had as lieve be a condemned man.

First and Sec. Serv. Wherefore? wherefore?

Third Serv. Why, here 's he that was wont to thwack our general, Caius Marcius.

First Serv. Why do you say, thwack our general?

Third Serv. I do not say, thwack our general; but he was always good enough for him.

Sec. Serv. Come, we are fellows and friends: he was ever too hard for him; I have heard him say so himself.

First Serv. He was too hard for him directly, to say the troth on 't: before Corioli he scotched him and notched him like a carbonado.

Sec. Serv. An he had been cannibally given, he might have broiled and eaten him too.

First Serv. But, more of thy news?

Third Serv. Why, he is so made on here within as if he were son and heir to Mars; set at upper end o' the table; no question asked him by any of the senators, but they stand bald before him. Our general himself makes a mistress of him; sanctifies himself with 's hand, and turns up the white o' the eye to his discourse. But the bottom of the news is, our general is cut i' the middle, and but one half of what he was yesterday; for the other has half, by the entreaty and grant of the whole table. He 'll go, he says, and sowl the porter of Rome gates by the ears: he will mow all down before him, and leave his passage poll'd.

Sec. Serv. And he 's as like to do 't as any man I can imagine.

Third Serv. Do 't! he will do 't; for, look you, sir, he has as many friends as enemies; which friends, sir, as it were, durst not, look you, sir, show themselves, as we term it, his friends whilst he 's in directitude.

First Serv. Directitude! what's that?

Third Serv. But when they shall see, sir, his crest up again and the man in blood, they will out of their burrows, like conies after rain, and revel all with him.

First Serv. But when goes this forward?

Third Serv. To-morrow; to-day; presently: you shall have the drum struck up this afternoon: 'tis, as it were, a parcel of their feast, and to be executed ere they wipe their lips.

Sec. Serv. Why, then we shall have a stirring world again. This peace is nothing, but to rust iron, increase tailors, and breed ballad-makers.

First Serv. Let me have war, say I; it exceeds peace as far as day does night; it's spritely, waking, audible, and full of vent. Peace is a very apoplexy, lethargy, mull'd, deaf, sleepy, insensible; a getter of more bastard children than war's a destroyer of men.

Sec. Serv. 'Tis so: and as war, in some sort, may be said to be a ravisher, so it cannot be denied but peace is a great maker of cuckolds.

First Serv. Ay, and it makes men hate one another.

Third Serv. Reason; because they then less need one another. The wars for my money. I hope to see Romans as cheap as Volscians. They are rising, they are rising.

First and Sec. Serv. In, in, in, in! [*Exeunt.*

SCENE VI

Rome. A public place.

Enter the two Tribunes, Sicinius and Brutus.

Sic. We hear not of him, neither need we fear him;
His remedies are tame i' the present peace
And quietness of the people, which before
Were in wild hurry. Here do we make his friends
Blush that the world goes well; who rather had,
Though they themselves did suffer by 't, behold
Dissentious numbers pestering streets than see
Our tradesmen singing in their shops and going
About their functions friendly.

Bru. We stood to 't in good time.

Enter Menenius.

Is this Menenius?

Sic. 'Tis he, 'tis he: O, he is grown most kind
Of late. Hail, sir!

Men. Hail to you both!

Sic. Your Coriolanus is not much miss'd,
But with his friends: the commonwealth doth stand;

And so would do, were he more angry at it.
Men. All 's well; and might have been much better, if
He could have temporized.
Sic. Where is he, hear you?
Men. Nay, I hear nothing: his mother and his wife
Hear nothing from him.

Enter three or four Citizens.

Citizens. The gods preserve you both!
Sic. God-den, our neighbours.
Bru. God-den to you all, god-den to you all.
First Cit. Ourselves, our wives, and children, on our knees,
Are bound to pray for you both.
Sic. Live, and thrive!
Bru. Farewell, kind neighbours: we wish'd Coriolanus
Had loved you as we did.
Citizens. Now the gods keep you!
Both Tri. Farewell, farewell. [*Exeunt Citizens.*
Sic. This is a happier and more comely time
Than when these fellows ran about the streets,
Crying confusion.
Bru. Caius Marcius was
A worthy officer i' the war, but insolent,
O'ercome with pride, ambitious past all thinking,
Self-loving,—
Sic. And affecting one sole throne,
Without assistance.
Men. I think not so.
Sic. We should by this, to all our lamentation,
If he had gone forth consul, found it so.
Bru. The gods have well prevented it, and Rome
Sits safe and still without him.

Enter an Ædile.

Æd. Worthy tribunes,
There is a slave, whom we have put in prison,
Reports, the Volsces with two several powers
Are enter'd in the Roman territories,
And with the deepest malice of the war
Destroy what lies before 'em.
Men. 'Tis Aufidius,
Who, hearing of our Marcius' banishment,
Thrusts forth his horns again into the world;
Which were inshell'd when Marcius stood for Rome,
And durst not once peep out.
Sic. Come, what talk you
Of Marcius?

Bru. Go see this rumourer whipp'd. It cannot be
The Volsces dare break with us.
Men. Cannot be!
We have record that very well it can,
And three examples of the like have been
Within my age. But reason with the fellow,
Before you punish him, where he heard this,
Lest you shall chance to whip your information,
And beat the messenger who bids beware
Of what is to be dreaded.
Sic. Tell not me:
I know this cannot be.
Bru. Not possible.

Enter a Messenger.

Mess. The nobles in great earnestness are going
All to the senate-house: some news is come
That turns their countenances.
Sic. 'Tis this slave;
Go whip him 'fore the people's eyes: his raising;
Nothing but his report.
Mess. Yes, worthy sir,
The slave's report is seconded; and more,
More fearful, is deliver'd.
Sic. What more fearful?
Mess. It is spoke freely out of many mouths—
How probable I do not know—that Marcius,
Join'd with Aufidius, leads a power 'gainst Rome,
And vows revenge as spacious as between
The young'st and oldest thing.
Sic. This is most likely!
Bru. Raised only, that the weaker sort may wish
Good Marcius home again.
Sic. The very trick on 't.
Men. This is unlikely:
He and Aufidius can no more atone
Than violentest contrariety.

Enter a second Messenger.

Sec. Mess. You are sent for to the senate:
A fearful army, led by Caius Marcius
Associated with Aufidius, rages
Upon our territories; and have already
O'erborne their way, consumed with fire, and took
What lay before them.

Enter Cominius.

Com. O, you have made good work!

Men. What news? what news?
Com. You have holp to ravish your own daughters, and
To melt the city leads upon your pates;
To see your wives dishonour'd to your noses,—
Men. What's the news? what's the news?
Com. Your temples burned in their cement, and
Your franchises, whereon you stood, confined
Into an auger's bore.
Men. Pray now, your news?—
You have made fair work, I fear me.—Pray, your news?—
If Marcius should be join'd with Volscians,—
Com. If!
He is their god: he leads them like a thing
Made by some other deity than nature,
That shapes man better; and they follow him,
Against us brats, with no less confidence
Than boys pursuing summer butterflies,
Or butchers killing flies.
Men. You have made good work,
You and your apron-men; you that stood so much
Upon the voice of occupation and
The breath of garlic-eaters!
Com. He'll shake your Rome about your ears.
Men. As Hercules
Did shake down mellow fruit. You have made fair work!
Bru. But is this true, sir?
Com. Ay; and you'll look pale
Before you find it other. All the regions
Do smilingly revolt; and who resist
Are mock'd for valiant ignorance,
And perish constant fools. Who is't can blame him?
Your enemies and his find something in him.
Men. We are all undone, unless
The noble man have mercy.
Com. Who shall ask it?
The tribunes cannot do't for shame; the people
Deserve such pity of him as the wolf
Does of the shepherds: for his best friends, if they
Should say 'Be good to Rome,' they charged him even
As those should do that had deserved his hate,
And therein show'd like enemies.
Men. 'Tis true:
If he were putting to my house the brand
That should consume it, I have not the face
To say 'Beseech you, cease.' You have made fair hands,

You and your crafts! you have crafted fair!

Com. You have brought
A trembling upon Rome such as was never
So incapable of help.

Both Tri. Say not, we brought it.

Men. How! was it we? we loved him; but, like beasts
And cowardly nobles, gave way unto your clusters,
Who did hoot him out o' the city.

Com. But I fear
They 'll roar him in again. Tullus Aufidius,
The second name of men, obeys his points
As if he were his officer: desperation
Is all the policy, strength and defence,
That Rome can make against them.

Enter a troop of Citizens.

Men. Here come the clusters.
And is Aufidius with him? You are they
That made the air unwholesome, when you cast
Your stinking greasy caps in hooting at
Coriolanus' exile. Now he 's coming;
And not a hair upon a soldier's head
Which will not prove a whip: as many coxcombs
As you threw caps up will he tumble down,
And pay you for your voices. 'Tis no matter;
If he could burn us all into one coal,
We have deserved it.

Citizens. Faith, we hear fearful news.

First Cit. For mine own part,
When I said, banish him, I said, 'twas pity.

Sec. Cit. And so did I.

Third Cit. And so did I; and, to say the truth, so did very many of us: that we did, we did for the best; and though we willingly consented to his banishment, yet it was against our will.

Com. Ye 're goodly things, you voices!

Men. You have made
Good work, you and your cry! Shall 's to the Capitol?

Com. O, ay, what else? [*Exeunt Cominius and Menenius.*

Sic. Go, masters, get you home; be not dismay'd:
These are a side that would be glad to have
This true which they so seem to fear. Go home,
And show no sign of fear.

First Cit. The gods be good to us! Come, masters, let 's home. I ever said we were i' the wrong when we banished him.

Sec. Cit. So did we all. But, come, let 's home. [*Exeunt Citizens.*

Bru. I do not like this news.
Sic. Nor I.
Bru. Let 's to the Capitol: would half my wealth
Would buy this for a lie!
Sic. Pray, let us go. [*Exeunt.*

Scene VII

A camp, at a small distance from Rome.
Enter Aufidius with his Lieutenant.

Auf. Do they still fly to the Roman?
Lieu. I do not know what witchcraft 's in him, but
Your soldiers use him as the grace 'fore meat,
Their talk at table and their thanks at end;
And you are darken'd in this action, sir,
Even by your own.
Auf. I cannot help it now,
Unless, by using means, I lame the foot
Of our design. He bears himself more proudlier,
Even to my person, than I thought he would
When first I did embrace him: yet his nature
In that 's no changeling; and I must excuse
What cannot be amended.
Lieu. Yet I wish, sir—
I mean for your particular—you had not
Join'd in commission with him; but either
Had borne the action of yourself, or else
To him had left it solely.
Auf. I understand thee well; and be thou sure,
When he shall come to his account, he knows not
What I can urge against him. Although it seems,
And so he thinks, and is no less apparent
To the vulgar eye, that he bears all things fairly,
And shows good husbandry for the Volscian state,
Fights dragon-like, and does achieve as soon
As draw his sword, yet he hath left undone
That which shall break his neck or hazard mine,
Whene'er we come to our account.
Lieu. Sir, I beseech you, think you he 'll carry Rome?
Auf. All places yield to him ere he sits down;
And the nobility of Rome are his:
The senators and patricians love him too:
The tribunes are no soldiers; and their people
Will be as rash in the repeal, as hasty
To expel him thence. I think he 'll be to Rome
As is the osprey to the fish, who takes it

By sovereignty of nature. First he was
A noble servant to them; but he could not
Carry his honours even: whether 'twas pride,
Which out of daily fortune ever taints
The happy man; whether defect of judgement,
To fail in the disposing of those chances
Which he was lord of; or whether nature,
Not to be other than one thing, not moving
From the casque to the cushion, but commanding peace
Even with the same austerity and garb
As he controll'd the war; but one of these—
As he hath spices of them all, not all,
For I dare so far free him—made him fear'd,
So hated, and so banish'd: but he has a merit,
To choke it in the utterance. So our virtues
Lie in the interpretation of the time;
And power, unto itself most commendable,
Hath not a tomb so evident as a chair
To extol what it hath done.
One fire drives out one fire; one nail, one nail;
Rights by rights fouler, strengths by strengths do fail.
Come, let 's away. When, Caius, Rome is thine,
Thou art poor'st of all; then shortly art thou mine. [*Exeunt*

ACT V—Scene I

Rome. A public place.

Enter Menenius, Cominius, Sicinius and Brutus, the two Tribunes, with others.

Men. No, I'll not go: you hear what he hath said
Which was sometime his general, who loved him
In a most dear particular. He call'd me father:
But what o' that? Go, you that banish'd him;
A mile before his tent fall down, and knee
The way into his mercy: nay, if he coy'd
To hear Cominius speak, I'll keep at home.

Com. He would not seem to know me.

Men. Do you hear?

Com. Yet one time he did call me by my name:
I urged our old acquaintance, and the drops
That we have bled together. Coriolanus
He would not answer to: forbad all names;
He was a kind of nothing, titleless,
Till he had forged himself a name o' the fire
Of burning Rome.

Men. Why, so: you have made good work!

A pair of tribunes that have rack'd for Rome,
To make coals cheap: a noble memory!

Com. I minded him how royal 'twas to pardon
When it was less expected: he replied,
It was a bare petition of a state
To one whom they had punish'd.

Men. Very well:
Could he say less?

Com. I offer'd to awaken his regard
For 's private friends: his answer to me was,
He could not stay to pick them in a pile
Of noisome musty chaff: he said, 'twas folly,
For one poor grain or two, to leave unburnt,
And still to nose the offence.

Men. For one poor grain or two!
I am one of those; his mother, wife, his child,
And this brave fellow too, we are the grains:
You are the musty chaff, and you are smelt
Above the moon: we must be burnt for you.

Sic. Nay, pray, be patient: if you refuse your aid
In this so never-needed help, yet do not
Upbraid 's with our distress. Be sure, if you
Would be your country's pleader, your good tongue,
More than the instant army we can make,
Might stop our countryman.

Men. No, I'll not meddle.

Sic. Pray you, go to him.

Men. What should I do?

Bru. Only make trial what your love can do
For Rome, towards Marcius.

Men. Well, and say that Marcius
Return me, as Cominius is return'd,
Unheard; what then?
But as a discontented friend, grief-shot
With his unkindness? say 't be so?

Sic. Yet your good will
Must have that thanks from Rome, after the measure
As you intended well.

Men. I'll undertake 't:
I think he'll hear me. Yet, to bite his lip
And hum at good Cominius, much unhearts me.
He was not taken well; he had not dined:
The veins unfill'd, our blood is cold, and then
We pout upon the morning, are unapt
To give or to forgive; but when we have stuff'd

These pipes and these conveyances of our blood
With wine and feeding, we have suppler souls
Than in our priest-like fasts: therefore I 'll watch him
Till he be dieted to my request,
And then I 'll set upon him.

Bru. You know the very road into his kindness,
And cannot lose your way.

Men. Good faith, I 'll prove him,
Speed how it will. I shall ere long have knowledge
Of my success. [*Exit.*

Com. He 'll never hear him.

Sic. Not?

Com. I tell you, he does sit in gold, his eye
Red as 'twould burn Rome; and his injury
The gaoler to his pity. I kneel'd before him;
'Twas very faintly he said 'Rise;' dismiss'd me
Thus, with his speechless hand: what he would do,
He sent in writing after me; what he would not,
Bound with an oath to yield to his conditions:
So that all hope is vain,
Unless his noble mother, and his wife;
Who, as I hear, mean to solicit him
For mercy to his country. Therefore, let 's hence,
And with our fair entreaties haste them on. [*Exeunt.*

Scene II

Entrance to the Volscian camp before Rome.
Two Sentinels on guard.
Enter to them, Menenius.

First Sen. Stay: whence are you?

Sec. Sen. Stand, and go back.

Men. You guard like men; 'tis well: but, by your leave,
I am an officer of state, and come
To speak with Coriolanus.

First Sen. From whence?

Men. From Rome.

First Sen. You may not pass, you must return: our general
Will no more hear from thence.

Sec. Sen. You 'll see your Rome embraced with fire, before
You 'll speak with Coriolanus.

Men. Good my friends,
If you have heard your general talk of Rome,
And of his friends there, it is lots to blanks
My name hath touch'd your ears: it is Menenius.

First Sen. Be it so; go back: the virtue of your name
Is not here passable.

Men. I tell thee, fellow,
Thy general is my lover: I have been
The book of his good acts, whence men have read
His fame unparallel'd haply amplified;
For I have ever verified my friends,
Of whom he's chief, with all the size that verity
Would without lapsing suffer: nay, sometimes,
Like to a bowl upon a subtle ground,
I have tumbled past the throw, and in his praise
Have almost stamp'd the leasing: therefore, fellow,
I must have leave to pass.

First Sen. Faith, sir, if you had told as many lies in his behalf as you have uttered words in your own, you should not pass here; no, though it were as virtuous to lie as to live chastely. Therefore go back.

Men. Prithee, fellow, remember my name is Menenius, always factionary on the party of your general.

Sec. Sen. Howsoever you have been his liar, as you say you have, I am one that, telling true under him, must say, you cannot pass. Therefore go back.

Men. Has he dined, canst thou tell? for I would not speak with him till after dinner.

First Sen. You are a Roman, are you?

Men. I am, as thy general is.

First Sen. Then you should hate Rome, as he does. Can you, when you have pushed out your gates the very defender of them, and, in a violent popular ignorance, given your enemy your shield, think to front his revenges with the easy groans of old women, the virginal palms of your daughters, or with the palsied intercession of such a decayed dotant as you seem to be? Can you think to blow out the intended fire your city is ready to flame in, with such weak breath as this? No, you are deceived; therefore, back to Rome, and prepare for your execution: you are condemned; our general has sworn you out of reprieve and pardon.

Men. Sirrah, if thy captain knew I were here, he would use me with estimation.

First Sen. Come, my captain knows you not.

Men. I mean, thy general.

First Sen. My general cares not for you. Back, I say, go; lest I let forth your half-pint of blood;—back,—that's the utmost of your having:—back.

Men. Nay, but, fellow, fellow,—

Enter Coriolanus and Aufidius.

Cor. What's the matter?

Men. Now, you companion, I'll say an errand for you: you shall know now that I am in estimation; you shall perceive that a Jack guardant cannot office me from my son Coriolanus: guess, but by my entertainment with him, if thou standest not i' the state of hanging, or of some death more long in spectatorship and crueller in suffering; behold now presently, and swoon for what's to come upon thee. The glorious gods sit in hourly synod about thy particular prosperity, and love thee no worse than thy old father Menenius does! O my son, my son! thou art preparing fire for us; look thee, here's water to quench it. I was hardly moved to come to thee; but being assured none but myself could move thee, I have been blown out of your gates with sighs; and conjure thee to pardon Rome and thy petitionary countrymen. The good gods assuage thy wrath, and turn the dregs of it upon this varlet here,—this, who, like a block, hath denied my access to thee.

Cor. Away!

Men. How! away!

Cor. Wife, mother, child, I know not. My affairs
Are servanted to others: though I owe
My revenge properly, my remission lies
In Volscian breasts. That we have been familiar,
Ingrate forgetfulness shall poison rather
Than pity note how much. Therefore be gone.
Mine ears against your suits are stronger than
Your gates against my force. Yet, for I loved thee,
Take this along; I writ it for thy sake,
And would have sent it. [*Gives him a letter.*] Another word,
I will not hear thee speak. This man, Aufidius, [Menenius,
Was my beloved in Rome: yet thou behold'st.

Auf. You keep a constant temper.

[*Exeunt Coriolanus and Aufidius.*

First Sen. Now, sir, is your name Menenius?

Sec. Sen. 'Tis a spell, you see, of much power: you know the way home again.

First Sen. Do you hear how we are shent for keeping your greatness back?

Sec. Sen. What cause, do you think, I have to swoon?

Men. I neither care for the world nor your general: for such things as you, I can scarce think there's any, ye're so slight. He that hath a will to die by himself fears it not from another: let your general do his worst. For you, be that you are, long; and your misery increase with your age! I say to you, as I was said to, Away! [*Exit.*

First Sen. A noble fellow, I warrant him.

Sec. Sen. The worthy fellow is our general: he's the rock, the oak not to be wind-shaken. [*Exeunt.*

Scene III

The tent of Coriolanus.

Enter Coriolanus, Aufidius, and others.

Cor. We will before the walls of Rome to-morrow
Set down our host. My partner in this action,
You must report to the Volscian lords how plainly
I have borne this business.

Auf. Only their ends
You have respected; stopp'd your ears against
The general suit of Rome; never admitted
A private whisper, no, not with such friends
That thought them sure of you.

Cor. This last old man,
Whom with a crack'd heart I have sent to Rome,
Loved me above the measure of a father,
Nay, godded me indeed. Their latest refuge
Was to send him; for whose old love I have,
Though I show'd sourly to him, once more offer'd
The first conditions, which they did refuse
And cannot now accept; to grace him only
That thought he could do more, a very little
I have yielded to: fresh embassies and suits,
Nor from the state nor private friends, hereafter
Will I lend ear to. [*Shout within.*] Ha! what shout is this?
Shall I be tempted to infringe my vow
In the same time 'tis made? I will not.

Enter, in mourning habits, Virgilia, Volumnia, leading young Marcius, Valeria, and Attendants.

My wife comes foremost; then the honour'd mould
Wherein this trunk was framed, and in her hand
The grandchild to her blood. But out, affection!
All bond and privilege of nature, break!
Let it be virtuous to be obstinate.
What is that curtsy worth? or those doves' eyes,
Which can make gods forsworn? I melt, and am not
Of stronger earth than others. My mother bows;
As if Olympus to a molehill should
In supplication nod: and my young boy
Hath an aspect of intercession, which

Great nature cries 'Deny not.' Let the Volsces
Plough Rome, and harrow Italy: I'll never
Be such a gosling to obey instinct; but stand,
As if a man were author of himself
And knew no other kin.

Vir. My lord and husband!

Cor. These eyes are not the same I wore in Rome.

Vir. The sorrow that delivers us thus changed
Makes you think so.

Cor. Like a dull actor now
I have forgot my part and I am out,
Even to a full disgrace. Best of my flesh,
Forgive my tyranny; but do not say,
For that 'Forgive our Romans.' O, a kiss
Long as my exile, sweet as my revenge!
Now, by the jealous queen of heaven, that kiss
I carried from thee, dear, and my true lip
Hath virgin'd it e'er since. You gods! I prate,
And the most noble mother of the world
Leave unsaluted: sink, my knee, i' the earth; [*Kneels.*
Of thy deep duty more impression show
Than that of common sons.

Vol. O, stand up blest!
Whilst, with no softer cushion than the flint,
I kneel before thee, and unproperly
Show duty, as mistaken all this while
Between the child and parent. [*Kneels.*

Cor. What is this?
Your knees to me? to your corrected son?
Then let the pebbles on the hungry beach
Fillip the stars; then let the mutinous winds
Strike the proud cedars 'gainst the fiery sun,
Murdering impossibility, to make
What cannot be, slight work.

Vol. Thou art my warrior;
I holp to frame thee. Do you know this lady?

Cor. The noble sister of Publicola,
The moon of Rome; chaste as the icicle
That's curdied by the frost from purest snow
And hangs on Dian's temple: dear Valeria!

Vol. This is a poor epitome of yours,
Which by the interpretation of full time
May show like all yourself.

Cor. The god of soldiers,
With the consent of supreme Jove, inform

Thy thoughts with nobleness, that thou mayst prove
To shame unvulnerable, and stick i' the wars
Like a great sea-mark, standing every flaw
And saving those that eye thee!

Vol. Your knee, sirrah.

Cor. That 's my brave boy!

Vol. Even he, your wife, this lady and myself
Are suitors to you.

Cor. I beseech you, peace:
Or, if you 'ld ask, remember this before:
The thing I have forsworn to grant may never
Be held by you denials. Do not bid me
Dismiss my soldiers, or capitulate
Again with Rome's mechanics: tell me not
Wherein I seem unnatural: desire not
To allay my rages and revenges with
Your colder reasons.

Vol. O, no more, no more!
You have said you will not grant us any thing;
For we have nothing else to ask, but that
Which you deny already: yet we will ask;
That, if you fail in our request, the blame
May hang upon your hardness: therefore hear us.

Cor. Aufidius, and you Volsces, mark; for we 'll
Hear nought from Rome in private. Your request?

Vol. Should we be silent and not speak, our raiment
And state of bodies would bewray what life
We have led since thy exile. Think with thyself
How more unfortunate than all living women
Are we come hither: since that thy sight, which should
Make our eyes flow with joy, hearts dance with comforts,
Constrains them weep and shake with fear and sorrow;
Making the mother, wife and child, to see
The son, the husband and the father, tearing
His country's bowels out. And to poor we
Thine enmity's most capital: thou barr'st us
Our prayers to the gods, which is a comfort
That all but we enjoy; for how can we,
Alas, how can we for our country pray,
Whereto we are bound, together with thy victory,
Whereto we are bound? alack, or we must lose
The country, our dear nurse, or else thy person,
Our comfort in the country. We must find
An evident calamity, though we had
Our wish, which side should win; for either thou

Must, as a foreign recreant, be led
With manacles thorough our streets, or else
Triumphantly tread on thy country's ruin,
And bear the palm for having bravely shed
Thy wife and children's blood. For myself, son,
I purpose not to wait on fortune till
These wars determine: if I cannot persuade thee
Rather to show a noble grace to both parts
Than seek the end of one, thou shalt no sooner
March to assault thy country than to tread—
Trust to 't, thou shalt not—on thy mother's womb,
That brought thee to this world.

Vir. Ay, and mine,
That brought you forth this boy, to keep your name
Living to time.

Boy. A' shall not tread on me;
I 'll run away till I am bigger, but then I 'll fight.

Cor. Not of a woman's tenderness to be,
Requires nor child nor woman's face to see.
I have sat too long. [*Rising.*

Vol. Nay, go not from us thus.
If it were so that our request did tend
To save the Romans, thereby to destroy
The Volsces whom you serve, you might condemn us,
As poisonous of your honour: no; our suit
Is, that you reconcile them: while the Volsces
May say 'This mercy we have show'd,' the Romans,
'This we received;' and each in either side
Give the all-hail to thee, and cry 'Be blest
For making up this peace!' Thou know'st, great son,
The end of war 's uncertain, but this certain,
That if thou conquer Rome, the benefit
Which thou shalt thereby reap is such a name
Whose repetition will be dogg'd with curses;
Whose chronicle thus writ: 'The man was noble,
But with his last attempt he wiped it out,
Destroy'd his country, and his name remains
To the ensuing age abhorr'd.' Speak to me, son:
Thou hast affected the fine strains of honour,
To imitate the graces of the gods;
To tear with thunder the wide cheeks o' the air,
And yet to charge thy sulphur with a bolt
That should but rive an oak. Why dost not speak?
Think'st thou it honourable for a noble man
Still to remember wrongs? Daughter, speak you:

He cares not for your weeping. Speak thou, boy:
Perhaps thy childishness will move him more
Than can our reasons. There 's no man in the world
More bound to 's mother, yet here he lets me prate
Like one i' the stocks. Thou hast never in thy life
Show'd thy dear mother any courtesy;
When she, poor hen, fond of no second brood,
Has cluck'd thee to the wars, and safely home,
Loaden with honour. Say my request 's unjust,
And spurn me back: but if it be not so,
Thou art not honest, and the gods will plague thee,
That thou restrain'st from me the duty which
To a mother's part belongs. He turns away:
Down, ladies; let us shame him with our knees.
To his surname Coriolanus 'longs more pride
Than pity to our prayers. Down: an end;
This is the last: so we will home to Rome,
And die among our neighbours. Nay, behold 's:
This boy, that cannot tell what he would have,
But kneels and holds up hands for fellowship,
Does reason our petition with more strength
Than thou hast to deny 't. Come, let us go:
This fellow had a Volscian to his mother;
His wife is in Corioli, and his child
Like him by chance. Yet give us our dispatch:
I am hush'd until our city be a-fire,
And then I 'll speak a little.

Cor. [*After holding her by the hand, silent*] O, mother, mother!
What have you done? Behold, the heavens do ope,
The gods look down, and this unnatural scene
They laugh at. O my mother, mother! O!
You have won a happy victory to Rome;
But, for your son, believe it, O, believe it,
Most dangerously you have with him prevail'd,
If not most mortal to him. But let it come.
Aufidius, though I cannot make true wars,
I 'll frame convenient peace. Now, good Aufidius,
Were you in my stead, would you have heard
A mother less? or granted less, Aufidius?

Auf. I was moved withal.

Cor. I dare be sworn you were:
And, sir, it is no little thing to make
Mine eyes to sweat compassion. But, good sir,
What peace you 'll make, advise me: for my part,
I 'll not to Rome, I 'll back with you; and pray you,

Stand to me in this cause. O mother! wife!

Auf. [*Aside*] I am glad thou hast set thy mercy and thy honour
At difference in thee: out of that I 'll work
Myself a former fortune. [*The Ladies make signs to Coriolanus.*

Cor. [*To Volumnia, Virgilia, &c.*] Ay, by and by:—
But we will drink together; and you shall bear
A better witness back than words, which we
On like conditions will have counter-seal'd.
Come, enter with us. Ladies, you deserve
To have a temple built you: all the swords
In Italy, and her confederate arms,
Could not have made this peace. [*Exeunt.*

Scene IV

Rome. A public place.

Enter Menenius and Sicinius.

Men. See you yond coign o' the Capitol, yond corner-stone?

Sic. Why, what of that?

Men. If it be possible for you to displace it with your little finger, there is some hope the ladies of Rome, especially his mother, may prevail with him. But I say there is no hope in 't: our throats are sentenced, and stay upon execution.

Sic. Is 't possible that so short a time can alter the condition of a man?

Men. There is differency between a grub and a butterfly; yet your butterfly was a grub. This Marcius is grown from man to dragon: he has wings; he 's more than a creeping thing.

Sic. He loved his mother dearly.

Men. So did he me: and he no more remembers his mother now than an eight-year-old horse. The tartness of his face sours ripe grapes: when he walks, he moves like an engine, and the ground shrinks before his treading: he is able to pierce a corslet with his eye; talks like a knell, and his hum is a battery. He sits in his state, as a thing made for Alexander. What he bids be done, is finished with his bidding. He wants nothing of a god but eternity and a heaven to throne in.

Sic. Yes, mercy, if you report him truly.

Men. I paint him in the character. Mark what mercy his mother shall bring from him: there is no more mercy in him than there is milk in a male tiger; that shall our poor city find: and all this is long of you.

Sic. The gods be good unto us!

Men. No, in such a case the gods will not be good unto us. When we banished him, we respected not them; and, he returning to break our necks, they respect not us.

Enter a Messenger.

Mess. Sir, if you 'ld save your life, fly to your house:
The plebeians have got your fellow-tribune,
And hale him up and down, all swearing, if
The Roman ladies bring not comfort home,
They 'll give him death by inches.

Enter another Messenger.

Sic. What 's the news?
Sec. Mess. Good news, good news; the ladies have prevail'd,
The Volscians are dislodged, and Marcius gone:
A merrier day did never yet greet Rome,
No, not the expulsion of the Tarquins.
Sic. Friend,
Art thou certain this is true? is it most certain?
Sec. Mess. As certain as I know the sun is fire:
Where have you lurk'd, that you make doubt of it?
Ne'er through an arch so hurried the blown tide,
As the recomforted through the gates. Why, hark you!
[*Trumpets; hautboys; drums beat; all together.*
The trumpets, sackbuts, psalteries and fifes,
Tabors and cymbals and the shouting Romans,
Make the sun dance. Hark you! [*A shout within.*
Men. This is good news:
I will go meet the ladies. This Volumnia
Is worth of consuls, senators, patricians,
A city full; of tribunes, such as you,
A sea and land full. You have pray'd well to-day:
This morning for ten thousand of your throats
I 'ld not have given a doit. Hark, how they joy!
[*Music still, with shouts.*
Sic. First, the gods bless you for your tidings; next,
Accept my thankfulness.
Sec. Mess. Sir, we have all
Great cause to give great thanks.
Sic. They are near the city?
Sec. Mess. Almost at point to enter.
Sic. We will meet them,
And help the joy. [*Exeunt.*

Scene V

The same. A street near the gate.

Enter two Senators with Volumnia, Virgilia, Valeria, &c. passing over the stage, followed by Patricians and others.

First Sen. Behold our patroness, the life of Rome!
Call all your tribes together, praise the gods,

And make triumphant fires; strew flowers before them:
Unshout the noise that banish'd Marcius,
Repeal him with the welcome of his mother;
Cry 'Welcome, ladies, welcome!'

All. Welcome, ladies,
Welcome! [*A flourish with drums and trumpets. Exeunt.*

Scene VI

Corioli. A public place.

Enter Tullus Aufidius, with Attendants.

Auf. Go tell the lords o' the city I am here:
Deliver them this paper: having read it,
Bid them repair to the market-place, where I,
Even in theirs and in the commons' ears,
Will vouch the truth of it. Him I accuse
The city ports by this hath enter'd, and
Intends to appear before the people, hoping
To purge himself with words: dispatch. [*Exeunt Attendants.*

Enter three or four Conspirators of Aufidius' faction.

Most welcome!

First Con. How is it with our general?

Auf. Even so
As with a man by his own alms empoison'd,
And with his charity slain.

Sec. Con. Most noble sir,
If you do hold the same intent wherein
You wish'd us parties, we'll deliver you
Of your great danger.

Auf. Sir, I cannot tell:
We must proceed as we do find the people.

Third Con. The people will remain uncertain whilst
'Twixt you there's difference; but the fall of either
Makes the survivor heir of all.

Auf. I know it,
And my pretext to strike at him admits
A good construction. I raised him, and I pawn'd
Mine honour for his truth: who being so heighten'd
He water'd his new plants with dews of flattery,
Seducing so my friends; and, to this end,
He bow'd his nature, never known before
But to be rough, unswayable and free.

Third Con. Sir, his stoutness
When he did stand for consul, which he lost
By lack of stooping,—

Auf. That I would have spoke of:
Being banish'd for 't, he came unto my hearth;
Presented to my knife his throat: I took him,
Made him joint-servant with me, gave him way
In all his own desires, nay, let him choose
Out of my files, his projects to accomplish,
My best and freshest men, served his designments
In mine own person, holp to reap the fame
Which he did end all his; and took some pride
To do myself this wrong: till at the last
I seem'd his follower, not partner, and
He waged me with his countenance, as if
I had been mercenary.

First Con. So he did, my lord:
The army marvell'd at it, and in the last,
When he had carried Rome and that we look'd
For no less spoil than glory—

Auf. There was it:
For which my sinews shall be stretch'd upon him.
At a few drops of women's rheum, which are
As cheap as lies, he sold the blood and labour
Of our great action: therefore shall he die,
And I 'll renew me in his fall. But hark!
[*Drums and trumpets sound, with great shouts of the people.*

First Con. Your native town you enter'd like a post,
And had no welcomes home; but he returns,
Splitting the air with noise.

Sec. Con. And patient fools,
Whose children he hath slain, their base throats tear
With giving him glory.

Third Con. Therefore, at your vantage,
Ere he express himself, or move the people
With what he would say, let him feel your sword,
Which we will second. When he lies along,
After your way his tale pronounced shall bury
His reasons with his body.

Auf. Say no more:
Here come the lords.

Enter the Lords of the city.

All the Lords. You are most welcome home.

Auf. I have not deserved it.
But, worthy lords, have you with heed perused
What I have written to you?

Lords. We have.

First Lord. And grieve to hear 't.

What faults he made before the last, I think
Might have found easy fines: but there to end
Where he was to begin, and give away
The benefit of our levies, answering us
With our own charge, making a treaty where
There was a yielding,—this admits no excuse.

Auf. He approaches: you shall hear him.

Enter Coriolanus, marching with drum and colours; the commoners being with him.

Cor. Hail, lords! I am return'd your soldier;
No more infected with my country's love
Than when I parted hence, but still subsisting
Under your great command. You are to know,
That prosperously I have attempted, and
With bloody passage led your wars even to
The gates of Rome. Our spoils we have brought home
Do more than counterpoise a full third part
The charges of the action. We have made peace,
With no less honour to the Antiates
Than shame to the Romans: and we here deliver,
Subscribed by the consuls and patricians,
Together with the seal o' the senate, what
We have compounded on.

Auf. Read it not, noble lords;
But tell the traitor, in the highest degree
He hath abused your powers.

Cor. Traitor! how now!

Auf. Ay, traitor, Marcius!

Cor. Marcius!

Auf. Ay, Marcius, Caius Marcius: dost thou think
I 'll grace thee with that robbery, thy stol'n name
Coriolanus, in Corioli?
You lords and heads o' the state, perfidiously
He has betray'd your business, and given up,
For certain drops of salt, your city Rome,
I say 'your city,' to his wife and mother;
Breaking his oath and resolution, like
A twist of rotten silk; never admitting
Counsel o' the war; but at his nurse's tears
He whined and roar'd away your victory;
That pages blush'd at him, and men of heart
Look'd wondering each at other.

Cor. Hear'st thou, Mars?

Auf. Name not the god, thou boy of tears!

Cor. Ha!

Auf. No more.
Cor. Measureless liar, thou hast made my heart
Too great for what contains it. 'Boy!' O slave!
Pardon me, lords, 'tis the first time that ever
I was forced to scold. Your judgements, my grave lords,
Must give this cur the lie: and his own notion—
Who wears my stripes impress'd upon him; that
Must bear my beating to his grave—shall join
To thrust the lie unto him.
First Lord. Peace, both, and hear me speak.
Cor. Cut me to pieces, Volsces; men and lads,
Stain all your edges on me. 'Boy!' false hound!
If you have writ your annals true, 'tis there,
That, like an eagle in a dove-cote, I
Flutter'd your Volscians in Corioli;
Alone I did it. 'Boy!'
Auf. Why, noble lords,
Will you be put in mind of his blind fortune,
Which was your shame, by this unholy braggart,
'Fore your own eyes and ears?
All Consp. Let him die for 't.
All the People. 'Tear him to pieces.' 'Do it presently.' 'He killed my son.' 'My daughter.' 'He killed my cousin Marcus.' 'He killed my father.'
Sec. Lord. Peace, ho! no outrage: peace!
The man is noble, and his fame folds-in
This orb o' the earth. His last offences to us
Shall have judicious hearing. Stand, Aufidius,
And trouble not the peace.
Cor. O that I had him,
With six Aufidiuses, or more, his tribe,
To use my lawful sword!
Auf. Insolent villain!
All Consp. Kill, kill, kill, kill, kill him!
[*The Conspirators draw, and kill Coriolanus: Aufidius stands on his body.*
Lords. Hold, hold, hold, hold!
Auf. My noble masters, hear me speak.
First Lord. O Tullus,—
Sec. Lord. Thou hast done a deed whereat valour will weep.
Third Lord. Tread not upon him. Masters all, be quiet;
Put up your swords.
Auf. My lords, when you shall know—as in this rage
Provoked by him, you cannot—the great danger
Which this man's life did owe you, you 'll rejoice

That he is thus cut off. Please it your honours
To call me to your senate, I 'll deliver
Myself your loyal servant, or endure
Your heaviest censure.

First Lord. Bear from hence his body;
And mourn you for him: let him be regarded
As the most noble corse that ever herald
Did follow to his urn.

Sec. Lord. His own impatience
Takes from Aufidius a great part of blame.
Let 's make the best of it.

Auf. My rage is gone,
And I am struck with sorrow. Take him up:
Help, three o' the chiefest soldiers; I 'll be one.
Beat thou the drum, that it speak mournfully:
Trail your steel pikes. Though in this city he
Hath widow'd and unchilded many a one,
Which to this hour bewail the injury,
Yet he shall have a noble memory.
Assist. [*Exeunt, bearing the body of Coriolanus. A dead march sounded.*

THE TRAGEDY OF JULIUS CÆSAR

DRAMATIS PERSONÆ

Julius Cæsar,
Octavius Cæsar, Marcus Antonius, M. Æmil. Lepidus, *triumvirs after the death of Julius Cæsar.*
Cicero, Publius, Popilius Lena, *senators.*
Marcus Brutus, Cassius, Casca, Trebonius, Ligarius, Decius Brutus, Metellu Cimber, Cinna, *conspirators against Julius Cæsar.*
Flavius and Marullus, *tribunes.*
Artemidorus of Cnidos, *a teacher of Rhetoric.*
A Soothsayer.
Cinna, *a poet.* Another Poet.
Lucilius, Titinius, Messala, Young Cato, Volumnius, *friends to Brutus and Cassius.*
Varro, Clitus, Claudius, Strato, Lucius, Dardanius, *servants to Brutus.*
Pindarus, *servant to Cassius.*

Calpurnia, *wife to Cæsar.*
Portia, *wife to Brutus.*

Senators, Citizens, Guards, Attendants, &c.

Scene : *Rome ; the neighbourhood of Sardis ; the neighbourhood of Philippi.*

ACT I—Scene I

Rome. A street.

Enter Flavius, Marullus, and certain Commoners.

Flav. Hence ! home, you idle creatures, get you home :
Is this a holiday ? what ! know you not,
Being mechanical, you ought not walk
Upon a labouring day without the sign
Of your profession ? Speak, what trade art thou ?

First Com. Why, sir, a carpenter.

Mar. Where is thy leather apron and thy rule ?
What dost thou with thy best apparel on ?
You, sir, what trade are you ?

Sec. Com. Truly, sir, in respect of a fine workman,
I am but, as you would say, a cobbler.

Mar. But what trade art thou ? answer me directly.

Sec Com. A trade, sir, that, I hope, I may use with a safe conscience ; which is indeed, sir, a mender of bad soles.

Mar. What trade, thou knave ? thou naughty knave, what trade ?

Sec. Com. Nay, I beseech you, sir, be not out with me : yet, if you be out, sir, I can mend you.

Mar. What mean'st thou by that ? mend me, thou saucy fellow !

Sec. Com. Why, sir, cobble you.

Flav. Thou art a cobbler, art thou ?

Sec. Com. Truly, sir, all that I live by is with the awl : I meddle with no tradesman's matters, nor women's matters, but with awl. I am indeed, sir, a surgeon to old shoes ; when they are in great danger, I re cover them. As proper men as ever trod upon neats-leather have gone upon my handiwork.

Flav. But wherefore art not in thy shop to-day?
Why dost thou lead these men about the streets?

Sec. Com. Truly, sir, to wear out their shoes, to get myself into more work. But indeed, sir, we make holiday, to see Cæsar and to rejoice in his triumph.

Mar. Wherefore rejoice? What conquest brings he home?
What tributaries follow him to Rome,
To grace in captive bonds his chariot-wheels?
You blocks, you stones, you worse than senseless things!
O you hard hearts, you cruel men of Rome,
Knew you not Pompey? Many a time and oft
Have you climb'd up to walls and battlements,
To towers and windows, yea, to chimney-tops,
Your infants in your arms, and there have sat
The live-long day with patient expectation
To see great Pompey pass the streets of Rome:
And when you saw his chariot but appear,
Have you not made an universal shout,
That Tiber trembled underneath her banks
To hear the replication of your sounds
Made in her concave shores?
And do you now put on your best attire?
And do you now cull out a holiday?
And do you now strew flowers in his way
That comes in triumph over Pompey's blood?
Be gone!
Run to your houses, fall upon your knees,
Pray to the gods to intermit the plague
That needs must light on this ingratitude.

Flav. Go, go, good countrymen, and, for this fault,
Assemble all the poor men of your sort;
Draw them to Tiber banks and weep your tears
Into the channel, till the lowest stream
Do kiss the most exalted shores of all.
[*Exeunt all the Commoners.*
See, whether their basest metal be not moved;
They vanish tongue-tied in their guiltiness.
Go you down that way towards the Capitol;
This way will I: disrobe the images,
If you do find them deck'd with ceremonies.

Mar. May we do so?
You know it is the feast of Lupercal.

Flav. It is no matter; let no images
Be hung with Cæsar's trophies. I'll about,
And drive away the vulgar from the streets:
So do you too, where you perceive them thick.
These growing feathers pluck'd from Cæsar's wing
Will make him fly an ordinary pitch,
Who else would soar above the view of men
And keep us all in servile fearfulness. [*Exeunt.*

Scene II

A public place.

Flourish. Enter Cæsar; Antony, for the course; Calpurnia, Portia, Decius, Cicero, Brutus, Cassius, and Casca; a great crowd following, among them a Soothsayer.

Cæs. Calpurnia!
Casca. Peace, ho! Cæsar speaks. [*Music ceases.*
Cæs. Calpurnia!
Cal. Here, my lord.
Cæs. Stand you directly in Antonius' way,
When he doth run his course. Antonius!
Ant. Cæsar, my lord?
Cæs. Forget not, in your speed, Antonius,
To touch Calpurnia; for our elders say,
The barren, touched in this holy chase,
Shake off their sterile curse.
Ant. I shall remember:
When Cæsar says 'do this,' it is perform'd.
Cæs. Set on, and leave no ceremony out. [*Flourish.*
Sooth. Cæsar!
Cæs. Ha! who calls?
Casca. Bid every noise be still: peace yet again!
Cæs. Who is it in the press that calls on me?
I hear a tongue, shriller than all the music,
Cry 'Cæsar.' Speak; Cæsar is turn'd to hear.
Sooth. Beware the ides of March.
Cæs. What man is that?
Bru. A soothsayer bids you beware the ides of March.
Cæs. Set him before me; let me see his face.
Cas. Fellow, come from the throng: look upon Cæsar.
Cæs. What say'st thou to me now? speak once again.
Sooth. Beware the ides of March.
Cæs. He is a dreamer; let us leave him: pass.
[*Sennet. Exeunt all but Brutus and Cassius.*
Cas. Will you go see the order of the course?
Bru. Not I.

Cas. I pray you, do.
Bru. I am not gamesome: I do lack some part
Of that quick spirit that is in Antony.
Let me not hinder, Cassius, your desires;
I'll leave you.
Cas. Brutus, I do observe you now of late:
I have not from your eyes that gentleness
And show of love as I was wont to have:
You bear too stubborn and too strange a hand
Over your friend that loves you.
Bru. Cassius,
Be not deceived: if I have veil'd my look,
I turn the trouble of my countenance
Merely upon myself. Vexed I am
Of late with passions of some difference,
Conceptions only proper to myself,
Which give some soil perhaps to my behaviours:
But let not therefore my good friends be grieved—
Among which number, Cassius, be you one—
Nor construe any further my neglect
Than that poor Brutus with himself at war
Forget the shows of love to other men.
Cas. Then, Brutus, I have much mistook your passion;
By means whereof this breast of mine hath buried
Thoughts of great value, worthy cogitations.
Tell me, good Brutus, can you see your face?
Bru. No, Cassius; for the eye sees not itself
But by reflection, by some other things.
Cas. 'Tis just:
And it is very much lamented, Brutus,
That you have no such mirrors as will turn
Your hidden worthiness into your eye,
That you might see your shadow. I have heard
Where many of the best respect in Rome,
Except immortal Cæsar, speaking of Brutus,
And groaning underneath this age's yoke,
Have wish'd that noble Brutus had his eyes.
Bru. Into what dangers would you lead me, Cassius,
That you would have me seek into myself
For that which is not in me?
Cas. Therefore, good Brutus, be prepared to hear:
And since you know you cannot see yourself
So well as by reflection, I your glass
Will modestly discover to yourself
That of yourself which you yet know not of.

And be not jealous on me, gentle Brutus:
Were I a common laugher, or did use
To stale with ordinary oaths my love
To every new protester; if you know
That I do fawn on men and hug them hard,
And after scandal them; or if you know
That I profess myself in banqueting
To all the rout, then hold me dangerous. [*Flourish and shout.*
Bru. What means this shouting? I do fear, the people
Choose Cæsar for their king.
Cas. Ay, do you fear it?
Then must I think you would not have it so.
Bru. I would not, Cassius, yet I love him well.
But wherefore do you hold me here so long?
What is it that you would impart to me?
If it be aught toward the general good,
Set honour in one eye and death i' the other,
And I will look on both indifferently:
For let the gods so speed me as I love
The name of honour more than I fear death.
Cas. I know that virtue to be in you, Brutus,
As well as I do know your outward favour.
Well, honour is the subject of my story.
I cannot tell what you and other men
Think of this life, but, for my single self,
I had as lief not be as live to be
In awe of such a thing as I myself.
I was born free as Cæsar; so were you:
We both have fed as well, and we can both
Endure the winter's cold as well as he:
For once, upon a raw and gusty day,
The troubled Tiber chafing with her shores,
Cæsar said to me 'Darest thou, Cassius, now
Leap in with me into this angry flood,
And swim to yonder point?' Upon the word,
Accoutred as I was, I plunged in
And bade him follow: so indeed he did.
The torrent roar'd, and we did buffet it
With lusty sinews, throwing it aside
And stemming it with hearts of controversy;
But ere we could arrive the point proposed,
Cæsar cried 'Help me, Cassius, or I sink!'
I, as Æneas our great ancestor
Did from the flames of Troy upon his shoulder
The old Anchises bear, so from the waves of Tiber

Did I the tired Cæsar: and this man
Is now become a god, and Cassius is
A wretched creature, and must bend his body
If Cæsar carelessly but nod on him.
He had a fever when he was in Spain,
And when the fit was on him, I did mark
How he did shake: 'tis true, this god did shake;
His coward lips did from their colour fly,
And that same eye whose bend doth awe the world
Did lose his lustre: I did hear him groan:
Ay, and that tongue of his that bade the Romans
Mark him and write his speeches in their books,
Alas, it cried, 'Give me some drink, Titinius,'
As a sick girl. Ye gods! it doth amaze me
A man of such a feeble temper should
So get the start of the majestic world
And bear the palm alone. [*Shout. Flourish.*

Bru. Another general shout!
I do believe that these applauses are
For some new honours that are heap'd on Cæsar.

Cas. Why, man, he doth bestride the narrow world
Like a Colossus, and we petty men
Walk under his huge legs and peep about
To find ourselves dishonourable graves.
Men at some time are masters of their fates:
The fault, dear Brutus, is not in our stars,
But in ourselves, that we are underlings.
Brutus, and Cæsar: what should be in that Cæsar?
Why should that name be sounded more than yours?
Write them together, yours is as fair a name;
Sound them, it doth become the mouth as well;
Weigh them, it is as heavy; conjure with 'em,
Brutus will start a spirit as soon as Cæsar.
Now, in the names of all the gods at once,
Upon what meat doth this our Cæsar feed,
That he is grown so great? Age, thou art shamed!
Rome, thou hast lost the breed of noble bloods!
When went there by an age, since the great flood,
But it was famed with more than with one man?
When could they say till now that talk'd of Rome
That her wide walls encompass'd but one man?
Now is it Rome indeed, and room enough,
When there is in it but one only man.
O, you and I have heard our fathers say
There was a Brutus once that would have brook'd

The eternal devil to keep his state in Rome
As easily as a king.

Bru. That you do love me, I am nothing jealous;
What you would work me to, I have some aim:
How I have thought of this and of these times,
I shall recount hereafter; for this present,
I would not, so with love I might entreat you,
Be any further moved. What you have said
I will consider; what you have to say
I will with patience hear, and find a time
Both meet to hear and answer such high things.
Till then, my noble friend, chew upon this:
Brutus had rather be a villager
Than to repute himself a son of Rome
Under these hard conditions as this time
Is like to lay upon us.

Cas. I am glad that my weak words
Have struck but thus much show of fire from Brutus.

Bru. The games are done, and Cæsar is returning.

Cas. As they pass by, pluck Casca by the sleeve;
And he will, after his sour fashion, tell you
What hath proceeded worthy note to-day.

Re-enter Cæsar and his Train.

Bru. I will do so: but, look you, Cassius,
The angry spot doth glow on Cæsar's brow,
And all the rest look like a chidden train:
Calpurnia's cheek is pale, and Cicero
Looks with such ferret and such fiery eyes
As we have seen him in the Capitol,
Being cross'd in conference by some senators.

Cas. Casca will tell us what the matter is.

Cæs. Antonius!

Ant. Cæsar?

Cæs. Let me have men about me that are fat,
Sleek-headed men, and such as sleep o' nights:
Yond Cassius has a lean and hungry look;
He thinks too much: such men are dangerous.

Ant. Fear him not, Cæsar; he 's not dangerous;
He is a noble Roman, and well given.

Cæs. Would he were fatter! but I fear him not:
Yet if my name were liable to fear,
I do not know the man I should avoid
So soon as that spare Cassius. He reads much;
He is a great observer, and he looks
Quite through the deeds of men: he loves no plays,

As thou dost, Antony; he hears no music:
Seldom he smiles, and smiles in such a sort
As if he mock'd himself, and scorn'd his spirit
That could be moved to smile at any thing.
Such men as he be never at heart's ease
Whiles they behold a greater than themselves,
And therefore are they very dangerous.
I rather tell thee what is to be fear'd
Than what I fear; for always I am Cæsar.
Come on my right hand, for this ear is deaf,
And tell me truly what thou think'st of him.

[*Sennet. Exeunt Cæsar and all his Train but Casca.*

Casca. You pull'd me by the cloak; would you speak with me?
Bru. Ay, Casca; tell us what hath chanced to-day,
That Cæsar looks so sad.
Casca. Why, you were with him, were you not?
Bru. I should not then ask Casca what had chanced.

Casca. Why, there was a crown offered him: and being offered him, he put it by with the back of his hand, thus: and then the people fell a-shouting.

Bru. What was the second noise for?

Casca. Why, for that too.

Cas. They shouted thrice: what was the last cry for?

Casca. Why for that too.

Bru. Was the crown offered him thrice?

Casca. Ay, marry, was 't, and he put it by thrice, every time gentler than other; and at every putting by mine honest neighbours shouted.

Cas. Who offered him the crown?

Casca. Why, Antony.

Bru. Tell us the manner of it, gentle Casca.

Casca. I can as well be hang'd as tell the manner of it: it was mere foolery; I did not mark it. I saw Mark Antony offer him a crown: yet 'twas not a crown neither, 'twas one of these coronets: and, as I told you, he put it by once: but for all that, to my thinking, he would fain have had it. Then he offered it to him again; then he put it by again: but, to my thinking, he was very loath to lay his fingers off it. And then he offered it the third time; he put it the third time by: and still as he refused it, the rabblement hooted and clapped their chopped hands and threw up their sweaty night-caps and uttered such a deal of stinking breath because Cæsar refused the crown, that it had almost choked Cæsar; for he swounded and fell down at it: and for mine own part,

I durst not laugh, for fear of opening my lips and receiving the bad air.

Cas. But, soft, I pray you : what, did Cæsar swound?

Casca. He fell down in the market-place and foamed at mouth and was speechless.

Bru. 'Tis very like : he hath the falling-sickness.

Cas. No, Cæsar hath it not : but you, and I,
And honest Casca, we have the falling-sickness.

Casca. I know not what you mean by that, but I am sure Cæsar fell down. If the tag-rag people did not clap him and hiss him according as he pleased and displeased them, as they use to do the players in the theatre, I am no true [man.

Bru. What said he when he came unto himself?

Casca. Marry, before he fell down, when he perceived the common herd was glad he refused the crown, he plucked me ope his doublet and offered them his throat to cut. An I had been a man of any occupation, if I would not have taken him at a word, I would I might go to hell among the rogues. And so he fell. When he came to himself again, he said, if he had done or said any thing amiss, he desired their worships to think it was his infirmity. Three or four wenches, where I stood, cried 'Alas, good soul!' and forgave him with all their hearts : but there 's no heed to be taken of them ; if Cæsar had stabbed their mothers, they would have done no less.

Bru. And after that, he came, thus sad, away?

Casca. Ay.

Cas. Did Cicero say any thing?

Casca. Ay, he spoke Greek.

Cas. To what effect?

Casca. Nay, an I tell you that, I'll ne'er look you i' the face again : but those that understood him smiled at one another and shook their heads ; but for mine own part, it was Greek to me. I could tell you more news too : Marullus and Flavius, for pulling scarfs off Cæsar's images, are put to silence. Fare you well. There was more foolery yet, if I could remember it.

Cas. Will you sup with me to-night, Casca?

Casca. No, I am promised forth.

Cas. Will you dine with me to-morrow?

Casca. Ay, if I be alive, and your mind hold, and your dinner worth the eating.

Cas. Good ; I will expect you.

Casca. Do so : farewell, both. [*Exit.*

Bru. What a blunt fellow is this grown to be!

He was quick metal when he went to school.
Cas. So is he now in execution
Of any bold or noble enterprise,
However he puts on this tardy form.
This rudeness is a sauce to his good wit,
Which gives men stomach to digest his words
With better appetite.
Bru. And so it is. For this time I will leave you:
To-morrow, if you please to speak with me,
I will come home to you, or, if you will,
Come home to me and I will wait for you.
Cas. I will do so: till then, think of the world. [*Exit Brutus.*
Well, Brutus, thou art noble; yet, I see,
Thy honourable metal may be wrought
From that it is disposed: therefore, it is meet
That noble minds keep ever with their likes;
For who so firm that cannot be seduced?
Cæsar doth bear me hard; but he loves Brutus:
If I were Brutus now and he were Cassius,
He should not humour me. I will this night,
In several hands, in at his windows throw,
As if they came from several citizens,
Writings, all tending to the great opinion
That Rome holds of his name, wherein obscurely
Cæsar's ambition shall be glanced at:
And after this let Cæsar seat him sure;
For we will shake him, or worse days endure. [*Exit.*

Scene III

A street.

Thunder and lightning. Enter, from opposite sides, Casca, with his sword drawn, and Cicero.

Cic. Good even, Casca: brought you Cæsar home?
Why are you breathless? and why stare you so?
Casca. Are not you moved, when all the sway of earth
Shakes like a thing unfirm? O Cicero,
I have seen tempests, when the scolding winds
Have rived the knotty oaks, and I have seen
The ambitious ocean swell and rage and foam,
To be exalted with the threatening clouds;
But never till to-night, never till now,
Did I go through a tempest dropping fire.
Either there is a civil strife in heaven,
Or else the world too saucy with the gods
Incenses them to send destruction.

Cic. Why, saw you any thing more wonderful?
Casca. A common slave—you know him well by sight—
Held up his left hand, which did flame and burn
Like twenty torches join'd, and yet his hand
Not sensible of fire remain'd unscorch'd.
Besides—I ha' not since put up my sword—
Against the Capitol I met a lion,
Who glazed upon me and went surly by
Without annoying me: and there were drawn
Upon a heap a hundred ghastly women
Transformed with their fear, who swore they saw
Men all in fire walk up and down the streets.
And yesterday the bird of night did sit
Even at noon-day upon the market-place,
Hooting and shrieking. When these prodigies
Do so conjointly meet, let not men say
'These are their reasons: they are natural:'
For, I believe, they are portentous things
Unto the climate that they point upon.
Cic. Indeed, it is a strange-disposed time:
But men may construe things after their fashion,
Clean from the purpose of the things themselves.
Comes Cæsar to the Capitol to-morrow?
Casca. He doth; for he did bid Antonius
Send word to you he would be there to-morrow.
Cic. Good night then, Casca: this disturbed sky
Is not to walk in.
Casca. Farewell, Cicero. [*Exit Cicero.*

Enter Cassius.

Cas. Who 's there?
Casca. A Roman.
Cas. Casca, by your voice.
Casca. Your ear is good. Cassius, what night is this!
Cas. A very pleasing night to honest men.
Casca. Who ever knew the heavens menace so?
Cas. Those that have known the earth so full of faults.
For my part, I have walk'd about the streets,
Submitting me unto the perilous night,
And thus unbraced, Casca, as you see,
Have bared my bosom to the thunder-stone;
And when the cross blue lightning seem'd to open
The breast of heaven, I did present myself
Even in the aim and very flash of it.
Casca. But wherefore did you so much tempt the heavens?
It is the part of men to fear and tremble

When the most mighty gods by tokens send
Such dreadful heralds to astonish us.

Cas. You are dull, Casca, and those sparks of life
That should be in a Roman you do want,
Or else you use not. You look pale and gaze
And put on fear and cast yourself in wonder,
To see the strange impatience of the heavens:
But if you would consider the true cause
Why all these fires, why all these gliding ghosts,
Why birds and beasts from quality and kind,
Why old men fool and children calculate,
Why all these things change from their ordinance,
Their natures and preformed faculties,
To monstrous quality, why, you shall find
That heaven hath infused them with these spirits
To make them instruments of fear and warning
Unto some monstrous state.
Now could I, Casca, name to thee a man
Most like this dreadful night,
That thunders, lightens, opens graves, and roars
As doth the lion in the Capitol,
A man no mightier than thyself or me
In personal action, yet prodigious grown
And fearful, as these strange eruptions are.

Casca. 'Tis Cæsar that you mean; is it not, Cassius?

Cas. Let it be who it is: for Romans now
Have thews and limbs like to their ancestors;
But, woe the while! our fathers' minds are dead,
And we are govern'd with our mothers' spirits;
Our yoke and sufferance show us womanish.

Casca. Indeed they say the senators to-morrow
Mean to establish Cæsar as a king;
And he shall wear his crown by sea and land,
In every place save here in Italy.

Cas. I know where I will wear this dagger then:
Cassius from bondage will deliver Cassius.
Therein, ye gods, ye make the weak most strong;
Therein, ye gods, you tyrants do defeat:
Nor stony tower, nor walls of beaten brass,
Nor airless dungeon, nor strong links of iron,
Can be retentive to the strength of spirit:
But life, being weary of these worldly bars,
Never lacks power to dismiss itself.
If I know this, know all the world besides,
That part of tyranny that I do bear

I can shake off at pleasure. [*Thunder still.*

Casca. So can I:
So every bondman in his own hand bears
The power to cancel his captivity.

Cas. And why should Cæsar be a tyrant then?
Poor man! I know he would not be a wolf
But that he sees the Romans are but sheep:
He were no lion, were not Romans hinds.
Those that with haste will make a mighty fire
Begin it with weak straws: what trash is Rome,
What rubbish and what offal, when it serves
For the base matter to illuminate
So vile a thing as Cæsar! But, O grief,
Where hast thou led me? I perhaps speak this
Before a willing bondman; then I know
My answer must be made. But I am arm'd,
And dangers are to me indifferent.

Casca. You speak to Casca, and to such a man
That is no fleering tell-tale. Hold, my hand:
Be factious for redress of all these griefs,
And I will set this foot of mine as far
As who goes farthest.

Cas. There 's a bargain made.
Now know you, Casca, I have moved already
Some certain of the noblest-minded Romans
To undergo with me an enterprise
Of honourable-dangerous consequence;
And I do know, by this they stay for me
In Pompey's porch: for now, this fearful night,
There is no stir or walking in the streets,
And the complexion of the element
In favour 's like the work we have in hand,
Most bloody, fiery, and most terrible.

Enter Cinna.

Casca. Stand close awhile, for here comes one in haste.

Cas. 'Tis Cinna; I do know him by his gait;
He is a friend. Cinna, where haste you so?

Cin. To find out you. Who 's that? Metellus Cimber?

Cas. No, it is Casca; one incorporate
To our attempts. Am I not stay'd for, Cinna?

Cin. I am glad on 't. What a fearful night is this!
There 's two or three of us have seen strange sights.

Cas. Am I not stay'd for? tell me.

Cin. Yes, you are.
O Cassius, if you could

But win the noble Brutus to our party—
Cas. Be you content: good Cinna, take this paper,
And look you lay it in the prætor's chair,
Where Brutus may but find it, and throw this
In at his window; set this up with wax
Upon old Brutus' statue: all this done,
Repair to Pompey's porch, where you shall find us.
Is Decius Brutus and Trebonius there?
Cin. All but Metellus Cimber; and he 's gone
To seek you at your house. Well, I will hie,
And so bestow these papers as you bade me.
Cas. That done, repair to Pompey's theatre. [*Exit Cinna.*
Come, Casca, you and I will yet ere day
See Brutus at his house: three parts of him
Is ours already, and the man entire
Upon the next encounter yields him ours.
Casca. O, he sits high in all the people's hearts;
And that which would appear offence in us
His countenance, like richest alchemy,
Will change to virtue and to worthiness.
Cas. Him and his worth and our great need of him
You have right well conceited. Let us go,
For it is after midnight, and ere day
We will awake him and be sure of him. [*Exeunt.*

ACT II—Scene I

Rome. Brutus's Orchard.

Enter Brutus.

Bru. What, Lucius, ho!
I cannot, by the progress of the stars,
Give guess how near to day. Lucius, I say!
I would it were my fault to sleep so soundly.
When, Lucius, when? awake, I say! what, Lucius!

Enter Lucius.

Luc. Call'd you, my lord?
Bru. Get me a taper in my study, Lucius:
When it is lighted, come and call me here.
Luc. I will, my lord. [*Exit.*
Bru. It must be by his death: and, for my part,
I know no personal cause to spurn at him,
But for the general. He would be crown'd:
How that might change his nature, there 's the question:
It is the bright day that brings forth the adder;
And that craves wary walking. Crown him?—that;—

And then, I grant, we put a sting in him,
That at his will he may do danger with.
The abuse of greatness is when it disjoins
Remorse from power: and, to speak truth of Cæsar,
I have not known when his affections sway'd
More than his reason. But 'tis a common proof,
That lowliness is young ambition's ladder,
Whereto the climber-upward turns his face;
But when he once attains the upmost round,
He then unto the ladder turns his back,
Looks in the clouds, scorning the base degrees
By which he did ascend: so Cæsar may;
Then, lest he may, prevent. And, since the quarrel
Will bear no colour for the thing he is,
Fashion it thus; that what he is, augmented,
Would run to these and these extremities:
And therefore think him as a serpent's egg
Which hatch'd would as his kind grow mischievous,
And kill him in the shell.

Re-enter Lucius.

Luc. The taper burneth in your closet, sir.
Searching the window for a flint I found
This paper thus seal'd up, and I am sure
It did not lie there when I went to bed. [*Gives him the letter.*

Bru. Get you to bed again; it is not day.
Is not to-morrow, boy, the ides of March?

Luc. I know not, sir.

Bru. Look in the calendar and bring me word.

Luc. I will, sir. [*Exit.*

Bru. The exhalations whizzing in the air
Give so much light that I may read by them.
[*Opens the letter and reads.*
'Brutus, thou sleep'st: awake and see thyself.
Shall Rome, &c. Speak, strike, redress.
Brutus, thou sleep'st: awake.'
Such instigations have been often dropp'd
Where I have took them up.
'Shall Rome, &c.' Thus must I piece it out:
Shall Rome stand under one man's awe? What, Rome?
My ancestors did from the streets of Rome
The Tarquin drive, when he was call'd a king.
'Speak, strike, redress.' Am I entreated
To speak and strike? O Rome, I make thee promise,
If the redress will follow, thou receivest
Thy full petition at the hand of Brutus!

Re-enter Lucius.

Luc. Sir, March is wasted fifteen days. [*Knocking within.*
Bru. 'Tis good. Go to the gate; somebody knocks.
[*Exit Lucius.*
Since Cassius first did whet me against Cæsar
I have not slept.
Between the acting of a dreadful thing
And the first motion, all the interim is
Like a phantasma or a hideous dream:
The Genius and the mortal instruments
Are then in council, and the state of man,
Like to a little kingdom, suffers then
The nature of an insurrection.

Re-enter Lucius.

Luc. Sir, 'tis your brother Cassius at the door,
Who doth desire to see you.
Bru. Is he alone?
Luc. No, sir, there are moe with him.
Bru. Do you know them?
Luc. No, sir; their hats are pluck'd about their ears,
And half their faces buried in their cloaks,
That by no means I may discover them
By any mark of favour.
Bru. Let 'em enter. [*Exit Lucius.*
They are the faction. O conspiracy,
Shamest thou to show thy dangerous brow by night,
When evils are most free? O, then, by day
Where wilt thou find a cavern dark enough
To mask thy monstrous visage? Seek none, conspiracy;
Hide it in smiles and affability:
For if thou path, thy native semblance on,
Not Erebus itself were dim enough
To hide thee from prevention.

Enter the conspirators, Cassius, Casca, Decius, Cinna, Metellus Cimber and Trebonius.

Cas. I think we are too bold upon your rest:
Good morrow, Brutus; do we trouble you?
Bru. I have been up this hour, awake all night.
Know I these men that come along with you?
Cas. Yes, every man of them; and no man here
But honours you; and every one doth wish
You had but that opinion of yourself
Which every noble Roman bears of you.
This is Trebonius.
Bru. He is welcome hither.

Cas. This, Decius Brutus.
Bru. He is welcome too.
Cas. This, Casca; this, Cinna; and this, Metellus Cimber.
Bru. They are all welcome.
What watchful cares do interpose themselves
Betwixt your eyes and night?
Cas. Shall I entreat a word? [*They whisper.*
Dec. Here lies the east: doth not the day break here?
Casca. No.
Cin. O, pardon, sir, it doth, and yon grey lines
That fret the clouds are messengers of day.
Casca. You shall confess that you are both deceived.
Here, as I point my sword, the sun arises;
Which is a great way growing on the south,
Weighing the youthful season of the year.
Some two months hence up higher toward the north
He first presents his fire, and the high east
Stands as the Capitol, directly here.
Bru. Give me your hands all over, one by one.
Cas. And let us swear our resolution.
Bru. No, not an oath; if not the face of men,
The sufferance of our souls, the time's abuse,—
If these be motives weak, break off betimes,
And every man hence to his idle bed;
So let high-sighted tyranny range on
Till each man drop by lottery. But if these,
As I am sure they do, bear fire enough
To kindle cowards and to steel with valour
The melting spirits of women, then, countrymen,
What need we any spur but our own cause
To prick us to redress? what other bond
Than secret Romans that have spoke the word,
And will not palter? and what other oath
Than honesty to honesty engaged
That this shall be or we will fall for it?
Swear priests and cowards and men cautelous,
Old feeble carrions and such suffering souls
That welcome wrongs; unto bad causes swear
Such creatures as men doubt: but do not stain
The even virtue of our enterprise,
Nor the insuppressive mettle of our spirits,
To think that or our cause or our performance
Did need an oath; when every drop of blood
That every Roman bears, and nobly bears,
Is guilty of a several bastardy

If he do break the smallest particle
Of any promise that hath pass'd from him.
Cas. But what of Cicero? shall we sound him?
I think he will stand very strong with us.
Casca. Let us not leave him out.
Cin. No, by no means.
Met. O, let us have him, for his silver hairs
Will purchase us a good opinion,
And buy men's voices to commend our deeds:
It shall be said his judgment ruled our hands;
Our youths and wildness shall no whit appear,
But all be buried in his gravity.
Bru. O, name him not: let us not break with him,
For he will never follow any thing
That other men begin.
Cas. Then leave him out.
Casca. Indeed he is not fit.
Dec. Shall no man else be touch'd but only Cæsar?
Cas. Decius, well urged: I think it is not meet
Mark Antony, so well beloved of Cæsar,
Should outlive Cæsar: we shall find of him
A shrewd contriver; and you know his means,
If he improve them, may well stretch so far
As to annoy us all: which to prevent,
Let Antony and Cæsar fall together.
Bru. Our course will seem too bloody, Caius Cassius,
To cut the head off and then hack the limbs,
Like wrath in death and envy afterwards;
For Antony is but a limb of Cæsar:
Let us be sacrificers, but not butchers, Caius.
We all stand up against the spirit of Cæsar,
And in the spirit of men there is no blood:
O, that we then could come by Cæsar's spirit,
And not dismember Cæsar? But, alas,
Cæsar must bleed for it! And, gentle friends,
Let 's kill him boldly, but not wrathfully;
Let 's carve him as a dish fit for the gods,
Not hew him as a carcass fit for hounds:
And let our hearts, as subtle masters do,
Stir up their servants to an act of rage
And after seem to chide 'em. This shall make
Our purpose necessary and not envious:
Which so appearing to the common eyes,
We shall be call'd purgers, not murderers.
And for Mark Antony, think not of him;

For he can do no more than Cæsar's arm
When Cæsar's head is off.
Cas. Yet I fear him,
For in the ingrafted love he bears to Cæsar—
Bru. Alas, good Cassius, do not think of him:
If he love Cæsar, all that he can do
Is to himself, take thought and die for Cæsar:
And that were much he should, for he is given
To sports, to wildness and much company.
Treb. There is no fear in him; let him not die;
For he will l ve and laugh at this hereafter.
[*Clock strikes.*
Bru. Peace! count the clock.
Cas. The clock hath stricken three.
Treb. 'Tis time to part.
Cas. But it is doubtful yet
Whether Cæsar will come forth to-day or no;
For he is superstitious grown of late,
Quite from the main opinion he held once
Of fantasy, of dreams and ceremonies:
It may be these apparent prodigies,
The unaccustom'd terror of this night
And the persuasion of his augurers,
May hold him from the Capitol to-day.
Dec. Never fear that: if he be so resolved,
I can o'ersway him; for he loves to hear
That unicorns may be betray'd with trees
And bears with glasses, elephants with holes,
Lions with toils and men with flatterers:
But when I tell him he hates flatterers,
He says he does, being then most flattered.
Let me work;
For I can give his humour the true bent,
And I will bring him to the Capitol.
Cas. Nay, we will all of us be there to fetch him.
Bru. By the eighth hour: is that the uttermost?
Cin. Be that the uttermost, and fail not then.
Met. Caius Ligarius doth bear Cæsar hard,
Who rated him for speaking well of Pompey:
I wonder none of you have thought of him.
Bru. Now, good Metellus, go along by him:
He loves me well, and I have given him reasons;
Send him but hither, and I 'll fashion him.
Cas. The morning comes upon 's: we 'll leave you, Brutus:
And, friends, disperse yourselves: but all remember

What you have said and show yourselves true Romans.
Bru. Good gentlemen, look fresh and merrily;
Let not our looks put on our purposes;
But bear it as our Roman actors do,
With untired spirits and formal constancy:
And so, good morrow to you every one.
[*Exeunt all but Brutus.*
Boy! Lucius! Fast asleep! It is no matter;
Enjoy the honey-heavy dew of slumber:
Thou hast no figures nor no fantasies,
Which busy care draws in the brains of men;
Therefore thou sleep'st so sound.

Enter Portia.

Por. Brutus, my lord!
Bru. Portia, what mean you? wherefore rise you now?
It is not for your health thus to commit
Your weak condition to the raw cold morning.
Por. Nor for yours neither. You 've ungently, Brutus,
Stole from my bed: and yesternight at supper
You suddenly arose and walk'd about,
Musing and sighing, with your arms across;
And when I ask'd you what the matter was,
You stared upon me with ungentle looks:
I urged you further; then you scratch'd your head,
And too impatiently stamp'd with your foot:
Yet I insisted, yet you answer'd not,
But with an angry wafture of your hand
Gave sign for me to leave you: so I did,
Fearing to strengthen that impatience
Which seem'd too much enkindled, and withal
Hoping it was but an effect of humour,
Which sometime hath his hour with every man.
It will not let you eat, nor talk, nor sleep,
And, could it work so much upon your shape
As it hath much prevail'd on your condition,
I should not know you, Brutus. Dear my lord,
Make me acquainted with your cause of grief.
Bru. I am not well in health, and that is all.
Por. Brutus is wise, and, were he not in health,
He would embrace the means to come by it.
Bru. Why, so I do: good Portia, go to bed.
Por. Is Brutus sick, and is it physical
To walk unbraced and suck up the humours
Of the dank morning? What, is Brutus sick,
And will he steal out of his wholesome bed,

To dare the vile contagion of the night,
And tempt the rheumy and unpurged air
To add unto his sickness? No, my Brutus;
You have some sick offence within your mind,
Which by the right and virtue of my place
I ought to know of: and, upon my knees,
I charm you, by my once commended beauty,
By all your vows of love and that great vow
Which did incorporate and make us one,
That you unfold to me, yourself, your half,
Why you are heavy, and what men to-night
Have had resort to you; for here have been
Some six or seven, who did hide their faces
Even from darkness.

Bru. Kneel not, gentle Portia.

Por. I should not need, if you were gentle Brutus.
Within the bond of marriage, tell me, Brutus,
Is it expected I should know no secrets
That appertain to you? Am I yourself
But, as it were, in sort or limitation,
To keep with you at meals, comfort your bed,
And talk to you sometimes? Dwell I but in the suburbs
Of your good pleasure? If it be no more,
Portia is Brutus' harlot, not his wife.

Bru. You are my true and honourable wife,
As dear to me as are the ruddy drops
That visit my sad heart.

Por. If this were true, then should I know this secret.
I grant I am a woman, but withal
A woman that Lord Brutus took to wife:
I grant I am a woman, but withal
A woman well reputed, Cato's daughter.
Think you I am no stronger than my sex,
Being so father'd and so husbanded?
Tell me your counsels, I will not disclose 'em:
I have made strong proof of my constancy,
Giving myself a voluntary wound
Here in the thigh: can I bear that with patience
And not my husband's secrets?

Bru. O ye gods,
Render me worthy of this noble wife! [*Knocking within.*
Hark, hark! one knocks: Portia, go in a while;
And by and by thy bosom shall partake
The secrets of my heart:
All my engagements I will construe to thee,

All the charactery of my sad brows.
Leave me with haste. [*Exit Portia.*] Lucius, who 's that [knocks?

Re-enter Lucius with Ligarius.

Luc. Here is a sick man that would speak with you.
Bru. Caius Ligarius, that Metellus spake of.
Boy, stand aside. Caius Ligarius! how?
Lig. Vouchsafe good morrow from a feeble tongue.
Bru. O, what a time have you chose out, brave Caius,
To wear a kerchief! Would you were not sick!
Lig. I am not sick, if Brutus have in hand
Any exploit worthy the name of honour.
Bru. Such an exploit have I in hand, Ligarius,
Had you a healthful ear to hear of it.
Lig. By all the gods that Romans bow before,
I here discard my sickness! Soul of Rome!
Brave son, derived from honourable loins!
Thou, like an exorcist, hast conjured up
My mortified spirit. Now bid me run,
And I will strive with things impossible,
Yea, get the better of them. What 's to do?
Bru. A piece of work that will make sick men whole.
Lig. But are not some whole that we must make sick?
Bru. That must we also. What it is, my Caius,
I shall unfold to thee, as we are going
To whom it must be done.
Lig. Set on your foot,
And with a heart new-fired I follow you,
To do I know not what: but it sufficeth
That Brutus leads me on.
Bru. Follow me then. [*Exeunt.*

Scene II

Cæsar's house.

Thunder and lightning. Enter Cæsar, in his night-gown.

Cæs. Nor heaven nor earth have been at peace to-night:
Thrice hath Calpurnia in her sleep cried out,
'Help, ho! they murder Cæsar!' Who 's within?

Enter a Servant.

Serv. My lord?
Cæs. Go bid the priests do present sacrifice.
And bring me their opinions of success.
Serv. I will, my lord. [*Exit*

Enter Calpurnia.

Cal. What mean you, Cæsar? think you to walk forth?

You shall not stir out of your house to-day.
Cæs. Cæsar shall forth: the things that threaten'd me
Ne'er look'd but on my back; when they shall see
The face of Cæsar, they are vanished.
Cal. Cæsar, I never stood on ceremonies,
Yet now they fright me. There is one within,
Besides the things that we have heard and seen,
Recounts most horrid sights seen by the watch.
A lioness hath whelped in the streets;
And graves have yawn'd, and yielded up their dead;
Fierce fiery warriors fight upon the clouds,
In ranks and squadrons and right form of war,
Which drizzled blood upon the Capitol;
The noise of battle hurtled in the air,
Horses did neigh and dying men did groan,
And ghosts did shriek and squeal about the streets.
O Cæsar! these things are beyond all use,
And I do fear them.
Cæs. What can be avoided
Whose end is purposed by the mighty gods?
Yet Cæsar shall go forth; for these predictions
Are to the world in general as to Cæsar.
Cal. When beggars die, there are no comets seen;
The heavens themselves blaze forth the death of princes.
Cæs. Cowards die many times before their death;
The valiant never taste of death but once.
Of all the wonders that I yet have heard,
It seems to me most strange that men should fear;
Seeing that death, a necessary end,
Will come when it will come.

Re-enter Servant.

What say the augurers?
Serv. They would not have you to stir forth to-day.
Plucking the entrails of an offering forth,
They could not find a heart within the beast.
Cæs. The gods do this in shame of cowardice:
Cæsar should be a beast without a heart
If he should stay at home to-day for fear.
No, Cæsar shall not: danger knows full well
That Cæsar is more dangerous than he:
We are two lions litter'd in one day,
And I the elder and more terrible:
And Cæsar shall go forth.
Cal. Alas, my lord,

Your wisdom is consumed in confidence.
Do not go forth to-day: call it my fear
That keeps you in the house and not your own.
We'll send Mark Antony to the senate-house,
And he shall say you are not well to-day:
Let me, upon my knee, prevail in this.

Cæs. Mark Antony shall say I am not well,
And, for thy humour, I will stay at home.

Enter Decius.

Here's Decius Brutus, he shall tell them so.

Dec. Cæsar, all hail! good morrow, worthy Cæsar:
I come to fetch you to the senate-house.

Cæs. And you are come in very happy time,
To bear my greeting to the senators
And tell them that I will not come to-day:
Cannot, is false, and that I dare not, falser:
I will not come to-day: tell them so, Decius.

Cal. Say he is sick.

Cæs. Shall Cæsar send a lie?
Have I in conquest stretch'd mine arm so far,
To be afeard to tell graybeards the truth?
Decius, go tell them Cæsar will not come.

Dec. Most mighty Cæsar, let me know some cause,
Lest I be laugh'd at when I tell them so.

Cæs. The cause is in my will: I will not come;
That is enough to satisfy the senate.
But, for your private satisfaction,
Because I love you, I will let you know.
Calpurnia here, my wife, stays me at home:
She dreamt to-night she saw my statuë,
Which like a fountain with an hundred spouts
Did run pure blood, and many lusty Romans
Came smiling and did bathe their hands in it:
And these does she apply for warnings and portents
And evils imminent, and on her knee
Hath begg'd that I will stay at home to-day.

Dec. This dream is all amiss interpreted;
It was a vision fair and fortunate:
Your statue spouting blood in many pipes,
In which so many smiling Romans bathed,
Signifies that from you great Rome shall suck
Reviving blood, and that great men shall press
For tinctures, stains, relics and cognizance.
This by Calpurnia's dream is signified.

Cæs. And this way have you well expounded it.

Dec. I have, when you have heard what I can say:
And know it now: the senate have concluded
To give this day a crown to mighty Cæsar.
If you shall send them word you will not come,
Their minds may change. Besides, it were a mock
Apt to be render'd, for some one to say
'Break up the senate till another time,
When Cæsar's wife shall meet with better dreams.'
If Cæsar hide himself, shall they not whisper
'Lo, Cæsar is afraid'?
Pardon me, Cæsar, for my dear dear love
To your proceeding bids me tell you this,
And reason to my love is liable.

Cæs. How foolish do your fears seem now, Calpurnia!
I am ashamed I did yield to them.
Give me my robe, for I will go.

Enter Publius, Brutus, Ligarius, Metellus, Casca, Trebonius, and Cinna.

And look where Publius is come to fetch me.

Pub. Good morrow, Cæsar.

Cæs. Welcome, Publius.
What, Brutus, are you stirr'd so early too?
Good morrow, Casca. Caius Ligarius,
Cæsar was ne'er so much your enemy
As that same ague which hath made you lean.
What is't o'clock?

Bru. Cæsar, 'tis strucken eight.

Cæs. I thank you for your pains and courtesy.

Enter Antony.

See! Antony, that revels long o' nights,
Is notwithstanding up. Good morrow, Antony.

Ant. So to most noble Cæsar.

Cæs. Bid them prepare within:
I am to blame to be thus waited for.
Now, Cinna: now, Metellus: what, Trebonius!
I have an hour's talk in store for you;
Remember that you call on me to-day:
Be near me, that I may remember you.

Treb. Cæsar, I will. [*Aside*] And so near will I be,
That your best friends shall wish I had been further.

Cæs. Good friends, go in and taste some wine with me;
And we like friends will straightway go together.

Bru. [*Aside*] That every like is not the same, O Cæsar,
The heart of Brutus yearns to think upon! [*Exeunt.*

Scene III

A street near the Capitol.

Enter Artemidorus, reading a paper.

Art. 'Cæsar, beware of Brutus; take heed of Cassius; come not near Casca; have an eye to Cinna; trust not Trebonius; mark well Metellus Cimber: Decius Brutus loves thee not: thou hast wronged Caius Ligarius. There is but one mind in all these men, and it is bent against Cæsar. If thou beest not immortal, look about you: security gives way to conspiracy. The mighty gods defend thee!

Thy lover, Artemidorus.'

Here will I stand till Cæsar pass along,
And as a suitor will I give him this.
My heart laments that virtue cannot live
Out of the teeth of emulation.
If thou read this, O Cæsar, thou mayst live;
If not, the Fates with traitors do contrive. [*Exit*

Scene IV

Another part of the same street, before the house of Brutus.

Enter Portia and Lucius.

Por. I prithee, boy, run to the senate-house;
Stay not to answer me, but get thee gone.
Why dost thou stay?
Luc. To know my errand, madam.
Por. I would have had thee there, and here again,
Ere I can tell thee what thou shouldst do there.
O constancy, be strong upon my side!
Set a huge mountain 'tween my heart and tongue!
I have a man's mind, but a woman's might.
How hard it is for women to keep counsel!
Art thou here yet?
Luc. Madam, what should I do?
Run to the Capitol, and nothing else?
And so return to you, and nothing else?
Por. Yes, bring me word, boy, if thy lord look well,
For he went sickly forth: and take good note
What Cæsar doth, what suitors press to him.
Hark, boy! what noise is that?
Luc. I hear none, madam.
Por. Prithee, listen well:
I heard a bustling rumour like a fray,
And the wind brings it from the Capitol.
Luc. Sooth, madam, I hear nothing.

Enter the Soothsayer.

Por. Come hither, fellow:
Which way hast thou been?
Sooth. At mine own house, good lady.
Por. What is 't o'clock?
Sooth. About the ninth hour, lady.
Por. Is Cæsar yet gone to the Capitol?
Sooth. Madam, not yet: I go to take my stand,
To see him pass on to the Capitol.
Por. Thou hast some suit to Cæsar, hast thou not?
Sooth. That I have, lady: if it will please Cæsar
To be so good to Cæsar as to hear me,
I shall beseech him to befriend himself.
Por. Why, know'st thou any harm 's intended towards him?
Sooth. None that I know will be, much that I fear may chance.
Good morrow to you. Here the street is narrow:
The throng that follows Cæsar at the heels,
Of senators, of prætors, common suitors,
Will crowd a feeble man almost to death:
I 'll get me to a place more void and there
Speak to great Cæsar as he comes along. [*Exit.*
Por. I must go in. Ay me, how weak a thing
The heart of woman is! O Brutus,
The heavens speed thee in thine enterprise!
Sure, the boy heard me. Brutus hath a suit
That Cæsar will not grant. O, I grow faint.
Run, Lucius, and commend me to my lord;
Say I am merry: come to me again,
And bring me word what he doth say to thee.
[*Exeunt severally.*

ACT III—Scene I

Rome. Before the Capitol; the Senate sitting above.

A crowd of people; among them Artemidorus and the Soothsayer. Flourish. Enter Cæsar, Brutus, Cassius, Casca, Decius, Metellus, Trebonius, Cinna, Antony, Lepidus, Popilius, Publius, and others.

Cæs. The ides of March are come.
Sooth. Ay, Cæsar; but not gone.
Art. Hail, Cæsar! read this schedule.
Dec. Trebonius doth desire you to o'er-read,
At your best leisure, this his humble suit.
Art. O Cæsar, read mine first; for mine 's a suit
That touches Cæsar nearer: read it, great Cæsar.
Cæs. What touches us ourself shall be last served.

Art. Delay not, Cæsar; read it instantly.
Cæs. What, is the fellow mad?
Pub. Sirrah, give place.
Cas. What, urge you your petitions in the street?
Come to the Capitol.

Cæsar goes up to the Senate-house, the rest following.

Pop. I wish your enterprise to-day may thrive.
Cas. What enterprise, Popilius?
Pop. Fare you well. [*Advances to Cæsar.*
Bru. What said Popilius Lena?
Cas. He wish'd to-day our enterprise might thrive.
I fear our purpose is discovered.
Bru. Look, how he makes to Cæsar: mark him.
Cas. Casca,
Be sudden, for we fear prevention.
Brutus, what shall be done? If this be known,
Cassius or Cæsar never shall turn back,
For I will slay myself.
Bru. Cassius, be constant:
Popilius Lena speaks not of our purposes;
For, look, he smiles, and Cæsar doth not change.
Cas. Trebonius knows his time; for, look you, Brutus,
He draws Mark Antony out of the way.
[*Exeunt Antony and Trebonius.*
Dec. Where is Metellus Cimber? Let him go,
And presently prefer his suit to Cæsar.
Bru. He is address'd: press near and second him.
Cin. Casca, you are the first that rears your hand.
Cæs. Are we all ready? What is now amiss
That Cæsar and his senate must redress?
Met. Most high, most mighty and most puissant Cæsar,
Metellus Cimber throws before thy seat
An humble heart:— [*Kneeling.*
Cæs. I must prevent thee, Cimber.
These couchings and these lowly courtesies
Might fire the blood of ordinary men,
And turn pre-ordinance and first decree
Into the law of children. Be not fond,
To think that Cæsar bears such rebel blood
That will be thaw'd from the true quality
With that which melteth fools, I mean, sweet words,
Low-crooked court'sies and base spaniel-fawning.
Thy brother by decree is banished:
If thou dost bend and pray and fawn for him,
I spurn thee like a cur out of my way.

Know, Cæsar doth not wrong, nor without cause
Will he be satisfied.

Met. Is there no voice more worthy than my own,
To sound more sweetly in great Cæsar's ear
For the repealing of my banish'd brother?

Bru. I kiss thy hand, but not in flattery, Cæsar,
Desiring thee that Publius Cimber may
Have an immediate freedom of repeal.

Cæs. What, Brutus!

Cas. Pardon, Cæsar; Cæsar, pardon:
As low as to thy foot doth Cassius fall,
To beg enfranchisement for Publius Cimber.

Cæs. I could be well moved, if I were as you;
If I could pray to move, prayers would move me:
But I am constant as the northern star,
Of whose true-fix'd and resting quality
There is no fellow in the firmament.
The skies are painted with unnumber'd sparks;
They are all fire and every one doth shine;
But there 's but one in all doth hold his place:
So in the world; 'tis furnish'd well with men,
And men are flesh and blood, and apprehensive;
Yet in the number I do know but one
That unassailable holds on his rank,
Unshaked of motion: and that I am he,
Let me a little show it, even in this;
That I was constant Cimber should be banish'd,
And constant do remain to keep him so.

Cin. O Cæsar,—

Cæs. Hence! wilt thou lift up Olympus?

Dec. Great Cæsar,—

Cæs. Doth not Brutus bootless kneel?

Casca. Speak, hands, for me!

[*Casca first, then the other Conspirators and Marcus Brutus stab Cæsar.*

Cæs. Et tu, Brute? Then fall, Cæsar! [*Dies.*

Cin. Liberty! freedom! Tyranny is dead!
Run hence, proclaim, cry it about the streets.

Cas. Some to the common pulpits, and cry out
'Liberty, freedom and enfranchisement!'

Bru. People, and senators, be not affrighted;
Fly not; stand still: ambition's debt is paid.

Casca. Go to the pulpit, Brutus.

Dec. And Cassius too.

Bru. Where 's Publius?

Cin. Here, quite confounded with this mutiny.
Met. Stand fast together, lest some friend of Cæsar's
Should chance—
Bru. Talk not of standing. Publius, good cheer;
There is no harm intended to your person,
Nor to no Roman else: so tell them, Publius.
Cas. And leave us, Publius; lest that the people
Rushing on us should do your age some mischief.
Bru. Do so: and let no man abide this deed
But we the doers.

Re-enter Trebonius.

Cas. Where is Antony?
Tre. Fled to his house amazed:
Men, wives and children stare, cry out and run
As it were doomsday.
Bru. Fates, we will know your pleasures:
That we shall die, we know; 'tis but the time,
And drawing days out, that men stand upon.
Cas. Why, he that cuts off twenty years of life
Cuts off so many years of fearing death.
Bru. Grant that, and then is death a benefit:
So are we Cæsar's friends, that have abridged
His time of fearing death. Stoop, Romans, stoop,
And let us bathe our hands in Cæsar's blood
Up to the elbows, and besmear our swords:
Then walk we forth, even to the market-place,
And waving our red weapons o'er our heads,
Let's all cry 'Peace, freedom and liberty!'
Cas. Stoop then and wash. How many ages hence
Shall this our lofty scene be acted over
In states unborn and accents yet unknown!
Bru. How many times shall Cæsar bleed in sport,
That now on Pompey's basis lies along
No worthier than the dust!
Cas. So oft as that shall be,
So often shall the knot of us be call'd
The men that gave their country liberty.
Dec. What, shall we forth?
Cas. Ay, every man away:
Brutus shall lead, and we will grace his heels
With the most boldest and best hearts of Rome.

Enter a Servant.

Bru. Soft! who comes here? A friend of Antony's.
Serv. Thus, Brutus, did my master bid me kneel;
Thus did Mark Antony bid me fall down;

And, being prostrate, thus he bade me say:
Brutus is noble, wise, valiant and honest;
Cæsar was mighty, bold, royal and loving:
Say I love Brutus and I honour him;
Say I fear'd Cæsar, honour'd him and loved him.
If Brutus will vouchsafe that Antony
May safely come to him and be resolved
How Cæsar hath deserved to lie in death,
Mark Antony shall not love Cæsar dead
So well as Brutus living, but will follow
The fortunes and affairs of noble Brutus
Thorough the hazards of this untrod state
With all true faith. So says my master Antony.

Bru. Thy master is a wise and valiant Roman;
I never thought him worse.
Tell him, so please him come unto this place,
He shall be satisfied and, by my honour,
Depart untouch'd.

Serv. I'll fetch him presently. [*Exit.*

Bru. I know that we shall have him well to friend.

Cas. I wish we may: but yet have I a mind
That fears him much, and my misgiving still
Falls shrewdly to the purpose.

Re-enter Antony.

Bru. But here comes Antony. Welcome, Mark Antony.

Ant. O mighty Cæsar! dost thou lie so low?
Are all thy conquests, glories, triumphs, spoils,
Shrunk to this little measure? Fare thee well.
I know not, gentlemen, what you intend,
Who else must be let blood, who else is rank:
If I myself, there is no hour so fit
As Cæsar's death's hour, nor no instrument
Of half that worth as those your swords, made rich
With the most noble blood of all this world.
I do beseech ye, if you bear me hard,
Now, whilst your purpled hands do reek and smoke,
Fulfil your pleasure. Live a thousand years,
I shall not find myself so apt to die:
No place will please me so, no mean of death,
As here by Cæsar, and by you cut off,
The choice and master spirits of this age.

Bru. O Antony, beg not your death of us.
Though now we must appear bloody and cruel,
As, by our hands and this our present act,
You see we do; yet see you but our hands

And this the bleeding business they have done:
Our hearts you see not; they are pitiful;
And pity to the general wrong of Rome—
As fire drives out fire, so pity pity—
Hath done this deed on Cæsar. For your part,
To you our swords have leaden points, Mark Antony:
Our arms in strength of malice, and our hearts
Of brothers' temper, do receive you in
With all kind love, good thoughts and reverence.

Cas. Your voice shall be as strong as any man's
In the disposing of new dignities.

Bru. Only be patient till we have appeased
The multitude, besides themselves with fear,
And then we will deliver you the cause
Why I, that did love Cæsar when I struck him,
Have thus proceeded.

Ant. I doubt not of your wisdom.
Let each man render me his bloody hand:
First, Marcus Brutus, will I shake with you;
Next, Caius Cassius, do I take your hand;
Now, Decius Brutus, yours; now yours, Metellus;
Yours, Cinna; and, my valiant Casca, yours;
Though last, not least in love, yours, good Trebonius.
Gentlemen all,—alas, what shall I say?
My credit now stands on such slippery ground,
That one of two bad ways you must conceit me,
Either a coward or a flatterer.
That I did love thee, Cæsar, O, 'tis true:
If then thy spirit look upon us now,
Shall it not grieve thee dearer than thy death,
To see thy Antony making his peace,
Shaking the bloody fingers of thy foes,
Most noble! in the presence of thy corse?
Had I as many eyes as thou hast wounds,
Weeping as fast as they stream forth thy blood,
It would become me better than to close
In terms of friendship with thine enemies.
Pardon me, Julius! Here wast thou bay'd, brave hart
Here didst thou fall, and here thy hunters stand,
Sign'd in thy spoil and crimson'd in thy lethe.
O world, thou wast the forest to this hart;
And this, indeed, O world, the heart of thee.
How like a deer strucken by many princes
Dost thou here lie!

Cas. Mark Antony,—

Ant. Pardon me, Caius Cassius:
The enemies of Cæsar shall say this;
Then, in a friend, it is cold modesty.
Cas. I blame you not for praising Cæsar so;
But what compact mean you to have with us?
Will you be prick'd in number of our friends,
Or shall we on, and not depend on you?
Ant. Therefore I took your hands, but was indeed
Sway'd from the point by looking down on Cæsar.
Friends am I with you all and love you all,
Upon this hope that you shall give me reasons
Why and wherein Cæsar was dangerous.
Bru. Or else were this a savage spectacle:
Our reasons are so full of good regard
That were you, Antony, the son of Cæsar,
You should be satisfied.
Ant. That's all I seek:
And am moreover suitor that I may
Produce his body to the market-place,
And in the pulpit, as becomes a friend,
Speak in the order of his funeral.
Bru. You shall, Mark Antony.
Cas. Brutus, a word with you.
[*Aside to Bru.*] You know not what you do: do not consent
That Antony speak in his funeral:
Know you how much the people may be moved
By that which he will utter?
Bru. By your pardon:
I will myself into the pulpit first,
And show the reason of our Cæsar's death:
What Antony shall speak, I will protest
He speaks by leave and by permission,
And that we are contented Cæsar shall
Have all true rites and lawful ceremonies.
It shall advantage more than do us wrong.
Cas. I know not what may fall; I like it not.
Bru. Mark Antony, here, take you Cæsar's body.
You shall not in your funeral speech blame us,
But speak all good you can devise of Cæsar,
And say you do't by our permission;
Else shall you not have any hand at all
About his funeral: and you shall speak
In the same pulpit whereto I am going,
After my speech is ended.
Ant. Be it so;

I do desire no more.
Bru. Prepare the body then, and follow us.
[*Exeunt all but Antony.*
Ant. O, pardon me, thou bleeding piece of earth,
That I am meek and gentle with these butchers!
Thou art the ruins of the noblest man
That ever lived in the tide of times.
Woe to the hand that shed this costly blood!
Over thy wounds now do I prophesy,
Which like dumb mouths do ope their ruby lips
To beg the voice and utterance of my tongue,
A curse shall light upon the limbs of men;
Domestic fury and fierce civil strife
Shall cumber all the parts of Italy;
Blood and destruction shall be so in use,
And dreadful objects so familiar,
That mothers shall but smile when they behold
Their infants quarter'd with the hands of war;
All pity choked with custom of fell deeds:
And Cæsar's spirit ranging for revenge,
With Ate by his side come hot from hell,
Shall in these confines with a monarch's voice
Cry 'Havoc,' and let slip the dogs of war;
That this foul deed shall smell above the earth
With carrion men, groaning for burial.
Enter a Servant.
You serve Octavius Cæsar, do you not?
Serv. I do, Mark Antony.
Ant. Cæsar did write for him to come to Rome.
Serv. He did receive his letters, and is coming;
And bid me say to you by word of mouth—
O Cæsar! [*Seeing the body.*
Ant. Thy heart is big; get thee apart and weep.
Passion, I see, is catching, for mine eyes,
Seeing those beads of sorrow stand in thine,
Began to water. Is thy master coming?
Serv. He lies to-night within seven leagues of Rome.
Ant. Post back with speed, and tell him what hath chanced:
Here is a mourning Rome, a dangerous Rome,
No Rome of safety for Octavius yet;
Hie hence, and tell him so. Yet stay awhile;
Thou shalt not back till I have borne this corse
Into the market-place: there shall I try,
In my oration, how the people take
The cruel issue of these bloody men;

According to the which, thou shalt discourse
To young Octavius of the state of things.
Lend me your hand. [*Exeunt with Cæsar's body.*

SCENE II

The Forum.

Enter Brutus and Cassius, and a throng of Citizens.

Citizens. We will be satisfied; let us be satisfied.

Bru. Then follow me, and give me audience, friends.
Cassius, go you into the other street,
And part the numbers.
Those that will hear me speak, let 'em stay here;
Those that will follow Cassius, go with him;
And public reasons shall be rendered
Of Cæsar's death.

First Cit. I will hear Brutus speak.

Sec. Cit. I will hear Cassius; and compare their reasons,
When severally we hear them rendered.

[*Exit Cassius, with some of the Citizens. Brutus goes into the pulpit.*

Third Cit. The noble Brutus is ascended: silence!

Bru. Be patient till the last.
Romans, countrymen, and lovers! hear me for my cause, and be silent, that you may hear: believe me for mine honour, and have respect for mine honour, that you may believe: censure me in your wisdom, and awake your senses, that you may the better judge. If there be any in this assembly, any dear friend of Cæsar's, to him I say that Brutus' love to Cæsar was no less than his. If then that friend demand why Brutus rose against Cæsar, this is my answer: not that I loved Cæsar less, but that I loved Rome more. Had you rather Cæsar were living, and die all slaves, than that Cæsar were dead, to live all freemen? As Cæsar loved me, I weep for him; as he was fortunate, I rejoice at it; as he was valiant, I honour him; but as he was ambitious, I slew him. There is tears for his love; joy for his fortune; honour for his valour; and death for his ambition. Who is here so base that would be a bondman? If any, speak; for him have I offended. Who is here so rude that would not be a Roman? If any, speak; for him have I offended. Who is here so vile that will not love his country? If any, speak; for him have I offended. I pause for a reply.

All. None, Brutus, none.

Bru. Then none have I offended. I have done no more to Cæsar than you shall do to Brutus. The question of his death is enrolled in the Capitol; his glory not extenuated, wherein he was worthy, nor his offences enforced, for which he suffered death.

Enter Antony and others, with Cæsar's body.

Here comes his body, mourned by Mark Antony: who, though he had no hand in his death, shall receive the benefit of his dying, a place in the commonwealth; as which of you shall not? With this I depart,—that, as I slew my best lover for the good of Rome, I have the same dagger for myself, when it shall please my country to need my death.

All. Live, Brutus! live, live!
First Cit. Bring him with triumph home unto his house.
Sec. Cit. Give him a statue with his ancestors.
Third Cit. Let him be Cæsar.
Fourth Cit. Cæsar's better parts
Shall be crown'd in Brutus.
First Cit. We'll bring him to his house with shouts and [clamours.
Bru. My countrymen,—
Sec. Cit. Peace! silence! Brutus speaks.
First Cit. Peace, ho!
Bru. Good Countryman, let me depart alone,
And, for my sake, stay here with Antony:
Do grace to Cæsar's corpse, and grace his speech
Tending to Cæsar's glories, which Mark Antony
By our permission is allow'd to make.
I do entreat you, not a man depart,
Save I alone, till Antony have spoke. [*Exit.*
First Cit. Stay, ho! and let us hear Mark Antony.
Third Cit. Let him go up into the public chair;
We'll hear him. Noble Antony, go up.
Ant. For Brutus' sake, I am beholding to you.
[*Goes into the pulpit.*
Fourth Cit. What does he say of Brutus?
Third Cit. He says, for Brutus' sake,
He finds himself beholding to us all.
Fourth Cit. 'Twere best he speak no harm of Brutus here.
First Cit. This Cæsar was a tyrant.
Third Cit. Nay, that's certain:
We are blest that Rome is rid of him.
Sec. Cit. Peace! let us hear what Antony can say.
Ant. You gentle Romans,—
All. Peace, ho! let us hear him.
Ant. Friends, Romans, countrymen, lend me your ears;
I come to bury Cæsar, not to praise him.
The evil that men do lives after them;

The good is oft interred with their bones;
So let it be with Cæsar. The noble Brutus
Hath told you Cæsar was ambitious:
If it were so, it was a grievous fault,
And grievously hath Cæsar answer'd it.
Here, under leave of Brutus and the rest,—
For Brutus is an honourable man;
So are they all, all honourable men,—
Come I to speak in Cæsar's funeral.
He was my friend, faithful and just to me:
But Brutus says he was ambitious;
And Brutus is an honourable man.
He hath brought many captives home to Rome,
Whose ransoms did the general coffers fill:
Did this in Cæsar seem ambitious?
When that the poor have cried, Cæsar hath wept:
Ambition should be made of sterner stuff:
Yet Brutus says he was ambitious;
And Brutus is an honourable man.
You all did see that on the Lupercal
I thrice presented him a kingly crown,
Which he did thrice refuse: was this ambition?
Yet Brutus says he was ambitious;
And, sure, he is an honourable man.
I speak not to disprove what Brutus spoke,
But here I am to speak what I do know.
You all did love him once, not without cause:
What cause withholds you then to mourn for him?
O judgement! thou art fled to brutish beasts,
And men have lost their reason. Bear with me;
My heart is in the coffin there with Cæsar,
And I must pause till it come back to me.

First Cit. Methinks there is much reason in his sayings.

Sec. Cit. If thou consider rightly of the matter,
Cæsar has had great wrong.

Third Cit. Has he, masters?
I fear there will a worse come in his place.

Fourth Cit. Mark'd ye his words? He would not take the crown;
Therefore 'tis certain he was not ambitious.

First Cit. If it be found so, some will dear abide it.

Sec. Cit. Poor soul! his eyes are red as fire with weeping.

Third Cit. There's not a nobler man in Rome than Antony.

Fourth Cit. Now mark him, he begins again to speak.

Ant. But yesterday the word of Cæsar might
Have stood against the world: now lies he there,

And none so poor to do him reverence.
O masters, if I were disposed to stir
Your hearts and minds to mutiny and rage,
I should do Brutus wrong and Cassius wrong,
Who, you all know, are honourable men:
I will not do them wrong; I rather choose
To wrong the dead, to wrong myself and you,
Than I will wrong such honourable men.
But here 's a parchment with the seal of Cæsar;
I found it in his closet; 'tis his will:
Let but the commons hear this testament—
Which, pardon me, I do not mean to read—
And they would go and kiss dead Cæsar's wounds
And dip their napkins in his sacred blood,
Yea, beg a hair of him for memory,
And, dying, mention it within their wills,
Bequeathing it as a rich legacy
Unto their issue.

Fourth Cit. We 'll hear the will: read it, Mark Antony.

All. The will, the will! we will hear Cæsar's will.

Ant. Have patience, gentle friends, I must not read it;
It is not meet you know how Cæsar loved you.
You are not wood, you are not stones, but men;
And, being men, hearing the will of Cæsar,
It will inflame you, it will make you mad:
'Tis good you know not that you are his heirs;
For if you should, O, what would come of it!

Fourth Cit. Read the will; we 'll hear it, Antony;
You shall read us the will, Cæsar's will.

Ant. Will you be patient? will you stay awhile?
I have o'ershot myself to tell you of it:
I fear I wrong the honourable men
Whose daggers have stabb'd Cæsar; I do fear it.

Fourth Cit. They were traitors: honourable men!

All. The will! the testament!

Sec. Cit. They were villains, murderers: the will! read the will.

Ant. You will compel me then to read the will?
Then make a ring about the corpse of Cæsar,
And let me show you him that made the will.
Shall I descend? and will you give me leave?

All. Come down.

Sec. Cit. Descend. [*He comes down from the pulpit.*

Third Cit. You shall have leave.

Fourth Cit. A ring; stand round.

First Cit. Stand from the hearse, stand from the body.

Sec. Cit. Room for Antony, most noble Antony.
Ant. Nay, press not so upon me; stand far off.
All. Stand back. Room! Bear back.
Ant. If you have tears, prepare to shed them now.
You all do know this mantle: I remember
The first time ever Cæsar put it on;
'Twas on a summer's evening, in his tent,
That day he overcame the Nervii:
Look, in this place ran Cassius' dagger through:
See what a rent the envious Casca made:
Through this the well-beloved Brutus stabb'd;
And as he pluck'd his cursed steel away,
Mark how the blood of Cæsar follow'd it,
As rushing out of doors, to be resolved
If Brutus so unkindly knock'd, or no:
For Brutus, as you know, was Cæsar's angel:
Judge, O you gods, how dearly Cæsar loved him!
This was the most unkindest cut of all;
For when the noble Cæsar saw him stab,
Ingratitude, more strong than traitors' arms,
Quite vanquish'd him: then burst his mighty heart;
And, in his mantle muffling up his face,
Even at the base of Pompey's statuë,
Which all the while ran blood, great Cæsar fell.
O, what a fall was there, my countrymen!
Then I, and you, and all of us fell down,
Whilst bloody treason flourish'd over us.
O, now you weep, and I perceive you feel
The dint of pity: these are gracious drops.
Kind souls, what weep you when you but behold
Our Cæsar's vesture wounded? Look you here,
Here is himself, marr'd, as you see, with traitors.
First Cit. O piteous spectacle!
Sec. Cit. O noble Cæsar!
Third Cit. O woful day!
Fourth Cit. O traitors, villains!
First Cit. O most bloody sight!
Sec. Cit. We will be revenged.
All. Revenge! About! Seek! Burn! Fire! Kill! Slay!
Let not a traitor live!
Ant. Stay, countrymen.
First Cit. Peace there! hear the noble Antony.
Sec. Cit. We'll hear him, we'll follow him, we'll die with him.
Ant. Good friends, sweet friends, let me not stir you up
To such a sudden flood of mutiny.

They that have done this deed are honourable;
What private griefs they have, alas, I know not,
That made them do it: they are wise and honourable,
And will, no doubt, with reasons answer you.
I come not, friends, to steal away your hearts:
I am no orator, as Brutus is;
But, as you know me all, a plain blunt man,
That love my friend; and that they know full well
That gave me public leave to speak of him:
For I have neither wit, nor words, nor worth,
Action, nor utterance, nor the power of speech,
To stir men's blood: I only speak right on;
I tell you that which you yourselves do know;
Show you sweet Cæsar's wounds, poor poor dumb mouths,
And bid them speak for me: but were I Brutus,
And Brutus Antony, there were an Antony
Would ruffle up your spirits, and put a tongue
In every wound of Cæsar, that should move
The stones of Rome to rise and mutiny.

All. We'll mutiny.

First Cit. We'll burn the house of Brutus.

Third Cit. Away, then! come, seek the conspirators.

Ant. Yet hear me, countrymen; yet hear me speak.

All. Peace, ho! Hear Antony. Most noble Antony!

Ant. Why, friends, you go to do you know not what:
Wherein hath Cæsar thus deserved your loves?
Alas, you know not; I must tell you then:
You have forgot the will I told you of.

All. Most true: the will! Let's stay and hear the will.

Ant. Here is the will, and under Cæsar's seal.
To every Roman citizen he gives,
To every several man, seventy-five drachmas.

Sec. Cit. Most noble Cæsar! we'll revenge his death.

Third Cit. O royal Cæsar!

Ant. Hear me with patience.

All. Peace, ho!

Moreover, he hath left you all his walks,
His private arbours and new-planted orchards,
On this side Tiber; he hath left them you,
And to your heirs for ever; common pleasures,
To walk abroad and recreate yourselves.
Here was a Cæsar! when comes such another?

First Cit. Never, never. Come, away, away!
We'll burn his body in the holy place,
And with the brands fire the traitors' houses.

Take up the body.
Sec. Cit. Go fetch fire.
Third Cit. Pluck down benches.
Fourth Cit. Pluck down forms, windows, any thing.
[*Exeunt Citizens with the body.*
Ant. Now let it work. Mischief, thou art afoot,
Take thou what course thou wilt.
Enter a Servant.
How now, fellow!
Serv. Sir, Octavius is already come to Rome.
Ant. Where is he?
Serv. He and Lepidus are at Cæsar's house.
Ant. And thither will I straight to visit him.
He comes upon a wish. Fortune is merry,
And in this mood will give us any thing.
Serv. I heard him say, Brutus and Cassius
Are rid like madmen through the gates of Rome.
Ant. Belike they had some notice of the people,
How I had moved them. Bring me to Octavius. [*Exeunt.*

Scene III

A street.

Enter Cinna the poet.

Cin. I dreamt to-night that I did feast with Cæsar,
And things unluckily charge my fantasy:
I have no will to wander forth of doors,
Yet something leads me forth.
Enter Citizens.
First Cit. What is your name?
Sec. Cit. Whither are you going?
Third Cit. Where do you dwell?
Fourth Cit. Are you a married man or a bachelor?
Sec. Cit. Answer every man directly.
First Cit. Ay, and briefly.
Fourth Cit. Ay, and wisely.
Third Cit. Ay, and truly, you were best.
Cin. What is my name? Whither am I going? Where do I dwell? Am I a married man or a bachelor? Then, to answer every man directly and briefly, wisely and truly: wisely I say, I am a bachelor.
Sec. Cit. That 's as much as to say, they are fools that marry: you 'll bear me a bang for that, I fear. Proceed; directly.
Cin. Directly, I am going to Cæsar's funeral.
First Cit. As a friend or an enemy?
Cin. As a friend.

Sec. Cit. That matter is answered directly.
Fourth Cit. For your dwelling, briefly.
Cin. Briefly, I dwell by the Capitol.
Third Cit. Your name, sir, truly.
Cin. Truly, my name is Cinna.
First Cit. Tear him to pieces; he 's a conspirator.
Cin. I am Cinna the poet, I am Cinna the poet.
Fourth Cit. Tear him for his bad verses, tear him for his bad [verses.
Cin. I am not Cinna the conspirator.
Fourth Cit. It is no matter, his name 's Cinna; pluck but his name out of his heart, and turn him going.
Third Cit. Tear him, tear him! Come, brands, ho! firebrands: to Brutus', to Cassius'; burn all: some to Decius' house, and some to Casca's; some to Ligarius'; away, go!
[*Exeunt.*

ACT IV—Scene I

A house in Rome.

Antony, Octavius, and Lepidus, seated at a table.

Ant. These many then shall die; their names are prick'd.
Oct. Your brother too must die; consent you, Lepidus?
Lep. I do consent—
Oct. Prick him down, Antony.
Lep. Upon condition Publius shall not live,
Who is your sister's son, Mark Antony.
Ant. He shall not live; look, with a spot I damn him.
But, Lepidus, go you to Cæsar's house;
Fetch the will hither, and we shall determine
How to cut off some charge in legacies.
Lep. What, shall I find you here?
Oct. Or here, or at the Capitol. [*Exit Lepidus.*
Ant. This is a slight unmeritable man,
Meet to be sent on errands: is it fit,
The three-fold world divided, he should stand
One of the three to share it?
Oct. So you thought him,
And took his voice who should be prick'd to die
In our black sentence and proscription.
Ant. Octavius, I have seen more days than you:
And though we lay these honours on this man,
To ease ourselves of divers slanderous loads,
He shall but bear them as the ass bears gold,
To groan and sweat under the business,
Either led or driven, as we point the way;

And having brought our treasure where we will,
Then take we down his load and turn him off,
Like to the empty ass, to shake his ears
And graze in commons.

Oct. You may do your will:
But he 's a tried and valiant soldier.

Ant. So is my horse, Octavius, and for that
I do appoint him store of provender:
It is a creature that I teach to fight,
To wind, to stop, to run directly on,
His corporal motion govern'd by my spirit.
And, in some taste, is Lepidus but so;
He must be taught, and train'd, and bid go forth;
A barren-spirited fellow; one that feeds
On abjects, orts and imitations,
Which, out of use and staled by other men,
Begin his fashion: do not talk of him
But as a property. And now, Octavius,
Listen great things: Brutus and Cassius
Are levying powers: we must straight make head:
Therefore let our alliance be combined,
Our best friends made, our means stretch'd;
And let us presently go sit in council,
How covert matters may be best disclosed,
And open perils surest answered.

Oct. Let us do so: for we are at the stake,
And bay'd about with many enemies;
And some that smile have in their hearts, I fear,
Millions of mischiefs. [*Exeunt.*

Scene II

Camp near Sardis. Before Brutus's tent.

Drum. Enter Brutus, Lucilius, Lucius, and Soldiers; Titinius and Pindarus meet them.

Bru. Stand, ho!

Lucil. Give the word, ho! and stand.

Bru. What now, Lucilius? is Cassius near?

Lucil. He is at hand; and Pindarus is come
To do you salutation from his master.

Bru. He greets me well. Your master, Pindarus,
In his own change, or by ill officers,
Hath given me some worthy cause to wish
Things done undone: but if he be at hand,
I shall be satisfied.

Pin. I do not doubt

But that my noble master will appear
Such as he is, full of regard and honour.
Bru. He is not doubted. A word, Lucilius,
How he received you: let me be resolved.
Lucil. With courtesy and with respect enough;
But not with such familiar instances,
Nor with such free and friendly conference,
As he hath used of old.
Bru. Thou hast described
A hot friend cooling: ever note, Lucilius,
When love begins to sicken and decay,
It useth an enforced ceremony.
There are no tricks in plain and simple faith:
But hollow men, like horses hot at hand,
Make gallant show and promise of their mettle;
But when they should endure the bloody spur,
They fall their crests and like deceitful jades
Sink in the trial. Comes his army on?
Lucil. They mean this night in Sardis to be quarter'd;
The greater part, the horse in general,
Are come with Cassius. [*Low march within.*
Bru. Hark! he is arrived:
March gently on to meet him.

Enter Cassius and his powers.

Cas. Stand, ho!
Bru. Stand, ho! Speak the word along.
First Sol. Stand!
Sec. Sol. Stand!
Third Sol. Stand!
Cas. Most noble brother, you have done me wrong.
Bru. Judge me, you gods! wrong I mine enemies?
And, if not so, how should I wrong a brother?
Cas. Brutus, this sober form of yours hides wrongs;
And when you do them—
Bru. Cassius, be content;
Speak your griefs softly: I do know you well.
Before the eyes of both our armies here,
Which should perceive nothing but love from us,
Let us not wrangle: bid them move away;
Then in my tent, Cassius, enlarge your griefs,
And I will give you audience.
Cas. Pindarus,
Bid our commanders lead their charges off
A little from this ground.
Bru. Lucilius, do you the like, and let no man

Come to our tent till we have done our conference.
Let Lucius and Titinius guard our door. [*Exeunt.*

SCENE III

Brutus's tent.

Enter Brutus and Cassius.

Cas. That you have wrong'd me doth appear in this:
You have condemn'd and noted Lucius Pella
For taking bribes here of the Sardians;
Wherein my letters, praying on his side,
Because I knew the man, were slighted off.
Bru. You wrong'd yourself to write in such a case.
Cas. In such a time as this it is not meet
That every nice offence should bear his comment.
Bru. Let me tell you, Cassius, you yourself
Are much condemn'd to have an itching palm,
To sell and mart your offices for gold
To undeservers.
Cas. I an itching palm!
You know that you are Brutus that speaks this,
Or, by the gods, this speech were else your last.
Bru. The name of Cassius honours this corruption,
And chastisement doth therefore hide his head.
Cas. Chastisement!
Bru. Remember March, the ides of March remember:
Did not great Julius bleed for justice' sake?
What villain touch'd his body, that did stab,
And not for justice? What, shall one of us,
That struck the foremost man of all this world
But for supporting robbers, shall we now
Contaminate our fingers with base bribes,
And sell the mighty space of our large honours
For so much trash as may be grasped thus?
I had rather be a dog, and bay the moon,
Than such a Roman.
Cas. Brutus, bait not me
I'll not endure it: you forget yourself,
To hedge me in; I am a soldier, I,
Older in practice, abler than yourself
To make conditions.
Bru. Go to; you are not, Cassius.
Cas. I am.
Bru. I say you are not.
Cas. Urge me no more, I shall forget myself;
Have mind upon your health, tempt me no farther.

Bru. Away, slight man!
Cas. Is 't possible?
Bru. Hear me, for I will speak.
Must I give way and room to your rash choler?
Shall I be frighted when a madman stares?
Cas. O ye gods, ye gods! must I endure all this?
Bru. All this! ay, more: fret till your proud heart break;
Go show your slaves how choleric you are,
And make your bondmen tremble. Must I budge?
Must I observe you? must I stand and crouch
Under your testy humour? By the gods,
You shall digest the venom of your spleen,
Though it do split you; for, from this day forth,
I 'll use you for my mirth, yea, for my laughter,
When you are waspish.
Cas. Is it come to this?
Bru. You say you are a better soldier:
Let it appear so; make you vaunting true,
And it shall please me well: for mine own part,
I shall be glad to learn of noble men.
Cas. You wrong me every way; you wrong me, Brutus;
I said, an elder soldier, not a better:
Did I say, better?
Bru. If you did, I care not.
Cas. When Cæsar lived, he durst not thus have moved me.
Bru. Peace, peace! you durst not so have tempted him.
Cas. I durst not!
Bru. No.
Cas. What, durst not tempt him!
Bru. For your life you durst not.
Cas. Do not presume too much upon my love;
I may do that I shall be sorry for.
Bru. You have done that you should be sorry for.
There is no terror, Cassius, in your threats;
For I am arm'd so strong in honesty,
That they pass by me as the idle wind
Which I respect not. I did send to you
For certain sums of gold, which you denied me:
For I can raise no money by vile means:
By heaven, I had rather coin my heart,
And drop my blood for drachmas, than to wring
From the hard hands of peasants their vile trash
By any indirection. I did send
To you for gold to pay my legions,
Which you denied me: was that done like Cassius?

Should I have answer'd Caius Cassius so?
When Marcus Brutus grows so covetous,
To lock such rascal counters from his friends,
Be ready, gods, with all your thunderbolts,
Dash him to pieces!
Cas. I denied you not.
Bru. You did.
Cas. I did not: he was but a fool
That brought my answer back. Brutus hath rived my heart:
A friend should bear his friend's infirmities,
But Brutus makes mine greater than they are.
Bru. I do not, till you practise them on me.
Cas. You love me not.
Bru. I do not like your faults.
Cas. A friendly eye could never see such faults.
Bru. A flatterer's would not, though they do appear
As huge as high Olympus.
Cas. Come, Antony, and young Octavius, come,
Revenge yourselves alone on Cassius,
For Cassius is aweary of the world;
Hated by one he loves; braved by his brother!
Check'd like a bondman; all his faults observed,
Set in a note-book, learn'd and conn'd by rote,
To cast into my teeth. O, I could weep
My spirit from mine eyes! There is my dagger,
And here my naked breast; within, a heart
Dearer than Plutus' mine, richer than gold;
If that thou be'st a Roman, take it forth;
I, that denied thee gold, will give my heart;
Strike, as thou didst at Cæsar; for I know,
When thou didst hate him worst, thou lovedst him better
Than ever thou lovedst Cassius.
Bru. Sheathe your dagger:
Be angry when you will, it shall have scope;
Do what you will, dishonour shall be humour.
O Cassius, you are yoked with a lamb,
That carries anger as the flint bears fire,
Who, much enforced, shows a hasty spark
And straight is cold again.
Cas. Hath Cassius lived
To be but mirth and laughter to his Brutus,
When grief and blood ill-temper'd vexeth him.
Bru. When I spoke that, I was ill-temper'd too.
Cas. Do you confess so much? Give me your hand.
Bru. And my heart too.

Cas. O Brutus!
Bru. What's the matter?
Cas. Have not you love enough to bear with me,
When that rash humour which my mother gave me
Makes me forgetful?
Bru. Yes, Cassius, and from henceforth,
When you are over-earnest with your Brutus,
He'll think your mother chides, and leave you so.
Poet. [*Within*] Let me go in to see the generals;
There is some grudge between 'em; 'tis not meet
They be alone.
Lucil. [*Within*] You shall not come to them.
Poet. [*Within*] Nothing but death shall stay me.

Enter Poet, followed by Lucilius, Titinius, and Lucius.

Cas. How now! what's the matter?
Poet. For shame, you generals! what do you mean?
Love, and be friends, as two such men should be;
For I have seen more years, I'm sure, than ye.
Cas. Ha, ha! how vilely doth this cynic rhyme!
Bru. Get you hence, sirrah; saucy fellow, hence!
Cas. Bear with him, Brutus; 'tis his fashion.
Bru. I'll know his humour when he knows his time:
What should the wars do with these jigging fools?
Companion, hence!
Cas. Away, away, be gone! [*Exit Poet.*
Bru. Lucilius and Titinius, bid the commanders
Prepare to lodge their companies to-night.
Cas. And come yourselves, and bring Messala with you
Immediately to us. [*Exeunt Lucilius and Titinius.*
Bru. Lucius, a bowl of wine! [*Exit Lucius.*
Cas. I did not think you could have been so angry.
Bru. O Cassius, I am sick of many griefs.
Cas. Of your philosophy you make no use,
If you give place to accidental evils.
Bru. No man bears sorrow better: Portia is dead.
Cas. Ha! Portia!
Bru. She is dead.
Cas. How 'scaped I killing when I cross'd you so?
O insupportable and touching loss!
Upon what sickness?
Bru. Impatient of my absence,
And grief that young Octavius with Mark Antony
Have made themselves so strong: for with her death
That tidings came: with this she fell distract,
And, her attendants absent, swallow'd fire.

Cas. And died so?
Bru. Even so.
Cas. O ye immortal gods!
Re-enter Lucius, with wine and taper.
Bru. Speak no more of her. Give me a bowl of wine.
In this I bury all unkindness, Cassius. [*Drinks.*
Cas. My heart is thirsty for that noble pledge.
Fill, Lucius, till the wine o'erswell the cup;
I cannot drink too much of Brutus' love. [*Drinks.*
Bru. Come in, Titinius! [*Exit Lucius.*
Re-enter Titinius, with Messala.
Welcome, good Messala.
Now sit we close about this taper here,
And call in question our necessities.
Cas. Portia, art thou gone?
Bru. No more, I pray you.
Messala, I have here received letters,
That young Octavius and Mark Antony
Come down upon us with a mighty power,
Bending their expedition toward Philippi.
Mes. Myself have letters of the self-same tenour.
Bru. With what addition?
Mes. That by proscription and bills of outlawry
Octavius, Antony and Lepidus,
Have put to death an hundred senators.
Bru. Therein our letters do not well agree;
Mine speak of seventy senators that died
By their proscriptions, Cicero being one.
Cas. Cicero one!
Mes. Cicero is dead,
And by that order of proscription.
Had you your letters from your wife, my lord?
Bru. No, Messala.
Mes. Nor nothing in your letters writ of her?
Bru. Nothing, Messala.
Mes. That, methinks, is strange.
Bru. Why ask you? hear you aught of her in yours?
Mes. No, my lord.
Bru. Now, as you are a Roman, tell me true.
Mes. Then like a Roman bear the truth I tell:
For certain she is dead, and by strange manner.
Bru. Why, farewell, Portia. We must die, Messala:
With meditating that she must die once
I have the patience to endure it now.
Mes. Even so great men great losses should endure.

Cas. I have as much of this in art as you,
But yet my nature could not bear it so.
Bru. Well, to our work alive. What do you think
Of marching to Philippi presently?
Cas. I do not think it good.
Bru. Your reason?
Cas. This it is:
'Tis better that the enemy seek us:
So shall he waste his means, weary his soldiers,
Doing himself offence; whilst we lying still
Are full of rest, defence and nimbleness.
Bru. Good reasons must of force give place to better.
The people 'twixt Philippi and this ground
Do stand but in a forced affection,
For they have grudged us contribution;
The enemy, marching along by them,
By them shall make a fuller number up,
Come on refresh'd, new-added and encouraged;
From which advantage shall we cut him off
If at Philippi we do face him there,
These people at our back.
Cas. Hear me, good brother.
Bru. Under your pardon. You must note beside
That we have tried the utmost of our friends,
Our legions are brim-full, our cause is ripe:
The enemy increaseth every day;
We, at the height, are ready to decline.
There is a tide in the affairs of men
Which taken at the flood leads on to fortune;
Omitted, all the voyage of their life
Is bound in shallows and in miseries.
On such a full sea are we now afloat,
And we must take the current when it serves,
Or lose our ventures.
Cas. Then, with your will, go on;
We'll along ourselves and meet them at Philippi.
Bru. The deep of night is crept upon our talk,
And nature must obey necessity;
Which we will niggard with a little rest.
There is no more to say?
Cas. No more. Good night:
Early to-morrow will we rise and hence.
Bru. Lucius! [*Re-enter Lucius.*] My gown. [*Exit Lucius.*]
Farewell, good Messala:
Good-night, Titinius: noble, noble Cassius,

Good night, and good repose.
Cas. O my dear brother!
This was an ill beginning of the night:
Never come such division 'tween our souls!
Let it not, Brutus.
Bru. Every thing is well.
Cas. Good night, my lord.
Bru. Good night, good brother.
Tit. Mes. Good night, Lord Brutus.
Bru. Farewell, every one.
[*Exeunt all but Brutus.*

Re-enter Lucius, with the gown.

Give me the gown. Where is thy instrument?
Luc. Here in the tent.
Bru. What, thou speak'st drowsily?
Poor knave, I blame thee not; thou art o'er-watch'd.
Call Claudius and some other of my men;
I'll have them sleep on cushions in my tent.
Luc. Varro and Claudius!

Enter Varro and Claudius.

Var. Calls my lord?
Bru. I pray you, sirs, lie in my tent and sleep;
It may be I shall raise you by and by
On business to my brother Cassius.
Var. So please you, we will stand and watch your pleasure.
Bru. I will not have it so: lie down, good sirs;
It may be I shall otherwise bethink me.
Look, Lucius, here's the book I sought for so;
I put it in the pocket of my gown.
[*Var. and Clau. lie down.*
Luc. I was sure your lordship did not give it me.
Bru. Bear with me, good boy, I am much forgetful.
Canst thou hold up thy heavy eyes awhile,
And touch thy instrument a strain or two?
Luc. Ay, my lord, an 't please you.
Bru. It does, my boy:
I trouble thee too much, but thou art willing.
Luc. It is my duty, sir.
Bru. I should not urge thy duty past thy might;
I know young bloods look for a time of rest.
Luc. I have slept, my lord, already.
Bru. It was well done; and thou shalt sleep again;
I will not hold thee long: if I do live,
I will be good to thee. [*Music, and a song.*
This is a sleepy tune. O murderous slumber,

Lay'st thou thy leaden mace upon my boy,
That plays thee music? Gentle knave, good night;
I will not do thee so much wrong to wake thee:
If thou dost nod, thou break'st thy instrument;
I 'll take it from thee; and, good boy, good night.
Let me see, let me see; is not the leaf turn'd down
Where I left reading? Here it is, I think. [*Sits down.*

Enter the Ghost of Cæsar.

How ill this taper burns! Ha! who comes here?
I think it is the weakness of mine eyes
That shapes this monstrous apparition.
It comes upon me. Art thou any thing?
Art thou some god, some angel, or some devil,
That makest my blood cold, and my hair to stare?
Speak to me what thou art.

Ghost. Thy evil spirit, Brutus.

Bru. Why comest thou?

Ghost. To tell thee thou shalt see me at Philippi.

Bru. Well; then I shall see thee again?

Ghost. Ay, at Philippi.

Bru. Why, I will see thee at Philippi then. [*Exit Ghost.*
Now I have taken heart thou vanishest.
Ill spirit, I would hold more talk with thee.
Boy, Lucius! Varro! Claudius! Sirs, awake! Claudius!

Luc. The strings, my lord, are false.

Bru. He thinks he still is at his instrument.
Lucius, awake!

Luc. My lord?

Bru. Didst thou dream, Lucius, that thou so criedst out?

Luc. My lord, I do not know that I did cry.

Bru. Yes, that thou didst: didst thou see any thing?

Luc. Nothing, my lord.

Bru. Sleep again, Lucius. Sirrah Claudius!
[*To Var.*] Fellow thou, awake!

Var. My lord?

Clau. My lord?

Bru. Why did you so cry out, sirs, in your sleep?

Var. Clau. Did we, my lord?

Bru. Ay: saw you any thing?

Var. No, my lord, I saw nothing.

Clau. Nor I, my lord.

Bru. Go and commend me to my brother Cassius;
Bid him set on his powers betimes before,
And we will follow.

Var. Clau. It shall be done, my lord. [*Exeunt.*

ACT V—Scene I

The plains of Philippi.

Enter Octavius, Antony, and their army.

Oct. Now, Antony, our hopes are answered:
You said the enemy would not come down,
But keep the hills and upper regions;
It proves not so: their battles are at hand;
They mean to warn us at Philippi here,
Answering before we do demand of them.

Ant. Tut, I am in their bosoms, and I know
Wherefore they do it: they could be content
To visit other places; and come down
With fearful bravery, thinking by this face
To fasten in our thoughts that they have courage;
But 'tis not so.

Enter a Messenger.

Mess. Prepare you, generals:
The enemy comes on in gallant show;
Their bloody sign of battle is hung out,
And something to be done immediately.

Ant. Octavius, lead your battle softly on,
Upon the left hand of the even field.

Oct. Upon the right hand I; keep thou the left.

Ant. Why do you cross me in this exigent?

Oct. I do not cross you; but I will do so. [*March.*

Drum. Enter Brutus, Cassius, and their Army; Lucilius, Titinius, Messala, and others.

Bru. They stand, and would have parley.

Cas. Stand fast, Titinius: we must out and talk.

Oct. Mark Antony, shall we give sign of battle?

Ant. No, Cæsar, we will answer on their charge.
Make forth; the generals would have some words.

Oct. Stir not until the signal.

Bru. Words before blows: is it so, countrymen?

Oct. Not that we love words better, as you do.

Bru. Good words are better than bad strokes, Octavius.

Ant. In your bad strokes, Brutus, you give good words:
Witness the hole you made in Cæsar's heart,
Crying 'Long live! hail Cæsar!'

Cas. Antony,
The posture of your blows are yet unknown;
But for your words, they rob the Hybla bees,
And leave them honeyless.

Ant. Not stingless too.
Bru. O, yes, and soundless too;
For you have stol'n their buzzing, Antony,
And very wisely threat before you sting.
Ant. Villains, you did not so, when your vile daggers
Hack'd one another in the sides of Cæsar:
You show'd your teeth like apes, and fawn'd like hounds,
And bow'd like bondmen, kissing Cæsar's feet;
Whilst damned Casca, like a cur, behind
Struck Cæsar on the neck. O you flatterers!
Cas. Flatterers! Now, Brutus, thank yourself:
This tongue had not offended so to-day,
If Cassius might have ruled.
Oct. Come, come, the cause: if arguing makes us sweat,
The proof of it will turn to redder drops.
Look;
I draw a sword against conspirators;
When think you that the sword goes up again?
Never, till Cæsar's three and thirty wounds
Be well avenged, or till another Cæsar
Have added slaughter to the sword of traitors.
Bru. Cæsar, thou canst not die by traitors' hands,
Unless thou bring'st them with thee.
Oct. So I hope
I was not born to die on Brutus' sword.
Bru. O, if thou wert the noblest of thy strain,
Young man, thou couldst not die more honourable.
Cas. A peevish schoolboy, worthless of such honour,
Join'd with a masker and a reveller!
Ant. Old Cassius still!
Oct. Come, Antony; away!
Defiance, traitors, hurl we in your teeth;
If you dare fight to-day, come to the field:
If not, when you have stomachs.
[*Exeunt Octavius, Antony, and their army.*
Cas. Why, now, blow wind, swell billow, and swim bark!
The storm is up, and all is on the hazard.
Bru. Ho, Lucilius! hark, a word with you.
Lucil. [*Standing forth*] My lord?
[*Brutus and Lucilius converse apart.*
Cas. Messala!
Mes. [*Standing forth*] What says my general?
Cas. Messala,
This is my birth-day; as this very day
Was Cassius born. Give me thy hand, Messala:

Be thou my witness that, against my will,
As Pompey was, am I compell'd to set
Upon one battle all our liberties.
You know that I held Epicurus strong,
And his opinion: now I change my mind,
And partly credit things that do presage.
Coming from Sardis, on our former ensign
Two mighty eagles fell, and there they perch'd,
Gorging and feeding from our soldiers' hands;
Who to Philippi here consorted us:
This morning are they fled away and gone;
And in their steads do ravens, crows and kites
Fly o'er our heads and downward look on us,
As we were sickly prey: their shadows seem
A canopy most fatal, under which
Our army lies, ready to give up the ghost.

Mes. Believe not so.

Cas. I but believe it partly,
For I am fresh of spirit and resolved
To meet all perils very constantly.

Bru. Even so, Lucilius.

Cas. Now, most noble Brutus,
The gods to-day stand friendly, that we may,
Lovers in peace, lead on our days to age!
But, since the affairs of men rest still incertain,
Let 's reason with the worst that may befall.
If we do lose this battle, then is this
The very last time we shall speak together:
What are you then determined to do?

Bru. Even by the rule of that philosophy
By which I did blame Cato for the death
Which he did give himself: I know not how,
But I do find it cowardly and vile,
For fear of what might fall, so to prevent
The time of life: arming myself with patience
To stay the providence of some high powers
That govern us below.

Cas. Then, if we lose this battle,
You are contented to be led in triumph
Thorough the streets of Rome?

Bru. No, Cassius, no: think not, thou noble Roman,
That ever Brutus will go bound to Rome;
He bears too great a mind. But this same day
Must end that work the ides of March begun;
And whether we shall meet again I know not.

Therefore our everlasting farewell take.
For ever, and for ever, farewell, Cassius!
If we do meet again, why, we shall smile;
If not, why then this parting was well made.
Cas. For ever and for ever farewell, Brutus!
If we do meet again, we 'll smile indeed;
If not, 'tis true this parting was well made.
Bru. Why then, lead on. O, that a man might know
The end of this day's business ere it come!
But it sufficeth that the day will end,
And then the end is known. Come, ho! away! [*Exeunt.*

SCENE II

The field of battle.

Alarum. Enter Brutus and Messala.

Bru. Ride, ride, Messala, ride, and give these bills
Unto the legions on the other side: [*Loud alarum.*
Let them set on at once; for I perceive
But cold demeanour in Octavius' wing,
And sudden push gives them the overthrow.
Ride, ride, Messala: let them all come down. [*Exeunt.*

SCENE III

Another part of the field.

Alarums. Enter Cassius and Titinius.

Cas. O, look, Titinius, look, the villains fly!
Myself have to mine own turn'd enemy:
This ensign here of mine was turning back;
I slew the coward, and did take it from him.
Tit. O Cassius, Brutus gave the word too early;
Who, having some advantage on Octavius,
Took it too eagerly: his soldiers fell to spoil,
Whilst we by Antony are all enclosed.

Enter Pindarus.

Pin. Fly further off, my lord, fly further off;
Mark Antony is in your tents, my lord:
Fly, therefore, noble Cassius, fly far off.
Cas. This hill is far enough. Look, look, Titinius;
Are those my tents where I perceive the fire?
Tit. They are, my lord.
Cas. Titinius, if thou lovest me,
Mount thou my horse and hide thy spurs in him,
Till he have brought thee up to yonder troops
And here again; that I may rest assured
Whether yond troops are friend or enemy.

Tit. I will be here again, even with a thought. [*Exit.*

Cas. Go, Pindarus, get higher on that hill;
My sight was ever thick; regard Titinius,
And tell me what thou notest about the field.
[*Pindarus ascends the hill.*
This day I breathed first: time is come round,
And where I did begin, there shall I end;
My life is run his compass. Sirrah, what news?

Pin. [*Above*] O my lord!

Cas. What news?

Pin. [*Above*] Titinius is enclosed round about
With horsemen, that make to him on the spur;
Yet he spurs on. Now they are almost on him.
Now, Titinius! Now some light. O, he lights too.
He's ta'en. [*Shout.*] And, hark! they shout for joy.

Cas. Come down; behold no more.
O, coward that I am, to live so long,
To see my best friend ta'en before my face!

Pindarus descends.

Come hither, sirrah:
In Parthia did I take thee prisoner;
And then I swore thee, saving of thy life,
That whatsoever I did bid thee do,
Thou shouldst attempt it. Come now, keep thine oath;
Now be a freeman; and with this good sword,
That ran through Cæsar's bowels, search this bosom.
Stand not to answer: here, take thou the hilts;
And when my face is cover'd, as 'tis now,
Guide thou the sword. [*Pindarus stabs him.*] Cæsar, thou art revenged,
Even with the sword that kill'd thee. [*Dies.*

Pin. So, I am free; yet would not so have been,
Durst I have done my will. O Cassius!
Far from this country Pindarus shall run,
Where never Roman shall take note of him. [*Exit.*

Re-enter Titinius with Messala.

Mes. It is but change, Titinius; for Octavius
Is overthrown by noble Brutus' power,
As Cassius' legions are by Antony.

Tit. These tidings will well comfort Cassius.

Mes. Where did you leave him?

Tit. All disconsolate,
With Pindarus his bondman, on this hill.

Mes. Is not that he that lies upon the ground?

Tit. He lies not like the living. O my heart!

Mes. Is not that he?

Tit. No, this was he, Messala,
But Cassius is no more. O setting sun,
As in thy red rays thou dost sink to night,
So in his red blood Cassius' day is set,
The sun of Rome is set! Our day is gone;
Clouds, dews and dangers come; our deeds are done!
Mistrust of my success hath done this deed.

Mes. Mistrust of good success hath done this deed.
O hateful error, melancholy's child,
Why dost thou show to the apt thoughts of men
The things that are not? O error, soon conceived,
Thou never comest unto a happy birth,
But kill'st the mother that engender'd thee!

Tit. What, Pindarus! where art thou, Pindarus?

Mes. Seek him, Titinius, whilst I go to meet
The noble Brutus, thrusting this report
Into his ears: I may say 'thrusting' it,
For piercing steel and darts envenomed
Shall be as welcome to the ears of Brutus
As tidings of this sight.

Tit. Hie you, Messala,
And I will seek for Pindarus the while. [*Exit Messala.*
Why didst thou send me forth, brave Cassius?
Did I not meet thy friends? and did not they
Put on my brows this wreath of victory,
And bid me give it thee? Didst thou not hear their shouts?
Alas, thou hast misconstrued every thing!
But, hold thee, take this garland on thy brow;
Thy Brutus bid me give it thee, and I
Will do his bidding. Brutus, come apace,
And see how I regarded Caius Cassius.
By your leave, gods: this is a Roman's part:
Come, Cassius' sword, and find Titinius' heart. [*Kills himself.*

Alarum. Re-enter Messala, with Brutus, young Cato, and others.

Bru. Where, where, Messala, doth his body lie?

Mes. Lo, yonder, and Titinius mourning it.

Bru. Titinius' face is upward.

Cato. He is slain.

Bru. O Julius Cæsar, thou art mighty yet!
Thy spirit walks abroad, and turns our swords
In our own proper entrails. [*Low alarums.*

Cato. Brave Titinius!
Look, whether he have not crown'd dead Cassius!

Bru. Are yet two Romans living such as these?

The last of all the Romans, fare thee well!
It is impossible that ever Rome
Should breed thy fellow. Friends, I owe moe tears
To this dead man than you shall see me pay.
I shall find time, Cassius, I shall find time.
Come therefore, and to Thasos send his body:
His funerals shall not be in our camp,
Lest it discomfort us. Lucilius, come,
And come, young Cato: let us to the field.
Labeo and Flavius, set our battles on.
'Tis three o'clock; and, Romans, yet ere night
We shall try fortune in a second fight. [*Exeunt.*

Scene IV

Another part of the field.

Alarum. Enter, fighting, Soldiers of both armies; then Brutus, young Cato, Lucilius, and others.

Bru. Yet, countrymen, O, yet hold up your heads!
Cato. What bastard doth not? Who will go with me?
I will proclaim my name about the field.
I am the son of Marcus Cato, ho!
A foe to tyrants, and my country's friend;
I am the son of Marcus Cato, ho!
Bru. And I am Brutus, Marcus Brutus, I;
Brutus, my country's friend; know me for Brutus! [*Exit.*
Lucil. O young and noble Cato, art thou down?
Why, now thou diest as bravely as Titinius,
And mayst be honour'd, being Cato's son.
First Sold. Yield, or thou diest.
Lucil. Only I yield to die:
[*Offering money*] There is so much that thou wilt kill me straight;
Kill Brutus, and be honour'd in his death.
First Sold. We must not. A noble prisoner!
Sec. Sold. Room, ho! Tell Antony, Brutus is ta'en.
First Sold. I'll tell the news. Here comes the general.

Enter Antony.

Brutus is ta'en, Brutus is ta'en, my lord.
Ant. Where is he?
Lucil. Safe, Antony; Brutus is safe enough:
I dare assure thee that no enemy
Shall ever take alive the noble Brutus:
The gods defend him from so great a shame!
When you do find him, or alive or dead,
He will be found like Brutus, like himself.
Ant. This is not Brutus, friend, but, I assure you,

A prize no less in worth: keep this man safe,
Give him all kindness: I had rather have
Such men my friends than enemies. Go on,
And see whether Brutus be alive or dead,
And bring us word unto Octavius' tent
How every thing is chanced. [*Exeunt.*

Scene V

Another part of the field.

Enter Brutus, Dardanius, Clitus, Strato, and Volumnius.

Bru. Come, poor remains of friends, rest on this rock.
Cli. Statilius show'd the torch-light, but, my lord,
He came not back: he is or ta'en or slain.
Bru. Sit thee down, Clitus: slaying is the word;
It is a deed in fashion. Hark thee, Clitus. [*Whispering.*
Cli. What, I, my lord? No, not for all the world.
Bru. Peace then, no words.
Cli. I'll rather kill myself.
Bru. Hark thee, Dardanius. [*Whispering.*
Dar. Shall I do such a deed?
Cli. O Dardanius!
Dar. O Clitus!
Cli. What ill request did Brutus make to thee?
Dar. To kill him, Clitus. Look, he meditates.
Cli. Now is that noble vessel full of grief,
That it runs over even at his eyes.
Bru. Come hither, good Volumnius; list a word.
Vol. What says my lord?
Bru. Why, this, Volumnius:
The ghost of Cæsar hath appear'd to me
Two several times by night; at Sardis once,
And this last night here in Philippi fields:
I know my hour is come.
Vol. Not so, my lord.
Bru. Nay, I am sure it is, Volumnius.
Thou seest the world, Volumnius, how it goes;
Our enemies have beat us to the pit: [*Low alarums.*
It is more worthy to leap in ourselves
Than tarry till they push us. Good Volumnius,
Thou know'st that we two went to school together:
Even for that our love of old, I prithee,
Hold thou my sword-hilts, whilst I run on it.
Vol. That's not an office for a friend, my lord. [*Alarum still.*
Cli. Fly, fly, my lord; there is no tarrying here.
Bru. Farewell to you; and you; and you, Volumnius.

Strato, thou hast been all this while asleep;
Farewell to thee too, Strato. Countrymen,
My heart doth joy that yet in all my life
I found no man but he was true to me.
I shall have glory by this losing day,
More than Octavius and Mark Antony
By this vile conquest shall attain unto.
So, fare you well at once; for Brutus' tongue
Hath almost ended his life's history:
Night hangs upon mine eyes; my bones would rest,
That have but labour'd to attain this hour.
[*Alarum. Cry within, 'Fly, fly, fly!'*

Cli. Fly, my lord, fly.

Bru. Hence! I will follow.
[*Exeunt Clitus, Dardanius, and Volumnius.*
I prithee, Strato, stay thou by thy lord:
Thou art a fellow of a good respect;
Thy life hath had some smatch of honour in it:
Hold then my sword, and turn away thy face,
While I do run upon it. Wilt thou, Strato?

Stra. Give me your hand first: fare you well, my lord.

Bru. Farewell, good Strato. [*Runs on his sword.*] Cæsar, now be still:
I kill'd not thee with half so good a will. [*Dies.*

Alarum. Retreat. Enter Octavius, Antony, Messala, Lucilius, and the army.

Oct. What man is that?

Mes. My master's man. Strato, where is thy master?

Stra. Free from the bondage you are in, Messala:
The conquerors can but make a fire of him;
For Brutus only overcame himself,
And no man else hath honour by his death.

Lucil. So Brutus should be found. I thank thee, Brutus,
That thou hast proved Lucilius' saying true.

Oct. All that served Brutus, I will entertain them.
Fellow, wilt thou bestow thy time with me?

Stra. Ay, if Messala will prefer me to you.

Oct. Do so, good Messala.

Mes. How died my master, Strato?

Stra. I held the sword, and he did run on it.

Mes. Octavius, then take him to follow thee,
That did the latest service to my master.

Ant. This was the noblest Roman of them all:
All the conspirators, save only he,
Did that they did in envy of great Cæsar;

He only, in a general honest thought
And common good to all, made one of them.
His life was gentle, and the elements
So mix'd in him that Nature might stand up
And say to all the world 'This was a man!'

Oct. According to his virtue let us use him,
With all respect and rites of burial.
Within my tent his bones to-night shall lie,
Most like a soldier, order'd honourably.
So call the field to rest, and let's away,
To part the glories of this happy day. [*Exeunt.*

THE TRAGEDY OF MACBETH

DRAMATIS PERSONÆ

DUNCAN, *king of Scotland.*
MALCOLM, DONALBAIN, } *his sons.*
MACBETH, BANQUO, } *generals of the King's army.*
MACDUFF, LENNOX, ROSS, MENTEITH, ANGUS, CAITHNESS, } *noblemen of Scotland.*
FLEANCE, *son to Banquo.*
SIWARD, *earl of Northumberland, general of the English forces.*
Young SIWARD, *his son.*
SEYTON, *an officer attending on Macbeth.*
Boy, *son to Macduff.*
An English Doctor.
A Scotch Doctor.
A Sergeant.
A Porter.
An Old Man.

Lady MACBETH.
Lady MACDUFF.
Gentlewoman attending on Lady Macbeth.

HECATE.
Three Witches.
Apparitions.

Lords, Gentlemen, Officers, Soldiers, Murderers, Attendants, and Messengers.

SCENE: *Scotland; England.*

ACT I—SCENE I

A desert place.

Thunder and Lightning. Enter three Witches.

First Witch. When shall we three meet again
In thunder, lightning, or in rain?
Sec. Witch. When the hurlyburly 's done,
When the battle 's lost and won.
Third Witch. That will be ere the set of sun.
First Witch. Where the place?
Sec. Witch. Upon the heath.
Third Witch. There to meet with Macbeth
First Witch. I come, Graymalkin.
All. Paddock calls:—anon!
Fair is foul, and foul is fair.
Hover through the fog and filthy air. [*Exeunt.*

SCENE II

A camp near Forres.

Alarum within. Enter Duncan, Malcolm, Donalbain, Lennox, with Attendants, meeting a bleeding Sergeant.

Dun. What bloody man is that? He can report,
As seemeth by his plight, of the revolt
The newest state.
Mal. This is the sergeant
Who like a good and hardy soldier fought
'Gainst my captivity. Hail, brave friend!
Say to the king the knowledge of the broil
As thou didst leave it.
Ser. Doubtful it stood;

As two spent swimmers, that do cling together
And choke their art. The merciless Macdonwald—
Worthy to be a rebel, for to that
The multiplying villanies of nature
Do swarm upon him—from the western isles
Of kerns and gallowglasses is supplied;
And fortune, on his damned quarrel smiling,
Show'd like a rebel's whore: but all 's too weak:
For brave Macbeth—well he deserves that name—
Disdaining fortune, with his brandish'd steel
Which smoked with bloody execution,
Like valour's minion carved out his passage
Till he faced the slave;
Which ne'er shook hands, nor bade farewell to him,
Till he unseam'd him from the nave to the chaps,
And fix'd his head upon our battlements.

Dun. O valiant cousin! worthy gentleman!

Ser. As whence the sun 'gins his reflection
Shipwrecking storms and direful thunders break,
So from that spring whence comfort seem'd to come
Discomfort swells. Mark, king of Scotland, mark:
No sooner justice had, with valour arm'd,
Compell'd these skipping kerns to trust their heels,
But the Norweyan lord, surveying vantage,
With furbish'd arms and new supplies of men,
Began a fresh assault.

Dun. Dismay'd not this
Our captains, Macbeth and Banquo?

Ser. Yes;
As sparrows eagles, or the hare the lion.
If I say sooth, I must report they were
As cannons overcharged with double cracks; so they
Doubly redoubled strokes upon the foe:
Except they meant to bathe in reeking wounds,
Or memorize another Golgotha,
I cannot tell—
But I am faint; my gashes cry for help.

Dun. So well thy words become thee as thy wounds;
They smack of honour both. Go get him surgeons.
[*Exit Sergeant, attended.*
Who comes here?

Enter Ross.

Mal. The worthy thane of Ross.

Len. What a haste looks through his eyes! So should he look
That seems to speak things strange.

Ross. God save the king!
Dun. Whence camest thou, worthy thane?
Ross. From Fife, great king;
Where the Norweyan banners flout the sky
And fan our people cold. Norway himself
With terrible numbers,
Assisted by that most disloyal traitor
The thane of Cawdor, began a dismal conflict;
Till that Bellona's bridegroom, lapp'd in proof,
Confronted him with self-comparisons,
Point against point rebellious, arm 'gainst arm,
Curbing his lavish spirit: and, to conclude,
The victory fell on us.
Dun. Great happiness!
Ross. That now
Sweno, the Norways' king, craves composition;
Nor would we deign him burial of his men
Till he disbursed, at Saint Colme's inch,
Ten thousand dollars to our general use.
Dun. No more that thane of Cawdor shall deceive
Our bosom interest: go pronounce his present death,
And with his former title greet Macbeth.
Ross. I'll see it done.
Dun. What he hath lost, noble Macbeth hath won. [*Exeunt.*

Scene III

A heath.

Thunder. Enter the three Witches.

First Witch. Where hast thou been, sister?
Sec. Witch. Killing swine.
Third Witch. Sister, where thou?
First Witch. A sailor's wife had chestnuts in her lap,
And mounch'd, and mounch'd, and mounch'd. 'Give me,' quoth I:
'Aroint thee, witch!' the rump-fed ronyon cries.
Her husband's to Aleppo gone, master o' the Tiger;
But in a sieve I'll thither sail,
And, like a rat without a tail,
I'll do, I'll do, and I'll do.
Sec. Witch. I'll give thee a wind.
First Witch. Thou 'rt kind.
Third Witch. And I another.
First Witch. I myself have all the other;
And the very ports they blow,
All the quarters that they know

I' the shipman's card.
I will drain him dry as hay:
Sleep shall neither night nor day
Hang upon his pent-house lid;
He shall live a man forbid:
Weary se'nnights nine times nine
Shall he dwindle, peak, and pine:
Though his bark cannot be lost,
Yet it shall be tempest-tost.
Look what I have.

Sec. Witch. Show me, show me.

First Witch. Here I have a pilot's thumb,
Wreck'd as homeward he did come. [*Drum within.*

Third Witch. A drum, a drum!
Macbeth doth come.

All. The weird sisters, hand in hand,
Posters of the sea and land,
Thus do go about, about:
Thrice to thine, and thrice to mine,
And thrice again, to make up nine.
Peace! the charm's wound up.

Enter Macbeth and Banquo.

Macb. So foul and fair a day I have not seen.

Ban. How far is 't call'd to Forres? What are these
So wither'd, and so wild in their attire,
That look not like the inhabitants o' the earth,
And yet are on 't? Live you? or are you aught
That man may question? You seem to understand me,
By each at once her choppy finger laying
Upon her skinny lips: you should be women,
And yet your beards forbid me to interpret
That you are so.

Macb. Speak, if you can: what are you?

First Witch. All hail, Macbeth! hail to thee, thane of Glamis!

Sec. Witch. All hail, Macbeth! hail to thee, thane of Cawdor!

Third Witch. All hail, Macbeth! thou shalt be king hereafter!

Ban. Good sir, why do you start, and seem to fear
Things that do sound so fair? I' the name of truth,
Are ye fantastical, or that indeed
Which outwardly ye show? My noble partner
You greet with present grace and great prediction
Of noble having and of royal hope,
That he seems rapt withal: to me you speak not:
If you can look into the seeds of time,
And say which grain will grow and which will not,

Speak then to me, who neither beg nor fear
Your favours nor your hate.
First Witch. Hail!
Sec. Witch. Hail!
Third Witch. Hail!
First Witch. Lesser than Macbeth, and greater.
Sec. Witch. Not so happy, yet much happier.
Third Witch. Thou shalt get kings, though thou be none:
So all hail, Macbeth and Banquo!
First Witch. Banquo and Macbeth, all hail!
Macb. Stay, you imperfect speakers, tell me more:
By Sinel's death I know I am thane of Glamis;
But how of Cawdor? the thane of Cawdor lives,
A prosperous gentleman; and to be king
Stands not within the prospect of belief,
No more than to be Cawdor. Say from whence
You owe this strange intelligence? or why
Upon this blasted heath you stop our way
With such prophetic greeting? Speak, I charge you.
[*Witches vanish.*
Ban. The earth hath bubbles as the water has,
And these are of them: whither are they vanish'd?
Macb. Into the air, and what seem'd corporal melted
As breath into the wind. Would they had stay'd!
Ban. Were such things here as we do speak about?
Or have we eaten on the insane root
That takes the reason prisoner!
Macb. Your children shall be kings.
Ban. You shall be king.
Macb. And thane of Cawdor too: went it not so?
Ban. To the selfsame tune and words. Who's here?
Enter Ross and Angus.
Ross. The king hath happily received, Macbeth,
The news of thy success: and when he reads
Thy personal venture in the rebels' fight,
His wonders and his praises do contend
Which should be thine or his: silenced with that,
In viewing o'er the rest o' the selfsame day,
He finds thee in the stout Norweyan ranks,
Nothing afeard of what thyself didst make,
Strange images of death. As thick as hail
Came post with post, and every one did bear
Thy praises in his kingdom's great defence,
And pour'd them down before him.
Ang. We are sent

To give thee, from our royal master, thanks;
Only to herald thee into his sight,
Not pay thee.

Ross. And for an earnest of a greater honour,
He bade me, from him, call thee thane of Cawdor:
In which addition, hail, most worthy thane!
For it is thine.

Ban. What, can the devil speak true?

Macb. The thane of Cawdor lives: why do you dress me
In borrow'd robes?

Ang. Who was the thane lives yet,
But under heavy judgement bears that life
Which he deserves to lose. Whether he was combined
With those of Norway, or did line the rebel
With hidden help and vantage, or that with both
He labour'd in his country's wreck, I know not;
But treasons capital, confess'd and proved,
Have overthrown him.

Macb. [*Aside*] Glamis, and thane of Cawdor:
The greatest is behind.—Thanks for your pains.—
Do you not hope your children shall be kings,
When those that gave the thane of Cawdor to me
Promised no less to them?

Ban. That, trusted home,
Might yet enkindle you unto the crown,
Besides the thane of Cawdor. But 'tis strange:
And oftentimes, to win us to our harm,
The instruments of darkness tell us truths,
Win us with honest trifles, to betray 's
In deepest consequence.
Cousins, a word, I pray you.

Macb. [*Aside*] Two truths are told,
As happy prologues to the swelling act
Of the imperial theme.—I thank you, gentlemen.—
[*Aside*] This supernatural soliciting
Cannot be ill; cannot be good: if ill,
Why hath it given me earnest of success,
Commencing in a truth? I am thane of Cawdor
If good, why do I yield to that suggestion
Whose horrid image doth unfix my hair
And make my seated heart knock at my ribs,
Against the use of nature? Present fears
Are less than horrible imaginings:
My thought, whose murder yet is but fantastical,
Shakes to my single state of man that function

Is smother'd in surmise, and nothing is
But what is not.

Ban. Look, how our partner's rapt.

Macb. [*Aside*] If chance will have me king, why, chance may
Without my stir. [crown me,

Ban. New honours come upon him,
Like our strange garments, cleave not to their mould
But with the aid of use.

Macb. [*Aside*] Come what come may,
Time and the hour runs through the roughest day.

Ban. Worthy Macbeth, we stay upon your leisure.

Macb. Give me your favour: my dull brain was wrought
With things forgotten. Kind gentlemen, your pains
Are register'd where every day I turn
The leaf to read them. Let us toward the king.
Think upon what hath chanced, and at more time,
The interim having weigh'd it, let us speak
Our free hearts each to other.

Ban. Very gladly.

Macb. Till then, enough. Come, friends. [*Exeunt.*

Scene IV

Forres. The palace.

Flourish. Enter Duncan, Malcolm, Donalbain, Lennox, and Attendants.

Dun. Is execution done on Cawdor? Are not
Those in commission yet return'd?

Mal. My liege,
They are not yet come back. But I have spoke
With one that saw him die, who did report
That very frankly he confess'd his treasons,
Implored your highness' pardon and set forth
A deep repentance: nothing in his life
Became him like the leaving it; he died
As one that had been studied in his death,
To throw away the dearest thing he owed
As 'twere a careless trifle.

Dun. There 's no art
To find the mind's construction in the face:
He was a gentleman on whom I built
An absolute trust.

Enter Macbeth, Banquo, Ross, and Angus.

O worthiest cousin!
The sin of my ingratitude even now

Was heavy on me: thou art so far before,
That swiftest wing of recompense is slow
To overtake thee. Would thou hadst less deserved,
That the proportion both of thanks and payment
Might have been mine! only I have left to say,
More is thy due than more than all can pay.

Macb. The service and the loyalty I owe,
In doing it, pays itself. Your highness' part
Is to receive our duties: and our duties
Are to your throne and state children and servants;
Which do but what they should, by doing every thing
Safe toward your love and honour.

Dun. Welcome hither:
I have begun to plant thee, and will labour
To make thee full of growing. Noble Banquo,
That hast no less deserved, nor must be known
No less to have done so: let me infold thee
And hold thee to my heart.

Ban. There if I grow,
The harvest is your own.

Dun. My plenteous joys,
Wanton in fulness, seek to hide themselves
In drops of sorrow. Sons, kinsmen, thanes,
And you whose places are the nearest, know,
We will establish our estate upon
Our eldest, Malcolm, when we name hereafter
The Prince of Cumberland: which honour must
Not unaccompanied invest him only,
But signs of nobleness, like stars, shall shine
On all deservers. From hence to Inverness,
And bind us further to you.

Macb. The rest is labour, which is not used for you:
I'll be myself the harbinger, and make joyful
The hearing of my wife with your approach;
So humbly take my leave.

Dun. My worthy Cawdor!

Macb. [*Aside*] The Prince of Cumberland! that is a step
On which I must fall down, or else o'erleap,
For in my way it lies. Stars, hide your fires;
Let not light see my black and deep desires:
The eye wink at the hand; yet let that be
Which the eye fears, when it is done, to see. [*Exit.*

Dun. True, worthy Banquo; he is full so valiant,
And in his commendations I am fed;
It is a banquet to me. Let's after him,

Whose care is gone before to bid us welcome:
It is a peerless kinsman. [*Flourish. Exeunt.*

SCENE V

Inverness. Macbeth's castle.

Enter Lady Macbeth, reading a letter.

Lady M. 'They met me in the day of success; and I have learned by the perfectest report, they have more in them than mortal knowledge. When I burned in desire to question them further, they made themselves air, into which they vanished. Whiles I stood rapt in the wonder of it, came missives from the king, who all-hailed me "Thane of Cawdor;" by which title, before, these weird sisters saluted me, and referred me to the coming on of time, with "Hail, king that shalt be!" This have I thought good to deliver thee, my dearest partner of greatness, that thou mightst not lose the dues of rejoicing, by being ignorant of what greatness is promised thee. Lay it to thy heart, and farewell.'
Glamis thou art, and Cawdor, and shalt be
What thou art promised: yet do I fear thy nature;
It is too full o' the milk of human kindness
To catch the nearest way: thou wouldst be great;
Art not without ambition, but without
The illness should attend it: what thou wouldst highly,
That wouldst thou holily; wouldst not play false,
And yet wouldst wrongly win: thou 'ldst have, great Glamis,
That which cries 'Thus thou must do, if thou have it;
And that which rather thou dost fear to do
Than wishest should be undone.' Hie thee hither,
That I may pour my spirits in thine ear,
And chastise with the valour of my tongue
All that impedes thee from the golden round,
Which fate and metaphysical aid doth seem
To have thee crown'd withal.

Enter a Messenger.

What is your tidings?

Mess. The king comes here to-night.

Lady M. Thou 'rt mad to say it:
Is not thy master with him? who, were 't so,
Would have inform'd for preparation.

Mess. So please you, it is true: our thane is coming:
One of my fellows had the speed of him,
Who, almost dead for breath, had scarcely more
Than would make up his message.

Lady M. Give him tending;

He brings great news. [*Exit Messenger.*
The raven himself is hoarse
That croaks the fatal entrance of Duncan
Under my battlements. Come, you spirits
That tend on mortal thoughts, unsex me here,
And fill me, from the crown to the toe, top-full
Of direst cruelty! make thick my blood,
Stop up the access and passage to remorse,
That no compunctious visitings of nature
Shake my fell purpose, nor keep peace between
The effect and it! Come to my woman's breasts,
And take my milk for gall, you murdering ministers,
Wherever in your sightless substances
You wait on nature's mischief! Come, thick night,
And pall thee in the dunnest smoke of hell,
That my keen knife see not the wound it makes,
Nor heaven peep through the blanket of the dark,
To cry 'Hold, hold!'

Enter Macbeth.

Great Glamis! worthy Cawdor!
Greater than both, by the all hail hereafter!
Thy letters have transported me beyond
This ignorant present, and I feel now
The future in the instant.

Macb. My dearest love,
Duncan comes here to-night.

Lady M. And when goes hence?

Macb. To-morrow, as he purposes.

Lady M. O, never
Shall sun that morrow see!
Your face, my thane, is as a book where men
May read strange matters. To beguile the time,
Look like the time; bear welcome in your eye,
Your hand, your tongue: look like the innocent flower,
But be the serpent under 't. He that's coming
Must be provided for: and you shall put
This night's great business into my dispatch;
Which shall to all our nights and days to come
Give solely sovereign sway and masterdom.

Macb. We will speak further.

Lady M. Only look up clear;
To alter favour ever is to fear:
Leave all the rest to me. [*Exeunt.*

Scene VI

Before Macbeth's castle.

Hautboys and torches. Enter Duncan, Malcolm, Donalbain, Banquo, Lennox, Macduff, Ross, Angus, and Attendants.

Dun. This castle hath a pleasant seat; the air
Nimbly and sweetly recommends itself
Unto our gentle senses.
Ban. This guest of summer,
The temple-haunting martlet, does approve
By his loved mansionry that the heaven's breath
Smells wooingly here: no jutty, frieze,
Buttress, nor coign of vantage, but this bird
Hath made his pendant bed and procreant cradle:
Where they most breed and haunt, I have observed
The air is delicate.

Enter Lady Macbeth.

Dun. See, see, our honour'd hostess!
The love that follows us sometime is our trouble,
Which still we thank as love. Herein I teach you
How you shall bid God 'ild us for your pains,
And thank us for your trouble.
Lady M. All our service
In every point twice done, and then done double,
Were poor and single business to contend
Against those honours deep and broad wherewith
Your majesty loads our house: for those of old,
And the late dignities heap'd up to them,
We rest your hermits.
Dun. Where 's the thane of Cawdor?
We coursed him at the heels, and had a purpose
To be his purveyor: but he rides well,
And his great love, sharp as his spur, hath holp him
To his home before us. Fair and noble hostess,
We are your guest to-night.
Lady M. Your servants ever
Have theirs, themselves, and what is theirs, in compt,
To make their audit at your highness' pleasure,
Still to return your own.
Dun. Give me your hand;
Conduct me to mine host: we love him highly,
And shall continue our graces towards him.
By your leave, hostess. [*Exeunt.*

Scene VII

Macbeth's castle.

Hautboys and torches. Enter a Sewer, and divers Servants with dishes and service, and pass over the stage. Then enter Macbeth.

Macb. If it were done when 'tis done, then 'twere well
It were done quickly: if the assassination
Could trammel up the consequence, and catch,
With his surcease, success; that but this blow
Might be the be-all and the end-all here,
But here, upon this bank and shoal of time,
We 'ld jump the life to come. But in these cases
We still have judgement here; that we but teach
Bloody instructions, which being taught return
To plague the inventor: this even-handed justice
Commends the ingredients of our poison'd chalice
To our own lips. He 's here in double trust:
First, as I am his kinsman and his subject,
Strong both against the deed; then, as his host,
Who should against his murderer shut the door,
Not bear the knife myself. Besides, this Duncan
Hath borne his faculties so meek, hath been
So clear in his great office, that his virtues
Will plead like angels trumpet-tongued against
The deep damnation of his taking-off;
And pity, like a naked new-born babe,
Striding the blast, or heaven's cherubin horsed
Upon the sightless couriers of the air,
Shall blow the horrid deed in every eye,
That tears shall drown the wind. I have no spur
To prick the sides of my intent, but only
Vaulting ambition, which o'erleaps itself
And falls on the other.

Enter Lady Macbeth.

How now! what news?

Lady M. He has almost supp'd: why have you left the chamber?
Macb. Hath he ask'd for me?
Lady M. Know you not he has?
Macb. We will proceed no further in this business:
He hath honour'd me of late; and I have bought
Golden opinions from all sorts of people,
Which would be worn now in their newest gloss,
Not cast aside so soon.
Lady M. Was the hope drunk

Wherein you dress'd yourself? hath it slept since?
And wakes it now, to look so green and pale
At what it did so freely? From this time
Such I account thy love. Art thou afeard
To be the same in thine own act and valour
As thou art in desire? Wouldst thou have that
Which thou esteem'st the ornament of life,
And live a coward in thine own esteem,
Letting 'I dare not' wait upon 'I would,'
Like the poor cat i' the adage?

Macb. Prithee, peace:
I dare do all that may become a man;
Who dares do more is none.

Lady M. What beast was 't then
That made you break this enterprize to me?
When you durst do it, then you were a man;
And, to be more than what you were, you would
Be so much more the man. Nor time nor place
Did then adhere, and yet you would make both:
They have made themselves, and that their fitness now
Does unmake you. I have given suck, and know
How tender 'tis to love the babe that milks me:
I would, while it was smiling in my face,
Have pluck'd my nipple from his boneless gums,
And dash'd the brains out, had I so sworn as you
Have done to this.

Macb. If we should fail?

Lady M. We fail!
But screw your courage to the sticking-place,
And we 'll not fail. When Duncan is asleep—
Whereto the rather shall his day's hard journey
Soundly invite him—his two chamberlains
Will I with wine and wassail so convince,
That memory, the warder of the brain,
Shall be a fume, and the receipt of reason
A limbec only: when in swinish sleep
Their drenched natures lie as in a death,
What cannot you and I perform upon
The unguarded Duncan? what not put upon
His spongy officers, who shall bear the guilt
Of our great quell?

Macb. Bring forth men-children only;
For thy undaunted mettle should compose
Nothing but males. Will it not be received,
When we have mark'd with blood those sleepy two

Of his own chamber, and used their very daggers,
That they have done 't?

Lady M. Who dares receive it other,
As we shall make our griefs and clamour roar
Upon his death?

Macb. I am settled, and bend up
Each corporal agent to this terrible feat.
Away, and mock the time with fairest show:
False face must hide what the false heart doth know.
[*Exeunt.*

ACT II—Scene I

Inverness. Court of Macbeth's castle.

Enter Banquo, and Fleance bearing a torch before him.

Ban. How goes the night, boy?

Fle. The moon is down; I have not heard the clock.

Ban. And she goes down at twelve.

Fle. I take 't, 'tis later, sir.

Ban. Hold, take my sword. There 's husbandry in heaven,
Their candles are all out. Take thee that too.
A heavy summons lies like lead upon me,
And yet I would not sleep. Merciful powers,
Restrain in me the cursed thoughts that nature
Gives way to in repose!

Enter Macbeth, and a Servant with a torch.

Give me my sword.
Who 's there?

Macb. A friend.

Ban. What, sir, not yet at rest? The king 's a-bed:
He hath been in unusual pleasure, and
Sent forth great largess to your offices:
This diamond he greets your wife withal,
By the name of most kind hostess; and shut up
In measureless content.

Macb. Being unprepared,
Our will became the servant to defect,
Which else should free have wrought.

Ban. All 's well.
I dreamt last night of the three weird sisters:
To you they have show'd some truth.

Macb. I think not of them:
Yet, when we can entreat an hour to serve,
We would spend it in some words upon that business,

If you would grant the time.
Ban. At your kind'st leisure.
Macb. If you shall cleave to my consent, when 'tis,
It shall make honour for you.
Ban. So I lose none
In seeking to augment it, but still keep
My bosom franchised and allegiance clear,
I shall be counsell'd.
Macb. Good repose the while!
Ban. Thanks, sir: the like to you!
[*Exeunt Banquo and Fleance.*
Macb. Go bid thy mistress, when my drink is ready,
She strike upon the bell. Get thee to bed. [*Exit Servant.*
Is this a dagger which I see before me,
The handle toward my hand? Come, let me clutch thee.
I have thee not, and yet I see thee still.
Art thou not, fatal vision, sensible
To feeling as to sight? or art thou but
A dagger of the mind, a false creation,
Proceeding from the heat-oppressed brain?
I see thee yet, in form as palpable
As this which now I draw.
Thou marshall'st me the way that I was going;
And such an instrument I was to use.
Mine eyes are made the fools o' the other senses,
Or else worth all the rest: I see thee still;
And on thy blade and dudgeon gouts of blood,
Which was not so before. There's no such thing:
It is the bloody business which informs
Thus to mine eyes. Now o'er the one half-world
Nature seems dead, and wicked dreams abuse
The curtain'd sleep; witchcraft celebrates
Pale Hecate's offerings; and wither'd murder,
Alarum'd by his sentinel, the wolf,
Whose howl 's his watch, thus with his stealthy pace,
With Tarquin's ravishing strides, towards his design
Moves like a ghost. Thou sure and firm-set earth,
Hear not my steps, which way they walk, for fear
Thy very stones prate of my whereabout,
And take the present horror from the time,
Which now suits with it. Whiles I threat, he lives:
Words to the heat of deeds too cold breath gives. [*A bell rings.*
I go, and it is done: the bell invites me.
Hear it not, Duncan, for it is a knell
That summons thee to heaven, or to hell. [*Exit.*

Scene II

The same.

Enter Lady Macbeth.

Lady M. That which hath made them drunk hath made me bold;
What hath quench'd them hath given me fire. Hark! Peace!
It was the owl that shriek'd, the fatal bellman,
Which gives the stern'st good-night. He is about it:
The doors are open, and the surfeited grooms
Do mock their charge with snores: I have drugg'd their possets,
That death and nature do contend about them,
Whether they live or die.

Macb. [*Within*] Who 's there? what, ho!

Lady M. Alack, I am afraid they have awaked
And 'tis not done: the attempt and not the deed
Confounds us. Hark! I laid their daggers ready;
He could not miss 'em. Had he not resembled
My father as he slept, I had done 't.

Enter Macbeth.

My husband!

Macb. I have done the deed. Didst thou not hear a noise?

Lady M. I heard the owl scream and the crickets cry.
Did not you speak?

Macb. When?

Lady M. Now.

Macb. As I descended?

Lady M. Ay.

Macb. Hark!
Who lies i' the second chamber?

Lady M. Donalbain.

Macb. This is a sorry sight. [*Looking on his hands.*

Lady M. A foolish thought, to say a sorry sight.

Macb. There 's one did laugh in 's sleep, and one cried 'Murder!'
That they did wake each other: I stood and heard them:
But they did say their prayers, and address'd them
Again to sleep.

Lady M. There are two lodged together.

Macb. One cried 'God bless us!' and 'Amen' the other,
As they had seen me with these hangman's hands:
Listening their fear, I could not say 'Amen,'
When they did say 'God bless us!'

Lady M. Consider it not so deeply.

Macb. But wherefore could not I pronounce 'Amen'?
I had most need of blessing, and 'Amen

Stuck in my throat.
Lady M. These deeds must not be thought
After these ways; so, it will make us mad.
Macb. Methought I heard a voice cry 'Sleep no more!
Macbeth does murder sleep'—the innocent sleep,
Sleep that knits up the ravell'd sleave of care,
The death of each day's life, sore labour's bath,
Balm of hurt minds, great nature's second course,
Chief nourisher in life's feast,—
Lady M. What do you mean?
Macb. Still it cried 'Sleep no more!' to all the house:
'Glamis hath murder'd sleep, and therefore Cawdor
Shall sleep no more: Macbeth shall sleep no more.'
Lady M. Who was it that thus cried? Why, worthy thane,
You do unbend your noble strength, to think
So brainsickly of things. Go get some water,
And wash this filthy witness from your hand.
Why did you bring these daggers from the place?
They must lie there: go carry them, and smear
The sleepy grooms with blood.
Macb. I'll go no more:
I am afraid to think what I have done;
Look on 't again I dare not.
Lady M. Infirm of purpose!
Give me the daggers: the sleeping and the dead
Are but as pictures: 'tis the eye of childhood
That fears a painted devil. If he do bleed,
I'll gild the faces of the grooms withal,
For it must seem their guilt. [*Exit. Knocking within.*
Macb. Whence is that knocking?
How is 't with me, when every noise appals me?
What hands are here? ha! they pluck out mine eyes!
Will all great Neptune's ocean wash this blood
Clean from my hand? No; this my hand will rather
The multitudinous seas incarnadine,
Making the green one red.

Re-enter Lady Macbeth.

Lady M. My hands are of your colour, but I shame
To wear a heart so white. [*Knocking within.*] I hear a
At the south entry: retire we to our chamber: [knocking
A little water clears us of this deed:
How easy is it then! Your constancy
Hath left you unattended. [*Knocking within.*] Hark! more
Get on your nightgown, lest occasion call us [knocking:

And show us to be watchers : be not lost
So poorly in your thoughts.

Macb. To know my deed, 'twere best not know myself.
[*Knocking within.*
Wake Duncan with thy knocking ! I would thou couldst !
[*Exeunt.*

SCENE III

The same.

Enter a Porter. Knocking within.

Porter. Here 's a knocking indeed ! If a man were porter of hell-gate, he should have old turning the key. [*Knocking within.*] Knock, knock, knock ! Who 's there, i' the name of Beelzebub ? Here 's a farmer, that hanged himself on th' expectation of plenty : come in time ; have napkins enow about you ; here you 'll sweat for 't. [*Knocking within.*] Knock, knock ! Who 's there, in th' other devil's name ? Faith, here 's an equivocator, that could swear in both the scales against either scale ; who committed treason enough for God's sake, yet could not equivocate to heaven : O, come in, equivocator. [*Knocking within.*] Knock, knock, knock ! Who 's there ? Faith, here 's an English tailor come hither, for stealing out of a French hose : come in, tailor ; here you may roast your goose. [*Knocking within.*] Knock, knock ; never at quiet ! What are you ? But this place is too cold for hell. I 'll devil-porter it no further : I had thought to have let in some of all professions, that go the primrose way to the everlasting bonfire. [*Knocking within.*] Anon, anon ! I pray you, remember the porter. [*Opens the gate.*

Enter Macduff and Lennox.

Macd. Was it so late, friend, ere you went to bed,
That you do lie so late ?

Port. Faith, sir, we were carousing till the second cock : and drink, sir, is a great provoker of three things.

Macd. What three things does drink especially provoke ?

Port. Marry, sir, nose-painting, sleep and urine. Lechery, sir, it provokes and unprovokes ; it provokes the desire, but it takes away the performance : therefore much drink may be said to be an equivocator with lechery : it makes him and it mars him ; it sets him on and it takes him off ; it persuades him and disheartens him ; makes him stand to and not stand to ; in conclusion, equivocates him in a sleep, and giving him the lie, leaves him.

Macd. I believe drink gave thee the lie last night.

Port. That it did, sir, i' the very throat on me: but I requited him for his lie, and, I think, being too strong for him, though he took up my leg sometime, yet I made a shift to cast him.

Macd. Is thy master stirring?

Enter Macbeth.

Our knocking has awaked him; here he comes.

Len. Good morrow, noble sir.

Macb. Good morrow, both.

Macd. Is the king stirring, worthy thane?

Macb. Not yet.

Macd. He did command me to call timely on him:
I had almost slipp'd the hour.

Macb. I'll bring you to him.

Macd. I know this is a joyful trouble to you;
But yet 'tis one.

Macb. The labour we delight in physics pain.
This is the door.

Macd. I'll make so bold to call,
For 'tis my limited service. [*Exit.*

Len. Goes the king hence to-day?

Macb. He does: he did appoint so.

Len. The night has been unruly: where we lay,
Our chimneys were blown down, and, as they say,
Lamentings heard i' the air, strange screams of death,
And prophesying with accents terrible
Of dire combustion and confused events
New hatch'd to the woful time: the obscure bird
Clamour'd the livelong night: some say, the earth
Was feverous and did shake.

Macb. 'Twas a rough night.

Len. My young remembrance cannot parallel
A fellow to it.

Re-enter Macduff.

Macd. O horror, horror, horror! Tongue nor heart
Cannot conceive nor name thee.

Macb.
Len. } What's the matter?

Macd. Confusion now hath made his masterpiece.
Most sacrilegious murder hath broke ope
The Lord's anointed temple, and stole thence
The life o' the building.

Macb. What is't you say? the life?

Len. Mean you his majesty?

Macd. Approach the chamber, and destroy your sight
With a new Gorgon: do not bid me speak;

See, and then speak yourselves.
[*Exeunt Macbeth and Lennox.*
Awake, awake!
Ring the alarum-bell. Murder and treason!
Banquo and Donalbain! Malcolm! awake!
Shake off this downy sleep, death's counterfeit,
And look on death itself! up, up, and see
The great doom's image! Malcolm! Banquo!
As from your graves rise up, and walk like sprites,
To countenance this horror. Ring the bell. [*Bell rings.*

Enter Lady Macbeth.

Lady M. What's the business,
That such a hideous trumpet calls to parley
The sleepers of the house? speak, speak!
Macd. O gentle lady,
'Tis not for you to hear what I can speak:
The repetition, in a woman's ear,
Would murder as it fell.

Enter Banquo.

O Banquo, Banquo!
Our royal master's murder'd.
Lady M. Woe, alas!
What, in our house?
Ban. Too cruel any where.
Dear Duff, I prithee, contradict thyself,
And say it is not so.

Re-enter Macbeth and Lennox, with Ross.

Macb. Had I but died an hour before this chance,
I had lived a blessed time; for from this instant
There's nothing serious in mortality:
All is but toys: renown and grace is dead;
The wine of life is drawn, and the mere lees
Is left this vault to brag of.

Enter Malcolm and Donalbain.

Don. What is amiss?
Macb. You are, and do not know't:
The spring, the head, the fountain of your blood
Is stopp'd; the very source of it is stopp'd.
Macd. Your royal father's murder'd.
Mal. O, by whom?
Len. Those of his chamber, as it seem'd, had done't:
Their hands and faces were all badged with blood;
So were their daggers, which unwiped we found
Upon their pillows:
They stared, and were distracted; no man's life

Was to be trusted with them.
Macb. O, yet I do repent me of my fury,
That I did kill them.
Macd. Wherefore did you so?
Macb. Who can be wise, amazed, temperate and furious,
Loyal and neutral, in a moment? No man:
The expedition of my violent love
Outrun the pauser reason. Here lay Duncan,
His silver skin laced with his golden blood,
And his gash'd stabs look'd like a breach in nature
For ruin's wasteful entrance: there, the murderers,
Steep'd in the colours of their trade, their daggers
Unmannerly breech'd with gore: who could refrain,
That had a heart to love, and in that heart
Courage to make 's love known?
Lady M. Help me hence, ho!
Macd. Look to the lady.
Mal. [*Aside to Don.*] Why do we hold our tongues,
That most may claim this argument for ours?
Don. [*Aside to Mal.*] What should be spoken here, where our fate,
Hid in an auger-hole, may rush, and seize us?
Let 's away;
Our tears are not yet brew'd.
Mal. [*Aside to Don.*] Nor our strong sorrow
Upon the foot of motion.
Ban. Look to the lady:
[*Lady Macbeth is carried out.*
And when we have our naked frailties hid,
That suffer in exposure, let us meet,
And question this most bloody piece of work,
To know it further. Fears and scruples shake us:
In the great hand of God I stand, and thence
Against the undivulged pretence I fight
Of treasonous malice.
Macd. And so do I.
All. So all.
Macb. Let 's briefly put on manly readiness,
And meet i' the hall together.
All. Well contented.
[*Exeunt all but Malcolm and Donalbain.*
Mal. What will you do? Let 's not consort with them;
To show an unfelt sorrow is an office
Which the false man does easy. I 'll to England.
Don. To Ireland, I; our separated fortune
Shall keep us both the safer: where we are

There 's daggers in men's smiles: the near in blood,
The nearer bloody.

Mal. This murderous shaft that 's shot
Hath not yet lighted, and our safest way
Is to avoid the aim. Therefore to horse;
And let us not be dainty of leave-taking,
But shift away: there 's warrant in that theft
Which steals itself when there 's no mercy left. [*Exeunt.*

Scene IV

Outside Macbeth's castle.

Enter Ross with an old Man.

Old M. Threescore and ten I can remember well;
Within the volume of which time I have seen
Hours dreadful and things strange, but this sore night
Hath trifled former knowings.

Ross. Ah, good father,
Thou seest, the heavens, as troubled with man's act,
Threaten his bloody stage: by the clock 'tis day,
And yet dark night strangles the travelling lamp:
Is 't night's predominance, or the day's shame,
That darkness does the face of earth entomb,
When living light should kiss it?

Old M. 'Tis unnatural,
Even like the deed that 's done. On Tuesday last
A falcon towering in her pride of place
Was by a mousing owl hawk'd at and kill'd.

Ross. And Duncan's horses—a thing most strange and certain—
Beauteous and swift, the minions of their race,
Turn'd wild in nature, broke their stalls, flung out,
Contending 'gainst obedience as they would make
War with mankind.

Old M. 'Tis said they eat each other.

Ross. They did so, to the amazement of mine eyes,
That look'd upon 't.

Enter Macduff.

Here comes the good Macduff.
How goes the world, sir, now?

Macd. Why, see you not?

Ross. Is 't known who did this more than bloody deed?

Macd. Those that Macbeth hath slain.

Ross. Alas, the day!
What good could they pretend?

Macd. They were suborn'd
Malcolm and Donalbain, the king's two sons,

Are stol'n away and fled, which puts upon them
Suspicion of the deed.
Ross. 'Gainst nature still:
Thriftless ambition, that wilt ravin up
Thine own life's means! Then 'tis most like
The sovereignty will fall upon Macbeth.
Macd. He is already named, and gone to Scone
To be invested.
Ross. Where is Duncan's body?
Macd. Carried to Colme-kill,
The sacred storehouse of his predecessors
And guardian of their bones.
Ross. Will you to Scone?
Macd. No, cousin, I'll to Fife.
Ross. Well, I will thither.
Macd. Well, may you see things well done there: adieu!
Lest our old robes sit easier than our new!
Ross. Farewell, father.
Old M. God's benison go with you, and with those
That would make good of bad and friends of foes! [*Exeunt.*

ACT III—Scene I

Forres. The palace.

Enter Banquo.

Ban. Thou hast it now: king, Cawdor, Glamis, all,
As the weird women promised, and I fear
Thou play'dst most foully for 't: yet it was said
It should not stand in thy posterity,
But that myself should be the root and father
Of many kings. If there come truth from them—
As upon thee, Macbeth, their speeches shine—
Why, by the verities on thee made good,
May they not be my oracles as well
And set me up in hope? But hush, no more.

Sennet sounded. Enter Macbeth, as king; Lady Macbeth, as queen; Lennox, Ross, Lords, Ladies, and Attendants.

Macb. Here 's our chief guest.
Lady M. If he had been forgotten,
It had been as a gap in our great feast,
And all-thing unbecoming.
Macb. To-night we hold a solemn supper, sir,
And I 'll request your presence.
Ban. Let your highness
Command upon me, to the which my duties

Are with a most indissoluble tie
For ever knit.

Macb. Ride you this afternoon?

Ban. Ay, my good lord.

Macb. We should have else desired your good advice,
Which still hath been both grave and prosperous,
In this day's council; but we'll take to-morrow.
Is't far you ride?

Ban. As far, my lord, as will fill up the time
'Twixt this and supper: go not my horse the better,
I must become a borrower of the night
For a dark hour or twain.

Macb. Fail not our feast.

Ban. My lord, I will not.

Macb. We hear our bloody cousins are bestow'd
In England and in Ireland, not confessing
Their cruel parricide, filling their hearers
With strange invention: but of that to-morrow,
When therewithal we shall have cause of state
Craving us jointly. Hie you to horse: adieu,
Till you return at night. Goes Fleance with you?

Ban. Ay, my good lord: our time does call upon 's.

Macb. I wish your horses swift and sure of foot
And so I do commend you to their backs.
Farewell. [*Exit Banquo.*
Let every man be master of his time
Till seven at night; to make society
The sweeter welcome, we will keep ourself
Till supper-time alone: while then, God be with you!
[*Exeunt all but Macbeth and an Attendant.*
Sirrah, a word with you: attend those men
Our pleasure?

Attend. They are, my lord, without the palace-gate.

Macb. Bring them before us. [*Exit Attendant.*
To be thus is nothing;
But to be safely thus: our fears in Banquo
Stick deep; and in his royalty of nature
Reigns that which would be fear'd: 'tis much he dares,
And, to that dauntless temper of his mind,
He hath a wisdom that doth guide his valour
To act in safety. There is none but he
Whose being I do fear: and under him
My Genius is rebuked, as it is said
Mark Antony's was by Cæsar. He chid the sisters,
When first they put the name of king upon me,

And bade them speak to him ; then prophet-like
They hail'd him father to a line of kings :
Upon my head they placed a fruitless crown
And put a barren sceptre in my gripe,
Thence to be wrench'd with an unlineal hand,
No son of mine succeeding. If't be so,
For Banquo's issue have I filed my mind ;
For them the gracious Duncan have I murder'd ;
Put rancours in the vessel of my peace
Only for them, and mine eternal jewel
Given to the common enemy of man,
To make them kings, the seed of Banquo kings !
Rather than so, come, fate, into the list,
And champion me to the utterance ! Who 's there ?

Re-enter Attendant, with two Murderers.

Now go to the door, and stay there till we call.
[*Exit Attendant.*
Was it not yesterday we spoke together ?

First Mur. It was, so please your highness.

Macb. Well, then, now
Have you consider'd of my speeches ? Know
That it was he in the times past which held you
So under fortune, which you thought had been
Our innocent self : this I made good to you
In our last conference ; pass'd in probation with you,
How you were borne in hand, how cross'd, the instruments,
Who wrought with them, and all things else that might
To half a soul and to a notion crazed
Say 'Thus did Banquo.'

First Mur. You made it known to us.

Macb. I did so ; and went further, which is now
Our point of second meeting. Do you find
Your patience so predominant in your nature,
That you can let this go ? Are you so gospell'd,
To pray for this good man and for his issue,
Whose heavy hand hath bow'd you to the grave
And beggar'd yours for ever ?

First Mur. We are men, my liege.

Macb. Ay, in the catalogue ye go for men ;
As hounds and greyhounds, mongrels, spaniels, curs,
Shoughs, water-rugs and demi-wolves, are clept
All by the name of dogs : the valued file
Distinguishes the swift, the slow, the subtle,
The housekeeper, the hunter, every one
According to the gift which bounteous nature

Hath in him closed, whereby he does receive
Particular addition, from the bill
That writes them all alike: and so of men.
Now if you have a station in the file,
Not i' the worst rank of manhood, say it,
And I will put that business in your bosoms
Whose execution takes your enemy off,
Grapples you to the heart and love of us,
Who wear our health but sickly in his life,
Which in his death were perfect.

Sec. Mur. I am one, my liege,
Whom the vile blows and buffets of the world
Have so incensed that I am reckless what
I do to spite the world.

First Mur. And I another
So weary with disasters, tugg'd with fortune,
That I would set my life on any chance,
To mend it or be rid on 't.

Macb. Both of you
Know Banquo was your enemy.

Both Mur. True, my lord.

Macb. So is he mine, and in such bloody distance
That every minute of his being thrusts
Against my near'st of life: and though I could
With barefaced power sweep him from my sight
And bid my will avouch it, yet I must not,
For certain friends that are both his and mine,
Whose loves I may not drop, but wail his fall
Who I myself struck down: and thence it is
That I to your assistance do make love,
Masking the business from the common eye
For sundry weighty reasons.

Sec. Mur. We shall, my lord,
Perform what you command us.

First Mur. Though our lives—

Macb. Your spirits shine through you. Within this hour at most
I will advise you where to plant yourselves,
Acquaint you with the perfect spy o' the time,
The moment on 't; for 't must be done to-night,
And something from the palace; always thought
That I require a clearness: and with him—
To leave no rubs nor botches in the work—
Fleance his son, that keeps him company,
Whose absence is no less material to me
Than is his father's, must embrace the fate

Of that dark hour. Resolve yourselves apart:
I'll come to you anon.
Both Mur. We are resolved, my lord.
Macb. I'll call upon you straight: abide within.
[*Exeunt Murderers.*
It is concluded: Banquo thy soul's flight,
If it find heaven, must find it out to-night. [*Exit.*

SCENE II

The palace.

Enter Lady Macbeth and a Servant.

Lady M. Is Banquo gone from court?
Serv. Ay, madam, but returns again to-night.
Lady M. Say to the king, I would attend his leisure
For a few words.
Serv. Madam, I will. [*Exit.*
Lady M. Nought's had, all's spent,
Where our desire is got without content:
'Tis safer to be that which we destroy
Than by destruction dwell in doubtful joy.

Enter Macbeth.

How now, my lord! why do you keep alone,
Of sorriest fancies your companions making;
Using those thoughts which should indeed have died
With them they think on? Things without all remedy
Should be without regard: what's done is done.
Macb. We have scotch'd the snake, not kill'd it:
She'll close and be herself, whilst our poor malice
Remains in danger of her former tooth.
But let the frame of things disjoint, both the worlds suffer,
Ere we will eat our meal in fear, and sleep
In the affliction of these terrible dreams
That shake us nightly: better be with the dead,
Whom we, to gain our peace, have sent to peace,
Than on the torture of the mind to lie
In restless ecstasy. Duncan is in his grave;
After life's fitful fever he sleeps well;
Treason has done his worst: nor steel, nor poison,
Malice domestic, foreign levy, nothing,
Can touch him further.
Lady M. Come on;
Gentle my lord, sleek o'er your rugged looks;
Be bright and jovial among your guests to-night.
Macb. So shall I, love; and so, I pray, be you:
Let your remembrance apply to Banquo;

Present him eminence, both with eye and tongue:
Unsafe the while, that we
Must lave our honours in these flattering streams,
And make our faces visards to our hearts,
Disguising what they are.

Lady M. You must leave this.

Macb. O, full of scorpions is my mind, dear wife!
Thou know'st that Banquo, and his Fleance, lives.

Lady M. But in them nature's copy 's not eterne.

Macb. There 's comfort yet; they are assailable;
Then be thou jocund: ere the bat hath flown
His cloister'd flight; ere to black Hecate's summons
The shard-borne beetle with his drowsy hums
Hath rung night's yawning peal, there shall be done
A deed of dreadful note.

Lady M. What 's to be done?

Macb. Be innocent of the knowledge, dearest chuck,
Till thou applaud the deed. Come, seeling night,
Scarf up the tender eye of pitiful day,
And with thy bloody and invisible hand
Cancel and tear to pieces that great bond
Which keeps me pale! Light thickens, and the crow
Makes wing to the rooky wood:
Good things of day begin to droop and drowse,
Whiles night's black agents to their preys do rouse.
Thou marvell'st at my words: but hold thee still;
Things bad begun make strong themselves by ill:
So, prithee, go with me. [*Exeunt.*

Scene III

A park near the palace.

Enter three Murderers.

First Mur. But who did bid thee join with us?

Third Mur. Macbeth.

Sec. Mur. He needs not our mistrust; since he delivers
Our offices, and what we have to do,
To the direction just.

First Mur. Then stand with us.
The west yet glimmers with some streaks of day:
Now spurs the lated traveller apace
To gain the timely inn, and near approaches
The subject of our watch.

Third Mur. Hark! I hear horses.

Ban. [*Within*] Give us a light there, ho!

Sec. Mur. Then 'tis he: the rest

That are within the note of expectation
Already are i' the court.

First Mur. His horses go about.

Third Mur. Almost a mile: but he does usually—
So all men do—from hence to the palace gate
Make it their walk.

Sec. Mur. A light, a light!

Enter Banquo, and Fleance with a torch.

Third Mur. 'Tis he.

First Mur. Stand to 't.

Ban. It will be rain to-night.

First Mur. Let it come down.

[*They set upon Banquo.*

Ban. O, treachery! Fly, good Fleance, fly, fly, fly!
Thou mayst revenge. O slave! [*Dies. Fleance escapes.*

Third Mur. Who did strike out the light?

First Mur. Was 't not the way?

Third Mur. There 's but one down; the son is fled.

Sec. Mur. We have lost
Best half of our affair.

First Mur. Well, let 's away and say how much is done.

[*Exeunt.*

Scene IV

Hall in the palace.

A banquet prepared. Enter Macbeth, Lady Macbeth, Ross, Lennox, Lords, and Attendants.

Macb. You know your own degrees; sit down: at first
And last a hearty welcome.

Lords. Thanks to your majesty.

Macb. Ourself will mingle with society
And play the humble host.
Our hostess keeps her state, but in best time
We will require her welcome.

Lady M. Pronounce it for me, sir, to all our friends,
For my heart speaks they are welcome.

Enter first Murderer to the door.

Macb. See, they encounter thee with their hearts' thanks.
Both sides are even: here I 'll sit i' the midst:
Be large in mirth; anon we 'll drink a measure
The table round. [*Approaching the door*] There 's blood upon [thy face.

Mur. 'Tis Banquo's then.

Macb. 'Tis better thee without than he within.
Is he dispatch'd?

Mur. My lord, his throat is cut; that I did for him.

Macb. Thou art the best o' the cut-throats: yet he 's good
That did the like for Fleance: if thou didst it,
Thou art the nonpareil.
Mur. Most royal sir,
Fleance is 'scaped.
Macb. [*Aside*] Then comes my fit again: I had else been [perfect,
Whole as the marble, founded as the rock,
As broad and general as the casing air:
But now I am cabin'd, cribb'd, confined, bound in
To saucy doubts and fears.—But Banquo 's safe?
Mur. Ay, my good lord: safe in a ditch he bides,
With twenty trenched gashes on his head;
The least a death to nature.
Macb. Thanks for that.
[*Aside*] There the grown serpent lies; the worm that 's fled
Hath nature that in time will venom breed,
No teeth for the present. Get thee gone: to-morrow
We 'll hear ourselves again. [*Exit Murderer*
Lady M. My royal lord,
You do not give the cheer: the feast is sold
That is not often vouch'd, while 'tis a making,
'Tis given with welcome: to feed were best at home;
From thence the sauce to meat is ceremony;
Meeting were bare without it.
Macb. Sweet remembrancer!
Now good digestion wait on appetite,
And health on both!
Len. May 't please your highness sit.
The Ghost of Banquo enters, and sits in Macbeth's place.
Macb. Here had we now our country's honour roof'd,
Were the graced person of our Banquo present;
Who may I rather challenge for unkindness
Than pity for mischance!
Ross. His absence, sir,
Lays blame upon his promise. Please 't your highness
To grace us with your royal company.
Macb. The table 's full.
Len. Here is a place reserved, sir.
Macb. Where?
Len. Here, my good lord. What is 't that moves your highness?
Macb. Which of you have done this?
Lords. What, my good lord?
Macb. Thou canst not say I did it: never shake
Thy gory locks at me.
Ross. Gentlemen, rise; his highness is not well.

Lady M. Sit, worthy friends: my lord is often thus,
And hath been from his youth: pray you, keep seat;
The fit is momentary; upon a thought
He will again be well: if much you note him,
You shall offend him and extend his passion:
Feed, and regard him not. Are you a man?

Macb. Ay, and a bold one, that dare look on that
Which might appal the devil.

Lady M. O proper stuff!
This is the very painting of your fear:
This is the air-drawn dagger which, you said,
Led you to Duncan. O, these flaws and starts,
Impostors to true fear, would well become
A woman's story at a winter's fire,
Authorized by her grandam. Shame itself!
Why do you make such faces? When all 's done,
You look but on a stool.

Macb. Prithee, see there! behold! look! lo! how say you?
Why, what care I? If thou canst nod, speak too.
If charnel-houses and our graves must send
Those that we bury back, our monuments
Shall be the maws of kites. [*Exit Ghost.*

Lady M. What, quite unmann'd in folly?

Macb. If I stand here, I saw him.

Lady M. Fie, for shame!

Macb. Blood hath been shed ere now, i' the olden time,
Ere humane statute purged the gentle weal;
Ay, and since too, murders have been perform'd
Too terrible for the ear: the time has been,
That, when the brains were out, the man would die,
And there an end; but now they rise again,
With twenty mortal murders on their crowns,
And push us from our stools: this is more strange
Than such a murder is.

Lady M. My worthy lord,
Your noble friends do lack you.

Macb. I do forget.
Do not muse at me, my most worthy friends;
I have a strange infirmity, which is nothing
To those that know me. Come, love and health to all;
Then I 'll sit down. Give me some wine, fill full.
I drink to the general joy o' the whole table,
And to our dear friend Banquo, whom we miss;
Would he were here! to all and him we thirst,
And all to all.

Lords. Our duties, and the pledge.

Re-enter Ghost.

Macb. Avaunt! and quit my sight! let the earth hide thee!
Thy bones are marrowless, thy blood is cold;
Thou hast no speculation in those eyes
Which thou dost glare with.

Lady M. Think of this, good peers,
But as a thing of custom: 'tis no other,
Only it spoils the pleasure of the time.

Macb. What man dare, I dare:
Approach thou like the rugged Russian bear,
The arm'd rhinoceros, or the Hyrcan tiger;
Take any shape but that, and my firm nerves
Shall never tremble: or be alive again,
And dare me to the desert with thy sword;
If trembling I inhabit then, protest me
The baby of a girl. Hence, horrible shadow!
Unreal mockery, hence! [*Exit Ghost.*
Why, so: being gone,
I am a man again. Pray you, sit still.

Lady M. You have displaced the mirth, broke the good meeting,
With most admired disorder.

Macb. Can such things be,
And overcome us like a summer's cloud,
Without our special wonder? You make me strange
Even to the disposition that I owe,
When now I think you can behold such sights,
And keep the natural ruby of your cheeks,
When mine is blanch'd with fear.

Ross. What sights, my lord?

Lady M. I pray you, speak not; he grows worse and worse;
Question enrages him: at once, good night:
Stand not upon the order of your going,
But go at once.

Len. Good night; and better health
Attend his majesty!

Lady M. A kind good night to all!

[*Exeunt all but Macbeth and Lady M.*

Macb. It will have blood: they say blood will have blood:
Stones have been known to move and trees to speak;
Augures and understood relations have
By maggot-pies and choughs and rooks brought forth
The secret'st man of blood. What is the night?

Lady M. Almost at odds with morning, which is which.

Macb. How say'st thou, that Macduff denies his person

At our great bidding?
Lady M. Did you send to him, sir?
Macb. I hear it by the way, but I will send:
There 's not a one of them but in his house
I keep a servant fee'd. I will to-morrow,
And betimes I will, to the weird sisters:
More shall they speak, for now I am bent to know,
By the worst means, the worst. For mine own good
All causes shall give way: I am in blood
Stepp'd in so far that, should I wade no more,
Returning were as tedious as go o'er:
Strange things I have in head that will to hand,
Which must be acted ere they may be scann'd.
Lady M. You lack the season of all natures, sleep.
Macb. Come, we 'll to sleep. My strange and self-abuse
Is the initiate fear that wants hard use:
We are yet but young in deed. [*Exeunt.*

Scene V

A heath.

Thunder. Enter the three Witches, meeting Hecate.

First Witch. Why, how now, Hecate! you look angerly.
Hec. Have I not reason, beldams as you are,
Saucy and over-bold? How did you dare
To trade and traffic with Macbeth
In riddles and affairs of death;
And I, the mistress of your charms,
The close contriver of all harms,
Was never call'd to bear my part,
Or show the glory of our art?
And, which is worse, all you have done
Hath been but for a wayward son,
Spiteful and wrathful; who, as others do,
Loves for his own ends, not for you.
But make amends now: get you gone,
And at the pit of Acheron
Meet me i' the morning: thither he
Will come to know his destiny:
Your vessels and your spells provide,
Your charms and every thing beside.
I am for the air; this night I 'll spend
Unto a dismal and a fatal end:
Great business must be wrought ere noon:
Upon the corner of the moon
There hangs a vaporous drop profound;

I 'll catch it ere it come to ground:
And that distill'd by magic sleights
Shall raise such artificial sprites
As by the strength of their illusion
Shall draw him on to his confusion:
He shall spurn fate, scorn death, and bear
His hopes 'bove wisdom, grace and fear:
And you all know security
Is mortals' chiefest enemy.
[*Music and a song within: 'Come away, come away,' &c.*
Hark! I am call'd; my little spirit, see,
Sits in a foggy cloud, and stays for me. [*Exit.*

First Witch. Come, let 's make haste; she 'll soon be back again. [*Exeunt.*

Scene VI

Forres. The palace.

Enter Lennox and another Lord.

Len. My former speeches have but hit your thoughts,
Which can interpret farther: only I say
Things have been strangely borne. The gracious Duncan
Was pitied of Macbeth: marry, he was dead:
And the right-valiant Banquo walk'd too late;
Whom, you may say, if 't please you, Fleance kill'd,
For Fleance fled: men must not walk too late.
Who cannot want the thought, how monstrous
It was for Malcolm and for Donalbain
To kill their gracious father? damned fact!
How it did grieve Macbeth! did he not straight,
In pious rage, the two delinquents tear,
That were the slaves of drink and thralls of sleep?
Was not that nobly done? Ay, and wisely too;
For 'twould have anger'd any heart alive
To hear the men deny 't. So that, I say,
He has borne all things well: and I do think
That, had he Duncan's sons under his key—
As, an 't please heaven, he shall not—they should find
What 'twere to kill a father; so should Fleance.
But, peace! for from broad words, and 'cause he fail'd
His presence at the tyrant's feast, I hear,
Macduff lives in disgrace: sir, can you tell
Where he bestows himself?

Lord. The son of Duncan,
From whom this tyrant holds the due of birth,
Lives in the English court, and is received

Of the most pious Edward with such grace
That the malevolence of fortune nothing
Takes from his high respect. Thither Macduff
Is gone to pray the holy king, upon his aid
To wake Northumberland and warlike Siward:
That by the help of these, with Him above
To ratify the work, we may again
Give to our tables meat, sleep to our nights,
Free from our feasts and banquets bloody knives,
Do faithful homage and receive free honours:
All which we pine for now: and this report
Hath so exasperate the king that he
Prepares for some attempt of war.

Len. Sent he to Macduff?

Lord. He did: and with an absolute 'Sir, not I,'
The cloudy messenger turns me his back,
And hums, as who should say 'You'll rue the time
That clogs me with this answer.'

Len. And that well might
Advise him to a caution, to hold what distance
His wisdom can provide. Some holy angel
Fly to the court of England and unfold
His message ere he come, that a swift blessing
May soon return to this our suffering country
Under a hand accursed!

Lord. I'll send my prayers with him.
[*Exeunt.*

ACT IV—SCENE I

A cavern. In the middle, a boiling cauldron.
Thunder. Enter the three Witches.

First Witch. Thrice the brinded cat hath mew'd.

Sec. Witch. Thrice and once the hedge-pig whined.

Third Witch. Harpier cries ''Tis time, 'tis time.'

First Witch. Round about the cauldron go:
In the poison'd entrails throw.
Toad, that under cold stone
Days and nights has thirty one
Swelter'd venom sleeping got,
Boil thou first i' the charmed pot.

All. Double, double toil and trouble;
Fire burn and cauldron bubble.

Sec. Witch. Fillet of a fenny snake,
In the cauldron boil and bake;
Eye of newt and toe of frog,

Wool of bat and tongue of dog,
Adder's fork and blind-worm's sting,
Lizard's leg and howlet's wing,
For a charm of powerful trouble,
Like a hell-broth boil and bubble.

All. Double, double toil and trouble;
Fire burn and cauldron bubble.

Third Witch. Scale of dragon, tooth of wolf,
Witches' mummy, maw and gulf
Of the ravin'd salt-sea shark,
Root of hemlock digg'd i' the dark,
Liver of blaspheming Jew,
Gall of goat and slips of yew
Sliver'd in the moon's eclipse,
Nose of Turk and Tartar's lips,
Finger of birth-strangled babe
Ditch-deliver'd by a drab,
Make the gruel thick and slab:
Add thereto a tiger's chaudron,
For the ingredients of our cauldron.

All. Double, double toil and trouble;
Fire burn and cauldron bubble.

Sec. Witch. Cool it with a baboon's blood,
Then the charm is firm and good.

Enter Hecate to the other three Witches.

Hec. O, well done! I commend your pains;
And every one shall share i' the gains:
And now about the cauldron sing,
Like elves and fairies in a ring,
Enchanting all that you put in.

[*Music and a song: 'Black spirits,' &c. Hecate retires.*

Sec. Witch. By the pricking of my thumbs,
Something wicked this way comes:
Open, locks,
Whoever knocks!

Enter Macbeth.

Macb. How now, you secret, black, and midnight hags!
What is 't you do?

All. A deed without a name.

Macb. I conjure you, by that which you profess,
Howe'er you come to know it, answer me:
Though you untie the winds and let them fight
Against the churches; though the yesty waves
Confound and swallow navigation up;
Though bladed corn be lodged and trees blown down;

Though castles topple on their warders' heads;
Though palaces and pyramids do slope
Their heads to their foundations; though the treasure
Of nature's germins tumble all together,
Even till destruction sicken; answer me
To what I ask you.

First Witch. Speak.

Sec. Witch. Demand.

Third Witch. We 'll answer.

First Witch. Say, if thou 'dst rather hear it from our mouths,
Or from our masters?

Macb. Call 'em, let me see 'em.

First Witch. Pour in sow's blood, that hath eaten
Her nine farrow; grease that 's sweaten
From the murderer's gibbet throw
Into the flame.

All. Come, high or low;
Thyself and office deftly show!

Thunder. First Apparition: an armed Head.

Macb. Tell me, thou unknown power,—

First Witch. He knows thy thought:
Hear his speech, but say thou nought.

First App. Macbeth! Macbeth! Macbeth! beware Macduff;
Beware the thane of Fife. Dismiss me: enough. [*Descends.*

Macb. Whate'er thou art, for thy good caution thanks;
Thou hast harp'd my fear aright: but one word more,—

First Witch. He will not be commanded: here's another,
More potent than the first.

Thunder. Second Apparition: a bloody Child.

Sec. App. Macbeth! Macbeth! Macbeth!

Macb. Had I three ears, I 'ld hear thee.

Sec. App. Be bloody, bold and resolute; laugh to scorn
The power of man, for none of woman born
Shall harm Macbeth. [*Descends.*

Macb. Then live, Macduff: what need I fear of thee?
But yet I 'll make assurance doubly sure,
And take a bond of fate: thou shalt not live;
That I may tell pale-hearted fear it lies,
And sleep in spite of thunder.

Thunder. Third Apparition: a Child crowned, with a tree in his hand.

What is this,
That rises like the issue of a king,
And wears upon his baby-brow the round
And top of sovereignty?

All. Listen, but speak not to 't.
Third App. Be lion-mettled, proud, and take no care
Who chafes, who frets, or where conspirers are:
Macbeth shall never vanquish'd be until
Great Birnam wood to high Dunsinane hill
Shall come against him. [*Descends.*
Macb. That will never be:
Who can impress the forest, bid the tree
Unfix his earth-bound root? Sweet bodements! good!
Rebellion's head, rise never, till the wood
Of Birnam rise, and our high-placed Macbeth
Shall live the lease of nature, pay his breath
To time and mortal custom. Yet my heart
Throbs to know one thing: tell me, if your art
Can tell so much: shall Banquo's issue ever
Reign in this kingdom?
All. Seek to know no more.
Macb. I will be satisfied: deny me this,
And an eternal curse fall on you! Let me know:
Why sinks that cauldron? and what noise is this? [*Hautboys.*
First Witch. Show!
Sec. Witch. Show!
Third Witch. Show!
All. Show his eyes, and grieve his heart;
Come like shadows, so depart!

A show of eight Kings, the last with a glass in his hand; Banquo's Ghost following.

Macb. Thou art too like the spirit of Banquo: down!
Thy crown does sear mine eye-balls. And thy hair,
Thou other gold-bound brow, is like the first.
A third is like the former. Filthy hags!
Why do you show me this? A fourth! Start, eyes!
What, will the line stretch out to the crack of doom?
Another yet! A seventh! I'll see no more:
And yet the eighth appears, who bears a glass
Which shows me many more; and some I see
That two-fold balls and treble sceptres carry:
Horrible sight! Now I see 'tis true;
For the blood-bolter'd Banquo smiles upon me,
And points at them for his. What, is this so?
First Witch. Ay, sir, all this is so: but why
Stands Macbeth thus amazedly?
Come, sisters, cheer we up his sprites,
And show the best of our delights:
I'll charm the air to give a sound,

While you perform your antic round,
That this great king may kindly say
Our duties did his welcome pay.
[*Music. The Witches dance, and then vanish, with Hecate.*

Macb. Where are they? Gone? Let this pernicious hour
Stand aye accursed in the calendar!
Come in, without there!

Enter Lennox.

Len. What 's your grace's will?

Macb. Saw you the weird sisters?

Len. No, my lord.

Macb. Came they not by you?

Len. No indeed, my lord.

Macb. Infected be the air whereon they ride,
And damn'd all those that trust them! I did hear
The galloping of horse: who was 't came by?

Len. 'Tis two or three, my lord, that bring you word
Macduff is fled to England.

Macb. Fled to England!

Len. Ay, my good lord.

Macb. [*Aside*] Time, thou anticipatest my dread exploits:
The flighty purpose never is o'ertook
Unless the deed go with it: from this moment
The very firstlings of my heart shall be
The firstlings of my hand. And even now,
To crown my thoughts with acts, be it thought and done:
The castle of Macduff I will surprise;
Seize upon Fife; give to the edge o' the sword
His wife, his babes, and all unfortunate souls
That trace him in his line. No boasting like a fool;
This deed I 'll do before this purpose cool:
But no more sights!—Where are these gentlemen?
Come, bring me where they are. [*Exeunt.*

SCENE II

Fife. Macduff's castle.

Enter Lady Macduff, her Son, and Ross.

L. Macd. What had he done, to make him fly the land?

Ross. You must have patience, madam.

L. Macd. He had none:
His flight was madness: when our actions do not,
Our fears do make us traitors.

Ross. You know not
Whether it was his wisdom or his fear.

L. Macd. Wisdom! to leave his wife, to leave his babes,

His mansion and his titles, in a place
From whence himself does fly? He loves us not;
He wants the natural touch: for the poor wren,
The most diminutive of birds, will fight,
Her young ones in her nest, against the owl.
All is the fear and nothing is the love;
As little is the wisdom, where the flight
So runs against all reason.

Ross. My dearest coz,
I pray you, school yourself: but, for your husband,
He is noble, wise, judicious, and best knows
The fits o' the season. I dare not speak much further:
But cruel are the times, when we are traitors
And do not know ourselves; when we hold rumour
From what we fear, yet know not what we fear,
But float upon a wild and violent sea
Each way and move. I take my leave of you:
Shall not be long but I 'll be here again:
Things at the worst will cease, or else climb upward
To what they were before. My pretty cousin,
Blessing upon you!

L. Macd. Father'd he is, and yet he 's fatherless.

Ross. I am so much a fool, should I stay longer,
It would be my disgrace and your discomfort:
I take my leave at once. [*Exit.*

L. Macd. Sirrah, your father 's dead:
And what will you do now? How will you live?

Son. As birds do, mother.

L. Macd. What, with worms and flies?

Son. With what I get, I mean; and so do they.

L. Macd. Poor bird! thou 'ldst never fear the net nor lime,
The pitfall nor the gin.

Son. Why should I, mother? Poor birds they are not set for.
My father is not dead, for all your saying.

L. Macd. Yes, he is dead: how wilt thou do for a father?

Son. Nay, how will you do for a husband?

L. Macd. Why, I can buy me twenty at any market.

Son. Then you 'll buy 'em to sell again.

L. Macd. Thou speak'st with all thy wit, and yet, i' faith,
With wit enough for thee.

Son. Was my father a traitor, mother?

L. Macd. Ay, that he was.

Son. What is a traitor?

L. Macd. Why, one that swears and lies.

Son. And be all traitors that do so?

L. Macd. Every one that does so is a traitor, and must be hanged.

Son. And must they all be hanged that swear and lie?

L. Macd. Every one.

Son. Who must hang them?

L. Macd. Why, the honest men.

Son. Then the liars and swearers are fools; for there are liars and swearers enow to beat the honest men and hang up them.

L. Macd. Now, God help thee, poor monkey!
But how wilt thou do for a father?

Son. If he were dead, you 'ld weep for him: if you would not, it were a good sign that I should quickly have a new father.

L. Macd. Poor prattler, how thou talk'st!

Enter a Messenger.

Mess. Bless you, fair dame! I am not to you known,
Though in your state of honour I am perfect.
I doubt some danger does approach you nearly:
If you will take a homely man's advice,
Be not found here; hence, with your little ones.
To fright you thus, methinks I am too savage;
To do worse to you were fell cruelty,
Which is too nigh your person. Heaven preserve you!
I dare abide no longer. [*Exit.*

L. Macd. Whither should I fly?
I have done no harm. But I remember now
I am in this earthly world, where to do harm
Is often laudable, to do good sometime
Accounted dangerous folly: why then, alas,
Do I put up that womanly defence,
To say I have done no harm?—What are these faces?

Enter Murderers.

First Mur. Where is your husband?

L. Macd. I hope, in no place so unsanctified
Where such as thou mayst find him.

First Mur. He 's a traitor.

Son. Thou liest, thou shag-ear'd villain!

First Mur. What, you egg! [*Stabbing him.*
Young fry of treachery!

Son. He has kill'd me, mother:
Run away, I pray you! [*Dies.*

[*Exit Lady Macduff, crying 'Murderer!' Exeunt murderers, following her.*

Scene III

England. Before the King's palace.

Enter Malcolm and Macduff.

Mal. Let us seek out some desolate shade, and there
Weep our sad bosoms empty.
Macd. Let us rather
Hold fast the mortal sword, and like good men
Bestride our down-fall'n birthdom: each new morn
New widows howl, new orphans cry, new sorrows
Strike heaven on the face, that it resounds
As if it felt with Scotland and yell'd out
Like syllable of dolour.
Mal. What I believe, I 'll wail;
What know, believe; and what I can redress,
As I shall find the time to friend, I will.
What you have spoke, it may be so perchance.
This tyrant, whose sole name blisters our tongues,
Was once thought honest: you have loved him well;
He hath not touch'd you yet. I am young; but something
You may deserve of him through me; and wisdom
To offer up a weak, poor, innocent lamb
To appease an angry god.
Macd. I am not treacherous.
Mal. But Macbeth is.
A good and virtuous nature may recoil
In an imperial charge. But I shall crave your pardon;
That which you are, my thoughts cannot transpose:
Angels are bright still, though the brightest fell:
Though all things foul would wear the brows of grace,
Yet grace must still look so.
Macd. I have lost my hopes.
Mal. Perchance even there where I did find my doubts.
Why in that rawness left you wife and child,
Those precious motives, those strong knots of love
Without leave-taking? I pray you,
Let not my jealousies be your dishonours,
But mine own safeties. You may be rightly just,
Whatever I shall think.
Macd. Bleed, bleed, poor country:
Great tyranny, lay thou thy basis sure,
For goodness dare not check thee: wear thou thy wrongs;
The title is affeer'd. Fare thee well, lord:
I would not be the villain that thou think'st
For the whole space that 's in the tyrant's grasp

And the rich East to boot.
Mal. Be not offended:
I speak not as in absolute fear of you.
I think our country sinks beneath the yoke;
It weeps, it bleeds, and each new day a gash
Is added to her wounds: I think withal
There would be hands uplifted in my right;
And here from gracious England have I offer
Of goodly thousands: but for all this,
When I shall tread upon the tyrant's head,
Or wear it on my sword, yet my poor country
Shall have more vices than it had before,
More suffer and more sundry ways than ever,
By him that shall succeed.
Macd. What should he be?
Mal. It is myself I mean: in whom I know
All the particulars of vice so grafted
That, when they shall be open'd, black Macbeth
Will seem as pure as snow, and the poor state
Esteem him as a lamb, being compared
With my confineless harms.
Macd. Not in the legions
Of horrid hell can come a devil more damn'd
In evils to top Macbeth.
Mal. I grant him bloody,
Luxurious, avaricious, false, deceitful,
Sudden, malicious, smacking of every sin
That has a name: but there 's no bottom, none,
In my voluptuousness: your wives, your daughters,
Your matrons, and your maids, could not fill up
The cistern of my lust, and my desire
All continent impediments would o'erbear,
That did oppose my will: better Macbeth
Than such an one to reign.
Macd. Boundless intemperance
In nature is a tyranny; it hath been
The untimely emptying of the happy throne,
And fall of many kings. But fear not yet
To take upon you what is yours: you may
Convey your pleasures in a spacious plenty,
And yet seem cold, the time you may so hoodwink:
We have willing dames enough; there cannot be
That vulture in you, to devour so many
As will to greatness dedicate themselves,
Finding it so inclined.

Mal. With this there grows
In my most ill-composed affection such
A stanchless avarice that, were I king,
I should cut off the nobles for their lands,
Desire his jewels and this other's house:
And my more-having would be as a sauce
To make me hunger more, that I should forge
Quarrels unjust against the good and loyal,
Destroying them for wealth.
Macd. This avarice
Sticks deeper, grows with more pernicious root
Than summer-seeming lust, and it hath been
The sword of our slain kings: yet do not fear;
Scotland hath foisons to fill up your will
Of your mere own: all these are portable,
With other graces weigh'd.
Mal. But I have none: the king-becoming graces,
As justice, verity, temperance, stableness,
Bounty, perseverance, mercy, lowliness,
Devotion, patience, courage, fortitude,
I have no relish of them, but abound
In the division of each several crime,
Acting it many ways. Nay, had I power, I should
Pour the sweet milk of concord into hell,
Uproar the universal peace, confound
All unity on earth.
Macd. O Scotland, Scotland!
Mal. If such a one be fit to govern, speak:
I am as I have spoken.
Macd. Fit to govern!
No, not to live. O nation miserable!
With an untitled tyrant bloody-scepter'd,
When shalt thou see thy wholesome days again,
Since that the truest issue of thy throne
By his own interdiction stands accursed,
And does blaspheme his breed? Thy royal father
Was a most sainted king: the queen that bore thee,
Oftener upon her knees than on her feet,
Died every day she lived. Fare thee well!
These evils thou repeat'st upon thyself
Have banish'd me from Scotland. O my breast,
Thy hope ends here!
Mal. Macduff, this noble passion,
Child of integrity, hath from my soul
Wiped the black scruples, reconciled my thoughts

To thy good truth and honour. Devilish Macbeth
By many of these trains hath sought to win me
Into his power; and modest wisdom plucks me
From over-credulous haste: but God above
Deal between thee and me! for even now
I put myself to thy direction, and
Unspeak mine own detraction; here abjure
The taints and blames I laid upon myself,
For strangers to my nature. I am yet
Unknown to woman, never was forsworn,
Scarcely have coveted what was mine own,
At no time broke my faith, would not betray
The devil to his fellow, and delight
No less in truth than life: my first false speaking
Was this upon myself: what I am truly,
Is thine and my poor country's to command:
Whither indeed, before thy here-approach,
Old Siward, with ten thousand warlike men,
Already at a point, was setting forth.
Now we'll together, and the chance of goodness
Be like our warranted quarrel! Why are you silent?

Macd. Such welcome and unwelcome things at once
'Tis hard to reconcile.

Enter a Doctor.

Mal. Well, more anon. Comes the king forth, I pray you?

Doct. Ay, sir; there are a crew of wretched souls
That stay his cure: their malady convinces
The great assay of art; but at his touch,
Such sanctity hath heaven given his hand,
They presently amend.

Mal. I thank you, doctor. [*Exit Doctor.*

Macd. What's the disease he means?

Mal. 'Tis call'd the evil:
A most miraculous work in this good king;
Which often, since my here-remain in England,
I have seen him do. How he solicits heaven,
Himself best knows: but strangely-visited people,
All swoln and ulcerous, pitiful to the eye,
The mere despair of surgery, he cures,
Hanging a golden stamp about their necks,
Put on with holy prayers: and 'tis spoken,
To the succeeding royalty he leaves
The healing benediction. With this strange virtue
He hath a heavenly gift of prophecy,
And sundry blessings hang about his throne

That speak him full of grace.

Enter Ross.

Macd. See, who comes here?
Mal. My countryman; but yet I know him not.
Macd. My ever gentle cousin, welcome hither.
Mal. I know him now: good God, betimes remove
The means that makes us strangers!
Ross. Sir, amen.
Macd. Stands Scotland where it did?
Ross. Alas, poor country!
Almost afraid to know itself! It cannot
Be call'd our mother, but our grave: where nothing,
But who knows nothing, is once seen to smile;
Where sighs and groans and shrieks that rend the air,
Are made, not mark'd; where violent sorrow seems
A modern ecstasy: the dead man's knell
Is there scarce ask'd for who; and good men's lives
Expire before the flowers in their caps,
Dying or ere they sicken.
Macd. O, relation
Too nice, and yet too true!
Mal. What 's the newest grief?
Ross. That of an hour's age doth hiss the speaker;
Each minute teems a new one.
Macd. How does my wife?
Ross. Why, well.
Macd. And all my children?
Ross. Well too.
Macd. The tyrant has not batter'd at their peace?
Ross. No; they were well at peace when I did leave 'em.
Macd. Be not a niggard of your speech: how goes 't?
Ross. When I came hither to transport the tidings,
Which I have heavily borne, there ran a rumour
Of many worthy fellows that were out;
Which was to my belief witness'd the rather,
For that I saw the tryant's power a-foot:
Now is the time of help; your eye in Scotland
Would create soldiers, make our women fight,
To doff their dire distresses.
Mal. Be 't their comfort
We are coming thither: gracious England hath
Lent us good Siward and ten thousand men;
An older and a better soldier none
That Christendom gives out.
Ross. Would I could answer

This comfort with the like! But I have words
That would be howl'd out in the desert air,
Where hearing should not latch them.

Macd. What concern they?
The general cause? or is it a fee-grief
Due to some single breast?

Ross. No mind that 's honest
But in it shares some woe, though the main part
Pertains to you alone.

Macd. If it be mine,
Keep it not from me, quickly let me have it.

Ross. Let not your ears despise my tongue for ever,
Which shall possess them with the heaviest sound
That ever yet they heard.

Macd. Hum! I guess at it.

Ross. Your castle is surprised; your wife and babes
Savagely slaughter'd: to relate the manner,
Were, on the quarry of these murder'd deer,
To add the death of you.

Mal. Merciful heaven!
What, man! ne'er pull your hat upon your brows;
Give sorrow words: the grief that does not speak
Whispers the o'erfraught heart, and bids it break.

Macd. My children too?

Ross. Wife, children, servants, all
That could be found.

Macd. And I must be from thence!
My wife kill'd too?

Ross. I have said.

Mal. Be comforted:
Let 's make us medicines of our great revenge,
To cure this deadly grief.

Macd. He has no children. All my pretty ones?
Did you say all? O hell-kite! All?
What, all my pretty chickens and their dam
At one fell swoop?

Mal. Dispute it like a man.

Macd. I shall do so;
But I must also feel it as a man:
I cannot but remember such things were,
That were most precious to me. Did heaven look on,
And would not take their part? Sinful Macduff,
They were all struck for thee! naught that I am,
Not for their own demerits, but for mine,
Fell slaughter on their souls: heaven rest them now!

Mal. Be this the whetstone of your sword: let grief
Convert to anger; blunt not the heart, enrage it.
Macd. O, I could play the woman with mine eyes,
And braggart with my tongue! But, gentle heavens,
Cut short all intermission; front to front
Bring thou this fiend of Scotland and myself;
Within my sword's length set him; if he 'scape,
Heaven forgive him too!
Mal. This tune goes manly.
Come, go we to the king; our power is ready;
Our lack is nothing but our leave. Macbeth
Is ripe for shaking, and the powers above
Put on their instruments. Receive what cheer you may;
The night is long that never finds the day. [*Exeunt.*

ACT V—Scene I

Dunsinane. Ante-room in the castle.

Enter a Doctor of Physic and a Waiting-Gentlewoman.

Doct. I have two nights watched with you, but can perceive no truth in your report. When was it she last walked?

Gent. Since his majesty went into the field, I have seen her rise from her bed, throw her nightgown upon her, unlock her closet, take forth paper, fold it, write upon 't, read it, afterwards seal it, and again return to bed; yet all this while in a most fast sleep.

Doct. A great perturbation in nature, to receive at once the benefit of sleep and do the effects of watching! In this slumbery agitation, besides her walking and other actual performances, what, at any time, have you heard her say?

Gent. That, sir, which I will not report after her.

Doct. You may to me, and 'tis most meet you should.

Gent. Neither to you nor any one, having no witness to confirm my speech.

Enter Lady Macbeth, with a taper.

Lo you, here she comes! This is her very guise, and, upon my life, fast asleep. Observe her; stand close.

Doct. How came she by that light?

Gent. Why, it stood by her: she has light by her continually; 'tis her command.

Doct. You see, her eyes are open.

Gent. Ay, but their sense is shut.

Doct. What is it she does now? Look, how she rubs her hands.

Gent. It is an accustomed action with her, to seem thus washing her hands: I have known her continue in this a quarter of an hour.

Lady M. Yet here 's a spot.

Doct. Hark! she speaks: I will set down what comes from her, to satisfy my remembrance the more strongly.

Lady M. Out, damned spot! out, I say! One: two: why, then 'tis time to do 't. Hell is murky. Fie, my lord, fie! a soldier, and afeard? What need we fear who knows it, when none can call our power to account? Yet who would have thought the old man to have had so much blood in him?

Doct. Do you mark that?

Lady M. The thane of Fife had a wife; where is she now? What, will these hands ne'er be clean? No more o' that, my lord, no more o' that: you mar all with this starting.

Doct. Go to, go to; you have known what you should not.

Gent. She has spoke what she should not, I am sure of that: heaven knows what she has known.

Lady M. Here 's the smell of the blood still: all the perfumes of Arabia will not sweeten this little hand. Oh, oh, oh!

Doct. What a sigh is there! The heart is sorely charged.

Gent. I would not have such a heart in my bosom for the dignity of the whole body.

Doct. Well, well, well,—

Gent. Pray God it be, sir.

Doct. This disease is beyond my practice: yet I have known those which have walked in their sleep who have died holily in their beds.

Lady M. Wash your hands; put on your nightgown; look not so pale: I tell you yet again, Banquo 's buried; he cannot come out on 's grave.

Doct. Even so?

Lady M. To bed, to bed; there 's knocking at the gate: come, come, come, come, give me your hand: what 's done cannot be undone: to bed, to bed, to bed. [*Exit.*

Doct. Will she go now to bed?

Gent. Directly.

Doct. Foul whisperings are abroad: unnatural deeds
Do breed unnatural troubles: infected minds
To their deaf pillows will discharge their secrets:
More needs she the divine than the physician.
God, God forgive us all! Look after her;
Remove from her the means of all annoyance,
And still keep eyes upon her. So good night:
My mind she has mated and amazed my sight:

I think, but dare not speak.
Gent. Good night, good doctor.
[*Exeunt.*

Scene II

The country near Dunsinane.

Drum and colours. Enter Menteith, Caithness, Angus, Lennox, and Soldiers.

Ment. The English power is near, led on by Malcolm,
His uncle Siward and the good Macduff:
Revenges burn in them; for their dear causes
Would to the bleeding and the grim alarm
Excite the mortified man.
Ang. Near Birnam wood
Shall we well meet them; that way are they coming.
Caith. Who knows if Donalbain be with his brother?
Len. For certain, sir, he is not: I have a file
Of all the gentry: there is Siward's son,
And many unrough youths, that even now
Protest their first of manhood.
Ment. What does the tyrant?
Caith. Great Dunsinane he strongly fortifies:
Some say he 's mad; others, that lesser hate him,
Do call it valiant fury: but, for certain,
He cannot buckle his distemper'd cause
Within the belt of rule.
Ang. Now does he feel
His secret murders sticking on his hands;
Now minutely revolts upbraid his faith-breach;
Those he commands move only in command,
Nothing in love: now does he feel his title
Hang loose about him, like a giant's robe
Upon a dwarfish thief.
Ment. Who then shall blame
His pester'd senses to recoil and start,
When all that is within him does condemn
Itself for being there?
Caith. Well, march we on,
To give obedience where 'tis truly owed:
Meet we the medicine of the sickly weal,
And with him pour we, in our country's purge,
Each drop of us.
Len. Or so much as it needs
To dew the sovereign flower and drown the weeds.
Make we our march towards Birnam. [*Exeunt, marching.*

Scene III

Dunsinane. A room in the castle.

Enter Macbeth, Doctor, and Attendants.

Macb. Bring me no more reports; let them fly all:
Till Birnam wood remove to Dunsinane
I cannot taint with fear. What 's the boy Malcolm?
Was he not born of woman? The spirits that know
All mortal consequences have pronounced me thus:
'Fear not, Macbeth; no man that 's born of woman
Shall e'er have power upon thee.' Then fly, false thanes,
And mingle with the English epicures:
The mind I sway by and the heart I bear
Shall never sag with doubt nor shake with fear.

Enter a Servant.

The devil damn thee black, thou cream-faced loon!
Where got'st thou that goose look?
Serv. There is ten thousand—
Macb. Geese, villain?
Serv. Soldiers, sir.
Macb. Go prick thy face and over-red thy fear,
Thou lily-liver'd boy. What soldiers, patch!
Death of my soul! those linen cheeks of thine
Are counsellors to fear. What soldiers, whey-face!
Serv. The English force, so please you.
Macb. Take thy face hence. [*Exit Servant.*
Seyton!—I am sick at heart,
When I behold—Seyton, I say!—This push
Will cheer me ever, or disseat me now.
I have lived long enough: my way of life
Is fall'n into the sear, the yellow leaf,
And that which should accompany old age,
As honour, love, obedience, troops of friends,
I must not look to have; but, in their stead,
Curses, not loud but deep, mouth-honour, breath,
Which the poor heart would fain deny, and dare not.
Seyton!

Enter Seyton.

Sey. What 's your gracious pleasure?
Macb. What news more?
Sey. All is confirm'd, my lord, which was reported.
Macb. I 'll fight, till from my bones my flesh be hack'd.
Give me my armour.
Sey. 'Tis not needed yet.
Macb. I 'll put it on.

Send out moe horses, skirr the country round;
Hang those that talk of fear. Give me mine armour.
How does your patient, doctor?
Doct. Not so sick, my lord,
As she is troubled with thick-coming fancies,
That keep her from her rest.
Macb. Cure her of that.
Canst thou not minister to a mind diseased,
Pluck from the memory a rooted sorrow,
Raze out the written troubles of the brain,
And with some sweet oblivious antidote
Cleanse the stuff'd bosom of that perilous stuff
Which weighs upon the heart?
Doct. Therein the patient
Must minister to himself.
Macb. Throw physic to the dogs, I 'll none of it.
Come, put mine armour on; give me my staff.
Seyton, send out. Doctor, the thanes fly from me.
Come, sir, dispatch. If thou couldst, doctor, cast
The water of my land, find her disease
And purge it to a sound and pristine health,
I would applaud thee to the very echo,
That should applaud again. Pull 't off, I say.
What rhubarb, senna, or what purgative drug,
Would scour these English hence? Hear'st thou of them?
Doct. Ay, my good lord; your royal preparation
Makes us hear something.
Macb. Bring it after me.
I will not be afraid of death and bane
Till Birnam forest come to Dunsinane.
Doct. [*Aside*] Were I from Dunsinane away and clear,
Profit again should hardly draw me here. [*Exeunt.*

Scene IV

Country near Birnam wood.

Drum and colours. Enter Malcolm, old Siward and his Son, Macduff, Menteith, Caithness, Angus, Lennox, Ross, and Soldiers, marching.

Mal. Cousins, I hope the days are near at hand
That chambers will be safe.
Ment. We doubt it nothing.
Siw. What wood is this before us?
Ment. The wood of Birnam.
Mal. Let every soldier hew him down a bough,
And bear 't before him: thereby shall we shadow

The numbers of our host, and make discovery
Err in report of us.

Soldiers. It shall be done.

Siw. We learn no other but the confident tyrant
Keeps still in Dunsinane, and will endure
Our setting down before 't.

Mal. 'Tis his main hope:
For where there is advantage to be given,
Both more and less have given him the revolt,
And none serve with him but constrained things
Whose hearts are absent too.

Macd. Let our just censures
Attend the true event, and put we on
Industrious soldiership.

Siw. The time approaches,
That will with due decision make us know
What we shall say we have and what we owe.
Thoughts speculative their unsure hopes relate,
But certain issue strokes must arbitrate:
Towards which advance the war. [*Exeunt, marching.*

Scene V

Dunsinane. Within the castle.

Enter Macbeth, Seyton, and Soldiers, with drum and colours.

Macb. Hang out our banners on the outward walls;
The cry is still 'They come:' our castle's strength
Will laugh a siege to scorn: here let them lie
Till famine and the ague eat them up:
Were they not forced with those that should be ours,
We might have met them dareful, beard to beard,
And beat them backward home. [*A cry of women within.*
What is that noise?

Sey. It is the cry of women, my good lord. [*Exit.*

Macb. I have almost forgot the taste of fears:
The time has been, my senses would have cool'd
To hear a night-shriek, and my ell of hair
Would at a dismal treatise rouse and stir
As life were in 't: I have supp'd full with horrors;
Direness, familiar to my slaughterous thoughts,
Cannot once start me.

Re-enter Seyton.

Wherefore was that cry?

Sey. The queen, my lord, is dead.

Macb. She should have died hereafter;
There would have been a time for such a word.

To-morrow, and to-morrow, and to-morrow,
Creeps in this petty pace from day to day,
To the last syllable of recorded time;
And all our yesterdays have lighted fools
The way to dusty death. Out, out, brief candle!
Life 's but a walking shadow, a poor player
That struts and frets his hour upon the stage
And then is heard no more: it is a tale
Told by an idiot, full of sound and fury,
Signifying nothing.

Enter a Messenger.

Thou comest to use thy tongue; thy story quickly.
Mess. Gracious my lord,
I should report that which I say I saw,
But know not how to do it.
Macb. Well, say, sir.
Mess. As I did stand my watch upon the hill,
I look'd toward Birnam, and anon, methought,
The wood began to move.
Macb. Liar and slave!
Mess. Let me endure your wrath, if 't be not so:
Within this three mile may you see it coming;
I say, a moving grove.
Macb. If thou speak'st false,
Upon the next tree shalt thou hang alive,
Till famine cling thee: if thy speech be sooth,
I care not if thou dost for me as much.
I pull in resolution, and begin
To doubt the equivocation of the fiend
That lies like truth: 'Fear not, till Birnam wood
Do come to Dunsinane;' and now a wood
Comes towards Dunsinane. Arm, arm, and out!
If this which he avouches does appear,
There is nor flying hence nor tarrying here.
I 'gin to be a-weary of the sun,
And wish the estate o' the world were now undone.
Ring the alarum-bell! Blow, wind! come, wrack!
At least we 'll die with harness on our back. [*Exeunt.*

Scene VI

Dunsinane. Before the castle.

Drum and colours. Enter Malcolm, old Siward, Macduff, and their Army, with boughs.

Mal. Now near enough; your leavy screens throw down,
And show like those you are. You, worthy uncle,

Shall, with my cousin, your right noble son,
Lead our first battle: worthy Macduff and we
Shall take upon 's what else remains to do,
According to our order.

Siw. Fare you well.
Do we but find the tyrant's power to-night,
Let us be beaten, if we cannot fight.

Macd. Make all our trumpets speak; give them all breath,
Those clamorous harbingers of blood and death. [*Exeunt.*

SCENE VII

Another part of the field.

Alarums. Enter Macbeth.

Macb. They have tied me to a stake; I cannot fly,
But bear-like I must fight the course. What 's he
That was not born of woman? Such a one
Am I to fear, or none.

Enter young Siward.

Yo. Siw. What is thy name?

Macb. Thou 'lt be afraid to hear it.

Yo. Siw. No; though thou call'st thyself a hotter name
Than any is in hell.

Macb. My name 's Macbeth.

Yo. Siw. The devil himself could not pronounce a title
More hateful to mine ear.

Macb. No, nor more fearful.

Yo. Siw. Thou liest, abhorred tyrant; with my sword
I 'll prove the lie thou speak'st.

[*They fight, and young Siward is slain.*

Macb. Thou wast born of woman.
But swords I smile at, weapons laugh to scorn,
Brandish'd by man that 's of a woman born. [*Exit.*

Alarums. Enter Macduff.

Macd. That way the noise is. Tyrant, show thy face!
If thou be'st slain and with no stroke of mine,
My wife and children's ghosts will haunt me still.
I cannot strike at wretched kerns, whose arms
Are hired to bear their staves: either thou, Macbeth,
Or else my sword, with an unbatter'd edge,
I sheathe again undeeded. There thou shouldst be;
By this great clatter, one of greatest note
Seems bruited: let me find him, fortune!
And more I beg not. [*Exit. Alarums.*

Enter Malcolm and old Siward.

Siw. This way, my lord; the castle 's gently render'd:

The tyrant's people on both sides do fight;
The noble thanes do bravely in the war;
The day almost itself professes yours,
And little is to do.

Mal. We have met with foes
That strike beside us.

Siw. Enter, sir, the castle.
[*Exeunt. Alarum.*

Scene VIII

Another part of the field.

Enter Macbeth.

Macb. Why should I play the Roman fool, and die
On mine own sword? whiles I see lives, the gashes
Do better upon them.

Enter Macduff.

Macd. Turn, hell-hound, turn!

Macb. Of all men else I have avoided thee:
But get thee back; my soul is too much charged
With blood of thine already.

Macd. I have no words:
My voice is in my sword, thou bloodier villain
Than terms can give thee out! [*They fight.*

Macb. Thou losest labour:
As easy mayst thou the intrenchant air
With thy keen sword impress as make me bleed:
Let fall thy blade on vulnerable crests;
I bear a charmed life, which must not yield
To one of woman born.

Macd. Despair thy charm,
And let the angel whom thou still hast served
Tell thee, Macduff was from his mother's womb
Untimely ripp'd.

Macb. Accursed be that tongue that tells me so,
For it hath cow'd my better part of man!
And be these juggling fiends no more believed,
That palter with us in a double sense;
That keep the word of promise to our ear,
And break it to our hope. I'll not fight with thee.

Macd. Then yield thee, coward,
And live to be the show and gaze o' the time:
We'll have thee, as our rarer monsters are,
Painted upon a pole, and underwrit,
'Here may you see the tyrant.'

Macb. I will not yield,

To kiss the ground before young Malcolm's feet,
And to be baited with the rabble's curse.
Though Birnam wood be come to Dunsinane,
And thou opposed, being of no woman born,
Yet I will try the last: before my body
I throw my warlike shield: lay on, Macduff;
And damn'd be him that first cries 'Hold, enough!'
[*Exeunt fighting. Alarums.*

Retreat. Flourish. Enter, with drum and colours, Malcolm, old Siward, Ross, the other Thanes, and Soldiers.

Mal. I would the friends we miss were safe arrived.
Siw. Some must go off: and yet, by these I see,
So great a day as this is cheaply bought.
Mal. Macduff is missing, and your noble son.
Ross. Your son, my lord, has paid a soldier's debt:
He only lived but till he was a man;
The which no sooner had his prowess confirm'd
In the unshrinking station where he fought,
But like a man he died.
Siw. Then he is dead?
Ross. Ay, and brought off the field: your cause of sorrow
Must not be measured by his worth, for then
It hath no end.
Siw. Had he his hurts before?
Ross. Ay, on the front.
Siw. Why then, God's soldier be he!
Had I as many sons as I have hairs,
I would not wish them to a fairer death:
And so his knell is knoll'd.
Mal. He's worth more sorrow,
And that I'll spend for him.
Siw. He's worth no more:
They say he parted well and paid his score:
And so God be with him! Here comes newer comfort.

Re-enter Macduff, with Macbeth's head.

Macd. Hail, king! for so thou art: behold, where stands
The usurper's cursed head: the time is free:
I see thee compass'd with thy kingdom's pearl,
That speak my salutation in their minds;
Whose voices I desire aloud with mine:
Hail, King of Scotland!
All. Hail, King of Scotland! [*Flourish.*
Mal. We shall not spend a large expense of time
Before we reckon with your several loves,
And make us even with you. My thanes and kinsmen,

Henceforth be earls, the first that ever Scotland
In such an honour named. What 's more to do,
Which would be planted newly with the time,
As calling home our exiled friends abroad
That fled the snares of watchful tyranny,
Producing forth the cruel ministers
Of this dead butcher and his fiend-like queen,
Who, as 'tis thought, by self and violent hands
Took off her life ; this, and what needful else
That calls upon us by the grace of Grace
We will perform in measure, time and place :
So thanks to all at once and to each one,
Whom we invite to see us crown'd at Scone.
[*Flourish. Exeunt.*

THE TRAGEDY OF HAMLET, PRINCE OF DENMARK

DRAMATIS PERSONÆ.

CLAUDIUS, *king of Denmark.*
HAMLET, *son to the late, and nephew to the present king.*
POLONIUS, *lord chamberlain.*
HORATIO, *friend to Hamlet.*
LAERTES, *son to Polonius.*
VOLTIMAND, CORNELIUS, ROSENCRANTZ, GUILDENSTERN, OSRIC, A Gentleman, } courtiers.
A Priest.
MARCELLUS, BERNARDO, } officers.
FRANCISCO, *a soldier.*
REYNALDO, *servant to Polonius.*
Players.
Two clowns, grave-diggers.
FORTINBRAS, *prince of Norway.*
A Captain.
English Ambassadors.

GERTRUDE, *queen of Denmark, and mother to Hamlet.*
OPHELIA, *daughter to Polonius.*

Lords, Ladies, Officers, Soldiers, Sailors, Messengers, and other Attendants
Ghost of Hamlet's Father.
SCENE: *Denmark.*

ACT I—SCENE I

Elsinore. A platform before the castle.

Francisco at his post. Enter to him Bernardo.

Ber. Who 's there?
Fran. Nay, answer me: stand, and unfold yourself.
Ber. Long live the king!
Fran. Bernardo?
Ber. He.
Fran. You come most carefully upon your hour.
Ber. 'Tis now struck twelve; get thee to bed, Francisco.
Fran. For this relief much thanks: 'tis bitter cold,
And I am sick at heart.
Ber. Have you had quiet guard?
Fran. Not a mouse stirring.
Ber. Well, good night.
If you do meet Horatio and Marcellus,
The rivals of my watch, bid them make haste.
Fran. I think I hear them. Stand, ho! Who is there?

Enter Horatio and Marcellus.

Hor. Friends to this ground.
Mar. And liegemen to the Dane.
Fran. Give you good night.
Mar. O, farewell, honest soldier:
Who hath relieved you?
Fran. Bernardo hath my place.
Give you good night. [*Exit.*
Mar. Holla! Bernardo!
Ber. Say,

What, is Horatio there?
Hor. A piece of him.
Ber. Welcome, Horatio; welcome, good Marcellus.
Mar. What, has this thing appear'd again to-night?
Ber. I have seen nothing.
Mar. Horatio says 'tis but our fantasy,
And will not let belief take hold of him
Touching this dreaded sight, twice seen of us:
Therefore I have entreated him along
With us to watch the minutes of this night,
That if again this apparition come,
He may approve our eyes and speak to it.
Hor. Tush, tush, 'twill not appear.
Ber. Sit down a while;
And let us once again assail your ears,
That are so fortified against our story,
What we have two nights seen.
Hor. Well, sit we down,
And let us hear Bernardo speak of this.
Ber. Last night of all,
When yond same star that 's westward from the pole
Had made his course to illume that part of heaven
Where now it burns, Marcellus and myself,
The bell then beating one,—

Enter Ghost.

Mar. Peace, break thee off; look, where it comes again!
Ber. In the same figure, like the king that 's dead.
Mar. Thou art a scholar; speak to it, Horatio.
Ber. Looks it not like the king? mark it, Horatio.
Hor. Most like: it harrows me with fear and wonder.
Ber. It would be spoke to.
Mar. Question it, Horatio.
Hor. What art thou, that usurp'st this time of night,
Together with that fair and warlike form
In which the majesty of buried Denmark
Did sometimes march? by heaven I charge thee, speak!
Mar. It is offended.
Ber. See, it stalks away!
Hor. Stay! speak, speak! I charge thee, speak! [*Exit Ghost.*
Mar. 'Tis gone, and will not answer.
Ber. How now, Horatio! you tremble and look pale:
Is not this something more than fantasy?
What think you on 't?
Hor. Before my God, I might not this believe
Without the sensible and true avouch

Of mine own eyes.
Mar. Is it not like the king?
Hor. As thou art to thyself:
Such was the very armour he had on
When he the ambitious Norway combated;
So frown'd he once, when, in an angry parle,
He smote the sledded Polacks on the ice.
'Tis strange.
Mar. Thus twice before, and jump at this dead hour,
With martial stalk hath he gone by our watch.
Hor. In what particular thought to work I know not;
But, in the gross and scope of my opinion,
This bodes some strange eruption to our state.
Mar. Good now, sit down, and tell me, he that knows,
Why this same strict and most observant watch
So nightly toils the subject of the land,
And why such daily cast of brazen cannon,
And foreign mart for implements of war;
Why such impress of shipwrights, whose sore task
Does not divide the Sunday from the week;
What might be toward, that this sweaty haste
Doth make the night joint-labourer with the day:
Who is 't that can inform me?
Hor. That can I;
At least the whisper goes so. Our last king,
Whose image even but now appear'd to us,
Was, as you know, by Fortinbras of Norway,
Thereto prick'd on by a most emulate pride,
Dared to the combat; in which our valiant Hamlet—
For so this side of our known world esteem'd him—
Did slay this Fortinbras; who by a seal'd compact,
Well ratified by law and heraldry,
Did forfeit, with his life, all those his lands
Which he stood seized of, to the conqueror:
Against the which, a moiety competent
Was gaged by our king; which had return'd
To the inheritance of Fortinbras,
Had he been vanquisher; as, by the same covenant
And carriage of the article design'd,
His fell to Hamlet. Now, sir, young Fortinbras,
Of unimproved metal hot and full,
Hath in the skirts of Norway here and there
Shark'd up a list of lawless resolutes,
For food and diet, to some enterprise
That hath a stomach in 't: which is no other—

As it doth well appear unto our state—
But to recover of us, by strong hand
And terms compulsatory, those foresaid lands
So by his father lost: and this, I take it,
Is the main motive of our preparations,
The source of this our watch and the chief head
Of this post-haste and romage in the land.

Ber. I think it be no other but e'en so:
Well may it sort, that this portentous figure
Comes armed through our watch, so like the king
That was and is the question of these wars.

Hor. A mote it is to trouble the mind's eye.
In the most high and palmy state of Rome,
A little ere the mightiest Julius fell,
The graves stood tenantless, and the sheeted dead
Did squeak and gibber in the Roman streets:
. . . .
As stars with trains of fire and dews of blood,
Disasters in the sun; and the moist star,
Upon whose influence Neptune's empire stands,
Was sick almost to doomsday with eclipse:
And even the like precurse of fierce events,
As harbingers preceding still the fates
And prologue to the omen coming on,
Have heaven and earth together demonstrated
Unto our climatures and countrymen.

Re-enter Ghost.

But soft, behold! lo, where it comes again!
I'll cross it, though it blast me. Stay, illusion!
If thou hast any sound, or use of voice,
Speak to me:
If there be any good thing to be done,
That may to thee do ease and grace to me,
Speak to me:
If thou art privy to thy country's fate,
Which, happily, foreknowing may avoid,
O, speak!
Of if thou hast uphoarded in thy life
Extorted treasure in the womb of earth,
For which, they say, you spirits oft walk in death,
Speak of it: stay, and speak! [*The cock crows.*] Stop it,
Marcellus.

Mar. Shall I strike at it with my partisan?

Hor. Do, if it will not stand.

Ber. 'Tis here!

Hor. 'Tis here!
Mar. 'Tis gone [*Exit Ghost.*
We do it wrong, being so majestical,
To offer it the show of violence;
For it is, as the air, invulnerable,
And our vain blows malicious mockery.
Ber. It was about to speak, when the cock crew.
Hor. And then it started like a guilty thing
Upon a fearful summons. I have heard,
The cock, that is the trumpet to the morn,
Doth with his lofty and shrill-sounding throat
Awake the god of day, and at his warning,
Whether in sea or fire, in earth or air,
The extravagant and erring spirit hies
To his confine: and of the truth herein
This present object made probation.
Mar. It faded on the crowing of the cock.
Some say that ever 'gainst that season comes
Wherein our Saviour's birth is celebrated,
The bird of dawning singeth all night long:
And then, they say, no spirit dare stir abroad,
The nights are wholesome, then no planets strike,
No fairy takes nor witch hath power to charm,
So hallow'd and so gracious is the time.
Hor. So have I heard and do in part believe it.
But look, the morn, in russet mantle clad,
Walks o'er the dew of yon high eastward hill:
Break we our watch up; and by my advice,
Let us impart what we have seen to-night
Unto young Hamlet; for, upon my life,
This spirit, dumb to us, will speak to him:
Do you consent we shall acquaint him with it,
As needful in our loves, fitting our duty?
Mar. Let's do't, I pray; and I this morning know
Where we shall find him most conveniently. [*Exeunt.*

Scene II

A room of state in the castle.

Flourish. Enter the King, Queen, Hamlet, Polonius, Laertes Voltimand, Cornelius, Lords, and Attendants.

King. Though yet of Hamlet our dear brother's death
The memory be green, and that it us befitted
To bear our hearts in grief and our whole kingdom
To be contracted in one brow of woe.
Yet so far hath discretion fought with nature

That we with wisest sorrow think on him,
Together with remembrance of ourselves.
Therefore our sometime sister, now our queen,
The imperial jointress to this warlike state,
Have we, as 'twere with a defeated joy,—
With an auspicious and a dropping eye,
With mirth in funeral and with dirge in marriage,
In equal scale weighing delight and dole,—
Taken to wife: nor have we herein barr'd
Your better wisdoms, which have freely gone
With this affair along. For all, our thanks.
Now follows, that you know, young Fortinbras,
Holding a weak supposal of our worth,
Or thinking by our late dear brother's death
Our state to be disjoint and out of frame,
Colleagued with this dream of his advantage,
He hath not fail'd to pester us with message,
Importing the surrender of those lands
Lost by his father, with all bonds of law,
To our most valiant brother. So much for him.
Now for ourself, and for this time of meeting:
Thus much the business is: we have here writ
To Norway, uncle of young Fortinbras,—
Who, impotent and bed-rid, scarcely hears
Of this his nephew's purpose,—to suppress
His further gait herein; in that the levies,
The lists and full proportions, are all made
Out of his subject: and we here dispatch
You, good Cornelius, and you, Voltimand,
For bearers of this greeting to old Norway,
Giving to you no further personal power
To business with the king more than the scope
Of these delated articles allow.
Farewell, and let your haste commend your duty.

Cor. }
Vol. } In that and all things will we show our duty.

King. We doubt it nothing: heartily farewell.

[*Exeunt Voltimand and Cornelius.*

And now, Laertes, what's the news with you?
You told us of some suit; what is't, Laertes?
You cannot speak of reason to the Dane,
And lose your voice: what wouldst thou beg, Laertes,
That shall not be my offer, not thy asking?
The head is not more native to the heart,
The hand more instrumental to the mouth,

Than is the throne of Denmark to thy father.
What wouldst thou have, Laertes?
Laer. My dread lord,
Your leave and favour to return to France,
From whence though willingly I came to Denmark,
To show my duty in your coronation,
Yet now, I must confess, that duty done,
My thoughts and wishes bend again toward France
And bow them to your gracious leave and pardon.
King. Have you your father's leave? What says Polonius?
Pol. He hath, my lord, wrung from me my slow leave
By laboursome petition, and at last
Upon his will I seal'd my hard consent:
I do beseech you, give him leave to go.
King. Take thy fair hour, Laertes; time be thine,
And thy best graces spend it at thy will!
But now, my cousin Hamlet, and my son,—
Ham. [*Aside*] A little more than kin, and less than kind.
King. How is it that the clouds still hang on you?
Ham. Not so, my lord; I am too much i' the sun.
Queen. Good Hamlet, cast thy nighted colour off,
And let thine eye look like a friend on Denmark.
Do not for ever with thy vailed lids
Seek for thy noble father in the dust:
Thou know'st 'tis common; all that lives must die,
Passing through nature to eternity.
Ham. Ay, madam, it is common.
Queen. If it be,
Why seems it so particular with thee?
Ham. Seems, madam! nay, it is; I know not 'seems.'
'Tis not alone my inky cloak, good mother,
Nor customary suits of solemn black,
Nor windy suspiration of forced breath,
No, nor the fruitful river in the eye,
Nor the dejected haviour of the visage,
Together with all forms, moods, shapes of grief,
That can denote me truly: these indeed seem,
For they are actions that a man might play:
But I have that within which passeth show;
These but the trappings and the suits of woe.
King. 'Tis sweet and commendable in your nature, Hamlet,
To give these mourning duties to your father:
But, you must know, your father lost a father,
That father lost, lost his, and the survivor bound
In filial obligation for some term

To do obsequious sorrow: but to persever
In obstinate condolement is a course
Of impious stubbornness; 'tis unmanly grief:
It shows a will most incorrect to heaven,
A heart unfortified, a mind impatient,
An understanding simple and unschool'd:
For what we know must be and is as common
As any the most vulgar thing to sense,
Why should we in our peevish opposition
Take it to heart? Fie! 'tis a fault to heaven,
A fault against the dead, a fault to nature,
To reason most absurd, whose common theme
Is death of fathers, and who still hath cried,
From the first corse till he that died to-day,
'This must be so.' We pray you, throw to earth
This unprevailing woe, and think of us
As of a father: for let the world take note,
You are the most immediate to our throne,
And with no less nobility of love
Than that which dearest father bears his son
Do I impart toward you. For your intent
In going back to school in Wittenberg,
It is most retrograde to our desire:
And we beseech you, bend you to remain
Here in the cheer and comfort of our eye,
Our chiefest courtier, cousin and our son.

Queen. Let not thy mother lose her prayers, Hamlet:
I pray thee, stay with us; go not to Wittenberg.

Ham. I shall in all my best obey you, madam.

King. Why, 'tis a loving and a fair reply:
Be as ourself in Denmark. Madam, come;
This gentle and unforced accord of Hamlet
Sits smiling to my heart: in grace whereof,
No jocund health that Denmark drinks to-day,
But the great cannon to the clouds shall tell,
And the king's rouse the heaven shall bruit again,
Re-speaking earthly thunder. Come away.
[*Flourish. Exeunt all but Hamlet.*

Ham. O, that this too too solid flesh would melt,
Thaw and resolve itself into a dew!
Or that the Everlasting had not fix'd
His canon 'gainst self-slaughter! O God! God!
How weary, stale, flat and unprofitable
Seem to me all the uses of this world!
Fie on 't! ah fie! 'tis an unweeded garden,

That grows to seed; things rank and gross in nature
Possess it merely. That it should come to this!
But two months dead! nay, not so much, not two:
So excellent a king; that was, to this,
Hyperion to a satyr: so loving to my mother,
That he might not beteem the winds of heaven
Visit her face too roughly. Heaven and earth!
Must I remember? why, she would hang on him,
As if increase of appetite had grown
By what it fed on: and yet, within a month—
Let me not think on 't—Frailty, thy name is woman!—
A little month, or ere those shoes were old
With which she follow'd my poor father's body,
Like Niobe, all tears:—why she, even she,—
O God! a beast that wants discourse of reason
Would have mourn'd longer,—married with my uncle
My father's brother, but no more like my father
Than I to Hercules: within a month;
Ere yet the salt of most unrighteous tears
Had left the flushing in her galled eyes,
She married. O, most wicked speed, to post
With such dexterity to incestuous sheets!
It is not, nor it cannot come to good:
But break, my heart, for I must hold my tongue!

Enter Horatio, Marcellus, and Bernardo.

Hor. Hail to your lordship!
Ham. I am glad to see you well:
Horatio,—or I do forget myself.
Hor. The same, my lord, and your poor servant ever.
Ham. Sir, my good friend; I 'll change that name with you:
And what make you from Wittenberg, Horatio?
Marcellus?
Mar. My good lord?
Ham. I am very glad to see you. [*To Ber.*] Good even, sir.
But what, in faith, make you from Wittenberg?
Hor. A truant disposition, good my lord.
Ham. I would not hear your enemy say so,
Nor shall you do my ear that violence,
To make it truster of your own report
Against yourself: I know you are no truant.
But what is your affair in Elsinore?
We 'll teach you to drink deep ere you depart.
Hor. My lord, I came to see your father's funeral.
Ham. I pray thee, do not mock me, fellow-student;
I think it was to see my mother's wedding.

Hor. Indeed, my lord, it follow'd hard upon.
Ham. Thrift, thrift, Horatio! the funeral baked-meats
Did coldly furnish forth the marriage tables.
Would I had met my dearest foe in heaven
Or ever I had seen that day, Horatio!
My father!—methinks I see my father.
Hor. O where, my lord?
Ham. In my mind's eye, Horatio.
Hor. I saw him once; he was a goodly king.
Ham. He was a man, take him for all in all,
I shall not look upon his like again.
Hor. My lord, I think I saw him yesternight.
Ham. Saw? who?
Hor. My lord, the king your father.
Ham. The king my father!
Hor. Season your admiration for a while
With an attent ear, till I may deliver,
Upon the witness of these gentlemen,
This marvel to you.
Ham. For God's love, let me hear.
Hor. Two nights together had these gentlemen,
Marcellus and Bernardo, on their watch,
In the dead vast and middle of the night,
Been thus encounter'd. A figure like your father,
Armed at point exactly, cap-a-pe,
Appears before them, and with solemn march
Goes slow and stately by them: thrice he walk'd
By their oppress'd and fear-surprised eyes,
Within his truncheon's length; whilst they, distill'd
Almost to jelly with the act of fear,
Stand dumb, and speak not to him. This to me
In dreadful secrecy impart they did;
And I with them the third night kept the watch:
Where, as they had deliver'd, both in time,
Form of the thing, each word made true and good,
The apparition comes: I knew your father;
These hands are not more like.
Ham. But where was this?
Mar. My lord, upon the platform where we watch'd.
Ham. Did you not speak to it?
Hor. My lord, I did,
But answer made it none: yet once methought
It lifted up its head and did address
Itself to motion, like as it would speak:
But even then the morning cock crew loud,

And at the sound it shrunk in haste away
And vanish'd from our sight.

Ham. 'Tis very strange.

Hor. As I do live, my honour'd lord, 'tis true,
And we did think it writ down in our duty
To let you know of it.

Ham. Indeed, indeed, sirs, but this troubles me.
Hold you the watch to-night?

Mar. } *Ber.* } We do, my lord.

Ham. Arm'd, say you?

Mar. } *Ber.* } Arm'd, my lord.

Ham. From top to toe?

Mar. } *Ber.* } My lord, from head to foot.

Ham. Then saw you not his face?

Hor. O, yes, my lord; he wore his beaver up.

Ham. What, look'd he frowningly?

Hor. A countenance more in sorrow than in anger.

Ham. Pale, or red?

Hor. Nay, very pale.

Ham. And fix'd his eyes upon you?

Hor. Most constantly.

Ham. I would I had been there.

Hor. It would have much amazed you.

Ham. Very like, very like. Stay'd it long?

Hor. While one with moderate haste might tell a hundred.

Mar. } *Ber.* } Longer, longer.

Hor. Not when I saw 't.

Ham. His beard was grizzled? no?

Hor. It was, as I have seen it in his life,
A sable silver'd.

Ham. I will watch to-night;
Perchance 'twill walk again.

Hor. I warrant it will.

Ham. If it assume my noble father's person,
I 'll speak to it, though hell itself should gape
And bid me hold my peace. I pray you all,
If you have hitherto conceal'd this sight,
Let it be tenable in your silence still,
And whatsoever else shall hap to-night,
Give it an understanding, but no tongue:
I will requite your loves. So fare you well:

Upon the platform, 'twixt eleven and twelve,
I 'll visit you.

All. Our duty to your honour.

Ham. Your loves, as mine to you: farewell.
[*Exeunt all but Hamlet.*
My father's spirit in arms! all is not well;
I doubt some foul play: would the night were come!
Till then sit still, my soul: foul deeds will rise,
Though all the earth o'erwhelm them, to men's eyes. [*Exit.*

Scene III

A room in Polonius's house.

Enter Laertes and Ophelia.

Laer. My necessaries are embark'd: farewell:
And, sister, as the winds give benefit
And convoy is assistant, do not sleep,
But let me hear from you.

Oph. Do you doubt that?

Laer. For Hamlet, and the trifling of his favour,
Hold it a fashion, and a toy in blood,
A violet in the youth of primy nature,
Forward, not permanent, sweet, not lasting,
The perfume and suppliance of a minute;
No more.

Oph. No more but so?

Laer. Think it no more:
For nature crescent does not grow alone
In thews and bulk; but, as this temple waxes,
The inward service of the mind and soul
Grows wide withal. Perhaps he loves you now;
And now no soil nor cautel doth besmirch
The virtue of his will: but you must fear,
His greatness weigh'd, his will is not his own;
For he himself is subject to his birth:
He may not, as unvalued persons do,
Carve for himself, for on his choice depends
The safety and health of this whole state,
And therefore must his choice be circumscribed
Unto the voice and yielding of that body
Whereof he is the head. Then if he says he loves you,
It fits your wisdom so far to believe it
As he in his particular act and place
May give his saying deed; which is no further
Than the main voice of Denmark goes withal.
Then weigh what loss your honour may sustain,

If with too credent ear you list his songs,
Or lose your heart, or your chaste treasure open
To his unmaster'd importunity.
Fear it, Ophelia, fear it, my dear sister,
And keep you in the rear of your affection,
Out of the shot and danger of desire.
The chariest maid is prodigal enough,
If she unmask her beauty to the moon:
Virtue itself 'scapes not calumnious strokes:
The canker galls the infants of the spring
Too oft before their buttons be disclosed,
And in the morn and liquid dew of youth
Contagious blastments are most imminent.
Be wary then; best safety lies in fear:
Youth to itself rebels, though none else near.

Oph. I shall the effect of this good lesson keep,
As watchman to my heart. But, good my brother,
Do not, as some ungracious pastors do,
Show me the steep and thorny way to heaven,
Whilst, like a puff'd and reckless libertine,
Himself the primrose path of dalliance treads
And recks not his own rede.

Laer. O, fear me not:
I stay too long: but here my father comes.

Enter Polonius.

A double blessing is a double grace;
Occasion smiles upon a second leave.

Pol. Yet here, Laertes! Aboard, aboard, for shame!
The wind sits in the shoulder of your sail,
And you are stay'd for. There; my blessing with thee!
And these few precepts in thy memory
Look thou character. Give thy thoughts no tongue,
Nor any unproportion'd thought his act.
Be thou familiar, but by no means vulgar.
Those friends thou hast, and their adoption tried,
Grapple them to thy soul with hoops of steel,
But do not dull thy palm with entertainment
Of each new-hatch'd unfledged comrade. Beware
Of entrance to a quarrel; but being in,
Bear 't, that the opposed may beware of thee.
Give every man thy ear, but few thy voice:
Take each man's censure, but reserve thy judgement.
Costly thy habit as thy purse can buy,
But not express'd in fancy; rich, not gaudy:
For the apparel oft proclaims the man;

And they in France of the best rank and station
Are of a most select and generous chief in that.
Neither a borrower nor a lender be:
For loan oft loses both itself and friend,
And borrowing dulls the edge of husbandry.
This above all: to thine own self be true,
And it must follow, as the night the day,
Thou canst not then be false to any man.
Farewell: my blessing season this in thee!

Laer. Most humbly do I take my leave, my lord.

Pol. The time invites you; go, your servants tend.

Laer. Farewell, Ophelia, and remember well
What I have said to you.

Oph. 'Tis in my memory lock'd,
And you yourself shall keep the key of it.

Laer. Farewell. [*Exit.*

Pol. What is 't, Ophelia, he hath said to you?

Oph. So please you, something touching the Lord Hamlet.

Pol. Marry, well bethought:
'Tis told me, he hath very oft of late
Given private time to you, and you yourself
Have of your audience been most free and bounteous:
If it be so—as so 'tis put on me,
And that in way of caution—I must tell you,
You do not understand yourself so clearly
As it behoves my daughter and your honour.
What is between you? give me up the truth.

Oph. He hath, my lord, of late made many tenders
Of his affection to me.

Pol. Affection! pooh! you speak like a green girl,
Unsifted in such perilous circumstance.
Do you believe his tenders, as you call them?

Oph. I do not know, my lord, what I should think.

Pol. Marry, I 'll teach you: think yourself a baby,
That you have ta'en these tenders for true pay,
Which are not sterling. Tender yourself more dearly;
Or—not to crack the wind of the poor phrase,
Running it thus—you 'll tender me a fool.

Oph. My lord, he hath importuned me with love
In honourable fashion.

Pol. Ay, fashion you may call it; go to, go to.

Oph. And hath given countenance to his speech, my lord,
With almost all the holy vows of heaven.

Pol. Ay, springes to catch woodcocks. I do know,
When the blood burns, how prodigal the soul

Lends the tongue vows: these blazes, daughter,
Giving more light than heat, extinct in both,
Even in their promise, as it is a-making,
You must not take for fire. From this time
Be something scanter of your maiden presence;
Set your entreatments at a higher rate
Than a command to parley. For Lord Hamlet,
Believe so much in him, that he is young,
And with a larger tether may he walk
Than may be given you: in few, Ophelia,
Do not believe his vows; for they are brokers,
Not of that dye which their investments show,
But mere implorators of unholy suits,
Breathing like sanctified and pious bawds,
The better to beguile. This is for all:
I would not, in plain terms, from this time forth,
Have you so slander any moment leisure,
As to give words or talk with the Lord Hamlet.
Look to 't, I charge you: come your ways.

Oph. I shall obey, my lord. [*Exeunt.*

Scene IV

The platform.

Enter Hamlet, Horatio, and Marcellus.

Ham. The air bites shrewdly; it is very cold.

Hor. It is a nipping and an eager air.

Ham. What hour now?

Hor. I think it lacks of twelve.

Mar. No, it is struck.

Hor. Indeed? I heard it not: it then draws near the season
Wherein the spirit held his wont to walk.
[*A flourish of trumpets, and ordnance shot off within.*
What doth this mean, my lord?

Ham. The king doth wake to-night and takes his rouse,
Keeps wassail, and the swaggering up-spring reels;
And as he drains his draughts of Rhenish down,
The kettle-drum and trumpet thus bray out
The triumph of his pledge.

Hor. Is it a custom?

Ham. Ay, marry, is 't:
But to my mind, though I am native here
And to the manner born, it is a custom
More honour'd in the breach than the observance.
This heavy-headed revel east and west
Makes us traduced and tax'd of other nations:

They clepe us drunkards, and with swinish phrase
Soil our addition; and indeed it takes
From our achievements, though perform'd at height,
The pith and marrow of our attribute.
So, oft it chances in particular men,
That for some vicious mole of nature in them,
As, in their birth,—wherein they are not guilty,
Since nature cannot choose his origin,—
By the o'ergrowth of some complexion,
Oft breaking down the pales and forts of reason,
Or by some habit that too much o'er-leavens
The form of plausive manners, that these men,—
Carrying, I say, the stamp of one defect,
Being nature's livery, or fortune's star,—
Their virtues else—be they as pure as grace,
As infinite as man may undergo—
Shall in the general censure take corruption
From that particular fault: the dram of eale
Doth all the noble substance of a doubt
To his own scandal.

Enter Ghost.

Hor. Look, my lord, it comes!

Ham. Angels and ministers of grace defend us!
Be thou a spirit of health or goblin damn'd,
Bring with thee airs from heaven or blasts from hell,
Be thy intents wicked or charitable,
Thou comest in such a questionable shape
That I will speak to thee: I'll call thee Hamlet,
King, father, royal Dane: O, answer me!
Let me not burst in ignorance; but tell
Why thy canonized bones, hearsed in death,
Have burst their cerements; why the sepulchre,
Wherein we saw thee quietly inurn'd,
Hath oped his ponderous and marble jaws,
To cast thee up again. What may this mean,
That thou, dead corse, again, in complete steel,
Revisit'st thus the glimpses of the moon,
Making night hideous; and we fools of nature
So horridly to shake our disposition
With thoughts beyond the reaches of our souls?
Say, why is this? wherefore? what should we do?

[*Ghost beckons Hamlet.*

Hor. It beckons you to go away with it,
As if it some impartment did desire
To you alone.

Mar. Look, with what courteous action
It waves you to a more removed ground:
But do not go with it.
Hor. No, by no means.
Ham. It will not speak; then I will follow it.
Hor. Do not, my lord.
Ham. Why, what should be the fear?
I do not set my life at a pin's fee;
And for my soul, what can it do to that,
Being a thing immortal as itself?
It waves me forth again: I'll follow it.
Hor. What if it tempt you toward the flood, my lord,
Or to the dreadful summit of the cliff
That beetles o'er his base into the sea,
And there assume some other horrible form,
Which might deprive your sovereignty of reason
And draw you into madness? think of it:
The very place puts toys of desperation,
Without more motive, into every brain
That looks so many fathoms to the sea
And hears it roar beneath.
Ham. It waves me still.
Go on; I'll follow thee.
Mar. You shall not go, my lord.
Ham. Hold off your hands
Hor. Be ruled; you shall not go.
Ham. My fate cries out,
And makes each petty artery in this body
As hardy as the Nemean lion's nerve.
Still am I call'd: unhand me, gentlemen;
By heaven, I'll make a ghost of him that lets me:
I say, away! Go on; I'll follow thee.
[*Exeunt Ghost and Hamlet.*
Hor. He waxes desperate with imagination.
Mar. Let's follow; 'tis not fit thus to obey him.
Hor. Have after. To what issue will this come?
Mar. Something is rotten in the state of Denmark.
Hor. Heaven will direct it.
Mar. Nay, let's follow him. [*Exeunt.*

Scene V

Another part of the platform.

Enter Ghost and Hamlet.

Ham. Whither wilt thou lead me? speak; I'll go no further.
Ghost. Mark me.

Ham. I will.
Ghost. My hour is almost come,
When I to sulphurous and tormenting flames
Must render up myself.
Ham. Alas, poor ghost!
Ghost. Pity me not, but lend thy serious hearing
To what I shall unfold.
Ham. Speak; I am bound to hear.
Ghost. So art thou to revenge, when thou shalt hear.
Ham. What?
Ghost. I am thy father's spirit;
Doom'd for a certain term to walk the night,
And for the day confined to fast in fires,
Till the foul crimes done in my days of nature
Are burnt and purged away. But that I am forbid
To tell the secrets of my prison-house,
I could a tale unfold whose lightest word
Would harrow up thy soul, freeze thy young blood,
Make thy two eyes, like stars, start from their spheres,
Thy knotted and combined locks to part
And each particular hair to stand an end,
Like quills upon the fretful porpentine:
But this eternal blazon must not be
To ears of flesh and blood. List, list, O, list!
If thou didst ever thy dear father love—
Ham. O God!
Ghost. Revenge his foul and most unnatural murder.
Ham. Murder!
Ghost. Murder most foul, as in the best it is,
But this most foul, strange, and unnatural.
Ham. Haste me to know 't, that I, with wings as swift
As meditation or the thoughts of love,
May sweep to my revenge.
Ghost. I find thee apt;
And duller shouldst thou be than the fat weed
That roots itself in ease on Lethe wharf,
Wouldst thou not stir in this. Now, Hamlet, hear:
'Tis given out that, sleeping in my orchard,
A serpent stung me; so the whole ear of Denmark
Is by a forged process of my death
Rankly abused: but know, thou noble youth,
The serpent that did sting thy father's life
Now wears his crown.
Ham. O my prophetic soul!
My uncle!

Ghost. Ay, that incestuous, that adulterate beast,
With witchcraft of his wit, with traitorous gifts,—
O wicked wit and gifts, that have the power
So to seduce!—won to his shameful lust
The will of my most seeming-virtuous queen:
O Hamlet, what a falling-off was there!
From me, whose love was of that dignity
That it went hand in hand even with the vow
I made to her in marriage; and to decline
Upon a wretch, whose natural gifts were poor
To those of mine!
But virtue, as it never will be moved,
Though lewdness court it in a shape of heaven,
So lust, though to a radiant angel link'd,
Will sate itself in a celestial bed
And prey on garbage.
But, soft! methinks I scent the morning air;
Brief let me be. Sleeping within my orchard,
My custom always of the afternoon,
Upon my secure hour thy uncle stole,
With juice of cursed hebenon in a vial,
And in the porches of my ears did pour
The leperous distilment; whose effect
Holds such an enmity with blood of man
That swift as quick-silver it courses through
The natural gates and alleys of the body;
And with a sudden vigour it doth posset
And curd, like eager droppings into milk,
The thin and wholesome blood: so did it mine;
And a most instant tetter bark'd about,
Most lazar-like, with vile and loathsome crust,
All my smooth body.
Thus was I, sleeping, by a brother's hand
Of life, of crown, of queen, at once dispatch'd
Cut off even in the blossoms of my sin,
Unhousel'd, disappointed, unaneled;
No reckoning made, but sent to my account
With all my imperfections on my head:
O, horrible! O, horrible! most horrible!
If thou hast nature in thee, bear it not;
Let not the royal bed of Denmark be
A couch for luxury and damned incest.
But, howsoever thou pursuest this act,
Taint not thy mind, nor let thy soul contrive
Against thy mother aught: leave her to heaven,

And to those thorns that in her bosom lodge,
To prick and sting her. Fare thee well at once!
The glow-worm shows the matin to be near,
And 'gins to pale his uneffectual fire:
Adieu, adieu, adieu! remember me. [*Exit.*

Ham. O all you host of heaven! O earth! what else?
And shall I couple hell? O, fie! Hold, hold, my heart;
And you, my sinews, grow not instant old,
But bear me stiffly up. Remember thee!
Ay, thou poor ghost, while memory holds a seat
In this distracted globe. Remember thee!
Yea, from the table of my memory
I'll wipe away all trivial fond records,
All saws of books, all forms, all pressures past,
That youth and observation copied there;
And thy commandment all alone shall live
Within the book and volume of my brain,
Unmix'd with baser matter: yes, by heaven!
O most pernicious woman!
O villain, villain, smiling, damned villain!
My tables,—meet it is I set it down,
That one may smile, and smile, and be a villain;
At least I'm sure it may be so in Denmark. [*Writing.*
So, uncle, there you are. Now to my word;
It is 'Adieu, adieu! remember me.'
I have sworn 't.

Hor., *Mar.* [*Within*] My lord, my lord!

Enter Horatio and Marcellus.

Mar. Lord Hamlet!

Hor. Heaven secure him!

Ham. So be it!

Mar. Illo, ho, ho, my lord!

Ham. Hillo, ho, ho, boy! come, bird, come.

Mar. How is 't, my noble lord?

Hor. What news, my lord?

Ham. O, wonderful!

Hor. Good my lord, tell it.

Ham. No; you will reveal it.

Hor. Not I, my lord, by heaven.

Mar. Nor I, my lord.

Ham. How say you, then; would heart of man once think it?
But you'll be secret?

Hor., *Mar.* Ay, by heaven, my lord.

Ham. There 's ne'er a villain dwelling in all Denmark
But he 's an arrant knave.
Hor. There needs no ghost, my lord, come from the grave
To tell us this.
Ham. Why, right; you are i' the right;
And so, without more circumstance at all,
I hold it fit that we shake hands and part:
You, as your business and desire shall point you;
For every man hath business and desire,
Such as it is; and for my own poor part,
Look you, I 'll go pray.
Hor. These are but wild and whirling words, my lord.
Ham. I 'm sorry they offend you, heartily;
Yes, faith, heartily.
Hor. There 's no offence, my lord.
Ham. Yes, by Saint Patrick, but there is, Horatio,
And much offence too. Touching this vision here,
It is an honest ghost, that let me tell you:
For your desire to know what is between us,
O'ermaster 't as you may. And now, good friends,
As you are friends, scholars and soldiers,
Give me one poor request.
Hor. What is 't, my lord? we will.
Ham. Never make known what you have seen to-night.
Hor. } *Mar.* } My lord, we will not.
Ham. Nay, but swear 't.
Hor. In faith,
My lord, not I.
Mar. Nor I, my lord, in faith.
Ham. Upon my sword.
Mar. We have sworn, my lord, already.
Ham. Indeed, upon my sword, indeed.
Ghost. [*Beneath*] Swear.
Ham. Ah, ha, boy! say'st thou so? art thou there, truepenny?
Come on: you hear this fellow in the cellarage:
Consent to swear.
Hor. Propose the oath, my lord.
Ham. Never to speak of this that you have seen,
Swear by my sword.
Ghost. [*Beneath*] Swear.
Ham. Hic et ubique? then we 'll shift our ground.
Come hither, gentlemen,
And lay your hands again upon my sword:
Never to speak of this that you have heard,

Swear by my sword.
Ghost. [*Beneath*] Swear.
Ham. Well said, old mole! canst work i' the earth so fast?
A worthy pioner! Once more remove, good friends.
Hor. O day and night, but this is wondrous strange!
Ham. And therefore as a stranger give it welcome.
There are more things in heaven and earth, Horatio,
Than are dreamt of in your philosophy.
But come;
Here, as before, never, so help you mercy,
How strange or odd soe'er I bear myself,
As I perchance hereafter shall think meet
To put an antic disposition on.
That you, at such times seeing me, never shall,
With arms encumber'd thus, or this head-shake,
Or by pronouncing of some doubtful phrase,
As 'Well, well, we know,' or 'We could, an if we would,'
Or 'If we list to speak,' or 'There be, an if they might,'
Or such ambiguous giving out, to note
That you know aught of me: this not to do,
So grace and mercy at your most need help you,
Swear.
Ghost. [*Beneath*] Swear.
Ham. Rest, rest, perturbed spirit! [*They swear.*] So, gentlemen,
With all my love I do commend me to you:
And what so poor a man as Hamlet is
May do, to express his love and friending to you,
God willing, shall not lack. Let us go in together;
And still your fingers on your lips, I pray.
The time is out of joint: O cursed spite,
That ever I was born to set it right!
Nay, come, let's go together. [*Exeunt.*

ACT II—Scene I

A room in Polonius's house.

Enter Polonius and Reynaldo.

Pol. Give him this money and these notes, Reynaldo.
Rey. I will, my lord.
Pol. You shall do marvellous wisely, good Reynaldo,
Before you visit him, to make inquire
Of his behaviour.
Rey. My lord, I did intend it.
Pol. Marry, well said, very well said. Look you, sir,
Inquire me first what Danskers are in Paris,

And how, and who, what means, and where they keep,
What company, at what expense, and finding
By this encompassment and drift of question
That they do know my son, come you more nearer
Than your particular demands will touch it:
Take you, as 'twere, some distant knowledge of him,
As thus, 'I know his father and his friends,
And in part him:' do you mark this, Reynaldo?

Rey. Ay, very well, my lord.

Pol. 'And in part him; but,' you may say, 'not well:
But if't be he I mean, he's very wild,
Addicted so and so;' and there put on him
What forgeries you please; marry, none so rank
As may dishonour him; take heed of that;
But, sir, such wanton, wild and usual slips
As are companions noted and most known
To youth and liberty.

Rey. As gaming, my lord.

Pol. Ay, or drinking, fencing, swearing, quarrelling,
Drabbing: you may go so far.

Rey. My lord, that would dishonour him.

Pol. Faith, no; as you may season it in the charge.
You must not put another scandal on him,
That he is open to incontinency;
That's not my meaning: but breathe his faults so quaintly
That they may seem the taints of liberty,
The flash and outbreak of a fiery mind,
A savageness in unreclaimed blood,
Of general assault.

Rey. But, my good lord,—

Pol. Wherefore should you do this?

Rey. Ay, my lord,
I would know that.

Pol. Marry, sir, here's my drift,
And I believe it is a fetch of warrant:
You laying these slight sullies on my son,
As 'twere a thing a little soil'd i' the working,
Mark you,
Your party in converse, him you would sound,
Having ever seen in the prenominate crimes
The youth you breathe of guilty, be assured
He closes with you in this consequence;
'Good sir,' or so, or 'friend,' or 'gentleman,'
According to the phrase or the addition
Of man and country.

Rey. Very good, my lord.
Pol. And then, sir, does he this—he does—what was I about to say? By the mass, I was about to say something: where did I leave?
Rey. At 'closes in the consequence,' at 'friend or so,' and ['gentleman.'
Pol. At 'closes in the consequence,' ay, marry;
He closes with you thus: 'I know the gentleman;
I saw him yesterday, or t' other day,
Or then, or then, with such, or such, and, as you say,
There was a' gaming, there o'ertook in 's rouse,
There falling out at tennis:' or perchance,
'I saw him enter such a house of sale,'
Videlicet, a brothel, or so forth.
See you now;
Your bait of falsehood takes this carp of truth:
And thus do we of wisdom and of reach,
With windlasses and with assays of bias,
By indirections find directions out:
So, by my former lecture and advice,
Shall you my son. You have me, have you not?
Rey. My lord, I have.
Pol. God be wi' ye; fare ye well.
Rey. Good, my lord!
Pol. Observe his inclination in yourself.
Rey. I shall, my lord.
Pol. And let him ply his music.
Rey. Well, my lord.
Pol. Farewell! [*Exit Reynaldo.*

Enter Ophelia.

How now, Ophelia! what 's the matter?
Oph. O, my lord, my lord, I have been so affrighted!
Pol. With what, i' the name of God?
Oph. My lord, as I was sewing in my closet,
Lord Hamlet, with his doublet all unbraced,
No hat upon his head, his stockings foul'd,
Ungarter'd and down-gyved to his ancle;
Pale as his shirt, his knees knocking each other,
And with a look so piteous in purport
As if he had been loosed out of hell
To speak of horrors, he comes before me.
Pol. Mad for thy love?
Oph. My lord, I do not know,
But truly I do fear it.
Pol. What said he?
Oph. He took m by the wrist and held me hard;

Then goes he to the length of all his arm,
And with his other hand thus o'er his brow,
He falls to such perusal of my face
As he would draw it. Long stay'd he so;
At last, a little shaking of mine arm,
And thrice his head thus waving up and down,
He raised a sigh so piteous and profound
As it did seem to shatter all his bulk
And end his being: that done, he lets me go:
And with his head over his shoulder turn'd,
He seem'd to find his way without his eyes;
For out o' doors he went without their helps,
And to the last bended their light on me.

Pol. Come, go with me: I will go seek the king.
This is the very ecstasy of love;
Whose violent property fordoes itself
And leads the will to desperate undertakings
As oft as any passion under heaven
That does afflict our natures. I am sorry.
What, have you given him any hard words of late?

Oph. No, my good lord, but, as you did command,
I did repel his letters and denied
His access to me.

Pol. That hath made him mad.
I am sorry that with better heed and judgement
I had not quoted him: I fear'd he did but trifle
And meant to wreck thee; but beshrew my jealousy!
By heaven, it is as proper to our age
To cast beyond ourselves in our opinions
As it is common for the younger sort
To lack discretion. Come, go we to the king:
This must be known; which, being kept close, might move
More grief to hide than hate to utter love.
Come. [*Exeunt.*

Scene II

A room in the castle.

Flourish. Enter King, Queen, Rosencrantz, Guildenstern, and Attendants.

King. Welcome, dear Rosencrantz and Guildenstern!
Moreover that we much did long to see you,
The need we have to use you did provoke
Our hasty sending. Something have you heard
Of Hamlet's transformation; so I call it,
Sith nor the exterior nor the inward man

Resembles that it was. What it should be,
More than his father's death, that thus hath put him
So much from the understanding of himself,
I cannot dream of: I entreat you both,
That, being of so young days brought up with him
And sith so neighbour'd to his youth and haviour,
That you vouchsafe your rest here in our court
Some little time: so by your companies
To draw him on to pleasures, and to gather
So much as from occasion you may glean,
Whether aught to us unknown afflicts him thus,
That open'd lies within our remedy.

Queen. Good gentlemen, he hath much talk'd of you,
And sure I am two men there are not living
To whom he more adheres. If it will please you
To show us so much gentry and good will
As to expend your time with us a while
For the supply and profit of our hope,
Your visitation shall receive such thanks
As fits a king's remembrance.

Ros. Both your majestics
Might, by the sovereign power you have of us,
Put your dread pleasures more into command
Than to entreaty.

Guil. But we both obey,
And here give up ourselves, in the full bent
To lay our service freely at your feet,
To be commanded.

King. Thanks, Rosencrantz and gentle Guildenstern.

Queen. Thanks, Guildenstern and gentle Rosencrantz:
And I beseech you instantly to visit
My too much changed son. Go, some of you,
And bring these gentlemen where Hamlet is.

Guil. Heavens make our presence and our practices
Pleasant and helpful to him!

Queen. Ay, amen!

[*Exeunt Rosencrantz, Guildenstern, and some Attendants.*

Enter Polonius.

Pol. The ambassadors from Norway, my good lord,
Are joyfully return'd.

King. Thou still hast been the father of good news.

Pol. Have I, my lord? I assure my good liege,
I hold my duty as I hold my soul,
Both to my God and to my gracious king:
And I do think, or else this brain of mine

Hunts not the trail of policy so sure
As it hath used to do, that I have found
The very cause of Hamlet's lunacy.
King. O, speak of that; that do I long to hear.
Pol. Give first admittance to the ambassadors;
My news shall be the fruit to that great feast.
King. Thyself do grace to them, and bring them in.
[*Exit Polonius.*
He tells me, my dear Gertrude, he hath found
The head and source of all your son's distemper.
Queen. I doubt it is no other but the main;
His father's death and our o'erhasty marriage.
King. Well, we shall sift him.
Re-enter Polonius, with Voltimand and Cornelius.
Welcome, my good friends!
Say, Voltimand, what from our brother Norway?
Volt. Most fair return of greetings and desires.
Upon our first, he sent out to suppress
His nephew's levies, which to him appear'd
To be a preparation 'gainst the Polack,
But better look'd into, he truly found
It was against your highness: whereat grieved,
That so his sickness, age and impotence
Was falsely borne in hand, sends out arrests
On Fortinbras; which he, in brief, obeys,
Receives rebuke from Norway, and in fine
Makes vow before his uncle never more
To give the assay of arms against your majesty.
Whereon old Norway, overcome with joy,
Gives him three thousand crowns in annual fee
And his commission to employ those soldiers,
So levied as before, against the Polack:
With an entreaty, herein further shown, [*Giving a paper.*
That it might please you to give quiet pass
Through your dominions for this enterprise,
On such regards of safety and allowance
As therein are set down.
King. It likes us well,
And at our more consider'd time we'll read,
Answer, and think upon this business.
Meantime we thank you for your well-took labour:
Go to your rest; at night we'll feast together:
Most welcome home! [*Exeunt Voltimand and Cornelius.*
Pol. This business is well ended.
My liege, and madam, to expostulate

What majesty should be, what duty is,
Why day is day, night night, and time is time,
Were nothing but to waste night, day and time.
Therefore, since brevity is the soul of wit
And tediousness the limbs and outward flourishes,
I will be brief. Your noble son is mad:
Mad call I it; for, to define true madness,
What is't but to be nothing else but mad?
But let that go.

Queen. More matter, with less art.

Pol. Madam, I swear I use no art at all.
That he is mad, 'tis true: 'tis true 'tis pity,
And pity 'tis 'tis true: a foolish figure;
But farewell it, for I will use no art.
Mad let us grant him then: and now remains
That we find out the cause of this effect,
Or rather say, the cause of this defect,
For this effect defective comes by cause:
Thus it remains and the remainder thus.
Perpend.
I have a daughter,—have while she is mine,—
Who in her duty and obedience, mark,
Hath given me this: now gather and surmise. [*Reads.*
'To the celestial, and my soul's idol, the most beautified Ophelia,'—
That's an ill phrase, a vile phrase; 'beautified' is a vile phrase; but you shall hear. Thus: [*Reads.*
'In her excellent white bosom, these,' &c.

Queen. Came this from Hamlet to her?

Pol. Good madam, stay awhile; I will be faithful. [*Reads.*
'Doubt thou the stars are fire;
Doubt that the sun doth move;
Doubt truth to be a liar;
But never doubt I love.

'O dear Ophelia, I am ill at these numbers; I have not art to reckon my groans: but that I love thee best, O most best, believe it. Adieu.

'Thine evermore, most dear lady, while this machine is to him, HAMLET.'

This in obedience hath my daughter shown me;
And more above, hath his solicitings,
As they fell out by time, by means and place,
All given to mine ear.

King. But how hath she
Received his love?

Pol. What do you think of me?
King. As of a man faithful and honourable.
Pol. I would fain prove so. But what might you think,
When I had seen this hot love on the wing,—
As I perceived it, I must tell you that,
Before my daughter told me,—what might you,
Or my dear majesty your queen here, think,
If I had play'd the desk or table-book,
Or given my heart a winking, mute and dumb,
Or look'd upon this love with idle sight;
What might you think? No, I went round to work,
And my young mistress thus I did bespeak:
'Lord Hamlet is a prince, out of thy star;
This must not be:' and then I prescripts gave her,
That she should lock herself from his resort,
Admit no messengers, receive no tokens.
Which done, she took the fruits of my advice;
And he repulsed, a short tale to make,
Fell into a sadness, then into a fast,
Thence to a watch, thence into a weakness,
Thence to a lightness, and by this declension,
Into the madness wherein now he raves
And all we mourn for.
King. Do you think this?
Queen. It may be, very like.
Pol. Hath there been such a time, I 'ld fain know that,
That I have positively said ''tis so,'
When it proved otherwise?
King. Not that I know.
Pol. [*Pointing to his head and shoulder*] Take this from this, if this be otherwise:
If circumstances lead me, I will find
Where truth is hid, though it were hid indeed
Within the centre.
King. How may we try it further?
Pol. You know, sometimes he walks for hours together
Here in the lobby.
Queen. So he does, indeed.
Pol. At such a time I'll loose my daughter to him:
Be you and I behind an arras then;
Mark the encounter: if he love her not,
And be not from his reason fall'n thereon,
Let me be no assistant for a state,
But keep a farm and carters.
King. We will try it.

Queen. But look where sadly the poor wretch comes reading.

Pol. Away, I do beseech you, both away:
I 'll board him presently.

[*Exeunt King, Queen, and Attendants.*

Enter Hamlet, reading.

O, give me leave: how does my good Lord Hamlet?

Ham. Well, God-a-mercy.

Pol. Do you know me, my lord?

Ham. Excellent well; you are a fishmonger.

Pol. Not I, my lord.

Ham. Then I would you were so honest a man.

Pol. Honest, my lord!

Ham. Ay, sir; to be honest, as this world goes, is to be one man picked out of ten thousand.

Pol. That 's very true, my lord.

Ham. For if the sun breed maggots in a dead dog, being a god kissing carrion—Have you a daughter?

Pol. I have, my lord.

Ham. Let her not walk i' the sun: conception is a blessing; but as your daughter may conceive,—friend, look to 't.

Pol. [*Aside*] How say you by that? Still harping on my daughter: yet he knew me not at first; he said I was a fishmonger: he is far gone: and truly in my youth I suffered much extremity for love; very near this. I 'll speak to him again.—What do you read, my lord?

Ham. Words, words, words.

Pol. What is the matter, my lord?

Ham. Between who?

Pol. I mean, the matter that you read, my lord.

Ham. Slanders, sir: for the satirical rogue says here that old men have grey beards, that their faces are wrinkled, their eyes purging thick amber and plum-tree gum, and that they have a plentiful lack of wit, together with most weak hams: all which, sir, though I most powerfully and potently believe, yet I hold it not honesty to have it thus set down; for yourself, sir, shall grow old as I am, if like a crab you could go backward.

Pol. [*Aside*] Though this be madness, yet there is method in 't.—Will you walk out of the air, my lord?

Ham. Into my grave.

Pol. Indeed, that 's out of the air. [*Aside*] How pregnant sometimes his replies are! a happiness that often madness hits on, which reason and sanity could not so prosperously be delivered of. I will leave him, and suddenly contrive the means of meeting between him and my daughter.—My honourable lord, I will most humbly take my leave of you.

Ham. You cannot, sir, take from me any thing that I will more willingly part withal: except my life, except my life, except my life.

Pol. Fare you well, my lord.

Ham. These tedious old fools!

Enter Rosencrantz and Guildenstern

Pol. You go to seek the Lord Hamlet; there he is.

Ros. [*To Polonius*] God save you, sir! [*Exit Polonius.*

Guil. My honoured lord!

Ros. My most dear lord!

Ham. My excellent good friends! How dost thou, Guildenstern? Ah, Rosencrantz! Good lads, how do you both?

Ros. As the indifferent children of the earth.

Guil. Happy, in that we are not over-happy;
On Fortune's cap we are not the very button.

Ham. Nor the soles of her shoe?

Ros. Neither, my lord.

Ham. Then you live about her waist, or in the middle of her favours?

Guil. Faith, her privates we.

Ham. In the secret parts of Fortune? O, most true; she is a strumpet. What 's the news?

Ros. None, my lord, but that the world 's grown honest.

Ham. Then is doomsday near: but your news is not true. Let me question more in particular: what have you, my good friends, deserved at the hands of Fortune, that she sends you to prison hither?

Guil. Prison, my lord!

Ham. Denmark 's a prison.

Ros. Then is the world one.

Ham. A goodly one; in which there are many confines, wards and dungeons, Denmark being one o' the worst.

Ros. We think not so, my lord.

Ham. Why, then 'tis none to you; for there is nothing either good or bad, but thinking makes it so: to me it is a prison.

Ros. Why, then your ambition makes it one; 'tis too narrow for your mind.

Ham. O God, I could be bounded in a nut-shell and count myself a king of infinite space, were it not that I have bad dreams.

Guil. Which dreams indeed are ambition; for the very substance of the ambitious is merely the shadow of a dream.

Ham. A dream itself is but a shadow.

Ros. Truly, and I hold ambition of so airy and light a quality that it is but a shadow's shadow.

Ham. Then are our beggars bodies, and our monarchs and outstretched heroes the beggars' shadows. Shall we to the court? for, by my fay, I cannot reason.

Ros.
Guil. } We 'll wait upon you.

Ham. No such matter: I will not sort you with the rest of my servants; for, to speak to you like an honest man, I am most dreadfully attended. But, in the beaten way of friendship, what make you at Elsinore?

Ros. To visit you, my lord; no other occasion.

Ham. Beggar that I am, I am even poor in thanks; but I thank you: and sure, dear friends, my thanks are too dear a halfpenny. Were you not sent for? Is it your own inclining? Is it a free visitation? Come, deal justly with me: come, come; nay, speak.

Guil. What should we say, my lord?

Ham. Why, any thing, but to the purpose. You were sent for; and there is a kind of confession in your looks, which your modesties have not craft enough to colour: I know the good king and queen have sent for you.

Ros. To what end, my lord?

Ham. That you must teach me. But let me conjure you, by the rights of our fellowship, by the consonancy of our youth, by the obligation of our ever-preserved love, and by what more dear a better proposer could charge you withal, be even and direct with me, whether you were sent for, or no.

Ros. [*Aside to Guil.*] What say you?

Ham. [*Aside*] Nay then, I have an eye of you.—If you love me, hold not off.

Guil. My lord, we were sent for.

Ham. I will tell you why; so shall my anticipation prevent your discovery, and your secrecy to the king and queen moult no feather. I have of late—but wherefore I know not—lost all my mirth, forgone all custom of exercises; and indeed it goes so heavily with my disposition that this goodly frame, the earth, seems to me a sterile promontory; this most excellent canopy, the air, look you, this brave o'erhanging firmament, this majestical roof fretted with golden fire, why, it appears no other thing to me than a foul and pestilent congregation of vapours. What a piece of work is a man! how noble in reason! how infinite in faculty! in form and moving how express and admirable! in action how like an angel! in apprehension how like a god! the beauty of the world! the paragon of animals! And yet, to me, what is this quintessence of dust? man delights not me; no, nor woman neither, though by your smiling you seem to say so.

Ros. My lord, there was no such stuff in my thoughts.

Ham. Why did you laugh then, when I said 'man delights not me'?

Ros. To think, my lord, if you delight not in man, what lenten entertainment the players shall receive from you: we coted them on the way; and hither are they coming, to offer you service.

Ham. He that plays the king shall be welcome; his majesty shall have tribute of me; the adventurous knight shall use his foil and target; the lover shall not sigh gratis; the humorous man shall end his part in peace; the clown shall make those laugh whose lungs are tickle o' the sere, and the lady shall say her mind freely, or the blank verse shall halt for 't. What players are they?

Ros. Even those you were wont to take such delight in, the tragedians of the city.

Ham. How chances it they travel? their residence, both in reputation and profit, was better both ways.

Ros. I think their inhibition comes by the means of the late [innovation.

Ham. Do they hold the same estimation they did when I was in the city? are they so followed?

Ros. No, indeed, are they not.

Ham. How comes it? do they grow rusty?

Ros. Nay, their endeavour keeps in the wonted pace: but there is, sir, an eyrie of children, little eyases, that cry out on the top of question and are most tyrannically clapped for 't: these are now the fashion, and so berattle the common stages—so they call them—that many wearing rapiers are afraid of goose-quills, and dare scarce come thither.

Ham. What, are they children? who maintains 'em? how are they escoted? Will they pursue the quality no longer than they can sing? will they not say afterwards, if they should grow themselves to common players,—as it is most like, if their means are no better,—their writers do them wrong, to make them exclaim against their own succession?

Ros. Faith, there has been much to do on both sides, and the nation holds it no sin to tarre them to controversy: there was for a while no money bid for argument unless the poet and the player went to cuffs in the question.

Ham. Is 't possible?

Guil. O, there has been much throwing about of brains.

Ham. Do the boys carry it away?

Ros. Ay, that they do, my lord; Hercules and his load too.

Ham. It is not very strange; for my uncle is king of Denmark, and those that would make mows at him while my father lived, give twenty, forty, fifty, a hundred ducats a-piece, for his picture in little. 'Sblood, there is something in this more than natural, if philosophy could find it out. [*Flourish of trumpets within.*

Guil. There are the players.

Ham. Gentlemen, you are welcome to Elsinore. Your hands, come then: the appurtenance of welcome is fashion and ceremony: let me comply with you in this garb, lest my extent to the players, which, I tell you, must show fairly outwards, should more appear like entertainment than yours. You are welcome: but my uncle-father and aunt-mother are deceived.

Guil. In what, my dear lord?

Ham. I am but mad north-north-west: when the wind is southerly I know a hawk from a handsaw.

Re-enter Polonius.

Pol. Well be with you, gentlemen!

Ham. Hark you, Guildenstern; and you too: at each ear a hearer: that great baby you see there is not yet out of his swaddling clouts.

Ros. Happily he's the second time come to them; for they say an old man is twice a child.

Ham. I will prophesy he comes to tell me of the players; mark it. You say right, sir: o' Monday morning; 'twas so, indeed.

Pol. My lord, I have news to tell you.

Ham. My lord, I have news to tell you. When Roscius was an actor in Rome,—

Pol. The actors are come hither, my lord.

Ham. Buz, buz!

Pol. Upon my honour,—

Ham. Then came each actor on his ass,—

Pol. The best actors in the world, either for tragedy, comedy, history, pastoral, pastoral-comical, historical-pastoral, tragical-historical, tragical-comical-historical-pastoral, scene individable, or poem unlimited: Seneca cannot be too heavy, nor Plautus too light. For the law of writ and the liberty, these are the only men.

Ham. O Jephthah, judge of Israel, what a treasure hadst thou!

Pol. What a treasure had he, my lord?

Ham. Why,

'One fair daughter, and no more,
The which he loved passing well.'

Pol. [*Aside*] Still on my daughter.

Ham. Am I not i' the right, old Jephthah?

Pol. If you call me Jephthah, my lord, I have a daughter that I love passing well.

Ham. Nay, that follows not.

Pol. What follows, then, my lord?

Ham. Why,

'As by lot, God wot,'

and then you know,

'It came to pass, as most like it was,'—

the first row of the pious chanson will show you more; for look, where my abridgement comes.

Enter four or five Players.

You are welcome, masters; welcome, all. I am glad to see thee well. Welcome, good friends. O, my old friend! Why thy face is valanced since I saw thee last; comest thou to beard me in Denmark? What, my young lady and mistress! By 'r lady, your ladyship is nearer to heaven than when I saw you last, by the altitude of a chopine. Pray God, your voice, like a piece of uncurrent gold, be not cracked within the ring. Masters, you are all welcome. We 'll e'en to 't like French falconers, fly at any thing we see: we 'll have a speech straight: come, give us a taste of your quality; come, a passionate speech.

First Play. What speech, my good lord?

Ham. I heard thee speak me a speech once, but it was never acted; or, if it was, not above once; for the play, I remember, pleased not the million; 'twas caviare to the general: but it was—as I received it, and others, whose judgements in such matters cried in the top of mine—an excellent play, well digested in the scenes, set down with as much modesty as cunning. I remember, one said there were no sallets in the lines to make the matter savoury, nor no matter in the phrase that might indict the author of affection; but called it an honest method, as wholesome as sweet, and by very much more handsome than fine. One speech in it I chiefly loved: 'twas Æneas' tale to Dido; and thereabout of it especially, where he speaks of Priam's slaughter: if it live in your memory, begin at this line; let me see, let me see;

'The rugged Pyrrhus, like th' Hyrcanian beast,'—

It is not so: it begins with 'Pyrrhus.'

'The rugged Pyrrhus, he whose sable arms,
Black as his purpose, did the night resemble
When he lay couched in the ominous horse,
Hath now this dread and black complexion smear'd
With heraldry more dismal: head to foot

Now is he total gules ; horridly trick'd
With blood of fathers, mothers, daughters, sons,
Baked and impasted with the parching streets
That lend a tyrannous and a damned light
To their lord's murder : roasted in wrath and fire,
And thus o'er-sized with coagulate gore,
With eyes like carbuncles, the hellish Pyrrhus
Old grandsire Priam seeks.'
So, proceed you.

Pol. 'Fore God, my lord, well spoken, with good accent and good discretion.

First Play. 'Anon he finds him
Striking too short at Greeks ; his antique sword,
Rebellious to his arm, lies where it falls,
Repugnant to command : unequal match'd,
Pyrrhus at Priam drives ; in rage strikes wide ;
But with the whiff and wind of his fell sword
The unnerved father falls. Then senseless Ilium,
Seeming to feel this blow, with flaming top
Stoops to his base, and with a hideous crash
Takes prisoner Pyrrhus' ear : for, lo ! his sword,
Which was declining on the milky head
Of reverend Priam, seem'd i' the air to stick :
So, as a painted tyrant, Pyrrhus stood,
And like a neutral to his will and matter,
Did nothing.
But as we often see, against some storm,
A silence in the heavens, the rack stand still,
The bold winds speechless and the orb below
As hush as death, anon the dreadful thunder
Doth rend the region, so after Pyrrhus' pause
Aroused vengeance sets him new a-work ;
And never did the Cyclops' hammers fall
On Mars's armour, forged for proof eterne,
With less remorse than Pyrrhus' bleeding sword
Now falls on Priam.
Out, out, thou strumpet, Fortune ! All you gods,
In general synod take away her power,
Break all the spokes and fellies from her wheel,
And bowl the round nave down the hill of heaven
As low as to the fiends !'

Pol. This is too long.

Ham. It shall to the barber's, with your beard.
Prithee, say on : he's for a jig or a tale of bawdry, or he sleeps : say on : come to Hecuba.

First Play. 'But who, O, who had seen the mobled queen—'

Ham. 'The mobled queen?'

Pol. That's good; 'mobled queen' is good.

First Play. 'Run barefoot up and down, threatening the flames
With bisson rheum; a clout upon that head
Where late the diadem stood; and for a robe,
About her lank and all o'er-teemed loins,
A blanket, in the alarm of fear caught up:
Who this had seen, with tongue in venom steep'd
'Gainst Fortune's state would treason have pronounced:
But if the gods themselves did see her then,
When she saw Pyrrhus make malicious sport
In mincing with his sword her husband's limbs,
The instant burst of clamour that she made,
Unless things mortal move them not at all,
Would have made milch the burning eyes of heaven
And passion in the gods.'

Pol. Look, whether he has not turned his colour and has tears in 's eyes. Prithee, no more.

Ham. 'Tis well; I'll have thee speak out the rest of this soon. Good my lord, will you see the players well bestowed? Do you hear, let them be well used, for they are the abstract and brief chronicles of the time: after your death you were better have a bad epitaph than their ill report while you live.

Pol. My lord, I will use them according to their desert.

Ham. God's bodykins, man, much better: use every man after his desert, and who shall 'scape whipping? Use them after your own honour and dignity: the less they deserve, the more merit is in your bounty. Take them in.

Pol. Come, sirs.

Ham. Follow him, friends: we'll hear a play to-morrow. [*Exit Polonius with all the Players but the First.*] Dost thou hear me, old friend; can you play the Murder of Gonzago?

First Play. Ay, my lord.

Ham. We'll ha't to-morrow night. You could, for a need, study a speech of some dozen or sixteen lines, which I would set down and insert in't, could you not?

First Play. Ay, my lord.

Ham. Very well. Follow that lord; and look you mock him not. [*Exit First Player.*] My good friends, I'll leave you till night: you are welcome to Elsinore.

Ros. Good my lord!

Ham. Ay, so, God be wi' ye! [*Exeunt Rosencrantz and Guildenstern.*] Now I am alone.

O, what a rogue and peasant slave am I!
Is it not monstrous that this player here,
But in a fiction, in a dream of passion,
Could force his soul so to his own conceit
That from her working all his visage wann'd;
Tears in his eyes, distraction in 's aspect,
A broken voice, and his whole function suiting
With forms to his conceit? and all for nothing!
For Hecuba!
What 's Hecuba to him, or he to Hecuba,
That he should weep for her? What would he do,
Had he the motive and the cue for passion
That I have? He would drown the stage with tears
And cleave the general ear with horrid speech,
Make mad the guilty and appal the free,
Confound the ignorant, and amaze indeed
The very faculties of eyes and ears.
Yet I,
A dull and muddy mettled rascal, peak,
Like John-a-dreams, unpregnant of my cause,
And can say nothing; no, not for a king,
Upon whose property and most dear life
A damn'd defeat was made. Am I a coward?
Who calls me villain? breaks my pate across?
Plucks off my beard, and blows it in my face?
Tweaks me by the nose? gives me the lie i' the throat,
As deep as to the lungs? who does me this?
Ha!
'Swounds, I should take it: for it cannot be
But I am pigeon-liver'd and lack gall
To make oppression bitter, or ere this
I should have fatted all the region kites
With this slave's offal: bloody, bawdy villain!
Remorseless, treacherous, lecherous, kindless villain!
O, vengeance!
Why, what an ass am I! This is most brave,
That I, the son of a dear father murder'd,
Prompted to my revenge by heaven and hell,
Must, like a whore, unpack my heart with words,
And fall a-cursing, like a very drab,
A scullion!
Fie upon 't! foh! About, my brain! Hum, I have heard
That guilty creatures, sitting at a play,
Have by the very cunning of the scene
Been struck so to the soul that presently

They have proclaim'd their malefactions;
For murder, though it have no tongue, will speak
With most miraculous organ. I 'll have these players
Play something like the murder of my father
Before mine uncle: I 'll observe his looks;
I 'll tent him to the quick: if he but blench,
I know my course. The spirit that I have seen
May be the devil; and the devil hath power
To assume a pleasing shape; yea, and perhaps
Out of my weakness and my melancholy,
As he is very potent with such spirits,
Abuses me to damn me. I 'll have grounds
More relative than this. The play 's the thing
Wherein I 'll catch the conscience of the king. [*Exit.*

ACT III—Scene I

A room in the castle.

Enter King, Queen, Polonius, Ophelia, Rosencrantz, and Guildenstern.

King. And can you, by no drift of circumstance,
Get from him why he puts on this confusion,
Grating so hardly all his days of quiet
With turbulent and dangerous lunacy?
Ros. He does confess he feels himself distracted,
But from what cause he will by no means speak.
Guil. Nor do we find him forward to be sounded;
But, with a crafty madness, keeps aloof,
When we would bring him on to some confession
Of his true state.
Queen. Did he receive you well?
Ros. Most like a gentleman.
Guil. But with much forcing of his disposition.
Ros. Niggard of question, but of our demands
Most free in his reply.
Queen. Did you assay him
To any pastime?
Ros. Madam, it so fell out that certain players
We o'er-raught on the way: of these we told him,
And there did seem in him a kind of joy
To hear of it: they are about the court,
And, as I think, they have already order
This night to play before him.
Pol. 'Tis most true:
And he beseech'd me to entreat your majesties

To hear and see the matter.

King. With all my heart; and it doth much content me
To hear him so inclined.
Good gentlemen, give him a further edge,
And drive his purpose on to these delights.

Ros. We shall, my lord. [*Exeunt Rosencrantz and Guildenstern.*

King. Sweet Gertrude, leave us too;
For we have closely sent for Hamlet hither,
That he, as 'twere by accident, may here
Affront Ophelia:
Her father and myself, lawful espials,
Will so bestow ourselves that, seeing unseen,
We may of their encounter frankly judge,
And gather by him, as he is behaved,
If 't be the affliction of his love or no
That thus he suffers for.

Queen. I shall obey you:
And for your part, Ophelia, I do wish
That your good beauties be the happy cause
Of Hamlet's wildness: so shall I hope your virtues
Will bring him to his wonted way again,
To both your honours.

Oph. Madam, I wish it may. [*Exit Queen.*

Pol. Ophelia, walk you here. Gracious, so please you,
We will bestow ourselves. [*To Ophelia*] Read on this book;
That show of such an exercise may colour
Your loneliness. We are oft to blame in this,—
'Tis too much proved—that with devotion's visage
And pious action we do sugar o'er
The devil himself.

King. [*Aside*] O, 'tis too true;
How smart a lash that speech doth give my conscience!
The harlot's cheek, beautied with plastering art,
Is not more ugly to the thing that helps it
Than is my deed to my most painted word:
O heavy burthen!

Pol. I hear him coming: let 's withdraw, my lord.
[*Exeunt King and Polonius.*

Enter Hamlet.

Ham. To be, or not to be: that is the question:
Whether 'tis nobler in the mind to suffer
The slings and arrows of outrageous fortune,
Or to take arms against a sea of troubles,
And by opposing end them. To die: to sleep;
No more; and by a sleep to say we end

The heart-ache, and the thousand natural shocks
That flesh is heir to, 'tis a consummation
Devoutly to be wish'd. To die, to sleep;
To sleep: perchance to dream: ay, there 's the rub;
For in that sleep of death what dreams may come,
When we have shuffled off this mortal coil,
Must give us pause: there 's the respect
That makes calamity of so long life;
For who would bear the whips and scorns of time.
The oppressor's wrong, the proud man's contumely,
The pangs of despised love, the law's delay,
The insolence of office, and the spurns
That patient merit of the unworthy takes,
When he himself might his quietus make
With a bare bodkin? who would fardels bear,
To grunt and sweat under a weary life,
But that the dread of something after death,
The undiscover'd country from whose bourn
No traveller returns, puzzles the will,
And makes us rather bear those ills we have
Than fly to others that we know not of?
Thus conscience does make cowards of us all,
And thus the native hue of resolution
Is sicklied o'er with the pale cast of thought,
And enterprises of great pitch and moment
With this regard their currents turn awry
And lose the name of action. Soft you now!
The fair Ophelia! Nymph, in thy orisons
Be all my sins remember'd.

Oph. Good my lord,
How does your honour for this many a day?

Ham. I humbly thank you: well, well, well.

Oph. My lord, I have remembrances of yours,
That I have longed long to re-deliver;
I pray you, now receive them.

Ham. No, not I:
I never gave you aught.

Oph. My honour'd lord, you know right well you did;
And with them words of so sweet breath composed
As made the things more rich: their perfume lost,
Take these again; for to the noble mind
Rich gifts wax poor when givers prove unkind.
There, my lord.

Ham. Ha, ha! are you honest?

Oph. My lord?

Ham. Are you fair?

Oph. What means your lordship?

Ham. That if you be honest and fair, your honesty should admit no discourse to your beauty.

Oph. Could beauty, my lord, have better commerce than with honesty?

Ham. Ay, truly; for the power of beauty will sooner transform honesty from what it is to a bawd than the force of honesty can translate beauty into his likeness: this was sometime a paradox, but now the time gives it proof. I did love you once.

Oph. Indeed, my lord, you made me believe so.

Ham. You should not have believed me; for virtue cannot so inoculate our old stock but we shall relish of it: I loved you not.

Oph. I was the more deceived.

Ham. Get thee to a nunnery: why wouldst thou be a breeder of sinners? I am myself indifferent honest; but yet I could accuse me of such things that it were better my mother had not borne me: I am very proud, revengeful, ambitious; with more offences at my beck than I have thoughts to put them in, imagination to give them shape, or time to act them in. What should such fellows as I do crawling between heaven and earth! We are arrant knaves all; believe none of us. Go thy ways to a nunnery. Where 's your father?

Oph. At home, my lord.

Ham. Let the doors be shut upon him, that he may play the fool no where but in 's own house. Farewell.

Oph. O, help him, you sweet heavens!

Ham. If thou dost marry, I 'll give thee this plague for thy dowry: be thou as chaste as ice, as pure as snow, thou shalt not escape calumny. Get thee to a nunnery, go: farewell. Or, if thou wilt needs marry, marry a fool; for wise men know well enough what monsters you make of them. To a nunnery, go; and quickly too. Farewell.

Oph. O heavenly powers, restore him!

Ham. I have heard of your paintings too, well enough; God hath given you one face, and you make yourselves another: you jig, you amble, and you lisp, and nick-name God's creatures, and make your wantonness your ignorance. Go to, I 'll no more on 't; it hath made me mad. I say, we will have no more marriages: those that are married already, all but one, shall live; the rest shall keep as they are. To a nunnery, go. [*Exit.*

Oph. O, what a noble mind is here o'erthrown!
The courtier's, soldier's, scholar's, eye, tongue, sword:
The expectancy and rose of the fair state,
The glass of fashion and the mould of form,

The observed of all observers, quite, quite down!
And I, of ladies most deject and wretched,
That suck'd the honey of his music vows,
Now see that noble and most sovereign reason,
Like sweet bells jangled, out of tune and harsh;
That unmatch'd form and feature of blown youth
Blasted with ecstasy: O, woe is me,
To have seen what I have seen, see what I see!

Re-enter King and Polonius.

King. Love! his affections do not that way tend;
Nor what he spake, though it lack'd form a little,
Was not like madness. There 's something in his soul
O'er which his melancholy sits on brood,
And I do doubt the hatch and the disclose
Will be some danger: which for to prevent,
I have in quick determination
Thus set it down:—he shall with speed to England,
For the demand of our neglected tribute:
Haply the seas and countries different
With variable objects shall expel
This something-settled matter in his heart,
Whereon his brains still beating puts him thus
From fashion of himself. What think you on 't?

Pol. It shall do well: but yet do I believe
The origin and commencement of his grief
Sprung from neglected love. How now, Ophelia!
You need not tell us what Lord Hamlet said;
We heard it all. My lord, do as you please;
But, if you hold it fit, after the play,
Let his queen mother all alone entreat him
To show his grief: let her be round with him;
And I 'll be placed, so please you, in the ear
Of all their conference. If she find him not,
To England send him, or confine him where
Your wisdom best shall think.

King. It shall be so:
Madness in great ones must not unwatch'd go. [*Exeunt.*

Scene II

A hall in the castle.

Enter Hamlet and Players.

Ham. Speak the speech, I pray you, as I pronounced it to you, trippingly on the tongue: but if you mouth it, as many of your players do, I had as lief the town-crier spoke my lines.

Nor do not saw the air too much with your hand, thus; but use all gently: for in the very torrent, tempest, and, as I may say, whirlwind of your passion, you must acquire and beget a temperance that may give it smoothness. O, it offends me to the soul to hear a robustious periwig-pated fellow tear a passion to tatters, to very rags, to split the ears of the groundlings, who, for the most part, are capable of nothing but inexplicable dumb-shows and noise: I would have such a fellow whipped for o'erdoing Termagant; it out-herods Herod: pray you, avoid it.

First Play. I warrant your honour.

Ham. Be not too tame neither, but let your own discretion be your tutor: suit the action to the word, the word to the action; with this special observance, that you o'erstep not the modesty of nature: for anything so overdone is from the purpose of playing, whose end, both at the first and now, was and is, to hold, as 'twere, the mirror up to nature; to show virtue her own feature, scorn her own image, and the very age and body of the time his form and pressure. Now this overdone or come tardy off, though it make the unskilful laugh, cannot but make the judicious grieve; the censure of the which one must in your allowance o'erweigh a whole theatre of others. O, there be players that I have seen play, and heard others praise, and that highly, not to speak it profanely, that neither having the accent of Christians nor the gait of Christian, pagan, nor man, have so strutted and bellowed, that I have thought some of nature's journeymen had made men, and not made them well, they imitated humanity so abominably.

First Play. I hope we have reformed that indifferently with us, sir.

Ham. O, reform it altogether. And let those that play your clowns speak no more than is set down for them: for there be of them that will themselves laugh, to set on some quantity of barren spectators to laugh too, though in the mean time some necessary question of the play be then to be considered: that 's villainous, and shows a most pitiful ambition in the fool that uses it. Go, make you ready. [*Exeunt Players.*

Enter Polonius, Rosencrantz, and Guildenstern.

How now, my lord! will the king hear this piece of work?

Pol. And the queen too, and that presently.

Ham. Bid the players make haste. [*Exit Polonius*

Will you two help to hasten them?

Ros.
Guil. } We will, my lord.

[*Exeunt Rosencrantz and Guildenstern.*

Ham. What ho! Horatio!

Enter Horatio.

Hor. Here, sweet lord, at your service.
Ham. Horatio, thou art e'en as just a man
As e'er my conversation coped withal.
Hor. O, my dear lord,—
Ham. Nay, do not think I flatter;
For what advancement may I hope from thee,
That no revenue hast but thy good spirits,
To feed and clothe thee? Why should the poor be flatter'd?
No, let the candied tongue lick absurd pomp,
And crook the pregnant hinges of the knee
Where thrift may follow fawning. Dost thou hear?
Since my dear soul was mistress of her choice,
And could of men distinguish, her election
Hath seal'd thee for herself: for thou hast been
As one, in suffering all, that suffers nothing;
A man that fortune's buffets and rewards
Hast ta'en with equal thanks: and blest are those
Whose blood and judgement are so well commingled
That they are not a pipe for fortune's finger
To sound what stop she please. Give me that man
That is not passion's slave, and I will wear him
In my heart's core, ay, in my heart of heart,
As I do thee. Something too much of this.
There is a play to-night before the king;
One scene of it comes near the circumstance
Which I have told thee of my father's death:
I prithee, when thou seest that act a-foot,
Even with the very comment of thy soul
Observe my uncle: if his occulted guilt
Do not itself unkennel in one speech,
It is a damned ghost that we have seen,
And my imaginations are as foul
As Vulcan's stithy. Give him heedful note;
For I mine eyes will rivet to his face,
And after we will both our judgements join
In censure of his seeming.
Hor. Well, my lord:
If he steal aught the whilst this play is playing,
And 'scape detecting, I will pay the theft.
Ham. They are coming to the play: I must be idle:

Get you a place.

Danish march. A flourish. Enter King, Queen, Polonius, Ophelia, Rosencrantz, Guildenstern, and other Lords attendant, with the Guard carrying torches.

King. How fares our cousin Hamlet?

Ham. Excellent, i' faith; of the chameleon's dish: I eat the air, promise-crammed: you cannot feed capons so.

King. I have nothing with this answer, Hamlet; these words are not mine.

Ham. No, nor mine now. [*To Polonius*] My lord, you played once i' the university, you say?

Pol. That did I, my lord, and was accounted a good actor.

Ham. What did you enact?

Pol. I did enact Julius Cæsar: I was killed i' the Capitol; Brutus killed me.

Ham. It was a brute part of him to kill so capital a calf there. Be the players ready?

Ros. Ay, my lord; they stay upon your patience.

Queen. Come hither, my dear Hamlet, sit by me.

Ham. No, good mother, here 's metal more attractive.

Pol. [*To the King*] O, ho! do you mark that?

Ham. Lady, shall I lie in your lap?

[*Lying down at Ophelia's feet.*

Oph. No, my lord.

Ham. I mean, my head upon your lap?

Oph. Ay, my lord.

Ham. Do you think I mean country matters?

Oph. I think nothing, my lord.

Ham. That 's a fair thought to lie between maids' legs.

Oph. What is, my lord?

Ham. Nothing.

Oph. You are merry, my lord.

Ham. Who, I?

Oph. Ay, my lord.

Ham. O God, your only jig-maker. What should a man do but be merry? for, look you, how cheerfully my mother looks, and my father died within 's two hours.

Oph. Nay, 'tis twice two months, my lord.

Ham. So long? Nay then, let the devil wear black, for I 'll have a suit of sables. O heavens! die two months ago, and not forgotten yet? Then there 's hope a great man's memory may outlive his life half a year: but, by 'r lady, he must build churches then; or else shall he suffer not thinking on, with the hobby-horse, whose epitaph is, 'For, O, for, O, the hobby-horse is forgot.'

Hautboys play. The dumb-show enters.

Enter a King and a Queen very lovingly; the Queen embracing him, and he her. She kneels, and makes show of protestation unto him. He takes her up, and declines his head upon her neck: lays him down upon a bank of flowers: she, seeing him asleep, leaves him. Anon comes in a fellow, takes off his crown, kisses it, and pours poison in the King's ears, and exit. The Queen returns; finds the King dead, and makes passionate action. The Poisoner, with some two or three Mutes, comes in again, seeming to lament with her. The dead body is carried away. The Poisoner wooes the Queen with gifts: she seems loath and unwilling awhile, but in the end accepts his love. [*Exeunt.*

Oph. What means this, my lord?

Ham. Marry, this is miching mallecho; it means mischief.

Oph. Belike this show imports the argument of the play.

Enter Prologue.

Ham. We shall know by this fellow: the players cannot keep counsel; they 'll tell all.

Oph. Will he tell us what this show meant?

Ham. Ay, or any show that you 'll show him: be not you ashamed to show, he 'll not shame to tell you what it means.

Oph. You are naught, you are naught: I 'll mark the play.

Pro. For us, and for our tragedy,
Here stooping to your clemency
We beg your hearing patiently.

Ham. Is this a prologue, or the posy of a ring?

Oph. 'Tis brief, my lord.

Ham. As woman's love.

Enter two Players, King and Queen.

P. King. Full thirty times hath Phœbus' cart gone round
Neptune's salt wash and Tellus' orbed ground,
And thirty dozen moons with borrowed sheen
About the world have times twelve thirties been,
Since love our hearts and Hymen did our hands
Unite commutual in most sacred bands.

P. Queen. So many journeys may the sun and moon
Make us again count o'er ere love be done!
But, woe is me, you are so sick of late,
So far from cheer and from your former state,
That I distrust you. Yet, though I distrust,
Discomfort you, my lord, it nothing must:
For women's fear and love holds quantity,
In neither aught, or in extremity.
Now, what my love is, proof hath made you know,

And as my love is sized, my fear is so:
Where love is great, the littlest doubts are fear,
Where little fears grow great, great love grows there.
P. King. Faith, I must leave thee, love, and shortly too;
My operant powers their functions leave to do:
And thou shalt live in this fair world behind,
Honour'd, beloved; and haply one as kind
For husband shalt thou—
P. Queen. O, confound the rest!
Such love must needs be treason in my breast:
In second husband let me be accurst!
None wed the second but who kill'd the first.
Ham. [*Aside*] Wormwood, wormwood.
P. Queen. The instances that second marriage move
Are base respects of thrift, but none of love:
A second time I kill my husband dead,
When second husband kisses me in bed.
P. King. I do believe you think what now you speak,
But what we do determine oft we break.
Purpose is but the slave to memory,
Of violent birth but poor validity:
Which now, like fruit unripe, sticks on the tree,
But fall unshaken when they mellow be.
Most necessary 'tis that we forget
To pay ourselves what to ourselves is debt:
What to ourselves in passion we propose,
The passion ending, doth the purpose lose.
The violence of either grief or joy
Their own enactures with themselves destroy:
Where joy most revels, grief doth most lament;
Grief joys, joy grieves, on slender accident.
This world is not for aye, nor 'tis not strange
That even our loves should with our fortunes change,
For 'tis a question left us yet to prove,
Whether love lead fortune or else fortune love.
The great man down, you mark his favourite flies;
The poor advanced makes friends of enemies:
And hitherto doth love on fortune tend;
For who not needs shall never lack a friend,
And who in want a hollow friend doth try
Directly seasons him his enemy.
But, orderly to end where I begun,
Our wills and fates do so contrary run,
That our devices still are overthrown,
Our thoughts are ours, their ends none of our own:

So think thou wilt no second husband wed,
But die thy thoughts when thy first lord is dead.

P. Queen. Nor earth to me give food nor heaven light!
Sport and repose lock from me day and night!
To desperation turn my trust and hope!
An anchor's cheer in prison be my scope!
Each opposite, that blanks the face of joy,
Meet what I would have well and it destroy!
Both here and hence pursue me lasting strife,
If, once a widow, ever I be wife!

Ham. If she should break it now!

P. King. 'Tis deeply sworn. Sweet, leave me here a while;
My spirits grow dull, and fain I would beguile
The tedious day with sleep. [*Sleeps.*

P. Queen. Sleep rock thy brain;
And never come mischance between us twain! [*Exit.*

Ham. Madam, how like you this play?

Queen. The lady doth protest too much, methinks.

Ham. O, but she 'll keep her word.

King. Have you heard the argument? Is there no offence in 't?

Ham. No, no, they do but jest, poison in jest; no offence i' the world.

King. What do you call the play?

Ham. The Mouse-trap. Marry, how? Tropically. This play is the image of a murder done in Vienna: Gonzago is the duke's name: his wife, Baptista: you shall see anon; 'tis a knavish piece of work; but what o' that? your majesty, and we that have free souls, it touches us not: let the galled jade wince, our withers are unwrung.

Enter Lucianus.

This is one Lucianus, nephew to the king.

Oph. You are as good as a chorus, my lord.

Ham. I could interpret between you and your love, if I could see the puppets dallying.

Oph. You are keen, my lord, you are keen.

Ham. It would cost you a groaning to take off my edge.

Oph. Still better and worse.

Ham. So you must take your husbands. Begin, murderer; pox, leave thy damnable faces, and begin. Come: the croaking raven doth bellow for revenge.

Luc. Thoughts black, hands apt, drugs fit, and time agreeing;
Confederate season, else no creature seeing;
Thou mixture rank, of midnight weeds collected,
With Hecate's ban thrice blasted, thrice infected,
Thy natural magic and dire property,

On wholesome life usurp immediately.

[*Pours the poison into the sleeper's ear.*

Ham. He poisons him i' the garden for his estate. His name 's Gonzago: the story is extant, and written in very choice Italian: you shall see anon how the murderer gets the love of Gonzago's wife.

Oph. The king rises.

Ham. What, frighted with false fire!

Queen. How fares my lord?

Pol. Give o'er the play.

King. Give me some light. Away!

Pol. Lights, lights, lights!

[*Exeunt all but Hamlet and Horatio.*

Ham. Why, let the stricken deer go weep,
The hart ungalled play;
For some must watch, while some must sleep:
Thus runs the world away.

Would not this, sir, and a forest of feathers—if the rest of my fortunes turn Turk with me—with two Provincial roses on my razed shoes, get me a fellowship in a cry of players, sir?

Hor. Half a share.

Ham. A whole one, I.
For thou dost know, O Damon dear,
This realm dismantled was
Of Jove himself; and now reigns here
A very, very—pajock.

Hor. You might have rhymed.

Ham. O good Horatio, I 'll take the ghost's word for a thousand pound. Didst perceive?

Hor. Very well, my lord.

Ham. Upon the talk of the poisoning?

Hor. I did very well note him.

Ham. Ah, ha! Come, some music! come, the recorders!
For if the king like not the comedy,
Why then, belike, he likes it not, perdy.
Come, some music!

Re-enter Rosencrantz and Guildenstern.

Guil. Good my lord, vouchsafe me a word with you.

Ham. Sir, a whole history.

Guil. The king, sir,—

Ham. Ay, sir, what of him?

Guil. Is in his retirement marvellous distempered.

Ham. With drink, sir?

Guil. No, my lord, rather with choler.

Ham. Your wisdom should show itself more richer to signify this to the doctor; for, for me to put him to his purgation would perhaps plunge him into far more choler.

Guil. Good my lord, put your discourse into some frame, and start not so wildly from my affair.

Ham. I am tame, sir: pronounce.

Guil. The queen, your mother, in most great affliction of spirit, hath sent me to you.

Ham. You are welcome.

Guil. Nay, good my lord, this courtesy is not of the right breed. If it shall please you to make me a wholesome answer, I will do your mother's commandment: if not, your pardon and my return shall be the end of my business.

Ham. Sir, I cannot.

Guil. What, my lord?

Ham. Make you a wholesome answer; my wit 's diseased: but, sir, such answer as I can make, you shall command; or rather, as you say, my mother: therefore no more, but to the matter: my mother, you say,—

Ros. Then thus she says; your behaviour hath struck her into amazement and admiration.

Ham. O wonderful son, that can so astonish a mother! But is there no sequel at the heels of this mother's admiration? Impart.

Ros. She desires to speak with you in her closet, ere you go to [bed.

Ham. We shall obey, were she ten times our mother. Have you any further trade with us?

Ros. My lord, you once did love me.

Ham. So I do still, by these pickers and stealers.

Ros. Good my lord, what is your cause of distemper? you do surely bar the door upon your own liberty, if you deny your griefs to your friend.

Ham. Sir, I lack advancement.

Ros. How can that be, when you have the voice of the king himself for your succession in Denmark?

Ham. Ay, sir, but 'while the grass grows,'—the proverb is something musty.

Re-enter Players with recorders.

O, the recorders! let me see one. To withdraw with you:—why do you go about to recover the wind of me, as if you would drive me into a toil?

Guil. O, my lord, if my duty be too bold, my love is too unmannerly.

Ham. I do not well understand that. Will you play upon this [pipe?

Guil. My lord, I cannot.

Ham. I pray you.

Guil. Believe me, I cannot.

Ham. I do beseech you.

Guil. I know no touch of it, my lord.

Ham. It is as easy as lying: govern these ventages with your fingers and thumb, give it breath with your mouth, and it will discourse most eloquent music. Look you, these are the stops.

Guil. But these cannot I command to any utterance of harmony; I have not the skill.

Ham. Why, look you now, how unworthy a thing you make of me! You would play upon me; you would seem to know my stops; you would pluck out the heart of my mystery; you would sound me from my lowest note to the top of my compass: and there is much music, excellent voice, in this little organ; yet cannot you make it speak. 'Sblood, do you think I am easier to be played on than a pipe? Call me what instrument you will, though you can fret me, yet you cannot play upon me.

Re-enter Polonius.

God bless you, sir!

Pol. My lord, the queen would speak with you, and presently.

Ham. Do you see yonder cloud that's almost in shape of a camel?

Pol. By the mass, and 'tis like a camel, indeed.

Ham. Methinks it is like a weasel.

Pol. It is backed like a weasel.

Ham. Or like a whale?

Pol. Very like a whale.

Ham. Then I will come to my mother by and by. They fool me to the top of my bent. I will come by and by.

Pol. I will say so. [*Exit Polonius.*

Ham. 'By and by' is easily said. Leave me, friends.

[*Exeunt all but Hamlet.*

'Tis now the very witching time of night,
When churchyards yawn, and hell itself breathes out
Contagion to this world: now could I drink hot blood,
And do such bitter business as the day
Would quake to look on. Soft! now to my mother.
O heart, lose not thy nature; let not ever
The soul of Nero enter this firm bosom:
Let me be cruel, not unnatural:
I will speak daggers to her, but use none;
My tongue and soul in this be hypocrites;
How in my words soever she be shent,
To give them seals never, my soul, consent! [*Exit*

Scene III

A room in the castle.

Enter King, Rosencrantz, and Guildenstern.

King. I like him not, nor stands it safe with us
To let his madness range. Therefore prepare you;
I your commission will forthwith dispatch,
And he to England shall along with you:
The terms of our estate may not endure
Hazard so near us as doth hourly grow
Out of his lunacies.

Guil. We will ourselves provide:
Most holy and religious fear it is
To keep those many many bodies safe
That live and feed upon your majesty.

Ros. The single and peculiar life is bound
With all the strength and armour of the mind
To keep itself from noyance; but much more
That spirit upon whose weal depends and rests
The lives of many. The cease of majesty
Dies not alone, but like a gulf doth draw
What's near it with it: it is a massy wheel,
Fix'd on the summit of the highest mount,
To whose huge spokes ten thousand lesser things
Are mortised and adjoin'd; which, when it falls,
Each small annexment, petty consequence,
Attends the boisterous ruin. Never alone
Did the king sigh, but with a general groan.

King. Arm you, I pray you, to this speedy voyage,
For we will fetters put about this fear,
Which now goes too free-footed.

Ros.
Guil. } We will haste us.

[*Exeunt Rosencrantz and Guildenstern.*

Enter Polonius.

Pol. My lord, he's going to his mother's closet:
Behind the arras I'll convey myself,
To hear the process: I'll warrant she'll tax him home:
And, as you said, and wisely was it said,
'Tis meet that some more audience than a mother,
Since nature makes them partial, should o'erhear
The speech, of vantage. Fare you well, my liege:
I'll call upon you ere you go to bed,
And tell you what I know.

King. Thanks, dear my lord.
[*Exit Polonius.*

O, my offence is rank, it smells to heaven;
It hath the primal eldest curse upon 't,
A brother's murder. Pray can I not,
Though inclination be as sharp as will:
My stronger guilt defeats my strong intent,
And like a man to double business bound,
I stand in pause where I shall first begin,
And both neglect. What if this cursed hand
Were thicker than itself with brother's blood,
Is there not rain enough in the sweet heavens
To wash it white as snow? Whereto serves mercy
But to confront the visage of offence?
And what 's in prayer but this two-fold force,
To be forestalled ere we come to fall,
Or pardon'd being down? Then I 'll look up;
My fault is past. But O, what form of prayer
Can serve my turn? 'Forgive me my foul murder?'
That cannot be, since I am still possess'd
Of those effects for which I did the murder,
My crown, mine own ambition and my queen.
May one be pardon'd and retain the offence?
In the corrupted currents of this world
Offence's gilded hand may shove by justice,
And oft 'tis seen the wicked prize itself
Buys out the law: but 'tis not so above;
There is no shuffling, there the action lies
In his true nature, and we ourselves compell'd
Even to the teeth and forehead of our faults
To give in evidence. What then? what rests?
Try what repentance can: what can it not?
Yet what can it when one can not repent?
O wretched state! O bosom black as death!
O limed soul, that struggling to be free
Art more engaged! Help, angels! make assay!
Bow, stubborn knees, and, heart with strings of steel,
Be soft as sinews of the new-born babe!
All may be well. [*Retires and kneels.*

Enter Hamlet.

Ham. Now might I do it pat, now he is praying;
And now I 'll do 't: and so he goes to heaven:
And so am I revenged. That would be scann'd;
A villain kills my father; and for that,
I, his sole son, do this same villain send

To heaven.
O, this is hire and salary, not revenge.
He took my father grossly, full of bread,
With all his crimes broad blown, as flush as May;
And how his audit stands who knows save heaven?
But in our circumstance and course of thought,
'Tis heavy with him: and am I then revenged,
To take him in the purging of his soul,
When he is fit and season'd for his passage?
No.
Up, sword, and know thou a more horrid hent:
When he is drunk, asleep, or in his rage,
Or in the incestuous pleasure of his bed;
At game, a-swearing, or about some act
That has no relish of salvation in 't;
Then trip him, that his heels may kick at heaven
And that his soul may be as damn'd and black
As hell, whereto it goes. My mother stays:
This physic but prolongs thy sickly days. [*Exit.*

King. [*Rising*] My words fly up, my thoughts remain below:
Words without thoughts never to heaven go. [*Exit.*

Scene IV

The Queen's closet.

Enter Queen and Polonius.

Pol. He will come straight. Look you lay home to him:
Tell him his pranks have been too broad to bear with,
And that your grace hath screen'd and stood between
Much heat and him. I'll sconce me even here.
Pray you, be round with him.

Ham. [*Within*] Mother, mother, mother!

Queen. I'll warrant you; fear me not. Withdraw, I hear him coming. [*Polonius hides behind the arras.*

Enter Hamlet.

Ham. Now, mother, what's the matter?

Queen. Hamlet, thou hast thy father much offended.

Ham. Mother, you have my father much offended.

Queen. Come, come, you answer with an idle tongue.

Ham. Go, go, you question with a wicked tongue.

Queen. Why, how now, Hamlet!

Ham. What's the matter now?

Queen. Have you forgot me?

Ham. No, by the rood, not so:
You are the queen, your husband's brother's wife;
And—would it were not so!—you are my mother.

Queen. Nay, then, I'll set those to you that can speak.
Ham. Come, come, and sit you down; you shall not budge;
You go not till I set you up a glass
Where you may see the inmost part of you.
Queen. What wilt thou do? thou wilt not murder me?
Help, help, ho!
Pol. [*Behind*] What, ho! help, help, help!
Ham. [*Drawing*] How now! a rat? Dead, for a ducat, dead!
[*Makes a pass through the arras.*
Pol. [*Behind*] O, I am slain! [*Falls and dies.*
Queen. O me, what hast thou done?
Ham. Nay, I know not: is it the king?
Queen. O, what a rash and bloody deed is this!
Ham. A bloody deed! almost as bad, good mother,
As kill a king, and marry with his brother.
Queen. As kill a king!
Ham. Ay, lady, 'twas my word.
[*Lifts up the arras and discovers Polonius.*
Thou wretched, rash, intruding fool, farewell!
I took thee for thy better: take thy fortune;
Thou find'st to be too busy is some danger.
Leave wringing of your hands: peace! sit you down,
And let me wring your heart: for so I shall,
If it be made of penetrable stuff;
If damned custom have not brass'd it so,
That it be proof and bulwark against sense.
Queen. What have I done, that thou darest wag thy tongue
In noise so rude against me?
Ham. Such an act
That blurs the grace and blush of modesty,
Calls virtue hypocrite, takes off the rose
From the fair forehead of an innocent love,
And sets a blister there; makes marriage vows
As false as dicers' oaths: O, such a deed
As from the body of contraction plucks
The very soul, and sweet religion makes
A rhapsody of words: heaven's face doth glow;
Yea, this solidity and compound mass,
With tristful visage, as against the doom,
Is thought-sick at the act.
Queen. Ay me, what act,
That roars so loud and thunders in the index?
Ham. Look here, upon this picture, and on this,
The counterfeit presentment of two brothers.
See what a grace was seated on this brow;

Hyperion's curls, the front of Jove himself,
An eye like Mars, to threaten and command;
A station like the herald Mercury
New-lighted on a heaven-kissing hill;
A combination and a form indeed,
Where every god did seem to set his seal
To give the world assurance of a man:
This was your husband. Look you now, what follows:
Here is your husband; like a mildew'd ear,
Blasting his wholesome brother. Have you eyes?
Could you on this fair mountain leave to feed,
And batten on this moor? Ha! have you eyes?
You cannot call it love, for at your age
The hey-day in the blood is tame, it 's humble,
And waits upon the judgement: and what judgement
Would step from this to this? Sense sure you have,
Else could you not have motion: but sure that sense
Is apoplex'd: for madness would not err,
Nor sense to ecstasy was ne'er so thrall'd
But it reserved some quantity of choice,
To serve in such a difference. What devil was 't
That thus hath cozen'd you at hoodman-blind?
Eyes without feeling, feeling without sight,
Ears without hands or eyes, smelling sans all,
Or but a sickly part of one true sense
Could not so mope.
O shame! where is thy blush? Rebellious hell,
If thou canst mutine in a matron's bones,
To flaming youth let virtue be as wax
And melt in her own fire: proclaim no shame
When the compulsive ardour gives the charge,
Since frost itself as actively doth burn,
And reason pandars will.

Queen. O Hamlet, speak no more:
Thou turn'st mine eyes into my very soul,
And there I see such black and grained spots
As will not leave their tinct.

Ham. Nay, but to live
In the rank sweat of an enseamed bed,
Stew'd in corruption, honeying and making love
Over the nasty sty,—

Queen. O, speak to me no more;
These words like daggers enter in my ears;
No more, sweet Hamlet!

Ham. A murderer and a villain;

A slave that is not twentieth part the tithe
Of your precedent lord; a vice of kings;
A cutpurse of the empire and the rule,
That from a shelf the precious diadem stole
And put it in his pocket!

Queen. No more!

Ham. A king of shreds and patches—

Enter Ghost.

Save me, and hover o'er me with your wings,
You heavenly guards! What would your gracious figure?

Queen. Alas, he 's mad!

Ham. Do you not come your tardy son to chide,
That, lapsed in time and passion, lets go by
The important acting of your dread command?
O, say!

Ghost. Do not forget: this visitation
Is but to whet thy almost blunted purpose.
But look, amazement on thy mother sits:
O, step between her and her fighting soul:
Conceit in weakest bodies strongest works:
Speak to her, Hamlet.

Ham. How is it with you, lady?

Queen. Alas, how is 't with you,
That you do bend your eye on vacancy
And with the incorporal air do hold discourse?
Forth at your eyes your spirits wildly peep;
And, as the sleeping soldiers in the alarm,
Your bedded hairs, like life in excrements,
Stand up and stand an end. O gentle son,
Upon the heat and flame of thy distemper
Sprinkle cool patience. Whereon do you look?

Ham. On him, on him! Look you how pale he glares!
His form and cause conjoin'd, preaching to stones,
Would make them capable. Do not look upon me,
Lest with this piteous action you convert
My stern effects: then what I have to do
Will want true colour; tears perchance for blood.

Queen. To whom do you speak this?

Ham. Do you see nothing there?

Queen. Nothing at all; yet all that is I see.

Ham. Nor did you nothing hear?

Queen. No, nothing but ourselves.

Ham. Why, look you there! look, how it steals away!
My father, in his habit as he lived!

Look, where he goes, even now, out at the portal.
[*Exit Ghost.*

Queen. This is the very coinage of your brain:
This bodiless creation ecstasy
Is very cunning in.

Ham. Ecstasy!
My pulse, as yours, doth temperately keep time,
And makes as healthful music: it is not madness
That I have utter'd: bring me to the test,
And I the matter will re-word, which madness
Would gambol from. Mother, for love of grace,
Lay not that flattering unction to your soul,
That not your trespass but my madness speaks:
It will but skin and film the ulcerous place,
Whiles rank corruption, mining all within,
Infects unseen. Confess yourself to heaven;
Repent what 's past, avoid what is to come,
And do not spread the compost on the weeds,
To make them ranker. Forgive me this my virtue,
For in the fatness of these pursy times
Virtue itself of vice must pardon beg,
Yea, curb and woo for leave to do him good.

Queen. O Hamlet, thou hast cleft my heart in twain.

Ham. O, throw away the worser part of it,
And live the purer with the other half.
Good night: but go not to my uncle's bed;
Assume a virtue, if you have it not.
That monster, custom, who all sense doth eat,
Of habits devil, is angel yet in this,
That to the use of actions fair and good
He likewise gives a frock or livery,
That aptly is put on. Refrain to-night,
And that shall lend a kind of easiness
To the next abstinence; the next more easy;
For use almost can change the stamp of nature,
And either . . . the devil, or throw him out
With wondrous potency. Once more, good night:
And when you are desirous to be blest,
I 'll blessing beg of you. For this same lord,
[*Pointing to Polonius.*
I do repent: but heaven hath pleased it so,
To punish me with this, and this with me,
That I must be their scourge and minister.
I will bestow him, and will answer well
The death I gave him. So, again, good night.

I must be cruel, only to be kind:
Thus bad begins, and worse remains behind.
One word more, good lady.

Queen. What shall I do?

Ham. Not this, by no means, that I bid you do:
Let the bloat king tempt you again to bed;
Pinch wanton on your cheek, call you his mouse;
And let him, for a pair of reechy kisses,
Or paddling in your neck with his damn'd fingers,
Make you to ravel all this matter out,
That I essentially am not in madness,
But mad in craft. 'Twere good you let him know;
For who, that's but a queen, fair, sober, wise,
Would from a paddock, from a bat, a gib,
Such dear concernings hide? who would do so?
No, in despite of sense and secrecy,
Unpeg the basket on the house's top,
Let the birds fly, and like the famous ape,
To try conclusions, in the basket creep
And break your own neck down.

Queen. Be thou assured, if words be made of breath
And breath of life, I have no life to breathe
What thou hast said to me.

Ham. I must to England; you know that?

Queen. Alack,
I had forgot: 'tis so concluded on.

Ham. There's letters seal'd: and my two schoolfellows,
Whom I will trust as I will adders fang'd,
They bear the mandate; they must sweep my way,
And marshal me to knavery. Let it work;
For 'tis the sport to have the enginer
Hoist with his own petar: and 't shall go hard
But I will delve one yard below their mines,
And blow them at the moon: O, 'tis most sweet
When in one line two crafts directly meet.
This man shall set me packing:
I'll lug the guts into the neighbour room.
Mother, good night. Indeed this counsellor
Is now most still, most secret and most grave,
Who was in life a foolish prating knave.
Come, sir, to draw toward an end with you.
Good night, mother.

[*Exeunt severally; Hamlet dragging in Polonius.*

ACT IV—Scene I

A room in the castle.

Enter King, Queen, Rosencrantz, and Guildenstern.

King. There 's matter in these sighs, these profound heaves:
You must translate: 'tis fit we understand them.
Where is your son?

Queen. Bestow this place on us a little while.
[*Exeunt Rosencrantz and Guildenstern.*
Ah, mine own lord, what have I seen to-night!

King. What, Gertrude? How does Hamlet?

Queen. Mad as the sea and wind, when both contend
Which is the mightier: in his lawless fit,
Behind the arras hearing something stir,
Whips out his rapier, cries 'A rat, a rat!'
And in this brainish apprehension kills
The unseen good old man.

King. O heavy deed!
It had been so with us, had we been there:
His liberty is full of threats to all,
To you yourself, to us, to every one.
Alas, how shall this bloody deed be answer'd?
It will be laid to us, whose providence
Should have kept short, restrain'd and out of haunt,
This mad young man: but so much was our love,
We would not understand what was most fit,
But, like the owner of a foul disease,
To keep it from divulging, let it feed
Even on the pith of life. Where is he gone?

Queen. To draw apart the body he hath kill'd:
O'er whom his very madness, like some ore
Among a mineral of metals base,
Shows itself pure; he weeps for what is done.

King. O Gertrude, come away!
The sun no sooner shall the mountains touch,
But we will ship him hence: and this vile deed
We must, with all our majesty and skill,
Both countenance and excuse. Ho, Guildenstern!

Re-enter Rosencrantz and Guildenstern.

Friends both, go join you with some further aid:
Hamlet in madness hath Polonius slain,
And from his mother's closet hath he dragg'd him:
Go seek him out; speak fair, and bring the body

Into the chapel. I pray you, haste in this.
[*Exeunt Rosencrantz and Guildenstern.*
Come, Gertrude, we 'll call up our wisest friends;
And let them know, both what we mean to do,
And what 's untimely done. . . .
Whose whisper o'er the world's diameter
As level as the cannon to his blank
Transports his poison'd shot, may miss our name
And hit the woundless air. O, come away!
My soul is full of discord and dismay. [*Exeunt.*

Scene II

Another room in the castle.

Enter Hamlet.

Ham. Safely stowed.

Ros., *Guil.* [*Within*] Hamlet! Lord Hamlet.

Ham. But soft, what noise? who calls on Hamlet?
O, here they come.

Enter Rosencrantz and Guildenstern.

Ros. What have you done, my lord, with the dead body?

Ham. Compounded it with dust, whereto 'tis kin.

Ros. Tell us where 'tis, that we may take it thence
And bear it to the chapel.

Ham. Do not believe it.

Ros. Believe what?

Ham. That I can keep your counsel and not mine own. Besides, to be demanded of a sponge! what replication should be made by the son of a king?

Ros. Take you me for a sponge, my lord?

Ham. Ay, sir; that soaks up the king's countenance, his rewards, his authorities. But such officers do the king best service in the end: he keeps them, like an ape, in the corner of his jaw; first mouthed, to be last swallowed: when he needs what you have gleaned, it is but squeezing you, and, sponge, you shall be dry again.

Ros. I understand you not, my lord.

Ham. I am glad of it: a knavish speech sleeps in a foolish ear.

Ros. My lord, you must tell us where the body is, and go with us to the king.

Ham. The body is with the king, but the king is not with the body. The king is a thing—

Guil. A thing, my lord?

Ham. Of nothing: bring me to him. Hide fox, and all after.
[*Exeunt.*

Scene III

Another room in the castle.

Enter King, attended.

King. I have sent to seek him, and to find the body.
How dangerous is it that this man goes loose!
Yet must not we put the strong law on him:
He 's loved of the distracted multitude,
Who like not in their judgement, but their eyes,
And where 'tis so, the offender's scourge is weigh'd,
But never the offence. To bear all smooth and even,
This sudden sending him away must seem
Deliberate pause: diseases desperate grown
By desperate appliance are relieved,
Or not at all.

Enter Rosencrantz.

How now! what hath befall'n?

Ros. Where the dead body is bestow'd, my lord,
We cannot get from him.

King. But where is he?

Ros. Without, my lord; guarded, to know your pleasure.

King. Bring him before us.

Ros. Ho, Guildenstern! bring in my lord.

Enter Hamlet and Guildenstern.

King. Now, Hamlet, where 's Polonius?

Ham. At supper.

King. At supper! where?

Ham. Not where he eats, but where he is eaten: a certain convocation of public worms are e'en at him. Your worm is your only emperor for diet: we fat all creatures else to fat us, and we fat ourselves for maggots: your fat king and your lean beggar is but variable service, two dishes, but to one table: that 's the end.

King. Alas, alas!

Ham. A man may fish with the worm that hath eat of a king, and eat of the fish that hath fed of that worm.

King. What dost thou mean by this?

Ham. Nothing but to show you how a king may go a progress through the guts of a beggar.

King. Where is Polonius?

Ham. In heaven; send thither to see: if your messenger find him not there, seek him i' the other place yourself. But indeed, if you find him not within this month, you shall nose him as you go up the stairs into the lobby.

King. Go seek him there. [*To some Attendants.*

Ham. He will stay till you come. [*Exeunt Attendants.*

King. Hamlet, this deed, for thine especial safety,
Which we do tender, as we dearly grieve
For that which thou hast done, must send thee hence
With fiery quickness: therefore prepare thyself;
The bark is ready and the wind at help,
The associates tend, and every thing is bent
For England.

Ham. For England?

King. Ay, Hamlet.

Ham. Good.

King. So is it, if thou knew'st our purposes.

Ham. I see a cherub that sees them. But, come; for England! Farewell, dear mother.

King. Thy loving father, Hamlet.

Ham. My mother: father and mother is man and wife; man and wife is one flesh, and so, my mother. Come, for England! [*Exit.*

King. Follow him at foot; tempt him with speed aboard;
Delay it not; I'll have him hence to-night:
Away! for every thing is seal'd and done
That else leans on the affair: pray you, make haste.
[*Exeunt Rosencrantz and Guildenstern.*
And, England, if my love thou hold'st at aught—
As my great power thereof may give thee sense,
Since yet thy cicatrice looks raw and red
After the Danish sword, and thy free awe
Pays homage to us—thou mayst not coldly set
Our sovereign process; which imports at full,
By letters congruing to that effect,
The present death of Hamlet. Do it, England;
For like the hectic in my blood he rages,
And thou must cure me: till I know 'tis done,
Howe'er my haps, my joys were ne'er begun. [*Exit.*

Scene IV

A plain in Denmark.

Enter Fortinbras, a Captain and Soldiers, marching.

For. Go, captain, from me greet the Danish king;
Tell him that by his license Fortinbras
Craves the conveyance of a promised march
Over his kingdom. You know the rendezvous.
If that his majesty would aught with us,
We shall express our duty in his eye;
And let him know so.

Cap. I will do't, my lord.
For. Go softly on. [*Exeunt Fortinbras and Soldiers.*
Enter Hamlet, Rosencrantz, Guildenstern, and others.
Ham. Good sir, whose powers are these?
Cap. They are of Norway, sir.
Ham. How purposed, sir, I pray you?
Cap. Against some part of Poland.
Ham. Who commands them, sir?
Cap. The nephew to old Norway, Fortinbras.
Ham. Goes it against the main of Poland, sir,
Or for some frontier?
Cap. Truly to speak, and with no addition,
We go to gain a little patch of ground
That hath in it no profit but the name.
To pay five ducats, five, I would not farm it;
Nor will it yield to Norway or the Pole
A ranker rate, should it be sold in fee.
Ham. Why, then the Polack never will defend it.
Cap. Yes, it is already garrison'd.
Ham. Two thousand souls and twenty thousand ducats
Will not debate the question of this straw:
This is the imposthume of much wealth and peace,
That inward breaks, and shows no cause without
Why the man dies. I humbly thank you, sir.
Cap. God be wi' you, sir. [*Exit.*
Ros. Will't please you go, my lord?
Ham. I'll be with you straight. Go a little before.
[*Exeunt all but Hamlet.*
How all occasions do inform against me,
And spur my dull revenge! What is a man,
If his chief good and market of his time
Be but to sleep and feed? a beast, no more.
Sure, he that made us with such large discourse,
Looking before and after, gave us not
That capability and god-like reason
To fust in us unused. Now, whether it be
Bestial oblivion, or some craven scruple
Of thinking too precisely on the event,—
A thought which, quarter'd, hath but one part wisdom
And ever three parts coward,—I do not know
Why yet I live to say 'this thing's to do,'
Sith I have cause, and will, and strength, and means,
To do't. Examples gross as earth exhort me:
Witness this army, of such mass and charge,
Led by a delicate and tender prince,

Whose spirit with divine ambition puff'd
Makes mouths at the invisible event,
Exposing what is mortal and unsure
To all that forture, death and danger dare,
Even for an egg-shell. Rightly to be great
Is not to stir without great argument,
But greatly to find quarrel in a straw
When honour 's at the stake. How stand I then,
That have a father kill'd, a mother stain'd,
Excitements of my reason and my blood,
And let all sleep, while to my shame I see
The imminent death of twenty thousand men,
That for a fantasy and trick of fame
Go to their graves like beds, fight for a plot
Whereon the numbers cannot try the cause,
Which is not tomb enough and continent
To hide the slain? O, from this time forth,
My thoughts be bloody, or be nothing worth! [*Exit.*

Scene V

Elsinore. A room in the castle.

Enter Queen, Horatio, and a Gentleman.

Queen. I will not speak with her.
Gent. She is importunate, indeed distract:
Her mood will needs be pitied.
Queen. What would she have?
Gent. She speaks much of her father, says she hears
There 's tricks i' the world, and hems and beats her heart,
Spurns enviously at straws; speaks things in doubt,
That carry but half sense: her speech is nothing,
Yet the unshaped use of it doth move
The hearers to collection; they aim at it,
And botch the words up fit to their own thoughts;
Which, as her winks and nods and gestures yield them,
Indeed would make one think there might be thought,
Though nothing sure, yet much unhappily.
Hor. 'Twere good she were spoken with, for she may strew
Dangerous conjectures in ill-breeding minds.
Queen. Let her come in. [*Exit Gentleman.*
[*Aside*] To my sick soul, as sin's true nature is,
Each toy seems prologue to some great amiss:
So full of artless jealousy is guilt,
It spills itself in fearing to be spilt.

Re-enter Gentleman, with Ophelia.

Oph. Where is the beauteous majesty of Denmark?

Queen. How now, Ophelia!

Oph. [*Sings*] How should I your true love know
From another one?
By his cockle hat and staff
And his sandal shoon.

Queen. Alas, sweet lady, what imports this song?

Oph. Say you? nay, pray you, mark.

[*Sings*] He is dead and gone, lady,
He is dead and gone;
At his head a grass-green turf,
At his heels a stone.

Oh, oh!

Queen. Nay, but Ophelia,—

Oph. Pray you, mark.

[*Sings*] White his shroud as the mountain snow,—

Enter King.

Queen. Alas, look here, my lord.

Oph. [*Sings*] Larded with sweet flowers;
Which bewept to the grave did go
With true-love showers.

King. How do you, pretty lady?

Oph. Well, God 'ild you! They say the owl was a baker's daughter. Lord, we know what we are, but know not what we may be. God be at your table!

King. Conceit upon her father.

Oph. Pray you, let 's have no words of this; but when they ask you what it means, say you this:

[*Sings*] To-morrow is Saint Valentine's day
All in the morning betime,
And I a maid at your window,
To be your Valentine.
Then up he rose, and donn'd his clothes,
And dupp'd the chamber-door;
Let in the maid, that out a maid
Never departed more.

King. Pretty Ophelia!

Oph. Indeed, la, without an oath, I 'll make an end on 't:

[*Sings*] By Gis and by Saint Charity,
Alack, and fie for shame!
Young men will do 't, if they come to 't;
By cock, they are to blame.
Quoth she, before you tumbled me,
You promised me to wed.

He answers :
So would I ha' done, by yonder sun,
An thou hadst not come to my bed.

King. How long hath she been thus ?

Oph. I hope all will be well. We must be patient : but I cannot choose but weep, to think they should lay him i' the cold ground. My brother shall know of it : and so I thank you for your good counsel. Come, my coach ! Good night, ladies ; good night, sweet ladies ; good night, good night. [*Exit.*

King. Follow her close ; give her good watch, I pray you. [*Exit Horatio.*
O, this is the poison of deep grief ; it springs
All from her father's death. O Gertrude, Gertrude,
When sorrows come, they come not single spies,
But in battalions ! First, her father slain :
Next, your son gone ; and he most violent author
Of his own just remove : the people muddied,
Thick and unwholesome in their thoughts and whispers,
For good Polonius' death ; and we have done but greenly,
In hugger-mugger to inter him : poor Ophelia
Divided from herself and her fair judgement,
Without the which we are pictures, or mere beasts :
Last, and as much containing as all these,
Her brother is in secret come from France,
Feeds on his wonder, keeps himself in clouds,
And wants not buzzers to infect his ear
With pestilent speeches of his father's death ;
Wherein necessity, of matter beggar'd,
Will nothing stick our person to arraign
In ear and ear. O my dear Gertrude, this,
Like to a murdering-piece, in many places
Gives me superfluous death. [*A noise within.*

Queen. Alack, what noise is this ?

King. Where are my Switzers ? Let them guard the door.

Enter another Gentleman.

What is the matter ?

Gent. Save yourself, my lord :
The ocean, overpeering of his list,
Eats not the flats with more impetuous haste
Than young Laertes, in a riotous head,
O'erbears your officers. The rabble call him lord ;
And, as the world were now but to begin,
Antiquity forgot, custom not known,
The ratifiers and props of every word,

They cry 'Choose we; Laertes shall be king!'
Caps, hands and tongues applaud it to the clouds,
'Laertes shall be king, Laertes king!'

Queen. How cheerfully on the false trail they cry!
O, this is counter, you false Danish dogs! [*Noise within.*

King. The doors are broke.

Enter Laertes, armed; Danes following.

Laer. Where is this king? Sirs, stand you all without.

Danes. No, let's come in.

Laer. I pray you, give me leave.

Danes. We will, we will. [*They retire without the door.*

Laer. I thank you: keep the door. O thou vile king,
Give me my father!

Queen. Calmly, good Laertes.

Laer. That drop of blood that's calm proclaims me bastard;
Cries cuckold to my father; brands the harlot
Even here, between the chaste unsmirched brows
Of my true mother.

King. What is the cause, Laertes,
That thy rebellion looks so giant-like?
Let him go, Gertrude; do not fear our person:
There's such divinity doth hedge a king,
That treason can but peep to what it would,
Acts little of his will. Tell me, Laertes,
Why thou art thus incensed: let him go, Gertrude:
Speak, man.

Laer. Where is my father?

King. Dead.

Queen. But not by him.

King. Let him demand his fill.

Laer. How came he dead? I'll not be juggled with:
To hell, allegiance! vows, to the blackest devil!
Conscience and grace, to the profoundest pit!
I dare damnation: to this point I stand,
That both the worlds I give to negligence,
Let come what comes; only I'll be revenged
Most throughly for my father.

King. Who shall stay you?

Laer. My will, not all the world:
And for my means, I'll husband them so well,
They shall go far with little.

King. Good Laertes,
If you desire to know the certainty
Of your dear father's death, is't writ in your revenge
That, swoopstake, you will draw both friend and foe,

Winner and loser?

Laer. None but his enemies.

King. Will you know them then?

Laer. To his good friends thus wide I 'll ope my arms;
And, like the kind life-rendering pelican,
Repast them with my blood.

King. Why, now you speak
Like a good child and a true gentleman.
That I am guiltless of your father's death,
And am most sensibly in grief for it,
It shall as level to your judgement pierce
As day does to your eye.

Danes. [*Within*] Let her come in.

Laer. How now! what noise is that?

Re-enter Ophelia.

O heat, dry up my brains! tears seven times salt,
Burn out the sense and virtue of mine eye!
By heaven, thy madness shall be paid with weight,
Till our scale turn the beam. O rose of May!
Dear maid, kind sister, sweet Ophelia!
O heavens! is 't possible a young maid's wits
Should be as mortal as an old man's life?
Nature is fine in love, and where 'tis fine
It sends some precious instance of itself
After the thing it loves.

Oph. [*Sings*] They bore him barefaced on the bier:
Hey non nonny, nonny, hey nonny:
And in his grave rain'd many a tear,—
Fare you well, my dove!

Laer Hadst thou thy wits, and didst persuade revenge,
It could not move thus.

Oph. [*Sings*] You must sing down a-down,
An you call him a-down-a.
O, how the wheel becomes it! It is the false steward, that stole his master's daughter.

Laer. This nothing 's more than matter.

Oph. There 's rosemary, that 's for remembrance: pray you, love, remember: and there is pansies, that 's for thoughts.

Laer. A document in madness; thoughts and remembrance fitted.

Oph. There 's fennel for you, and columbines: there 's rue for you: and here 's some for me: we may call it herb of grace o' Sundays: O, you must wear your rue with a difference. There 's a daisy: I would give you some violets, but they

withered all when my father died: they say a' made a good end,—
[*Sings*] For bonnie sweet Robin is all my joy.

Laer. Thought and affliction, passion, hell itself,
She turns to favour and to prettiness.

Oph. [*Sings*] And will a' not come again?
And will a' not come again?
No, no, he is dead,
Go to thy death-bed,
He never will come again.

His beard was as white as snow,
All flaxen was his poll:
He is gone, he is gone,
And we cast away moan:
God ha' mercy on his soul!

And of all Christian souls, I pray God. God be wi' you. [*Exit.*

Laer. Do you see this, O God?

King. Laertes, I must commune with your grief,
Or you deny me right. Go but apart,
Make choice of whom your wisest friends you will.
And they shall hear and judge 'twixt you and me:
If by direct or by collateral hand
They find us touch'd, we will our kingdom give,
Our crown, our life, and all that we call ours,
To you in satisfaction; but if not,
Be you content to lend your patience to us,
And we shall jointly labour with your soul
To give it due content.

Laer. Let this be so;
His means of death, his obscure funeral,
No trophy, sword, nor hatchment o'er his bones,
No noble rite nor formal ostentation,
Cry to be heard, as 'twere from heaven to earth,
That I must call't in question.

King. So you shall;
And where the offence is let the great axe fall.
I pray you, go with me. [*Exeunt.*

Scene VI

Another room in the castle.

Enter Horatio and a Servant.

Hor. What are they that would speak with me?

Serv. Sea-faring men, sir: they say they have letters for you.

Hor. Let them come in. [*Exit Servant.*

I do not know from what part of the world
I should be greeted, if not from Lord Hamlet.

Enter Sailors.

First Sail. God bless you, sir.

Hor. Let him bless thee too.

First Sail. He shall, sir, an 't please him. There 's a letter for you, sir; it comes from the ambassador that was bound for England; if your name be Horatio, as I am let to know it is.

Hor. [*Reads*] 'Horatio, when thou shalt have overlooked this, give these fellows some means to the king: they have letters for him. Ere we were two days old at sea, a pirate of very warlike appointment gave us chase. Finding ourselves too slow of sail, we put on a compelled valour, and in the grapple I boarded them: on the instant they got clear of our ship; so I alone became their prisoner. They have dealt with me like thieves of mercy: but they knew what they did; I am to do a good turn for them. Let the king have the letters I have sent; and repair thou to me with as much speed as thou wouldest fly death. I have words to speak in thine ear will make thee dumb; yet are they much too light for the bore of the matter. These good fellows will bring thee where I am. Rosencrantz and Guildenstern hold their course for England: of them I have much to tell thee. Farewell.

'He that thou knowest thine, HAMLET.'

Come, I will make you way for these your letters;
And do 't the speedier, that you may direct me
To him from whom you brought them. [*Exeunt.*

SCENE VII

Another room in the castle.

Enter King and Laertes.

King. Now must your conscience my acquittance seal,
And you must put me in your heart for friend,
Sith you have heard, and with a knowing ear,
That he which hath your noble father slain
Pursued my life.

Laer. It well appears: but tell me
Why you proceeded not against these feats,
So crimeful and so capital in nature,
As by your safety, wisdom, all things else,
You mainly were stirr'd up.

King. O, for two special reasons,
Which may to you perhaps seem much unsinew'd,
But yet to me they 're strong. The queen his mother

Lives almost by his looks; and for myself—
My virtue or my plague, be it either which—
She 's so conjunctive to my life and soul,
That, as the star moves not but in his sphere,
I could not but by her. The other motive,
Why to a public count I might not go,
Is the great love the general gender bear him;
Who, dipping all his faults in their affection,
Would, like the spring that turneth wood to stone,
Convert his gyves to graces; so that my arrows,
Too slightly timber'd for so loud a wind,
Would have reverted to my bow again
And not where I had aim'd them.

Laer. And so have I a noble father lost;
A sister driven into desperate terms,
Whose worth, if praises may go back again,
Stood challenger on mount of all the age
For her perfections: but my revenge will come.

King. Break not your sleeps for that: you must not think
That we are made of stuff so flat and dull
That we can let our beard be shook with danger
And think it pastime. You shortly shall hear more:
I loved your father, and we love ourself;
And that, I hope, will teach you to imagine—

Enter a Messenger with letters.

How now! what news?

Mess. Letters, my lord, from Hamlet:
This to your majesty; this to the queen.

King. From Hamlet! who brought them?

Mess. Sailors, my lord, they say; I saw them not:
They were given me by Claudio; he received them
Of him that brought them.

King. Laertes, you shall hear them.
Leave us. [*Exit Messenger.*
[*Reads*] 'High and mighty, You shall know I am set naked on your kingdom. To-morrow shall I beg leave to see your kingly eyes: when I shall, first asking your pardon thereunto, recount the occasion of my sudden and more strange return.
'HAMLET.'
What should this mean? Are all the rest come back?
Or is it some abuse, and no such thing?

Laer. Know you the hand?

King. 'Tis Hamlet's character. 'Naked'!
And in a postscript here, he says 'alone'.
Can you advise me?

Laer. I 'm lost in it, my lord. But let him come;
It warms the very sickness in my heart,
That I shall live and tell him to his teeth,
'Thus didest thou.'
King. If it be so, Laertes,—
As how should it be so? how otherwise?—
Will you be ruled by me?
Laer. Ay, my lord;
So you will not o'errule me to a peace.
King. To thine own peace. If he be now return'd,
As checking at his voyage, and that he means
No more to undertake it, I will work him
To an exploit now ripe in my device,
Under the which he shall not choose but fall:
And for his death no wind of blame shall breathe;
But even his mother shall uncharge the practice,
And call it accident.
Laer. My lord, I will be ruled;
The rather, if you could devise it so
That I might be the organ.
King. It falls right.
You have been talk'd of since your travel much,
And that in Hamlet's hearing, for a quality
Wherein, they say, you shine: your sum of parts
Did not together pluck such envy from him,
As did that one, and that in my regard
Of the unworthiest siege.
Laer. What part is that, my lord?
King. A very riband in the cap of youth,
Yet needful too; for youth no less becomes
The light and careless livery that it wears
Than settled age his sables and his weeds,
Importing health and graveness. Two months since,
Here was a gentleman of Normandy:—
I 've seen myself, and served against, the French,
And they can well on horseback: but this gallant
Had witchcraft in 't; he grew unto his seat,
And to such wondrous doing brought his horse
As had he been incorpsed and demi-natured
With the brave beast: so far he topp'd my thought
That I, in forgery of shapes and tricks,
Come short of what he did.
Laer. A Norman was 't?
King. A Norman.
Laer. Upon my life, Lamond.

King. The very same.
Laer. I know him well: he is the brooch indeed
And gem of all the nation.
King. He made confession of you,
And gave you such a masterly report,
For art and exercise in your defence,
And for your rapier most especial,
That he cried out, 'twould be a sight indeed
If one could match you: the scrimers of their nation,
He swore, had neither motion, guard, nor eye,
If you opposed them. Sir, this report of his
Did Hamlet so envenom with his envy
That he could nothing do but wish and beg
Your sudden coming o'er, to play with him.
Now, out of this—
Laer. What out of this, my lord?
King. Laertes, was your father dear to you?
Or are you like the painting of a sorrow,
A face without a heart?
Laer. Why ask you this?
King. Not that I think you did not love your father,
But that I know love is begun by time,
And that I see, in passages of proof,
Time qualifies the spark and fire of it.
There lives within the very flame of love
A kind of wick or snuff that will abate it;
And nothing is at a like goodness still,
For goodness, growing to a plurisy,
Dies in his own too much: that we would do
We should do when we would; for this 'would' changes
And hath abatements and delays as many
As there are tongues, are hands, are accidents,
And then this 'should' is like a spendthrift sigh,
That hurts by easing. But, to the quick o' the ulcer:
Hamlet comes back: what would you undertake,
To show yourself your father's son in deed
More than in words?
Laer. To cut his throat i' the church.
King. No place indeed should murder sanctuarize;
Revenge should have no bounds. But, good Laertes,
Will you do this, keep close within your chamber.
Hamlet return'd shall know you are come home:
We'll put on those shall praise your excellence
And set a double varnish on the fame
The Frenchman gave you; bring you in fine together

And wager on your heads: he, being remiss,
Most generous and free from all contriving,
Will not peruse the foils, so that with ease,
Or with a little shuffling, you may choose
A sword unbated, and in a pass of practice
Requite him for your father.

Laer. I will do 't;
And for that purpose I 'll anoint my sword.
I bought an unction of a mountebank,
So mortal that but dip a knife in it,
Where it draws blood no cataplasm so rare,
Collected from all simples that have virtue
Under the moon, can save the thing from death
That is but scratch'd withal: I 'll touch my point
With this contagion, that, if I gall him slightly,
It may be death.

King. Let 's further think of this;
Weigh what convenience both of time and means
May fit us to our shape: if this should fail,
And that our drift look through our bad performance,
'Twere better not assay'd: therefore this project
Should have a back or second, that might hold
If this did blast in proof. Soft! let me see:
We 'll make a solemn wager on your cunnings:
I ha 't:
When in your motion you are hot and dry—
As make your bouts more violent to that end—
And that he calls for drink, I 'll have prepared him
A chalice for the nonce; whereon but sipping,
If he by chance escape your venom'd stuck,
Our purpose may hold there. But stay, what noise?

Enter Queen.

How now, sweet queen!

Queen. One woe doth tread upon another's heel,
So fast they follow: your sister 's drown'd, Laertes.

Laer. Drown'd! O, where?

Queen. There is a willow grows aslant a brook,
That shows his hoar leaves in the glassy stream;
There with fantastic garlands did she come
Of crow-flowers, nettles, daisies, and long purples,
That liberal shepherds give a grosser name,
But our cold maids do dead men's fingers call them:
There, on the pendent boughs her coronet weeds
Clambering to hang, an envious sliver broke;
When down her weedy trophies and herself

Fell in the weeping brook. Her clothes spread wide,
And mermaid-like a while they bore her up:
Which times she chanted snatches of old tunes,
As one incapable of her own distress,
Or like a creature native and indued
Unto that element: but long it could not be
Till that her garments, heavy with their drink,
Pull'd the poor wretch from her melodious lay
To muddy death.

Laer. Alas, then she is drown'd!

Queen. Drown'd, drown'd.

Laer. Too much of water hast thou, poor Ophelia,
And therefore I forbid my tears: but yet
It is our trick; nature her custom holds,
Let shame say what it will: when these are gone,
The woman will be out. Adieu, my lord:
I have a speech of fire that fain would blaze,
But that this folly douts it. [*Exit.*

King. Let 's follow, Gertrude:
How much I had to do to calm his rage!
Now fear I this will give it start again;
Therefore let 's follow. [*Exeunt.*

ACT V—Scene I

A churchyard.

Enter two Clowns, with spades, &c.

First Clo. Is she to be buried in Christian burial that wilfully seeks her own salvation?

Sec. Clo. I tell thee she is; and therefore make her grave straight: the crowner hath sat on her, and finds it Christian burial.

First Clo. How can that be, unless she drowned herself in her own defence?

Sec. Clo. Why, 'tis found so.

First Clo. It must be 'se offendendo;' it cannot be else. For here lies the point: if I drown myself wittingly, it argues an act: and an act hath three branches; it is, to act, to do, to perform: argal, she drowned herself wittingly.

Sec. Clo. Nay, but hear you, goodman delver.

First Clo. Give me leave. Here lies the water; good: here stands the man; good: if the man go to this water and drown himself, it is, will he, nill he, he goes; mark you that; but if the water come to him and drown him, he drowns not himself: argal, he that is not guilty of his own death shortens not his own life.

Sec. Clo. But is this law?

First Clo. Ay, marry, is 't; crowner's quest law.

Sec. Clo. Will you ha' the truth on 't? If this had not been a gentlewoman, she should have been buried out o' Christian burial.

First Clo. Why, there thou say'st: and the more pity that great folk should have countenance in this world to drown or hang themselves, more than their even Christian. Come, my spade. There is no ancient gentlemen but gardeners, ditchers and grave-makers: they hold up Adam's profession.

Sec. Clo. Was he a gentleman?

First Clo. A' was the first that ever bore arms.

Sec. Clo. Why, he had none.

First Clo. What, art a heathen? How dost thou understand the Scripture? The Scripture says Adam digged: could he dig without arms? I'll put another question to thee: if thou answerest me not to the purpose, confess thyself—

Sec. Clo. Go to.

First Clo. What is he that builds stronger than either the mason, the shipwright, or the carpenter?

Sec. Clo. The gallows-maker; for that frame outlives a thousand tenants.

First Clo. I like thy wit well, in good faith: the gallows does well; but how does it well? it does well to those that do ill: now, thou dost ill to say the gallows is built stronger than the church: argal, the gallows may do well to thee. To 't again, come.

Sec. Clo. 'Who builds stronger than a mason, a shipwright, or a carpenter?'

First Clo. Ay, tell me that, and unyoke.

Sec. Clo. Marry, now I can tell.

First Clo. To 't.

Sec. Clo. Mass, I cannot tell.

Enter Hamlet and Horatio, afar off.

First Clo. Cudgel thy brains no more about it, for your dull ass will not mend his pace with beating, and when you are asked this question next, say 'a grave-maker:' the houses that he makes last till doomsday. Go, get thee to Yaughan; fetch me a stoup of liquor. [*Exit Sec. Clown.*

[*He digs, and sings.*

In youth, when I did love, did love,
Methought it was very sweet,
To contract, O, the time, for-a my behove,
O, methought, there-a was nothing-a meet.

Ham. Has this fellow no feeling of his business, that he sings at grave-making?

Hor. Custom hath made it in him a property of easiness.

Ham. 'Tis e'en so: the hand of little employment hath the daintier sense.

First Clo. [*Sings*] But age, with his stealing steps,
Hath claw'd me in his clutch,
And hath shipped me intil the land,
As if I had never been such.
[*Throws up a skull.*

Ham. That skull had a tongue in it, and could sing once: how the knave jowls it to the ground, as if it were Cain's jaw-bone, that did the first murder! It might be the pate of a politician, which this ass now o'er-reaches; one that would circumvent God, might it not?

Hor. It might, my lord.

Ham. Or of a courtier, which could say 'Good morrow, sweet lord! How dost thou, sweet lord?' This might be my lord such-a-one, that praised my lord such-a-one's horse, when he meant to beg it; might it not?

Hor. Ay, my lord.

Ham. Why, e'en so: and now my Lady Worm's; chapless, and knocked about the mazzard with a sexton's spade: here's fine revolution, an we had the trick to see't. Did these bones cost no more the breeding, but to play at loggats with 'em; mine ache to think on't.

First Clo. [*Sings*] A pick-axe, and a spade, a spade,
For and a shrouding sheet:
O, a pit of clay for to be made
For such a guest is meet.
[*Throws up another skull.*

Ham. There's another: why may not that be the skull of a lawyer? Where be his quiddities now, his quillets, his cases, his tenures, and his tricks? why does he suffer this rude knave now to knock him about the sconce with a dirty shovel, and will not tell him of his action of battery? Hum! This fellow might be in's time a great buyer of land, with his statutes, his recognizances, his fines, his double vouchers, his recoveries: is this the fine of his fines and the recovery of his recoveries, to have his fine pate full of fine dirt? will his vouchers vouch him no more of his purchases, and double ones too, than the length and breadth of a pair of indentures? The very conveyances of his lands will hardly lie in this box; and must the inheritor himself have no more, ha?

Hor. Not a jot more, my lord.

Ham. Is not parchment made of sheep-skins?

Hor. Ay, my lord, and of calf-skins too.

Ham. They are sheep and calves which seek out assurance in that. I will speak to this fellow. Whose grave 's this, sirrah?

First Clo. Mine, sir.

[*Sings*] O, a pit of clay for to be made
For such a guest is meet.

Ham. I think it be thine indeed, for thou liest in 't.

First Clo. You lie out on 't, sir, and therefore 'tis not yours: for my part, I do not lie in 't, and yet it is mine.

Ham. Thou dost lie in 't, to be in 't and say it is thine: 'tis for the dead, not for the quick; therefore thou liest.

First Clo. 'Tis a quick lie, sir; 'twill away again, from me to you.

Ham. What man dost thou dig it for?

First Clo. For no man, sir.

Ham. What woman then?

First Clo. For none neither.

Ham. Who is to be buried in 't?

First Clo. One that was a woman, sir; but, rest her soul, she 's [dead.

Ham. How absolute the knave is! we must speak by the card, or equivocation will undo us. By the Lord, Horatio, this three years I have taken note of it; the age is grown so picked that the toe of the peasant comes so near the heel of the courtier, he galls his kibe. How long hast thou been a grave-maker?

First Clo. Of all the days i' the year, I came to 't that day that our last King Hamlet o'ercame Fortinbras.

Ham. How long is that since?

First Clo. Cannot you tell that? every fool can tell that: it was that very day that young Hamlet was born; he that is mad, and sent into England.

Ham. Ay, marry, why was he sent into England?

First Clo. Why, because a' was mad; a' shall recover his wits there; or, if a' do not, 'tis no great matter there.

Ham. Why?

First Clo. 'Twill not be seen in him there; there the men are as mad as he.

Ham. How came he mad?

First Clo. Very strangely, they say.

Ham. How 'strangely'?

First Clo. Faith, e'en with losing his wits.

Ham. Upon what ground?

First Clo. Why, here in Denmark: I have been sexton here, man and boy, thirty years.

Ham. How long will a man lie i' the earth ere he rot?

First Clo. I' faith, if a' be not rotten before a' die—as we have many pocky corses now-a-days, that will scarce hold the laying in—a' will last you some eight year or nine year: a tanner will last you nine year.

Ham. Why he more than another?

First Clo. Why, sir, his hide is so tanned with his trade that a' will keep out water a great while; and your water is a sore decayer of your whoreson dead body. Here 's a skull now: this skull has lain in the earth three and twenty years.

Ham. Whose was it?

First Clo. A whoreson mad fellow's it was: whose do you think it was?

Ham. Nay, I know not.

First Clo. A pestilence on him for a mad rogue! a' poured a flagon of Rhenish on my head once. This same skull, sir, was Yorick's skull, the king's jester.

Ham. This?

First Clo. E'en that.

Ham. Let me see. [*Takes the skull.*] Alas, poor Yorick! I knew him, Horatio: a fellow of infinite jest, of most excellent fancy: he hath borne me on his back a thousand times; and now how abhorred in my imagination it is! my gorge rises at it. Here hung those lips that I have kissed I know not how oft. Where be your gibes now? your gambols? your songs? your flashes of merriment, that were wont to set the table on a roar? Not one now, to mock your own grinning? quite chop-fallen? Now get you to my lady's chamber, and tell her, let her paint an inch thick, to this favour she must come; make her laugh at that. Prithee, Horatio, tell me one thing.

Hor. What 's that, my lord?

Ham. Dost thou think Alexander looked o' this fashion i' the earth?

Hor. E'en so.

Ham. And smelt so? pah! [*Puts down the skull.*

Hor. E'en so, my lord.

Ham. To what base uses we may return, Horatio! Why may not imagination trace the noble dust of Alexander, till he find it stopping a bung-hole?

Hor. 'Twere to consider too curiously, to consider so.

Ham. No, faith, not a jot; but to follow him thither with modesty enough and likelihood to lead it: as thus: Alexander died, Alexander was buried, Alexander returneth into dust; the dust is earth; of earth we make loam; and why of that loam, whereto he was converted, might they not stop a beer-barrel?

Imperious Cæsar, dead and turn'd to clay,
Might stop a hole to keep the wind away:
O, that that earth, which kept the world in awe,
Should patch a wall to expel the winter's flaw!

But soft! but soft! aside: here comes the king.

Enter Priests, &c., in procession; the Corpse of Ophelia, Laertes and Mourners following; King, Queen, their trains, &c.

The queen, the courtiers: who is this they follow?
And with such maimed rites? This doth betoken
The corse they follow did with desperate hand
Fordo its own life: 'twas of some estate.
Couch we awhile, and mark. [*Retiring with Horatio*

Laer. What ceremony else?

Ham. That is Laertes, a very noble youth: mark.

Laer. What ceremony else?

First Priest. Her obsequies have been as far enlarged
As we have warranty: her death was doubtful;
And, but that great command o'ersways the order
She should in ground unsanctified have lodged
Till the last trumpet; for charitable prayers,
Shards, flints and pebbles should be thrown on her:
Yet here she is allow'd her virgin crants,
Her maiden strewments and the bringing home
Of bell and burial.

Laer. Must there no more be done?

First Priest. No more be done:
We should profane the service of the dead
To sing a requiem and such rest to her
As to peace-parted souls.

Laer. Lay her i' the earth:
And from her fair and unpolluted flesh
May violets spring! I tell thee, churlish priest,
A ministering angel shall my sister be,
When thou liest howling.

Ham. What, the fair Ophelia!

Queen. [*Scattering flowers*] Sweets to the sweet: farewell!
I hoped thou shouldst have been my Hamlet's wife;
I thought thy bride-bed to have deck'd, sweet maid,
And not have strew'd thy grave.

Laer. O, treble woe
Fall ten times treble on that cursed head

Whose wicked deed thy most ingenious sense
Deprived thee of! Hold off the earth a while,
Till I have caught her once more in mine arms:
[*Leaps into the grave.*
Now pile your dust upon the quick and dead,
Till of this flat a mountain you have made
To o'ertop old Pelion or the skyish head
Of blue Olympus.

Ham. [*Advancing*] What is he whose grief
Bears such an emphasis? whose phrase of sorrow
Conjures the wandering stars and makes them stand
Like wonder-wounded hearers? This is I,
Hamlet the Dane. [*Leaps into the grave.*

Laer. The devil take thy soul! [*Grappling with him.*

Ham. Thou pray'st not well.
I prithee, take thy fingers from my throat;
For, though I am not splenitive and rash,
Yet have I in me something dangerous,
Which let thy wisdom fear. Hold off thy hand.

King. Pluck them asunder.

Queen. Hamlet, Hamlet!

All. Gentlemen,—

Hor. Good my lord, be quiet.
[*The Attendants part them, and they come out of the grave.*

Ham. Why, I will fight with him upon this theme
Until my eyelids will no longer wag.

Queen. O my son, what theme?

Ham. I loved Ophelia: forty thousand brothers
Could not, with all their quantity of love,
Make up my sum. What wilt thou do for her?

King. O, he is mad, Laertes.

Queen. For love of God, forbear him.

Ham. 'Swounds, show me what thou 'lt do:
Woo 't weep? woo 't fight? woo 't fast? woo 't tear thyself?
Woo 't drink up eisel? eat a crocodile?
I 'll do 't. Dost thou come here to whine?
To outface me with leaping in her grave?
Be buried quick with her, and so will I:
And, if thou prate of mountains, let them throw
Millions of acres on us, till our ground,
Singeing his pate against the burning zone,
Make Ossa like a wart! Nay, an thou 'lt mouth,
I 'll rant as well as thou.

Queen. This is mere madness:
And thus a while the fit will work on him;

Anon, as patient as the female dove
When that her golden couplets are disclosed,
His silence will sit drooping.

Ham. Hear you, sir;
What is the reason that you use me thus?
I loved you ever: but it is no matter;
Let Hercules himself do what he may,
The cat will mew, and dog will have his day. [*Exit.*

King. I pray thee, good Horatio, wait upon him. [*Exit Horatio.*
[*To Laertes*] Strengthen your patience in our last night's speech;
We 'll put the matter to the present push.
Good Gertrude, set some watch over your son.
This grave shall have a living monument:
An hour of quiet shortly shall we see;
Till then, in patience our proceeding be. [*Exeunt.*

Scene II

A hall in the castle.

Enter Hamlet and Horatio.

Ham. So much for this, sir: now shall you see the other;
You do remember all the circumstance?

Hor. Remember it, my lord!

Ham. Sir, in my heart there was a kind of fighting,
That would not let me sleep: methought I lay
Worse than the mutines in the bilboes. Rashly,
And praised be rashness for it, let us know,
Our indiscretion sometime serves us well
When our deep plots do pall; and that should learn us
There 's a divinity that shapes our ends,
Rough-hew them how we will.

Hor. That is most certain.

Ham. Up from my cabin,
My sea-gown scarf'd about me, in the dark
Groped I to find out them; had my desire,
Finger'd their packet, and in fine withdrew
To mine own room again; making so bold,
My fears forgetting manners, to unseal
Their grand commission; where I found, Horatio,—
O royal knavery!—an exact command,
Larded with many several sorts of reasons,
Importing Denmark's health and England's too,
With ho! such bugs and goblins in my life,
That, on the supervise, no leisure bated,
No, not to stay the grinding of the axe,
My head should be struck off.

Hor. Is 't possible?
Ham. Here 's the commission: read it at more leisure.
But wilt thou hear now how I did proceed?
Hor. I beseech you.
Ham. Being thus be-netted round with villanies,—
Or I could make a prologue to my brains,
They had begun the play,—I sat me down;
Devised a new commission; wrote it fair:
I once did hold it, as our statists do,
A baseness to write fair, and labour'd much
How to forget that learning; but, sir, now
It did me yeomen's service: wilt thou know
The effect of what I wrote?
Hor. Ay, good my lord.
Ham. An earnest conjuration from the king,
As England was his faithful tributary,
As love between them like the palm might flourish,
As peace should still her wheaten garland wear
And stand a comma 'tween their amities,
And many such-like 'As' es of great charge,
That, on the view and knowing of these contents
Without debatement further, more or less,
He should the bearers put to sudden death,
Not shriving-time allow'd.
Hor. How was this seal'd?
Ham. Why, even in that was heaven ordinant.
I had my father's signet in my purse,
Which was the model of that Danish seal:
Folded the writ up in the form of the other;
Subscribed it; gave 't the impression; placed it safely,
The changeling never known. Now, the next day
Was our sea-fight; and what to this was sequent
Thou know'st already.
Hor. So Guildenstern and Rosencrantz go to 't.
Ham. Why, man, they did make love to this employment;
They are not near my conscience; their defeat
Does by their own insinuation grow:
'Tis dangerous when the baser nature comes
Between the pass and fell incensed points
Of mighty opposites.
Hor. Why, what a king is this!
Ham. Does it not, think'st thee, stand me now upon—
He that hath kill'd my king, and whored my mother;
Popp'd in between the election and my hopes;
Thrown out his angle for my proper life,

And with such cozenage—is 't not perfect conscience,
To quit him with this arm? and is 't not to be damn'd,
To let this canker of our nature come
In further evil?

Hor. It must be shortly known to him from England
What is the issue of the business there.

Ham. It will be short: the interim is mine;
And a man's life 's no more than to say 'One.'
But I am very sorry, good Horatio,
That to Laertes I forgot myself;
For, by the image of my cause, I see
The portraiture of his: I 'll court his favours:
But, sure, the bravery of his grief did put me
Into a towering passion.

Hor. Peace! who comes here?

Enter Osric.

Osr. Your lordship is right welcome back to Denmark.

Ham. I humbly thank you, sir. Dost know this water-fly?

Hor. No, my good lord.

Ham. Thy state is the more gracious, for 'tis a vice to know him. He hath much land, and fertile: let a beast be lord of beasts, and his crib shall stand at the king's mess: 'tis a chough, but, as I say, spacious in the possession of dirt.

Osr. Sweet lord, if your lordship were at leisure, I should impart a thing to you from his majesty.

Ham. I will receive it, sir, with all diligence of spirit. Put your bonnet to his right use; 'tis for the head.

Osr. I thank your lordship, it is very hot.

Ham. No, believe me, 'tis very cold; the wind is northerly.

Osr. It is indifferent cold, my lord, indeed.

Ham. But yet methinks it is very sultry and hot, or my complexion—

Osr. Exceedingly, my lord; it is very sultry, as 'twere,—I cannot tell how. But, my lord, his majesty bade me signify to you that he has laid a great wager on your head: sir, this is the matter—

Ham. I beseech you, remember—

[*Hamlet moves him to put on his hat.*

Osr. Nay, good my lord; for mine ease, in good faith. Sir, here is newly come to court Laertes; believe me, an absolute gentleman, full of most excellent differences, of very soft society and great showing: indeed, to speak feelingly of him, he is the card or calendar of gentry, for you shall find in him the continent of what part a gentleman would see.

Ham. Sir, his definement suffers no perdition in you; though, I know, to divide him inventorially would dizzy the arithmetic of memory, and yet but yaw neither, in respect of his quick sail. But in the verity of extolment, I take him to be a soul of great article, and his infusion of such dearth and rareness, as, to make true diction of him, his semblable is his mirror, and who else would trace him, his umbrage, nothing [more.

Osr. Your lordship speaks most infallibly of him.

Ham. The concernancy, sir? why do we wrap the gentleman in our more rawer breath?

Osr. Sir?

Hor. Is 't not possible to understand in another tongue? You will do 't, sir, really.

Ham. What imports the nomination of this gentleman?

Osr. Of Laertes?

Hor. His purse is empty already; all 's golden words are spent.

Ham. Of him, sir.

Osr. I know you are not ignorant—

Ham. I would you did, sir; yet, in faith, if you did, it would not much approve me. Well, sir?

Osr. You are not ignorant of what excellence Laertes is—

Ham. I dare not confess that, lest I should compare with him in excellence; but, to know a man well, were to know himself.

Osr. I mean, sir, for his weapon; but in the imputation laid on him by them, in his meed he 's unfellowed.

Ham. What 's his weapon?

Osr. Rapier and dagger.

Ham. That 's two of his weapons: but, well.

Osr. The king, sir, hath wagered with him six Barbary horses: against the which he has imponed, as I take it, six French rapiers and poniards, with their assigns, as girdle, hanger, and so: three of the carriages, in faith, are very dear to fancy, very responsive to the hilts, most delicate carriages, and of very liberal conceit.

Ham. What call you the carriages?

Hor. I knew you must be edified by the margent ere you had [done.

Osr. The carriages, sir, are the hangers.

Ham. The phrase would be more germane to the matter if we could carry a cannon by our sides: I would it might be hangers till then. But, on: six Barbary horses against six French swords, their assigns, and three liberal-conceited carriages; that 's the French bet against the Danish. Why is this 'imponed,' as you call it?

Osr. The king, sir, hath laid, sir, that in a dozen passes between yourself and him, he shall not exceed you three hits: he hath laid on twelve for nine; and it would come to immediate trial if your lordship would vouchsafe the answer.

Ham. How if I answer 'no'?

Osr. I mean, my lord, the opposition of your person in trial.

Ham. Sir, I will walk here in the hall: if it please his majesty, it is the breathing time of day with me; let the foils be brought, the gentleman willing, and the king hold his purpose, I will win for him an I can; if not, I will gain nothing but my shame and the odd hits.

Osr. Shall I redeliver you e'en so?

Ham. To this effect, sir, after what flourish your nature will.

Osr. I commend my duty to your lordship.

Ham. Yours, yours. [*Exit Osric.*] He does well to commend it himself; there are no tongues else for 's turn.

Hor. This lapwing runs away with the shell on his head.

Ham. He did comply with his dug before he sucked it. Thus has he—and many more of the same breed that I know the drossy age dotes on—only got the tune of the time and outward habit of encounter; a kind of yesty collection, which carries them through and through the most fond and winnowed opinions; and do but blow them to their trial, the bubbles are out.

Enter a Lord.

Lord. My lord, his majesty commended him to you by young Osric, who brings back to him, that you attend him in the hall: he sends to know if your pleasure hold to play with Laertes, or that you will take longer time.

Ham. I am constant to my purposes; they follow the king's pleasure: if his fitness speaks, mine is ready; now or whensoever, provided I be so able as now.

Lord. The king and queen and all are coming down.

Ham. In happy time.

Lord. The queen desires you to use some gentle entertainment to Laertes before you fall to play.

Ham. She well instructs me. [*Exit Lord.*

Hor. You will lose this wager, my lord.

Ham. I do not think so; since he went into France, I have been in continual practice; I shall win at the odds. But thou wouldst not think how ill all 's here about my heart: but it is no matter.

Hor. Nay, good my lord,—

Ham. It is but foolery; but it is such a kind of gain-giving as would perhaps trouble a woman.

Hor. If your mind dislike any thing, obey it. I will forestal their repair hither, and say you are not fit.

Ham. Not a whit; we defy augury: there is special providence in the fall of a sparrow. If it be now, 'tis not to come; if it be not to come, it will be now; if it be not now, yet it will come: the readiness is all; since no man has aught of what he leaves, what is 't to leave betimes? Let be.

Enter King, Queen, Laertes, and Lords, Osric and other Attendants with foils and gauntlets; a table and flagons of wine on it.

King. Come, Hamlet, come, and take this hand from me.
[*The King puts Laertes' hand into Hamlet's.*

Ham. Give me your pardon, sir: I 've done you wrong;
But pardon 't, as you are a gentleman.
This presence knows,
And you must needs have heard, how I am punish'd
With sore distraction. What I have done,
That might your nature, honour and exception
Roughly awake, I here proclaim was madness.
Was 't Hamlet wrong'd Laertes? Never Hamlet:
If Hamlet from himself be ta'en away,
And when he 's not himself does wrong Laertes,
Then Hamlet does it not, Hamlet denies it.
Who does it then? His madness: if 't be so,
Hamlet is of the faction that is wrong'd;
His madness is poor Hamlet's enemy.
Sir, in this audience,
Let my disclaiming from a purposed evil
Free me so far in your most generous thoughts,
That I have shot mine arrow o'er the house,
And hurt my brother.

Laer. I am satisfied in nature,
Whose motive, in this case, should stir me most
To my revenge: but in my terms of honour
I stand aloof, and will no reconcilement,
Till by some elder masters of known honour
I have a voice and precedent of peace,
To keep my name ungored. But till that time
I do receive your offer'd love like love
And will not wrong it.

Ham. I embrace it freely,
And will this brother's wager frankly play.
Give us the foils. Come on.

Laer. Come, one for me.

Ham. I 'll be your foil, Laertes: in mine ignorance
Your skill shall, like a star i' the darkest night,
Stick fiery off indeed.

Laer. You mock me, sir.

Ham. No, by this hand.

King. Give them the foils, young Osric. Cousin Hamlet,
You know the wager?
Ham. Very well, my lord;
Your grace has laid the odds o' the weaker side.
King. I do not fear it; I have seen you both:
But since he is better'd, we have therefore odds.
Laer. This is too heavy; let me see another.
Ham. This likes me well. These foils have all a length?
[*They prepare to play*.
Osr. Ay, my good lord.
King. Set me the stoups of wine upon that table.
If Hamlet give the first or second hit,
Or quit in answer of the third exchange,
Let all the battlements their ordnance fire;
The king shall drink to Hamlet's better breath;
And in the cup an union shall he throw,
Richer than that which four successive kings
In Denmark's crown have worn. Give me the cups;
And let the kettle to the trumpet speak,
The trumpet to the cannoneer without,
The cannons to the heavens, the heaven to earth,
'Now the king drinks to Hamlet.' Come, begin;
And you, the judges, bear a wary eye.
Ham. Come on, sir.
Laer. Come, my lord. [*They play*.
Ham. One.
Laer. No.
Ham Judgement.
Osr. A hit, a very palpable hit.
Laer. Well; again.
King. Stay; give me drink. Hamlet, this pearl is thine;
Here 's to thy health.
[*Trumpets sound, and cannon shot off within*.
Give him the cup.
Ham. I 'll play this bout first; set it by a while.
Come. [*They play*.] Another hit; what say you?
Laer. A touch, a touch, I do confess.
King. Our son shall win.
Queen. He 's fat and scant of breath.
Here, Hamlet, take my napkin, rub thy brows:
The queen carouses to thy fortune, Hamlet.
Ham. Good madam!
King. Gertrude, do not drink.
Queen. I will, my lord; I pray you pardon me.
King. [*Aside*] It is the poison'd cup; it is too late.

Ham. I dare not drink yet, madam; by and by.
Queen. Come, let me wipe thy face.
Laer. My lord, I'll hit him now.
King. I do not think 't.
Laer. [*Aside*] And yet it is almost against my conscience.
Ham. Come, for the third, Laertes: you but dally;
I pray you, pass with your best violence;
I am afeard you make a wanton of me.
Laer. Say you so? come on. [*They play.*
Osr. Nothing, neither way.
Laer. Have at you now!
[*Laertes wounds Hamlet; then, in scuffling, they change rapiers, and Hamlet wounds Laertes.*
King. Part them; they are incensed.
Ham. Nay, come, again. [*The Queen falls.*
Osr. Look to the queen there, ho!
Hor. They bleed on both sides. How is it, my lord?
Osr. How is 't, Laertes?
Laer. Why, as a woodcock to mine own springe, Osric;
I am justly kill'd with mine own treachery.
Ham. How does the queen?
King. She swounds to see them bleed.
Queen. No, no, the drink, the drink,—O my dear Hamlet,—
The drink, the drink! I am poison'd. [*Dies.*
Ham. O villany! Ho! let the door be lock'd:
Treachery! seek it out. [*Laertes falls.*
Laer. It is here, Hamlet: Hamlet, thou art slain;
No medicine in the world can do thee good,
In thee there is not half an hour of life;
The treacherous instrument is in thy hand,
Unbated and envenom'd: the foul practice
Hath turn'd itself on me; lo, here I lie,
Never to rise again: thy mother's poison'd:
I can no more: the king, the king 's to blame.
Ham. The point envenom'd too!
Then, venom, to thy work. [*Stabs the King.*
All. Treason! treason!
King. O, yet defend me, friends; I am but hurt.
Ham. Here, thou incestuous, murderous, damned Dane,
Drink off this potion: is thy union here?
Follow my mother. [*King dies.*
Laer. He is justly served;
It is a poison temper'd by himself.
Exchange forgiveness with me, noble Hamlet:
Mine and my father's death come not upon thee,

Nor thine on me! [*Dies.*

Ham. Heaven make thee free of it! I follow thee.
I am dead, Horatio. Wretched queen, adieu!
You that look pale and tremble at this chance,
That are but mutes or audience to this act,
Had I but time—as this fell sergeant, death,
Is strict in his arrest—O, I could tell you—
But let it be. Horatio, I am dead!
Thou livest; report me and my cause aright
To the unsatisfied.

Hor. Never believe it:
I am more an antique Roman than a Dane:
Here 's yet some liquor left.

Ham. As thou 'rt a man,
Give me the cup: let go; by heaven, I 'll have 't.
O good Horatio, what a wounded name,
Things standing thus unknown, shall live behind me!
If thou didst ever hold me in thy heart,
Absent thee from felicity a while,
And in this harsh world draw thy breath in pain,
To tell my story. [*March afar off, and shot within.*
What warlike noise is this?

Osr. Young Fortinbras, with conquest come from Poland,
To the ambassadors of England gives
This warlike volley.

Ham. O, I die, Horatio;
The potent poison quite o'er-crows my spirit:
I cannot live to hear the news from England;
But I do prophesy the election lights
On Fortinbras: he has my dying voice;
So tell him, with the occurrents, more and less,
Which have solicited. The rest is silence. [*Dies.*

Hor. Now cracks a noble heart. Good night, sweet prince,
And flights of angels sing thee to thy rest! [*March within.*
Why does the drum come hither?

Enter Fortinbras, and the English Ambassadors, with drum, colours, and Attendants.

Fort. Where is this sight?

Hor. What is it you would see?
If aught of woe or wonder, cease your search.

Fort. This quarry cries on havoc. O proud death,
What feast is toward in thine eternal cell,
That thou so many princes at a shot
So bloodily hast struck?

First Amb. The sight is dismal;

And our affairs from England come too late:
The ears are senseless that should give us hearing,
To tell him his commandment is fulfill'd,
That Rosencrantz and Guildenstern are dead:
Where should we have our thanks?
Hor. Not from his mouth
Had it the ability of life to thank you:
He never gave commandment for their death.
But since, so jump upon this bloody question,
You from the Polack wars, and you from England,
Are here arrived, give order that these bodies
High on a stage be placed to the view;
And let me speak to the yet unknowing world
How these things came about: so shall you hear
Of carnal, bloody and unnatural acts,
Of accidental judgements, casual slaughters,
Of deaths put on by cunning and forced cause,
And, in this upshot, purposes mistook
Fall'n on the inventors' heads: all this can I
Truly deliver.
Fort. Let us haste to hear it,
And call the noblest to the audience.
For me, with sorrow I embrace my fortune:
I have some rights of memory in this kingdom,
Which now to claim my vantage doth invite me.
Hor. Of that I shall have also cause to speak,
And from his mouth whose voice will draw on more:
But let this same be presently perform'd,
Even while men's minds are wild; lest more mischance
On plots and errors happen.
Fort. Let four captains
Bear Hamlet, like a soldier, to the stage;
For he was likely, had he been put on,
To have proved most royally: and, for his passage,
The soldiers' music and the rites of war
Speak loudly for him.
Take up the bodies: such a sight as this
Becomes the field, but here shows much amiss.
Go, bid the soldiers shoot.
[*A dead march. Exeunt, bearing off the bodies: after which a peal of ordnance is shot off.*

THE TRAGEDY OF KING LEAR

DRAMATIS PERSONÆ

LEAR, *king of Britain.*
KING OF FRANCE.
DUKE OF BURGUNDY.
DUKE OF CORNWALL.
DUKE OF ALBANY.
EARL OF KENT.
EARL OF GLOUCESTER.
EDGAR, *son to Gloucester.*
EDMUND, *bastard son to Gloucester.*
CURAN, *a courtier.*
Old Man, tenant to Gloucester.
Doctor.
Fool.
OSWALD, *steward to Goneril.*
A captain employed by Edmund.
Gentleman attendant on Cordelia.
Herald.
Servants to Cornwall.
GONERIL, REGAN, CORDELIA, *daughters to Lear.*

Knights of Lear's train, Captains, Messengers, Soldiers, and Attendants.

SCENE : *Britain.*

ACT I—SCENE I

King Lear's palace.

Enter Kent, Gloucester, and Edmund.

Kent. I thought the king had more affected the Duke of Albany than Cornwall.

Glou. It did always seem so to us: but now, in the division of the kingdom, it appears not which of the dukes he values most; for equalities are so weighed that curiosity in neither can make choice of either's moiety.

Kent. Is not this your son, my lord?

Glou. His breeding, sir, hath been at my charge: I have so often blushed to acknowledge him that now I am brazed to it.

Kent. I cannot conceive you.

Glou. Sir, this young fellow's mother could: whereupon she grew round-wombed, and had indeed, sir, a son for her cradle ere she had a husband for her bed. Do you smell a fault?

Kent. I cannot wish the fault undone, the issue of it being so proper.

Glou. But I have, sir, a son by order of law, some year elder than this, who yet is no dearer in my account: though this knave came something saucily into the world before he was sent for, yet was his mother fair; there was good sport at his making, and the whoreson must be acknowledged. Do you know this noble gentleman, Edmund?

Edm. No, my lord.

Glou. My lord of Kent: remember him hereafter as my honourable friend.

Edm. My services to your lordship.

Kent. I must love you, and sue to know you better.

Edm. Sir, I shall study deserving.

Glou. He hath been out nine years, and away he shall again. The king is coming.

Sennet. Enter one bearing a coronet, King Lear, Cornwall, Albany, Goneril, Regan, Cordelia, and Attendants.

Lear. Attend the lords of France and Burgundy, Gloucester.

Glou. I shall, my liege. [*Exeunt Gloucester and Edmund.*

Lear. Meantime we shall express our darker purpose.
Give me the map there. Know we have divided
In three our kingdom: and 'tis our fast intent
To shake all cares and business from our age,
Conferring them on younger strengths, while we
Unburthen'd crawl toward death. Our son of Cornwall,
And you, our no less loving son of Albany,
We have this hour a constant will to publish
Our daughters' several dowers, that future strife
May be prevented now. The princes, France and Burgundy,
Great rivals in our youngest daughter's love,
Long in our court have made their amorous sojourn,
And here are to be answer'd. Tell me, my daughters,
Since now we will divest us both of rule,
Interest of territory, cares of state,
Which of you shall we say doth love us most?
That we our largest bounty may extend
Where nature doth with merit challenge. Goneril,
Our eldest-born, speak first.

Gon. Sir, I love you more than words can wield the matter,
Dearer than eye-sight, space and liberty,
Beyond what can be valued, rich or rare,
No less than life, with grace, health, beauty, honour,
As much as child e'er loved or father found;
A love that makes breath poor and speech unable;
Beyond all manner of so much I love you.

Cor. [*Aside*] What shall Cordelia do? Love, and be silent.

Lear. Of all these bounds, even from this line to this,
With shadowy forests and with champains rich'd,
With plenteous rivers and wide-skirted meads,
We make thee lady. To thine and Albany's issue
Be this perpetual. What says our second daughter,
Our dearest Regan, wife to Cornwall? Speak.

Reg. I am made of that self metal as my sister,
And prize me at her worth. In my true heart
I find she names my very deed of love;
Only she comes too short: that I profess
Myself an enemy to all other joys
Which the most precious square of sense possesses,
And find I am alone felicitate
In your dear highness' love.

Cor. [*Aside*] Then poor Cordelia!
And yet not so, since I am sure my love 's
More ponderous than my tongue.

Lear. To thee and thine hereditary ever
Remain this ample third of our fair kingdom,
No less in space, validity and pleasure,
Than that conferr'd on Goneril. Now, our joy,
Although the last, not least, to whose young love
The vines of France and milk of Burgundy
Strive to be interess'd, what can you say to draw
A third more opulent than your sisters? Speak.

Cor. Nothing, my lord.

Lear. Nothing!

Cor. Nothing.

Lear. Nothing will come of nothing: speak again.

Cor. Unhappy that I am, I cannot heave
My heart into my mouth: I love your majesty
According to my bond; nor more nor less.

Lear. How, how, Cordelia! mend your speech a little,
Lest it may mar your fortunes.

Cor. Good my lord,
You have begot me, bred me, loved me: I
Return those duties back as are right fit,
Obey you, love you, and most honour you.
Why have my sisters husbands, if they say
They love you all? Haply, when I shall wed,
That lord whose hand must take my plight shall carry
Half my love with him, half my care and duty:
Sure, I shall never marry like my sisters,
To love my father all.

Lear. But goes thy heart with this?

Cor. Ay, good my lord.

Lear. So young, and so untender?

Cor. So young, my lord, and true.

Lear. Let it be so; thy truth then be thy dower:
For, by the sacred radiance of the sun,
The mysteries of Hecate, and the night;
By all the operation of the orbs
From whom we do exist and cease to be;
Here I disclaim all my paternal care,
Propinquity and property of blood,
And as a stranger to my heart and me
Hold thee from this for ever. The barbarous Scythian,
Or he that makes his generation messes
To gorge his appetite, shall to my bosom

Be as well neighbour'd, pitied and relieved,
As thou my sometime daughter.

Kent. Good my liege,—

Lear. Peace, Kent!
Come not between the dragon and his wrath.
I loved her most, and thought to set my rest
On her kind nursery. Hence, and avoid my sight!
So be my grave my peace, as here I give
Her father's heart from her! Call France. Who stirs?
Call Burgundy. Cornwall and Albany,
With my two daughters' dowers digest this third:
Let pride, which she calls plainness, marry her.
I do invest you jointly with my power,
Pre-eminence and all the large effects
That troop with majesty. Ourself, by monthly course,
With reservation of an hundred knights
By you to be sustain'd, shall our abode
Make with you by due turns. Only we still retain
The name and all the additions to a king;
The sway, revenue, execution of the rest,
Beloved sons, be yours: which to confirm,
This coronet part betwixt you.

Kent. Royal Lear,
Whom I have ever honour'd as my king,
Loved as my father, as my master follow'd,
As my great patron thought on in my prayers,—

Lear. The bow is bent and drawn; make from the shaft.

Kent. Let it fall rather, though the fork invade
The region of my heart: be Kent unmannerly,
When Lear is mad. What wouldst thou do, old man?
Think'st thou that duty shall have dread to speak,
When power to flattery bows? To plainness honour's bound,
When majesty stoops to folly. Reverse thy doom,
And in thy best consideration check
This hideous rashness: answer my life my judgement,
Thy youngest daughter does not love thee least;
Nor are those empty-hearted whose low sound
Reverbs no hollowness.

Lear. Kent, on thy life, no more.

Kent. My life I never held but as a pawn
To wage against thy enemies, nor fear to lose it,
Thy safety being the motive.

Lear. Out of my sight!

Kent. See better, Lear, and let me still remain
The true blank of thine eye.

Lear. Now, by Apollo,—
Kent. Now, by Apollo, king,
Thou swear'st thy gods in vain.
Lear. O, vassal! miscreant!
[*Laying his hand on his sword.*
Alb.
Corn. Dear sir, forbear.
Kent. Do;
Kill thy physician, and the fee bestow
Upon the foul disease. Revoke thy doom;
Or, whilst I can vent clamour from my throat,
I'll tell thee thou dost evil.
Lear. Hear me, recreant!
On thy allegiance, hear me!
Since thou hast sought to make us break our vow,
Which we durst never yet, and with strain'd pride
To come between our sentence and our power,
Which nor our nature nor our place can bear,
Our potency made good, take thy reward.
Five days we do allot thee, for provision
To shield thee from diseases of the world,
And on the sixth to turn thy hated back
Upon our kingdom: if on the tenth day following
Thy banish'd trunk be found in our dominions,
The moment is thy death. Away! By Jupiter,
This shall not be revoked.
Kent. Fare thee well, king: sith thus thou wilt appear,
Freedom lives hence, and banishment is here.
[*To Cordelia*] The gods to their dear shelter take thee, maid,
That justly think'st and hast most rightly said!
[*To Regan and Goneril*] And your large speeches may your deeds approve,
That good effects may spring from words of love.
Thus Kent, O princes, bids you all adieu;
He'll shape his old course in a country new. [*Exit.*

Flourish. Re-enter Gloucester, with France, Burgundy, and Attendants.

Glou. Here's France and Burgundy, my noble lord.
Lear. My lord of Burgundy,
We first address towards you, who with this king
Hath rivall'd for our daughter: what, in the least,
Will you require in present dower with her,
Or cease your quest of love?
Bur. Most royal majesty,
I crave no more than what your highness offer'd,

Nor will you tender less.

Lear. Right noble Burgundy,
When she was dear to us, we did hold her so;
But now her price is fall'n. Sir, there she stands:
If aught within that little seeming substance,
Or all of it, with our displeasure pierced,
And nothing more, may fitly like your grace,
She 's there, and she is yours.

Bur. I know no answer.

Lear. Will you, with those infirmities she owes,
Unfriended, new adopted to our hate,
Dower'd with our curse and stranger'd with our oath,
Take her, or leave her?

Bur. Pardon me, royal sir;
Election makes not up on such conditions.

Lear. Then leave her, sir; for, by the power that made me,
I tell you all her wealth. [*To France*] For you, great king,
I would not from your love make such a stray,
To match you where I hate; therefore beseech you
To avert your liking a more worthier way
Than on a wretch whom nature is ashamed
Almost to acknowledge hers.

France. This is most strange,
That she, that even but now was your best object,
The argument of your praise, balm of your age,
Most best, most dearest, should in this trice of time
Commit a thing so monstrous, to dismantle
So many folds of favour. Sure, her offence
Must be of such unnatural degree
That monsters it, or your fore-vouch'd affection
Fall'n into taint: which to believe of her,
Must be a faith that reason without miracle
Could never plant in me.

Cor. I yet beseech your majesty,--
If for I want that glib and oily art,
To speak and purpose not, since what I well intend,
I'll do 't before I speak,—that you make known
It is no vicious blot, murder, or foulness,
No unchaste action, or dishonour'd step,
That hath deprived me of your grace and favour;
But even for want of that for which I am richer,
A still-soliciting eye, and such a tongue
As I am glad I have not, though not to have it
Hath lost me in your liking.

Lear. Better thou

Hadst not been born than not to have pleased me better.
France. Is it but this? a tardiness in nature
Which often leaves the history unspoke
That it intends to do? My lord of Burgundy,
What say you to the lady? Love 's not love
When it is mingled with regards that stand
Aloof from the entire point. Will you have her?
She is herself a dowry.
Bur. Royal Lear,
Give but that portion which yourself proposed,
And here I take Cordelia by the hand,
Duchess of Burgundy.
Lear. Nothing: I have sworn; I am firm.
Bur. I am sorry then you have so lost a father
That you must lose a husband.
Cor. Peace be with Burgundy!
Since that respects of fortune are his love,
I shall not be his wife.
France. Fairest Cordelia, that art most rich being poor,
Most choice forsaken, and most loved despised,
Thee and thy virtues here I seize upon:
Be it lawful I take up what 's cast away.
Gods, gods! 'tis strange that from their cold'st neglect
My love should kindle to inflamed respect.
Thy dowerless daughter, king, thrown to my chance,
Is queen of us, of ours, and our fair France:
Not all the dukes of waterish Burgundy
Can buy this unprized precious maid of me.
Bid them farewell, Cordelia, though unkind:
Thou losest here, a better where to find.
Lear. Thou hast her, France: let her be thine, for we
Have no such daughter, nor shall ever see
That face of hers again. Therefore be gone
Without our grace, our love, our benison.
Come, noble Burgundy.
[*Flourish. Exeunt all but France, Goneril, Regan, and Cordelia.*
France. Bid farewell to your sisters.
Cor. The jewels of our father, with wash'd eyes
Cordelia leaves you: I know you what you are;
And, like a sister, am most loath to call
Your faults as they are named. Use well our father:
To your professed bosoms I commit him:
But yet, alas, stood I within his grace,
I would prefer him to a better place.
So farewell to you both.

Reg. Prescribe not us our duties.
Gon. Let your study
Be to content your lord, who hath received you
At fortune's alms. You have obedience scanted,
And well are worth the want that you have wanted.
Cor. Time shall unfold what plaited cunning hides:
Who cover faults, at last shame them derides.
Well may you prosper!
France. Come, my fair Cordelia.
[*Exeunt France and Cordelia.*

Gon. Sister, it is not a little I have to say of what most nearly appertains to us both. I think our father will hence to-night.

Reg. That 's most certain, and with you; next month with us.

Gon. You see how full of changes his age is; the observation we have made of it hath not been little: he always loved our sister most; and with what poor judgement he hath now cast her off appears too grossly.

Reg. 'Tis the infirmity of his age; yet he hath ever but slenderly known himself.

Gon. The best and soundest of his time hath been but rash; then must we look to receive from his age, not alone the imperfections of long ingrafted condition, but therewithal the unruly waywardness that infirm and choleric years bring with them.

Reg. Such unconstant starts are we like to have from him as this of Kent's banishment.

Gon. There is further compliment of leave-taking between France and him. Pray you, let 's hit together: if our father carry authority with such dispositions as he bears, this last surrender of his will but offend us.

Reg. We shall further think on 't.

Gon. We must do something, and i' the heat. [*Exeunt.*

Scene II

The Earl of Gloucester's castle.

Enter Edmund, with a letter.

Edm. Thou, nature, art my goddess; to thy law
My services are bound. Wherefore should I
Stand in the plague of custom, and permit
The curiosity of nations to deprive me,
For that I am some twelve or fourteen moonshines
Lag of a brother? Why bastard? wherefore base?
When my dimensions are as well compact,
My mind as generous and my shape as true,
As honest madam's issue? Why brand they us

With base? with baseness? bastardy? base, base?
Who in the lusty stealth of nature take
More composition and fierce quality
Than doth, within a dull, stale, tired bed,
Go to the creating a whole tribe of fops,
Got 'tween asleep and wake? Well then,
Legitimate Edgar, I must have your land:
Our father's love is to the bastard Edmund
As to the legitimate: fine word, 'legitimate'!
Well, my legitimate, if this letter speed
And my invention thrive, Edmund the base
Shall top the legitimate. I grow; I prosper:
Now, gods, stand up for bastards!

Enter Gloucester.

Glou. Kent banish'd thus! and France in choler parted!
And the king gone to-night! subscribed his power!
Confined to exhibition! All this done
Upon the gad! Edmund, how now! what news?

Edm. So please your lordship, none. [*Putting up the letter.*

Glou. Why so earnestly seek you to put up that letter?

Edm. I know no news, my lord.

Glou. What paper were you reading?

Edm. Nothing, my lord.

Glou. No? What needed then that terrible dispatch of it into your pocket? the quality of nothing hath not such need to hide itself. Let's see: come, if it be nothing, I shall not need spectacles.

Edm. I beseech you, sir, pardon me: it is a letter from my brother, that I have not all o'er-read; and for so much as I have perused, I find it not fit for your o'er-looking.

Glou. Give me the letter, sir.

Edm. I shall offend, either to detain or give it. The contents, as in part I understand them, are to blame.

Glou Let's see, let's see.

Edm. I hope, for my brother's justification, he wrote this but as an essay or taste of my virtue.

Glou. [*Reads*] 'This policy and reverence of age makes the world bitter to the best of our times; keeps our fortunes from us till our oldness cannot relish them. I begin to find an idle and fond bondage in the oppression of aged tyranny; who sways, not as it hath power, but as it is suffered. Come to me, that of this I may speak more. If our father would sleep till I waked him, you should enjoy half his revenue for ever, and live the beloved of your brother, EDGAR.' Hum! Conspiracy!—'Sleep till I waked him, you should enjoy half his revenue,—My son Edgar! Had he a hand to write this? a heart and brain to breed it in? When came this to you? who brought it?

Edm. It was not brought me, my lord; there 's the cunning of it; I found it thrown in at the casement of my closet.

Glou. You know the character to be your brother's?

Edm. If the matter were good, my lord, I durst swear it were his; but, in respect of that, I would fain think it were not.

Glou. It is his.

Edm. It is his hand, my lord; but I hope his heart is not in the [contents.

Glou. Hath he never heretofore sounded you in this business?

Edm. Never, my lord: but I have heard him oft maintain it to be fit, that, sons at perfect age, and fathers declining, the father should be as ward to the son, and the son manage his revenue.

Glou. O villain, villain! His very opinion in the letter! Abhorred villain! Unnatural, detested, brutish villain! worse than brutish! Go, sirrah, seek him; ay, apprehend him: abominable villain! Where is he?

Edm. I do not well know, my lord. If it shall please you to suspend your indignation against my brother till you can derive from him better testimony of his intent, you should run a certain course; where, if you violently proceed against him, mistaking his purpose, it would make a great gap in your own honour and shake in pieces the heart of his obedience. I dare pawn down my life for him that he hath wrote this to feel my affection to your honour and to no further pretence of danger.

Glou. Think you so?

Edm. If your honour judge it meet, I will place you where you shall hear us confer of this, and by an auricular assurance have your satisfaction, and that without any further delay than this very evening.

Glou. He cannot be such a monster—

Edm. Nor is not, sure.

Glou. To his father, that so tenderly and entirely loves him. Heaven and earth! Edmund, seek him out; wind me into him, I pray you: frame the business after your own wisdom. I would unstate myself, to be in a due resolution.

Edm. I will seek him, sir, presently, convey the business as I shall find means, and acquaint you withal.

Glou. These late eclipses in the sun and moon portend no good to us: though the wisdom of nature can reason it thus and thus, yet nature finds itself scourged by the sequent effects: love cools, friendship falls off, brothers divide: in cities, mutinies; in countries, discord; in palaces, treason; and the bond cracked 'twixt son and father. This villain of mine comes under the prediction; there's son against father: the king falls from bias of nature; there's father against child. We have seen the best of our time: machinations, hollowness, treachery and all ruinous disorders follow us disquietly to our graves. Find out this villain, Edmund; it shall lose thee nothing; do it carefully. And the noble and true-hearted Kent banished! his offence, honesty! 'Tis strange. [*Exit.*

Edm. This is the excellent foppery of the world, that when we are sick in fortune—often the surfeit of our own behaviour—we make guilty of our disasters the sun, the moon and the stars: as if we were villains by necessity, fools by heavenly compulsion; knaves, thieves and treachers, by spherical predominance; drunkards, liars and adulterers, by an enforced obedience of planetary influence; and all that we are evil in, by a divine thrusting on: an admirable evasion of whoremaster man, to lay his goatish disposition to the charge of a star! My father compounded with my mother under the dragon's tail, and my nativity was under Ursa major; so that it follows I am rough and lecherous. Tut, I should have been that I am, had the maidenliest star in the firmament twinkled on my bastardizing. Edgar—

Enter Edgar.

And pat he comes like the catastrophe of the old comedy: my cue is villainous melancholy, with a sigh like Tom o' Bedlam. O, these eclipses do portend these divisions! fa, sol, la, mi.

Edg. How now, brother Edmund! what serious contemplation are you in?

Edm. I am thinking, brother, of a prediction I read this other day, what should follow these eclipses.

Edg. Do you busy yourself about that?

Edm. I promise you, the effects he writ of succeed unhappily; as of unnaturalness between the child and the parent; death, dearth, dissolutions of ancient amities; divisions in state, menaces and maledictions against king and nobles; needless diffidences, banishment of friends, dissipation of cohorts, nuptial breaches, and I know not what.

Edg. How long have you been a sectary astronomical?

Edm. Come, come; when saw you my father last?

Edg. Why, the night gone by.

Edm. Spake you with him?

Edg. Ay, two hours together.

Edm. Parted you in good terms? Found you no displeasure in him by word or countenance?

Edg. None at all.

Edm. Bethink yourself wherein you may have offended him: and at my entreaty forbear his presence till some little time hath qualified the heat of his displeasure, which at this instant so rageth in him that with the mischief of your person it would scarcely allay.

Edg. Some villain hath done me wrong.

Edm. That 's my fear. I pray you, have a continent forbearance till the speed of his rage goes slower, and, as I say, retire with me to my lodging, from whence I will fitly bring you to hear my lord speak: pray ye, go; there 's my key: if you do stir abroad, go armed.

Edg. Armed, brother!

Edm. Brother, I advise you to the best: go armed: I am no honest man if there be any good meaning towards you: I have told you what I have seen and heard; but faintly, nothing like the image and horror of it: pray you, away.

Edg. Shall I hear from you anon?

Edm. I do serve you in this business. [*Exit Edgar.*
A credulous father, and a brother noble,
Whose nature is so far from doing harms
That he suspects none; on whose foolish honesty
My practices ride easy. I see the business.
Let me, if not by birth, have lands by wit:
All with me 's meet that I can fashion fit. [*Exit.*

Scene III

The Duke of Albany's palace.

Enter Goneril and Oswald, her steward.

Gon. Did my father strike my gentleman for chiding of his fool?

Osw. Yes, madam.

Gon. By day and night he wrongs me; every hour
He flashes into one gross crime or other,
That sets us all at odds: I 'll not endure it:
His knights grow riotous, and himself upbraids us
On every trifle. When he returns from hunting,
I will not speak with him; say I am sick:
If you come slack of former services,
You shall do well; the fault of it I 'll answer.

Osw. He 's coming, madam; I hear him. [*Horns within.*

Gon. Put on what weary negligence you please,
You and your fellows; I 'ld have it come to question:
If he distaste it, let him to our sister,
Whose mind and mine, I know, in that are one,
Not to be over-ruled. Idle old man,

That still would manage those authorities
That he hath given away! Now, by my life,
Old fools are babes again, and must be used
With checks as flatteries, when they are seen abused.
Remember what I tell you.

Osw. Very well, madam.

Gon. And let his knights have colder looks among you;
What grows of it, no matter; advise your fellows so:
I would breed from hence occasions, and I shall,
That I may speak: I'll write straight to my sister,
To hold my very course. Prepare for dinner. [*Exeunt.*

Scene IV

A hall in the same.

Enter Kent, disguised.

Kent. If but as well I other accents borrow,
That can my speech defuse, my good intent
May carry through itself to that full issue
For which I razed my likeness. Now, banish'd Kent,
If thou canst serve where thou dost stand condemn'd,
So may it come, thy master whom thou lovest
Shall find thee full of labours.

Horns within. Enter Lear, Knights, and Attendants.

Lear. Let me not stay a jot for dinner; go get it ready. [*Exit an Attendant.*] How now! what art thou?

Kent. A man, sir.

Lear. What dost thou profess? What wouldst thou with us?

Kent. I do profess to be no less than I seem; to serve him truly that will put me in trust; to love him that is honest; to converse with him that is wise and says little; to fear judgement; to fight when I cannot choose, and to eat no fish.

Lear. What art thou?

Kent. A very honest-hearted fellow, and as poor as the king.

Lear. If thou be as poor for a subject as he is for a king, thou art poor enough. What wouldst thou?

Kent. Service.

Lear. Who wouldst thou serve?

Kent. You.

Lear. Dost thou know me, fellow?

Kent. No, sir; but you have that in your countenance which I would fain call master.

Lear. What's that?

Kent. Authority.

Lear. What services canst thou do?

Kent. I can keep honest counsel, ride, run, mar a curious tale in telling it, and deliver a plain message bluntly: that which ordinary men are fit for, I am qualified in, and the best of me is diligence.

Lear. How old art thou?

Kent. Not so young, sir, to love a woman for singing, nor so old to dote on her for any thing: I have years on my back forty eight.

Lear. Follow me; thou shalt serve me: if I like thee no worse after dinner, I will not part from thee yet. Dinner, ho, dinner! Where's my knave? my fool? Go you, and call my fool hither. [*Exit an Attendant.*

Enter Oswald.

You, you, sirrah, where's my daughter?

Osw. So please you,— [*Exit.*

Lear. What says the fellow there? Call the clot-poll back. [*Exit a Knight.*] Where's my fool, ho? I think the world 's asleep.

Re-enter Knight.

How now! where's that mongrel?

Knight. He says, my lord, your daughter is not well.

Lear. Why came not the slave back to me when I called him?

Knight. Sir, he answered me in the roundest manner, he would not.

Lear. He would not!

Knight. My lord, I know not what the matter is; but, to my judgement, your highness is not entertained with that ceremonious affection as you were wont; there's a great abatement of kindness appears as well in the general dependants as in the duke himself also and your daughter.

Lear. Ha! sayest thou so?

Knight. I beseech you, pardon me, my lord, if I be mistaken; for my duty cannot be silent when I think your highness wronged.

Lear. Thou but rememberest me of mine own conception: I have perceived a most faint neglect of late; which I have rather blamed as mine own jealous curiosity than as a very pretence and purpose of unkindness: I will look further into 't. But where's my fool? I have not seen him these two days.

Knight. Since my young lady's going into France, sir, the fool hath much pined away.

Lear. No more of that; I have noted it well. Go you, and tell my daughter I would speak with her. [*Exit an Attendant.*] Go you, call hither my fool. [*Exit an Attendant.*

Re-enter Oswald.

O, you sir, you, come you hither, sir: who am I, sir?

Osw. My lady's father.

Lear. My lady's father! my lord's knave: you whoreson dog! you slave! you cur!

Osw. I am none of these, my lord; I beseech your pardon.

Lear. Do you bandy looks with me, you rascal? [*Striking him.*

Osw. I'll not be struck, my lord.

Kent. Nor tripped neither, you base foot-ball player. [*Tripping up his heels.*

Lear. I thank thee, fellow; thou servest me, and I'll love thee.

Kent. Come, sir, arise, away! I'll teach you differences: away, away! If you will measure your lubber's length again, tarry: but away! go to; have you wisdom? so. [*Pushes Oswald out.*

Lear. Now, my friendly knave, I thank thee: there's earnest of thy service. [*Giving Kent money.*

Enter Fool.

Fool. Let me hire him too: here's my coxcomb. [*Offering Kent his cap.*

Lear. How now, my pretty knave! how dost thou?

Fool. Sirrah, you were best take my coxcomb.

Kent. Why, fool?

Fool. Why, for taking one's part that's out of favour: nay, as thou canst not smile as the wind sits, thou'lt catch cold shortly: there, take my coxcomb: why, this fellow hath banished two on's daughters, and done the third a blessing against his will; if thou follow him, thou must needs wear my coxcomb. How now, nuncle! Would I had two coxcombs and two daughters!

Lear. Why, my boy?

Fool. If I gave them all my living, I'ld keep my coxcombs myself. There's mine; beg another of thy daughters.

Lear. Take heed, sirrah; the whip.

Fool. Truth's a dog must to kennel; he must be whipped out, when Lady the brach may stand by the fire and stink.

Lear. A pestilent gall to me!

Fool. Sirrah, I'll teach thee a speech.

Lear. Do.

Fool. Mark it, nuncle:

Have more than thou showest,
Speak less than thou knowest,
Lend less than thou owest,
Ride more than thou goest,
Learn more than thou trowest,

Set less than thou throwest;
Leave thy drink and thy whore,
And keep in-a-door,
And thou shalt have more
Than two tens to a score.

Kent. This is nothing, fool.

Fool. Then 'tis like the breath of an unfee'd lawyer, you gave me nothing for 't. Can you make no use of nothing, nuncle?

Lear. Why, no, boy; nothing can be made out of nothing.

Fool. [*To Kent*] Prithee, tell him, so much the rent of his land comes to: he will not believe a fool.

Lear. A bitter fool!

Fool. Dost thou know the difference, my boy, between a bitter fool and a sweet fool?

Lear. No, lad; teach me.

Fool. That lord that counsell'd thee
To give away thy land,
Come place him here by me;
Do thou for him stand:
The sweet and bitter fool
Will presently appear;
The one in motley here,
The other found out there.

Lear. Dost thou call me fool, boy?

Fool. All thy other titles thou hast given away; that thou wast born with.

Kent. This is not altogether fool, my lord.

Fool. No, faith, lords and great men will not let me; if I had a monopoly out, they would have part on 't: and ladies too, they will not let me have all the fool to myself; they 'll be snatching. Give me an egg, nuncle, and I 'll give thee two crowns.

Lear. What two crowns shall they be?

Fool. Why, after I have cut the egg in the middle and eat up the meat, the two crowns of the egg. When thou clovest thy crown i' the middle and gavest away both parts, thou borest thine ass on thy back o'er the dirt: thou hadst little wit in thy bald crown when thou gavest thy golden one away. If I speak like myself in this, let him be whipped that first finds it so.

[*Singing*] Fools had ne'er less wit in a year;
For wise men are grown foppish,
And know not how their wits to wear,
Their manners are so apish.

Lear. When were you wont to be so full of songs, sirrah?

Fool. I have used it, nuncle, ever since thou madest thy daughters thy mother: for when thou gavest them the rod and puttest down thine own breeches,

[*Singing*] Then they for sudden joy did weep,
And I for sorrow sung,
That such a king should play bo-peep,
And go the fools among.

Prithee, nuncle, keep a schoolmaster that can teach thy fool to lie: I would fain learn to lie.

Lear. An you lie, sirrah, we 'll have you whipped.

Fool. I marvel what kin thou and thy daughters are: they 'll have me whipped for speaking true, thou 'lt have me whipped for lying, and sometimes I am whipped for holding my peace. I had rather be any kind o' thing than a fool: and yet I would not be thee, nuncle; thou hast pared thy wit o' both sides and left nothing i' the middle. Here comes one o' the parings.

Enter Goneril.

Lear. How now, daughter! what makes that frontlet on? Methinks you are too much of late i' the frown.

Fool. Thou wast a pretty fellow when thou hadst no need to care for her frowning; now thou art an O without a figure: I am better than thou art now; I am a fool, thou art nothing. [*To Gon.*] Yes, forsooth, I will hold my tongue; so your face bids me, though you say nothing.

Mum, mum:
He that keeps nor crust nor crumb,
Weary of all, shall want some.

[*Pointing to Lear*] That 's a shealed peascod.

Gon. Not only, sir, this your all-licensed fool,
But other of your insolent retinue
Do hourly carp and quarrel, breaking forth
In rank and not to be endured riots. Sir,
I had thought, by making this well known unto you,
To have found a safe redress; but now grow fearful,
By what yourself too late have spoke and done,
That you protect this course and put it on
By your allowance; which if you should, the fault
Would not 'scape censure, nor the redresses sleep,
Which, in the tender of a wholesome weal,
Might in their working do you that offence
Which else were shame, that then necessity
Will call discreet proceeding.

Fool. For, you know, nuncle,
The hedge-sparrow fed the cuckoo so long,
That it had its head bit off by its young.
So out went the candle, and we were left darkling.

Lear. Are you our daughter?

Gon. Come, sir,
I would you would make use of that good wisdom
Whereof I know you are fraught, and put away
These dispositions that of late transform you
From what you rightly are.

Fool. May not an ass know when the cart draws the horse? Whoop, Jug! I love thee.

Lear. Doth any here know me? This is not Lear:
Doth Lear walk thus? speak thus? Where are his eyes?
Either his notion weakens, his discernings
Are lethargied—Ha! waking? 'tis not so.
Who is it that can tell me who I am?

Fool. Lear's shadow.

Lear. I would learn that; for, by the marks of sovereignty, knowledge and reason, I should be false persuaded I had daughters.

Fool. Which they will make an obedient father.

Lear. Your name, fair gentlewoman?

Gon. This admiration, sir, is much o' the savour
Of other your new pranks. I do beseech you
To understand my purposes aright:
As you are old and reverend, you should be wise.
Here do you keep a hundred knights and squires;
Men so disorder'd, so debosh'd and bold,
That this our court, infected with their manners,
Shows like a riotous inn: epicurism and lust
Make it more like a tavern or a brothel
Than a graced palace. The shame itself doth speak
For instant remedy: be then desired
By her that else will take the thing she begs
A little to disquantity your train,
And the remainder that shall still depend,
To be such men as may besort your age,
Which know themselves and you.

Lear. Darkness and devils!
Saddle my horses; call my train together.
Degenerate bastard! I 'll not trouble thee:
Yet have I left a daughter.

Gon. You strike my people, and your disorder'd rabble
Make servants of their betters.

Enter Albany.

Lear. Woe, that too late repents,—[*To Alb.*] O, sir, are you come?
Is it your will? Speak, sir. Prepare my horses.
Ingratitude, thou marble-hearted fiend,
More hideous when thou show'st thee in a child
Than the sea-monster!

Alb. Pray, sir, be patient.

Lear. [*To Gon.*] Detested kite! thou liest.
My train are men of choice and rarest parts,
That all particulars of duty know,
And in the most exact regard support
The worships of their name. O most small fault,
How ugly didst thou in Cordelia show!
That, like an engine, wrench'd my frame of nature
From the fix'd place, drew from my heart all love
And added to the gall. O Lear, Lear, Lear!
Beat at this gate, and let thy folly in [*Striking his head.*
And thy dear judgement out! Go, go, my people.

Alb. My lord, I am guiltless, as I am ignorant
Of what hath moved you.

Lear. It may be so, my lord.
Hear, nature, hear; dear goddess, hear!
Suspend thy purpose, if thou didst intend
To make this creature fruitful:
Into her womb convey sterility:
Dry up in her the organs of increase,
And from her derogate body never spring
A babe to honour her! If she must teem,
Create her child of spleen, that it may live
And be a thwart disnatured torment to her.
Let it stamp wrinkles in her brow of youth;
With cadent tears fret channels in her cheeks;
Turn all her mother's pains and benefits
To laughter and contempt; that she may feel
How sharper than a serpent's tooth it is
To have a thankless child! Away, away! [*Exit.*

Alb. Now, gods that we adore, whereof comes this?

Gon. Never afflict yourself to know the cause,
But let his disposition have that scope
That dotage gives it.

Re-enter Lear.

Lear. What, fifty of my followers at a clap!
Within a fortnight!

Alb. What 's the matter, sir?

Lear. I 'll tell thee. [*To Gon.*] Life and death! I am ashamed

That thou hast power to shake my manhood thus;
That these hot tears, which break from me perforce,
Should make thee worth them. Blasts and fogs upon thee!
The untented woundings of a father's curse
Pierce every sense about thee! Old fond eyes,
Beweep this cause again, I 'll pluck ye out
And cast you with the waters that you lose
To temper clay. Yea, is it come to this?
Let it be so: yet have I left a daughter,
Who, I am sure, is kind and comfortable:
When she shall hear this of thee, with her nails
She 'll flay thy wolvish visage. Thou shalt find
That I 'll resume the shape which thou dost think
I have cast off for ever: thou shalt, I warrant thee.
[*Exeunt Lear, Kent, and Attendants.*

Gon. Do you mark that, my lord?

Alb. I cannot be so partial, Goneril,
To the great love I bear you,—

Gon. Pray you, content. What, Oswald, ho!
[*To the Fool*] You, sir, more knave than fool, after your master.

Fool. Nuncle Lear, nuncle Lear, tarry; take the fool with thee.
A fox, when one has caught her,
And such a daughter,
Should sure to the slaughter,
If my cap would buy a halter:
So the fool follows after. [*Exit.*

Gon. This man hath had good counsel: a hundred knights!
'Tis politic and safe to let him keep
At point a hundred knights: yes, that on every dream,
Each buzz, each fancy, each complaint, dislike,
He may enguard his dotage with their powers
And hold our lives in mercy. Oswald, I say!

Alb. Well, you may fear too far.

Gon. Safer than trust too far:
Let me still take away the harms I fear,
Not fear still to be taken: I know his heart.
What he hath utter'd I have writ my sister:
If she sustain him and his hundred knights,
When I have show'd the unfitness,—

Re-enter Oswald.

How now, Oswald!
What, have you writ that letter to my sister?

Osw. Yes, madam.

Gon. Take you some company, and away to horse:
Inform her full of my particular fear,

And thereto add such reasons of your own
As may compact it more. Get you gone;
And hasten your return. [*Exit Oswald.*] No, no, my lord,
This milky gentleness and course of yours
Though I condemn not, yet, under pardon,
You are much more attask'd for want of wisdom
Than praised for harmful mildness.

Alb. How far your eyes may pierce I cannot tell:
Striving to better, oft we mar what's well.

Gon. Nay, then—

Alb. Well, well; the event. [*Exeunt.*

Scene V

Court before the same.

Enter Lear, Kent, and Fool.

Lear. Go you before to Gloucester with these letters. Acquaint my daughter no further with any thing you know than comes from her demand out of the letter. If your diligence be not speedy, I shall be there afore you.

Kent. I will not sleep, my lord, till I have delivered your letter. [*Exit.*

Fool. If a man's brains were in 's heels, were 't not in danger of kibes?

Lear. Ay, boy.

Fool. Then, I prithee, be merry; thy wit shall ne'er go slip-shod.

Lear. Ha, ha, ha!

Fool. Shalt see thy other daughter will use thee kindly; for though she 's as like this as a crab 's like an apple, yet I can tell what I can tell.

Lear. Why, what canst thou tell, my boy?

Fool. She will taste as like this as a crab does to a crab. Thou canst tell why one's nose stands i' the middle on 'is face?

Lear. No.

Fool. Why, to keep one's eyes of either side 's nose, that what a man cannot smell out he may spy into.

Lear. I did her wrong—

Fool. Canst tell how an oyster makes his shell?

Lear. No.

Fool. Nor I neither; but I can tell why a snail has a house.

Lear. Why?

Fool. Why to put 's head in; not to give it away to his daughters, and leave his horns without a case.

Lear. I will forget my nature.—So kind a father!—Be my horses ready?

Fool. Thy asses are gone about 'em. The reason why the seven stars are no more than seven is a pretty reason.

Lear. Because they are not eight?

Fool. Yes, indeed: thou wouldst make a good fool.

Lear. To take 't again perforce! Monster ingratitude!

Fool. If thou wert my fool, nuncle, I 'ld have thee beaten for being old before thy time.

Lear. How 's that?

Fool. Thou shouldst not have been old till thou hadst been [wise.

Lear. O, let me not be mad, not mad, sweet heaven!
Keep me in temper: I would not be mad!

Enter Gentleman.

How now! are the horses ready?

Gent. Ready, my lord.

Lear. Come, boy.

Fool. She that 's a maid now and laughs at my departure
Shall not be a maid long, unless things be cut shorter.
[*Exeunt.*

ACT II—Scene I

The Earl of Gloucester's castle.

Enter Edmund and Curan, meeting.

Edm. Save thee, Curan.

Cur. And you, sir. I have been with your father, and given him notice that the Duke of Cornwall and Regan his duchess will be here with him this night.

Edm. How comes that?

Cur. Nay, I know not. You have heard of the news abroad, I mean the whispered ones, for they are yet but ear-kissing arguments?

Edm. Not I: pray you, what are they?

Cur. Have you heard of no likely wars toward, 'twixt the Dukes of Cornwall and Albany?

Edm. Not a word.

Cur. You may do then in time. Fare you well, sir. [*Exit.*

Edm. The duke be here to-night? The better! best!
This weaves itself perforce into my business.
My father hath set guard to take my brother;
And I have one thing, of a queasy question,
Which I must act: briefness and fortune, work!
Brother, a word; descend: brother, I say!

Enter Edgar.

My father watches: O sir, fly this place;
Intelligence is given where you are hid;

You have now the good advantage of the night:
Have you not spoken 'gainst the Duke of Cornwall?
He 's coming hither, now, i' the night, i' the haste,
And Regan with him: have you nothing said
Upon his party 'gainst the Duke of Albany?
Advise yourself.

Edg. I am sure on 't, not a word.

Edm. I hear my father coming: pardon me:
In cunning I must draw my sword upon you:
Draw: seem to defend yourself: now quit you well.
Yield: come before my father. Light, ho, here!
Fly, brother. Torches, torches! So farewell.
[*Exit Edgar.*
Some blood drawn on me would beget opinion
[*Wounds his arm.*
Of my more fierce endeavour: I have seen drunkards
Do more than this in sport. Father, father!
Stop, stop! No help?

Enter Gloucester, and Servants with torches.

Glou. Now, Edmund, where 's the villain?

Edm. Here stood he in the dark, his sharp sword out,
Mumbling of wicked charms, conjuring the moon
To stand 's auspicious mistress.

Glou. But where is he?

Edm. Look, sir, I bleed.

Glou. Where is the villain, Edmund?

Edm. Fled this way, sir. When by no means he could—

Glou. Pursue him, ho!—Go after. [*Exeunt some Servants.*]
'By no means' what?

Edm. Persuade me to the murder of your lordship;
But that I told him the revenging gods
'Gainst parricides did all their thunders bend,
Spoke with how manifold and strong a bond
The child was bound to the father; sir, in fine,
Seeing how loathly opposite I stood
To his unnatural purpose, in fell motion
With his prepared sword he charges home
My unprovided body, lanced mine arm:
But when he saw my best alarum'd spirits
Bold in the quarrel's right, roused to the encounter,
Or whether gasted by the noise I made,
Full suddenly he fled.

Glou. Let him fly far:
Not in this land shall he remain uncaught:
And found—dispatch. The noble duke my master,

My worthy arch and patron, comes to-night:
By his authority I will proclaim it,
That he which finds him shall deserve our thanks,
Bringing the murderous caitiff to the stake;
He that conceals him, death.

Edm. When I dissuaded him from his intent
And found him pight to do it, with curst speech
I threaten'd to discover him: he replied,
'Thou unpossessing bastard! dost thou think,
If I would stand against thee, could the reposure
Of any trust, virtue, or worth, in thee
Make thy words faith'd? No: what I should deny—
As this I would; ay, though thou didst produce
My very character—I 'ld turn it all
To thy suggestion, plot, and damned practice:
And thou must make a dullard of the world,
If they not thought the profits of my death
Were very pregnant and potential spurs
To make thee seek it.'

Glou. Strong and fasten'd villain!
Would he deny his letter? I never got him. [*Tucket within.*
Hark, the duke's trumpets! I know not why he comes.
All ports I 'll bar; the villain shall not 'scape;
The duke must grant me that: besides, his picture
I will send far and near, that all the kingdom
May have due note of him; and of my land,
Loyal and natural boy, I 'll work the means
To make thee capable.

Enter Cornwall, Regan, and Attendants.

Corn. How now, my noble friend! since I came hither,
Which I can call but now, I have heard strange news.

Reg. If it be true, all vengeance comes too short
Which can pursue the offender. How dost, my lord?

Glou. O, madam, my old heart is crack'd, is crack'd!

Reg. What, did my father's godson seek your life?
He whom my father named? your Edgar?

Glou. O, lady, lady, shame would have it hid!

Reg. Was he not companion with the riotous knights
That tend upon my father?

Glou. I know not, madam: 'tis too bad, too bad.

Edm. Yes, madam, he was of that consort.

Reg. No marvel then, though he were ill affected:
'Tis they have put him on the old man's death,
To have the waste and spoil of his revenues.
I have this present evening from my sister

Been well inform'd of them, and with such cautions
That if they come to sojourn at my house,
I 'll not be there.

Corn. Nor I, assure thee, Regan.
Edmund, I hear that you have shown your father
A child-like office.

Edm. 'Twas my duty, sir.

Glou. He did bewray his practice, and received
This hurt you see, striving to apprehend him.

Corn. Is he pursued?

Glou. Ay, my good lord.

Corn. If he be taken, he shall never more
Be fear'd of doing harm: make your own purpose,
How in my strength you please. For you, Edmund,
Whose virtue and obedience doth this instant
So much commend itself, you shall be ours:
Natures of such deep trust we shall much need:
You we first seize on.

Edm. I shall serve you, sir,
Truly, however else.

Glou. For him I thank your grace.

Corn. You know not why we came to visit you,—

Reg. Thus out of season, threading dark-eyed night:
Occasions, noble Gloucester, of some poise,
Wherein we must have use of your advice:
Our father he hath writ, so hath our sister,
Of differences, which I least thought it fit
To answer from our home; the several messengers
From hence attend dispatch. Our good old friend,
Lay comforts to your bosom, and bestow
Your needful counsel to our business,
Which craves the instant use.

Glou. I serve you, madam:
Your graces are right welcome. [*Flourish. Exeunt.*

Scene II

Before Gloucester's castle.

Enter Kent and Oswald, severally.

Osw. Good dawning to thee, friend: art of this house?

Kent. Ay.

Osw. Where may we set our horses?

Kent. I' the mire.

Osw. Prithee, if thou lovest me, tell me.

Kent. I love thee not.

Osw. Why then I care not for thee.

Kent. If I had thee in Lipsbury pinfold, I would make thee care for me.

Osw. Why dost thou use me thus? I know thee not.

Kent. Fellow, I know thee.

Osw. What dost thou know me for?

Kent. A knave; a rascal; an eater of broken meats; a base, proud, shallow, beggarly, three-suited, hundred-pound, filthy, worsted-stocking knave; a lily-livered, action-taking knave; a whoreson, glass-gazing, superserviceable, finical rogue; one-trunk-inheriting slave; one that wouldst be a bawd in way of good service, and art nothing but the composition of a knave, beggar, coward, pandar, and the son and heir of a mongrel bitch: one whom I will beat into clamorous whining, if thou deniest the least syllable of thy addition.

Osw. Why, what a monstrous fellow art thou, thus to rail on one that is neither known of thee nor knows thee!

Kent. What a brazen-faced varlet art thou, to deny thou knowest me! Is it two days ago since I tripped up thy heels and beat thee before the king? Draw, you rogue: for, though it be night, yet the moon shines; I'll make a sop o' the moonshine of you: draw, you whoreson cullionly barber-monger, draw. [*Drawing his sword.*

Osw. Away! I have nothing to do with thee.

Kent. Draw, you rascal: you come with letters against the king, and take vanity the puppet's part against the royalty of her father: draw, you rogue, or I'll so carbonado your shanks: draw, you rascal; come your ways.

Osw. Help, ho! murder! help!

Kent. Strike, you slave; stand, rogue; stand, you neat slave, strike. [*Beating him.*

Osw. Help, ho! murder! murder!

Enter Edmund, with his rapier drawn, Cornwall, Regan, Gloucester, and Servants.

Edm. How now! What's the matter? [*Parting them.*

Kent. With you, goodman boy, an you please: come, I'll flesh you; come on young master.

Glou. Weapons! arms! What's the matter here?

Corn. Keep peace, upon your lives;
He dies that strikes again. What is the matter?

Reg. The messengers from our sister and the king.

Corn. What is your difference? speak.

Osw. I am scarce in breath, my lord.

Kent. No marvel, you have so bestirred your valour. You cowardly rascal, nature disclaims in thee: a tailor made thee.

Corn. Thou art a strange fellow: a tailor make a man?

Kent. Ay, a tailor, sir: a stone-cutter or a painter could not have made him so ill, though he had been but two hours at the trade.

Corn. Speak yet, how grew your quarrel?

Osw. This ancient ruffian, sir, whose life I have spared at suit of his gray beard,—

Kent. Thou whoreson zed! thou unnecessary letter! My lord, if you will give me leave, I will tread this unbolted villain into mortar, and daub the walls of a jakes with him. Spare my gray beard, you wagtail?

Corn. Peace, sirrah!
You beastly knave, know you no reverence?

Kent. Yes, sir; but anger hath a privilege.

Corn. Why art thou angry?

Kent. That such a slave as this should wear a sword,
Who wears no honesty. Such smiling rogues as these,
Like rats, oft bite the holy cords a-twain
Which are too intrinse to unloose; smooth every passion
That in the natures of their lords rebel;
Bring oil to fire, snow to their colder moods;
Renege, affirm, and turn their halcyon beaks
With every gale and vary of their masters,
Knowing nought, like dogs, but following.
A plague upon your epileptic visage!
Smile you my speeches, as I were a fool?
Goose, if I had you upon Sarum plain,
I 'ld drive ye cackling home to Camelot.

Corn. What, art thou mad, old fellow?

Glou. How fell you out? say that.

Kent. No contraries hold more antipathy
Than I and such a knave.

Corn. Why dost thou call him knave? What is his fault?

Kent. His countenance likes me not.

Corn. No more perchance does mine, nor his, nor hers.

Kent. Sir, 'tis my occupation to be plain:
I have seen better faces in my time
Than stands on any shoulder that I see
Before me at this instant.

Corn. This is some fellow,
Who, having been praised for bluntness, doth affect
A saucy roughness, and constrains the garb
Quite from his nature: he cannot flatter, he,—
An honest mind and plain,—he must speak truth!
An they will take it, so; if not, he 's plain.
These kind of knaves I know, which in this plainness
Harbour more craft and more corrupter ends

Than twenty silly ducking observants
That stretch their duties nicely.

Kent. Sir, in good faith, in sincere verity,
Under the allowance of your great aspect,
Whose influence, like the wreath of radiant fire
On flickering Phœbus' front,—

Corn. What mean'st by this?

Kent. To go out of my dialect, which you discommend so much. I know, sir, I am no flatterer: he that beguiled you in a plain accent was a plain knave; which, for my part, I will not be, though I should win your displeasure to entreat me to 't.

Corn. What was the offence you gave him?

Osw. I never gave him any:
It pleased the king his master very late
To strike at me, upon his misconstruction;
When he, conjunct, and flattering his displeasure,
Tripp'd me behind; being down, insulted, rail'd,
And put upon him such a deal of man,
That worthied him, got praises of the king
For him attempting who was self-subdued,
And in the fleshment of this dread exploit
Drew on me here again.

Kent. None of these rogues and cowards
But Ajax is their fool.

Corn. Fetch forth the stocks!
You stubborn ancient knave, you reverend braggart,
We'll teach you—

Kent. Sir, I am too old to learn:
Call not your stocks for me: I serve the king,
On whose employment I was sent to you:
You shall do small respect, show too bold malice
Against the grace and person of my master,
Stocking his messenger.

Corn. Fetch forth the stocks! As I have life and honour,
There shall he sit till noon.

Reg. Till noon! till night, my lord, and all night too.

Kent. Why, madam, if I were your father's dog,
You should not use me so.

Reg. Sir, being his knave, I will.

Corn. This is a fellow of the self-same colour
Our sister speaks of. Come, bring away the stocks!
[*Stocks brought out.*

Glou. Let me beseech your grace not to do so:
His fault is much, and the good king his master

Will check him for 't: your purposed low correction
Is such as basest and contemned'st wretches
For pilferings and most common trespasses
Are punish'd with: the king must take it ill,
That he, so slightly valued in his messenger,
Should have him thus restrain'd.

Corn. I 'll answer that.

Reg. My sister may receive it much more worse,
To have her gentleman abused, assaulted,
For following her affairs. Put in his legs.
[*Kent is put in the stocks.*
Come, my good lord, away.
[*Exeunt all but Gloucester and Kent.*

Glou. I am sorry for thee, friend; 'tis the duke's pleasure,
Whose disposition, all the world well knows,
Will not be rubb'd nor stopp'd: I 'll entreat for thee.

Kent. Pray, do not, sir: I have watch'd and travell'd hard;
Some time I shall sleep out, the rest I 'll whistle.
A good man's fortune may grow out at heels:
Give you good morrow!

Glou. The duke 's to blame in this! 'twill be ill taken. [*Exit.*

Kent. Good king, that must approve the common saw,
Thou out of heaven's benediction comest
To the warm sun!
Approach, thou beacon to this under globe,
That by thy comfortable beams I may
Peruse this letter! Nothing almost sees miracles
But misery: I know 'tis from Cordelia,
Who hath most fortunately been inform'd
Of my obscured course; and shall find time
From this enormous state, seeking to give
Losses their remedies. All weary and o'er-watch'd,
Take vantage, heavy eyes, not to behold
This shameful lodging.
Fortune, good night: smile once more; turn thy wheel!
[*Sleeps.*

Scene III

A wood.

Enter Edgar.

Edg. I heard myself proclaim'd;
And by the happy hollow of a tree
Escaped the hunt. No port is free; no place,
That guard and most unusual vigilance
Does not attend my taking. Whiles I may 'scape

I will preserve myself: and am bethought
To take the basest and most poorest shape
That ever penury in contempt of man
Brought near to beast: my face I 'll grime with filth,
Blanket my loins, elf all my hair in knots,
And with presented nakedness out-face
The winds and persecutions of the sky.
The country gives me proof and precedent
Of Bedlam beggars, who with roaring voices
Strike in their numb'd and mortified bare arms
Pins, wooden pricks, nails, sprigs of rosemary;
And with this horrible object, from low farms,
Poor pelting villages, sheep-cotes and mills,
Sometime with lunatic bans, sometime with prayers,
Enforce their charity. Poor Turlygod! poor Tom!
That 's something yet: Edgar I nothing am. [*Exit.*

Scene IV

Before Gloucester's castle. Kent in the stocks.

Enter Lear, Fool, and Gentleman.

Lear. 'Tis strange that they should so depart from home,
And not send back my messenger.
Gent. As I learn'd,
The night before there was no purpose in them
Of this remove.
Kent. Hail to thee, noble master!
Lear. Ha!
Makest thou this shame thy pastime?
Kent. No, my lord.

Fool. Ha, ha! he wears cruel garters. Horses are tied by the heads, dogs and bears by the neck, monkeys by the loins, and men by the legs: when a man's over-lusty at legs, then he wears wooden nether-stocks.

Lear. What 's he that hath so much thy place mistook
To set thee here?
Kent. It is both he and she;
Your son and daughter.
Lear. No.
Kent. Yes.
Lear. No, I say.
Kent. I say, yea.
Lear. No, no, they would not.
Kent. Yes, they have.
Lear. By Jupiter, I swear, no.
Kent. By Juno, I swear, ay.

Lear. They durst not do 't;
They could not, would not do 't; 'tis worse than murder,
To do upon respect such violent outrage:
Resolve me with all modest haste which way
Thou mightst deserve, or they impose, this usage,
Coming from us.
Kent. My lord, when at their home
I did commend your highness' letters to them,
Ere I was risen from the place that show'd
My duty kneeling, came there a reeking post,
Stew'd in his haste, half breathless, panting forth
From Goneril his mistress salutations;
Deliver'd letters, spite of intermission,
Which presently they read: on whose contents
They summon'd up their meiny, straight took horse;
Commanded me to follow and attend
The leisure of their answer; gave me cold looks:
And meeting here the other messenger,
Whose welcome, I perceived, had poison'd mine—
Being the very fellow that of late
Display'd so saucily against your highness—
Having more man than wit about me, drew:
He raised the house with loud and coward cries.
Your son and daughter found this trespass worth
The shame which here it suffers.
Fool. Winter 's not gone yet, if the wild geese fly that way
Fathers that wear rags
Do make their children blind;
But fathers that bear bags
Shall see their children kind.
Fortune, that arrant whore,
Ne'er turns the key to the poor.
But, for all this, thou shalt have as many dolours for thy daughters as thou canst tell in a year.
Lear. O, how this mother swells up toward my heart!
Hysterica passio, down, thou climbing sorrow,
Thy element 's below! Where is this daughter?
Kent. With the earl, sir, here within.
Lear. Follow me not; stay here. [*Exit.*
Gent. Made you no more offence but what you speak of?
Kent. None.
How chance the king comes with so small a train?
Fool. An thou hadst been set i' the stocks for that question, thou hadst well deserved it.
Kent. Why, fool?

Fool. We 'll set thee to school to an ant, to teach thee there 's no labouring i' the winter. All that follow their noses are led by their eyes but blind men; and there 's not a nose among twenty but can smell him that 's stinking. Let go thy hold when a great wheel runs down a hill, lest it break thy neck with following it; but the great one that goes up the hill, let him draw thee after. When a wise man gives thee better counsel, give me mine again: I would have none but knaves follow it, since a fool gives it.

That sir which serves and seeks for gain,
    And follows but for form,
Will pack when it begins to rain,
    And leave thee in the storm.
But I will tarry; the fool will stay,
    And let the wise man fly:
The knave turns fool that runs away;
    The fool no knave, perdy.

Kent. Where learned you this, fool?

Fool. Not i' the stocks, fool.

Re-enter Lear, with Gloucester.

Lear. Deny to speak with me? They are sick? they are weary?
They have travell'd all the night? Mere fetches;
The images of revolt and flying off.
Fetch me a better answer.

Glou. My dear lord,
You know the fiery quality of the duke;
How unremoveable and fix'd he is
In his own course.

Lear. Vengeance! plague! death! confusion!
Fiery? what quality? Why, Gloucester, Gloucester,
I 'ld speak with the Duke of Cornwall and his wife.

Glou. Well, my good lord, I have inform'd them so.

Lear. Inform'd them! Dost thou understand me, man?

Glou. Ay, my good lord.

Lear. The king would speak with Cornwall; the dear father
Would with his daughter speak, commands her service:
Are they inform'd of this? My breath and blood!
'Fiery'? 'the fiery duke'? Tell the hot duke that—
No, but not yet: may be he is not well:
Infirmity doth still neglect all office
Whereto our health is bound; we are not ourselves
When nature being oppress'd commands the mind
To suffer with the body: I'll forbear;
And am fall'n out with my more headier will,
To take the indisposed and sickly fit

For the sound man. [*Looking on Kent*] Death on my state!
Should he sit here? This act persuades me [wherefore
That this remotion of the duke and her
Is practice only. Give me my servant forth.
Go tell the duke and 's wife I 'ld speak with them,
Now, presently: bid them come forth and hear me,
Or at their chamber-door I 'll beat the drum
Till it cry sleep to death.

Glou. I would have all well betwixt you. [*Exit.*

Lear. O me, my heart, my rising heart! But down!

Fool. Cry to it, nuncle, as the cockney did to the eels when she put 'em i' the paste alive; she knapped 'em o' the coxcombs with a stick, and cried 'Down, wantons, down!' 'Twas her brother that, in pure kindness to his horse, buttered his hay.

Re-enter Gloucester, with Cornwall, Regan, and Servants.

Lear. Good morrow to you both.

Corn. Hail to your grace! [*Kent is set at liberty.*

Reg. I am glad to see your highness.

Lear. Regan, I think you are; I know what reason
I have to think so: If thou shouldst not be glad,
I would divorce me from thy mother's tomb,
Sepulchring an adultress. [*To Kent*] O, are you free?
Some other time for that. Beloved Regan,
Thy sister 's naught: O Regan, she hath tied
Sharp-tooth'd unkindness, like a vulture, here:
[*Points to his heart.*
I can scarce speak to thee; thou 'lt not believe
With how depraved a quality—O Regan!

Reg. I pray you, sir, take patience: I have hope
You less know how to value her desert
Than she to scant her duty.

Lear. Say, how is that?

Reg. I cannot think my sister in the least
Would fail her obligation: if, sir, perchance
She have restrain'd the riots of your followers,
'Tis on such ground and to such wholesome end
As clears her from all blame.

Lear. My curses on her!

Reg. O, sir, you are old;
Nature in you stands on the very verge
Of her confine: you should be ruled and led
By some discretion that discerns your state
Better than you yourself. Therefore I pray you
That to our sister you do make return;
Say you have wrong'd her, sir.

Lear. Ask her forgiveness?
Do you but mark how this becomes the house:
[*Kneeling*] 'Dear daughter, I confess that I am old;
Age is unnecessary: on my knees I beg
That you 'll vouchsafe me raiment, bed and food.'
Reg. Good sir, no more; these are unsightly tricks:
Return you to my sister.
Lear. [*Rising*] Never, Regan:
She hath abated me of half my train;
Look'd black upon me; struck me with her tongue,
Most serpent-like, upon the very heart:
All the stored vengeances of heaven fall
On her ingrateful top! Strike her young bones,
You taking airs, with lameness.
Corn. Fie, sir, fie!
Lear. You nimble lightnings, dart your blinding flames
Into her scornful eyes. Infect her beauty,
You fen-suck'd fogs, drawn by the powerful sun
To fall and blast her pride.
Reg. O the blest gods! so will you wish on me,
When the rash mood is on.
Lear. No, Regan, thou shalt never have my curse:
Thy tender-hefted nature shall not give
Thee o'er to harshness: her eyes are fierce, but thine
Do comfort and not burn. 'Tis not in thee
To grudge my pleasures, to cut off my train,
To bandy hasty words, to scant my sizes,
And in conclusion to oppose the bolt
Against my coming in: thou better know'st
The offices of nature, bond of childhood,
Effects of courtesy, dues of gratitude;
Thy half o' the kingdom hast thou not forgot,
Wherein I thee endow'd.
Reg. Good sir, to the purpose.
Lear. Who put my man i' the stocks? [*Tucket within.*
Corn. What trumpet 's that?
Reg. I know 't; my sister's: this approves her letter,
That she would soon be here.

Enter Oswald.

Is your lady come?
Lear. This is a slave whose easy-borrow'd pride
Dwells in the fickle grace of her he follows.
Out, varlet, from my sight!
Corn. What means your grace?
Lear. Who stock'd my servant? Regan, I have good hope

Thou didst not know on 't. Who comes here?

Enter Goneril.

O heavens,
If you do love old men, if your sweet sway
Allow obedience, if yourselves are old,
Make it your cause; send down, and take my part!
[*To Gon.*] Art not ashamed to look upon this beard?
O Regan, wilt thou take her by the hand?

Gon. Why not by the hand, sir? How have I offended?
All 's not offence that indiscretion finds
And dotage terms so.

Lear. O sides, you are too tough;
Will you yet hold? How came my man i' the stocks?

Corn. I set him there, sir: but his own disorders
Deserved much less advancement.

Lear. You! did you?

Reg. I pray you, father, being weak, seem so.
If, till the expiration of your month,
You will return and sojourn with my sister,
Dismissing half your train, come then to me:
I am now from home and out of that provision
Which shall be needful for your entertainment.

Lear. Return to her, and fifty men dismiss'd?
No, rather I abjure all roofs, and choose
To wage against the enmity o' the air,
To be a comrade with the wolf and owl,—
Necessity's sharp pinch! Return with her?
Why, the hot-blooded France, that dowerless took
Our youngest born, I could as well be brought
To knee his throne, and, squire-like, pension beg
To keep base life afoot. Return with her?
Persuade me rather to be slave and sumpter
To this detested groom. [*Pointing at Oswald.*

Gon. At your choice, sir.

Lear. I prithee, daughter, do not make me mad:
I will not trouble thee, my child; farewell:
We 'll no more meet, no more see one another:
But yet thou art my flesh, my blood, my daughter;
Or rather a disease that 's in my flesh,
Which I must needs call mine: thou art a boil,
A plague-sore, an embossed carbuncle,
In my corrupted blood. But I 'll not chide thee;
Let shame come when it will, I do not call it:
I do not bid the thunder-bearer shoot,
Nor tell tales of thee to high-judging Jove:

Mend when thou canst; be better at thy leisure:
I can be patient; I can stay with Regan,
I and my hundred knights.

Reg. Not altogether so:
I look'd not for you yet, nor am provided
For your fit welcome. Give ear, sir, to my sister;
For those that mingle reason with your passion
Must be content to think you old, and so—
But she knows what she does.

Lear. Is this well spoken?

Reg. I dare avouch it, sir: what, fifty followers?
Is it not well? What should you need of more?
Yea, or so many, sith that both charge and danger
Speak 'gainst so great a number? How in one house
Should many people under two commands
Hold amity? 'Tis hard, almost impossible.

Gon. Why might not you, my lord, receive attendance
From those that she calls servants or from mine?

Reg. Why not, my lord? If then they chanced to slack you,
We could control them. If you will come to me,
For now I spy a danger, I entreat you,
To bring but five and twenty: to no more
Will I give place or notice.

Lear. I gave you all—

Reg. And in good time you gave it.

Lear. Made you my guardians, my depositaries,
But kept a reservation to be follow'd
With such a number. What, must I come to you
With five and twenty, Regan? said you so?

Reg. And speak 't again, my lord; no more with me.

Lear. Those wicked creatures yet do look well-favour'd,
When others are more wicked; not being the worst
Stands in some rank of praise. [*To Gon.*] I'll go with thee:
Thy fifty yet doth double five and twenty,
And thou art twice her love.

Gon. Hear me, my lord:
What need you five and twenty, ten, or five,
To follow in a house where twice so many
Have a command to tend you?

Reg. What need one?

Lear. O, reason not the need: our basest beggars
Are in the poorest thing superfluous:
Allow not nature more than nature needs,
Man's life's as cheap as beast's: thou art a lady;
If only to go warm were gorgeous,

Why, nature needs not what thou gorgeous wear'st,
Which scarcely keeps thee warm. But for true need,—
You heavens, give me that patience, patience I need!
You see me here, you gods, a poor old man,
As full of grief as age; wretched in both:
If it be you that stirs these daughters' hearts
Against their father, fool me not so much
To bear it tamely; touch me with noble anger,
And let not woman's weapons, water-drops,
Stain my man's cheeks! No, you unnatural hags,
I will have such revenges on you both
That all the world shall—I will do such things,—
What they are, yet I know not, but they shall be
The terrors of the earth. You think I'll weep;
No, I'll not weep:
I have full cause of weeping; but this heart
Shall break into a hundred thousand flaws,
Or ere I'll weep. O fool, I shall go mad!
[*Exeunt Lear, Gloucester, Kent, and Fool.*

Corn. Let us withdraw; 'twill be a storm. [*Storm and tempest.*

Reg. This house is little: the old man and his people
Cannot be well bestow'd.

Gon. 'Tis his own blame; hath put himself from rest,
And must needs taste his folly.

Reg. For his particular, I'll receive him gladly,
But not one follower.

Gon. So am I purposed.
Where is my lord of Gloucester?

Corn. Follow'd the old man forth: he is return'd.

Re-enter Gloucester.

Glou. The king is in high rage.

Corn. Whither is he going?

Glou. He calls to horse; but will I know not whither.

Corn. 'Tis best to give him way; he leads himself.

Gon. My lord, entreat him by no means to stay.

Glou. Alack, the night comes on, and the bleak winds
Do sorely ruffle; for many miles about
There's scarce a bush.

Reg. O, sir, to wilful men
The injuries that they themselves procure
Must be their schoolmasters. Shut up your doors:
He is attended with a desperate train;
And what they may incense him to, being apt
To have his ear abused, wisdom bids fear.

Corn. Shut up your doors, my lord; 'tis a wild night:
My Regan counsels well: come out o' the storm. [*Exeunt.*

ACT III—Scene I

A heath.

Storm still. Enter Kent and a Gentleman, meeting.

Kent. Who 's there, besides foul weather?
Gent. One minded like the weather, most unquietly.
Kent. I know you. Where 's the king?
Gent. Contending with the fretful elements;
Bids the wind blow the earth into the sea,
Or swell the curled waters 'bove the main,
That things might change or cease; tears his white hair,
Which the impetuous blasts, with eyeless rage
Catch in their fury, and make nothing of;
Strives in his little world of man to out-scorn
The to-and-fro-conflicting wind and rain.
This night, wherein the cub-drawn bear would couch,
The lion and the belly-pinched wolf
Keep their fur dry, unbonneted he runs,
And bids what will take all.
Kent. But who is with him?
Gent. None but the fool; who labours to out-jest
His heart-struck injuries.
Kent. Sir, I do know you;
And dare, upon the warrant of my note,
Commend a dear thing to you. There is division,
Although as yet the face of it be cover'd
With mutual cunning, 'twixt Albany and Cornwall;
Who have—as who have not, that their great stars
Throned and set high?—servants, who seem no less,
Which are to France the spies and speculations
Intelligent of our state: what hath been seen,
Either in snuffs and packings of the dukes,
Or the hard rein which both of them have borne
Against the old kind king, or something deeper
Whereof perchance these are but furnishings,—
But true it is, from France there comes a power
Into this scatter'd kingdom; who already,
Wise in our negligence, have secret feet
In some of our best ports, and are at point
To show their open banner. Now to you:
If on my credit you dare build so far
To make your speed to Dover, you shall find

Some that will thank you, making just report
Of how unnatural and bemadding sorrow
The king hath cause to plain.
I am a gentleman of blood and breeding,
And from some knowledge and assurance offer
This office to you.

Gent. I will talk further with you.

Kent. No, do not.
For confirmation that I am much more
Than my out-wall, open this purse and take
What it contains. If you shall see Cordelia,—
As fear not but you shall,—show her this ring,
And she will tell you who your fellow is
That yet you do not know. Fie on this storm!
I will go seek the king.

Gent. Give me your hand:
Have you no more to say?

Kent. Few words, but, to effect, more than all yet;
That when we have found the king,—in which your pain
That way, I 'll this,—he that first lights on him
Holla the other. [*Exeunt severally.*

SCENE II

Another part of the heath. Storm still.

Enter Lear and Fool.

Lear. Blow, winds, and crack your cheeks! rage! blow!
You cataracts and hurricanoes, spout
Till you have drench'd our steeples, drown'd the cocks!
You sulphurous and thought-executing fires,
Vaunt-couriers to oak-cleaving thunderbolts,
Singe my white head! And thou, all-shaking thunder,
Smite flat the thick rotundity o' the world!
Crack nature's moulds, all germins spill at once
That make ingrateful man!

Fool. O nuncle, court holy-water in a dry house is better than this rain-water out o' door. Good nuncle, in, and ask thy daughters' blessing: here 's a night pities neither wise man nor fool.

Lear. Rumble thy bellyful! Spit, fire! spout, rain.
Nor rain, wind, thunder, fire, are my daughters:
I tax not you, you elements, with unkindness;
I never gave you kingdom, call'd you children,
You owe me no subscription: then let fall
Your horrible pleasure; here I stand, your slave,
A poor, infirm, weak and despised old man:

But yet I call you servile ministers,
That have with two pernicious daughters join'd
Your high-engender'd battles 'gainst a head
So old and white as this. O! O! 'tis foul!

Fool. He that has a house to put 's head in has a good head-[piece.
The cod-piece that will house
Before the head has any,
The head and he shall louse
So beggars marry many.
The man that makes his toe
What he his heart should make
Shall of a corn cry woe,
And turn his sleep to wake.
For there was never yet fair woman but she made mouths in [a glass.

Lear. No, I will be the pattern of all patience;
I will say nothing.

Enter Kent.

Kent. Who 's there?

Fool. Marry, here 's grace and a cod-piece; that 's a wise man [and a fool.

Kent. Alas, sir, are you here? things that love night
Love not such nights as these; the wrathful skies
Gallow the very wanderers of the dark,
And make them keep their caves: since I was man,
Such sheets of fire, such bursts of horrid thunder,
Such groans of roaring wind and rain, I never
Remember to have heard: man's nature cannot carry
The affliction nor the fear.

Lear. Let the great gods,
That keep this dreadful pother o'er our heads,
Find out their enemies now. Tremble, thou wretch,
That hast within thee undivulged crimes,
Unwhipp'd of justice: hide thee, thou bloody hand;
Thou perjured, and thou simular man of virtue
That art incestuous: caitiff, to pieces shake,
That under covert and convenient seeming
Hast practised on man's life: close pent-up guilts,
Rive your concealing continents and cry
These dreadful summoners grace. I am a man
More sinn'd against than sinning.

Kent. Alack, bare-headed!
Gracious my lord, hard by here is a hovel;
Some friendship will it lend you 'gainst the tempest:
Repose you there; while I to this hard house—
More harder than the stones whereof 'tis raised;
Which even but now, demanding after you,

Denied me to come in—return, and force
Their scanted courtesy.

Lear. My wits begin to turn.
Come on, my boy: how dost, my boy? art cold?
I am cold myself. Where is this straw, my fellow?
The art of our necessities is strange,
That can make vile things precious. Come, your hovel.
Poor fool and knave, I have one part in my heart
That 's sorry yet for thee.

Fool. [*Singing*]
He that has and a little tiny wit,—
With hey, ho, the wind and the rain,—
Must make content with his fortunes fit,
For the rain it raineth every day.

Lear. True, my good boy. Come, bring us to this hovel.
[*Exeunt Lear and Kent.*

Fool. This is a brave night to cool a courtezan.
I 'll speak a prophecy ere I go:
When priests are more in word than matter;
When brewers mar their malt with water;
When nobles are their tailors' tutors;
No heretics burn'd, but wenches' suitors;
When every case in law is right;
No squire in debt, nor no poor knight;
When slanders do not live in tongues,
Nor cutpurses come not to throngs;
When usurers tell their gold i' the field,
And bawds and whores do churches build
Then shall the realm of Albion
Come to great confusion:
Then comes the time, who lives to see 't,
That going shall be used with feet.
This prophecy Merlin shall make; for I live before his time.
[*Exit.*

SCENE III

Gloucester's castle.

Enter Gloucester and Edmund.

Glou. Alack, alack, Edmund, I like not this unnatural dealing. When I desired their leave that I might pity him, they took from me the use of mine own house; charged me, on pain of their perpetual displeasure, neither to speak of him, entreat for him, nor any way sustain him.

Edm. Most savage and unnatural!

Glou. Go to; say you nothing. There 's a division betwixt

the dukes, and a worse matter than that: I have received a letter this night; 'tis dangerous to be spoken; I have locked the letter in my closet: these injuries the king now bears will be revenged home; there is part of a power already footed; we must incline to the king. I will seek him and privily relieve him: go you, and maintain talk with the duke, that my charity be not of him perceived: if he ask for me, I am ill and gone to bed. Though I die for it, as no less is threatened me, the king my old master must be relieved. There is some strange thing toward, Edmund; pray you, be careful. [*Exit.*

Edm. This courtesy, forbid thee, shall the duke
Instantly know, and of that letter too:
This seems a fair deserving, and must draw me
That which my father loses; no less than all:
The younger rises when the old doth fall. [*Exit.*

Scene IV

The heath. Before a hovel.

Enter Lear, Kent, and Fool.

Kent. Here is the place, my lord: good my lord, enter:
The tyranny of the open night 's too rough
For nature to endure. [*Storm still.*
Lear. Let me alone.
Kent. Good my lord, enter here.
Lear. Wilt break my heart?
Kent. I had rather break mine own. Good my lord, enter.
Lear. Thou think'st 'tis much that this contentious storm
Invades us to the skin: so 'tis to thee;
But where the greater malady is fix'd
The lesser is scarce felt. Thou 'ldst shun a bear,
But if thy flight lay toward the raging sea
Thou 'ldst meet the bear i' the mouth. When the mind 's free
The body 's delicate: the tempest in my mind
Doth from my senses take all feeling else
Save what beats there. Filial ingratitude!
Is it not as this mouth should tear this hand
For lifting food to 't? But I will punish home.
No, I will weep no more. In such a night
To shut me out! Pour on; I will endure.
In such a night as this! O Regan, Goneril!
Your old kind father, whose frank heart gave you all,—
O that way madness lies; let me shun that;
No more of that.
Kent. Good my lord, enter here.

Lear. Prithee, go in thyself; seek thine own ease:
This tempest will not give me leave to ponder
On things would hurt me more. But I'll go in.
[*To the Fool*] In, boy; go first. You houseless poverty,—
Nay, get thee in. I'll pray, and then I'll sleep. [*Fool goes in.*
Poor naked wretches, wheresoe'er you are,
That bide the pelting of this pitiless storm,
How shall your houseless heads and unfed sides,
Your loop'd and window'd raggedness, defend you
From seasons such as these? O, I have ta'en
Too little care of this! Take physic, pomp;
Expose thyself to feel what wretches feel,
That thou mayst shake the superflux to them
And show the heavens more just.

Edg. [*Within*] Fathom and half, fathom and half!
Poor Tom! [*The Fool runs out from the hovel.*

Fool. Come not in here, nuncle, here 's a spirit.
Help me, help me!

Kent. Give me thy hand. Who 's there?

Fool. A spirit, a spirit: he says his name 's poor Tom.

Kent. What art thou that dost grumble there i' the straw?
Come forth.

Enter Edgar disguised as a madman.

Edg. Away! the foul fiend follows me!
'Through the sharp hawthorn blows the cold wind.'
Hum! go to thy cold bed and warm thee.

Lear. Hast thou given all to thy two daughters?
And art thou come to this?

Edg. Who gives any thing to poor Tom? whom the foul fiend hath led through fire and through flame, through ford and whirlpool, o'er bog and quagmire; that hath laid knives under his pillow and halters in his pew; set ratsbane by his porridge; made him proud of heart, to ride on a bay trotting-horse over four-inched bridges, to course his own shadow for a traitor. Bless thy five wits! Tom 's a-cold. O, do de, do de, do de. Bless thee from whirlwinds, starblasting, and taking! Do poor Tom some charity, whom the foul fiend vexes. There could I have him now, and there, and there again, and there. [*Storm still.*

Lear. What, have his daughters brought him to this pass?
Couldst thou save nothing? Didst thou give them all?

Fool. Nay, he reserved a blanket, else we had been all shamed

Lear. Now, all the plagues that in the pendulous air
Hang fated o'er men's faults light on thy daughters!

Kent. He hath no daughters, sir.

Lear. Death, traitor! nothing could have subdued nature
To such a lowness but his unkind daughters.
Is it the fashion that discarded fathers
Should have thus little mercy on their flesh?
Judicious punishment! 'twas this flesh begot
Those pelican daughters.

Edg. Pillicock sat on Pillicock-hill:
Halloo, halloo, loo, loo!

Fool. This cold night will turn us all to fools and madmen.

Edg. Take heed o' the foul fiend: obey thy parents; keep thy word justly; swear not; commit not with man's sworn spouse; set not thy sweet heart on proud array. Tom 's a-cold.

Lear. What hast thou been?

Edg. A serving-man, proud in heart and mind; that curled my hair; wore gloves in my cap; served the lust of my mistress' heart and did the act of darkness with her; swore as many oaths as I spake words and broke them in the sweet face of heaven: one that slept in the contriving of lust and waked to do it: wine loved I deeply, dice dearly, and in woman out-paramoured the Turk: false of heart, light of ear, bloody of hand; hog in sloth, fox in stealth, wolf in greediness, dog in madness, lion in prey. Let not the creaking of shoes nor the rustling of silks betray thy poor heart to woman: keep thy foot out of brothels, thy hand out of plackets, thy pen from lenders' books, and defy the foul fiend.
'Still through the hawthorn blows the cold wind.'
Says suum, mun, ha, no, nonny.
Dolphin my boy, my boy, sessa! let him trot by. [*Storm still.*

Lear. Why, thou wert better in thy grave than to answer with thy uncovered body this extremity of the skies. Is man no more than this? Consider him well. Thou owest the worm no silk, the beast no hide, the sheep no wool, the cat no perfume. Ha! here 's three on 's are sophisticated. Thou art the thing itself: unaccommodated man is no more but such a poor, bare, forked animal as thou art. Off, off, you lendings! come, unbutton here. [*Tearing off his clothes.*

Fool. Prithee, nuncle, be contented; 'tis a naughty night to swim in. Now a little fire in a wild field were like an old lecher's heart, a small spark, all the rest on 's body cold. Look, here comes a walking fire.

Enter Gloucester, with a torch.

Edg. This is the foul fiend Flibbertigibbet: he begins at curfew and walks till the first cock; he gives the web and the pin, squints the eye and makes the hare-lip; mildews the white wheat and hurts the poor creature of earth.

Saint Withold footed thrice the 'old;
He met the night-mare and her nine-fold;
Bid her alight,
And her troth plight,
And aroint thee, witch, aroint thee!

Kent. How fares your grace?

Lear. What's he?

Kent. Who's there? What is't you seek?

Glou. What are you there? Your names?

Edg. Poor Tom, that eats the swimming frog, the toad, the tadpole, the wall-newt and the water; that in the fury of his heart, when the foul fiend rages, eats cow-dung for sallets; swallows the old rat and the ditch-dog; drinks the green mantle of the standing pool; who is whipped from tithing to tithing, and stock-punished, and imprisoned; who hath had three suits to his back, six shirts to his body, horse to ride and weapon to wear;

But mice and rats and such small deer
Have been Tom's food for seven long year.

Beware my follower. Peace, Smulkin; peace, thou fiend!

Glou. What, hath your grace no better company?

Edg. The prince of darkness is a gentleman; Modo he's call'd, and Mahu.

Glou. Our flesh and blood is grown so vile, my lord,
That it doth hate what gets it.

Edg. Poor Tom's a-cold.

Glou. Go in with me: my duty cannot suffer
To obey in all your daughters' hard commands:
Though their injunction be to bar my doors
And let this tyrannous night take hold upon you,
Yet have I ventured to come seek you out
And bring you where both fire and food is ready.

Lear. First let me talk with this philosopher.
What is the cause of thunder?

Kent. Good my lord, take his offer; go into the house.

Lear. I'll talk a word with this same learned Theban.
What is your study?

Edg. How to prevent the fiend and to kill vermin.

Lear. Let me ask you one word in private.

Kent. Importune him once more to go, my lord;
His wits begin to unsettle.

Glou. Canst thou blame him? [*Storm still.*
His daughters seek his death; ah, that good Kent!
He said it would be thus, poor banish'd man!
Thou say'st the king grows mad; I'll tell thee, friend,

I am almost mad myself: I had a son,
Now outlaw'd from my blood; he sought my life,
But lately, very late: I loved him, friend,
No father his son dearer: truth to tell thee,
The grief hath crazed my wits. What a night 's this!
I do beseech your grace,—

Lear. O, cry you mercy, sir.
Noble philosopher, your company.

Edg. Tom 's a-cold.

Glou. In, fellow, there, into the hovel; keep thee warm.

Lear. Come, let 's in all.

Kent. This way, my lord.

Lear. With him;
I will keep still with my philosopher.

Kent. Good my lord, soothe him; let him take the fellow.

Glou. Take him you on.

Kent. Sirrah, come on; go along with us.

Lear. Come, good Athenian.

Glou. No words, no words: hush.

Edg. Child Rowland to the dark tower came:
His word was still 'Fie, foh, and fum,
I smell the blood of a British man.' [*Exeunt.*

Scene V

Gloucester's castle.

Enter Cornwall and Edmund.

Corn. I will have my revenge ere I depart his house.

Edm. How, my lord, I may be censured, that nature thus gives way to loyalty, something fears me to think of.

Corn. I now perceive, it was not altogether your brother's evil disposition made him seek his death, but a provoking merit, set a-work by a reproveable badness in himself.

Edm. How malicious is my fortune, that I must repent to be just! This is the letter he spoke of, which approves him an intelligent party to the advantages of France. O heavens! that this treason were not, or not I the detector!

Corn. Go with me to the duchess.

Edm. If the matter of this paper be certain, you have mighty business in hand.

Corn. True or false, it hath made thee earl of Gloucester. Seek out where thy father is, that he may be ready for our apprehension.

Edm. [*Aside*] If I find him comforting the king, it will stuff his suspicion more fully.—I will persever in my course of loyalty, though the conflict be sore between that and my blood.

Corn. I will lay trust upon thee, and thou shalt find a dearer father in my love. [*Exeunt.*

Scene VI

A chamber in a farmhouse adjoining the castle.

Enter Gloucester, Lear, Kent, Fool, and Edgar.

Glou. Here is better than the open air; take it thankfully. I will piece out the comfort with what addition I can: I will not be long from you.

Kent. All the power of his wits have given way to his impatience: the gods reward your kindness! [*Exit Gloucester.*

Edg. Frateretto calls me, and tells me Nero is an angler in the lake of darkness. Pray, innocent, and beware the foul fiend.

Fool. Prithee, nuncle, tell me whether a madman be a gentleman or a yeoman.

Lear. A king, a king!

Fool. No, he 's a yeoman that has a gentleman to his son, for he 's a mad yeoman that sees his son a gentleman before him.

Lear. To have a thousand with red burning spits
Come hissing in upon 'em,—

Edg. The foul fiend bites my back.

Fool. He 's mad that trusts in the tameness of a wolf, a horse's health, a boy's love, or a whore's oath.

Lear. It shall be done; I will arraign them straight.
[*To Edgar*] Come, sit thou here, most learned justicer;
[*To the Fool*] Thou, sapient sir, sit here. Now, you she foxes!

Edg. Look, where he stands and glares! Wantest thou eyes at trial, madam?
Come o'er the bourn, Bessy, to me.

Fool. Her boat hath a leak,
And she must not speak
Why she dares not come over to thee.

Edg. The foul fiend haunts poor Tom in the voice of a nightingale. Hopdance cries in Tom's belly for two white herring. Croak not, black angel; I have no food for thee.

Kent. How do you, sir? Stand you not so amazed:
Will you lie down and rest upon the cushions?

Lear. I 'll see their trial first. Bring in the evidence.
[*To Edgar*] Thou robed man of justice, take thy place;
[*To the Fool*] And thou, his yoke-fellow of equity,
Bench by his side. [*To Kent*] You are o' the commission;
Sit you too.

Edg. Let us deal justly.

Sleepest or wakest thou, jolly shepherd:
Thy sheep be in the corn;
And for one blast of thy minikin mouth,
Thy sheep shall take no harm.
Pur! the cat is gray.

Lear. Arraign her first; 'tis Goneril. I here take my oath before this honourable assembly, she kicked the poor king her father.

Fool. Come hither, mistress. Is your name Goneril?

Lear. She cannot deny it.

Fool. Cry you mercy, I took you for a joint-stool.

Lear. And here 's another, whose warp'd looks proclaim
What store her heart is made on. Stop her there!
Arms, arms, sword, fire! Corruption in the place!
False justicer, why hast thou let her 'scape?

Edg. Bless thy five wits!

Kent. O pity! Sir, where is the patience now,
That you so oft have boasted to retain!

Edg. [*Aside*] My tears begin to take his part so much,
They 'll mar my counterfeiting.

Lear. The little dogs and all,
Tray, Blanch, and Sweet-heart, see, they bark at me.

Edg. Tom will throw his head at them. Avaunt, you curs!
Be thy mouth or black or white,
Tooth that poisons if it bite;
Mastiff, greyhound, mongrel grim,
Hound or spaniel, brach or lym,
Or bobtail tike or trundle-tail,
Tom will make them weep and wail:
For, with throwing thus my head,
Dogs leap the hatch, and all are fled.
Do de, de, de. Sessa! Come, march to wakes and fairs and market-towns. Poor Tom, thy horn is dry.

Lear. Then let them anatomize Regan; see what breeds about her heart. Is there any cause in nature that makes these hard hearts? [*To Edgar*] You sir, I entertain for one of my hundred; only I do not like the fashion of your garments. You will say they are Persian attire; but let them be changed.

Kent. Now, good my lord, lie here and rest awhile.

Lear. Make no noise, make no noise; draw the curtains: so, so, so. We 'll go to supper i' the morning. So, so, so.

Fool. And I 'll go to bed at noon.

Re-enter Gloucester.

Glou. Come hither, friend: where is the king my master?

Kent. Here, sir; but trouble him not: his wits are gone.

Glou. Good friend, I prithee, take him in thy arms;
I have o'erheard a plot of death upon him:
There is a litter ready; lay him in 't,
And drive toward Dover, friend, where thou shalt meet
Both welcome and protection. Take up thy master:
If thou shouldst dally half an hour, his life,
With thine and all that offer to defend him,
Stand in assured loss. Take up, take up,
And follow me, that will to some provision
Give thee quick conduct.

Kent. Oppressed nature sleeps.
This rest might yet have balm'd thy broken sinews,
Which, if convenience will not allow,
Stand in hard cure. [*To the Fool*] Come, help to bear thy master;
Thou must not stay behind.

Glou. Come, come away.

[*Exeunt all but Edgar.*

Edg. When we our betters see bearing our woes,
We scarcely think our miseries our foes.
Who alone suffers suffers most i' the mind,
Leaving free things and happy shows behind:
But then the mind much sufferance doth o'erskip,
When grief hath mates, and bearing fellowship.
How light and portable my pain seems now,
When that which makes me bend makes the king bow,
He childed as I father'd! Tom, away!
Mark the high noises, and thyself bewray
When false opinion, whose wrong thought defiles thee,
In thy just proof repeals and reconciles thee.
What will hap more to-night, safe 'scape the king!
Lurk, lurk. [*Exit.*

Scene VII

Gloucester's castle.

Enter Cornwall, Regan, Goneril, Edmund, and Servants.

Corn. Post speedily to my lord your husband; show him this letter: the army of France is landed. Seek out the traitor Gloucester. [*Exeunt some of the Servants.*

Reg. Hang him instantly.

Gon. Pluck out his eyes.

Corn. Leave him to my displeasure. Edmund, keep you our sister company: the revenges we are bound to take upon your traitorous father are not fit for your beholding. Advise the duke, where you are going, to a most festinate preparation: we are bound to the like. Our posts shall be swift and intelligent betwixt us. Farewell, dear sister: farewell, my lord of Gloucester.

Enter Oswald.

How now! where 's the king?
Osw. My lord of Gloucester hath convey'd him hence:
Some five or six and thirty of his knights,
Hot questrists after him, met him at gate;
Who, with some other of the lord's dependants,
Are gone with him toward Dover; where they boast
To have well-armed friends.
Corn. Get horses for your mistress.
Gon. Farewell, sweet lord, and sister.
Corn. Edmund, farewell.

[*Exeunt Goneril, Edmund, and Oswald.*

Go seek the traitor Gloucester.
Pinion him like a thief, bring him before us.

[*Exeunt other Servants.*

Though well we may not pass upon his life
Without the form of justice, yet our power
Shall do a courtesy to our wrath, which men
May blame but not control. Who 's there? the traitor?

Enter Gloucester, brought in by two or three.

Reg. Ingrateful fox! 'tis he.
Corn. Bind fast his corky arms.
Glou. What mean your graces? Good my friends, consider
You are my guests: do me no foul play, friends.
Corn. Bind him, I say. [*Servants bind him.*
Reg. Hard, hard. O filthy traitor!
Glou. Unmerciful lady as you are, I 'm none.
Corn. To this chair bind him. Villain, thou shalt find—

[*Regan plucks his beard.*

Glou. By the kind gods, 'tis most ignobly done
To pluck me by the beard.
Reg. So white, and such a traitor!
Glou. Naughty lady,
These hairs which thou dost ravish from my chin
Will quicken and accuse thee: I am your host:
With robbers' hands my hospitable favours
You should not ruffle thus. What will you do?
Corn. Come, sir, what letters had you late from France?
Reg. Be simple answerer, for we know the truth.
Corn. And what confederacy have you with the traitors
Late footed in the kingdom?
Reg. To whose hands have you sent the lunatic king?
Speak.

Glou. I have a letter guessingly set down,
Which came from one that 's of a neutral heart,
And not from one opposed.
Corn. Cunning.
Reg. And false.
Corn. Where hast thou sent the king?
Glou. To Dover.
Reg. Wherefore to Dover? Wast thou not charged at peril—
Corn. Wherefore to Dover? Let him first answer that.
Glou. I am tied to the stake, and I must stand the course.
Reg. Wherefore to Dover, sir?
Glou. Because I would not see thy cruel nails
Pluck out his poor old eyes, nor thy fierce sister
In his anointed flesh stick boarish fangs.
The sea, with such a storm as his bare head
In hell-black night endured, would have buoy'd up,
And quench'd the stelled fires:
Yet, poor old heart, he holp the heavens to rain.
If wolves had at thy gate howl'd that stern time,
Thou shouldst have said, 'Good porter, turn the key,
All cruels else subscribed: but I shall see
The winged vengeance overtake such children.
Corn. See 't shalt thou never. Fellows, hold the chair.
Upon these eyes of thine I 'll set my foot.
Glou. He that will think to live till he be old,
Give me some help! O cruel! O you gods.
Reg. One side will mock another; the other too.
Corn. If you see vengeance—
First Serv. Hold your hand, my lord:
I have served you ever since I was a child;
But better service have I never done you
Than now to bid you hold.
Reg. How now, you dog!
First Serv. If you did wear a beard upon your chin,
I 'ld shake it on this quarrel. What do you mean?
Corn. My villain! [*They draw and fight.*
First Serv. Nay, then, come on, and take the chance of anger.
Reg. Give me thy sword. A peasant stand up thus!
[*Takes a sword and runs at him behind.*
First Serv. O, I am slain! My lord, you have one eye left
To see some mischief on him. O! [*Dies.*
Corn. Lest it see more, prevent it. Out, vile jelly!
Where is thy lustre now?
Glou. All dark and comfortless. Where 's my son Edmund?
Edmund, enkindle all the sparks of nature,

To quit this horrid act.
Reg. Out, treacherous villain!
Thou call'st on him that hates thee: it was he
That made the overture of thy treasons to us;
Who is too good to pity thee.
Glou. O my follies! Then Edgar was abused.
Kind gods, forgive me that, and prosper him!
Reg. Go thrust him out at gates, and let him smell
His way to Dover. [*Exit one with Gloucester.*] How is 't, my lord? how look you?
Corn. I have received a hurt: follow me, lady.
Turn out that eyeless villain: throw this slave
Upon the dunghill. Regan, I bleed apace:
Untimely comes this hurt: give me your arm.
[*Exit Cornwall, led by Regan.*
Sec. Serv. I 'll never care what wickedness I do,
If this man come to good.
Third Serv. If she live long,
And in the end meet the old course of death,
Women will all turn monsters.
Sec. Serv. Let 's follow the old earl, and get the Bedlam
To lead him where he would: his roguish madness
Allows itself to any thing.
Third Serv. Go thou: I 'll fetch some flax and whites of eggs
To apply to his bleeding face. Now, heaven help him!
[*Exeunt severally.*

ACT IV—Scene I

The heath.

Enter Edgar.

Edg. Yet better thus, and known to be contemn'd,
Than still contemn'd and flatter'd. To be worst,
The lowest and most dejected thing of fortune,
Stands still in esperance, lives not in fear:
The lamentable change is from the best;
The worst returns to laughter. Welcome then,
Thou unsubstantial air that I embrace!
The wretch that thou hast blown unto the worst
Owes nothing to thy blasts. But who comes here?

Enter Gloucester, led by an Old Man.

My father, poorly led? World, world, O world!
But that thy strange mutations make us hate thee,
Life would not yield to age.

Old Man. O, my good lord, I have been your tenant, and your father's tenant, these fourscore years.

Glou. Away, get thee away; good friend, be gone:
Thy comforts can do me no good at all;
Thee they may hurt.

Old Man. Alack, sir, you cannot see your way.

Glou. I have no way and therefore want no eyes;
I stumbled when I saw: full oft 'tis seen,
Our means secure us, and our mere defects
Prove our commodities. Ah, dear son Edgar,
The food of thy abused father's wrath!
Might I but live to see thee in my touch,
I 'ld say I had eyes again!

Old Man. How now! Who 's there?

Edg. [*Aside*] O gods! Who is 't can say 'I am at the worst'?
I am worse than e'er I was.

Old Man. 'Tis poor mad Tom.

Edg. [*Aside*] And worse I may be yet: the worst is not
So long as we can say 'This is the worst.'

Old Man. Fellow, where goest?

Glou. Is it a beggar-man?

Old Man. Madman and beggar too.

Glou. He has some reason, else he could not beg.
I' the last night's storm I such a fellow saw,
Which made me think a man a worm: my son
Came then into my mind, and yet my mind
Was then scarce friends with him: I have heard more since.
As flies to wanton boys, are we to the gods;
They kill us for their sport.

Edg. [*Aside*] How should this be?
Bad is the trade that must play fool to sorrow,
Angering itself and others. Bless thee, master!

Glou. Is that the naked fellow?

Old Man. Ay, my lord.

Glou. Then, prithee, get thee gone: if for my sake
Thou wilt o'ertake us hence a mile or twain
I' the way toward Dover, do it for ancient love;
And bring some covering for this naked soul,
Who I'll entreat to lead me.

Old Man. Alack, sir, he is mad.

Glou. 'Tis the times' plague, when madmen lead the blind.
Do as I bid thee, or rather do thy pleasure;
Above the rest, be gone.

Old Man. I'll bring him the best 'parel that I have,
Come on 't what will. [*Exit.*

Glou. Sirrah, naked fellow,—

Edg. Poor Tom 's a-cold. [*Aside*] I cannot daub it further.

Glou. Come hither, fellow.

Edg. [*Aside*] And yet I must.—Bless thy sweet eyes, they bleed.

Glou. Know'st thou the way to Dover?

Edg. Both stile and gate, horse-way and foot-path. Poor Tom hath been scared out of his good wits. Bless thee, good man's son, from the foul fiend! Five fiends have been in poor Tom at once; of lust, as Obidicut; Hobbididence, prince of dumbness; Mahu, of stealing; Modo, of murder; Flibbertigibbet, of mopping and mowing; who since possesses chambermaids and waiting-women. So, bless thee, master!

Glou. Here, take this purse, thou whom the heavens' plagues
Have humbled to all strokes: that I am wretched
Makes thee the happier. Heavens, deal so still!
Let the superfluous and lust-dieted man,
That slaves your ordinance, that will not see
Because he doth not feel, feel your power quickly;
So distribution should undo excess
And each man have enough. Dost thou know Dover?

Edg. Ay, master.

Glou. There is a cliff whose high and bending head
Looks fearfully in the confined deep:
Bring me but to the very brim of it,
And I 'll repair the misery thou dost bear
With something rich about me: from that place
I shall no leading need.

Edg. Give me thy arm:
Poor Tom shall lead thee. [*Exeunt.*

Scene II

Before the Duke of Albany's palace.

Enter Goneril and Edmund.

Gon. Welcome, my lord: I marvel our mild husband
Not met us on the way.

Enter Oswald.

Now, where 's your master?

Osw. Madam, within; but never man so changed.
I told him of the army that was landed;
He smiled at it: I told him you were coming;
His answer was, 'The worse:' of Gloucester's treachery
And of the loyal service of his son
When I inform'd him, then he call'd me sot
And told me I had turn'd the wrong side out:
What most he should dislike seems pleasant to him;

What like, offensive.

Gon. [*To Edm.*] Then shall you go no further.
It is the cowish terror of his spirit,
That dares not undertake: he 'll not feel wrongs,
Which tie him to an answer. Our wishes on the way
May prove effects. Back, Edmund, to my brother;
Hasten his musters and conduct his powers:
I must change arms at home and give the distaff
Into my husband's hands. This trusty servant
Shall pass between us: ere long you are like to hear,
If you dare venture in your own behalf,
A mistress's command. Wear this; spare speech;
[*Giving a favour.*
Decline your head: this kiss, if it durst speak,
Would stretch thy spirits up into the air:
Conceive, and fare thee well.

Edm. Yours in the ranks of death.

Gon. My most dear Gloucester!
[*Exit Edmund.*
O, the difference of man and man!
To thee a woman's services are due:
My fool usurps my body.

Osw. Madam, here comes my lord.
[*Exit.*

Enter Albany.

Gon. I have been worth the whistle.

Alb. O Goneril!
You are not worth the dust which the rude wind
Blows in your face. I fear your disposition:
That nature which contemns it origin
Cannot be border'd certain in itself;
She that herself will sliver and disbranch
From her material sap, perforce must wither
And come to deadly use.

Gon. No more; the text is foolish.

Alb. Wisdom and goodness to the vile seem vile:
Filths savour but themselves. What have you done?
Tigers, not daughters, what have you perform'd?
A father, and a gracious aged man,
Whose reverence even the head-lugg'd bear would lick,
Most barbarous, most degenerate! have you madded.
Could my good brother suffer you to do it?
A man, a prince, by him so benefited!
If that the heavens do not their visible spirits
Send quickly down to tame these vile offences,

It will come,
Humanity must perforce prey on itself,
Like monsters of the deep.

Gon. Milk-liver'd man!
That bear'st a cheek for blows, a head for wrongs;
Who hast not in thy brows an eye discerning
Thine honour from thy suffering; that not know'st
Fools do those villains pity who are punish'd
Ere they have done their mischief. Where 's thy drum?
France spreads his banners in our noiseless land,
With plumed helm thy state begins to threat,
Whiles thou, a moral fool, sit'st still and criest
'Alack, why does he so?'

Alb. See thyself, devil!
Proper deformity seems not in the fiend
So horrid as in woman.

Gon. O vain fool!

Alb. Thou changed and self-cover'd thing, for shame,
Be-monster not thy feature. Were 't my fitness
To let these hands obey my blood,
They are apt enough to dislocate and tear
Thy flesh and bones: howe'er thou art a fiend,
A woman's shape doth shield thee.

Gon. Marry, your manhood! mew!

Enter a Messenger.

Alb. What news?

Mess. O, my good lord, the Duke of Cornwall 's dead,
Slain by his servant, going to put out
The other eye of Gloucester.

Alb. Gloucester's eyes!

Mess. A servant that he bred, thrill'd with remorse,
Opposed against the act, bending his sword
To his great master; who thereat enraged
Flew on him and amongst them fell'd him dead,
But not without that harmful stroke which since
Hath pluck'd him after.

Alb. This shows you are above,
You justicers, that these our nether crimes
So speedily can venge. But, O poor Gloucester!
Lost he his other eye?

Mess. Both, both, my lord.
This letter, madam, craves a speedy answer;
'Tis from your sister.

Gon. [*Aside*] One way I like this well;
But being widow, and my Gloucester with her,

May all the building in my fancy pluck
Upon my hateful life: another way,
The news is not so tart.—I 'll read, and answer. [*Exit.*

Alb. Where was his son when they did take his eyes?

Mess. Come with my lady hither.

Alb. He is not here.

Mess. No, my good lord; I met him back again.

Alb. Knows he the wickedness?

Mess. Ay, my good lord; 'twas he inform'd against him,
And quit the house on purpose, that their punishment
Might have the freer course.

Alb. Gloucester, I live
To thank thee for the love thou show'dst the king,
And to revenge thine eyes. Come hither, friend:
Tell me what more thou know'st. [*Exeunt.*

Scene III

The French camp near Dover.

Enter Kent and a Gentleman.

Kent. Why the King of France is so suddenly gone back know you the reason?

Gent. Something he left imperfect in the state which since his coming forth is thought of, which imports to the kingdom so much fear and danger that his personal return was most required and necessary.

Kent. Who hath he left behind him general?

Gent. The Marshal of France, Monsieur La Far.

Kent. Did your letters pierce the queen to any demonstration of grief?

Gent. Ay, sir; she took them, read them in my presence,
And now and then an ample tear trill'd down
Her delicate cheek: it seem'd she was a queen
Over her passion, who most rebel-like
Sought to be king o'er her.

Kent. O, then it moved her.

Gent. Not to a rage: patience and sorrow strove
Who should express her goodliest. You have seen
Sunshine and rain at once: her smiles and tears
Were like a better way: those happy smilets
That play'd on her ripe lip seem'd not to know
What guests were in her eyes; which parted thence
As pearls from diamonds dropp'd. In brief,
Sorrow would be a rarity most beloved,
If all could so become it.

Kent. Made she no verbal question?

Gent. Faith, once or twice she heaved the name of 'father'

Pantingly forth, as if it press'd her heart;
Cried 'Sisters! sisters! Shame of ladies! sisters!
Kent! father! sisters! What, i' the storm! i' the night?
Let pity not be believed!' There she shook
The holy water from her heavenly eyes,
And clamour moisten'd: then away she started
To deal with grief alone.

Kent. It is the stars,
The stars above us, govern our conditions;
Else one self mate and mate could not beget
Such different issues. You spoke not with her since?

Gent. No.

Kent. Was this before the king return'd?

Gent. No, since.

Kent. Well, sir, the poor distress'd Lear 's i' the town;
Who sometime in his better tune remembers
What we are come about, and by no means
Will yield to see his daughter.

Gent. Why, good sir?

Kent. A sovereign shame so elbows him: his own unkindness
That stripp'd her from his benediction, turn'd her
To foreign casualties, gave her dear rights
To his dog-hearted daughters: these things sting
His mind so venomously that burning shame
Detains him from Cordelia.

Gent. Alack, poor gentleman!

Kent. Of Albany's and Cornwall's powers you heard not?

Gent. 'Tis so; they are afoot.

Kent. Well, sir, I 'll bring you to our master Lear,
And leave you to attend him: some dear cause
Will in concealment wrap me up awhile;
When I am known aright, you shall not grieve
Lending me this acquaintance. I pray you, go
Along with me. [*Exeunt.*

Scene IV

The same. A tent.

Enter, with drum and colours, Cordelia, Doctor, and Soldiers.

Cor. Alack, 'tis he: why, he was met even now
As mad as the vex'd sea; singing aloud;
Crown'd with rank fumiter and furrow-weeds,
With bur-docks, hemlock, nettles, cuckoo-flowers,
Darnel, and all the idle weeds that grow
In our sustaining corn. A century send forth;
Search every acre in the high-grown field,

And bring him to our eye. [*Exit an Officer.*] What can man's wisdom
In the restoring his bereaved sense?
He that helps him take all my outward worth.

Doct. There is means, madam:
Our foster-nurse of nature is repose,
The which he lacks: that to provoke in him,
Are many simples operative, whose power
Will close the eye of anguish.

Cor. All blest secrets,
All you unpublish'd virtues of the earth,
Spring with my tears! be aidant and remediate
In the good man's distress! Seek, seek for him;
Lest his ungovern'd rage dissolve the life
That wants the means to lead it.

Enter a Messenger.

Mess. News, madam;
The British powers are marching hitherward.

Cor. 'Tis known before; our preparation stands
In expectation of them. O dear father,
It is thy business that I go about;
Therefore great France
My mourning and important tears hath pitied.
No blown ambition doth our arms incite,
But love, dear love, and our aged father's right:
Soon may I hear and see him! [*Exeunt*

Scene V

Gloucester's castle.

Enter Regan and Oswald.

Reg. But are my brother's powers set forth?

Osw. Ay, madam.

Reg. Himself in person there?

Osw. Madam, with much ado;
Your sister is the better soldier.

Reg. Lord Edmund spake not with your lord at home?

Osw. No, madam.

Reg. What might import my sister's letter to him?

Osw. I know not, lady.

Reg. Faith, he is posted hence on serious matter.
It was great ignorance, Gloucester's eyes being out,
To let him live: where he arrives he moves
All hearts against us: Edmund, I think, is gone,
In pity of his misery, to dispatch
His nighted life; moreover, to descry
The strength o' the enemy.

Osw. I must needs after him, madam, with my letter.
Reg. Our troops set forth to-morrow: stay with us;
The ways are dangerous.
Osw. I may not, madam:
My lady charged my duty in this business.
Reg. Why should she write to Edmund? Might not you
Transport her purposes by word? Belike,
Something—I know not what: I 'll love thee much,
Let me unseal the letter.
Osw. Madam, I had rather—
Reg. I know your lady does not love her husband;
I am sure of that: and at her late being here
She gave strange œillades and most speaking looks
To noble Edmund. I know you are of her bosom.
Osw. I, madam?
Reg. I speak in understanding: you are; I know 't:
Therefore I do advise you, take this note:
My lord is dead; Edmund and I have talk'd;
And more convenient is he for my hand
Than for your lady's: you may gather more.
If you do find him, pray you, give him this;
And when your mistress hears thus much from you,
I pray, desire her call her wisdom to her.
So, fare you well.
If you do chance to hear of that blind traitor,
Preferment falls on him that cuts him off.
Osw. Would I could meet him, madam! I should show
What party I do follow.
Reg. Fare thee well. [*Exeunt.*

Scene VI

Fields near Dover.

Enter Gloucester, and Edgar dressed like a peasant.

Glou. When shall we come to the top of that same hill?
Edg. You do climb up it now: look, how we labour.
Glou. Methinks the ground is even.
Edg. Horrible steep.
Hark, do you hear the sea?
Glou. No, truly.
Edg. Why then your other senses grow imperfect
By your eyes' anguish.
Glou. So may it be indeed:
Methinks thy voice is alter'd, and thou speak'st
In better phrase and matter than thou didst.
Edg. You 're much deceived: in nothing am I changed

But in my garments.
Glou. Methinks you're better spoken.
Edg. Come on, sir; here's the place: stand still. How fearful
And dizzy 'tis to cast one's eyes so low!
The crows and choughs that wing the midway air
Show scarce so gross as beetles: half way down
Hangs one that gathers samphire, dreadful trade!
Methinks he seems no bigger than his head:
The fishermen that walk upon the beach
Appear like mice; and yond tall anchoring bark
Diminish'd to her cock; her cock, a buoy
Almost too small for sight: the murmuring surge
That on the unnumber'd idle pebbles chafes
Cannot be heard so high. I'll look no more,
Lest my brain turn and the deficient sight
Topple down headlong.
Glou. Set me where you stand.
Edg. Give me your hand: you are now within a foot
Of the extreme verge: for all beneath the moon
Would I not leap upright.
Glou. Let go my hand.
Here, friend, 's another purse; in it a jewel
Well worth a poor man's taking: fairies and gods
Prosper it with thee! Go thou further off;
Bid me farewell, and let me hear thee going.
Edg. Now fare you well, good sir.
Glou. With all my heart.
Edg. Why I do trifle thus with his despair
Is done to cure it.
Glou. [*Kneeling*] O you mighty gods!
This world I do renounce, and in your sights
Shake patiently my great affliction off:
If I could bear it longer and not fall
To quarrel with your great opposeless wills,
My snuff and loathed part of nature should
Burn itself out. If Edgar live, O bless him!
Now fellow, fare thee well. [*He falls forward.*
Edg. Gone, sir: farewell.
And yet I know not how conceit may rob
The treasury of life, when life itself
Yields to the theft: had he been where he thought,
By this had thought been past. Alive or dead?
Ho, you sir! friend! Hear you, sir! speak!
Thus might he pass indeed: yet he revives.
What are you, sir?

Glou. Away, and let me die.
Edg. Hadst thou been aught but gossamer, feathers, air,
So many fathom down precipitating,
Thou 'dst shiver'd like an egg: but thou dost breathe;
Hast heavy substance; bleed'st not; speak'st; art sound.
Ten masts at each make not the altitude
Which thou hast perpendicularly fell:
Thy life 's a miracle. Speak yet again.
Glou. But have I fall'n, or no?
Edg. From the dread summit of this chalky bourn.
Look up a-height; the shrill-gorged lark so far
Cannot be seen or heard: do but look up.
Glou. Alack, I have no eyes.
Is wretchedness deprived that benefit,
To end itself by death? 'Twas yet some comfort,
When misery could beguile the tyrant's rage
And frustrate his proud will.
Edg. Give me your arm:
Up: so. How is 't? Feel you your legs? You stand.
Glou. Too well, too well.
Edg. This is above all strangeness.
Upon the crown o' the cliff, what thing was that
Which parted from you?
Glou. A poor unfortunate beggar.
Edg. As I stood here below, methought his eyes
Were two full moons; he had a thousand noses,
Horns whelk'd and waved like the enridged sea:
It was some fiend; therefore, thou happy father,
Think that the clearest gods, who make them honours
Of men's impossibilities, have preserved thee.
Glou. I do remember now: henceforth I 'll bear
Affliction till it do cry out itself
'Enough, enough,' and die. That thing you speak of,
I took it for a man; often 'twould say
'The fiend, the fiend:' he led me to that place.
Edg. Bear free and patient thoughts. But who comes here?
Enter Lear, fantastically dressed with wild flowers.
The safer sense will ne'er accommodate
His master thus.
Lear. No, they cannot touch me for coining; I am the king [himself.
Edg. O thou side-piercing sight!
Lear. Nature 's above art in that respect. There 's your press-money. That fellow handles his bow like a crow-keeper; draw me a clothier's yard. Look, look, a mouse! Peace, peace; this piece of toasted cheese will do 't. There 's my

gauntlet; I 'll prove it on a giant. Bring up the brown bills. O, well flown, bird! i' the clout, i' the clout: hewgh! Give the word.

Edg. Sweet marjoram.

Lear. Pass.

Glou. I know that voice.

Lear. Ha! Goneril, with a white beard! They flattered me like a dog, and told me I had white hairs in my beard ere the black ones were there. To say 'ay' and 'no' to every thing that I said! 'Ay' and 'no' too was no good divinity. When the rain came to wet me once and the wind to make me chatter; when the thunder would not peace at my bidding; there I found 'em, there I smelt 'em out. Go to, they are not men o' their words: they told me I was every thing; 'tis a lie, I am not ague-proof.

Glou. The trick of that voice I do well remember:
Is 't not the king?

Lear. Ay, every inch a king:
When I do stare, see how the subject quakes.
I pardon that man's life. What was thy cause?
Adultery?
Thou shalt not die: die for adultery! No:
The wren goes to 't, and the small gilded fly
Does lecher in my sight.
Let copulation thrive; for Gloucester's bastard son
Was kinder to his father than my daughters
Got 'tween the lawful sheets.
To 't, luxury, pell mell! for I lack soldiers.
Behold yond simpering dame,
Whose face between her forks presages snow,
That minces virtue and does shake the head
To hear of pleasure's name;
The fitchew, nor the soiled horse, goes to 't
With a more riotous appetite.
Down from the waist they are Centaurs,
Though women all above:
But to the girdle do the gods inherit,
Beneath is all the fiends';
There 's hell, there 's darkness, there 's the sulphurous pit,
Burning, scalding, stench, consumption; fie, fie, fie! pah, pah! Give me an ounce of civet, good apothecary, to sweeten my imagination: there 's money for thee.

Glou. O, let me kiss that hand!

Lear. Let me wipe it first; it smells of mortality.

Glou. O ruin'd piece of nature! This great world

Shall so wear out to nought. Dost thou know me?

Lear. I remember thine eyes well enough. Dost thou squiny at me? No, do thy worst, blind Cupid; I'll not love. Read thou this challenge; mark but the penning on't.

Glou. Were all the letters suns, I could not see one.

Edg. I would not take this from report: it is,
And my heart breaks at it.

Lear. Read.

Glou. What, with the case of eyes?

Lear. O, ho, are you there with me? No eyes in your head, nor no money in your purse? Your eyes are in a heavy case, your purse in a light: yet you see how this world goes.

Glou. I see it feelingly.

Lear. What, art mad? A man may see how this world goes with no eyes. Look with thine ears: see how yond justice rails upon yond simple thief. Hark, in thine ear: change places, and, handy-dandy, which is the justice, which is the thief? Thou hast seen a farmer's dog bark at a beggar?

Glou. Ay, sir.

Lear. And the creature run from the cur? There thou mightst behold the great image of authority: a dog's obeyed in office.
Thou rascal beadle, hold thy bloody hand!
Why dost thou lash that whore? Strip thine own back;
Thou hotly lust'st to use her in that kind
For which thou whip'st her. The usurer hangs the cozener.
Through tatter'd clothes small vices do appear;
Robes and furr'd gowns hide all. Plate sin with gold,
And the strong lance of justice hurtless breaks;
Arm it in rags, a pigmy's straw does pierce it.
None does offend, none, I say, none; I'll able 'em:
Take that of me, my friend, who have the power
To seal the accuser's lips. Get thee glass eyes,
And, like a scurvy politician, seem
To see the things thou dost not.
Now, now, now, now: pull off my boots: harder, harder: so.

Edg. O, matter and impertinency mix'd!
Reason in madness!

Lear. If thou wilt weep my fortunes, take my eyes.
I know thee well enough; thy name is Gloucester:
Thou must be patient; we came crying hither:
Thou know'st, the first time that we smell the air,
We wawl and cry. I will preach to thee: mark.

Glou. Alack, alack the day!

Lear. When we are born, we cry that we are come
To this great stage of fools. This's a good block.

It were a delicate stratagem, to shoe
A troop of horse with felt: I 'll put 't in proof;
And when I have stol'n upon these sons-in-law,
Then, kill, kill, kill, kill, kill, kill!

Enter a Gentleman, with Attendants.

Gent. O, here he is: lay hand upon him. Sir,
Your most dear daughter—
Lear. No rescue? What, a prisoner? I am even
The natural fool of fortune. Use me well;
You shall have ransom. Let me have a surgeon;
I am cut to the brains.
Gent. You shall have any thing.
Lear. No seconds? all myself?
Why, this would make a man a man of salt,
To use his eyes for garden water-pots,
Aye, and laying autumn's dust.
Gent. Good sir,—
Lear. I will die bravely, like a smug bridegroom. What!
I will be jovial: come, come; I am a king,
My masters, know you that.
Gent. You are a royal one, and we obey you.
Lear. Then there 's life in 't. Nay, an you get it, you shall get it by running. Sa, sa, sa, sa.
[*Exit running; Attendants follow.*
Gent. A sight most pitiful in the meanest wretch,
Past speaking of in a king! Thou hast one daughter,
Who redeems nature from the general curse
Which twain have brought her to.
Edg. Hail, gentle sir.
Gent. Sir, speed you: what 's your will?
Edg. Do you hear aught, sir, of a battle toward?
Gent. Most sure and vulgar: every one hears that,
Which can distinguish sound.
Edg. But, by your favour,
How near 's the other army?
Gent. Near and on speedy foot; the main descry
Stands on the hourly thought.
Edg. I thank you, sir: that 's all.
Gent. Though that the queen on special cause is here,
Her army is moved on.
Edg. I thank you, sir. [*Exit Gent.*
Glou. You ever-gentle gods, take my breath from me;
Let not my worser spirit tempt me again
To die before you please!
Edg. Well pray you, father.

Glou. Now, good sir, what are you?

Edg. A most poor man, made tame to fortune's blows;
Who, by the art of known and feeling sorrows,
Am pregnant to good pity. Give me your hand,
I'll lead you to some biding.

Glou. Hearty thanks;
The bounty and the benison of heaven
To boot, and boot!

Enter Oswald.

Osw. A proclaim'd prize! Most happy!
That eyeless head of thine was first framed flesh,
To raise my fortunes. Thou old unhappy traitor,
Briefly thyself remember: the sword is out
That must destroy thee.

Glou. Now let thy friendly hand
Put strength enough to 't. [*Edgar interposes.*

Osw. Wherefore, bold peasant,
Darest thou support a publish'd traitor? Hence!
Lest that the infection of his fortune take
Like hold on thee. Let go his arm.

Edg. Chill not let go, zir, without vurther 'casion.

Osw. Let go, slave, or thou diest!

Edg. Good gentleman, go your gait, and let poor volk pass. An chud ha' been zwaggered out of my life, 'twould not ha' been zo long as 'tis by a vortnight. Nay, come not near th' old man; keep out, che vor ye, or I 'se try whether your costard or my ballow be the harder: chill be plain with you.

Osw. Out, dunghill! [*They fight.*

Edg. Chill pick your teeth, zir: come; no matter vor your foins.
[*Oswald falls.*

Osw. Slave thou hast slain me. Villain, take my purse:
If ever thou wilt thrive, bury my body;
And give the letters which thou find'st about me
To Edmund earl of Gloucester; seek him out
Upon the British party. O, untimely death!
Death! [*Dies.*

Edg. I know thee well: a serviceable villain,
As duteous to the vices of thy mistress
As badness would desire.

Glou. What, is he dead?

Edg. Sit you down, father; rest you.
Let 's see these pockets: the letters that he speaks of
May be my friends. He 's dead; I am only sorry
He had no other deathsman. Let us see:
Leave, gentle wax; and, manners, blame us not:

To know our enemies' minds, we 'ld rip their hearts;
Their papers, is more lawful.

[*Reads*] 'Let our reciprocal vows be remembered. You have many opportunities to cut him off: if your will want not, time and place will be fruitfully offered. There is nothing done, if he return the conqueror: then am I the prisoner, and his bed my gaol; from the loathed warmth whereof deliver me, and supply the place for your labour.

'Your—wife, so I would say—
'affectionate servant,
'GONERIL.'

O undistinguish'd space of woman's will!
A plot upon her virtuous husband's life;
And the exchange my brother! Here, in the sands,
Thee I'll rake up, the post unsanctified
Of murderous lechers; and in the mature time
With this ungracious paper strike the sight
Of the death-practised duke: for him 'tis well
That of thy death and business I can tell.

Glou. The king is mad: how stiff is my vile sense,
That I stand up, and have ingenious feeling
Of my huge sorrows! Better I were distract:
So should my thoughts be sever'd from my griefs,
And woes by wrong imaginations lose
The knowledge of themselves. [*Drum afar off.*

Edg. Give me your hand:
Far off, methinks, I hear the beaten drum:
Come, father, I'll bestow you with a friend. [*Exeunt.*

SCENE VII

A tent in the French camp. Lear on a bed asleep, soft music playing; Gentleman, and others attending.

Enter Cordelia, Kent, and Doctor.

Cor. O thou good Kent, how shall I live and work,
To match thy goodness? My life will be too short,
And every measure fail me.

Kent. To be acknowledged, madam, is o'erpaid.
All my reports go with the modest truth,
Nor more nor clipp'd, but so.

Cor. Be better suited:
These weeds are memories of those worser hours:
I prithee, put them off.

Kent. Pardon me, dear madam;
Yet to be known shortens my made intent:
My boon I make it, that you know me not

Till time and I think meet.
Cor. Then be 't so, my good lord. [*To the Doctor*] How does the king?
Doct. Madam, sleeps still.
Cor. O you kind gods,
Cure this great breach in his abused nature!
The untuned and jarring senses, O, wind up
Of this child-changed father!
Doct. So please your majesty
That we may wake the king: he hath slept long.
Cor. Be govern'd by your knowledge, and proceed
I' the sway of your own will. Is he array'd?
Gent. Ay, madam; in the heaviness of his sleep
We put fresh garments on him.
Doct. Be by, good madam, when we do awake him;
I doubt not of his temperance.
Cor. Very well.
Doct. Please you, draw near. Louder the music there!
Cor. O my dear father! Restoration hang
Thy medicine on my lips, and let this kiss
Repair those violent harms that my two sisters
Have in thy reverence made!
Kent. Kind and dear princess!
Cor. Had you not been their father, these white flakes
Had challenged pity of them. Was this a face
To be opposed against the warring winds?
To stand against the deep dread-bolted thunder?
In the most terrible and nimble stroke
Of quick, cross lightning? to watch—poor perdu!—
With this thin helm? Mine enemy's dog,
Though he had bit me, should have stood that night
Against my fire; and wast thou fain, poor father,
To hovel thee with swine and rogues forlorn,
In short and musty straw? Alack, alack!
'Tis wonder that thy life and wits at once
Had not concluded all. He wakes; speak to him.
Doct. Madam, do you; 'tis fittest.
Cor. How does my royal lord? How fares your majesty?
Lear. You do me wrong to take me out o' the grave:
Thou art a soul in bliss; but I am bound
Upon a wheel of fire, that mine own tears
Do scald like molten lead.
Cor. Sir, do you know me?
Lear. You are a spirit, I know: when did you die?
Cor. Still, still, far wide!

Doct. He 's scarce awake : let him alone awhile.
Lear. Where have I been? Where am I? Fair daylight?
I am mightily abused. I should e'en die with pity,
To see another thus. I know not what to say.
I will not swear these are my hands : let 's see;
I feel this pin prick. Would I were assured
Of my condition!
Cor. O, look upon me, sir,
And hold your hands in benediction o'er me.
No, sir, you must not kneel.
Lear. Pray, do not mock me :
I am a very foolish fond old man,
Fourscore and upward, not an hour more nor less;
And, to deal plainly,
I fear I am not in my perfect mind.
Methinks I should know you and know this man;
Yet I am doubtful; for I am mainly ignorant
What place this is, and all the skill I have
Remembers not these garments, nor I know not
Where I did lodge last night. Do not laugh at me;
For, as I am a man, I think this lady
To be my child Cordelia.
Cor. And so I am, I am.
Lear. Be your tears wet? yes, faith. I pray, weep not:
If you have poison for me, I will drink it.
I know you do not love me; for your sisters
Have, as I do remember, done me wrong:
You have some cause, they have not.
Cor. No cause, no cause.
Lear. Am I in France?
Kent. In your own kingdom, sir.
Lear. Do not abuse me.
Doct. Be comforted, good madam : the great rage,
You see, is kill'd in him : and yet it is danger
To make him even o'er the time he has lost.
Desire him to go in; trouble him no more
Till further settling.
Cor. Will 't please your highness walk?
Lear. You must bear with me.
Pray you now, forget and forgive: I am old and foolish.
[*Exeunt all but Kent and Gentleman.*
Gent. Holds it true, sir, that the Duke of Cornwall was so slain?
Kent. Most certain, sir.
Gent. Who is conductor of his people?
Kent. As 'tis said, the bastard son of Gloucester.

Gent. They say Edgar, his banished son, is with the Earl of Kent in Germany.

Kent. Report is changeable. 'Tis time to look about; the powers of the kingdom approach apace.

Gent. The arbitrement is like to be bloody. Fare you well, sir. [*Exit.*

Kent. My point and period will be throughly wrought,
Or well or ill, as this day's battle 's fought. [*Exit.*

ACT V—SCENE I

The British camp near Dover.

Enter, with drum and colours, Edmund, Regan, Gentlemen, and Soldiers.

Edm. Know of the duke if his last purpose hold,
Or whether since he is advised by aught
To change the course: he 's full of alteration
And self-reproving: bring his constant pleasure.
[*To a Gentleman, who goes out.*

Reg. Our sister's man is certainly miscarried.

Edm. 'Tis to be doubted, madam.

Reg. Now, sweet lord,
You know the goodness I intend upon you:
Tell me, but truly, but then speak the truth,
Do you not love my sister?

Edm. In honour'd love.

Reg. But have you never found my brother's way
To the forfended place?

Edm. That thought abuses you.

Reg. I am doubtful that you have been conjunct
And bosom'd with her, as far as we call hers.

Edm. No, by mine honour, madam.

Reg. I never shall endure her: dear my lord,
Be not familiar with her.

Edm. Fear me not.—
She and the duke her husband!

Enter, with drum and colours, Albany, Goneril, and Soldiers.

Gon. [*Aside*] I had rather lose the battle than that sister
Should loosen him and me.

Alb. Our very loving sister, well be-met.
Sir, this I hear; the king is come to his daughter,
With others whom the rigour of our state
Forced to cry out. Where I could not be honest,
I never yet was valiant: for this business,
It toucheth us, as France invades our land,
Not bolds the king, with others, whom, I fear,

Most just and heavy causes make oppose.
Edm. Sir, you speak nobly.
Reg. Why is this reason'd?
Gon. Combine together 'gainst the enemy;
For these domestic and particular broils
Are not the question here.
Alb. Let 's then determine
With the ancient of war on our proceedings.
Edm. I shall attend you presently at your tent.
Reg. Sister, you 'll go with us?
Gon. No.
Reg. 'Tis most convenient; pray you, go with us.
Gon. [*Aside*] O, ho, I know the riddle.—I will go.

As they are going out, enter Edgar disguised.

Edg. If e'er your grace had speech with man so poor,
Hear me one word.
Alb. I 'll overtake you. Speak.
[*Exeunt all but Albany and Edgar.*
Edg. Before you fight the battle, ope this letter.
If you have victory, let the trumpet sound
For him that brought it: wretched though I seem,
I can produce a champion that will prove
What is avouched there. If you miscarry,
Your business of the world hath so an end,
And machination ceases. Fortune love you!
Alb. Stay till I have read the letter.
Edg. I was forbid it.
When time shall serve, let but the herald cry,
And I 'll appear again.
Alb. Why, fare thee well: I will o'erlook thy paper.
[*Exit Edgar.*

Re-enter Edmund.

Edm. The enemy 's in view: draw up your powers.
Here is the guess of their true strength and forces
By diligent discovery; but your haste
Is now urged on you.
Alb. We will greet the time. [*Exit.*
Edm. To both these sisters have I sworn my love;
Each jealous of the other, as the stung
Are of the adder. Which of them shall I take?
Both? one? or neither? Neither can be enjoy'd,
If both remain alive: to take the widow
Exasperates, makes mad her sister Goneril;
And hardly shall I carry out my side,
Her husband being alive. Now then we 'll use

His countenance for the battle; which being done,
Let her who would be rid of him devise
His speedy taking off. As for the mercy
Which he intends to Lear and to Cordelia,
The battle done, and they within our power,
Shall never see his pardon; for my state
Stands on me to defend, not to debate. [*Exit.*

SCENE II

A field between the two camps.

Alarum within. Enter, with drum and colours, Lear, Cordelia, and Soldiers, over the stage; and exeunt.

Enter Edgar and Gloucester.

Edg. Here, father, take the shadow of this tree
For your good host; pray that the right may thrive:
If ever I return to you again,
I 'll bring you comfort.
Glou. Grace go with you, sir!
[*Exit Edgar.*

Alarum and retreat within. Re-enter Edgar.

Edg. Away, old man; give me thy hand; away!
King Lear hath lost, he and his daughter ta'en;
Give me thy hand; come on.
Glou. No further, sir; a man may rot even here.
Edg. What, in ill thoughts again? Men must endure
Their going hence, even as their coming hither:
Ripeness is all: come on.
Glou. And that 's true too. [*Exeunt.*

SCENE III

The British camp near Dover.

Enter, in conquest, with drum and colours, Edmund; Lear and Cordelia, as prisoners; Captain, Soldiers, &c.

Edm. Some officers take them away: good guard,
Until their greater pleasures first be known
That are to censure them.
Cor. We are not the first
Who with best meaning have incurr'd the worst.
For thee, oppressed king, am I cast down;
Myself could else out-frown false fortune's frown.
Shall we not see these daughters and these sisters?
Lear. No, no, no, no! Come, let 's away to prison:
We two alone will sing like birds i' the cage:

When thou dost ask me blessing, I 'll kneel down
And ask of thee forgiveness : so we 'll live,
And pray, and sing, and tell old tales, and laugh
At gilded butterflies, and hear poor rogues
Talk of court news ; and we 'll talk with them too,
Who loses and who wins, who 's in, who 's out;
And take upon 's the mystery of things,
As if we were God's spies : and we 'll wear out,
In a wall'd prison, packs and sects of great ones
That ebb and flow by the moon.

Edm. Take them away

Lear. Upon such sacrifices, my Cordelia,
The gods themselves throw incense. Have I caught thee?
He that parts us shall bring a brand from heaven,
And fire us hence like foxes. Wipe thine eyes;
The good-years shall devour them, flesh and fell,
Ere they shall make us weep : we 'll see 'em starve first.
Come. [*Exeunt Lear and Cordelia, guarded.*

Edm. Come hither, captain; hark.
Take thou this note : go follow them to prison :
One step I have advanced thee; if thou dost
As this instructs thee, thou dost make thy way
To noble fortunes : know thou this, that men
Are as the time is : to be tender-minded
Does not become a sword : thy great employment
Will not bear question ; either say thou 'lt do 't,
Or thrive by other means.

Capt. I 'll do 't, my lord.

Edm. About it ; and write happy when thou hast done.
Mark ; I say, instantly, and carry it so
As I have set it down.

Capt. I cannot draw a cart, nor eat dried oats ;
If it be a man's work, I 'll do 't. [*Exit.*

Flourish. Enter Albany, Goneril, Regan, another Captain, and Soldiers.

Alb. Sir, you have shown to-day your valiant strain,
And fortune led you well : you have the captives
That were the opposites of this day's strife :
We do require them of you, so to use them
As we shall find their merits and our safety
May equally determine.

Edm. Sir, I thought it fit
To send the old and miserable king
To some retention and appointed guard ;
Whose age has charms in it, whose title more,

To pluck the common bosom on his side,
And turn our impress'd lances in our eyes
Which do command them. With him I sent the queen:
My reason all the same; and they are ready
To-morrow or at further space to appear
Where you shall hold your session. At this time
We sweat and bleed: the friend hath lost his friend;
And the best quarrels, in the heat, are cursed
By those that feel their sharpness.
The question of Cordelia and her father
Requires a fitter place.

Alb. Sir, by your patience,
I hold you but a subject of this war,
Not as a brother.

Reg. That 's as we list to grace him.
Methinks our pleasure might have been demanded,
Ere you had spoke so far. He led our powers,
Bore the commission of my place and person;
The which immediacy may well stand up
And call itself your brother.

Gon. Not so hot:
In his own grace he doth exalt himself
More than in your addition.

Reg. In my rights,
By me invested, he compeers the best.

Gon. That were the most, if he should husband you.

Reg. Jesters do oft prove prophets.

Gon. Holla, holla!
That eye that told you so look'd but a-squint.

Reg. Lady, I am not well; else I should answer
From a full-flowing stomach. General,
Take thou my soldiers, prisoners, patrimony;
Dispose of them, of me; the walls are thine:
Witness the world, that I create thee here
My lord and master.

Gon. Mean you to enjoy him?

Alb. The let-alone lies not in your good will.

Edm. Nor in thine, lord.

Alb. Half-blooded fellow, yes.

Reg. [*To Edmund*] Let the drum strike, and prove my title [thine.

Alb. Stay yet; hear reason. Edmund, I arrest thee
On capital treason; and in thine attaint
This gilded serpent [*pointing to Gon.*]. For your claim, fair
I bar it in the interest of my wife; [sister,
'Tis she is sub-contracted to this lord,

And I, her husband, contradict your bans.
If you will marry, make your loves to me;
My lady is bespoke.

Gon. An interlude!

Alb. Thou art arm'd, Gloucester: let the trumpet sound:
If none appear to prove upon thy person
Thy heinous, manifest, and many treasons,
There is my pledge [*throwing down a glove*]: I'll prove it on [thy heart,
Ere I taste bread, thou art in nothing less
Than I have here proclaim'd thee.

Reg. Sick, O, sick!

Gon. [*Aside*] If not, I'll ne'er trust medicine.

Edm. [*Throwing down a glove*] There's my exchange: what in the world he is
That names me traitor, villain-like he lies:
Call by thy trumpet: he that dares approach,
On him, on you,—who not?—I will maintain
My truth and honour firmly.

Alb. A herald, ho!

Edm. A herald, ho, a herald!

Alb. Trust to thy single virtue; for thy soldiers,
All levied in my name, have in my name
Took their discharge.

Reg. My sickness grows upon me.

Alb. She is not well; convey her to my tent. [*Exit Regan, led.*

Enter a Herald.

Come hither, herald,—Let the trumpet sound,—
And read out this.

Capt. Sound, trumpet! [*A trumpet sounds.*

Her. [*Reads*] 'If any man of quality or degree within the lists of the army will maintain upon Edmund, supposed Earl of Gloucester, that he is a manifold traitor, let him appear by the third sound of the trumpet: he is bold in his defence.'

Edm. Sound! [*First trumpet.*

Her. Again! [*Second trumpet.*

Her. Again! [*Third trumpet.*

[*Trumpet answers within.*

Enter Edgar, at the third sound, armed, with a trumpet before him.

Alb. Ask him his purposes, why he appears
Upon this call o' the trumpet.

Her. What are you?
Your name, your quality? and why you answer
This present summons?

Edg. Know, my name is lost;
By treason's tooth bare-gnawn and canker-bit:
Yet am I noble as the adversary
I come to cope.
Alb. Which is that adversary?
Edg. What 's he that speaks for Edmund, Earl of Gloucester?
Edm. Himself: what say'st thou to him?
Edg. Draw thy sword,
That if my speech offend a noble heart,
Thy arm may do thee justice: here is mine.
Behold, it is the privilege of mine honours,
My oath, and my profession: I protest,
Maugre thy strength, youth, place and eminence,
Despite thy victor sword and fire-new fortune,
Thy valour and thy heart, thou art a traitor,
False to thy gods, thy brother and thy father,
Conspirant 'gainst this high illustrious prince,
And from the extremest upward of thy head
To the descent and dust below thy foot,
A most toad-spotted traitor. Say thou 'No,'
This sword, this arm and my best spirits are bent
To prove upon thy heart, whereto I speak,
Thou liest.
Edm. In wisdom I should ask thy name,
But since thy outside looks so fair and warlike
And that thy tongue some say of breeding breathes,
What safe and nicely I might well delay
By rule of knighthood, I disdain and spurn:
Back do I toss these treasons to thy head;
With the hell-hated lie o'erwhelm thy heart;
Which for they yet glance by and scarcely bruise,
This sword of mine shall give them instant way,
Where they shall rest for ever. Trumpets, speak!
[*Alarums. They fight. Edmund falls.*
Alb. Save him, save him!
Gon. This is practice, Gloucester:
By the law of arms thou wast not bound to answer
An unknown opposite; thou art not vanquish'd,
But cozen'd and beguiled.
Alb. Shut your mouth, dame,
Or with this paper shall I stop it. Hold, sir;
Thou worse than any name, read thine own evil.
No tearing, lady; I perceive you know it.
Gon. Say, if I do, the laws are mine, not thine:
Who can arraign me for 't?

Alb. Most monstrous!
Know'st thou this paper?
Gon. Ask me not what I know. [*Exit.*
Alb. Go after her: she's desperate; govern her.
Edm. What you have cnarged me with, that have I done;
And more, much more; the time will bring it out:
'Tis past, and so am I. But what art thou
That hast this fortune on me? If thou 'rt noble,
I do forgive thee.
Edg. Let's exchange charity.
I am no less in blood than thou art, Edmund;
If more, the more thou hast wrong'd me.
My name is Edgar, and thy father's son.
The gods are just, and of our pleasant vices
Make instruments to plague us:
The dark and vicious place where thee he got
Cost him his eyes.
Edm. Thou hast spoken right, 'tis true;
The wheel is come full circle; I am here.
Alb. Methought thy very gait did prophesy
A royal nobleness: I must embrace thee:
Let sorrow split my heart, if ever I
Did hate thee or thy father!
Edg. Worthy prince, I know 't.
Alb. Where have you hid yourself?
How have you known the miseries of your father?
Edg. By nursing them, my lord. List a brief tale;
And when 'tis told, O, that my heart would burst!
The bloody proclamation to escape
That follow'd me so near,—O, our lives' sweetness:
That we the pain of death would hourly die
Rather than die at once!—taught me to shift
Into a madman's rags, to assume a semblance
That very dogs disdain'd: and in this habit
Met I my father with his bleeding rings,
Their precious stones new lost; became his guide,
Led him, begg'd for him, saved him from despair;
Never—O fault!—reveal'd myself unto him,
Until some half-hour past, when I was arm'd;
Not sure, though hoping, of this good success,
I ask'd his blessing, and from first to last
Told him my pilgrimage: but his flaw'd heart,—
Alack, too weak the conflict to support!—
'Twixt two extremes of passion, joy and grief,
Burst smilingly.

Edm. This speech of yours hath moved me,
And shall perchance do good: but speak you on;
You look as you had something more to say.
Alb. If there be more, more woful, hold it in;
For I am almost ready to dissolve,
Hearing of this.
Edg. This would have seem'd a period
To such as love not sorrow; but another,
To amplify too much, would make much more,
And top extremity.
Whilst I was big in clamour, came there in a man,
Who, having seen me in my worst estate,
Shunn'd my abhorr'd society; but then, finding
Who 'twas that so endured, with his strong arms
He fasten'd on my neck, and bellow'd out
As he 'ld burst heaven; threw him on my father;
Told the most piteous tale of Lear and him
That ever ear received: which in recounting
His grief grew puissant, and the strings of life
Began to crack: twice then the trumpet sounded,
And there I left him tranced.
Alb. But who was this?
Edg. Kent, sir, the banish'd Kent; who in disguise
Follow'd his enemy king, and did him service
Improper for a slave.

Enter a Gentleman, with a bloody knife.

Gent. Help, help, O, help!
Edg. What kind of help?
Alb. Speak, man.
Edg. What means this bloody knife?
Gent. 'Tis hot, it smokes;
It came even from the heart of—O, she 's dead!
Alb. Who dead? speak, man.
Gent. Your lady, sir, your lady: and her sister
By her is poisoned; she hath confess'd it.
Edm. I was contracted to them both: all three
Now marry in an instant.
Edg. Here comes Kent.
Alb. Produce the bodies, be they alive or dead.
[*Exit Gentleman.*
This judgement of the heavens, that makes us tremble,
Touches us not with pity.

Enter Kent.

O, is this he?
The time will not allow the compliment

Which very manners urges.

Kent. I am come
To bid my king and master aye good night:
Is he not here?

Alb. Great thing of us forgot!
Speak, Edmund, where 's the king? and where 's Cordelia?
See'st thou this object, Kent?

[*The bodies of Goneril and Regan are brought in.*

Kent. Alack, why thus?

Edm. Yet Edmund was beloved:
The one the other poison'd for my sake,
And after slew herself.

Alb. Even so. Cover their faces.

Edm. I pant for life: some good I mean to do,
Despite of mine own nature. Quickly send,
Be brief in it, to the castle; for my writ
Is on the life of Lear and on Cordelia:
Nay, send in time.

Alb. Run, run, O, run!

Edg. To who, my lord? Who hath the office? send
Thy token of reprieve.

Edm. Well thought on: take my sword,
Give it the captain.

Alb. Haste thee, for thy life. [*Exit Edgar.*

Edm. He hath commission from thy wife and me
To hang Cordelia in the prison, and
To lay the blame upon her own despair,
That she fordid herself.

Alb. The gods defend her! Bear him hence awhile.

[*Edmund is borne off.*

Re-enter Lear, with Cordelia dead in his arms; Edgar, Captain, and others following.

Lear. Howl, howl, howl, howl! O, you are men of stones:
Had I your tongues and eyes, I 'ld use them so
That heaven's vault should crack. She 's gone for ever
I know when one is dead and when one lives;
She 's dead as earth. Lend me a looking-glass;
If that her breath will mist or stain the stone,
Why, then she lives.

Kent. Is this the promised end?

Edg. Or image of that horror?

Alb. Fall and cease.

Lear. This feather stirs; she lives. If it be so,
It is a chance which does redeem all sorrows
That ever I have felt.

Kent. [*Kneeling*] O my good master!
Lear. Prithee, away.
Edg. 'Tis noble Kent, your friend.
Lear. A plague upon you, murderers, traitors all!
I might have saved her; now she 's gone for ever!
Cordelia, Cordelia! stay a little. Ha!
What is 't thou say'st? Her voice was ever soft,
Gentle and low, an excellent thing in woman.
I kill'd the slave that was a-hanging thee.
Capt. 'Tis true, my lords, he did.
Lear. Did I not, fellow?
I have seen the day, with my good biting falchion
I would have made them skip: I am old now,
And these same crosses spoil me. Who are you?
Mine eyes are not o' the best: I 'll tell you straight.
Kent. If fortune brag of two she loved and hated,
One of them we behold.
Lear. This is a dull sight. Are you not Kent?
Kent. The same,
Your servant Kent. Where is your servant Caius?
Lear. He 's a good fellow, I can tell you that;
He 'll strike, and quickly too: he 's dead and rotten.
Kent. No, my good lord; I am the very man—
Lear. I 'll see that straight.
Kent. That from your first of difference and decay
Have follow'd your sad steps.
Lear. You are welcome hither.
Kent. Nor no man else: all 's cheerless, dark and deadly
Your eldest daughters have fordone themselves,
And desperately are dead.
Lear. Ay, so I think.
Alb. He knows not what he says, and vain is it
That we present us to him.
Edg. Very bootless.

Enter a Captain.

Capt. Edmund is dead, my lord.
Alb. That 's but a trifle here.
You lords and noble friends, know our intent.
What comfort to this great decay may come
Shall be applied: for us, we will resign,
During the life of this old majesty,
To him our absolute power: [*To Edgar and Kent*] you, to your rights;
With boot, and such addition as your honours
Have more than merited. All friends shall taste

The wages of their virtue, and all foes
The cup of their deservings. O, see, see!

Lear. And my poor fool is hang'd! No, no, no life!
Why should a dog, a horse, a rat, have life,
And thou no breath at all? Thou 'lt come no more,
Never, never, never, never, never!
Pray you, undo this button: thank you, sir.
Do you see this? Look on her, look, her lips,
Look there, look there! [*Dies.*

Edg. He faints. My lord, my lord!

Kent. Break, heart; I prithee, break!

Edg. Look up, my lord.

Kent. Vex not his ghost: O, let him pass! he hates him
That would upon the rack of this tough world
Stretch him out longer.

Edg. He is gone indeed.

Kent. The wonder is he hath endured so long:
He but usurp'd his life.

Alb. Bear them from hence. Our present business
Is general woe. [*To Kent and Edgar*] Friends of my soul, you twain
Rule in this realm and the gored state sustain.

Kent. I have a journey, sir, shortly to go;
My master calls me, I must not say no.

Alb. The weight of this sad time we must obey,
Speak what we feel, not what we ought to say.
The oldest hath borne most: we that are young
Shall never see so much, nor live so long.
[*Exeunt, with a dead march.*

THE TRAGEDY OF OTHELLO, THE MOOR OF VENICE

DRAMATIS PERSONÆ

DUKE OF VENICE.
BRABANTIO, *a senator.*
Other Senators.
GRATIANO, *brother to Brabantio.*
LODOVICO, *kinsman to Brabantio.*
OTHELLO, *a noble Moor in the service of the Venetian state.*
CASSIO, *his lieutenant.*
IAGO, *his ancient.*
RODERIGO, *a Venetian gentleman.*
MONTANO, *Othello's predecessor in the government of Cyprus.*
Clown, servant to Othello.

DESDEMONA, *daughter to Brabantio and wife to Othello.*
EMILIA, *wife to Iago.*
BIANCA, *mistress to Cassio.*

Sailor, Messenger, Herald, Officers, Gentlemen, Musicians, and Attendants.

SCENE: *Venice: a seaport in Cyprus.*

ACT I—SCENE I

Venice. A street.

Enter Roderigo and Iago.

Rod. Tush, never tell me; I take it much unkindly
That thou, Iago, who hast had my purse
As if the strings were thine, shouldst know of this.
Iago. 'Sblood, but you will not hear me:
If ever I did dream of such a matter,
Abhor me.
Rod. Thou told'st me thou didst hold him in thy hate.
Iago. Despise me, if I do not. Three great ones of the city,
In personal suit to make me his lieutenant,
Off-capp'd to him: and, by the faith of man,
I know my price, I am worth no worse a place:
But he, as loving his own pride and purposes,
Evades them, with a bombast circumstance
Horribly stuff'd with epithets of war;
And, in conclusion,
Nonsuits my mediators; for, 'Certes,' says he,
'I have already chose my officer.'
And what was he?
Forsooth, a great arithmetician,
One Michael Cassio, a Florentine,
A fellow almost damn'd in a fair wife;
That never set a squadron in the field,
Nor the division of a battle knows
More than a spinster; unless the bookish theoric,
Wherein the toged consuls can propose
As masterly as he: mere prattle without practice
Is all his soldiership. But he, sir, had the election:
And I, of whom his eyes had seen the proof

At Rhodes, at Cyprus, and on other grounds
Christian and heathen, must be be-lee'd and calm'd
By debitor and creditor: this counter-caster,
He, in good time, must his lieutenant be,
And I—God bless the mark!—his Moorship's ancient.

Rod. By heaven, I rather would have been his hangman.

Iago. Why, there 's no remedy; 'tis the curse of service,
Preferment goes by letter and affection,
And not by old gradation, where each second
Stood heir to the first. Now, sir, be judge yourself
Whether I in any just term am affined
To love the Moor.

Rod. I would not follow him then.

Iago. O, sir, content you;
I follow him to serve my turn upon him:
We cannot all be masters, nor all masters
Cannot be truly follow'd. You shall mark
Many a duteous and knee-crooking knave,
That doting on his own obsequious bondage
Wears out his time, much like his master's ass,
For nought but provender, and when he 's old, cashier'd:
Whip me such honest knaves. Others there are
Who, trimm'd in forms and visages of duty,
Keep yet their hearts attending on themselves,
And throwing but shows of service on their lords
Do well thrive by them, and when they have lined their coats
Do themselves homage: these fellows have some soul,
And such a one do I profess myself.
For, sir,
It is as sure as you are Roderigo,
Were I the Moor, I would not be Iago:
In following him, I follow but myself;
Heaven is my judge, not I for love and duty,
But seeming so, for my peculiar end:
For when my outward action doth demonstrate
The native act and figure of my heart
In compliment extern, 'tis not long after
But I will wear my heart upon my sleeve
For daws to peck at: I am not what I am.

Rod. What a full fortune does the thick lips owe,
If he can carry 't thus!

Iago. Call up her father,
Rouse him: make after him, poison his delight,
Proclaim him in the streets; incense her kinsmen,
And, though he in a fertile climate dwell,

Plague him with flies: though that his joy be joy,
Yet throw such changes of vexation on 't
As it may lose some colour.

Rod. Here is her father's house; I 'll call aloud.

Iago. Do; with like timorous accent and dire yell
As when, by night and negligence, the fire
Is spied in populous cities.

Rod. What, ho, Brabantio! Signior Brabantio, ho!

Iago. Awake! what, ho, Brabantio! thieves! thieves! thieves!
Look to your house, your daughter and your bags!
Thieves! thieves!

Brabantio appears above, at a window.

Bra. What is the reason of this terrible summons?
What is the matter there?

Rod. Signior, is all your family within?

Iago. Are your doors lock'd?

Bra. Why, wherefore ask you this?

Iago. 'Zounds, sir, you 're robb'd; for shame, put on your gown;
Your heart is burst, you have lost half your soul;
Even now, now, very now, an old black ram
Is tupping your white ewe. Arise, arise;
Awake the snorting citizens with the bell,
Or else the devil will make a grandsire of you;
Arise, I say.

Bra. What, have you lost your wits?

Rod. Most reverend signior, do you know my voice?

Bra. Not I: what are you?

Rod. My name is Roderigo.

Bra. The worser welcome:
I have charged thee not to haunt about my doors.
In honest plainness thou hast heard me say
My daughter is not for thee; and now, in madness,
Being full of supper and distempering draughts,
Upon malicious bravery, dost thou come
To start my quiet.

Rod. Sir, sir, sir,—

Bra. But thou must needs be sure
My spirit and my place have in them power
To make this bitter to thee.

Rod. Patience, good sir.

Bra. What tell'st thou me of robbing? this is Venice;
My house is not a grange.

Rod. Most grave Brabantio,
In simple and pure soul I come to you.

Iago. 'Zounds, sir, you are one of those that will not serve

God, if the devil bid you. Because we come to do you service and you think we are ruffians, you 'll have your daughter covered with a Barbary horse; you 'll have your nephews neigh to you; you 'll have coursers for cousins, and gennets for germans.

Bra. What profane wretch art thou?

Iago. I am one, sir, that comes to tell you your daughter and the Moor are now making the beast with two backs.

Bra. Thou art a villain.

Iago. You are—a senator.

Bra. This thou shalt answer; I know thee, Roderigo.

Rod. Sir, I will answer any thing. But, I beseech you,
If 't be your pleasure and most wise consent,
As partly I find it is, that your fair daughter,
At this odd-even and dull watch o' the night,
Transported with no worse nor better guard
But with a knave of common hire, a gondolier,
To the gross clasps of a lascivious Moor,—
If this be known to you, and your allowance,
We then have done you bold and saucy wrongs;
But if you know not this, my manners tell me
We have your wrong rebuke. Do not believe
That, from the sense of all civility,
I thus would play and trifle with your reverence:
Your daughter, if you have not given her leave,
I say again, hath made a gross revolt,
Tying her duty, beauty, wit and fortunes,
In an extravagant and wheeling stranger
Of here and every where. Straight satisfy yourself:
If she be in her chamber or your house,
Let loose on me the justice of the state
For thus deluding you.

Bra. Strike on the tinder, ho!
Give me a taper! call up all my people!
This accident is not unlike my dream:
Belief of it oppresses me already.
Light, I say! light! [*Exit above.*

Iago. Farewell; for I must leave you:
It seems not meet, nor wholesome to my place,
To be produced—as, if I stay, I shall—
Against the Moor: for I do know, the state,
However this may gall him with some check,
Cannot with safety cast him; for he 's embark'd
With such loud reason to the Cyprus wars,
Which even now stand in act, that, for their souls,

Another of his fathom they have none
To lead their business: in which regard,
Though I do hate him as I do hell pains,
Yet for necessity of present life,
I must show out a flag and sign of love,
Which is indeed but sign. That you shall surely find him,
Lead to the Sagittary the raised search;
And there will I be with him. So farewell. [*Exit.*

Enter, below, Brabantio, in his night-gown, and Servants with torches.

Bra. It is too true an evil: gone she is;
And what's to come of my despised time
Is nought but bitterness. Now, Roderigo,
Where didst thou see her? O unhappy girl!
With the Moor, say'st thou? Who would be a father!
How didst thou know 'twas she? O, she deceives me
Past thought! What said she to you? Get more tapers.
Raise all my kindred. Are they married, think you?

Rod. Truly, I think they are.

Bra. O heaven! How got she out? O treason of the blood!
Fathers, from hence trust not your daughters' minds
By what you see them act. Is there not charms
By which the property of youth and maidhood
May be abused? Have you not read, Roderigo,
Of some such thing?

Rod. Yes, sir, I have indeed.

Bra. Call up my brother. O, would you had had her!
Some one way, some another. Do you know
Where we may apprehend her and the Moor?

Rod. I think I can discover him, if you please
To get good guard and go along with me.

Bra. Pray you, lead on. At every house I'll call;
I may command at most. Get weapons, ho!
And raise some special officers of night.
On, good Roderigo; I'll deserve your pains. [*Exeunt.*

Scene II

Another street.

Enter Othello, Iago, and Attendants with torches.

Iago. Though in the trade of war I have slain men,
Yet do I hold it very stuff o' the conscience
To do no contrived murder: I lack iniquity
Sometimes to do me service: nine or ten times
I had thought to have yerk'd him here under under the ribs.

Oth. 'Tis better as it is.

Iago. Nay, but he prated
And spoke such scurvy and provoking terms
Against your honour,
That, with the little godliness I have,
I did full hard forbear him. But I pray you, sir,
Are you fast married? Be assured of this,
That the magnifico is much beloved,
And hath in his effect a voice potential
As double as the duke's: he will divorce you,
Or put upon you what restraint and grievance
The law, with all his might to enforce it on,
Will give him cable.

Oth. Let him do his spite:
My services, which I have done the signiory,
Shall out-tongue his complaints. 'Tis yet to know—
Which, when I know that boasting is an honour,
I shall promulgate—I fetch my life and being
From men of royal siege, and my demerits
May speak unbonneted to as proud a fortune
As this that I have reach'd: for know, Iago,
But that I love the gentle Desdemona,
I would not my unhoused free condition
Put into circumscription and confine
For the sea's worth. But, look! what lights come yond?

Iago. Those are the raised father and his friends:
You were best go in.

Oth. Not I; I must be found:
My parts, my title and my perfect soul,
Shall manifest me rightly. Is it they?

Iago. By Janus, I think no.

Enter Cassio, and certain Officers with torches.

Oth. The servants of the duke, and my lieutenant.
The goodness of the night upon you, friends!
What is the news?

Cas. The duke does greet you, general,
And he requires your haste-post-haste appearance,
Even on the instant.

Oth. What is the matter, think you?

Cas. Something from Cyprus, as I may divine:
It is a business of some heat: the galleys
Have sent a dozen sequent messengers
This very night at one another's heels;
And many of the consuls, raised and met,
Are at the duke's already: you have been hotly call'd for;
When, being not at your lodging to be found,

The senate hath sent about three several quests
To search you out.

Oth. 'Tis well I am found by you.
I will but spend a word here in the house,
And go with you. [*Exit.*

Cas. Ancient, what makes he here?

Iago. Faith, he to-night hath boarded a land carack:
If it prove lawful prize, he 's made for ever.

Cas. I do not understand.

Iago. He 's married.

Cas. To who?

Re-enter Othello.

Iago. Marry, to—Come, captain, will you go?

Oth. Have with you.

Cas. Here comes another troop to seek for you.

Iago. It is Brabantio: general, be advised;
He comes to bad intent.

Enter Brabantio, Roderigo, and Officers with torches and weapons.

Oth. Holla! stand there!

Rod. Signior, it is the Moor.

Bra. . Down with him, thief!
[*They draw on both sides.*

Iago. You, Roderigo! come, sir, I am for you.

Oth. Keep up your bright swords, for the dew will rust them.
Good signior, you shall more command with years
Than with your weapons.

Bra. O thou foul thief, where hast thou stow'd my daughter?
Damn'd as thou art, thou hast enchanted her;
For I 'll refer me to all things of sense,
If she in chains of magic were not bound,
Whether a maid so tender, fair and happy,
So opposite to marriage that she shunn'd
The wealthy curled darlings of our nation,
Would ever have, to incur a general mock,
Run from her guardage to the sooty bosom
Of such a thing as thou, to fear, not to delight.
Judge me the world, if 'tis not gross in sense
That thou hast practised on her with foul charms,
Abused her delicate youth with drugs or minerals
That weaken motion: I 'll have 't disputed on;
'Tis probable, and palpable to thinking.
I therefore apprehend and do attach thee
For an abuser of the world, a practiser
Of arts inhibited and out of warrant.
Lay hold upon him: if he do resist,

Subdue him at his peril.

Oth. Hold your hands,
Both you of my inclining and the rest:
Were it my cue to fight, I should have known it
Without a prompter. Where will you that I go
To answer this your charge?

Bra. To prison, till fit time
Of law and course of direct session
Call thee to answer.

Oth. What if I do obey?
How may the duke be therewith satisfied,
Whose messengers are here about my side,
Upon some present business of the state
To bring me to him?

First Off. 'Tis true, most worthy signior;
The duke 's in council, and your noble self,
I am sure, is sent for.

Bra. How! the duke in council!
In this time of the night! Bring him away:
Mine 's not an idle cause: the duke himself,
Or any of my brothers of the state,
Cannot but feel this wrong as 'twere their own;
For if such actions may have passage free,
Bond-slaves and pagans shall our statesmen be. [*Exeunt.*

Scene III

A council-chamber.

The Duke and Senators sitting at a table; Officers attending.

Duke. There is no composition in these news
That gives them credit.

First Sen. Indeed they are disproportion'd;
My letters say a hundred and seven galleys.

Duke. And mine, a hundred and forty.

Sec. Sen. And mine, two hundred:
But though they jump not on a just account,—
As in these cases, where the aim reports,
'Tis oft with difference,—yet do they all confirm
A Turkish fleet, and bearing up to Cyprus.

Duke. Nay, it is possible enough to judgement:
I do not so secure me in the error,
But the main article I do approve
In fearful sense.

Sailor. [*Within*] What, ho! what, ho! what, ho!

First Off. A messenger from the galleys.

Enter Sailor.

Duke. Now, what 's the business?
Sail. The Turkish preparation makes for Rhodes;
So was I bid report here to the state
By Signior Angelo.
Duke. How say you by this change?
First Sen. This cannot be,
By no assay of reason: 'tis a pageant
To keep us in false gaze. When we consider
The importancy of Cyprus to the Turk,
And let ourselves again but understand
That as it more concerns the Turk than Rhodes,
So may he with more facile question bear it,
For that it stands not in such warlike brace,
But altogether lacks the abilities
That Rhodes is dress'd in: if we make thought of this,
We must not think the Turk is so unskilful
To leave that latest which concerns him first,
Neglecting an attempt of ease and gain,
To wake and wage a danger profitless.
Duke. Nay, in all confidence, he 's not for Rhodes.
First Off. Here is more news.

Enter a Messenger.

Mess. The Ottomites, reverend and gracious,
Steering with due course toward the isle of Rhodes
Have there injointed them with an after fleet.
First Sen. Ay, so I thought. How many, as you guess?
Mess. Of thirty sail: and now they do re-stem
Their backward course, bearing with frank appearance
Their purposes toward Cyprus. Signior Montano,
Your trusty and most valiant servitor,
With his free duty recommends you thus,
And prays you to believe him.
Duke. 'Tis certain then for Cyprus.
Marcus Luccicos, is not he in town?
First Sen. He 's now in Florence.
Duke. Write from us to him; post-post-haste dispatch.
First Sen. Here comes Brabantio and the valiant Moor.

Enter Brabantio, Othello, Iago, Roderigo, and Officers.

Duke. Valiant Othello, we must straight employ you
Against the general enemy Ottoman.
[*To Brabantio*] I did not see you; welcome, gentle signior;
We lack'd your counsel and your help to-night.
Bra. So did I yours. Good your grace, pardon me;
Neither my place nor aught I heard of business

Hath raised me from my bed, nor doth the general care
Take hold on me; for my particular grief
Is of so flood-gate and o'erbearing nature
That it engluts and swallows other sorrows,
And it is still itself.

Duke. Why, what 's the matter?

Bra. My daughter! O, my daughter!

All. Dead?

Bra. Ay, to me;
She is abused, stol'n from me and corrupted
By spells and medicines bought of mountebanks;
For nature so preposterously to err,
Being not deficient, blind, or lame of sense,
Sans witchcraft could not.

Duke. Whoe'er he be that in this foul proceeding
Hath thus beguiled your daughter of herself
And you of her, the bloody book of law
You shall yourself read in the bitter letter
After your own sense, yea, though our proper son
Stood in your action.

Bra. Humbly I thank your grace.
Here is the man, this Moor; whom now, it seems,
Your special mandate for the state-affairs
Hath hither brought.

All. We are very sorry for 't.

Duke. [*To Othello*] What in your own part can you say to this?

Bra. Nothing, but this is so.

Oth. Most potent, grave, and reverend signiors,
My very noble and approved good masters,
That I have ta'en away this old man's daughter,
It is most true; true, I have married her:
The very head and front of my offending
Hath this extent, no more. Rude am I in my speech,
And little blest with the soft phrase of peace;
For since these arms of mine had seven years' pith,
Till now some nine moons wasted, they have used
Their dearest action in the tented field;
And little of this great world can I speak,
More than pertains to feats of broil and battle;
And therefore little shall I grace my cause
In speaking for myself. Yet, by your gracious patience,
I will a round unvarnish'd tale deliver
Of my whole course of love; what drugs, what charms,
What conjuration and what mighty magic—
For such proceeding I am charged withal—

I won his daughter.
Bra. A maiden never bold;
Of spirit so still and quiet that her motion
Blush'd at herself; and she—in spite of nature,
Of years, of country, credit, every thing—
To fall in love with what she fear'd to look on!
It is a judgement maim'd and most imperfect,
That will confess perfection so could err
Against all rules of nature; and must be driven
To find out practices of cunning hell,
Why this should be. I therefore vouch again,
That with some mixtures powerful o'er the blood,
Or with some dram conjured to this effect,
He wrought upon her.
Duke. To vouch this, is no proof,
Without more certain and more overt test
Than these thin habits and poor likelihoods
Of modern seeming do prefer against him.
First Sen. But, Othello, speak:
Did you by indirect and forced courses
Subdue and poison this young maid's affections?
Or came it by request, and such fair question
As soul to soul affordeth?
Oth. I do beseech you,
Send for the lady to the Sagittary,
And let her speak of me before her father:
If you do find me foul in her report,
The trust, the office I do hold of you,
Not only take away, but let your sentence
Even fall upon my life.
Duke. Fetch Desdemona hither.
Oth. Ancient, conduct them; you best know the place.
[*Exeunt Iago and Attendants.*
And till she come, as truly as to heaven
I do confess the vices of my blood,
So justly to your grave ears I'll present
How I did thrive in this fair lady's love
And she in mine.
Duke. Say it, Othello.
Oth. Her father loved me, oft invited me,
Still questioned me the story of my life
From year to year, the battles, sieges, fortunes,
That I have pass'd.
I ran it through, even from my boyish days
To the very moment that he bade me tell it:

Wherein I spake of most disastrous chances,
Of moving accidents by flood and field,
Of hair-breadth 'scapes i' the imminent deadly breach,
Of being taken by the insolent foe,
And sold to slavery, of my redemption thence,
And portance in my travels' history:
Wherein of antres vast and deserts idle,
Rough quarries, rocks, and hills whose heads touch heaven,
It was my hint to speak,—such was the process;
And of the Cannibals that each other eat,
The Anthropophagi, and men whose heads
Do grow beneath their shoulders. This to hear
Would Desdemona seriously incline:
But still the house-affairs would draw her thence;
Which ever as she could with haste dispatch,
She 'ld come again, and with a greedy ear
Devour up my discourse: which I observing,
Took once a pliant hour, and found good means
To draw from her a prayer of earnest heart
That I would all my pilgrimage dilate,
Whereof by parcels she had something heard,
But not intentively: I did consent,
And often did beguile her of her tears
When I did speak of some distressful stroke
That my youth suffer'd. My story being done,
She gave me for my pains a world of sighs:
She swore, in faith, 'twas strange, 'twas passing strange;
'Twas pitiful, 'twas wondrous pitiful:
She wish'd she had not heard it, yet she wish'd
That heaven had made her such a man: she thank'd me,
And bade me, if I had a friend that loved her,
I should but teach him how to tell my story,
And that would woo her. Upon this hint I spake:
She loved me for the dangers I had pass'd,
And I loved her that she did pity them.
This only is the witchcraft I have used.
Here comes the lady; let her witness it.

Enter Desdemona, Iago, and Attendants.

Duke. I think this tale would win my daughter too.
Good Brabantio,
Take up this mangled matter at the best:
Men do their broken weapons rather use
Than their bare hands.

Bra. I pray you, hear her speak:
If she confess that she was half the wooer,

Destruction on my head, if my bad blame
Light on the man! Come hither, gentle mistress:
Do you perceive in all this noble company
Where most you owe obedience?

Des. My noble father,
I do perceive here a divided duty:
To you I am bound for life and education;
My life and education both do learn me
How to respect you; you are the lord of duty,
I am hitherto your daughter: but here 's my husband,
And so much duty as my mother show'd
To you, preferring you before her father,
So much I challenge that I may profess
Due to the Moor my lord.

Bra. God be with you! I have done.
Please it your grace, on to the state-affairs:
I had rather to adopt a child than get it.
Come hither, Moor:
I here do give thee that with all my heart,
Which, but thou hast already, with all my heart
I would keep from thee. For your sake, jewel,
I am glad at soul I have no other child;
For thy escape would teach me tyranny,
To hang clogs on them. I have done, my lord.

Duke. Let me speak like yourself, and lay a sentence
Which, as a grise or step, may help these lovers
Into your favour.
When remedies are past, the griefs are ended
By seeing the worst, which late on hopes depended.
To mourn a mischief that is past and gone
Is the next way to draw new mischief on.
What cannot be preserved when fortune takes,
Patience her injury a mockery makes.
The robb'd that smiles steals something from the thief;
He robs himself that spends a bootless grief.

Bra. So let the Turk of Cyprus us beguile;
We lose it not so long as we can smile.
He bears the sentence well, that nothing bears
But the free comfort which from thence he hears;
But he bears both the sentence and the sorrow,
That, to pay grief, must of poor patience borrow.
These sentences, to sugar or to gall,
Being strong on both sides, are equivocal:
But words are words; I never yet did hear
That the bruised heart was pierced through the ear.

I humbly beseech you, proceed to the affairs of state.

Duke. The Turk with a most mighty preparation makes for Cyprus. Othello, the fortitude of the place is best known to you; and though we have there a substitute of most allowed sufficiency, yet opinion, a sovereign mistress of effects, throws a more safer voice on you: you must therefore be content to slubber the gloss of your new fortunes with this more stubborn and boisterous expedition.

Oth. The tyrant custom, most grave senators,
Hath made the flinty and steel couch of war
My thrice-driven bed of down: I do agnize
A natural and prompt alacrity
I find in hardness; and do undertake
These present wars against the Ottomites.
Most humbly therefore bending to your state,
I crave fit disposition for my wife,
Due reference of place and exhibition,
With such accommodation and besort
As levels with her breeding.

Duke. If you please,
Be 't at her father's.

Bra. I 'll not have it so.

Oth. Nor I.

Des. Nor I, I would not there reside,
To put my father in impatient thoughts
By being in his eye. Most gracious duke,
To my unfolding lend your prosperous ear,
And let me find a charter in your voice
To assist my simpleness.

Duke. What would you, Desdemona?

Des. That I did love the Moor to live with him,
My downright violence and storm of fortunes
May trumpet to the world: my heart 's subdued
Even to the very quality of my lord:
I saw Othello's visage in his mind,
And to his honours and his valiant parts
Did I my soul and fortunes consecrate.
So that, dear lords, if I be left behind,
A moth of peace, and he go to the war,
The rites for which I love him are bereft me,
And I a heavy interim shall support
By his dear absence. Let me go with him.

Oth. Let her have your voices.
Vouch with me, heaven, I therefore beg it not,
To please the palate of my appetite;

Nor to comply with heat—the young affects
In me defunct—and proper satisfaction;
But to be free and bounteous to her mind:
And heaven defend your good souls, that you think
I will your serious and great business scant
For she is with me. No, when light-wing'd toys
Of feather'd Cupid seel with wanton dullness
My speculative and officed instruments,
That my disports corrupt and taint my business,
Let housewives make a skillet of my helm,
And all indign and base adversities
Make head against my estimation!

Duke. Be it as you shall privately determine,
Either for her stay or going: the affair cries haste,
And speed must answer 't; you must hence to-night.

Des. To-night, my lord?

Duke. This night.

Oth. With all my heart.

Duke. At nine i' the morning here we'll meet again.
Othello, leave some officer behind,
And he shall our commission bring to you;
With such things else of quality and respect
As doth import you.

Oth. So please your grace, my ancient;
A man he is of honesty and trust:
To his conveyance I assign my wife,
With what else needful your good grace shall think
To be sent after me.

Duke. Let it be so.
Good night to every one. [*To Brab.*] And, noble signior,
If virtue no delighted beauty lack,
Your son-in-law is far more fair than black.

First Sen. Adieu, brave Moor; use Desdemona well.

Bra. Look to her, Moor, if thou hast eyes to see:
She has deceived her father, and may thee.

[*Exeunt Duke, Senators, Officers, &c.*

Oth. My life upon her faith! Honest Iago,
My Desdemona must I leave to thee:
I prithee, let thy wife attend on her;
And bring them after in the best advantage.
Come, Desdemona; I have but an hour
Of love, of worldly matters and direction,
To spend with thee: we must obey the time.

[*Exeunt Othello and Desdemona.*

Rod. Iago!

Iago. What say'st thou, noble heart?

Rod. What will I do, thinkest thou?

Iago. Why, go to bed and sleep.

Rod. I will incontinently drown myself.

Iago. If thou dost, I shall never love thee after. Why, thou silly gentleman!

Rod. It is silliness to live when to live is torment; and then have we a prescription to die when death is our physician.

Iago. O villanous! I have looked upon the world for four times seven years; and since I could distinguish betwixt a benefit and an injury, I never found man that knew how to love himself. Ere I would say I would drown myself for the love of a guinea-hen, I would change my humanity with a baboon.

Rod. What should I do? I confess it is my shame to be so fond; but it is not in my virtue to amend it.

Iago. Virtue! a fig! 'tis in ourselves that we are thus or thus. Our bodies are gardens; to the which our wills are gardeners: so that if we will plant nettles or sow lettuce, set hyssop and weed up thyme, supply it with one gender of herbs or distract it with many, either to have it sterile with idleness or manured with industry, why, the power and corrigible authority of this lies in our wills. If the balance of our lives had not one scale of reason to poise another of sensuality, the blood and baseness of our natures would conduct us to most preposterous conclusions: but we have reason to cool our raging motions, our carnal stings, our unbitted lusts; whereof I take this, that you call love, to be a sect or scion.

Rod. It cannot be.

Iago. It is merely a lust of the blood and a permission of the will. Come, be a man: drown thyself! drown cats and blind puppies. I have professed me thy friend, and I confess me knit to thy deserving with cables of perdurable toughness: I could never better stead thee than now. Put money in thy purse; follow thou the wars; defeat thy favour with an usurped beard; I say, put money in thy purse. It cannot be that Desdemona should long continue her love to the Moor—put money in thy purse—nor he his to her: it was a violent commencement, and thou shalt see an answerable sequestration; put but money in thy purse. These Moors are changeable in their wills:—fill thy purse with money. The food that to him now is as luscious as locusts, shall be to him shortly as bitter as coloquintida. She must change for youth: when she is sated with his body, she will find the error of her choice: she must have change, she must: therefore put money in thy purse. If thou wilt needs damn thyself, do it a more delicate way than drowning. Make all the money thou canst: if sanctimony and a frail vow betwixt an erring barbarian and a supersubtle Venetian be not too hard for my wits and all the tribe of hell, thou shalt enjoy her; therefore make money. A pox of drowning thyself! it is clean out of the way: seek thou rather to be hanged in compassing thy joy than to be drowned and go without her.

Rod. Wilt thou be fast to my hopes, if I depend on the issue?

Iago. Thou art sure of me: go, make money: I have told thee often, and I re-tell thee again and again, I hate the Moor: my cause is hearted; thine hath no less reason. Let us be conjunctive in our revenge against him: if thou canst cuckold him, thou dost thyself a pleasure, me a sport. There are many events in the womb of time, which will be delivered. Traverse; go; provide thy money. We will have more of this to-morrow. Adieu.

Rod. Where shall we meet i' the morning?

Iago. At my lodging.

Rod. I'll be with thee betimes.

Iago. Go to; farewell. Do you hear, Roderigo?

Rod. What say you?

Iago. No more of drowning, do you hear?

Rod. I am changed: I'll go sell all my land. [*Exit.*

Iago. Thus do I ever make my fool my purse;
For I mine own gain'd knowledge should profane,
If I would time expend with such a snipe
But for my sport and profit. I hate the Moor;
And it is thought abroad that 'twixt my sheets
He has done my office: I know not if 't be true;
But I for mere suspicion in that kind
Will do as if for surety. He holds me well:
The better shall my purpose work on him.
Cassio's a proper man: let me see now;
To get his place, and to plume up my will
In double knavery—How, how?—Let's see:—
After some time, to abuse Othello's ear
That he is too familiar with his wife.
He hath a person and a smooth dispose
To be suspected; framed to make women false.
The Moor is of a free and open nature,
That thinks men honest that but seem to be so;
And will as tenderly be led by the nose

As asses are.
I have 't. It is engender'd. Hell and night
Must bring this monstrous birth to the world's light. [*Exit.*

ACT II—Scene I

A sea-port in Cyprus. An open place near the quay.

Enter Montano and two Gentlemen.

Mon. What from the cape can you discern at sea?
First Gent. Nothing at all: it is a high-wrought flood;
I cannot, 'twixt the heaven and the main,
Descry a sail.
Mon. Methinks the wind hath spoke aloud at land;
A fuller blast ne'er shook our battlements:
If it hath ruffian'd so upon the sea,
What ribs of oak, when mountains melt on them,
Can hold the mortise? What shall we hear of this?
Sec. Gent. A segregation of the Turkish fleet:
For do but stand upon the foaming shore,
The chidden billow seems to pelt the clouds;
The wind-shaked surge, with high and monstrous mane,
Seems to cast water on the burning bear,
And quench the guards of the ever-fixed pole:
I never did like molestation view
On the enchafed flood.
Mon. If that the Turkish fleet
Be not enshelter'd and embay'd, they are drown'd;
It is impossible to bear it out.

Enter a third Gentleman.

Third Gent. News, lads! our wars are done.
The desperate tempest hath so bang'd the Turks,
That their designment halts: a noble ship of Venice
Hath seen a grievous wreck and sufferance
On most part of their fleet.
Mon. How! is this true?
Third Gent. The ship is here put in,
A Veronesa; Michael Cassio,
Lieutenant to the warlike Moor Othello,
Is come on shore: the Moor himself at sea,
And is in full commission here for Cyprus.
Mon. I am glad on 't; 'tis a worthy governor.
Third Gent. But this same Cassio, though he speak of comfort
Touching the Turkish loss, yet he looks sadly
And prays the Moor be safe; for they were parted
With foul and violent tempest.

Mon. Pray heavens he be;
For I have served him, and the man commands
Like a full soldier. Let's to the seaside, ho!
As well to see the vessel that's come in
As to throw out our eyes for brave Othello,
Even till we make the main and the aerial blue
An indistinct regard.

Third Gent. Come, let's do so;
For every minute is expectancy
Of more arrivance.

Enter Cassio.

Cas. Thanks, you the valiant of this warlike isle,
That so approve the Moor! O, let the heavens
Give him defence against the elements,
For I have lost him on a dangerous sea.

Mon. Is he well shipp'd?

Cas. His bark is stoutly timber'd, and his pilot
Of very expert and approved allowance;
Therefore my hopes, not surfeited to death,
Stand in bold cure. [*A cry within:* 'A sail, a sail, a sail!'

Enter a fourth Gentleman.

Cas. What noise?

Fourth Gent. The town is empty; on the brow o' the sea
Stand ranks of people, and they cry 'A sail!'

Cas. My hopes do shape him for the governor. [*Guns heard.*

Sec. Gent. They do discharge their shot of courtesy:
Our friends at least.

Cas. I pray you, sir, go forth,
And give us truth who 'tis that is arrived.

Sec. Gent. I shall. [*Exit.*

Mon. But, good lieutenant, is your general wived?

Cas. Most fortunately: he hath achieved a maid
That paragons description and wild fame;
One that excels the quirks of blazoning pens,
And in the essential vesture of creation
Does tire the ingener.

Re-enter second Gentleman.

How now! who has put in?

Sec. Gent. 'Tis one Iago, ancient to the general.

Cas. He has had most favourable and happy speed:
Tempests themselves, high seas, and howling winds,
The gutter'd rocks, and congregated sands,
Traitors ensteep'd to clog the guiltless keel,
As having sense of beauty, do omit
Their moral natures, letting go safely by

The divine Desdemona.
Mon. What is she?
Cas. She that I spake of, our great captain's captain,
Left in the conduct of the bold Iago;
Whose footing here anticipates our thoughts
A se'nnight's speed. Great Jove, Othello guard,
And swell his sail with thine own powerful breath,
That he may bless this bay with his tall ship,
Make love's quick pants in Desdemona's arms,
Give renew'd fire to our extincted spirits,
And bring all Cyprus comfort.

Enter Desdemona, Emilia, Iago, Roderigo, and Attendants.

O, behold,
The riches of the ship is come on shore!
Ye men of Cyprus, let her have your knees.
Hail to thee, lady! and the grace of heaven,
Before, behind thee, and on every hand,
Enwheel thee round!
Des. I thank you, valiant Cassio.
What tidings can you tell me of my lord?
Cas. He is not yet arrived: nor know I aught
But that he 's well and will be shortly here.
Des. O, but I fear—How lost you company?
Cas. The great contention of the sea and skies
Parted our fellowship—But, hark! a sail.
[*A cry within:* 'A sail, a sail!' *Guns heard.*
Sec. Gent. They give their greeting to the citadel;
This likewise is a friend.
Cas. See for the news. [*Exit Gentleman.*
Good ancient, you are welcome. [*To Emilia*] Welcome, mistress:
Let it not gall your patience, good Iago,
That I extend my manners; 'tis my breeding
That gives me this bold show of courtesy. [*Kissing her.*
Iago. Sir, would she give you so much of her lips
As of her tongue she oft bestows on me,
You 'ld have enough.
Des. Alas, she has no speech.
Iago. In faith, too much;
I find it still when I have list to sleep:
Marry, before your ladyship, I grant,
She puts her tongue a little in her heart
And chides with thinking.
Emil. You have little cause to say so.
Iago. Come on, come on; you are pictures out of doors,
Bells in your parlours, wild-cats in your kitchens,

Saints in your injuries, devils being offended,
Players in your housewifery, and housewives in your beds.
Des. O, fie upon thee, slanderer!
Iago. Nay, it is true, or else I am a Turk:
You rise to play, and go to bed to work.
Emil. You shall not write my praise.
Iago. No, let me not.
Des. What wouldst thou write of me, if thou shouldst praise [me?
Iago. O gentle lady, do not put me to 't;
For I am nothing if not critical.
Des. Come on, assay—There 's one gone to the harbour?
Iago. Ay, madam.
Des. I am not merry; but I do beguile
The thing I am by seeming otherwise.
Come, how wouldst thou praise me?
Iago. I am about it; but indeed my invention
Comes from my pate as birdlime does from frize;
It plucks out brains and all: but my Muse labours,
And thus she is deliver'd.
If she be fair and wise, fairness and wit,
The one 's for use, the other useth it.
Des. Well praised! How if she be black and witty?
Iago. If she be black, and thereto have a wit,
She 'll find a white that shall her blackness fit.
Des. Worse and worse.
Emil. How if fair and foolish?
Iago. She never yet was foolish that was fair;
For even her folly help'd her to an heir.
Des. These are old fond paradoxes to make fools laugh i' the alehouse. What miserable praise hast thou for her that 's foul and foolish?
Iago. There 's none so foul, and foolish thereunto,
But does foul pranks which fair and wise ones do.
Des. O heavy ignorance! thou praisest the worst best. But what praise couldst thou bestow on a deserving woman indeed, one that in the authority of her merit did justly put on the vouch of very malice itself?
Iago. She that was ever fair and never proud,
Had tongue at will and yet was never loud,
Never lack'd gold and yet went never gay,
Fled from her wish and yet said 'Now I may;'
She that, being anger'd, her revenge being nigh,
Bade her wrong stay and her displeasure fly;
She that in wisdom never was so frail
To change the cod's head for the salmon's tail;

She that could think and ne'er disclose her mind,
See suitors following and not look behind;
She was a wight, if ever such wight were,—

Des. To do what?

Iago. To suckle fools and chronicle small beer.

Des. O most lame and impotent conclusion! Do not learn of him, Emilia, though he be thy husband. How say you, Cassio? is he not a most profane and liberal counsellor?

Cas. He speaks home, madam: you may relish him more in the soldier than in the scholar.

Iago. [*Aside*] He takes her by the palm: ay, well said, whisper: with as little a web as this will I ensnare as great a fly as Cassio. Ay, smile upon her, do; I will gyve thee in thine own courtship. You say true; 'tis so, indeed: if such tricks as these strip you out of your lieutenantry, it had been better you had not kissed your three fingers so oft, which now again you are most apt to play the sir in. Very good; well kissed! and excellent courtesy! 'tis so, indeed. Yet again your fingers to your lips? would they were clyster-pipes for your sake!—[*Trumpet within.*] The Moor! I know his trumpet.

Cas. 'Tis truly so.

Des. Let's meet him and receive him.

Cas. Lo, where he comes!

Enter Othello and Attendants.

Oth. O my fair warrior!

Des. My dear Othello!

Oth. It gives me wonder great as my content
To see you here before me. O my soul's joy!
If after every tempest come such calms,
May the winds blow till they have waken'd death!
And let the labouring bark climb hills of seas
Olympus-high, and duck again as low
As hell's from heaven! If it were now to die,
'Twere now to be most happy; for I fear,
My soul hath her content so absolute
That not another comfort like to this
Succeeds in unknown fate.

Des. The heavens forbid
But that our loves and comforts should increase,
Even as our days do grow!

Oth. Amen to that, sweet powers!
I cannot speak enough of this content;
It stops me here; it is too much of joy:
And this, and this, the greatest discords be [*Kissing her.*

That e'er our hearts shall make!

Iago. [*Aside*] O, you are well tuned now!
But I 'll set down the pegs that make this music,
As honest as I am.

Oth. Come, let us to the castle.
News, friends; our wars are done, the Turks are drown'd.
How does my old acquaintance of this isle?
Honey, you shall be well desired in Cyprus;
I have found great love amongst them. O my sweet,
I prattle out of fashion, and I dote
In mine own comforts. I prithee, good Iago,
Go to the bay, and disembark my coffers:
Bring thou the master to the citadel;
He is a good one, and his worthiness
Does challenge much respect. Come, Desdemona,
Once more well met at Cyprus.

[*Exeunt all but Iago and Roderigo.*

Iago. Do thou meet me presently at the harbour. Come hither. If thou be'st valiant—as, they say, base men being in love have then a nobility in their natures more than is native to them—list me. The lieutenant to-night watches on the court of guard. First, I must tell thee this: Desdemona is directly in love with him.

Rod. With him! why, 'tis not possible.

Iago. Lay thy finger thus, and let thy soul be instructed. Mark me with what violence she first loved the Moor, but for bragging and telling her fantastical lies: and will she love him still for prating? let not thy discreet heart think it. Her eye must be fed; and what delight shall she have to look on the devil? When the blood is made dull with the act of sport, there should be, again to inflame it and to give satiety a fresh appetite, loveliness in favour, sympathy in years, manners and beauties; all which the Moor is defective in: now, for want of these required conveniences, her delicate tenderness will find itself abused, begin to heave the gorge, disrelish and abhor the Moor; very nature will instruct her in it and compel her to some second choice. Now, sir, this granted—as it is a most pregnant and unforced position—who stands so eminently in the degree of this fortune as Cassio does? a knave very voluble; no further conscionable than in putting on the mere form of civil and humane seeming, for the better compassing of his salt and most hidden loose affection? why, none; why, none: a slipper and subtle knave; a finder out of occasions; that has an eye can stamp and counterfeit advantages, though true advantage never present itself: a devilish knave! Besides, the knave is handsome, young, and hath all those requisites in him that folly and green minds look after: a pestilent complete knave; and the woman hath found him already.

Rod. I cannot believe that in her; she 's full of most blest [condition.

Iago. Blest fig's-end! the wine she drinks is made of grapes: if she had been blest, she would never have loved the Moor: blest pudding! Didst thou not see her paddle with the palm of his hand? didst not mark that?

Rod. Yes, that I did; but that was but courtesy.

Iago. Lechery, by this hand; an index and obscure prologue to the history of lust and foul thoughts. They met so near with their lips that their breaths embraced together. Villanous thoughts, Roderigo! when these mutualities so marshal the way, hard at hand comes the master and main exercise, the incorporate conclusion: pish! But, sir, be you ruled by me: I have brought you from Venice. Watch you to-night; for the command, I'll lay't upon you: Cassio knows you not: I'll not be far from you: do you find some occasion to anger Cassio, either by speaking too loud, or tainting his discipline, or from what other course you please, which the time shall more favourably minister.

Rod. Well.

Iago. Sir, he is rash and very sudden in choler, and haply may strike at you: provoke him, that he may; for even out of that will I cause these of Cyprus to mutiny; whose qualification shall come into no true taste again but by the displanting of Cassio. So shall you have a shorter journey to your desires by the means I shall then have to prefer them, and the impediment most profitably removed, without the which there were no expectation of our prosperity.

Rod. I will do this, if I can bring it to any opportunity.

Iago. I warrant thee. Meet me by and by at the citadel: I must fetch his necessaries ashore. Farewell.

Rod. Adieu. [*Exit.*

Iago. That Cassio loves her, I do well believe it;
That she loves him, 'tis apt and of great credit:
The Moor, howbeit that I endure him not,
Is of a constant, loving, noble nature;
And I dare think he 'll prove to Desdemona
A most dear husband. Now, I do love her too,
Not out of absolute lust, though peradventure
I stand accountant for as great a sin,
But partly led to diet my revenge,
For that I do suspect the lusty Moor

Hath leap'd into my seat: the thought whereof
Doth like a poisonous mineral gnaw my inwards;
And nothing can or shall content my soul
Till I am even'd with him, wife for wife;
Or failing so, yet that I put the Moor
At least into a jealousy so strong
That judgement cannot cure. Which thing to do,
If this poor trash of Venice, whom I trash
For his quick hunting, stand the putting on,
I 'll have our Michael Cassio on the hip,
Abuse him to the Moor in the rank garb;
For I fear Cassio with my night-cap too;
Make the Moor thank me, love me and reward me,
For making him egregiously an ass
And practising upon his peace and quiet
Even to madness. 'Tis here, but yet confused:
Knavery's plain face is never seen till used. [*Exit.*

Scene II

A street.

Enter a Herald with a proclamation; People following.

Her. It is Othello's pleasure, our noble and valiant general, that upon certain tidings now arrived, importing the mere perdition of the Turkish fleet, every man put himself into triumph; some to dance, some to make bonfires, each man to what sport and revels his addiction leads him: for, besides these beneficial news, it is the celebration of his nuptial. So much was his pleasure should be proclaimed. All offices are open, and there is full liberty of feasting from this present hour of five till the bell have told eleven. Heaven bless the isle of Cyprus and our noble general Othello! [*Exeunt.*

Scene III

A hall in the castle.

Enter Othello, Desdemona, Cassio, and Attendants.

Oth. Good Michael, look you to the guard to-night:
Let 's teach ourselves that honourable stop,
Not to outsport discretion.

Cas. Iago hath direction what to do;
But notwithstanding with my personal eye
Will I look to 't.

Oth. Iago is most honest.
Michael, good night: to-morrow with your earliest
Let me have speech with you. Come, my dear love,
The purchase made, the fruits are to ensue;

That profit 's yet to come 'tween me and you.
Good night. [*Exeunt Othello, Desdemona, and Attendants.*

Enter Iago.

Cas. Welcome, Iago; we must to the watch.

Iago. Not this hour, lieutenant; 'tis not yet ten o' the clock. Our general cast us thus early for the love of his Desdemona; who let us not therefore blame: he hath not yet made wanton the night with her, and she is sport for Jove.

Cas. She 's a most exquisite lady.

Iago. And, I 'll warrant her, full of game.

Cas. Indeed she 's a most fresh and delicate creature.

Iago. What an eye she has! methinks it sounds a parley to provocation.

Cas. An inviting eye; and yet methinks right modest.

Iago. And when she speaks, is it not an alarum to love?

Cas. She is indeed perfection.

Iago. Well, happiness to their sheets! Come, lieutenant, I have a stoup of wine; and here without are a brace of Cyprus gallants that would fain have a measure to the health of black Othello.

Cas. Not to-night, good Iago: I have very poor and unhappy brains for drinking: I could well wish courtesy would invent some other custom of entertainment.

Iago. O, they are our friends; but one cup: I 'll drink for you.

Cas. I have drunk but one cup to-night, and that was craftily qualified too, and behold what innovation it makes here: I am unfortunate in the infirmity, and dare not task my weakness with any more.

Iago. What, man! 'tis a night of revels: the gallants desire it.

Cas. Where are they?

Iago. Here at the door; I pray you, call them in.

Cas. I 'll do 't; but it dislikes me. [*Exit.*

Iago. If I can fasten but one cup upon him,
With that which he hath drunk to-night already,
He 'll be as full of quarrel and offence
As my young mistress' dog. Now my sick fool Roderigo,
Whom love hath turn'd almost the wrong side out,
To Desdemona hath to-night caroused
Potations pottle-deep; and he 's to watch:
Three lads of Cyprus, noble swelling spirits,
That hold their honours in a wary distance,
The very elements of this warlike isle,
Have I to-night fluster'd with flowing cups,
And they watch too. Now, 'mongst this flock of drunkards,
Am I to put our Cassio in some action

That may offend the isle. But here they come:
If consequence do but approve my dream,
My boat sails freely, both with wind and stream.

Re-enter Cassio; with him Montano and Gentlemen; Servants following with wine.

Cas. 'Fore God, they have given me a rouse already.

Mon. Good faith, a little one; not past a pint, as I am a [soldier.

Iago. Some wine, ho!

[*Sings*]　And let me the canakin clink, clink,
And let me the canakin clink:
A soldier's a man;
A life's but a span;
Why then let a soldier drink.

Some wine, boys!

Cas. 'Fore God, an excellent song.

Iago. I learned it in England, where indeed they are most potent in potting: your Dane, your German, and your swag-bellied Hollander,—Drink, ho!—are nothing to your English.

Cas. Is your Englishman so expert in his drinking?

Iago. Why, he drinks you with facility your Dane dead drunk; he sweats not to overthrow your Almain; he gives your Hollander a vomit ere the next pottle can be filled.

Cas. To the health of our general!

Mon. I am for it, lieutenant, and I'll do you justice.

Iago. O sweet England!

[*Sings*]　King Stephen was a worthy peer,
His breeches cost him but a crown;
He held them sixpence all too dear,
With that he call'd the tailor lown.

He was a wight of high renown,
And thou art but of low degree:
'Tis pride that pulls the country down;
Then take thine auld cloak about thee.

Some wine, ho!

Cas. Why, this is a more exquisite song than the other.

Iago. Will you hear 't again?

Cas. No; for I hold him to be unworthy of his place that does those things. Well: God's above all; and there be souls must be saved, and there be souls must not be saved.

Iago. It's true, good lieutenant.

Cas. For mine own part—no offence to the general, nor any man of quality—I hope to be saved.

Iago. And so do I too, lieutenant.

Cas. Ay, but, by your leave, not before me; the lieutenant is to be saved before the ancient. Let's have no more of this; let's to our affairs. God forgive us our sins! Gentlemen, let's look to our business. Do not think, gentlemen, I am drunk: this is my ancient: this is my right hand, and this is my left. I am not drunk now; I can stand well enough, and speak well enough.

All. Excellent well.

Cas. Why, very well then; you must not think then that I am drunk. [*Exit.*

Mon. To the platform, masters; come, let's set the watch.

Iago. You see this fellow that is gone before;
He is a soldier fit to stand by Cæsar
And give direction: and do but see his vice;
'Tis to his virtue a just equinox,
The one as long as the other: 'tis pity of him.
I fear the trust Othello puts him in
On some odd time of his infirmity
Will shake this island.

Mon. But is he often thus?

Iago. 'Tis evermore the prologue to his sleep:
He'll watch the horologe a double set,
If drink rock not his cradle.

Mon. It were well
The general were put in mind of it.
Perhaps he sees it not, or his good nature
Prizes the virtue that appears in Cassio
And looks not on his evils: is not this true?

Enter Roderigo.

Iago. [*Aside to him*] How now, Roderigo!
I pray you, after the lieutenant; go. [*Exit Roderigo.*

Mon. And 'tis great pity that the noble Moor
Should hazard such a place as his own second
With one of an ingraft infirmity:
It were an honest action to say
So to the Moor.

Iago. Not I, for this fair island:
I do love Cassio well, and would do much
To cure him of this evil:—But, hark! what noise?
[*A cry within:* 'Help! help!'

Re-enter Cassio, driving in Roderigo.

Cas. 'Zounds! you rogue! you rascal!

Mon. What's the matter, lieutenant?

Cas. A knave teach me my duty! But I'll beat the knave into [a wicker bottle.

Rod. Beat me!

Cas. Dost thou prate, rogue? [*Striking Roderigo.*
Mon. Nay, good lieutenant; I pray you, sir, hold your hand.
Cas. Let me go, sir, or I'll knock you o'er the mazzard.
Mon. Come, come, you're drunk.
Cas. Drunk! [*They fight.*
Iago. [*Aside to Roderigo*] Away, I say; go out and cry a mutiny. [*Exit Roderigo.*
Nay, good lieutenant! God's will, gentlemen!
Help, ho!—Lieutenant,—sir,—Montano,—sir;—
Help, masters!—Here's a goodly watch indeed! [*A bell rings.*
Who's that that rings the bell?—Diablo, ho!
The town will rise: God's will, lieutenant, hold;
You will be shamed for ever.

Re-enter Othello and Attendants.

Oth. What is the matter here?
Mon. 'Zounds, I bleed still; I am hurt to the death. [*Faints.*
Oth. Hold, for your lives!
Iago. Hold, ho! Lieutenant,—sir,—Montano,—gentlemen,—
Have you forgot all sense of place and duty?
Hold! the general speaks to you; hold, hold, for shame!
Oth. Why, how now, ho! from whence ariseth this?
Are we turn'd Turks, and to ourselves do that
Which heaven hath forbid the Ottomites?
For Christian shame, put by this barbarous brawl:
He that stirs next to carve for his own rage
Holds his soul light; he dies upon his motion.
Silence that dreadful bell: it frights the isle
From her propriety. What is the matter, masters?
Honest Iago, that look'st dead with grieving,
Speak, who began this? on thy love, I charge thee.
Iago. I do not know: friends all but now, even now,
In quarter, and in terms like bride and groom
Devesting them for bed; and then, but now,
As if some planet had unwitted men,
Swords out, and tilting one at other's breast,
In opposition bloody. I cannot speak
Any beginning to this peevish odds;
And would in action glorious I had lost
Those legs that brought me to a part of it!
Oth. How comes it, Michael, you are thus forgot?
Cas. I pray you, pardon me; I cannot speak.
Oth. Worthy Montano, you were wont be civil;
The gravity and stillness of your youth
The world hath noted, and your name is great
In mouths of wisest censure: what's the matter,

That you unlace your reputation thus,
And spend your rich opinion for the name
Of a night-brawler? give me answer to it.

Mon. Worthy Othello, I am hurt to danger:
Your officer, Iago, can inform you—
While I spare speech, which something now offends me—
Of all that I do know: nor know I aught
By me that 's said or done amiss this night;
Unless self-charity be sometimes a vice,
And to defend ourselves it be a sin
When violence assails us.

Oth. Now, by heaven,
My blood begins my safer guides to rule,
And passion, having my best judgement collied,
Assays to lead the way: if I once stir,
Or do but lift this arm, the best of you
Shall sink in my rebuke. Give me to know
How this foul rout began, who set it on,
And he that is approved in this offence,
Though he had twinn'd with me, both at a birth,
Shall lose me. What! in a town of war,
Yet wild, the people's hearts brimful of fear,
To manage private and domestic quarrel,
In night, and on the court and guard of safety!
'Tis monstrous. Iago, who began 't?

Mon. If partially affined, or leagued in office,
Thou dost deliver more or less than truth,
Thou art no soldier.

Iago. Touch me not so near:
I had rather have this tongue cut from my mouth
Than it should do offence to Michael Cassio;
Yet, I persuade myself, to speak the truth
Shall nothing wrong him. Thus it is, general.
Montano and myself being in speech,
There comes a fellow crying out for help,
And Cassio following him with determined sword,
To execute upon him. Sir, this gentleman
Steps in to Cassio and entreats his pause:
Myself the crying fellow did pursue,
Lest by his clamour—as it so fell out—
The town might fall in fright: he, swift of foot,
Outran my purpose; and I return'd the rather
For that I heard the clink and fall of swords,
And Cassio high in oath; which till to-night
I ne'er might say before. When I came back—

For this was brief—I found them close together,
At blow and thrust; even as again they were
When you yourself did part them.
More of this matter cannot I report:
But men are men; the best sometimes forget:
Though Cassio did some little wrong to him,
As men in rage strike those that wish them best,
Yet surely Cassio, I believe, received
From him that fled some strange indignity,
Which patience could not pass.

Oth. I know, Iago,
Thy honesty and love doth mince this matter,
Making it light to Cassio. Cassio, I love thee;
But never more be officer of mine.

Re-enter Desdemona, attended.

Look, if my gentle love be not raised up!
I 'll make thee an example.

Des. What 's the matter?

Oth. All 's well now, sweeting; come away to bed.
Sir, for your hurts, myself will be your surgeon:
[*To Montano, who is led off.*
Lead him off.
Iago, look with care about the town,
And silence those whom this vile brawl distracted.
Come, Desdemona: 'tis the soldiers' life
To have their balmy slumbers waked with strife.
[*Exeunt all but Iago and Cassio.*

Iago. What, are you hurt, lieutenant?

Cas. Ay, past all surgery.

Iago. Marry, heaven forbid!

Cas. Reputation, reputation, reputation! O, I have lost my reputation! I have lost the immortal part of myself, and what remains is bestial. My reputation, Iago, my reputation!

Iago. As I am an honest man, I thought you had received some bodily wound; there is more sense in that than in reputation. Reputation is an idle and most false imposition; oft got without merit and lost without deserving: you have lost no reputation at all, unless you repute yourself such a loser. What, man! there are ways to recover the general again: you are but now cast in his mood, a punishment more in policy than in malice; even so as one would beat his offenceless dog to affright an imperious lion: sue to him again, and he 's yours.

Cas. I will rather sue to be despised than to deceive so good a commander with so slight, so drunken, and so indiscreet an officer. Drunk? and speak parrot? and squabble? swagger? swear? and discourse fustian with one's own shadow? O thou invisible spirit of wine, if thou hast no name to be known by, let us call thee devil!

Iago. What was he that you followed with your sword? What had he done to you?

Cas. I know not.

Iago. Is 't possible?

Cas. I remember a mass of things, but nothing distinctly; a quarrel, but nothing wherefore. O God, that men should put an enemy in their mouths to steal away their brains! that we should, with joy, pleasance, revel and applause, transform ourselves into beasts!

Iago. Why, but you are now well enough: how came you thus recovered?

Cas. It hath pleased the devil drunkenness to give place to the devil wrath: one unperfectness shows me another, to make me frankly despise myself.

Iago. Come, you are too severe a moraler: as the time, the place, and the condition of this country stands, I could heartily wish this had not befallen; but since it is as it is, mend it for your own good.

Cas. I will ask him for my place again; he shall tell me I am a drunkard! Had I as many mouths as Hydra, such an answer would stop them all. To be now a sensible man, by and by a fool, and presently a beast! O strange! Every inordinate cup is unblest, and the ingredient is a devil.

Iago. Come, come, good wine is a good familiar creature, if it be well used: exclaim no more against it. And, good lieutenant, I think you think I love you.

Cas. I have well approved it, sir. I drunk!

Iago. You or any man living may be drunk at some time man. I'll tell you what you shall do. Our general's wife is now the general. I may say so in this respect, for that he hath devoted and given up himself to the contemplation, mark and denotement of her parts and graces: confess yourself freely to her; importune her help to put you in your place again: she is of so free, so kind, so apt, so blessed a disposition, she holds it a vice in her goodness not to do more than she is requested: this broken joint between you and her husband entreat her to splinter; and, my fortunes against any lay worth naming, this crack of your love shall grow stronger than it was before.

Cas. You advise me well.

Iago. I protest, in the sincerity of love and honest kindness.

Cas. I think it freely; and betimes in the morning I will

beseech the virtuous Desdemona to undertake for me: I am desperate of my fortunes if they check me here.

Iago. You are in the right. Good night, lieutenant;
I must to the watch.

Cas. Good night, honest Iago. [*Exit.*

Iago. And what's he then that says I play the villain?
When this advice is free I give and honest,
Probal to thinking, and indeed the course
To win the Moor again? For 'tis most easy
The inclining Desdemona to subdue
In any honest suit. She's framed as fruitful
As the free elements. And then for her
To win the Moor, were 't to renounce his baptism,
All seals and symbols of redeemed sin,
His soul is so enfetter'd to her love,
That she may make, unmake, do what she list,
Even as her appetite shall play the god
With his weak function. How am I then a villain
To counsel Cassio to this parallel course,
Directly to his good? Divinity of hell!
When devils will the blackest sins put on,
They do suggest at first with heavenly shows,
As I do now: for whiles this honest fool
Plies Desdemona to repair his fortunes,
And she for him pleads strongly to the Moor,
I'll pour this pestilence into his ear,
That she repeals him for her body's lust;
And by how much she strives to do him good,
She shall undo her credit with the Moor.
So will I turn her virtue into pitch;
And out of her own goodness make the net
That shall enmesh them all.

Enter Roderigo.

How now, Roderigo!

Rod. I do follow here in the chase, not like a hound that hunts, but one that fills up the cry. My money is almost spent; I have been to-night exceedingly well cudgelled; and I think the issue will be, I shall have so much experience for my pains; and so, with no money at all and a little more wit, return again to Venice.

Iago. How poor are they that have not patience!
What wound did ever heal but by degrees?
Thou know'st we work by wit and not by witchcraft,
And wit depends on dilatory time.
Does 't not go well? Cassio hath beaten thee,

And thou by that small hurt hast cashier'd Cassio:
Though other things grow fair against the sun,
Yet fruits that blossom first will first be ripe:
Content thyself awhile. By the mass, 'tis morning;
Pleasure and action make the hours seem short.
Retire thee; go where thou art billeted:
Away, I say; thou shalt know more hereafter:
Nay, get thee gone. [*Exit Rod.*] Two things are to be [done:
My wife must move for Cassio to her mistress;
I 'll set her on;
Myself the while to draw the Moor apart,
And bring him jump when he may Cassio find
Soliciting his wife: ay, that 's the way;
Dull not device by coldness and delay. [*Exit.*

ACT III—Scene I

Before the castle.

Enter Cassio and some Musicians.

Cas. Masters, play here; I will content your pains;
Something that 's brief; and bid 'Good-morrow, general.' [*Music.*

Enter Clown.

Clo. Why, masters, have your instruments been in Naples, that they speak i' the nose thus?

First Mus. How, sir, how?

Clo. Are these, I pray you, wind-instruments?

First Mus. Ay, marry, are they, sir.

Clo. O, thereby hangs a tail.

First Mus. Whereby hangs a tale, sir?

Clo. Marry, sir, by many a wind-instrument that I know. But, masters, here 's money for you: and the general so likes your music, that he desires you, for love's sake, to make no more noise with it.

First Mus. Well, sir, we will not.

Clo. If you have any music that may not be heard, to 't again: but, as they say, to hear music the general does not greatly care.

First Mus. We have none such, sir.

Clo. Then put up your pipes in your bag, for I 'll away: go; vanish into air; away! [*Exeunt Musicians.*

Cas. Dost thou hear, my honest friend?

Clo. No, I hear not your honest friend; I hear you.

Cas. Prithee, keep up thy quillets. There 's a poor piece of gold for thee: if the gentlewoman that attends the general's wife be stirring, tell her there's one Cassio entreats her a little favour of speech: wilt thou do this?

Clo. She is stirring, sir: if she will stir hither, I shall seem to notify unto her.

Cas. Do, good my friend. [*Exit Clown.*

Enter Iago.

In happy time, Iago.

Iago. You have not been a-bed, then?

Cas. Why, no; the day had broke
Before we parted. I have made bold, Iago,
To send in to your wife: my suit to her
Is, that she will to virtuous Desdemona
Procure me some access.

Iago. I'll send her to you presently;
And I'll devise a mean to draw the Moor
Out of the way, that your converse and business
May be more free.

Cas. I humbly thank you for't. [*Exit Iago.*] I never knew
A Florentine more kind and honest.

Enter Emilia.

Emil. Good morrow, good lieutenant: I am sorry
For your displeasure; but all will sure be well.
The general and his wife are talking of it,
And she speaks for you stoutly: the Moor replies,
That he you hurt is of great fame in Cyprus
And great affinity, and that in wholesome wisdom
He might not but refuse you; but he protests he loves you,
And needs no other suitor but his likings
To take the safest occasion by the front
To bring you in again.

Cas. Yet, I beseech you,
If you think fit, or that it may be done,
Give me advantage of some brief discourse
With Desdemona alone.

Emil. Pray you, come in:
I will bestow you where you shall have time
To speak your bosom freely.

Cas. I am much bound to you.
[*Exeunt.*

Scene II

A room in the castle.

Enter Othello, Iago, and Gentlemen.

Oth. These letters give, Iago, to the pilot;
And by him do my duties to the senate:
That done, I will be walking on the works;

Repair there to me.
Iago. Well, my good lord, I'll do 't.
Oth. This fortification, gentlemen, shall we see 't?
Gent. We'll wait upon your lordship. [*Exeunt.*

Scene III

The garden of the castle.

Enter Desdemona, Cassio, and Emilia.

Des. Be thou assured, good Cassio, I will do
All my abilities in thy behalf.
Emil. Good madam, do: I warrant it grieves my husband
As if the case were his.
Des. O, that's an honest fellow. Do not doubt, Cassio,
But I will have my lord and you again
As friendly as you were.
Cas. Bounteous madam,
Whatever shall become of Michael Cassio,
He's never any thing but your true servant.
Des. I know 't: I thank you. You do love my lord:
You have known him long; and be you well assured
He shall in strangeness stand no farther off
Than in a politic distance.
Cas. Ay, but, lady,
That policy may either last so long,
Or feed upon such nice and waterish diet,
Or breed itself so out of circumstance,
That, I being absent and my place supplied,
My general will forget my love and service.
Des. Do not doubt that; before Emilia here
I give thee warrant of thy place: assure thee,
If I do avow a friendship, I'll perform it
To the last article: my lord shall never rest;
I'll watch him tame and talk him out of patience;
His bed shall seem a school, his board a shrift;
I'll intermingle every thing he does
With Cassio's suit: therefore be merry, Cassio;
For thy solicitor shall rather die
Than give thy cause away.

Enter Othello and Iago, at a distance.

Emil. Madam, here comes my lord.
Cas. Madam, I'll take my leave.
Des. Nay, stay and hear me speak.
Cas. Madam, not now: I am very ill at ease,
Unfit for mine own purposes.
Des. Well, do your discretion. [*Exit Cassio*

Iago. Ha! I like not that.
Oth. What dost thou say?
Iago. Nothing, my lord: or if—I know not what.
Oth. Was not that Cassio parted from my wife?
Iago. Cassio, my lord! No, sure, I cannot think it,
That he would steal away so guilty-like,
Seeing you coming.
Oth. I do believe 'twas he.
Des. How now, my lord!
I have been talking with a suitor here.
A man that languishes in your displeasure.
Oth. Who is't you mean?
Des. Why, your lieutenant, Cassio. Good my lord,
If I have any grace or power to move you,
His present reconciliation take;
For if he be not one that truly loves you,
That errs in ignorance and not in cunning,
I have no judgement in an honest face:
I prithee, call him back.
Oth. Went he hence now?
Des. Ay, sooth; so humbled,
That he hath left part of his grief with me,
To suffer with him. Good love, call him back.
Oth. Not now, sweet Desdemona; some other time.
Des. But shall't be shortly?
Oth. The sooner, sweet, for you.
Des. Shall't be to-night at supper?
Oth. No, not to-night.
Des. To-morrow dinner then?
Oth. I shall not dine at home;
I meet the captains at the citadel.
Des. Why then to-morrow night; or Tuesday morn:
On Tuesday noon, or night; on Wednesday morn:
I prithee, name the time; but let it not
Exceed three days: in faith, he's penitent;
And yet his trespass, in our common reason—
Save that, they say, the wars must make examples
Out of their best—is not almost a fault
To incur a private check. When shall he come?
Tell me, Othello: I wonder in my soul,
What you would ask me, that I should deny,
Or stand so mammering on. What! Michael Cassio,
That came a-wooing with you, and so many a time
When I have spoke of you dispraisingly
Hath ta'en your part; to have so much to do

To bring him in! Trust me, I could do much—
Oth. Prithee, no more: let him come when he will;
I will deny thee nothing.
Des. Why, this is not a boon;
'Tis as I should entreat you wear your gloves,
Or feed on nourishing dishes, or keep you warm,
Or sue to you to do a peculiar profit
To your own person: nay, when I have a suit
Wherein I mean to touch your love indeed,
It shall be full of poise and difficult weight,
And fearful to be granted.
Oth. I will deny thee nothing:
Whereon, I do beseech thee, grant me this,
To leave me but a little to myself.
Des. Shall I deny you? no: farewell, my lord.
Oth. Farewell, my Desdemona: I'll come to thee straight.
Des. Emilia, come. Be as your fancies teach you;
Whate'er you be, I am obedient.
[*Exeunt Desdemona and Emilia.*
Oth. Excellent wretch! Perdition catch my soul,
But I do love thee! and when I love thee not,
Chaos is come again.
Iago. My noble lord,—
Oth. What dost thou say, Iago?
Iago. Did Michael Cassio, when you woo'd my lady,
Know of your love?
Oth. He did, from first to last: why dost thou ask?
Iago. But for a satisfaction of my thought;
No further harm.
Oth. Why of thy thought, Iago?
Iago. I did not think he had been acquainted with her.
Oth. O, yes, and went between us very oft.
Iago. Indeed!
Oth. Indeed! ay, indeed: discern'st thou aught in that?
Is he not honest?
Iago. Honest, my lord!
Oth. Honest! ay, honest.
Iago. My lord, for aught I know.
Oth. What dost thou think?
Iago. Think, my lord!
Oth. Think, my lord! By heaven, he echoes me,
As if there were some monster in his thought
Too hideous to be shown. Thou dost mean something:
I heard thee say even now, thou likedst not that,
When Cassio left my wife: what didst not like?

And when I told thee he was of my counsel
In my whole course of wooing, thou criedst 'Indeed!'
And didst contract and purse thy brow together,
As if thou then hadst shut up in thy brain
Some horrible conceit: if thou dost love me,
Show me thy thought.

Iago. My lord, you know I love you.

Oth. I think thou dost;
And for I know thou 'rt full of love and honesty
And weigh'st thy words before thou givest them breath,
Therefore these stops of thine fright me the more:
For such things in a false disloyal knave
Are tricks of custom; but in a man that 's just
They 're close delations, working from the heart,
That passion cannot rule.

Iago. For Michael Cassio,
I dare be sworn I think that he is honest.

Oth. I think so too.

Iago. Men should be what they seem;
Or those that be not, would they might seem none!

Oth. Certain, men should be what they seem.

Iago. Why then I think Cassio 's an honest man.

Oth. Nay, yet there 's more in this:
I prithee, speak to me as to thy thinkings,
As thou dost ruminate, and give thy worst of thoughts
The worst of words.

Iago. Good my lord, pardon me:
Though I am bound to every act of duty,
I am not bound to that all slaves are free to.
Utter my thoughts? Why, say they are vile and false;
As where 's that palace whereinto foul things
Sometimes intrude not? who has a breast so pure,
But some uncleanly apprehensions
Keep leets and law-days, and in session sit
With meditations lawful?

Oth. Thou dost conspire against thy friend, Iago,
If thou but think'st him wrong'd and makest his ear
A stranger to thy thoughts.

Iago. I do beseech you—
Though I perchance am vicious in my guess,
As, I confess, it is my nature's plague
To spy into abuses, and oft my jealousy
Shapes faults that are not—that your wisdom yet,
From one that so imperfectly conceits,
Would take no notice, nor build yourself a trouble

Out of his scattering and unsure observance.
It were not for your quiet nor your good,
Nor for my manhood, honesty, or wisdom,
To let you know my thoughts.

Oth. What dost thou mean?

Iago. Good name in man and woman, dear my lord,
Is the immediate jewel of their souls:
Who steals my purse steals trash; 'tis something, nothing;
'Twas mine, 'tis his, and has been slave to thousands;
But he that filches from me my good name
Robs me of that which not enriches him
And makes me poor indeed.

Oth. By heaven, I'll know thy thoughts.

Iago. You cannot, if my heart were in your hand;
Nor shall not, whilst 'tis in my custody.

Oth. Ha!

Iago. O, beware, my lord, of jealousy;
It is the green-eyed monster, which doth mock
The meat it feeds on: that cuckold lives in bliss
Who, certain of his fate, loves not his wronger;
But, O, what damned minutes tells he o'er
Who dotes, yet doubts, suspects, yet strongly loves!

Oth. O misery!

Iago. Poor and content is rich, and rich enough;
But riches fineless is as poor as winter
To him that ever fears he shall be poor:
Good heaven, the souls of all my tribe defend
From jealousy!

Oth. Why, why is this!
Think'st thou I'ld make a life of jealousy,
To follow still the changes of the moon
With fresh suspicions? No; to be once in doubt
Is once to be resolved: exchange me for a goat,
When I shall turn the business of my soul
To such exsufflicate and blown surmises,
Matching thy inference. 'Tis not to make me jealous
To say my wife is fair, feeds well, loves company,
Is free of speech, sings, plays and dances well;
Where virtue is, these are more virtuous:
Nor from mine own weak merits will I draw
The smallest fear or doubt of her revolt;
For she had eyes, and chose me. No, Iago,
I'll see before I doubt; when I doubt, prove;
And on the proof, there is no more but this,
Away at once with love or jealousy!

Iago. I am glad of it; for now I shall have reason
To show the love and duty that I bear you
With franker spirit: therefore, as I am bound,
Receive it from me. I speak not yet of proof.
Look to your wife: observe her well with Cassio;
Wear your eye thus, not jealous nor secure:
I would not have your free and noble nature
Out of self-bounty be abused; look to 't:
I know our country disposition well;
In Venice they do let heaven see the pranks
They dare not show their husbands; their best conscience
Is not to leave 't undone, but keep 't unknown.
Oth. Dost thou say so?
Iago. She did deceive her father, marrying you;
And when she seem'd to shake and fear your looks,
She loved them most.
Oth. And so she did.
Iago. Why, go to then;
She that so young could give out such a seeming,
To seel her father's eyes up close as oak—
He thought 'twas witchcraft—but I am much to blame;
I humbly do beseech you of your pardon
For too much loving you.
Oth. I am bound to thee for ever.
Iago. I see this hath a little dash'd your spirits.
Oth. Not a jot, not a jot.
Iago. I' faith, I fear it has.
I hope you will consider what is spoke
Comes from my love; but I do see you 're moved:
I am to pray you not to strain my speech
To grosser issues nor to larger reach
Than to suspicion.
Oth. I will not.
Iago. Should you do so, my lord,
My speech should fall into such vile success
As my thoughts aim not at. Cassio 's my worthy friend—
My lord, I see you 're moved.
Oth. No, not much moved:
I do not think but Desdemona 's honest.
Iago. Long live she so! and long live you to think so!
Oth. And yet, how nature erring from itself—
Iago. Ay, there 's the point: as—to be bold with you—
Not to affect many proposed matches
Of her own clime, complexion and degree,
Whereto we see in all things nature tends—

Foh! one may smell in such a will most rank,
Foul disproportion, thoughts unnatural.
But pardon me: I do not in position
Distinctly speak of her; though I may fear
Her will, recoiling to her better judgement,
May fall to match you with her country forms,
And happily repent.
Oth. Farewell, farewell:
If more thou dost perceive, let me know more;
Set on thy wife to observe: leave me, Iago.
Iago. [*Going*] My lord, I take my leave.
Oth. Why did I marry? This honest creature doubtless
Sees and knows more, much more, than he unfolds.
Iago. [*Returning*] My lord, I would I might entreat your honour
To scan this thing no further; leave it to time:
Though it be fit that Cassio have his place,
For sure he fills it up with great ability,
Yet, if you please to hold him off awhile,
You shall by that perceive him and his means:
Note if your lady strain his entertainment
With any strong or vehement importunity;
Much will be seen in that. In the mean time,
Let me be thought too busy in my fears—
As worthy cause I have to fear I am—
And hold her free, I do beseech your honour.
Oth. Fear not my government.
Iago. I once more take my leave. [*Exit.*
Oth. This fellow 's of exceeding honesty,
And knows all qualities, with a learned spirit,
Of human dealings. If I do prove her haggard,
Though that her jesses were my dear heart-strings,
I 'ld whistle her off and let her down the wind
To prey at fortune. Haply, for I am black
And have not those soft parts of conversation
That chamberers have, or for I am declined
Into the vale of years,—yet that 's not much—
She 's gone; I am abused, and my relief
Must be to loathe her. O curse of marriage,
That we can call these delicate creatures ours,
And not their appetites! I had rather be a toad,
And live upon the vapour of a dungeon,
Than keep a corner in the thing I love
For others' uses. Yet, 'tis the plague of great ones;
Prerogatived are they less than the base;
'Tis destiny unshunnable, like death:

Even then this forked plague is fated to us
When we do quicken. Desdemona comes:

Re-enter Desdemona and Emilia.

If she be false, O, then heaven mocks itself!
I 'll not believe 't.

Des. How now, my dear Othello!
Your dinner, and the generous islanders
By you invited, do attend your presence.

Oth. I am to blame.

Des. Why do you speak so faintly?
Are you not well?

Oth. I have a pain upon my forehead here.

Des. Faith, that 's with watching; 'twill away again:
Let me but bind it hard, within this hour
It will be well.

Oth. Your napkin is too little;

[*He puts the handkerchief from him; and she drops it.*

Let it alone. Come, I 'll go in with you.

Des. I am very sorry that you are not well.

[*Exeunt Othello and Desdemona.*

Emil. I am glad I have found this napkin:
This was her first remembrance from the Moor:
My wayward husband hath a hundred times
Woo'd me to steal it; but she so loves the token,
For he conjured her she should ever keep it,
That she reserves it evermore about her
To kiss and talk to. I 'll have the work ta'en out,
And give 't Iago: what he will do with it
Heaven knows, not I;
I nothing but to please his fantasy.

Re-enter Iago.

Iago. How now! what do you do here alone?

Emil. Do not you chide; I have a thing for you.

Iago. A thing for me? it is a common thing—

Emil. Ha!

Iago. To have a foolish wife.

Emil. O, is that all? What will you give me now
For that same handkerchief?

Iago. What handkerchief?

Emil. What handkerchief!
Why, that the Moor first gave to Desdemona;
That which so often you did bid me steal.

Iago. Hast stol'n it from her?

Emil. No, faith! she let it drop by negligence,
And, to the advantage, I being here took 't up.

Look, here it is.
Iago. A good wench; give it me.
Emil. What will you do with 't, that you have been so earnest
To have me filch it?
Iago. [*Snatching it*] Why, what 's that to you?
Emil. If 't be not for some purpose of import,
Give 't me again: poor lady, she 'll run mad
When she shall lack it.
Iago. Be not acknown on 't; I have use for it.
Go, leave me. [*Exit Emilia.*
I will in Cassio's lodging lose this napkin.
And let him find it. Trifles light as air
Are to the jealous confirmations strong
As proofs of holy writ: this may do something.
The Moor already changes with my poison:
Dangerous conceits are in their natures poisons:
Which at the first are scarce found to distaste,
But with a little act upon the blood
Burn like the mines of sulphur. I did say so:
Look, where he comes!

Re-enter Othello.

Not poppy, nor mandragora,
Nor all the drowsy syrups of the world,
Shall ever medicine thee to that sweet sleep
Which thou owedst yesterday.
Oth. Ha! ha! false to me?
Iago. Why, how now, general! no more of that.
Oth. Avaunt! be gone! thou hast set me on the rack:
I swear 'tis better to be much abused
Than but to know 't a little.
Iago. How now, my lord!
Oth. What sense had I of her stol'n hours of lust?
I saw 't not, thought it not, it harm'd not me:
I slept the next night well, was free and merry;
I found not Cassio's kisses on her lips:
He that is robb'd, not wanting what is stol'n,
Let him not know 't and he 's not robbed at all.
Iago. I am sorry to hear this.
Oth. I had been happy, if the general camp,
Pioners and all, had tasted her sweet body,
So I had nothing known. O, now for ever
Farewell the tranquil mind! farewell content!
Farewell the plumed troop and the big wars
That make ambition virtue! O, farewell,
Farewell the neighing steed and the shrill trump,

The spirit-stirring drum, the ear-piercing fife,
The royal banner and all quality,
Pride, pomp and circumstance of glorious war!
And, O you mortal engines, whose rude throats
The immortal Jove's dread clamours counterfeit,
Farewell! Othello's occupation 's gone!

Iago. Is 't possible, my lord?

Oth. Villain, be sure thou prove my love a whore;
Be sure of it; give me the ocular proof;
Or, by the worth of man's eternal soul,
Thou hadst been better have been born a dog
Than answer my waked wrath!

Iago. Is 't come to this?

Oth. Make me to see 't; or at the least so prove it,
That the probation bear no hinge nor loop
To hang a doubt on; or woe upon thy life!

Iago. My noble lord,—

Oth. If thou dost slander her and torture me,
Never pray more; abandon all remorse;
On horror's head horrors accumulate;
Do deeds to make heaven weep, all earth amazed;
For nothing canst thou to damnation add
Greater than that.

Iago. O grace! O heaven defend me!
Are you a man? have you a soul or sense?
God be wi' you; take mine office. O wretched fool,
That livest to make thine honesty a vice!
O monstrous world! Take note, take note, O world,
To be direct and honest is not safe.
I thank you for this profit, and from hence
I 'll love no friend sith love breeds such offence.

Oth. Nay, stay: thou shouldst be honest.

Iago. I should be wise; for honesty 's a fool,
And loses that it works for.

Oth. By the world,
I think my wife be honest, and think she is not;
I think that thou art just, and think thou art not:
I 'll have some proof. Her name, that was as fresh
As Dian's visage, is now begrimed and black
As mine own face. If there be cords, or knives,
Poison, or fire, or suffocating streams,
I 'll not endure it. Would I were satisfied!

Iago. I see, sir, you are eaten up with passion:
I do repent me that I put it to you.
You would be satisfied?

Oth. Would! nay, I will.
Iago. And may: but, how? how satisfied, my lord?
Would you, the supervisor, grossly gape on?
Behold her topp'd?
Oth. Death and damnation! O!
Iago. It were a tedious difficulty, I think,
To bring them to that prospect; damn them then,
If ever mortal eyes do see them bolster
More than their own! What then? how then?
What shall I say? Where 's satisfaction?
It is impossible you should see this,
Were they as prime as goats, as hot as monkeys,
As salt as wolves in pride, and fools as gross
As ignorance made drunk. But yet, I say,
If imputation and strong circumstances,
Which lead directly to the door of truth,
Will give you satisfaction, you may have 't.
Oth. Give me a living reason she 's disloyal.
Iago. I do not like the office:
But sith I am enter'd in this cause so far,
Prick'd to 't by foolish honesty and love,
I will go on. I lay with Cassio lately,
And being troubled with a raging tooth,
I could not sleep.
There are a kind of men so loose of soul,
That in their sleeps will mutter their affairs:
One of this kind is Cassio:
In sleep I heard him say 'Sweet Desdemona,
Let us be wary, let us hide our loves;'
And then, sir, would he gripe and wring my hand,
Cry 'O sweet creature!' and then kiss me hard,
As if he pluck'd up kisses by the roots,
That grew upon my lips: then laid his leg
Over my thigh, and sigh'd and kiss'd, and then
Cried 'Cursed fate that gave thee to the Moor!'
Oth. O monstrous! monstrous!
Iago. Nay, this was but his dream
Oth. But this denoted a foregone conclusion:
'Tis a shrewd doubt, though it be but a dream.
Iago. And this may help to thicken other proofs
That do demonstrate thinly.
Oth. I 'll tear her all to pieces.
Iago. Nay, but be wise: yet we see nothing done;
She may be honest yet. Tell me but this;
Have you not sometimes seen a handkerchief

Spotted with strawberries in your wife's hand?
Oth. I gave her such a one; 'twas my first gift.
Iago. I know not that: but such a handkerchief—
I am sure it was your wife's—did I to-day
See Cassio wipe his beard with.
Oth. If it be that,—
Iago. If it be that, or any that was hers,
It speaks against her with the other proofs.
Oth. O, that the slave had forty thousand lives!
One is too poor, too weak for my revenge.
Now do I see 'tis true. Look here, Iago;
All my fond love thus do I blow to heaven:
'Tis gone.
Arise, black vengeance, from thy hollow cell!
Yield up, O love, thy crown and hearted throne
To tyrannous hate! Swell, bosom, with thy fraught,
For 'tis of aspics' tongues!
Iago. Yet be content.
Oth. O, blood, blood, blood!
Iago. Patience, I say; your mind perhaps may change.
Oth. Never, Iago. Like to the Pontic sea,
Whose icy current and compulsive course
Ne'er feels retiring ebb, but keeps due on
To the Propontic and the Hellespont;
Even so my bloody thoughts, with violent pace,
Shall ne'er look back, ne'er ebb to humble love,
Till that a capable and wide revenge
Swallow them up. Now, by yond marble heaven,
In the due reverence of a sacred vow [*Kneels.*
I here engage my words.
Iago. Do not rise yet. [*Kneels.*
Witness, you ever-burning lights above,
You elements that clip us round about,
Witness that here Iago doth give up
The execution of his wit, hands, heart,
To wrong'd Othello's service! Let him command,
And to obey shall be in me remorse,
What bloody business ever. [*They rise.*
Oth. I greet thy love,
Not with vain thanks, but with acceptance bounteous,
And will upon the instant put thee to 't:
Within these three days let me hear thee say
That Cassio's not alive.
Iago. My friend is dead; 'tis done at your request:
But let her live.

Oth. Damn her, lewd minx! O, damn her!
Come, go with me apart; I will withdraw,
To furnish me with some swift means of death
For the fair devil. Now art thou my lieutenant.
Iago. I am your own for ever. [*Exeunt.*

Scene IV

Before the castle.

Enter Desdemona, Emilia, and Clown.

Des. Do you know, sirrah, where Lieutenant Cassio lies?

Clo. I dare not say he lies any where.

Des. Why, man?

Clo. He 's a soldier; and for one to say a soldier lies, is stabbing.

Des. Go to: where lodges he?

Clo. To tell you where he lodges, is to tell you where I lie.

Des. Can any thing be made of this?

Clo. I know not where he lodges; and for me to devise a lodging, and say he lies here or he lies there, were to lie in mine own throat.

Des. Can you inquire him out and be edified by report?

Clo. I will catechize the world for him; that is, make questions and by them answer.

Des. Seek him, bid him come hither: tell him I have moved my lord on his behalf and hope all will be well.

Clo. To do this is within the compass of man's wit, and therefore I will attempt the doing it. [*Exit.*

Des. Where should I lose that handkerchief, Emilia?
Emil. I know not, madam.
Des. Believe me, I had rather have lost my purse
Full of crusadoes: and, but my noble Moor
Is true of mind and made of no such baseness
As jealous creatures are, it were enough
To put him to ill thinking.
Emil. Is he not jealous?
Des. Who, he? I think the sun where he was born
Drew all such humours from him.
Emil. Look, where he comes.
Des. I will not leave him now till Cassio
Be call'd to him.

Enter Othello.

How is 't with you, my lord?
Oth. Well, my good lady. [*Aside*] O, hardness to dissemble!
How do you, Desdemona?
Des. Well, my good lord.
Oth. Give me your hand: this hand is moist, my lady.

Des. It yet has felt no age nor known no sorrow.
Oth. This argues fruitfulness and liberal heart:
Hot, hot, and moist: this hand of yours requires
A sequester from liberty, fasting and prayer,
Much castigation, exercise devout;
For here 's a young and sweating devil here,
That commonly rebels. 'Tis a good hand,
A frank one.
Des. You may, indeed, say so;
For 'twas that hand that gave away my heart.
Oth. A liberal hand: the hearts of old gave hands;
But our new heraldry is hands, not hearts.
Des. I cannot speak of this. Come now, your promise.
Oth. What promise, chuck?
Des. I have sent to bid Cassio come speak with you.
Oth. I have a salt and sorry rheum offends me;
Lend me thy handkerchief.
Des. Here, my lord.
Oth. That which I gave you.
Des. I have it not about me.
Oth. Not?
Des. No, indeed, my lord.
Oth. That 's a fault. That handkerchief
Did an Egyptian to my mother give;
She was a charmer, and could almost read
The thoughts of people: she told her, while she kept it
'Twould make her amiable and subdue my father
Entirely to her love, but if she lost it
Or made a gift of it, my father's eye
Should hold her loathed and his spirits should hunt
After new fancies; she dying gave it me,
And bid me, when my fate would have me wife,
To give it her. I did so: and take heed on 't;
Make it a darling like your precious eye;
To lose 't or give 't away were such perdition
As nothing else could match.
Des. Is 't possible?
Oth. 'Tis true: there 's magic in a web of it:
A sibyl, that had number'd in the world
The sun to course two hundred compasses,
In her prophetic fury sew'd the work;
The worms were hallow'd that did breed the silk;
And it was dyed in mummy which the skilful
Conserved of maidens' hearts.
Des. Indeed! is 't true?

Oth. Most veritable; therefore look to 't well.
Des. Then would to God that I had never seen 't!
Oth. Ha! wherefore?
Des. Why do you speak so startingly and rash?
Oth. Is 't lost? is 't gone? speak, is it out o' the way?
Des. Heaven bless us!
Oth. Say you?
Des. It is not lost; but what an if it were?
Oth. How!
Des. I say, it is not lost.
Oth. Fetch 't, let me see it.
Des. Why, so I can, sir, but I will not now.
This is a trick to put me from my suit:
Pray you, let Cassio be received again.
Oth. Fetch me the handkerchief: my mind misgives.
Des. Come, come;
You 'll never meet a more sufficient man.
Oth. The handkerchief!
Des. I pray, talk me of Cassio.
Oth. The handkerchief!
Des. A man that all his time
Hath founded his good fortunes on your love,
Shared dangers with you,—
Oth. The handkerchief!
Des. In sooth, you are to blame.
Oth. Away! [*Exit.*
Emil. Is not this man jealous?
Des. I ne'er saw this before.
Sure there 's some wonder in this handkerchief:
I am most unhappy in the loss of it.
Emil. 'Tis not a year or two shows us a man:
They are all but stomachs and we all but food;
They eat us hungerly, and when they are full
They belch us. Look you, Cassio and my husband.

Enter Cassio and Iago.

Iago. There is no other way; 'tis she must do 't:
And, lo, the happiness! go and importune her.
Des. How now, good Cassio! what 's the news with you?
Cas. Madam, my former suit: I do beseech you
That by your virtuous means I may again
Exist, and be a member of his love
Whom I with all the office of my heart
Entirely honour: I would not be delay'd.
If my offence be of such mortal kind,
That nor my service past nor present sorrows

Nor purposed merit in futurity
Can ransom me into his love again,
But to know so must be my benefit;
So shall I clothe me in a forced content
And shut myself up in some other course
To fortune's alms.

Des. Alas, thrice-gentle Cassio!
My advocation is not now in tune;
My lord is not my lord, nor should I know him
Were he in favour as in humour alter'd.
So help me every spirit sanctified,
As I have spoken for you all my best
And stood within the blank of his displeasure
For my free speech! You must awhile be patient:
What I can do I will; and more I will
Than for myself I dare: let that suffice you.

Iago. Is my lord angry?

Emil. He went hence but now,
And certainly in strange unquietness.

Iago. Can he be angry? I have seen the cannon,
When it hath blown his ranks into the air,
And, like the devil, from his very arm
Puff'd his own brother; and can he be angry?
Something of moment then: I will go meet him:
There 's matter in 't indeed if he be angry.

Des. I prithee, do so. [*Exit Iago.*
Something sure of state,
Either from Venice some unhatch'd practice
Made demonstrable here in Cyprus to him,
Hath puddled his clear spirit; and in such cases
Men's natures wrangle with inferior things,
Though great ones are their object. 'Tis even so;
For let our finger ache, and it indues
Our other healthful members even to that sense
Of pain: nay, we must think men are not gods,
Nor of them look for such observancy
As fits the bridal. Beshrew me much, Emilia,
I was, unhandsome warrior as I am,
Arraigning his unkindness with my soul;
But now I find I had suborn'd the witness,
And he 's indicted falsely.

Emil. Pray heaven it be state-matters, as you think,
And no conception nor no jealous toy
Concerning you.

Des. Alas the day, I never gave him cause!

Emil. But jealous souls will not be answer'd so;
They are not ever jealous for the cause,
But jealous for they are jealous: 'tis a monster
Begot upon itself, born on itself.
Des. Heaven keep that monster from Othello's mind!
Emil. Lady, amen.
Des. I will go seek him. Cassio, walk hereabout:
If I do find him fit, I 'll move your suit,
And seek to effect it to my uttermost.
Cas. I humbly thank your ladyship.
[*Exeunt Desdemona and Emilia.*
Enter Bianca.
Bian. Save you, friend Cassio!
Cas. What make you from home?
How is it with you, my most fair Bianca?
I' faith, sweet love, I was coming to your house.
Bian. And I was going to your lodging, Cassio,
What, keep a week away? seven days and nights?
Eight score eight hours? and lovers' absent hours,
More tedious than the dial eight score times?
O weary reckoning!
Cas. Pardon me, Bianca;
I have this while with leaden thoughts been press'd;
But I shall in a more continuate time
Strike off this score of absence. Sweet Bianca,
[*Giving her Desdemona's handkerchief.*
Take me this work out.
Bian. O Cassio, whence came this?
This is some token from a newer friend:
To the felt absence now I feel a cause:
Is 't come to this? Well, well.
Cas. Go to, woman!
Throw your vile guesses in the devil's teeth,
From whence you have them. You are jealous now
That this is from some mistress, some remembrance:
No, by my faith, Bianca.
Bian. Why, whose is it?
Cas. I know not, sweet: I found it in my chamber.
I like the work well: ere it be demanded—
As like enough it will—I 'ld have it copied:
Take it, and do 't; and leave me for this time.
Bian. Leave you! wherefore?
Cas. I do attend here on the general;
And think it no addition, nor my wish,
To have him see me woman'd.

Bian. Why, I pray you?
Cas. Not that I love you not.
Bian. But that you do not love me.
I pray you, bring me on the way a little;
And say if I shall see you soon at night.
Cas. 'Tis but a little way that I can bring you;
For I attend here: but I'll see you soon.
Bian. 'Tis very good; I must be circumstanced. [*Exeunt.*

ACT IV—Scene I

Cyprus. Before the castle.

Enter Othello and Iago.

Iago. Will you think so?
Oth. Think so, Iago!
Iago. What,
To kiss in private?
Oth. An unauthorized kiss.
Iago. Or to be naked with her friend in bed
An hour or more, not meaning any harm?
Oth. Naked in bed, Iago, and not mean harm!
It is hypocrisy against the devil:
They that mean virtuously and yet do so,
The devil their virtue tempts and they tempt heaven.
Iago. So they do nothing, 'tis a venial slip:
But if I give my wife a handkerchief—
Oth. What then?
Iago. Why, then, 'tis hers, my lord; and being hers,
She may, I think, bestow 't on any man.
Oth. She is protectress of her honour too:
May she give that?
Iago. Her honour is an essence that 's not seen;
They have it very oft that have it not:
But for the handkerchief—
Oth. By heaven, I would most gladly have forgot it:
Thou said'st—O, it comes o'er my memory,
As doth the raven o'er the infected house,
Boding to all—he had my handkerchief.
Iago. Ay, what of that?
Oth. That 's not so good now.
Iago. What,
If I had said I had seen him do you wrong?
Or heard him say—as knaves be such abroad,
Who having, by their own importunate suit,
Or voluntary dotage of some mistress,

Convinced or supplied them, cannot choose
But they must blab—

Oth. Hath he said anything?

Iago. He hath, my lord; but be you well assured,
No more than he 'll unswear.

Oth. What hath he said?

Iago. Faith, that he did—I know not what he did.

Oth. What, what?

Iago. Lie—

Oth. With her?

Iago. With her, on her; what you will.

Oth. Lie with her! lie on her!—We say lie on her, when they belie her.—Lie with her! 'Zounds, that 's fulsome! Handkerchief—confessions—handkerchief!—To confess, and be hanged for his labour; first, to be hanged, and then to confess. I tremble at it. Nature would not invest herself in such shadowing passion without some instruction. It is not words that shakes me thus. Pish! Noses, ears and lips. Is 't possible?—Confess?—Handkerchief?—O devil!
[*Falls in a trance.*

Iago. Work on,
My medicine, work! Thus credulous fools are caught:
And many worthy and chaste dames even thus,
All guiltless, meet reproach. What, ho! my lord!
My lord, I say! Othello!

Enter Cassio.

How now, Cassio!

Cas. What 's the matter?

Iago. My lord is fall'n into an epilepsy:
This is his second fit; he had one yesterday.

Cas. Rub him about the temples.

Iago. No, forbear;
The lethargy must have his quiet course:
If not, he foams at mouth, and by and by
Breaks out to savage madness. Look, he stirs:
Do you withdraw yourself a little while,
He will recover straight: when he is gone,
I would on great occasion speak with you. [*Exit Cassio.*
How is it, general? have you not hurt your head?

Oth. Dost thou mock me?

Iago. I mock you! no, by heaven.
Would you would bear your fortune like a man!

Oth. A horned man 's a monster and a beast.

Iago. There 's many a beast then in a populous city
And many a civil monster.

Oth. Did he confess it?
Iago. Good sir, be a man;
Think every bearded fellow that 's but yoked
May draw with you: there 's millions now alive
That nightly lie in those unproper beds
Which they dare swear peculiar: your case is better.
O, 'tis the spite of hell, the fiend's arch-mock,
To lip a wanton in a secure couch,
And to suppose her chaste! No, let me know;
And knowing what I am, I know what she shall be.
Oth. O, thou art wise; 'tis certain.
Iago. Stand you awhile apart;
Confine yourself but in a patient list.
Whilst you were here o'erwhelmed with your grief—
A passion most unsuiting such a man—
Cassio came hither: I shifted him away,
And laid good 'scuse upon your ecstasy;
Bade him anon return and here speak with me;
The which he promised. Do but encave yourself,
And mark the fleers, the gibes and notable scorns,
That dwell in every region of his face;
For I will make him tell the tale anew,
Where, how, how oft, how long ago and when
He hath and is again to cope your wife:
I say, but mark his gesture. Marry, patience;
Or I shall say you are all in all in spleen,
And nothing of a man.
Oth. Dost thou hear, Iago?
I will be found most cunning in my patience;
But—dost thou hear?—most bloody.
Iago. That 's not amiss
But yet keep time in all. Will you withdraw?
[*Othello retires.*
Now will I question Cassio of Bianca,
A housewife that by selling her desires
Buys herself bread and clothes: it is a creature
That dotes on Cassio; as 'tis the strumpet's plague
To beguile many and be beguiled by one.
He, when he hears of her, cannot refrain
From the excess of laughter. Here he comes.

Re-enter Cassio.

As he shall smile, Othello shall go mad;
And his unbookish jealousy must construe
Poor Cassio's smiles, gestures and light behaviour,
Quite in the wrong. How do you now, lieutenant?

Cas. The worser that you give me the addition
Whose want even kills me.
Iago. Ply Desdemona well, and you are sure on 't.
Now, if this suit lay in Bianca's power,
How quickly should you speed!
Cas. Alas, poor caitiff!
Oth. Look, how he laughs already!
Iago. I never knew a woman love man so.
Cas. Alas, poor rogue! I think, i' faith, she loves me.
Oth. Now he denies it faintly and laughs it out.
Iago. Do you hear, Cassio?
Oth. Now he importunes him
To tell it o'er: go to; well said, well said.
Iago. She gives it out that you shall marry her:
Do you intend it?
Cas. Ha, ha, ha!
Oth. Do you triumph, Roman? do you triumph?
Cas. I marry her! what, a customer! I prithee, bear some charity to my wit; do not think it so unwholesome. Ha, ha, ha!
Oth. So, so, so, so: they laugh that win.
Iago. Faith, the cry goes that you shall marry her.
Cas. Prithee, say true.
Iago. I am a very villain else.
Oth. Have you scored me? Well.
Cas. This is the monkey's own giving out: she is persuaded I will marry her, out of her own love and flattery, not out of my promise.
Oth. Iago beckons me; now he begins the story.
Cas. She was here even now: she haunts me in every place. I was the other day talking on the sea-bank with certain Venetians; and thither comes the bauble, and, by this hand, she falls me thus about my neck—
Oth. Crying 'O dear Cassio!' as it were: his gesture imports it.
Cas. So hangs and lolls and weeps upon me; so hales and pulls me: ha, ha, ha!
Oth. Now he tells how she plucked him to my chamber. O, I see that nose of yours, but not that dog I shall throw it to.
Cas. Well, I must leave her company.
Iago. Before me! look, where she comes.
Cas. 'Tis such another fitchew! marry, a perfumed one.

Enter Bianca.

What do you mean by this haunting of me?
Bian. Let the devil and his dam haunt you! What did you mean by that same handkerchief you gave me even now! I was a fine fool to take it. I must take out the work? A

likely piece of work, that you should find it in your chamber, and not know who left it there! This is some minx's token, and I must take out the work? There; give it your hobby-horse: wheresoever you had it, I 'll take out no work on 't.

Cas. How now, my sweet Bianca! how now! how now!

Oth. By heaven, that should be my handkerchief!

Bian. An you 'll come to supper to-night, you may; an you will not, come when you are next prepared for. [*Exit.*

Iago. After her, after her.

Cas. Faith, I must; she 'll rail i' the street else.

Iago. Will you sup there?

Cas. Faith, I intend so.

Iago. Well, I may chance to see you; for I would very fain speak with you.

Cas. Prithee, come; will you?

Iago. Go to; say no more. [*Exit Cassio.*

Oth. [*Advancing*] How shall I murder him, Iago?

Iago. Did you perceive how he laughed at his vice?

Oth. O Iago!

Iago. And did you see the handkerchief?

Oth. Was that mine?

Iago. Yours, by this hand: and to see how he prizes the foolish woman your wife! she gave it him, and he hath given it his whore.

Oth. I would have him nine years a-killing. A fine woman! a fair woman! a sweet woman!

Iago. Nay, you must forget that.

Oth. Ay, let her rot, and perish, and be damned to-night; for she shall not live: no, my heart is turned to stone; I strike it, and it hurts my hand. O, the world hath not a sweeter creature: she might lie by an emperor's side, and command him tasks.

Iago. Nay, that 's not your way.

Oth. Hang her! I do but say what she is: so delicate with her needle: an admirable musician: O, she will sing the savageness out of a bear: of so high and plenteous wit and invention:—

Iago. She 's the worse for all this.

Oth. O, a thousand thousand times: and then, of so gentle a condition!

Iago. Ay, too gentle.

Oth. Nay, that 's certain: but yet the pity of it, Iago! O Iago, the pity of it, Iago!

Iago. If you are so fond over her iniquity, give her patent to offend; for, if it touch not you, it comes near nobody.

Oth. I will chop her into messes: cuckold me!

Iago. O, 'tis foul in her.
Oth. With mine officer!
Iago. That 's fouler.
Oth. Get me some poison, Iago; this night. I 'll not expostulate with her, lest her body and beauty unprovide my mind again: this night, Iago.
Iago. Do it not with poison, strangle her in her bed, even the bed she hath contaminated.
Oth. Good, good: the justice of it pleases: very good.
Iago. And for Cassio, let me be his undertaker: you shall hear more by midnight.
Oth. Excellent good. [*A trumpet within*.] What trumpet is that same?
Iago. Something from Venice, sure. 'Tis Lodovico
Come from the duke: and, see, your wife is with him.

Enter Lodovico, Desdemona, and Attendants.

Lod. God save the worthy general!
Oth. With all my heart, sir.
Lod. The duke and senators of Venice greet you.
[*Gives him a letter.*
Oth. I kiss the instrument of their pleasures.
[*Opens the letter, and reads.*
Des. And what 's the news, good cousin Lodovico?
Iago. I am very glad to see you, signior;
Welcome to Cyprus.
Lod. I thank you. How does Lieutenant Cassio?
Iago. Lives, sir.
Des. Cousin, there 's fall'n between him and my lord
An unkind breach: but you shall make all well.
Oth. Are you sure of that?
Des. My lord?
Oth. [*Reads*] 'This fail you not to do, as you will—'
Lod. He did not call; he 's busy in the paper.
Is there division 'twixt my lord and Cassio?
Des. A most unhappy one: I would do much
To atone them, for the love I bear to Cassio.
Oth. Fire and brimstone!
Des. My lord?
Oth. Are you wise?
Des. What, is he angry?
Lod. May be the letter moved him;
For, as I think, they do command him home,
Deputing Cassio in his government.
Des. By my troth, I am glad on 't.
Oth. Indeed?

Des. My lord?
Oth. I am glad to see you mad.
Des. Why, sweet Othello?
Oth. Devil! [*Striking her.*
Des. I have not deserved this.
Lod. My lord, this would not be believed in Venice,
Though I should swear I saw 't: 'tis very much:
Make her amends; she weeps.
Oth. O devil, devil!
If that the earth could teem with woman's tears,
Each drop she falls would prove a crocodile.
Out of my sight!
Des. I will not stay to offend you. [*Going*
Lod. Truly, an obedient lady:
I do beseech your lordship, call her back.
Oth. Mistress!
Des. My lord?
Oth. What would you with her, sir?
Lod. Who, I, my lord?
Oth. Ay; you did wish that I would make her turn:
Sir, she can turn and turn, and yet go on,
And turn again; and she can weep, sir, weep;
And she 's obedient, as you say, obedient,
Very obedient. Proceed you in your tears.
Concerning this, sir,—O well-painted passion!—
I am commanded home. Get you away;
I 'll send for you anon. Sir, I obey the mandate,
And will return to Venice. Hence, avaunt!
[*Exit Desdemona.*
Cassio shall have my place. And, sir, to-night,
I do entreat that we may sup together:
You are welcome, sir, to Cyprus. Goats and monkeys! [*Exit.*
Lod. Is this the noble Moor whom our full senate
Call all in all sufficient? This the nature
Whom passion could not shake? whose solid virtue
The shot of accident nor dart of chance
Could neither graze nor pierce?
Iago. He is much changed.
Lod. Are his wits safe? is he not light of brain?
Iago. He 's that he is: I may not breathe my censure
What he might be: if what he might he is not,
I would to heaven he were!
Lod. What, strike his wife.
Iago. Faith, that was not so well; yet would I knew
That stroke would prove the worst!

Lod. Is it his use?
Or did the letters work upon his blood,
And new create this fault?
Iago. Alas, alas!
It is not honesty in me to speak
What I have seen and known. You shall observe him,
And his own courses will denote him so
That I may save my speech: do but go after,
And mark how he continues.
Lod. I am sorry that I am deceived in him. [*Exeunt.*

Scene II

A room in the castle.

Enter Othello and Emilia.

Oth. You have seen nothing, then?
Emil. Nor ever heard, nor ever did suspect.
Oth. Yes, you have seen Cassio and she together.
Emil. But then I saw no harm, and then I heard
Each syllable that breath made up between them.
Oth. What, did they never whisper?
Emil. Never, my lord.
Oth. Nor send you out o' the way?
Emil. Never.
Oth. To fetch her fan, her gloves, her mask, nor nothing?
Emil. Never, my lord.
Oth. That 's strange.
Emil. I durst, my lord, to wager she is honest,
Lay down my soul at stake: if you think other,
Remove your thought; it doth abuse your bosom.
If any wretch have put this in your head,
Let heaven requite it with the serpent's curse!
For if she be not honest, chaste and true,
There 's no man happy; the purest of their wives
Is foul as slander.
Oth. Bid her come hither: go. [*Exit Emilia.*
She says enough: yet she 's a simple bawd
That cannot say as much. This is a subtle whore,
A closet lock and key of villanous secrets:
And yet she 'll kneel and pray; I have seen her do 't.

Enter Desdemona with Emilia.

Des. My lord, what is your will?
Oth. Pray, chuck, come hither
Des. What is your pleasure?
Oth. Let me see your eyes
Look in my face.

Des. What horrible fancy's this?
Oth. [*To Emilia*] Some of your function, mistress,
Leave procreants alone and shut the door;
Cough, or cry hem, if any body come:
Your mystery, your mystery: nay, dispatch. [*Exit Emilia.*
Des. Upon my knees, what doth your speech import?
I understand a fury in your words,
But not the words.
Oth. Why, what art thou?
Des. Your wife, my lord; your true and loyal wife.
Oth. Come, swear it, damn thyself;
Lest, being like one of heaven, the devils themselves
Should fear to seize thee: therefore be double-damn'd;
Swear thou art honest.
Des. Heaven doth truly know it.
Oth. Heaven truly knows that thou art false as hell.
Des. To whom, my lord? with whom? how am I false?
Oth. O Desdemona! Away! away! away!
Des. Alas the heavy day! Why do you weep?
Am I the motive of these tears, my lord?
If haply you my father do suspect
An instrument of this your calling back,
Lay not your blame on me: if you have lost him,
Why, I have lost him too.
Oth. Had it pleased heaven
To try me with affliction; had they rain'd
All kinds of sores and shames on my bare head,
Steep'd me in poverty to the very lips,
Given to captivity me and my utmost hopes,
I should have found in some place of my soul
A drop of patience: but, alas, to make me
A fixed figure for the time of scorn
To point his slow unmoving finger at!
Yet could I bear that too; well, very well:
But there, where I have garner'd up my heart,
Where either I must live or bear no life,
The fountain from the which my current runs,
Or else dries up; to be discarded thence!
Or keep it as a cistern for foul toads
To knot and gender in! Turn thy complexion there,
Patience, thou young and rose-lipp'd cherubin,
Ay, there, look grim as hell!
Des. I hope my noble lord esteems me honest.
Oth. O, ay; as summer flies are in the shambles,
That quicken even with blowing. O thou weed,

Who art so lovely fair and smell'st so sweet
That the sense aches at thee, would thou hadst ne'er been [born!
Des. Alas, what ignorant sin have I committed?
Oth. Was this fair paper, this most goodly book,
Made to write 'whore' upon? What committed!
Committed! O thou public commoner!
I should make very forges of my cheeks,
That would to cinders burn up modesty,
Did I but speak thy deeds. What committed!
Heaven stops the nose at it, and the moon winks;
The bawdy wind, that kisses all it meets,
Is hush'd within the hollow mine of earth,
And will not hear it. What committed!
Impudent strumpet!
Des. By heaven, you do me wrong.
Oth. Are not you a strumpet?
Des. No, as I am a Christian:
If to preserve this vessel for my lord
From any other foul unlawful touch
Be not to be a strumpet, I am none.
Oth. What, not a whore?
Des. No, as I shall be saved.
Oth. Is 't possible?
Des. O, heaven forgive us!
Oth. I cry you mercy then:
I took you for that cunning whore of Venice
That married with Othello. [*Raising his voice*] You, mistress
That have the office opposite to Saint Peter,
And keep the gate of hell!

Re-enter Emilia.

You, you, ay, you!
We have done our course; there 's money for your pains:
I pray you, turn the key, and keep our counsel. [*Exit.*
Emil. Alas, what does this gentleman conceive?
How do you, madam? how do you, my good lady?
Des. Faith, half asleep.
Emil. Good madam, what 's the matter with my lord?
Des. With who?
Emil. Why, with my lord, madam.
Des. Who is thy lord?
Emil. He that is yours, sweet lady.
Des. I have none: do not talk to me, Emilia;
I cannot weep, nor answer have I none
But what should go by water. Prithee, to-night
Lay on my bed my wedding sheets: remember;

And call thy husband hither.
Emil. Here 's a change indeed! [*Exit.*
Des. 'Tis meet I should be used so, very meet.
How have I been behaved, that he might stick
The small'st opinion on my least misuse?

Re-enter Emilia, with Iago.

Iago. What is your pleasure, madam? How is 't with you?
Des. I cannot tell. Those that do teach young babes
Do it with gentle means and easy tasks:
He might have chid me so; for, in good faith,
I am a child to chiding.
Iago. What 's the matter, lady?
Emil. Alas, Iago, my lord hath so bewhored her,
Thrown such despite and heavy terms upon her,
As true hearts cannot bear.
Des. Am I that name, Iago?
Iago. What name, fair lady?
Des. Such as she says my lord did say I was.
Emil. He call'd her whore: a beggar in his drink
Could not have laid such terms upon his callet.
Iago. Why did he so?
Des. I do not know: I am sure I am none such.
Iago. Do not weep, do not weep. Alas the day!
Emil. Hath she forsook so many noble matches,
Her father and her country and her friends,
To be call'd whore? would it not make one weep?
Des. It is my wretched fortune.
Iago. Beshrew him for 't!
How comes this trick upon him?
Des. Nay, heaven doth know.
Emil. I will be hang'd, if some eternal villain,
Some busy and insinuating rogue,
Some cogging, cozening slave, to get some office,
Have not devised this slander; I 'll be hang'd else.
Iago. Fie, there is no such man; it is impossible.
Des. If any such there be, heaven pardon him!
Emil. A halter pardon him! and hell gnaw his bones?
Why should he call her whore? who keeps her company?
What place? what time? what form? what likelihood?
The Moor 's abused by some most villanous knave,
Some base notorious knave, some scurvy fellow.
O heaven, that such companions thou 'ldst unfold,
And put in every honest hand a whip
To lash the rascals naked through the world
Even from the east to the west!

Iago. Speak within door.
Emil. O, fie upon them! Some such squire he was
That turn'd your wit the seamy side without,
And made you to suspect me with the Moor.
Iago. You are a fool; go to.
Des. O good Iago,
What shall I do to win my lord again?
Good friend, go to him; for, by this light of heaven,
I know not how I lost him. Here I kneel:
If e'er my will did trespass 'gainst his love
Either in discourse of thought or actual deed,
Or that mine eyes, mine ears, or any sense,
Delighted them in any other form,
Or that I do not yet, and ever did,
And ever will, though he do shake me off
To beggarly divorcement, love him dearly,
Comfort foreswear me! Unkindness may do much;
And his unkindness may defeat my life,
But never taint my love. I cannot say 'whore':
It doth abhor me now I speak the word;
To do the act that might the addition earn
Not the world's mass of vanity could make me.
Iago. I pray you, be content; 'tis but his humour:
The business of the state does him offence,
And he does chide with you.
Des. If 'twere no other,—
Iago. 'Tis but so, I warrant. [*Trumpets within.*
Hark, how these instruments summon to supper!
The messengers of Venice stay the meat:
Go in, and weep not; all things shall be well.
[*Exeunt Desdemona and Emilia.*

Enter Roderigo.

How now, Roderigo!
Rod. I do not find that thou dealest justly with me.
Iago. What in the contrary?
Rod. Every day thou daffest me with some device, Iago; and rather, as it seems to me now, keepest from me all conveniency than suppliest me with the least advantage of hope. I will indeed no longer endure it; nor am I yet persuaded to put up in peace what already I have foolishly suffered.
Iago. Will you hear me, Roderigo?
Rod. Faith, I have heard too much; for your words and performances are no kin together.
Iago. You charge me most unjustly.
Rod. With nought but truth. I have wasted myself out of my

means. The jewels you have had from me to deliver to Desdemona would half have corrupted a votarist: you have told me she hath received them and returned me expectations and comforts of sudden respect and acquaintance; but I find none.

Iago. Well; go to; very well.

Rod. Very well! go to! I cannot go to, man; nor 'tis not very well: by this hand, I say 'tis very scurvy, and begin to find myself fopped in it.

Iago. Very well.

Rod. I tell you 'tis not very well. I will make myself known to Desdemona: if she will return me my jewels, I will give over my suit and repent my unlawful solicitation; if not, assure yourself I will seek satisfaction of you.

Iago. You have said now.

Rod. Ay, and said nothing but what I protest intendment of doing.

Iago. Why, now I see there's mettle in thee; and even from this instant do build on thee a better opinion than ever before. Give me thy hand, Roderigo: thou hast taken against me a most just exception; but yet, I protest, I have dealt most directly in thy affair.

Rod. It hath not appeared.

Iago. I grant indeed it hath not appeared, and your suspicion is not without wit and judgement. But, Roderigo, if thou hast that in thee indeed, which I have greater reason to believe now than ever, I mean purpose, courage and valour, this night show it: if thou the next night following enjoy not Desdemona, take me from this world with treachery and devise engines for my life.

Rod. Well, what is it? is it within reason and compass?

Iago. Sir, there is especial commission come from Venice to depute Cassio in Othello's place.

Rod. Is that true? why then Othello and Desdemona return again to Venice.

Iago. O, no; he goes into Mauritania, and takes away with him the fair Desdemona; unless his abode be lingered here by some accident: wherein none can be so determinate as the removing of Cassio.

Rod. How do you mean, removing of him?

Iago. Why, by making him uncapable of Othello's place; knocking out his brains.

Rod. And that you would have me to do?

Iago. Ay, if you dare do yourself a profit and a right. He sups to-night with a harlotry, and thither will I go to him: he knows not yet of his honourable fortune. If you will watch his going thence, which I will fashion to fall out between twelve and one, you may take him at your pleasure: I will be near to second your attempt, and he shall fall between us. Come, stand not amazed at it, but go along with me; I will show you such a necessity in his death that you shall think yourself bound to put it on him. It is now high supper-time, and the night grows to waste: about it.

Rod. I will hear further reason for this.

Iago. And you shall be satisfied. [*Exeunt.*

Scene III

Another room in the castle.

Enter Othello, Lodovico, Desdemona, Emilia, and Attendants.

Lod. I do beseech you, sir, trouble yourself no further.

Oth. O, pardon me; 'twill do me good to walk.

Lod. Madam, good night; I humbly thank your ladyship.

Des. Your honour is most welcome.

Oth. Will you walk, sir?
O,—Desdemona,—

Des. My lord?

Oth. Get you to bed on the instant; I will be returned forth with: dismiss your attendant there: look it be done.

Des. I will, my lord. [*Exeunt Othello, Lodovico, and Attendants.*

Emil. How goes it now? he looks gentler than he did.

Des. He says he will return incontinent:
He hath commanded me to go to bed,
And bade me to dismiss you.

Emil. Dismiss me!

Des. It was his bidding; therefore, good Emilia,
Give me my nightly wearing, and adieu;
We must not now displease him.

Emil. I would you had never seen him!

Des. So would not I: my love doth so approve him,
That even his stubbornness, his checks, his frowns,—
Prithee, unpin me,—have grace and favour in them.

Emil. I have laid those sheets you bade me on the bed.

Des. All 's one. Good faith, how foolish are our minds!
If I do die before thee, prithee, shroud me
In one of those same sheets.

Emil. Come, come, you talk.

Des. My mother had a maid call'd Barbara:
She was in love; and he she loved proved mad
And did forsake her: she had a song of 'willow;'
An old thing 'twas, but it express'd her fortune,
And she died singing it: that song to-night
Will not go from my mind; I have much to do

But to go hang my head all at one side
And sing it like poor Barbara. Prithee, dispatch.

Emil. Shall I go fetch your night-gown?

Des. No, unpin me here.
This Lodovico is a proper man.

Emil. A very handsome man.

Des. He speaks well.

Emil. I know a lady in Venice would have walked barefoot to Palestine for a touch of his nether lip.

Des. [*Singing*] The poor soul sat sighing by a sycamore tree,
Sing all a green willow;
Her hand on her bosom, her head on her knee,
Sing willow, willow, willow:
The fresh streams ran by her, and murmur'd her moans;
Sing willow, willow, willow;
Her salt tears fell from her, and soften'd the stones;—
Lay by these:—
[*Singing*] Sing willow, willow, willow;
Prithee, hie thee; he 'll come anon:—
[*Singing*] Sing all a green willow must be my garland.
Let nobody blame him; his scorn I approve,—
Nay, that 's not next. Hark! who is 't that knocks?

Emil. It 's the wind.

Des. [*Singing*] I call'd my love false love; but what said he then?
Sing willow, willow, willow:
If I court moe women, you 'll couch with moe men
So get thee gone; good night. Mine eyes do itch;
Doth that bode weeping?

Emil. 'Tis neither here nor there.

Des. I have heard it said so. O, these men, these men!
Dost thou in conscience think,—tell me, Emilia,—
That there be women do abuse their husbands
In such gross kind?

Emil. There be some such, no question

Des. Wouldst thou do such a deed for all the world?

Emil. Why, would not you?

Des. No, by this heavenly light!

Emil. Nor I neither by this heavenly light; I might do 't as well i' the dark.

Des. Wouldst thou do such a deed for all the world?

Emil. The world 's a huge thing: it is a great price
For a small vice.

Des. In troth, I think thou wouldst not.

Emil. In troth, I think I should; and undo 't when I had done. Marry, I would not do such a thing for a joint-ring, nor for measures of lawn, nor for gowns, petticoats, nor caps, nor any petty exhibition; but, for the whole world,—why, who would not make her husband a cuckold to make him a monarch? I should venture purgatory for 't.

Des. Beshrew me, if I would do such a wrong
For the whole world.

Emil. Why, the wrong is but a wrong i' the world; and having the world for your labour, 'tis a wrong in your own world, and you might quickly make it right.

Des. I do not think there is any such woman.

Emil. Yes, a dozen; and as many to the vantage as would store the world they played for.
But I do think it is their husbands' faults
If wives do fall: say that they slack their duties
And pour our treasures into foreign laps,
Or else break out in peevish jealousies,
Throwing restraint upon us, or say they strike us,
Or scant our former having in despite,
Why, we have galls, and though we have some grace,
Yet have we some revenge. Let husbands know
Their wives have sense like them: they see and smell
And have their palates both for sweet and sour,
As husbands have. What is it that they do
When they change us for others? Is it sport?
I think it is: and doth affection breed it?
I think it doth: is 't frailty that thus errs?
It is so too: and have not we affections,
Desires for sport, and frailty, as men have?
Then let them use us well: else let them know,
The ills we do, their ills instruct us so.

Des. Good night, good night: heaven me such uses send,
Not to pick bad from bad, but by bad mend! [*Exeunt.*

ACT V—Scene I

Cyprus. A street.

Enter Iago and Roderigo.

Iago. Here, stand behind this bulk; straight will he come:
Wear thy good rapier bare, and put it home:
Quick, quick; fear nothing; I'll be at thy elbow:
It makes us, or it mars us; think on that,
And fix most firm thy resolution.

Rod. Be near at hand; I may miscarry in 't.

Iago. Here, at thy hand: be bold, and take thy stand. [*Retires.*

Rod. I have no great devotion to the deed;

And yet he hath given me satisfying reasons:
'Tis but a man gone. Forth, my sword: he dies.

Iago. I have rubb'd this young quat almost to the sense,
And he grows angry. Now, whether he kill Cassio,
Or Cassio him, or each do kill the other,
Every way makes my gain: live Roderigo,
He calls me to a restitution large
Of gold and jewels that I bobb'd from him,
As gifts to Desdemona:
It must not be: if Cassio do remain,
He hath a daily beauty in his life
That makes me ugly; and besides, the Moor
May unfold me to him; there stand I in much peril:
No, he must die. Be 't so. I hear him coming.

Enter Cassio.

Rod. I know his gait; 'tis he. Villain, thou diest!
[*Makes a pass at Cassio.*

Cas. That thrust had been mine enemy indeed,
But that my coat is better than thou know'st:
I will make proof of thine. [*Draws, and wounds Roderigo.*

Rod. O, I am slain!
[*Iago from behind wounds Cassio in the leg, and exit.*

Cas. I am maim'd for ever. Help, ho! murder! murder! [*Falls.*

Enter Othello.

Oth. The voice of Cassio: Iago keeps his word.

Rod. O, villain that I am!

Oth. It is even so.

Cas. O, help, ho! light! a surgeon!

Oth. 'Tis he. O brave Iago, honest and just,
That hast such noble sense of thy friend's wrong!
Thou teachest me. Minion, your dear lies dead,
And your unblest fate hies: strumpet, I come!
Forth of my heart those charms, thine eyes, are blotted:
Thy bed lust-stain'd shall with lust's blood be spotted. [*Exit.*

Enter Lodovico and Gratiano.

Cas. What, ho! no watch? no passage? murder! murder!

Gra. 'Tis some mischance; the cry is very direful.

Cas. O, help!

Lod. Hark!

Rod. O wretched villain!

Lod. Two or three groan: it is a heavy night:
These may be counterfeits: let 's think 't unsafe
To come into the cry without more help.

Rod. Nobody come? then shall I bleed to death.

Lod. Hark!

Re-enter Iago, with a light.

Gra. Here 's one comes in his shirt, with light and weapons.
Iago. Who 's there? whose noise is this that cries on murder?
Lod. We do not know.
Iago. Did not you hear a cry?
Cas. Here, here! for heaven's sake, help me!
Iago. What 's the matter?
Gra. This is Othello's ancient, as I take it.
Lod. The same indeed; a very valiant fellow.
Iago. What are you here that cry so grievously?
Cas. Iago? O, I am spoil'd, undone by villains!
Give me some help.
Iago. O me, lieutenant! what villains have done this?
Cas. I think that one of them is hereabout,
And cannot make away.
Iago. O treacherous villains?
What are you there? come in and give some help.
[*To Lodovico and Gratiano.*
Rod. O, help me here!
Cas. That 's one of them.
Iago. O murderous slave! O villain!
[*Stabs Roderigo.*
Rod. O damn'd Iago! O inhuman dog!
Iago. Kill men i' the dark! Where be these bloody thieves?
How silent is this town! Ho! murder! murder!
What may you be? are you of good or evil?
Lod. As you shall prove us, praise us.
Iago. Signior Lodovico?
Lod. He, sir.
Iago. I cry you mercy. Here 's Cassio hurt by villains.
Gra. Cassio!
Iago. How is 't, brother?
Cas. My leg is cut in two.
Iago. Marry, heaven forbid!
Light, gentlemen: I 'll bind it with my shirt.

Enter Bianca.

Bian. What is the matter, ho? who is 't that cried?
Iago. Who is 't that cried!
Bian. O my dear Cassio! my sweet Cassio! O Cassio, Cassio, [Cassio!
Iago. O notable strumpet! Cassio, may you suspect
Who they should be that have thus mangled you?
Cas. No.
Gra. I am sorry to find you thus: I have been to seek you.
Iago. Lend me a garter. So. O, for a chair,
To bear him easily hence!

Bian. Alas, he faints! O Cassio, Cassio, Cassio!
Iago. Gentlemen all, I do suspect this trash
To be a party in this injury.
Patience awhile, good Cassio. Come, come;
Lend me a light. Know we this face or no?
Alas, my friend and my dear countryman
Roderigo? no:—yes, sure: O heaven! Roderigo.
Gra. What, of Venice?
Iago. Even he, sir: did you know him?
Gra. Know him! ay.
Iago. Signior Gratiano? I cry you gentle pardon;
These bloody accidents must excuse my manners,
That so neglected you.
Gra. I am glad to see you.
Iago. How do you, Cassio? O, a chair, a chair?
Gra. Roderigo! [the chair:
Iago. He, he, 'tis he. [*A chair brought in.*] O, that's well said;
Some good man bear him carefully from hence;
I'll fetch the general's surgeon. [*To Bianca*] For you, mistress,
Save you your labour. He that lies slain here, Cassio,
Was my dear friend: what malice was between you?
Cas. None in the world; nor do I know the man.
Iago. [*To Bian.*] What, look you pale? O, bear him out o' the air. [*Cassio and Roderigo are borne off.*
Stay you, good gentlemen. Look you pale, mistress?
Do you perceive the gastness of her eye?
Nay, if you stare, we shall hear more anon.
Behold her well; I pray you, look upon her:
Do you see, gentlemen? nay, guiltiness will speak,
Though tongues were out of use.

Enter Emilia.

Emil. 'Las, what's the matter? what's the matter, husband?
Iago. Cassio hath here been set on in the dark
By Roderigo, and fellows that are 'scaped:
He's almost slain, and Roderigo dead.
Emil. Alas, good gentleman! alas, good Cassio!
Iago. This is the fruit of whoring. Prithee, Emilia,
Go know of Cassio where he supp'd to-night.
What, do you shake at that?
Bian. He supp'd at my house; but I therefore shake not.
Iago. O, did he so? I charge you, go with me.
Emil. Fie, fie upon thee, strumpet!
Bian. I am no strumpet; but of life as honest
As you that thus abuse me.
Emil. As I! foh! fie upon thee!

Iago. Kind gentlemen, let 's go see poor Cassio dress'd.
Come, mistress, you must tell 's another tale.
Emilia, run you to the citadel,
And tell my lord and lady what hath happ'd!
Will you go on? I pray. [*Aside*] This is the night
That either makes me or fordoes me quite. [*Exeunt.*

SCENE II

A bedchamber in the castle: Desdemona in bed asleep; a light burning.

Enter Othello.

Oth. It is the cause, it is the cause, my soul:
Let me not name it to you, you chaste stars!
It is the cause. Yet I 'll not shed her blood,
Nor scar that whiter skin of hers than snow
And smooth as monumental alabaster.
Yet she must die, else she 'll betray more men.
Put out the light, and then put out the light:
If I quench thee, thou flaming minister,
I can again thy former light restore,
Should I repent me: but once put out thy light,
Thou cunning'st pattern of excelling nature,
I know not where is that Promethean heat
That can thy light relume. When I have pluck'd the rose,
I cannot give it vital growth again,
It must needs wither: I 'll smell it on the tree. [*Kissing her.*
Ah, balmy breath, that dost almost persuade
Justice to break her sword! One more, one more:
Be thus when thou art dead, and I will kill thee,
And love thee after: once more, and this the last:
So sweet was ne'er so fatal. I must weep,
But they are cruel tears: this sorrow 's heavenly;
It strikes where it doth love. She wakes.
Des. Who 's there? Othello?
Oth. Ay, Desdemona.
Des. Will you come to bed, my lord?
Oth. Have you pray'd to-night, Desdemona?
Des. Ay, my lord.
Oth. If you bethink yourself of any crime
Unreconciled as yet to heaven and grace,
Solicit for it straight.
Des. Alas, my lord, what may you mean by that?
Oth. Well, do it, and be brief; I will walk by:
I would not kill thy unprepared spirit;
No; heaven forfend! I would not kill thy soul.

Des. Talk you of killing?
Oth. Ay, I do.
Des. Then heaven have mercy on me!
Oth. Amen, with all my heart!
Des. If you say so, I hope you will not kill me.
Oth. Hum!
Des. And yet I fear you; for you are fatal then
When your eyes roll so: why I should fear I know not,
Since guiltiness I know not; but yet I feel I fear.
Oth. Think on thy sins.
Des. They are loves I bear to you.
Oth. Ay, and for that thou diest.
Des. That death 's unnatural that kills for loving.
Alas, why gnaw you so your nether lip?
Some bloody passion shakes your very frame:
These are portents; but yet I hope, I hope,
They do not point on me.
Oth. Peace, and be still!
Des. I will so. What 's the matter?
Oth. That handkerchief which I so loved and gave thee
Thou gavest to Cassio.
Des. No, by my life and soul!
Send for the man, and ask him.
Oth. Sweet soul, take heed,
Take heed of perjury; thou art on thy death-bed.
Des. Ay, but not yet to die.
Oth. Yes, presently:
Therefore confess thee freely of thy sin;
For to deny each article with oath
Cannot remove nor choke the strong conception
That I do groan withal. Thou art to die.
Des. Then Lord have mercy on me!
Oth. I say, amen.
Des. And have you mercy too! I never did
Offend you in my life; never loved Cassio
But with such general warranty of heaven
As I might love: I never gave him token.
Oth. By heaven, I saw my handkerchief in 's hand.
O perjured woman! thou dost stone my heart,
And makest me call what I intend to do
A murder, which I thought a sacrifice:
I saw the handkerchief.
Des. He found it then;
I never gave it him: send for him hither;
Let him confess a truth.

Oth. He hath confess'd.
Des. What, my lord?
Oth. That he hath used thee.
Des. How? unlawfully?
Oth. Ay.
Des. He will not say so.
Oth. No, his mouth is stopp'd;
Honest Iago hath ta'en order for 't.
Des. O, my fear interprets! what, is he dead?
Oth. Had all his hairs been lives, my great revenge
Had stomach for them all.
Des. Alas, he is betray'd, and I undone!
Oth. Out, strumpet! weep'st thou for him to my face?
Des. O, banish me, my lord, but kill me not!
Oth. Down, strumpet!
Des. Kill me to-morrow; let me live to-night!
Oth. Nay, if you strive,—
Des. But half an hour!
Oth. Being done, there is no pause.
Des. But while I say one prayer!
Oth. It is too late. [*He stifles her.*
Emil. [*Within*] My lord, my lord! what, ho! my lord, my lord!
Oth. What noise is this? Not dead? not yet quite dead?
I that am cruel am yet merciful;
I would not have thee linger in thy pain:
So, so.
Emil. [*Within*] What, ho! my lord, my lord!
Oth. Who 's there?
Emil. [*Within*] O, good my lord, I would speak a word with you!
Oth. Yes: 'tis Emilia. By and by. She 's dead.
'Tis like she comes to speak of Cassio's death.
The noise was here. Ha! no more moving?
Still as the grave. Shall she come in? were 't good?
I think she stirs again. No. What 's best to do?
If she come in, she 'll sure speak to my wife:
My wife! my wife! what wife? I have no wife.
O, insupportable! O heavy hour!
Methinks it should be now a huge eclipse
Of sun and moon, and that the affrighted globe
Should yawn at alteration.
Emil. [*Within*] I do beseech you
That I may speak with you, O, good my lord!
Oth. I had forgot thee: O, come in, Emilia.
Soft; by and by. Let me the curtains draw.

Where art thou? [*Unlocks the door.*

Enter Emilia.

What 's the matter with thee now?

Emil. O, my good lord, yonder 's foul murders done!
Oth. What, now?
Emil. But now, my lord.
Oth. It is the very error of the moon;
She comes more nearer earth than she was wont
And makes men mad.
Emil. Cassio, my lord, hath kill'd a young Venetian
Call'd Roderigo.
Oth. Roderigo kill'd!
And Cassio kill'd!
Emil. No, Cassio is not kill'd.
Oth. Not Cassio kill'd! then murder 's out of tune.
And sweet revenge grows harsh.
Des. O, falsely, falsely murder'd!
Emil. Alas, what cry is that?
Oth. That! what?
Emil. Out, and alas! that was my lady's voice.
Help! help, ho! help! O lady, speak again!
Sweet Desdemona! O sweet mistress, speak!
Des. A guiltless death I die.
Emil. O, who hath done this deed?
Des. Nobody; I myself. Farewell:
Commend me to my kind lord: O, farewell! [*Dies.*
Oth. Why, how should she be murder'd?
Emil. Alas, who knows?
Oth. You heard her say herself, It was not I.
Emil. She said so: I must needs report the truth.
Oth. She 's like a liar gone to burning hell:
'Twas I that kill'd her.
Emil. O, the more angel she,
And you the blacker devil!
Oth. She turn'd to folly, and she was a whore.
Emil. Thou dost belie her, and thou art a devil.
Oth. She was false as water.
Emil. Thou art rash as fire, to say
That she was false: O, she was heavenly true!
Oth. Cassio did top her; ask thy husband else.
O, I were damn'd beneath all depth in hell,
But that I did proceed upon just grounds
To this extremity. Thy husband knew it all.
Emil. My husband!
Oth. Thy husband.

Emil. That she was false to wedlock?
Oth. Ay, with Cassio. Nay, had she been true,
If heaven would make me such another world
Of one entire and perfect chrysolite,
I 'ld not have sold her for it.
Emil. My husband!
Oth. Ay, 'twas he that told me first:
An honest man he is, and hates the slime
That sticks on filthy deeds.
Emil. My husband!
Oth. What needs this iteration, woman? I say thy husband.
Emil. O mistress, villany hath made mocks with love!
My husband say that she was false!
Oth. He, woman;
I say thy husband: dost understand the word?
My friend, thy husband, honest, honest Iago.
Emil. If he say so, may his pernicious soul
Rot half a grain a day! he lies to the heart:
She was too fond of her most filthy bargain.
Oth. Ha!
Emil. Do thy worst:
This deed of thine is no more worthy heaven
Than thou wast worthy her.
Oth. Peace, you were best.
Emil. Thou hast not half that power to do me harm
As I have to be hurt. O gull! O dolt!
As ignorant as dirt! thou hast done a deed—
I care not for thy sword; I'll make thee known,
Though I lost twenty lives. Help! help, ho! help
The Moor hath kill'd my mistress! Murder! murder

Enter Montano, Gratiano, Iago, and others.

Mon. What is the matter? How now, general!
Emil. O, are you come, Iago? you have done well,
That men must lay their murders on your neck.
Gra. What is the matter?
Emil. Disprove this villain, if thou be'st a man:
He says thou told'st him that his wife was false:
I know thou didst not, thou 'rt not such a villain.
Speak, for my heart is full.
Iago. I told him what I thought, and told no more
Than what he found himself was apt and true.
Emil. But did you ever tell him she was false?
Iago. I did.
Emil. You told a lie, an odious, damned lie;
Upon my soul, a lie, a wicked lie!

She false with Cassio! Did you say with Cassio?
Iago. With Cassio, mistress. Go to, charm your tongue.
Emil. I will not charm my tongue; I am bound to speak:
My mistress here lies murder'd in her bed,—
All. O heavens forfend!
Emil. And your reports have set the murder on.
Oth. Nay, stare not, masters: it is true indeed.
Gra. 'Tis a strange truth.
Mon. O monstrous act!
Emil. Villany, villany, villany!
I think upon't: I think: I smell't: O villany!
I thought so then: I'll kill myself for grief:
O villany, villany!
Iago. What, are you mad? I charge you, get you home.
Emil. Good gentlemen, let me have leave to speak:
'Tis proper I obey him, but not now.
Perchance, Iago, I will ne'er go home.
Oth. O! O! O! [*Falling on the bed.*
Emil. Nay, lay thee down and roar;
For thou hast kill'd the sweetest innocent
That e'er did lift up eye.
Oth. [*Rising*] O, she was foul!
I scarce did know you, uncle: there lies your niece,
Whose breath indeed these hands have newly stopp'd:
I know this act shows horrible and grim.
Gra. Poor Desdemona! I am glad thy father's dead:
Thy match was mortal to him, and pure grief
Shore his old thread in twain: did he live now,
This sight would make him do a desperate turn,
Yea, curse his better angel from his side,
And fall to reprobation.
Oth. 'Tis pitiful; but yet Iago knows
That she with Cassio hath the act of shame
A thousand times committed; Cassio confess'd it:
And she did gratify his amorous works
With that recognizance and pledge of love
Which I first gave her; I saw it in his hand:
It was a handkerchief, an antique token
My father gave my mother.
Emil. O heaven! O heavenly powers!
Iago. 'Zounds! hold your peace.
Emil. 'Twill out, 'twill out. I peace!
No, I will speak as liberal as the north:
Let heaven and men and devils, let them all,
All, all, cry shame against me, yet I'll speak.

Iago. Be wise, and get you home.
Emil. I will not.
[*Iago offers to stab Emilia.*
Gra. Fie!
Your sword upon a woman!
Emil. O thou dull Moor! that handkerchief thou speak'st of
I found by fortune and did give my husband;
For often with a solemn earnestness,
More than indeed belong'd to such a trifle,
He begg'd of me to steal it.
Iago. Villanous whore!
Emil. She gives it Cassio! no, alas, I found it,
And I did give 't my husband.
Iago. Filth, thou liest!
Emil. By heaven, I do not, I do not, gentlemen.
O murderous coxcomb! what should such a fool
Do with so good a wife?
Oth. Are there no stones in heaven
But what serve for the thunder? Precious villain!
[*He runs at Iago: Iago, from behind, stabs Emilia, and exit.*
Gra. The woman falls; sure, he hath kill'd his wife.
Emil. Ay, ay: O, lay me by my mistress' side.
Gra. He 's gone, but his wife 's kill'd.
Mon. 'Tis a notorious villain. Take you this weapon,
Which I have here recover'd from the Moor:
Come, guard the door without; let him not pass,
But kill him rather. I 'll after that same villain,
For 'tis a damned slave.
[*Exeunt all but Othello and Emilia.*
Oth. I am not valiant neither,
But every puny whipster gets my sword.
But why should honour outlive honesty?
Let it go all.
Emil. What did thy song bode, lady?
Hark, canst thou hear me? I will play the swan,
And die in music. [*Singing*] Willow, willow, willow.
Moor, she was chaste; she loved thee, cruel Moor;
So come my soul to bliss, as I speak true;
So speaking as I think, I die, I die. [*Dies.*
Oth. I have another weapon in this chamber;
It is a sword of Spain, the ice-brook's temper.—
O, here it is. Uncle, I must come forth.
Gra. [*Within*] If thou attempt it, it will cost thee dear:
Thou hast no weapon, and perforce must suffer.
Oth. Look in upon me then, and speak with me,

Or naked as I am, I will assault thee.

Re-enter Gratiano.

Gra. What is the matter?

Oth. Behold, I have a weapon;
A better never did itself sustain
Upon a soldier's thigh: I have seen the day
That with this little arm and this good sword
I have made my way through more impediments
Than twenty times your stop: but, O vain boast!
Who can control his fate? 'tis not so now.
Be not afraid, though you do see me weapon'd;
Here is my journey's end, here is my butt
And very sea-mark of my utmost sail.
Do you go back dismay'd? 'tis a lost fear:
Man but a rush against Othello's breast,
And he retires. Where should Othello go?
Now, how dost thou look now? O ill-starr'd wench!
Pale as thy smock! when we shall meet at compt,
This look of thine will hurl my soul from heaven,
And fiends will snatch at it. Cold, cold, my girl!
Even like thy chastity. O cursed slave!
Whip me, ye devils,
From the possession of this heavenly sight!
Blow me about in winds! roast me in sulphur!
Wash me in steep-down gulfs of liquid fire!
O Desdemona! Desdemona! dead!
Oh! Oh! Oh!

Enter Lodovico, Montano, Cassio carried in a chair, and Officers with Iago, prisoner.

Lod. Where is this rash and most unfortunate man?

Oth. That's he that was Othello: here I am.

Lod. Where is that viper? bring the villain forth.

Oth. I look down towards his feet; but that's a fable.
If that thou be'st a devil, I cannot kill thee. [*Wounds Iago.*

Lod. Wrench his sword from him.

Iago. I bleed, sir, but not kill'd.

Oth. I am not sorry neither: I'ld have thee live;
For, in my sense, 'tis happiness to die.

Lod. O thou Othello, that wert once so good,
Fall'n in the practice of a damned slave,
What shall be said to thee?

Oth. Why, any thing:
An honourable murderer, if you will;
For nought did I in hate, but all in honour.

Lod. This wretch hath part confess'd his villany:

Did you and he consent in Cassio's death?
Oth. Ay.
Cas. Dear general, I never gave you cause.
Oth. I do believe it, and I ask your pardon.
Will you, I pray, demand that demi-devil
Why he hath thus ensnared my soul and body?
Iago. Demand me nothing; what you know, you know:
From this time forth I never will speak word.
Lod. What, not to pray?
Gra. Torments will ope your lips.
Oth. Well, thou dost best.
Lod. Sir, you shall understand what hath befall'n,
Which, as I think, you know not. Here is a letter
Found in the pocket of the slain Roderigo,
And here another: the one of them imports
The death of Cassio to be undertook
By Roderigo.
Oth. O villain!
Cas. Most heathenish and most gross!
Lod. Now here 's another discontented paper,
Found in his pocket too; and this, it seems,
Roderigo meant to have sent this damned villain;
But that, belike, Iago in the interim
Came in and satisfied him.
Oth. O the pernicious caitiff!
How came you, Cassio, by that handkerchief
That was my wife's?
Cas. I found it in my chamber:
And he himself confess'd but even now
That there he dropp'd it for a special purpose
Which wrought to his desire.
Oth. O fool! fool! fool!
Cas. There is besides in Roderigo's letter,
How he upbraids Iago, that he made him
Brave me upon the watch; whereon it came
That I was cast: and even but now he spake
After long seeming dead, Iago hurt him,
Iago set him on.
Lod. You must forsake this room, and go with us:
Your power and your command is taken off,
And Cassio rules in Cyprus. For this slave,
If there be any cunning cruelty
That can torment him much and hold him long
It shall be his. You shall close prisoner rest,
Till that the nature of your fault be known

To the Venetian state. Come, bring away.
Oth. Soft you; a word or two before you go.
I have done the state some service, and they know 't.
No more of that. I pray you, in your letters,
When you shall these unlucky deeds relate,
Speak of me as I am; nothing extenuate,
Nor set down aught in malice: then must you speak
Of one that loved not wisely but too well;
Of one not easily jealous, but, being wrought,
Perplex'd in the extreme; of one whose hand,
Like the base Indian, threw a pearl away
Richer than all his tribe; of one whose subdued eyes,
Albeit unused to the melting mood,
Drop tears as fast as the Arabian trees
Their medicinal gum. Set you down this;
And say besides, that in Aleppo once,
Where a malignant and a turban'd Turk
Beat a Venetian and traduced the state,
I took by the throat the circumcised dog
And smote him, thus. [*Stabs himself.*
Lod. O bloody period!
Gra. All that 's spoke is marr'd.
Oth. I kiss'd thee ere I kill'd thee: no way but this,
Killing myself, to die upon a kiss.
[*Falls on the bed, and dies.*
Cas. This did I fear, but thought he had no weapon;
For he was great of heart.
Lod. [*To Iago*] O Spartan dog,
More fell than anguish, hunger, or the sea!
Look on the tragic loading of this bed;
This is thy work: the object poisons sight;
Let it be hid. Gratiano, keep the house,
And seize upon the fortunes of the Moor,
For they succeed on you. To you, lord governor,
Remains the censure of this hellish villain,
The time, the place, the torture: O, enforce it!
Myself will straight aboard, and to the state
This heavy act with heavy heart relate. [*Exeunt.*

ANTONY AND CLEOPATRA

DRAMATIS PERSONÆ

ANTONY, OCTAVIUS CÆSAR, LEPIDUS, *triumvirs.*
SEXTUS POMPEIUS.
DOMITIUS ENOBARBUS, VENTIDIUS, EROS, SCARUS, DERCETAS, DEMETRIUS, PHILO, *friends to Antony.*
MÆCENAS, AGRIPPA, DOLABELLA, PROCULEIUS, THYREUS, GALLUS, *friends to Cæsar.*
MENAS, MENECRATES, *friends to Sextus Pompeius.*
VARRIUS, *friend to Sextus Pompeius.*
TAURUS, *lieutenant-general to Cæsar.*
CANIDIUS, *lieutenant-general to Antony.*
SILIUS, *an officer in Ventidius's army.*
EUPHRONIUS, *an ambassador from Antony to Cæsar.*
ALEXAS, MARDIAN, *a eunuch,* SELEUCUS, DIOMEDES, *attendants on Cleopatra.*
A Soothsayer.
A Clown.

CLEOPATRA, *queen of Egypt.*
OCTAVIA, *sister to Cæsar, and wife to Antony.*
CHARMIAN, IRAS, *attendants on Cleopatra.*

Officers, Soldiers, Messengers, and other Attendants.
SCENE: *In several parts of the Roman Empire.*

ACT I—SCENE I

Alexandria. A room in Cleopatra's palace.

Enter Demetrius and Philo.

Phi. Nay, but this dotage of our general's
O'erflows the measure: those his goodly eyes,
That o'er the files and musters of the war
Have glow'd like plated Mars, now bend, now turn,
The office and devotion of their view
Upon a tawny front: his captain's heart,
Which in the scuffles of great fights hath burst
The buckles on his breast, reneges all temper,
And is become the bellows and the fan
To cool a gipsy's lust.

Flourish. Enter Antony, Cleopatra, her Ladies, the train, with Eunuchs fanning her.

Look, where they come:
Take but good note, and you shall see in him
The triple pillar of the world transform'd
Into a strumpet's fool: behold and see.

Cleo. If it be love indeed, tell me how much.
Ant. There 's beggary in the love that can be reckon'd.
Cleo. I 'll set a bourn how far to be beloved.
Ant. Then must thou needs find out new heaven, new earth.

Enter an Attendant.

Att. News, my good lord, from Rome.
Ant. Grates me: the sum.

Cleo. Nay, hear them, Antony:
Fulvia perchance is angry; or, who knows
If the scarce-bearded Cæsar have not sent
His powerful mandate to you, 'Do this, or this
Take in that kingdom, and enfranchise that;
Perform 't, or else we damn thee.'
Ant. How, my love!
Cleo. Perchance! nay, and most like:
You must not stay here longer, your dismission
Is come from Cæsar; therefore hear it, Antony.
Where 's Fulvia's process? Cæsar's I would say? both?
Call in the messengers. As I am Egypt's queen,
Thou blushest, Antony, and that blood of thine
Is Cæsar's homager: else so thy cheek pays shame
When shrill-tongued Fulvia scolds. The messengers!
Ant. Let Rome in Tiber melt, and the wide arch
Of the ranged empire fall! Here is my space.
Kingdoms are clay: our dungy earth alike
Feeds beast as man: the nobleness of life
Is to do thus; when such a mutual pair [*Embracing.*
And such a twain can do 't, in which I bind,
On pain of punishment, the world to weet
We stand up peerless.
Cleo. Excellent falsehood!
Why did he marry Fulvia, and not love her?
I 'll seem the fool I am not; Antony
Will be himself.
Ant. But stirr'd by Cleopatra.
Now, for the love of Love and her soft hours,
Let 's not confound the time with conference harsh:
There 's not a minute of our lives should stretch
Without some pleasure now. What sport to-night?
Cleo. Hear the ambassadors.
Ant. Fie, wrangling queen
Whom every thing becomes, to chide, to laugh,
To weep; whose every passion fully strives
To make itself, in thee, fair and admired!
No messenger but thine; and all alone
To-night we 'll wander through the streets and note
The qualities of people. Come, my queen;
Last night you did desire it. Speak not to us.
[*Exeunt Ant. and Cleo. with their train.*
Dem. Is Cæsar with Antonius prized so slight?
Phi. Sir, sometimes, when he is not Antony,
He comes too short of that great property

Which still should go with Antony.

Dem. I am full sorry
That he approves the common liar, who
Thus speaks of him at Rome: but I will hope
Of better deeds to-morrow. Rest you happy! [*Exeunt.*

Scene II

The same. Another room.

Enter Charmian, Iras, Alexas, and a Soothsayer.

Char. Lord Alexas, sweet Alexas, most any thing Alexas, almost most absolute Alexas, where 's the soothsayer that you praised so to the queen? O, that I knew this husband, which, you say, must charge his horns with garlands!

Alex. Soothsayer!

Sooth. Your will?

Char. Is this the man? Is 't you, sir, that know things?

Sooth. In nature's infinite book of secrecy
A little I can read.

Alex. Show him your hand.

Enter Enobarbus.

Eno. Bring in the banquet quickly; wine enough
Cleopatra's health to drink.

Char. Good sir, give me good fortune.

Sooth. I make not, but foresee.

Char. Pray then, foresee me one.

Sooth. You shall be yet far fairer than you are.

Char. He means in flesh.

Iras. No, you shall paint when you are old.

Char. Wrinkles forbid!

Alex. Vex not his prescience; be attentive.

Char. Hush!

Sooth. You shall be more beloving than beloved.

Char. I had rather heat my liver with drinking.

Alex. Nay, hear him.

Char. Good now, some excellent fortune! Let me be married to three kings in a forenoon, and widow them all: let me have a child at fifty, to whom Herod of Jewry may do homage: find me to marry me with Octavius Cæsar, and companion me with my mistress.

Sooth. You shall outlive the lady whom you serve.

Char. O excellent! I love long life better than figs.

Sooth. You have seen and proved a fairer former fortune
Than that which is to approach.

Char. Then belike my children shall have no names: prithee, how many boys and wenches must I have?

Sooth. If every of your wishes had a womb,
And fertile every wish, a million.

Char. Out, fool! I forgive thee for a witch.

Alex. You think none but your sheets are privy to your wishes.

Char. Nay, come, tell Iras hers.

Alex. We 'll know all our fortunes.

Eno. Mine and most of our fortunes to-night shall be—drunk [to bed.

Iras. There 's a palm presages chastity, if nothing else.

Char. E'en as the o'erflowing Nilus presageth famine.

Iras. Go, you wild bedfellow, you cannot soothsay.

Char. Nay, if an oily palm be not a fruitful prognostication, I cannot scratch mine ear. Prithee, tell her but a worky-day [fortune.

Sooth. Your fortunes are alike.

Iras. But how, but how? give me particulars.

Sooth. I have said.

Iras. Am I not an inch of fortune better than she?

Char. Well, if you were but an inch of fortune better than I, where would you choose it?

Iras. Not in my husband's nose.

Char. Our worser thoughts heavens mend! Alexas,—come, his fortune, his fortune! O, let him marry a woman that cannot go, sweet Isis, I beseech thee! and let her die too, and give him a worse! and let worse follow worse, till the worst of all follow him laughing to his grave, fifty-fold a cuckold! Good Isis, hear me this prayer, though thou deny me a matter of more weight; good Isis, I beseech thee!

Iras. Amen. Dear goddess, hear that prayer of the people! for, as it is a heart-breaking to see a handsome man loose-wived, so it is a deadly sorrow to behold a foul knave uncuckolded: therefore, dear Isis, keep decorum, and fortune him accordingly!

Char. Amen.

Alex. Lo, now, if it lay in their hands to make me a cuckold, they would make themselves whores, but they 'ld do 't!

Eno. Hush! here comes Antony.

Char. Not he; the queen.

Enter Cleopatra.

Cleo. Saw you my lord?

Eno. No, lady.

Cleo. Was he not here?

Char. No, madam.

Cleo. He was disposed to mirth; but on the sudden
A Roman thought has struck him. Enobarbus!

Eno. Madam?

Cleo. Seek him, and bring him hither. Where 's Alexas?

Alex. Here, at your service. My lord approaches.
Cleo. We will not look upon him: go with us. [*Exeunt.*

Enter Antony with a Messenger and Attendants.

Mess. Fulvia thy wife first came into the field.
Ant. Against my brother Lucius?
Mess. Ay:
But soon that war had end, and the time's state
Made friends of them, jointing their force 'gainst Cæsar,
Whose better issue in the war from Italy
Upon the first encounter drave them.
Ant. Well, what worst?
Mess. The nature of bad news infects the teller.
Ant. When it concerns the fool or coward. On:
Things that are past are done with me. 'Tis thus;
Who tells me true, though in his tale lie death,
I hear him as he flatter'd.
Mess. Labienus—
This is stiff news—hath with his Parthian force
Extended Asia from Euphrates,
His conquering banner shook from Syria
To Lydia and to Ionia,
Whilst—
Ant. Antony, thou wouldst say,—
Mess. O, my lord!
Ant. Speak to me home, mince not the general tongue:
Name Cleopatra as she is call'd in Rome;
Rail thou in Fulvia's phrase, and taunt my faults
With such full license as both truth and malice
Have power to utter. O, then we bring forth weeds
When our quick minds lie still, and our ills told us
Is as our earing. Fare thee well awhile.
Mess. At your noble pleasure. [*Exit.*
Ant. From Sicyon, ho, the news! Speak there!
First Att. The man from Sicyon, is there such an one?
Sec. Att. He stays upon your will.
Ant. Let him appear.
These strong Egyptian fetters I must break,
Or lose myself in dotage.

Enter another Messenger.

What are you?
Sec. Mess. Fulvia thy wife is dead.
Ant. Where died she?
Sec. Mess. In Sicyon:
Her length of sickness, with what else more serious
Importeth thee to know, this bears. [*Gives a letter.*

Ant. Forbear me. [*Exit Sec. Messenger.*
There 's a great spirit gone! Thus did I desire it:
What our contempts do often hurl from us,
We wish it ours again; the present pleasure,
By revolution lowering, does become
The opposite of itself: she 's good, being gone;
The hand could pluck her back that shoved her on.
I must from this enchanting queen break off:
Ten thousand harms, more than the ills I know,
My idleness doth hatch. How now! Enobarbus!

Re-enter Enobarbus.

Eno. What 's your pleasure, sir?

Ant. I must with haste from hence.

Eno. Why then we kill all our women. We see how mortal an unkindness is to them; if they suffer our departure, death 's the word.

Ant. I must be gone.

Eno. Under a compelling occasion let women die: it were pity to cast them away for nothing; though, between them and a great cause, they should be esteemed nothing. Cleopatra, catching but the least noise of this, dies instantly; I have seen her die twenty times upon far poorer moment: I do think there is mettle in death, which commits some loving act upon her, she hath such a celerity in dying.

Ant. She is cunning past man's thought.

Eno. Alack, sir, no; her passions are made of nothing but the finest part of pure love: we cannot call her winds and waters sighs and tears; they are greater storms and tempests than almanacs can report: this cannot be cunning in her; if it be, she makes a shower of rain as well as Jove.

Ant. Would I had never seen her!

Eno. O, sir, you had then left unseen a wonderful piece of work; which not to have been blest withal would have discredited your travel.

Ant. Fulvia is dead.

Eno. Sir?

Ant. Fulvia is dead.

Eno. Fulvia!

Ant. Dead.

Eno. Why, sir, give the gods a thankful sacrifice. When it pleaseth their deities to take the wife of a man from him, it shows to man the tailors of the earth, comforting therein, that when old robes are worn out there are members to make new. If there were no more women but Fulvia, then had you indeed a cut, and the case to be lamented; this grief is crowned with consolation; your old smock brings forth a new petticoat: and indeed the tears live in an onion that should water this sorrow.

Ant. The business she hath broached in the state cannot endure my absence.

Eno. And the business you have broached here cannot be without you; especially that of Cleopatra's, which wholly depends on your abode.

Ant. No more light answers. Let our officers
Have notice what we purpose. I shall break
The cause of our expedience to the queen
And get her leave to part. For not alone
The death of Fulvia, with more urgent touches,
Do strongly speak to us, but the letters too
Of many our contriving friends in Rome
Petition us at home: Sextus Pompeius
Hath given the dare to Cæsar and commands
The empire of the sea: our slippery people,
Whose love is never link'd to the deserver
Till his deserts are past, begin to throw
Pompey the Great and all his dignities
Upon his son; who, high in name and power,
Higher than both in blood and life, stands up
For the main soldier: whose quality, going on,
The sides o' the world may danger. Much is breeding,
Which, like the courser's hair, hath yet but life
And not a serpent's poison. Say, our pleasure,
To such whose place is under us, requires
Our quick remove from hence.

Eno. I shall do 't. [*Exeunt.*

Scene III

The same. Another room.

Enter Cleopatra, Charmian, Iras, and Alexas.

Cleo. Where is he?

Char. I did not see him since.

Cleo. See where he is, who 's with him, what he does:
I did not send you: if you find him sad,
Say I am dancing; if in mirth, report
That I am sudden sick: quick, and return. [*Exit Alexas.*

Char. Madam, methinks, if you did love him dearly,
You do not hold the method to enforce
The like from him.

Cleo. What should I do, I do not?

Char. In each thing give him way, cross him in nothing.

Cleo. Thou teachest like a fool: the way to lose him.
Char. Tempt him not so too far; I wish, forbear:
In time we hate that which we often fear.
But here comes Antony.

Enter Antony.

Cleo. I am sick and sullen.
Ant. I am sorry to give breathing to my purpose,—
Cleo. Help me away, dear Charmian; I shall fall:
It cannot be thus long, the sides of nature
Will not sustain it.
Ant. Now, my dearest queen,—
Cleo. Pray you, stand farther from me.
Ant. What 's the matter?
Cleo. I know, by that same eye, there 's some good news.
What says the married woman? You may go:
Would she had never given you leave to come!
Let her not say 'tis I that keep you here,
I have no power upon you; hers you are.
Ant. The gods best know—
Cleo. O, never was there queen
So mightily betray'd! yet at the first
I saw the treasons planted.
Ant. Cleopatra,—
Cleo. Why should I think you can be mine and true,
Though you in swearing shake the throned gods,
Who have been false to Fulvia? Riotous madness,
To be entangled with those mouth-made vows,
Which break themselves in swearing!
Ant. Most sweet queen,—
Cleo. Nay, pray you, seek no colour for your going,
But bid farewell, and go: when you sued staying,
Then was the time for words: no going then;
Eternity was in our lips and eyes,
Bliss in our brows' bent, none our parts so poor
But was a race of heaven: they are so still,
Or thou, the greatest soldier of the world,
Art turn'd the greatest liar.
Ant. How now, lady!
Cleo. I would I had thy inches; thou shouldst know
There were a heart in Egypt.
Ant. Hear me, queen:
The strong necessity of time commands
Our services awhile: but my full heart
Remains in use with you. Our Italy
Shines o'er with civil swords: Sextus Pompeius

Makes his approaches to the port of Rome:
Equality of two domestic powers
Breed scrupulous faction: the hated, grown to strength,
Are newly grown to love: the condemn'd Pompey,
Rich in his father's honour, creeps apace
Into the hearts of such as have not thrived
Upon the present state, whose numbers threaten;
And quietness grown sick of rest would purge
By any desperate change. My more particular,
And that which most with you should safe my going,
Is Fulvia's death.

Cleo. Though age from folly could not give me freedom,
It does from childishness: can Fulvia die?

Ant. She's dead, my queen:
Look here, and at thy sovereign leisure read
The garboils she awaked: at the last, best;
See when and where she died.

Cleo. O most false love!
Where be the sacred vials thou shouldst fill
With sorrowful water? Now I see, I see,
In Fulvia's death, how mine received shall be.

Ant. Quarrel no more, but be prepared to know
The purposes I bear, which are, or cease,
As you shall give the advice. By the fire
That quickens Nilus' slime, I go from hence
Thy soldier, servant, making peace or war
As thou affect'st.

Cleo. Cut my lace, Charmian, come;
But let it be: I am quickly ill and well,
So Antony loves.

Ant. My precious queen, forbear;
And give true evidence to his love, which stands
An honourable trial.

Cleo. So Fulvia told me.
I prithee, turn aside and weep for her;
Then bid adieu to me, and say the tears
Belong to Egypt: good now, play one scene
Of excellent dissembling, and let it look
Like perfect honour.

Ant. You'll heat my blood: no more.

Cleo. You can do better yet; but this is meetly.

Ant. Now, by my sword,—

Cleo. And target. Still he mends;
But this is not the best. Look, prithee, Charmian,
How this Herculean Roman does become

The carriage of his chafe.
Ant. I'll leave you, lady.
Cleo. Courteous lord, one word.
Sir, you and I must part, but that's not it:
Sir, you and I have loved, but there's not it:
That you know well: something it is I would,—
O, my oblivion is a very Antony,
And I am all forgotten.
Ant. But that your royalty
Holds idleness your subject, I should take you
For idleness itself.
Cleo. 'Tis sweating labour
To bear such idleness so near the heart
As Cleopatra this. But, sir, forgive me,
Since my becomings kill me when they do not
Eye well to you. Your honour calls you hence;
Therefore be deaf to my unpitied folly,
And all the gods go with you! Upon your sword
Sit laurel victory! and smooth success
Be strew'd before your feet!
Ant. Let us go. Come;
Our separation so abides and flies,
That thou residing here go'st yet with me,
And I hence fleeing here remain with thee.
Away! [*Exeunt.*

Scene IV

Rome. Cæsar's house.

Enter Octavius Cæsar, reading a letter, Lepidus, and their train.

Cæs. You may see, Lepidus, and henceforth know,
It is not Cæsar's natural vice to hate
Our great competitor: from Alexandria
This is the news: he fishes, drinks and wastes
The lamps of night in revel: is not more manlike
Than Cleopatra, nor the queen of Ptolemy
More womanly than he: hardly gave audience, or
Vouchsafed to think he had partners: you shall find there
A man who is the abstract of all faults
That all men follow.
Lep. I must not think there are
Evils enow to darken all his goodness:
His faults in him seem as the spots of heaven
More fiery by night's blackness, hereditary
Rather than purchased, what he cannot change

Than what he chooses.
Cæs. You are too indulgent. Let us grant it is not
Amiss to tumble on the bed of Ptolemy,
To give a kingdom for a mirth, to sit
And keep the turn of tippling with a slave,
To reel the streets at noon and stand the buffet
With knaves that smell of sweat: say this becomes him,—
As his composure must be rare indeed
Whom these things cannot blemish,—yet must Antony
No way excuse his soils, when we do bear
So great weight in his lightness. If he fill'd
His vacancy with his voluptuousness,
Full surfeits and the dryness of his bones
Call on him for 't: but to confound such time
That drums him from his sport and speaks as loud
As his own state and ours, 'tis to be chid
As we rate boys, who, being mature in knowledge,
Pawn their experience to their present pleasure,
And so rebel to judgement.

Enter a Messenger.

Lep. Here 's more news.
Mess. Thy biddings have been done; and every hour,
Most noble Cæsar, shalt thou have report
How 'tis abroad. Pompey is strong at sea;
And it appears he is beloved of those
That only have fear'd Cæsar: to the ports
The discontents repair, and men's reports
Give him much wrong'd.
Cæs. I should have known no less:
It had been taught us from the primal state,
That he which is was wish'd until he were;
And the ebb'd man, ne'er loved till ne'er worth love,
Comes dear'd by being lack'd. This common body,
Like to a vagabond flag upon the stream,
Goes to and back, lackeying the varying tide,
To rot itself with motion.
Mess. Cæsar, I bring thee word,
Menecrates and Menas, famous pirates,
Make the sea serve them, which they ear and wound
With keels of every kind; many hot inroads
They make in Italy; the borders maritime
Lack blood to think on 't, and flush youth revolt:
No vessel can peep forth, but 'tis as soon
Taken as seen; for Pompey's name strikes more

Than could his war resisted.

Cæs. Antony,
Leave thy lascivious wassails. When thou once
Wast beaten from Modena, where thou slew'st
Hirtius and Pansa, consuls, at thy heel
Did famine follow; whom thou fought'st against
Though daintily brought up, with patience more
Than savages could suffer: thou didst drink
The stale of horses and the gilded puddle
Which beasts would cough at: thy palate then did deign
The roughest berry on the rudest hedge;
Yea, like the stag, when snow the pasture sheets,
The barks of trees thou browsedst. On the Alps
It is reported thou didst eat strange flesh,
Which some did die to look on: and all this—
It wounds thine honour that I speak it now—
Was borne so like a soldier that thy cheek
So much as lank'd not.

Lep. 'Tis pity of him.

Cæs. Let his shames quickly
Drive him to Rome: 'tis time we twain
Did show ourselves i' the field; and to that end
Assemble we immediate council: Pompey
Thrives in our idleness.

Lep. To-morrow, Cæsar,
I shall be furnish'd to inform you rightly
Both what by sea and land I can be able
To front this present time.

Cæs. Till which encounter,
It is my business too. Farewell.

Lep. Farewell, my lord: what you shall know meantime
Of stirs abroad, I shall beseech you, sir,
To let me be partaker.

Cæs. Doubt not, sir;
I knew it for my bond. [*Exeunt.*

Scene V

Alexandria. Cleopatra's palace.

Enter Cleopatra, Charmian, Iras, and Mardian.

Cleo. Charmian!

Char. Madam?

Cleo. Ha, ha!
Give me to drink mandragora.

Char. Why, madam?

Cleo. That I might sleep out this great gap of time
My Antony is away.
Char. You think of him too much.
Cleo. O, 'tis treason!
Char. Madam, I trust, not so.
Cleo. Thou, eunuch Mardian!
Mar. What 's your highness' pleasure?
Cleo. Not now to hear thee sing; I take no pleasure
In aught an eunuch has: 'tis well for thee,
That, being unseminar'd, thy freer thoughts
May not fly forth of Egypt. Hast thou affections?
Mar. Yes, gracious madam.
Cleo. Indeed!
Mar. Not in deed, madam; for I can do nothing
But what indeed is honest to be done:
Yet have I fierce affections, and think
What Venus did with Mars.
Cleo. O Charmian,
Where think'st thou he is now? Stands he, or sits he?
Or does he walk? or is he on his horse?
O happy horse, to bear the weight of Antony!
Do bravely, horse! for wot'st thou whom thou movest?
The demi-Atlas of this earth, the arm
And burgonet of men. He 's speaking now,
Or murmuring, 'Where 's my serpent of old Nile?'
For so he calls me: now I feed myself
With most delicious poison. Think on me,
That am with Phœbus' amorous pinches black
And wrinkled deep in time! Broad-fronted Cæsar,
When thou wast here above the ground, I was
A morsel for a monarch: and great Pompey
Would stand and make his eyes grow in my brow;
There would he anchor his aspect and die
With looking on his life.

Enter Alexas.

Alex. Sovereign of Egypt, hail!
Cleo. How much unlike art thou Mark Antony!
Yet, coming from him, that great medicine hath
With his tinct gilded thee.
How goes it with my brave Mark Antony?
Alex. Last thing he did, dear queen,
He kiss'd—the last of many doubled kisses—
This orient pearl. His speech sticks in my heart.
Cleo. Mine ear must pluck it thence.

Alex. 'Good friend,' quoth he,
'Say, the firm Roman to great Egypt sends
This treasure of an oyster; at whose foot,
To mend the petty present, I will piece
Her opulent throne with kingdoms; all the east,
Say thou, shall call her mistress.' So he nodded,
And soberly did mount an arm-gaunt steed,
Who neigh'd so high, that what I would have spoke
Was beastly dumb'd by him.
Cleo. What, was he sad or merry?
Alex. Like to the time o' the year between the extremes
Of hot and cold, he was nor sad nor merry.
Cleo. O well divided disposition! Note him,
Note him, good Charmian, 'tis the man; but note him:
He was not sad, for he would shine on those
That make their looks by his; he was not merry,
Which seem'd to tell them his remembrance lay
In Egypt with his joy; but between both.
O heavenly mingle! Be'st thou sad or merry,
The violence of either thee becomes,
So does it no man else. Met'st thou my posts?
Alex. Ay, madam, twenty several messengers:
Why do you send so thick?
Cleo. Who 's born that day
When I forget to send to Antony,
Shall die a beggar. Ink and paper, Charmian.
Welcome, my good Alexas. Did I, Charmian,
Ever love Cæsar so?
Char. O that brave Cæsar!
Cleo. Be choked with such another emphasis!
Say, the brave Antony.
Char. The valiant Cæsar!
Cleo. By Isis, I will give thee bloody teeth,
If thou with Cæsar paragon again
My man of men.
Char. By your most gracious pardon,
I sing but after you.
Cleo. My salad days,
When I was green in judgement: cold in blood,
To say as I said then! But come, away;
Get me ink and paper:
He shall have every day a several greeting,
Or I 'll unpeople Egypt. [*Exeunt.*

ACT II—Scene I

Messina. Pompey's house.

Enter Pompey, Menecrates, and Menas, in warlike manner.

Pom. If the great gods be just, they shall assist
The deeds of justest men.
Mene. Know, worthy Pompey,
That what they do delay, they not deny.
Pom. Whiles we are suitors to their throne, decays
The thing we sue for.
Mene. We, ignorant of ourselves,
Beg often our own harms, which the wise powers
Deny us for our good; so find we profit
By losing of our prayers.
Pom. I shall do well:
The people love me, and the sea is mine;
My powers are crescent, and my auguring hope
Says it will come to the full. Mark Antony
In Egypt sits at dinner, and will make
No wars without doors: Cæsar gets money where
He loses hearts: Lepidus flatters both,
Of both is flatter'd, but he neither loves,
Nor either cares for him.
Men. Cæsar and Lepidus
Are in the field: a mighty strength they carry.
Pom. Where have you this? 'tis false.
Men. From Silvius, sir.
Pom. He dreams: I know they are in Rome together,
Looking for Antony. But all the charms of love,
Salt Cleopatra, soften thy waned lip!
Let witchcraft join with beauty, lust with both!
Tie up the libertine in a field of feasts,
Keep his brain fuming; Epicurean cooks
Sharpen with cloyless sauce his appetite;
That sleep and feeding may prorogue his honour
Even till a Lethe'd dulness!

Enter Varrius.

How now, Varrius!
Var. This is most certain that I shall deliver:
Mark Antony is every hour in Rome
Expected: since he went from Egypt 'tis
A space for farther travel.
Pom. I could have given less matter
A better ear. Menas, I did not think

This amorous surfeiter would have donn'd his helm
For such a petty war: his soldiership
Is twice the other twain: but let us rear
The higher our opinion, that our stirring
Can from the lap of Egypt's widow pluck
The ne'er-lust-wearied Antony.

Men. I cannot hope
Cæsar and Antony shall well greet together:
His wife that 's dead did trespasses to Cæsar;
His brother warr'd upon him; although, I think,
Not moved by Antony.

Pom. I know not, Menas,
How lesser enmities may give way to greater.
Were 't not that we stand up against them all,
'Twere pregnant they should square between themselves;
For they have entertained cause enough
To draw their swords: but how the fear of us
May cement their divisions and bind up
The petty difference, we yet not know.
Be 't as our gods will have 't! It only stands
Our lives upon to use our strongest hands.
Come, Menas. [*Exeunt.*

Scene II

Rome. The house of Lepidus.

Enter Enobarbus and Lepidus.

Lep. Good Enobarbus, 'tis a worthy deed,
And shall become you well, to entreat your captain
To soft and gentle speech.

Eno. I shall entreat him
To answer like himself: if Cæsar move him,
Let Antony look over Cæsar's head
And speak as loud as Mars. By Jupiter,
Were I the wearer of Antonius' beard,
I would not shave 't to-day.

Lep. 'Tis not a time
For private stomaching.

Eno. Every time
Serves for the matter that is then born in 't.

Lep. But small to greater matters must give way.

Eno. Not if the small come first.

Lep. Your speech is passion:
But, pray you, stir no embers up. Here comes
The noble Antony.

Enter Antony and Ventidius.

Eno. And yonder, Cæsar.

Enter Cæsar, Mæcenas, and Agrippa.

Ant. If we compose well here, to Parthia:
Hark, Ventidius.

Cæs. I do not know,
Mæcenas; ask Agrippa.

Lep. Noble friends,
That which combined us was most great, and let not
A leaner action rend us. What 's amiss,
May it be gently heard: when we debate
Our trivial difference loud, we do commit
Murder in healing wounds: then, noble partners,
The rather for I earnestly beseech,
Touch you the sourest points with sweetest terms,
Nor curstness grow to the matter.

Ant. 'Tis spoken well.
Were we before our armies and to fight,
I should do thus. [*Flourish.*

Cæs. Welcome to Rome.

Ant. Thank you.

Cæs. Sit.

Ant. Sit, sir.

Cæs. Nay, then.

Ant. I learn, you take things ill which are not so,
Or being, concern you not.

Cæs. I must be laugh'd at,
If, or for nothing or a little, I
Should say myself offended, and with you
Chiefly i' the world; more laugh'd at, that I should
Once name you derogately, when to sound your name
It not concern'd me.

Ant. My being in Egypt, Cæsar,
What was 't to you?

Cæs. No more than my residing here at Rome
Might be to you in Egypt: yet, if you there
Did practise on my state, your being in Egypt
Might be my question.

Ant. How intend you, practised?

Cæs. You may be pleased to catch at mine intent
By what did here befal me. Your wife and brother
Made wars upon me, and their contestation
Was theme for you, you were the word of war.

Ant. You do mistake your business; my brother never
Did urge me in his act: I did inquire it,

And have my learning from some true reports
That drew their swords with you. Did he not rather
Discredit my authority with yours,
And make the wars alike against my stomach,
Having alike your cause? of this my letters
Before did satisfy you. If you 'll patch a quarrel,
As matter whole you have not to make it with,
It must not be with this.

Cæs. You praise yourself
By laying defects of judgement to me, but
You patch'd up your excuses.

Ant. Not so, not so;
I know you could not lack, I am certain on 't,
Very necessity of this thought, that I,
Your partner in the cause 'gainst which he fought,
Could not with graceful eyes attend those wars
Which fronted mine own peace. As for my wife,
I would you had her spirit in such another:
The third o' the world is yours, which with a snaffle
You may pace easy, but not such a wife.

Eno. Would we had all such wives, that the men might go to wars with the women!

Ant. So much uncurbable, her garboils, Cæsar,
Made out of her impatience, which not wanted
Shrewdness of policy too, I grieving grant
Did you too much disquiet: for that you must
But say, I could not help it.

Cæs. I wrote to you
When rioting in Alexandria; you
Did pocket up my letters, and with taunts
Did gibe my missive out of audience.

Ant. Sir,
He fell upon me ere admitted: then
Three kings I had newly feasted and did want
Of what I was i' the morning: but next day
I told him of myself, which was as much
As to have ask'd him pardon. Let this fellow
Be nothing of our strife; if we contend,
Out of our question wipe him.

Cæs. You have broken
The article of your oath, which you shall never
Have tongue to charge me with.

Lep. Soft, Cæsar!

Ant. No, Lepidus, let him speak:
The honour is sacred which he talks on now,

Supposing that I lack'd it. But on, Cæsar;
The article of my oath.

Cæs. To lend me arms and aid when I required them;
The which you both denied.

Ant. Neglected rather,
And then when poison'd hours had bound me up
From mine own knowledge. As nearly as I may,
I 'll play the penitent to you: but mine honesty
Shall not make poor my greatness, nor my power
Work without it. Truth is that Fulvia,
To have me out of Egypt, made wars here;
For which myself, the ignorant motive, do
So far ask pardon as befits mine honour
To stoop in such a case.

Lep. 'Tis noble spoken.

Mæc. If it might please you, to enforce no further
The griefs between ye: to forget them quite
Were to remember that the present need
Speaks to atone you.

Lep. Worthily spoken, Mæcenas.

Eno. Or, if you borrow one another's love for the instant, you may, when you hear no more words of Pompey, return it again: you shall have time to wrangle in when you have nothing else to do.

Ant. Thou art a soldier only: speak no more.

Eno. That truth should be silent I had almost forgot.

Ant. You wrong this presence; therefore speak no more.

Eno. Go to, then; your considerate stone.

Cæs. I do not much dislike the matter, but
The manner of his speech; for 't cannot be
We shall remain in friendship, our conditions
So differing in their acts. Yet, if I knew
What hoop should hold us stanch, from edge to edge
O' the world I would pursue it.

Agr. Give me leave, Cæsar.

Cæs. Speak, Agrippa.

Agr. Thou hast a sister by the mother's side,
Admired Octavia: great Mark Antony
Is now a widower.

Cæs. Say not so, Agrippa:
If Cleopatra heard you, your reproof
Were well deserved of rashness.

Ant. I am not married, Cæsar: let me hear
Agrippa further speak.

Agr. To hold you in perpetual amity,

To make you brothers and to knit your hearts
With an unslipping knot, take Antony
Octavia to his wife; whose beauty claims
No worse a husband than the best of men,
Whose virtue and whose general graces speak
That which none else can utter. By this marriage
All little jealousies which now seem great,
And all great fears which now import their dangers,
Would then be nothing: truths would be tales,
Where now half tales be truths: her love to both
Would each to other and all loves to both
Draw after her. Pardon what I have spoke,
For 'tis a studied, not a present thought,
By duty ruminated.

Ant. Will Cæsar speak?

Cæs. Not till he hears how Antony is touch'd
With what is spoke already.

Ant. What power is in Agrippa,
If I would say, 'Agrippa, be it so,'
To make this good?

Cæs. The power of Cæsar, and
His power unto Octavia.

Ant. May I never
To this good purpose, that so fairly shows,
Dream of impediment! Let me have thy hand:
Further this act of grace; and from this hour
The heart of brothers govern in our loves
And sway out great designs!

Cæs. There is my hand.
A sister I bequeath you, whom no brother
Did ever love so dearly: let her live
To join our kingdoms and our hearts; and never
Fly off our loves again!

Lep. Happily, amen!

Ant. I did not think to draw my sword 'gainst Pompey;
For he hath laid strange courtesies and great
Of late upon me: I must thank him only,
Lest my remembrance suffer ill report;
At heel of that, defy him.

Lep. Time calls upon 's:
Of us must Pompey presently be sought,
Or else he seeks out us.

Ant. Where lies he?

Cæs. About the Mount Misenum.

Ant. What 's his strength

By land?

Cæs. Great and increasing: but by sea
He is an absolute master.

Ant. So is the fame.
Would we had spoke together! Haste we for it:
Yet, ere we put ourselves in arms, dispatch we
The business we have talk'd of.

Cæs. With most gladness;
And do invite you to my sister's view,
Whither straight I'll lead you.

Ant. Let us, Lepidus,
Not lack your company.

Lep. Noble Antony,
Not sickness should detain me.

[*Flourish. Exeunt Cæsar, Antony, and Lepidus.*

Mæc. Welcome from Egypt, sir.

Eno. Half the heart of Cæsar, worthy Mæcenas!
My honourable friend, Agrippa!

Agr. Good Enobarbus!

Mæc. We have cause to be glad that matters are so well digested. You stayed well by 't in Egypt.

Eno. Ay, sir; we did sleep day out of countenance, And made the night light with drinking.

Mæc. Eight wild-boars roasted whole at a breakfast, and but twelve persons there; is this true?

Eno. This was but as a fly by an eagle: we had much more monstrous matter of feast, which worthily deserved noting.

Mæc. She 's a most triumphant lady, if report be square to her.

Eno. When she first met Mark Antony, she pursed up his heart, upon the river of Cydnus.

Agr. There she appeared indeed, or my reporter devised well [for her.

Eno. I will tell you.
The barge she sat in, like a burnish'd throne,
Burn'd on the water: the poop was beaten gold;
Purple the sails, and so perfumed that
The winds were love-sick with them; the oars were silver,
Which to the tune of flutes kept stroke and made
The water which they beat to follow faster,
As amorous of their strokes. For her own person,
It beggar'd all description: she did lie
In her pavilion, cloth-of-gold of tissue,
O'er-picturing that Venus where we see
The fancy out-work nature: on each side her
Stood pretty dimpled boys, like smiling Cupids,
With divers-colour'd fans, whose wind did seem

To glow the delicate cheeks which they did cool,
And what they undid did.

Agr. O, rare for Antony!

Eno. Her gentlewomen, like the Nereides,
So many mermaids, tended her i' the eyes,
And made their bends adornings: at the helm
A seeming mermaid steers: the silken tackle
Swell with the touches of those flower-soft hands,
That yarely frame the office. From the barge
A strange invisible perfume hits the sense
Of the adjacent wharfs. The city cast
Her people out upon her; and Antony,
Enthroned i' the market-place, did sit alone,
Whistling to the air; which, but for vacancy,
Had gone to gaze on Cleopatra too,
And made a gap in nature.

Agr. Rare Egyptian!

Eno. Upon her landing, Antony sent to her,
Invited her to supper: she replied,
It should be better he became her guest,
Which she entreated: our courteous Antony,
Whom ne'er the word of 'No' woman heard speak,
Being barber'd ten times o'er, goes to the feast,
And, for his ordinary, pays his heart
For what his eyes eat only.

Agr. Royal wench!
She made great Cæsar, lay his sword to bed:
He plough'd her, and she cropp'd.

Eno. I saw her once
Hop forty paces through the public street;
And having lost her breath, she spoke, and panted,
That she did make defect perfection,
And, breathless, power breathe forth.

Mæc. Now Antony must leave her utterly.

Eno. Never; he will not:
Age cannot wither her, nor custom stale
Her infinite variety: other women cloy
The appetites they feed, but she makes hungry
Where most she satisfies: for vilest things
Become themselves in her, that the holy priests
Bless her when she is riggish.

Mæc. If beauty, wisdom, modesty, can settle
The heart of Antony, Octavia is

Agr. A blessed lottery to him.
Let us go.

Good Enobarbus, make yourself my guest
Whilst you abide here.

Eno. Humbly, sir, I thank you. [*Exeunt.*

Scene III

The same. Cæsar's house.

Enter Antony, Cæsar, Octavia between them, and Attendants.

Ant. The world and my great office will sometimes
Divide me from your bosom.

Octa. All which time
Before the gods my knee shall bow my prayers
To them for you.

Ant. Good night, sir. My Octavia,
Read not my blemishes in the world's report:
I have not kept my square; but that to come
Shall all be done by the rule. Good night, dear lady.
Good night, sir.

Cæs. Good night. [*Exeunt all but Antony.*

Enter Soothsayer.

Ant. Now, sirrah, you do wish yourself in Egypt?

Sooth. Would I had never come from thence, nor you thither!

Ant. If you can, your reason?

Sooth. I see it in
My notion, have it not in my tongue: but yet
Hie you to Egypt again.

Ant. Say to me,
Whose fortunes shall rise higher, Cæsar's or mine?

Sooth. Cæsar's.
Therefore, O Antony, stay not by his side:
Thy demon, that thy spirit which keeps thee, is
Noble, courageous, high, unmatchable,
Where Cæsar's is not; but near him thy angel
Becomes a fear, as being o'erpower'd: therefore
Make space enough between you.

Ant. Speak this no more.

Sooth. To none but thee; no more but when to thee.
If thou dost play with him at any game,
Thou art sure to lose; and, of that natural luck,
He beats thee 'gainst the odds: thy lustre thickens,
When he shines by: I say again, thy spirit
Is all afraid to govern thee near him,
But he away, 'tis noble.

Ant. Get thee gone:
Say to Ventidius I would speak with him. [*Exit Soothsayer.*
He shall to Parthia. Be it art or hap,

He hath spoken true: the very dice obey him,
And in our sports my better cunning faints
Under his chance: if we draw lots, he speeds;
His cocks do win the battle still of mine
When it is all to nought, and his quails ever
Beat mine, inhoop'd, at odds. I will to Egypt:
And though I make this marriage for my peace,
I' the east my pleasure lies.

Enter Ventidius.

O, come, Ventidius,
You must to Parthia: your commission's ready;
Follow me, and receive 't. [*Exeunt.*

Scene IV

The same. A street.

Enter Lepidus, Mæcenas, and Agrippa.

Lep. Trouble yourselves no further: pray you, hasten
Your generals after.

Agr. Sir, Mark Antony
Will e'en but kiss Octavia, and we 'll follow.

Lep. Till I shall see you in your soldier's dress,
Which will become you both, farewell.

Mæc. We shall,
As I conceive the journey, be at the Mount
Before you, Lepidus.

Lep. Your way is shorter;
My purposes do draw me much about:
You 'll win two days upon me.

Mæc., *Agr.* Sir, good success!

Lep. Farewell. [*Exeunt.*

Scene V

Alexandria. Cleopatra's palace.

Enter Cleopatra, Charmian, Iras, and Alexas.

Cleo. Give me some music; music, moody food
Of us that trade in love.

All. The music, ho!

Enter Mardian the Eunuch.

Cleo. Let it alone; let 's to billiards: come, Charmian.

Char. My arm is sore: best play with Mardian.

Cleo. As well a woman with an eunuch play'd
As with a woman. Come, you 'll play with me, sir?

Mar. As well as I can, madam.

Cleo. And when good will is show'd, though 't come too short,

The actor may plead pardon. I 'll none now:
Give me mine angle; we 'll to the river: there,
My music playing far off, I will betray
Tawny-finn'd fishes; my bended hook shall pierce
Their slimy jaws, and as I draw them up,
I 'll think them every one an Antony,
And say 'Ah, ha! you 're caught.'

Char. 'Twas merry when
You wager'd on your angling; when your diver
Did hang a salt-fish on his hook, which he
With fervency drew up.

Cleo. That time—O times!—
I laugh'd him out of patience, and that night
I laugh'd him into patience; and next morn,
Ere the ninth hour, I drunk him to his bed;
Then put my tires and mantles on him, whilst
I wore his sword Philippan.

Enter a Messenger.

O, from Italy!
Ram thou thy fruitful tidings in mine ears,
That long time have been barren.

Mess. Madam, madam,—

Cleo. Antonius dead! If thou say so, villain,
Thou kill'st thy mistress: but well and free,
If thou so yield him, there is gold, and here
My bluest veins to kiss: a hand that kings
Have lipp'd, and trembled kissing.

Mess. First, madam, he is well.

Cleo. Why, there 's more gold.
But, sirrah, mark, we use
To say the dead are well: bring it to that,
The gold I give thee will I melt and pour
Down thy ill-uttering throat.

Mess. Good madam, hear me.

Cleo. Well, go to, I will;
But there 's no goodness in thy face: if Antony
Be free and healthful,—so tart a favour
To trumpet such good tidings! If not well,
Thou shouldst come like a Fury crown'd with snakes,
Not like a formal man.

Mess. Will 't please you hear me?

Cleo. I have a mind to strike thee ere thou speak'st:
Yet, if thou say Antony lives, is well,
Or friends with Cæsar, or not captive to him,
I'll set thee in a shower of gold, and hail

Rich pearls upon thee.
Mess. Madam, he 's well.
Cleo. Well said.
Mess. And friends with Cæsar.
Cleo. Thou 'rt an honest man.
Mess. Cæsar and he are greater friends than ever.
Cleo. Make thee a fortune from me.
Mess. But yet, madam,—
Cleo. I do not like 'But yet,' it does allay
The good precedence; fie upon 'But yet'!
'But yet' is as a gaoler to bring forth
Some monstrous malefactor. Prithee, friend,
Pour out the pack of matter to mine ear,
The good and bad together: he 's friends with Cæsar,
In state of health, thou say'st, and thou say'st, free.
Mess. Free, madam! no; I made no such report:
He 's bound unto Octavia.
Cleo. For what good turn?
Mess. For the best turn i' the bed.
Cleo. I am pale, Charmian.
Mess. Madam, he 's married to Octavia.
Cleo. The most infectious pestilence upon thee!
[*Strikes him down.*
Mess. Good madam, patience.
Cleo. What say you? Hence,
[*Strikes him again.*
Horrible villain! or I 'll spurn thine eyes
Like balls before me; I 'll unhair thy head:
[*She hales him up and down.*
Thou shalt be whipp'd with wire, and stew'd in brine,
Smarting in lingering pickle.
Mess. Gracious madam,
I that do bring the news made not the match.
Cleo. Say 'tis not so, a province I will give thee
And make thy fortunes proud: the blow thou hadst
Shall make thy peace for moving me to rage,
And I will boot thee with what gift beside
Thy modesty can beg.
Mess. He 's married, madam.
Cleo. Rogue, thou hast lived too long. [*Draws a knife.*
Mess. Nay, then I 'll run.
What mean you, madam? I have made no fault. [*Exit.*
Char. Good madam, keep yourself within yourself:
The man is innocent.
Cleo. Some innocents 'scape not the thunderbolt.

Melt Egypt into Nile! and kindly creatures
Turn all to serpents! Call the slave again:
Though I am mad, I will not bite him: call.

Char. He is afeard to come.

Cleo. I will not hurt him.

[*Exit Charmian.*

These hands do lack nobility, that they strike
A meaner than myself; since I myself
Have given myself the cause.

Re-enter Charmian and Messenger.

Come hither, sir.
Though it be honest, it is never good
To bring bad news: give to a gracious message
An host of tongues, but let ill tidings tell
Themselves when they be felt.

Mess. I have done my duty.

Cleo. Is he married?
I cannot hate thee worser than I do,
If thou again say 'Yes.'

Mess. He's married, madam.

Cleo. The gods confound thee! dost thou hold there still?

Mess. Should I lie, madam?

Cleo. O, I would thou didst,
So half my Egypt were submerged and made
A cistern for scaled snakes! Go get thee hence:
Hadst thou Narcissus in thy face, to me
Thou wouldst appear most ugly. He is married?

Mess. I crave your highness' pardon.

Cleo. He is married?

Mess. Take no offence that I would not offend you:
To punish me for what you make me do
Seems much unequal: he's married to Octavia.

Cleo. O, that his fault should make a knave of thee,
That art not what thou'rt sure of! Get thee hence:
The merchandise which thou hast brought from Rome
Are all too dear for me: lie they upon thy hand,
And be undone by 'em! [*Exit Messenger.*

Char. Good your highness, patience.

Cleo. In praising Antony, I have dispraised Cæsar.

Char. Many times, madam.

Cleo. I am paid for 't now.
Lead me from hence;
I faint: O Iras, Charmian! 'tis no matter.
Go to the fellow, good Alexas; bid him
Report the feature of Octavia, her years,

Her inclination; let him not leave out
The colour of her hair: bring me word quickly. [*Exit Alexas.*
Let him for ever go: let him not—Charmian,
Though he be painted one way like a Gorgon,
The other way 's a Mars. [*To Mardian*] Bid you Alexas
Bring me word how tall she is. Pity me, Charmian,
But do not speak to me. Lead me to my chamber. [*Exeunt.*

Scene VI

Near Misenum.

Flourish. Enter Pompey and Menas from one side, with drum and trumpet: at another, Cæsar, Antony, Lepidus, Enobarbus, Mæcenas, with Soldiers marching.

Pom. Your hostages I have, so have you mine;
And we shall talk before we fight.
Cæs. Most meet
That first we come to words; and therefore have we
Our written purposes before us sent;
Which, if thou hast consider'd, let us know
If 'twill tie up thy discontented sword
And carry back to Sicily much tall youth
That else must perish here.
Pom. To you all three,
The senators alone of this great world,
Chief factors for the gods, I do not know
Wherefore my father should revengers want,
Having a son and friends; since Julius Cæsar,
Who at Philippi the good Brutus ghosted,
There saw you labouring for him. What was 't
That moved pale Cassius to conspire, and what
Made the all-honour'd honest Roman, Brutus,
With the arm'd rest, courtiers of beautous freedom,
To drench the Capitol, but that they would
Have one man but a man? And that is it
Hath made me rig my navy, at whose burthen
The anger'd ocean foams; with which I meant
To scourge the ingratitude that despiteful Rome
Cast on my noble father.
Cæs. Take your time.
Ant. Thou canst not fear us, Pompey, with thy sails;
We 'll speak with thee at sea: at land, thou know'st
How much we do o'ercount thee.
Pom. At land indeed
Thou dost o'ercount me of my father's house:

But since the cuckoo builds not for himself,
Remain in 't as thou mayst.

Lep. Be pleased to tell us—
For this is from the present—how you take
The offers we have sent you.

Cæs. There 's the point.

Ant. Which do not be entreated to, but weigh
What it is worth embraced.

Cæs. And what may follow,
To try a larger fortune.

Pom. You have made me offer
Of Sicily, Sardinia; and I must
Rid all the sea of pirates; then, to send
Measures of wheat to Rome! this 'greed upon
To part with unhack'd edges and bear back
Our targes undinted.

Cæs., *Ant.*, *Lep.* That 's our offer.

Pom. Know then.
I came before you here a man prepared
To take this offer: but Mark Antony
Put me to some impatience: though I lose
The praise of it by telling, you must know,
When Cæsar and your brother were at blows,
Your mother came to Sicily and did find
Her welcome friendly.

Ant. I have heard it, Pompey,
And am well studied for a liberal thanks
Which I do owe you.

Pom. Let me have your hand:
I did not think, sir, to have met you here.

Ant. The beds i' the east are soft; and thanks to you,
That call'd me timelier than my purpose hither;
For I have gain'd by 't.

Cæs. Since I saw you last,
There is a change upon you.

Pom. Well, I know not
What counts harsh fortune casts upon my face;
But in my bosom shall she never come,
To make my heart her vassal.

Lep. Well met here.

Pom. I hope so, Lepidus. Thus we are agreed
I crave our composition may be written
And seal'd between us.

Cæs. That 's the next to do.
Pom. We 'll feast each other ere we part, and let 's
Draw lots who shall begin.
Ant. That will I, Pompey.
Pom. No, Antony, take the lot:
But, first or last, your fine Egyptian cookery
Shall have the fame. I have heard that Julius Cæsar
Grew fat with feasting there.
Ant. You have heard much.
Pom. I have fair meanings, sir.
Ant. And fair words to them.
Pom. Then so much have I heard:
And I have heard, Apollodorus carried—
Eno. No more of that: he did so.
Pom. What, I pray you?
Eno. A certain queen to Cæsar in a mattress.
Pom. I know thee now: how farest thou, soldier?
Eno. Well;
And well am like to do, for I perceive
Four feasts are toward.
Pom. Let me shake thy hand;
I never hated thee: I have seen thee fight,
When I have envied thy behaviour.
Eno. Sir,
I never loved you much, but I ha' praised ye
When you have well deserved ten times as much
As I have said you did.
Pom. Enjoy thy plainness,
It nothing ill becomes thee.
Aboard my galley I invite you all:
Will you lead, lords?
Cæs. *Ant.* *Lep.* Show us the way, sir.
Pom. Come.
[*Exeunt all but Menas and Enobarbus.*
Men. [*Aside*] Thy father, Pompey, would ne'er have made this treaty.—You and I have known, sir.
Eno. At sea, I think.
Men. We have, sir.
Eno. You have done well by water.
Men. And you by land.
Eno. I will praise any man that will praise me; though it cannot be denied what I have done by land.
Men. Nor what I have done by water.

Eno. Yes, something you can deny for your own safety: you have been a great thief by sea.

Men. And you by land.

Eno. There I deny my land service. But give me your hand Menas: if our eyes had authority, here they might take two thieves kissing.

Men. All men's faces are true, whatsoe'er their hands are.

Eno. But there is never a fair woman has a true face.

Men. No slander; they steal hearts.

Eno. We came hither to fight with you.

Men. For my part, I am sorry it is turned to a drinking. Pompey doth this day laugh away his fortune.

Eno. If he do, sure he cannot weep 't back again.

Men. You 've said, sir. We looked not for Mark Antony here: pray you, is he married to Cleopatra?

Eno. Cæsar's sister is called Octavia.

Men. True, sir; she was the wife of Caius Marcellus.

Eno. But she is now the wife of Marcus Antonius.

Men. Pray ye, sir?

Eno. 'Tis true.

Men. Then is Cæsar and he for ever knit together.

Eno. If I were bound to divine of this unity, I would not prophesy so.

Men. I think the policy of that purpose made more in the marriage than the love of the parties.

Eno. I think so too. But you shall find, the band that seems to tie their friendship together will be the very strangler of their amity: Octavia is of a holy, cold and still conversation.

Men. Who would not have his wife so?

Eno. Not he that himself is not so; which is Mark Antony. He will to his Egyptian dish again: then shall the sighs of Octavia blow the fire up in Cæsar; and, as I said before, that which is the strength of their amity shall prove the immediate author of their variance. Antony will use his affection where it is: he married but his occasion here.

Men. And thus it may be. Come, sir, will you aboard? I have a health for you.

Eno. I shall take it, sir: we have used our throats in Egypt.

Men. Come, let 's away. [*Exeunt.*

Scene VII

On board Pompey's galley, off Misenum.

Music plays. Enter two or three Servants, with a banquet.

First Serv. Here they 'll be, man. Some o' their plants are ill-rooted already; the least wind i' the world will blow them down.

Sec. Serv. Lepidus is high-coloured.

First Serv. They have made him drink alms-drink.

Sec. Serv. As they pinch one another by the disposition, he cries out 'No more;' reconciles them to his entreaty and himself to the drink.

First Serv. But it raises the greater war between him and his discretion.

Sec. Serv. Why, this it is to have a name in great men's fellowship: I had as lief have a reed that will do me no service as a partisan I could not heave.

First Serv. To be called into a huge sphere, and not to be seen to move in 't, are the holes where eyes should be, which pitifully disaster the cheeks.

A sennet sounded. Enter Cæsar, Antony, Lepidus, Pompey, Agrippa, Mæcenas, Enobarbus, Menas, with other captains.

Ant. [*To Cæsar*] Thus do they, sir: they take the flow o' the [Nile
By certain scales i' the pyramid; they know,
By the height, the lowness, or the mean, if dearth
Or foison follow: the higher Nilus swells,
The more it promises: as it ebbs, the seedsman
Upon the slime and ooze scatters his grain,
And shortly comes to harvest.

Lep. You 've strange serpents there.

Ant. Ay, Lepidus.

Lep. Your serpent of Egypt is bred now of your mud by the operation of your sun: so is your crocodile.

Ant. They are so.

Pom. Sit,—and some wine! A health to Lepidus!

Lep. I am not so well as I should be, but I 'll ne'er out.

Eno. Not till you have slept; I fear me you 'll be in till then.

Lep. Nay, certainly, I have heard the Ptolemies pyramises are very goodly things; without contradiction, I have heard that

Men. [*Aside to Pom.*] Pompey, a word.

Pom. [*Aside to Men.*] Say in mine ear: what is 't?

Men. [*Aside to Pom.*] Forsake thy seat, I do beseech thee [captain,
And hear me speak a word.

Pom. [*Aside to Men.*] Forbear me till anon.—
This wine for Lepidus?

Lep. What manner o' thing is your crocodile?

Ant. It is shaped, sir, like itself; and it is as broad as it hath breadth: it is just so high as it is, and moves with its own organs: it lives by that which nourisheth it; and the elements once out of it, it transmigrates.

Lep. What colour is it of?

Ant. Of its own colour too.
Lep. 'Tis a strange serpent.
Ant. 'Tis so. And the tears of it are wet.
Cæs. Will this description satisfy him?
Ant. With the health that Pompey gives him, else he is a very [epicure.
Pom. [*Aside to Men.*] Go hang, sir, hang! Tell me of that? [away!
Do as I bid you.—Where 's this cup I call'd for?
Men. [*Aside to Pom.*] If for the sake of merit thou wilt hear me,
Rise from thy stool.
Pom. [*Aside to Men.*] I think thou 'rt mad. The matter?
[*Rises, and walks aside.*
Men. I have ever held my cap off to thy fortunes.
Pom. Thou hast served me with much faith. What 's else to [say?
Be jolly, lords.
Ant. These quick-sands, Lepidus,
Keep off them, for you sink.
Men. Wilt thou be lord of all the world?
Pom. What say'st thou?
Men. Wilt thou be lord of the whole world? That 's twice.
Pom. How should that be?
Men. But entertain it,
And, though thou think me poor, I am the man
Will give thee all the world.
Pom. Hast thou drunk well?
Men. No, Pompey, I have kept me from the cup.
Thou art, if thou darest be, the earthly Jove:
Whate'er the ocean pales, or sky inclips,
Is thine, if thou wilt ha 't.
Pom. Show me which way.
Men. These three world-sharers, these competitors,
Are in thy vessel: let me cut the cable;
And, when we are put off, fall to their throats:
All there is thine.
Pom. Ah, this thou shouldst have done,
And not have spoke on 't! In me 'tis villany;
In thee 't had been good service. Thou must know,
'Tis not my profit that does lead mine honour;
Mine honour, it. Repent that e'er thy tongue
Hath so betray'd thine act: being done unknown,
I should have found it afterwards well done,
But must condemn it now. Desist, and drink.
Men. [*Aside*] For this
I 'll never follow thy pall'd fortunes more.
Who seeks, and will not take when once 'tis offer'd,
Shall never find it more.

Pom. This health to Lepidus!
Ant. Bear him ashore. I 'll pledge it for him, Pompey.
Eno. Here 's to thee, Menas!
Men. Enobarbus, welcome!
Pom. Fill till the cup be hid.
Eno. There 's a strong fellow, Menas.
[*Pointing to the Attendant who carries off Lepidus.*
Men. Why?
Eno. A' bears the third part of the world, man; see'st not?
Men. The third part then is drunk: would it were all,
That it might go on wheels!
Eno. Drink thou; increase the reels.
Men. Come.
Pom. This is not yet an Alexandrian feast.
Ant. It ripens towards it. Strike the vessels, ho!
Here 's to Cæsar!
Cæs. I could well forbear 't.
It 's monstrous labour, when I wash my brain
And it grows fouler.
Ant. Be a child o' the time.
Cæs. Possess it, I 'll make answer:
But I had rather fast from all four days
Than drink so much in one.
Eno. [*To Antony*] Ha, my brave emperor!
Shall we dance now the Egyptian Bacchanals,
And celebrate our drink?
Pom. Let 's ha 't, good soldier.
Ant. Come, let 's all take hands,
Till that the conquering wine hath steep'd our sense
In soft and delicate Lethe.
Eno. All take hands.
Make battery to our ears with the loud music:
The while I 'll place you: then the boy shall sing;
The holding every man shall bear as loud
As his strong sides can volley.
[*Music plays. Enobarbus places them hand in hand.*

THE SONG.

Come, thou monarch of the vine,
Plumpy Bacchus with pink eyne!
In thy fats our cares be drown'd,
With thy grapes our hairs be crown'd:
Cup us, till the world go round,
Cup us, till the world go round!

Cæs. What would you more? Pompey, good night. Good brother,
Let me request you off: our graver business
Frowns at this levity. Gentle lords, let's part;
You see we have burnt our cheeks: strong Enobarb
Is weaker than the wine; and mine own tongue
Splits what it speaks: the wild disguise hath almost
Antick'd us all. What needs more words? Good night.
Good Antony, your hand.

Pom. I'll try you on the shore.

Ant. And shall, sir: give's your hand.

Pom. O Antony,
You have my father's house,—But, what? we are friends.
Come, down into the boat.

Eno. Take heed you fall not.
[*Exeunt all but Enobarbus and Menas.*
Menas, I'll not on shore.

Men. No, to my cabin.
These drums! these trumpets, flutes! what!
Let Neptune hear we bid a loud farewell
To these great fellows: sound and be hang'd, sound out!
[*Sound a flourish, with drums.*

Eno. Hoo! says-a'. There's my cap.

Men. Hoo! Noble captain, come. [*Exeunt.*

ACT III—Scene I

A plain in Syria.

Enter Ventidius as it were in triumph, with Silius, and other Romans, Officers, and soldiers; the dead body of Pacorus borne before him.

Ven. Now, darting Parthia, art thou struck; and now
Pleased fortune does of Marcus Crassus' death
Make me revenger. Bear the king's son's body
Before our army. Thy Pacorus, Orodes,
Pays this for Marcus Crassus.

Sil. Noble Ventidius,
Whilst yet with Parthian blood thy sword is warm,
The fugitive Parthians follow; spur through Media,
Mesopotamia, and the shelters whither
The routed fly: so thy grand captain Antony
Shall set thee on triumphant chariots and
Put garlands on thy head.

Ven. O Silius, Silius,
I have done enough: a lower place note well,

May make too great an act; for learn this, Silius,
Better to leave undone than by our deed
Acquire too high a fame when him we serve 's away.
Cæsar and Antony have ever won
More in their officer than person: Sossius,
One of my place in Syria, his lieutenant,
For quick accumulation of renown,
Which he achieved by the minute, lost his favour.
Who does i' the wars more than his captain can
Becomes his captain's captain: and ambition,
The soldier's virtue, rather makes choice of loss
Than gain which darkens him.
I could do more to do Antonius good,
But 'twould offend him, and in his offence
Should my performance perish.

Sil. Thou hast, Ventidius, that
Without the which a soldier and his sword
Grants scarce distinction. Thou wilt write to Antony?

Ven. I 'll humbly signify what in his name,
That magical word of war, we have effected;
How, with his banners and his well-paid ranks,
The ne'er-yet-beaten horse of Parthia
We have jaded out o' the field.

Sil. Where is he now?

Ven. He purposeth to Athens: whither, with what haste
The weight we must convey with 's will permit,
We shall appear before him. On, there; pass along!
[*Exeunt.*

Scene II

Rome. An ante-chamber in Cæsar's house.

Enter Agrippa at one door, and Enobarbus at another.

Agr. What, are the brothers parted?

Eno. They have dispatch'd with Pompey; he is gone;
The other three are sealing. Octavia weeps
To part from Rome; Cæsar is sad, and Lepidus
Since Pompey's feast, as Mena says, is troubled
With the green sickness.

Agr. 'Tis a noble Lepidus.

Eno. A very fine one: O, how he loves Cæsar!

Agr. Nay, but how dearly he adores Mark Antony!

Eno. Cæsar? Why, he 's the Jupiter of men.

Agr. What 's Antony? The god of Jupiter.

Eno. Spake you of Cæsar? How! the nonpareil!

Agr. O Antony! O thou Arabian bird!

Eno. Would you praise Cæsar, say 'Cæsar': go no further.
Agr. Indeed, he plied them both with excellent praises.
Eno. But he loves Cæsar best; yet he loves Antony:
Ho! hearts, tongues, figures, scribes, bards, poets, cannot
Think, speak, cast, write, sing, number—ho!—
His love to Antony. But as for Cæsar,
Kneel down, kneel down, and wonder.
Agr. Both he loves.
Eno. They are his shards, and he their beetle. [*Trumpet within.*]
This is to horse. Adieu, noble Agrippa. [So;
Agr. Good fortune, worthy soldier, and farewell.

Enter Cæsar, Antony, Lepidus, and Octavia.

Ant. No further, sir.
Cæs. You take from me a great part of myself;
Use me well in 't. Sister, prove such a wife
As my thoughts make thee, and as my farthest band
Shall pass on thy approof. Most noble Antony,
Let not the piece of virtue which is set
Betwixt us as the cement of our love,
To keep it builded, be the ram to batter
The fortress of it; for better might we
Have loved without this mean, if on both parts
This be not cherish'd.
Ant. Make me not offended
In your distrust.
Cæs. I have said.
Ant. You shall not find,
Though you be therein curious, the least cause
For what you seem to fear: so, the gods keep you,
And make the hearts of Romans serve your ends!
We will here part.
Cæs. Farewell, my dearest sister, fare thee well:
The elements be kind to thee, and make
Thy spirits all of comfort! fare thee well.
Octa. My noble brother!
Ant. The April's in her eyes: it is love's spring,
And these the showers to bring it on. Be cheerful.
Octa. Sir, look well to my husband's house, and—
Cæs. What,
Octavia?
Octa. I 'll tell you in your ear.
Ant. Her tongue will not obey her heart, nor can
Her heart inform her tongue, the swan's down-feather,
That stands upon the swell at full of tide
And neither way inclines.

Eno. [*Aside to Agr.*] Will Cæsar weep?
Agr. [*Aside to Eno.*] He has a cloud in 's face.
Eno. [*Aside to Agr.*] He were the worse for that, were he a horse;
So is he, being a man.
Agr. [*Aside to Eno.*] Why, Enobarbus,
When Antony found Julius Cæsar dead,
He cried almost to roaring; and he wept
When at Philippi he found Brutus slain.
Eno. [*Aside to Agr.*] That year indeed he was troubled with a rheum;
What willingly he did confound he wail'd,
Believe 't, till I wept too.
Cæs. No, sweet Octavia,
You shall hear from me still; the time shall not
Out-go my thinking on you.
Ant. Come, sir, come;
I 'll wrestle with you in my strength of love:
Look, here I have you; thus I let you go,
And give you to the gods.
Cæs. Adieu; be happy!
Lep. Let all the number of the stars give light
To thy fair way!
Cæs. Farewell, farewell! [*Kisses Octavia.*
Ant. Farewell!
[*Trumpets sound. Exeunt.*

Scene III

Alexandria. Cleopatra's palace.

Enter Cleopatra, Charmain, Iras, and Alexas.

Cleo. Where is the fellow?
Alex. Half afeard to come.
Cleo. Go to, go to.

Enter Messenger.

Come hither, sir.
Alex. Good majesty,
Herod of Jewry dare not look upon you
But when you are well pleased.
Cleo. That Herod's head
I 'll have: but how, when Antony is gone
Through whom I might command it? Come thou near.
Mess. Most gracious majesty,—
Cleo. Didst thou behold
Octavia?
Mess. Ay, dread queen.
Cleo. Where?
Mess. Madam, in Rome

I look'd her in the face, and saw her led
Between her brother and Mark Antony.
Cleo. Is she as tall as me?
Mess. She is not, madam.
Cleo. Didst hear her speak? is she shrill-tongued or low?
Mess. Madam, I heard her speak; she is low-voiced.
Cleo. That's not so good. He cannot like her long.
Char. Like her! O Isis! 'tis impossible.
Cleo. I think so, Charmian: dull of tongue and dwarfish.
What majesty is in her gait? Remember,
If e'er thou look'dst on majesty.
Mess. She creeps:
Her motion and her station are as one;
She shows a body rather than a life,
A statue than a breather.
Cleo. Is this certain?
Mess. Or I have no observance.
Char. Three in Egypt
Cannot make better note.
Cleo. He's very knowing;
I do perceive't: there's nothing in her yet:
The fellow has good judgement.
Char. Excellent.
Cleo. Guess at her years, I prithee.
Mess. Madam,
She was a widow—
Cleo. Widow! Charmian, hark.
Mess. And I do think she's thirty.
Cleo. Bear'st thou her face in mind? is't long or round?
Mess. Round even to faultiness.
Cleo. For the most part, too, they are foolish that are so.
Her hair, what colour?
Mess. Brown, madam: and her forehead
As low as she would wish it.
Cleo. There's gold for thee.
Thou must not take my former sharpness ill:
I will employ thee back again; I find thee
Most fit for business: go make thee ready;
Our letters are prepared. [*Exit Messenger.*
Char. A proper man.
Cleo. Indeed, he is so: I repent me much
That so I harried him. Why, methinks, by him,
This creature's no such thing.
Char. Nothing, madam.
Cleo. The man hath seen some majesty, and should know.

Char. Hath he seen majesty? Isis else defend,
And serving you so long!
Cleo. I have one thing more to ask him yet, good Charmian:
But 'tis no matter; thou shalt bring him to me
Where I will write. All may be well enough.
Char. I warrant you, madam. [*Exeunt.*

Scene IV

Athens. A room in Antony's house.
Enter Antony and Octavia.

Ant. Nay, nay, Octavia, not only that,
That were excusable, that and thousands more
Of semblable import, but he hath waged
New wars 'gainst Pompey; made his will, and read it
To public ear:
Spoke scantly of me: when perforce he could not
But pay me terms of honour, cold and sickly
He vented them; most narrow measure lent me;
When the best hint was given him, he not took 't,
Or did it from his teeth.
Octa. O my good lord,
Believe not all; or, if you must believe,
Stomach not all. A more unhappy lady,
If this division chance, ne'er stood between,
Praying for both parts:
The good gods will mock me presently,
When I shall pray, 'O, bless my lord and husband!'
Undo that prayer, by crying out as loud,
'O, bless my brother!' Husband win, win brother,
Prays, and destroys the prayer; no midway
'Twixt these extremes at all.
Ant. Gentle Octavia,
Let your best love draw to that point, which seeks
Best to preserve it; if I lose mine honour,
I lose myself: better I were not yours
Than yours so branchless. But, as you requested,
Yourself shall go between 's: the mean time, lady,
I 'll raise the preparation of a war
Shall stain your brother: make your soonest haste;
So your desires are yours.
Octa. Thanks to my lord.
The Jove of power make me most weak, most weak,
Your reconciler! Wars 'twixt your twain would be
As if the world should cleave, and that slain men
Should solder up the rift.

Ant. When it appears to you where this begins,
Turn your displeasure that way; for our faults
Can never be so equal, that your love
Can equally move with them. Provide your going;
Choose your own company, and command what cost
Your heart has mind to. [*Exeunt.*

Scene V

The same. Another room.

Enter Enobarbus and Eros, meeting.

Eno. How now, friend Eros!

Eros. There's strange news come, sir.

Eno. What, man?

Eros. Cæsar and Lepidus have made wars upon Pompey.

Eno. This is old: what is the success?

Eros. Cæsar, having made use of him in the wars 'gainst Pompey, presently denied him rivality; would not let him partake in the glory of the action: and not resting here, accuses him of letters he had formerly wrote to Pompey; upon his own appeal, seizes him: so the poor third is up, till death enlarge his confine.

Eno. Then, world, thou hast a pair of chaps, no more;
And throw between them all the food thou hast,
They'll grind the one the other. Where's Antony?

Eros. He's walking in the garden—thus; and spurns
The rush that lies before him; cries 'Fool Lepidus!'
And threats the throat of that his officer
That murder'd Pompey.

Eno. Our great navy's rigg'd.

Eros. For Italy and Cæsar. More, Domitius;
My lord desires you presently: my news
I might have told hereafter.

Eno. 'Twill be naught:
But let it be. Bring me to Antony.

Eros. Come, sir. [*Exeunt.*

Scene VI

Rome. Cæsar's house.

Enter Cæsar, Agrippa, and Mæcenas.

Cæs. Contemning Rome, he has done all this, and more,
In Alexandria: here's the manner of't:
I' the market-place, on a tribunal silver'd
Cleopatra and himself in chairs of gold
Were publicly enthroned: at the feet sat
Cæsarion, whom they call my father's son,

And all the unlawful issue that their lust
Since then hath made between them. Unto her
He gave the stablishment of Egypt; made her
Of lower Syria, Cyprus, Lydia,
Absolute queen.
Mæc. This in the public eye?
Cæs. I' the common show-place, where they exercise.
His sons he there proclaim'd the kings of kings:
Great Media, Parthia, and Armenia,
He gave to Alexander; to Ptolemy he assign'd
Syria, Cilicia and Phœnicia: she
In the habiliments of the goddess Isis
That day appear'd, and oft before gave audience,
As 'tis reported, so.
Mæc. Let Rome be thus
Inform'd.
Agr. Who, queasy with his insolence
Already, will their good thoughts call from him.
Cæs. The people know it, and have now received
His accusations.
Agr. Who does he accuse?
Cæs. Cæsar: and that, having in Sicily
Sextus Pompeius spoil'd, we had not rated him
His part o' the isle: then does he say, he lent me
Some shipping unrestored: lastly, he frets
That Lepidus of the triumvirate
Should be deposed; and, being, that we detain
All his revenue.
Agr. Sir, this should be answer'd.
Cæs. 'Tis done already, and the messenger gone.
I have told him, Lepidus was grown too cruel;
That he his high authority abused
And did deserve his change: for what I have conquer'd,
I grant him part; but then, in his Armenia
And other of his conquer'd kingdoms, I
Demand the like.
Mæc. He'll never yield to that.
Cæs. Nor must not then be yielded to in this.

Enter Octavia, with her train.

Octa. Hail, Cæsar, and my lord! hail, most dear Cæsar!
Cæs. That ever I should call thee castaway!
Octa. You have not call'd me so, nor have you cause.
Cæs. Why have you stol'n upon us thus? You come not
Like Cæsar's sister: the wife of Antony
Should have an army for an usher, and

The neighs of borse to tell of her approach
Long ere she did appear; the trees by the way
Should have borne men; and expectation fainted,
Longing for what it had not; nay, the dust
Should have ascended to the roof of heaven,
Raised by your populous troops: but you are come
A market-maid to Rome; and have prevented
The ostentation of our love, which, left unshown,
Is often left unloved: we should have met you
By sea and land, supplying every stage
With an augmented greeting.

Octa. Good my lord,
To come thus was I not constrain'd, but did it
On my free will. My lord, Mark Antony,
Hearing that you prepared for war, acquainted
My grieved ear withal; whereon, I begg'd
His pardon for return.

Cæs. Which soon he granted,
Being an obstruct 'tween his lust and him.

Octa. Do not say so, my lord.

Cæs. I have eyes upon him,
And his affairs come to me on the wind.
Where is he now?

Octa. My lord, in Athens.

Cæs. No, my most wronged sister; Cleopatra
Hath nodded him to her. He hath given his empire
Up to a whore; who now are levying
The kings o' the earth for war: he hath assembled
Bocchus, the king of Libya; Archelaus,
Of Cappadocia; Philadelphos, king
Of Paphlagonia; the Thracian king, Adallas;
King Malchus of Arabia; King of Pont;
Herod of Jewry; Mithridates, king
Of Comagene; Polemon and Amyntas,
The kings of Mede and Lycaonia,
With a more larger list of sceptres.

Octa. Ay me, most wretched,
That have my heart parted betwixt two friends
That do afflict each other!

Cæs. Welcome hither:
Your letters did withhold our breaking forth,
Till we perceived both how you were wrong led
And we in negligent danger. Cheer your heart:
Be you not troubled with the time, which drives
O'er your content these strong necessities;

But let determined things to destiny
Hold unbewail'd their way. Welcome to Rome;
Nothing more dear to me. You are abused
Beyond the mark of thought: and the high gods,
To do you justice, make them ministers
Of us and those that love you. Best of comfort;
And ever welcome to us.
Agr. Welcome, lady.
Mæc. Welcome, dear madam.
Each heart in Rome does love and pity you:
Only the adulterous Antony, most large
In his abominations, turns you off;
And gives his potent regiment to a trull,
That noises it against us.
Octa. Is it so, sir?
Cæs. Most certain. Sister, welcome: pray you,
Be ever known to patience: my dear'st sister! [*Exeunt.*

Scene VII

Near Actium. Antony's camp.

Enter Cleopatra and Enobarbus.

Cleo. I will be even with thee, doubt it not.
Eno. But why, why, why?
Cleo. Thou hast forspoke my being in these wars,
And say'st it is not fit.
Eno. Well, is it, is it?
Cleo. If not denounced against us, why should not we
Be there in person?
Eno. [*Aside*] Well, I could reply:
If we should serve with horse and mares together,
The horse were merely lost; the mares would bear
A soldier and his horse.
Cleo. What is 't you say?
Eno. Your presence needs must puzzle Antony;
Take from his heart, take from his brain, from 's time,
What should not then be spared. He is already
Traduced for levity; and 'tis said in Rome
That Photinus, an eunuch and your maids
Manage this war.
Cleo. Sink Rome, and their tongues rot
That speak against us! A charge we bear i' the war,
And, as the president of my kingdom, will
Appear there for a man. Speak not against it;
I will not stay behind.
Eno. Nay, I have done.

Here comes the emperor.

Enter Antony and Canidius.

Ant. Is it not strange, Canidius,
That from Tarentum and Brundusium
He could so quickly cut the Ionian sea,
And take in Toryne? You have heard on 't, sweet?

Cleo. Celerity is never more admired
Than by the negligent.

Ant. A good rebuke,
Which might have well becomed the best of men,
To taunt at slackness. Canidius, we
Will fight with him by sea.

Cleo. By sea: what else?

Can. Why will my lord do so?

Ant. For that he dares us to 't.

Eno. So hath my lord dared him to single fight.

Can. Ay, and to wage this battle at Pharsalia,
Where Cæsar fought with Pompey: but these offers,
Which serve not for his vantage, he shakes off,
And so should you.

Eno. Your ships are not well mann'd,
Your mariners are muleters, reapers, people
Ingross'd by swift impress; in Cæsar's fleet
Are those that often have 'gainst Pompey fought:
Their ships are yare, yours heavy: no disgrace
Shall fall you for refusing him at sea,
Being prepared for land.

Ant. By sea, by sea.

Eno. Most worthy sir, you therein throw away
The absolute soldiership you have by land,
Distract your army, which doth most consist
Of war-mark'd footmen, leave unexecuted
Your own renowned knowledge, quite forgo
The way which promises assurance, and
Give up yourself merely to chance and hazard
From firm security.

Ant. I'll fight at sea.

Cleo. I have sixty sails, Cæsar none better.

Ant. Our overplus of shipping will we burn;
And, with the rest full-mann'd, from the head of Actium
Beat the approaching Cæsar. But if we fail,
We then can do 't at land.

Enter a Messenger.

Thy business?

Mess. The news is true, my lord; he is descried;

Cæsar has taken Toryne.
Ant. Can he be there in person? 'tis impossible;
Strange that his power should be. Canidius,
Our nineteen legions thou shalt hold by land,
And our twelve thousand horse. We'll to our ship:
Away, my Thetis!

Enter a Soldier.

How now, worthy soldier?
Sold. O noble emperor, do not fight by sea;
Trust not to rotten planks. Do you misdoubt
This sword and these my wounds? Let the Egyptians
And the Phœnicians go a-ducking: we
Have used to conquer, standing on the earth
And fighting foot to foot.
Ant. Well, well: away!

[*Exeunt Antony, Cleopatra, and Enobarbus.*

Sold. By Hercules, I think I am i' the right.
Can. Soldier, thou art: but his whole action grows
Not in the power on 't: so our leader 's led,
And we are women's men.
Sold. You keep by land
The legions and the horse whole, do you not?
Can. Marcus Octavius, Marcus Justeius,
Publicola and Cælius, are for sea:
But we keep whole by land. This speed of Cæsar's
Carries beyond belief.
Sold. While he was yet in Rome,
His power went out in such distractions as
Beguiled all spies.
Can. Who 's his lieutenant, hear you?
Sold. They say, one Taurus.
Can. Well I know the man.

Enter a Messenger.

Mess. The emperor calls Canidius.
Can. With news the time 's with labour, and throes forth
Each minute some. [*Exeunt.*

Scene VIII

A plain near Actium.

Enter Cæsar, and Taurus, with his army, marching.

Cæs. Taurus!
Taur. My lord?
Cæs. Strike not by land; keep whole: provoke not battle,
Till we have done at sea. Do not exceed

The prescript of this scroll: our fortune lies
Upon this jump. [*Exeunt.*

Scene IX

Another part of the plain.

Enter Antony and Enobarbus.

Ant. Set we our squadrons on yond side o' the hill,
In eye of Cæsar's battle; from which place
We may the number of the ships behold,
And so proceed accordingly. [*Exeunt.*

Scene X

Another part of the plain.

Enter Canidius, marching with his land army one way; and Taurus, the lieutenant of Cæsar, with his army, the other way. After their going in, is heard the noise of a sea-fight.

Alarum. Enter Enobarbus.

Eno. Naught, naught, all naught! I can behold no longer!
The Antoniad, the Egyptian admiral,
With all their sixty, fly and turn the rudder:
To see 't mine eyes are blasted.

Enter Scarus.

Scar. Gods and goddesses,
All the whole synod of them!

Eno. What 's thy passion?

Scar. The greater cantle of the world is lost
With very ignorance; we have kiss'd away
Kingdoms and provinces.

Eno. How appears the fight?

Scar. On our side like the token'd pestilence,
Where death is sure. Yon ribaudred nag of Egypt—
Whom leprosy o'ertake!—i' the midst o' the fight,
When vantage like a pair of twins appear'd,
Both as the same, or rather ours the elder,—
The breese upon her, like a cow in June!—
Hoists sails and flies.

Eno. That I beheld:
Mine eyes did sicken at the sight, and could not
Endure a further view.

Scar. She once being loof'd,
The noble ruin of her magic, Antony,
Claps on his sea-wing, and like a doting mallard,
Leaving the fight in height, flies after her:
I never saw an action of such shame;
Experience, manhood honour, ne'er before

Did violate so itself.
Eno. Alack, alack!
Enter Canidius.
Can. Our fortune on the sea is out of breath,
And sinks most lamentably. Had our general
Been what he knew himself, it had gone well:
O, he has given example for our flight
Most grossly by his own!
Eno. Ay, are you thereabouts? Why then good night,
Indeed.
Can. Toward Peloponnesus are they fled.
Scar. 'Tis easy to 't; and there I will attend
What further comes.
Can. To Cæsar will I render
My legions and my horse: six kings already
Show me the way of yielding.
Eno. I 'll yet follow
The wounded chance of Antony, though my reason
Sits in the wind against me. [*Exeunt.*

SCENE XI

Alexandria. Cleopatra's palace.

Enter Antony with Attendants.

Ant. Hark! the land bids me tread no more upon 't;
It is ashamed to bear me. Friends, come hither:
I am so lated in the world that I
Have lost my way for ever. I have a ship
Laden with gold; take that, divide it; fly,
And make your peace with Cæsar.
All. Fly! not we.
Ant. I have fled myself, and have instructed cowards
To run and show their shoulders. Friends, be gone;
I have myself resolved upon a course
Which has no need of you; be gone:
My treasure 's in the harbour, take it. O,
I follow'd that I blush to look upon:
My very hairs do mutiny, for the white
Reprove the brown for rashness, and they them
For fear and doting. Friends, be gone: you shall
Have letters from me to some friends that will
Sweep your way for you. Pray you, look not sad,
Nor make replies of loathness; take the hint
Which my despair proclaims; let that be left
Which leaves itself: to the sea-side straightway:
I will possess you of that ship and treasure.

Leave me, I pray, a little: pray you now:
Nay, do so; for indeed I have lost command,
Therefore I pray you: I'll see you by and by. [*Sits down.*

Enter Cleopatra led by Charmian and Iras; Eros following.

Eros. Nay, gentle madam, to him, comfort him.
Iras. Do, most dear queen.
Char. Do! why, what else?
Cleo. Let me sit down. O Juno!
Ant. No, no, no, no, no.
Eros. See you here, sir?
Ant. O fie, fie, fie!
Char. Madam!
Iras. Madam, O good empress!
Eros. Sir, sir!
Ant. Yes, my lord, yes; he at Philippi kept
His sword e'en like a dancer; while I struck
The lean and wrinkled Cassius; and 'twas I
That the mad Brutus ended: he alone
Dealt on lieutenantry and no practice had
In the brave squares of war: yet now—No matter.
Cleo. Ah! stand by.
Eros. The queen, my lord, the queen.
Iras. Go to him, madam, speak to him:
He is unqualitied with very shame.
Cleo. Well then, sustain me: O!
Eros. Most noble sir, arise; the queen approaches:
Her head 's declined, and death will seize her, but
Your comfort makes the rescue.
Ant. I have offended reputation,
A most unnoble swerving.
Eros. Sir, the queen.
Ant. O, whither hast thou led me, Egypt? See,
How I convey my shame out of thine eyes
By looking back what I have left behind
Stroy'd in dishonour.
Cleo. O my lord, my lord,
Forgive my fearful sails! I little thought
You would have follow'd.
Ant. Egypt, thou knew'st too well
My heart was to thy rudder tied by the strings,
And thou shouldst tow me after: o'er my spirit
Thy full supremacy thou knew'st, and that
Thy beck might from the bidding of the gods
Command me.
Cleo. O, my pardon!

Ant. Now I must
To the young man send humble treaties, dodge
And palter in the shifts of lowness; who
With half the bulk o' the world play'd as I pleased,
Making and marring fortunes. You did know
How much you were my conqueror, and that
My sword, made weak by my affection, would
Obey it on all cause.
Cleo. Pardon, pardon!
Ant. Fall not a tear, I say; one of them rates
All that is won and lost: give me a kiss;
Even this repays me. We sent our schoolmaster;
Is he come back? Love, I am full of lead.
Some wine, within there, and our viands! Fortune knows
We scorn her most when most she offers blows. [*Exeunt.*

SCENE XII

Egypt. Cæsar's camp.

Enter Cæsar, Dolabella, Thyreus, with others.

Cæs. Let him appear that 's come from Antony.
Know you him?
Dol. Cæsar, 'tis his schoolmaster:
An argument that he is pluck'd, when hither
He sends so poor a pinion of his wing,
Which had superfluous kings for messengers
Not many moons gone by.

Enter Euphronius, ambassador from Antony.

Cæs. Approach, and speak.
Euph. Such as I am, I come from Antony:
I was of late as petty to his ends
As is the morn-dew on the myrtle-leaf
To his grand sea.
Cæs. Be 't so: declare thine office.
Euph. Lord of his fortunes he salutes thee, and
Requires to live in Egypt: which not granted,
He lessens his requests, and to thee sues
To let him breathe between the heavens and earth,
A private man in Athens: this for him.
Next, Cleopatra does confess thy greatness;
Submits her to thy might, and of thee craves
The circle of the Ptolemies for her heirs,
Now hazarded to thy grace.
Cæs. For Antony,
I have no ears to his request. The queen
Of audience nor desire shall fail, so she

From Egypt drive her all-disgraced friend,
Or take his life there: this if she perform,
She shall not sue unheard. So to them both.

Euph. Fortune pursue thee!

Cæs. Bring him through the bands.
[*Exit Euphronius.*

[*To Thyreus*] To try thy eloquence, now 'tis time: dispatch;
From Antony win Cleopatra: promise,
And in our name, what she requires; add more,
From thine invention, offers: women are not
In their best fortunes strong, but want will perjure
The ne'er-touch'd vestal: try thy cunning, Thyreus;
Make thine own edict for thy pains, which we
Will answer as a law.

Thyr. Cæsar, I go.

Cæs. Observe how Antony becomes his flaw,
And what thou think'st his very action speaks
In every power that moves.

Thyr. Cæsar, I shall. [*Exeunt.*

Scene XIII

Alexandria. Cleopatra's palace.

Enter Cleopatra, Enobarbus, Charmian, and Iras.

Cleo. What shall we do, Enobarbus?

Eno. Think, and die.

Cleo. Is Antony or we in fault for this?

Eno. Antony only, that would make his will
Lord of his reason. What though you fled
From that great face of war, whose several ranges
Frighted each other, why should he follow?
The itch of his affection should not then
Have nick'd his captainship; at such a point,
When half to half the world opposed, he being
The mered question: 'twas a shame no less
Than was his loss, to course your flying flags
And leave his navy gazing.

Cleo. Prithee, peace.

Enter Antony, with Euphronius the Ambassador.

Ant. Is that his answer?

Euph. Ay, my lord.

Ant. The queen shall then have courtesy, so she
Will yield us up.

Euph. He says so.

Ant. Let her know't.
To the boy Cæsar send this grizzled head,

And he will fill thy wishes to the brim
With principalities.
Cleo. That head, my lord?
Ant. To him again: tell him he wears the rose
Of youth upon him, from which the world should note
Something particular: his coin, ships, legions,
May be a coward's, whose ministers would prevail
Under the service of a child as soon
As i' the command of Cæsar: I dare him therefore
To lay his gay comparisons apart
And answer me declined, sword against sword,
Ourselves alone. I'll write it: follow me.
[*Exeunt Antony and Euphronius.*
Eno. [*Aside*] Yes, like enough, high-battled Cæsar will
Unstate his happiness and be staged to the show
Against a sworder! I see men's judgements are
A parcel of their fortunes, and things outward
Do draw the inward quality after them,
To suffer all alike. That he should dream,
Knowing all measures, the full Cæsar will
Answer his emptiness! Cæsar, thou hast subdued
His judgement too.

Enter an Attendant.

Att. A messenger from Cæsar.
Cleo. What, no more ceremony? See, my women,
Against the blown rose may they stop their nose
That kneel'd unto the buds. Admit him, sir. [*Exit Attend.*
Eno. [*Aside*] Mine honesty and I begin to square.
The loyalty well held to fools does make
Our faith mere folly: yet he that can endure
To follow with allegiance a fall'n lord
Does conquer him that did his master conquer,
And earns a place i' the story.

Enter Thyreus.

Cleo. Cæsar's will?
Thyr. Hear it apart.
Cleo. None but friends: say boldly.
Thyr. So, haply, are they friends to Antony.
Eno. He needs as many, sir, as Cæsar has,
Or needs not us. If Cæsar please, our master
Will leap to be his friend: for us, you know,
Whose he is we are, and that is Cæsar's.
Thyr. So.
Thus then, thou most renown'd: Cæsar entreats

Not to consider in what case thou stand'st
Further than he is Cæsar.
Cleo. Go on: right royal.
Thyr. He knows that you embrace not Antony
As you did love, but as you fear'd him.
Cleo. O!
Thyr. The scars upon your honour therefore he
Does pity as constrained blemishes,
Not as deserved.
Cleo. He is a god and knows
What is most right: mine honour was not yielded,
But conquer'd merely.
Eno. [*Aside*] To be sure of that,
I will ask Antony. Sir, sir, thou art so leaky
That we must leave thee to thy sinking, for
Thy dearest quit thee. [*Exit.*
Thyr. Shall I say to Cæsar
What you require of him? for he partly begs
To be desired to give. It much would please him,
That of his fortunes you should make a staff
To lean upon: but it would warm his spirits,
To hear from me you had left Antony,
And put yourself under his shrowd,
The universal landlord.
Cleo. What 's your name?
Thyr. My name is Thyrcus.
Cleo. Most kind messenger,
Say to great Cæsar this: in deputation
I kiss his conquering hand: tell him, I am prompt
To lay my crown at 's feet, and there to kneel:
Tell him, from his all-obeying breath I hear
The doom of Egypt.
Thyr. 'Tis your noblest course.
Wisdom and fortune combating together,
If that the former dare but what it can,
No chance may shake it. Give me grace to lay
My duty on your hand.
Cleo. Your Cæsar's father oft,
When he hath mused of taking kingdoms in,
Bestow'd his lips on that unworthy place,
As it rain'd kisses.

Re-enter Antony and Enobarbus.

Ant. Favours, by Jove that thunders
What art thou, fellow?

Thyr. One that but performs
The bidding of the fullest man and worthiest
To have command obey'd.
Eno. [*Aside*] You will be whipp'd.
Ant. Approach, there! Ah, you kite! Now, gods and devils!
Authority melts from me: of late, when I cried 'Ho!'
Like boys unto a muss, kings would start forth,
And cry 'Your will?' Have you no ears?
I am Antony yet.

Enter Attendants.

Take hence this Jack, and whip him.
Eno. [*Aside*] 'Tis better playing with a lion's whelp
Than with an old one dying.
Ant. Moon and stars!
Whip him. Were 't twenty of the greatest tributaries
That do acknowledge Cæsar, should I find them
So saucy with the hand of she here,—what 's her name,
Since she was Cleopatra? Whip him, fellows,
Till, like a boy, you see him cringe his face,
And whine aloud for mercy: take him hence.
Thyr. Mark Antony,—
Ant. Tug him away: being whipp'd,
Bring him again: this Jack of Cæsar's shall
Bear us an errand to him. [*Exeunt Attendants, with Thyreus.*
You were half blasted ere I knew you: ha!
Have I my pillow left unpress'd in Rome,
Forborne the getting of a lawful race,
And by a gem of women, to be abused
By one that looks on feeders?
Cleo. Good, my lord,—
Ant. You have been a boggler ever:
But when we in our viciousness grow hard—
O misery on 't!—the wise gods seel our eyes;
In our own filth drop our clear judgements; make us
Adore our errors; laugh at 's while we strut
To our confusion.
Cleo. O, is 't come to this?
Ant. I found you as a morsel cold upon
Dead Cæsar's trencher; nay, you were a fragment
Of Cneius Pompey's; besides what hotter hours,
Unregister'd in vulgar fame, you have
Luxuriously pick'd out: for I am sure,
Though you can guess what temperance should be,
You know not what it is.
Cleo. Wherefore is this?

Ant. To let a fellow what will take rewards
And say 'God quit you!' be familiar with
My playfellow, your hand, this kingly seal
And plighter of high hearts! O, that I were
Upon the hill of Basan, to outroar
The horned herd! for I have savage cause;
And to proclaim it civilly, were like
A halter'd neck which does the hangman thank
For being yare about him.

Re-enter Attendants, with Thyreus.

Is he whipp'd?
First Att. Soundly, my lord.
Ant. Cried he? and begg'd he pardon?
First Att. He did ask favour.
Ant. If that thy father live, let him repent
Thou wast not made his daughter; and be thou sorry
To follow Cæsar in his triumph, since
Thou hast been whipp'd for following him: henceforth
The white hand of a lady fever thee,
Shake thou to look on 't. Get thee back to Cæsar,
Tell him thy entertainment: look thou say
He makes me angry with him; for he seems
Proud and disdainful, harping on what I am,
Not what he knew I was: he makes me angry;
And at this time most easy 'tis to do 't,
When my good stars that were my former guides
Have empty left their orbs and shot their fires
Into the abysm of hell. If he mislike
My speech and what is done, tell him he has
Hipparchus, my enfranched bondman, whom
He may at pleasure whip, or hang, or torture,
As he shall like, to quit me: urge it thou:
Hence with thy stripes, begone! [*Exit Thyreus.*
Cleo. Have you done yet?
Ant. Alack, our terrene moon
Is now eclipsed, and it portends alone
The fall of Antony.
Cleo. I must stay his time.
Ant. To flatter Cæsar, would you mingle eyes
With one that ties his points?
Cleo. Not know me yet?
Ant. Cold-hearted toward me?
Cleo. Ah, dear, if I be so,
From my cold heart let heaven engender hail,

And poison it in the source, and the first stone
Drop in my neck: as it determines, so
Dissolve my life! The next Cæsarion smite!
Till by degrees the memory of my womb,
Together with my brave Egyptians all,
By the discandying of this pelleted storm
Lie graveless, till the flies and gnats of Nile
Have buried them for prey!

Ant. I am satisfied.
Cæsar sits down in Alexandria, where
I will oppose his fate. Our force by land
Hath nobly held; our sever'd navy too
Have knit again, and fleet, threatening most sea-like.
Where hast thou been, my heart? Dost thou hear, lady?
If from the field I shall return once more
To kiss these lips, I will appear in blood;
I and my sword will earn our chronicle:
There's hope in't yet.

Cleo. That's my brave lord!

Ant. I will be treble-sinew'd, hearted, breath'd,
And fight maliciously: for when mine hours
Were nice and lucky, men did ransom lives
Of me for jests: but now I'll set my teeth,
And send to darkness all that stop me. Come,
Let's have one other gaudy night: call to me
All my sad captains; fill our bowls once more:
Let's mock the midnight bell.

Cleo. It is my birth-day:
I had thought to have held it poor, but since my lord
Is Antony again, I will be Cleopatra.

Ant. We will yet do well.

Cleo. Call all his noble captains to my lord.

Ant. Do so, we'll speak to them; and to-night I'll force
The wine peep through their scars. Come on, my queen;
There's sap in't yet. The next time I do fight
I'll make death love me, for I will contend
Even with his pestilent scythe. [*Exeunt all but Enobarbus.*

Eno. Now he'll outstare the lightning. To be furious
Is to be frighted out of fear; and in that mood
The dove will peck the estridge; and I see still,
A diminution in our captain's brain
Restores his heart: when valour plays on reason,
It eats the sword it fights with. I will seek
Some way to leave him. [*Exit.*

ACT IV—Scene I

Before Alexandria. Cæsar's camp.

Enter Cæsar, Agrippa, and Mæcenas, with his army: Cæsar reading a letter.

Cæs. He calls me boy, and chides as he had power
To beat me out of Egypt; my messenger
He hath whipp'd with rods; dares me to personal combat,
Cæsar to Antony. Let the old ruffian know
I have many other ways to die, meantime
Laugh at his challenge.

Mæc. Cæsar must think,
When one so great begins to rage, he's hunted
Even to falling. Give him no breath, but now
Make boot of his distraction. Never anger
Made good guard for itself.

Cæs. Let our best heads
Know that to-morrow the last of many battles
We mean to fight. Within our files there are,
Of those that served Mark Antony but late,
Enough to fetch him in. See it done:
And feast the army; we have store to do 't,
And they have earn'd the waste. Poor Antony! [*Exeunt.*

Scene II

Alexandria. Cleopatra's palace.

Enter Antony, Cleopatra, Enobarbus, Charmian, Iras, Alexas, with others.

Ant. He will not fight with me, Domitius?

Eno. No.

Ant. Why should he not?

Eno. He thinks, being twenty times of better fortune,
He is twenty men to one.

Ant. To-morrow, soldier,
By sea and land I'll fight: or I will live,
Or bathe my dying honour in the blood
Shall make it live again. Woo 't thou fight well?

Eno. I'll strike, and cry 'Take all.'

Ant. Well said; come on.
Call forth my household servants: let's to-night
Be bounteous at our meal.

Enter three or four Servitors.

Give me thy hand,
Thou hast been rightly honest;—so hast thou;—
Thou,—and thou,—and thou: you have served me well,

And kings have been your fellows.
Cleo. [*Aside to Eno.*] What means this?
Eno. [*Aside to Cleo.*] 'Tis one of those odd tricks which sorrow
Out of the mind. [shoots
Ant. And thou art honest too.
I wish I could be made so many men,
And all of you clapp'd up together in
An Antony, that I might do you service
So good as you have done.
Serv. The gods forbid!
Ant. Well, my good fellows, wait on me to-night:
Scant not my cups, and make as much of me
As when mine empire was your fellow too
And suffer'd my command.
Cleo. [*Aside to Eno.*] What does he mean?
Eno. [*Aside to Cleo.*] To make his followers weep.
Ant. Tend me to-night:
May be it is the period of your duty:
Haply you shall not see me more; or if,
A mangled shadow: perchance to-morrow
You'll serve another master. I look on you
As one that takes his leave. Mine honest friends,
I turn you not away; but, like a master
Married to your good service, stay till death:
Tend me to-night two hours, I ask no more,
And the gods yield you for 't!
Eno. What mean you, sir,
To give them this discomfort? Look, they weep,
And I, an ass, am onion-eyed: for shame,
Transform us not to women.
Ant. Ho, ho, ho!
Now the witch take me, if I meant it thus!
Grace grow where those drops fall! My hearty friends,
You take me in too dolorous a sense;
For I spake to you for your comfort, did desire you
To burn this night with torches: know, my hearts,
I hope well of to-morrow, and will lead you
Where rather I'll expect victorious life
Than death and honour. Let's to supper, come,
And drown consideration. [*Exeunt.*

Scene III

The same. Before the palace.

Enter two Soldiers to their guard.

First Sold. Brother, good night: to-morrow is the day.

Sec. Sold. It will determine one way: fare you well.
Heard you of nothing strange about the streets?
First Sold. Nothing. What news?
Sec. Sold. Belike 'tis but a rumour. Good night to you.
First Sold. Well, sir, good night.

Enter two other Soldiers.

Sec. Sold. Soldiers, have careful watch.
Third Sold. And you. Good night, good night.

[*They place themselves in every corner of the stage.*

Fourth Sold. Here we: and if to-morrow
Our navy thrive, I have an absolute hope
Our landmen will stand up.
Third Sold. 'Tis a brave army,
And full of purpose.

Music of hautboys as under the stage.

Fourth Sold. Peace! what noise?
First Sold. List, list!
Sec. Sold. Hark!
First Sold. Music i' the air.
Third Sold. Under the earth.
Fourth Sold. It signs well, does it not?
Third Sold. No.
First Sold. Peace, I say!
What should this mean?
Sec. Sold. 'Tis the god Hercules, whom Antony loved,
Now leaves him.
First Sold. Walk; let 's see if other watchmen
Do hear what we do.
Sec. Sold. How now, masters!
All. [*Speaking together*] How now! How now! Do you hear [this?
First Sold. Ay; is 't not strange?
Third Sold. Do you hear, masters? do you hear?
First Sold. Follow the noise so far as we have quarter;
Let 's see how it will give off.
All. Content. 'Tis strange. [*Exeunt.*

Scene IV

The same. A room in the palace.

Enter Antony and Cleopatra, Charmian and others attending.

Ant. Eros! mine armour, Eros!
Cleo. Sleep a little.
Ant. No, my chuck. Eros, come; mine armour, Eros!

Enter Eros with armour.

Come, good fellow, put mine iron on:

If fortune be not ours to-day, it is
Because we brave her: come.

Cleo. Nay, I'll help too.
What's this for?

Ant. Ah, let be, let be! thou art
The armourer of my heart: false, false; this, this.

Cleo. Sooth, la, I'll help: thus it must be.

Ant. Well, well;
We shall thrive now. Seest thou, my good fellow?
Go put on thy defences.

Eros. Briefly, sir.

Cleo. Is not this buckled well?

Ant. Rarely, rarely:
He that unbuckles this, till we do please
To daff't for our repose, shall hear a storm.
Thou fumblest, Eros; and my queen's a squire
More tight at this than thou: dispatch. O love,
That thou couldst see my wars to-day, and knew'st
The royal occupation! thou shouldst see
A workman in't.

Enter an armed Soldier.

Good morrow to thee; welcome:
Thou look'st like him that knows a warlike charge:
To business that we love we rise betime,
And go to't with delight.

Sold. A thousand, sir,
Early though't be, have on their riveted trim,
And at the port expect you. [*Shout. Trumpets flourish.*

Enter Captains and Soldiers.

Capt. The morn is fair. Good morrow, general.

All. Good morrow, general.

Ant. 'Tis well blown, lads:
This morning, like the spirit of a youth
That means to be of note, begins betimes.
So, so; come, give me that: this way; well said.
Fare thee well, dame, whate'er becomes of me:
This is a soldier's kiss: rebukeable
And worthy shameful check it were, to stand
On more mechanic compliment; I'll leave thee
Now like a man of steel. You that will fight,
Follow me close; I'll bring you to't. Adieu.

[*Exeunt Antony, Eros, Captains, and Soldiers.*

Char. Please you, retire to your chamber.

Cleo. Lead me.
He goes forth gallantly. That he and Cæsar might

Determine this great war in single fight!
Then Antony—but now—Well, on. [*Exeunt.*

SCENE V

Alexandria. Antony's camp.

Trumpets sound. Enter Antony and Eros; a Soldier meeting them.

Sold. The gods make this a happy day to Antony!
Ant. Would thou and those thy scars had once prevail'd
To make me fight at land!
Sold. Hadst thou done so,
The kings that have revolted and the soldier
That has this morning left thee would have still
Follow'd thy heels.
Ant. Who 's gone this morning?
Sold. Who!
One ever near thee: call for Enobarbus,
He shall not hear thee, or from Cæsar's camp
Say 'I am none of thine.'
Ant. What say'st thou?
Sold. Sir,
He is with Cæsar.
Eros. Sir, his chests and treasure
He has not with him.
Ant. Is he gone?
Sold. Most certain.
Ant. Go, Eros, send his treasure after; do it;
Detain no jot, I charge thee: write to him—
I will subscribe—gentle adieus and greetings;
Say that I wish he never find more cause
To change a master. O, my fortunes have
Corrupted honest men! Dispatch. Enobarbus! [*Exeunt.*

SCENE VI

Alexandria. Cæsar's camp.

Flourish. Enter Cæsar with Agrippa, Enobarbus, and others.

Cæs. Go forth, Agrippa, and begin the fight:
Our will is Antony be took alive;
Make it so known.
Agr. Cæsar, I shall. [*Exit.*
Cæs. The time of universal peace is near:
Prove this a prosperous day, the three-nook'd world
Shall bear the olive freely.

Enter a Messenger.

Mess. Antony

Is come into the field.
Cæs. Go charge Agrippa
Plant those that have revolted in the van,
That Antony may seem to spend his fury
Upon himself. [*Exeunt all but Enobarbus.*
Eno. Alexas did revolt, and went to Jewry
On affairs of Antony; there did persuade
Great Herod to incline himself to Cæsar
And leave his master Antony: for this pains
Cæsar hath hang'd him. Canidius and the rest
That fell away have entertainment, but
No honourable trust. I have done ill;
Of which I do accuse myself so sorely
That I will joy no more.

Enter a Soldier of Cæsar's.

Sold. Enobarbus, Antony
Hath after thee sent all thy treasure, with
His bounty overplus: the messenger
Came on my guard, and at thy tent is now
Unloading of his mules.
Eno. I give it you.
Sold. Mock not, Enobarbus:
I tell you true: best you safed the bringer
Out of the host; I must attend mine office,
Or would have done 't myself. Your emperor
Continues still a Jove. [*Exit.*
Eno. I am alone the villain of the earth,
And feel I am so most. O Antony,
Thou mine of bounty, how wouldst thou have paid
My better service, when my turpitude
Thou dost so crown with gold! This blows my heart:
If swift thought break it not, a swifter mean
Shall outstrike thought: but thought will do 't, I feel.
I fight against thee! No: I will go seek
Some ditch wherein to die; the foul'st best fits
My latter part of life. [*Exit.*

Scene VII

Field of battle between the camps.

Alarum. Drums and trumpets. Enter Agrippa and others.

Agr. Retire, we have engaged ourselves too far:
Cæsar himself has work, and our oppression
Exceeds what we expected. [*Exeunt.*

Alarums. Enter Antony, and Scarus wounded.

Scar. O my brave emperor, this is fought indeed!

Had we done so at first, we had droven them home
With clouts about their heads.

Ant. Thou bleed'st apace.

Scar. I had a wound here that was like a T,
But now 'tis made an H. [*Retreat afar off.*

Ant. They do retire.

Scar. We 'll beat 'em into bench-holes: I have yet
Room for six scotches more.

Enter Eros.

Eros. They are beaten, sir, and our advantage serves
For a fair victory.

Scar. Let us score their backs
And snatch 'em up, as we take hares, behind:
'Tis sport to maul a runner.

Ant. I will reward thee
Once for thy spritely comfort, and ten-fold
For thy good valour. Come thee on.

Scar. I'll halt after. [*Exeunt.*

Scene VIII

Under the walls of Alexandria.

Alarum. Enter Antony, in a march; Scarus, with others.

Ant. We have beat him to his camp: run one before,
And let the queen know of our gests. To-morrow,
Before the sun shall see 's, we 'll spill the blood
That has to-day escaped. I thank you all;
For doughty-handed are you, and have fought
Not as you served the cause, but as 't had been
Each man 's like mine; you have shown all Hectors.
Enter the city, clip your wives, your friends,
Tell them your feats; whilst they with joyful tears
Wash the congealment from your wounds and kiss
The honour'd gashes whole. [*To Scarus*] Give me thy hand;

Enter Cleopatra, attended.

To this great fairy I 'll commend thy acts,
Make her thanks bless thee. O thou day o' the world,
Chain mine arm'd neck; leap thou, attire and all,
Through proof of harness to my heart, and there
Ride on the pants triumphing!

Cleo. Lord of lords!
O infinite virtue, comest thou smiling from
The world's great snare uncaught?

Ant. My nightingale,
We have beat them to their beds. What, girl! though grey
Do something mingle with our younger brown, yet ha' we

A brain that nourishes our nerves and can
Get goal for goal of youth. Behold this man;
Commend unto his lips thy favouring hand:
Kiss it, my warrior: he hath fought to-day
As if a god in hate of mankind had
Destroy'd in such a shape.
Cleo. I'll give thee, friend,
An armour all of gold; it was a king's.
Ant. He has deserved it, were it carbuncled
Like holy Phœbus' car. Give me thy hand:
Through Alexandria make a jolly march;
Bear our hack'd targets like the men that owe them:
Had our great palace the capacity
To camp this host, we all would sup together
And drink carouses to the next day's fate,
Which promises royal peril. Trumpeters,
With brazen din blast you the city's ear;
Make mingle with our rattling tabourines;
That heaven and earth may strike their sounds together,
Applauding our approach. [*Exeunt.*

Scene IX

Cæsar's camp.

Sentinels at their post.

First Sold. If we be not relieved within this hour,
We must return to the court of guard: the night
Is shiny, and they say we shall embattle
By the second hour i' the morn.
Sec. Sold. This last day was
A shrewd one to's.

Enter Enobarbus.

Eno. O, bear me witness, night,—
Third Sold. What man is this?
Sec. Sold. Stand close, and list him.
Eno. Be witness to me, O thou blessed moon,
When men revolted, shall upon record
Bear hateful memory, poor Enobarbus did
Before thy face repent!
First Sold. Enobarbus!
Third Sold. Peace!
Hark further.
Eno. O sovereign mistress of true melancholy,
The poisonous damp of night disponge upon me,
That life, a very rebel to my will,
May hang no longer on me: throw my heart

Against the flint and hardness of my fault;
Which, being dried with grief, will break to powder,
And finish all foul thoughts. O Antony,
Nobler than my revolt is infamous,
Forgive me in thine own particular,
But let the world rank me in register
A master-leaver and a fugitive:
O Antony! O Antony! [*Dies.*

Sec. Sold. Let 's speak to him.

First Sold. Let 's hear him, for the things he speaks
May concern Cæsar.

Third Sold. Let 's do so. But he sleeps.

First Sold. Swoons rather; for so bad a prayer as his
Was never yet for sleep.

Sec. Sold. Go we to him.

Third Sold. Awake, sir, awake; speak to us.

Sec. Sold. Hear you, sir?

First Sold. The hand of death hath raught him. [*Drums afar off.*] Hark! the drums.
Demurely wake the sleepers. Let us bear him
To the court of guard; he is of note: our hour
Is fully out.

Third Sold. Come on, then; he may recover yet.
[*Exeunt with the body.*

Scene X

Between the two camps.

Enter Antony and Scarus, with their army.

Ant. Their preparation is to-day by sea;
We please them not by land.

Scar. For both, my lord.

Ant. I would they 'ld fight i' the fire or i' the air;
We 'ld fight there to. But this it is; our foot
Upon the hills adjoining to the city
Shall stay with us: order for sea is given;
They have put forth the haven. . . . .
Where their appointment we may best discover.
And look on their endeavour. [*Exeunt.*

Scene XI

Another part of the same.

Enter Cæsar, and his army.

Cæs. But being charged, we will be still by land,
Which, as I take 't, we shall; for his best force

Is forth to man his galleys. To the vales,
And hold our best advantage. [*Exeunt.*

Scene XII

Hills adjoining to Alexandria.

Enter Antony and Scarus.

Ant. Yet they are not join'd: where yond pine does stand,
I shall discover all: I 'll bring thee word
Straight, how 'tis like to go. [*Exit.*
Scar. Swallows have built
In Cleopatra's sails their nests: the augurers
Say they know not, they cannot tell; look grimly
And dare not speak their knowledge. Antony
Is valiant, and dejected, and by starts
His fretted fortunes give him hope, and fear,
Of what he has, and has not.
[*Alarum afar off, as at a sea-fight.*

Re-enter Antony.

Ant. All is lost;
This foul Egyptian hath betrayed me:
My fleet hath yielded to the foe; and yonder
They cast their caps up and carouse together
Like friends long lost. Triple-turn'd whore! 'tis thou
Has sold me to this novice, and my heart
Makes only wars on thee. Bid them all fly;
For when I am revenged upon my charm,
I have done all. Bid them all fly; begone. [*Exit Scarus.*
O sun, thy uprise shall I see no more:
Fortune and Antony part here, even here
Do we shake hands. All come to this? The hearts
That spaniel'd me at heels, to whom I gave
Their wishes, do discandy, melt their sweets
On blossoming Cæsar; and this pine is bark'd,
That overtopp'd them all. Betray'd I am.
O this false soul of Egypt! this grave charm,
Whose eye beck'd forth my wars and call'd them home,
Whose bosom was my crownet, my chief end,
Like a right gipsy hath at fast and loose
Beguiled me to the very heart of loss.
What, Eros, Eros!

Enter Cleopatra.

Ah, thou spell! Avaunt!
Cleo. Why is my lord enraged against his love?
Ant. Vanish, or I shall give thee thy deserving,
And blemish Cæsar's triumph. Let him take thee,

And hoist thee up to the shouting plebeians:
Follow his chariot, like the greatest spot
Of all thy sex: most monster-like, be shown
For poor'st diminutives, for doits; and let
Patient Octavia plough thy visage up
With her prepared nails. [*Exit Cleopatra.*
'Tis well thou 'rt gone,
If it be well to live; but better 'twere
Thou fell'st into my fury, for one death
Might have prevented many. Eros, ho!
The shirt of Nessus is upon me: teach me,
Alcides, thou mine ancestor, thy rage:
Let me lodge Lichas on the horns o' the moon,
And with those hands that grasp'd the heaviest club
Subdue my worthiest self. The witch shall die:
To the young Roman boy she hath sold me, and I fall
Under this plot: she dies for 't. Eros, ho! [*Exit.*

Scene XIII

Alexandria. Cleopatra's palace.

Enter Cleopatra, Charmian, Iras, and Mardian.

Cleo. Help me, my women! O, he is more mad
Than Telamon for his shield; the boar of Thessaly
Was never so emboss'd.
Char. To the monument!
There lock yourself, and send him word you are dead.
The soul and body rive not more in parting
Than greatness going off.
Cleo. To the monument!
Mardian, go tell him I have slain myself;
Say that the last I spoke was 'Antony,'
And word it, prithee, piteously: hence, Mardian,
And bring me how he takes my death. To the monument!
[*Exeunt.*

Scene XIV

The same. Another room.

Enter Antony and Eros.

Ant. Eros, thou yet behold'st me?
Eros. Ay, noble lord.
Ant. Sometime we see a cloud that 's dragonish,
A vapour sometime like a bear or lion,
A tower'd citadel, a pendent rock,
A forked mountain, or blue promontory
With trees upon 't, that nod unto the world

And mock our eyes with air: thou hast seen these signs;
They are black vesper's pageants.

Eros. Ay, my lord.

Ant. That which is now a horse, even with a thought
The rack dislimns and makes it indistinct
As water is in water.

Eros. It does, my lord.

Ant. My good knave Eros, now thy captain is
Even such a body: here I am Antony,
Yet cannot hold this visible shape, my knave.
I made these wars for Egypt; and the queen—
Whose heart I thought I had, for she had mine,
Which, whilst it was mine, had annex'd unto 't
A million moe, now lost,—she, Eros, has
Pack'd cards with Cæsar, and false-play'd my glory
Unto an enemy's triumph.
Nay, weep not, gentle Eros; there is left us
Ourselves to end ourselves.

Enter Mardian.

O, thy vile lady!
She has robb'd me of my sword.

Mar. No, Antony;
My mistress loved thee, and her fortunes mingled
With thine entirely.

Ant. Hence, saucy eunuch; peace!
She hath betray'd me, and shall die the death.

Mar. Death of one person can be paid but once,
And that she has discharged: what thou wouldst do
Is done unto thy hand: the last she spake
Was 'Antony! most noble Antony!'
Then in the midst a tearing groan did break
The name of Antony; it was divided
Between her heart and lips: she render'd life,
Thy name so buried in her.

Ant. Dead then?

Mar. Dead.

Ant. Unarm, Eros; the long day's task is done,
And we must sleep. [*To Mar.*] That thou depart'st hence [safe,
Does pay thy labour richly; go. [*Exit Mardian.*
Off, pluck off:
The seven-fold shield of Ajax cannot keep
The battery from my heart. O, cleave, my sides!
Heart, once be stronger than thy continent,
Crack thy frail case! Apace, Eros, apace!
No more a soldier. Bruised pieces, go;

You have been nobly borne. From me awhile. [*Exit Eros.*
I will o'ertake thee, Cleopatra, and
Weep for my pardon. So it must be, for now
All length is torture: since the torch is out,
Lie down and stray no farther: now all labour
Mars what it does; yea, very force entangles
Itself with strength: seal then, and all is done.
Eros!—I come, my queen. Eros!—Stay for me:
Where souls do couch on flowers, we 'll hand in hand,
And with our sprightly port make the ghosts gaze:
Dido and her Æneas shall want troops,
And all the haunt be ours. Come, Eros, Eros!

Re-enter Eros.

Eros. What would my lord?
Ant. Since Cleopatra died
I have lived in such dishonour that the gods
Detest my baseness. I, that with my sword
Quarter'd the world, and o'er green Neptune's back
With ships made cities, condemn myself to lack
The courage of a woman; less noble mind
Than she which by her death our Cæsar tells
'I am conqueror of myself.' Thou art sworn, Eros,
That, when the exigent should come—which now
Is come indeed—when I should see behind me
The inevitable prosecution of
Disgrace and horror, that, on my command,
Thou then wouldst kill me: do 't; the time is come:
Thou strikest not me, 'tis Cæsar thou defeat'st.
Put colour in thy cheek.
Eros. The gods withhold me!
Shall I do that which all the Parthian darts,
Though enemy, lost aim and could not?
Ant. Eros,
Wouldst thou be window'd in great Rome, and see
Thy master thus with pleach'd arms, bending down
His corrigible neck, his face subdued
To penetrative shame, whilst the wheel'd seat
Of fortunate Cæsar, drawn before him, branded
His baseness that ensued?
Eros. I would not see 't.
Ant. Come, then; for with a wound I must be cured.
Draw that thy honest sword, which thou hast worn
Most useful for thy country.
Eros. O, sir, pardon me!
Ant. When I did make thee free, sworest thou not then

To do this when I bade thee? Do it at once;
Or thy precedent services are all
But accidents unpurposed. Draw, and come.

Eros. Turn from me then that noble countenance,
Wherein the worship of the whole world lies.

Ant. Lo thee! [*Turning from him.*

Eros. My sword is drawn.

Ant. Then let it do at once
The thing why thou hast drawn it.

Eros. My dear master,
My captain, and my emperor, let me say,
Before I strike this bloody stroke, farewell.

Ant. 'Tis said, man; and farewell.

Eros. Farewell, great chief. Shall I strike now?

Ant. Now, Eros.

Eros. Why, there then: thus I do escape the sorrow
Of Antony's death. [*Kills himself.*

Ant. Thrice-nobler than myself!
Thou teachest me, O valiant Eros, what
I should and thou couldst not. My queen and Eros
Have by their brave instruction got upon me
A nobleness in record: but I will be
A bridegroom in my death, and run into't
As to a lover's bed. Come then; and, Eros,
Thy master dies thy scholar: to do thus
[*Falling on his sword.*
I learn'd of thee. How! not dead? not dead?
The guard, ho! O, dispatch me!

Enter Dercetas and Guard.

First Guard. What 's the noise?

Ant. I have done my work ill, friends: O, make an end
Of what I have begun.

Sec. Guard. The star is fall'n.

First Guard. And time is at his period.

All. Alas, and woe!

Ant. Let him that loves me strike me dead.

First Guard. Not I.

Sec. Guard. Nor I.

Third Guard. Nor any one. [*Exeunt Guard.*

Der. Thy death and fortunes bid thy followers fly.
This sword but shown to Cæsar, with this tidings,
Shall enter me with him.

Enter Diomedes.

Dio. Where 's Antony?

Der. There, Diomed, there.

Dio. Lives he?
Wilt thou not answer, man? [*Exit Dercetas.*
Ant. Art thou there, Diomed? Draw thy sword, and give me
Sufficing strokes for death.
Dio. Most absolute lord,
My mistress Cleopatra sent me to thee.
Ant. When did she send thee?
Dio. Now, my lord.
Ant. Where is she?
Dio. Lock'd in her monument. She had a prophesying fear
Of what hath come to pass: for when she saw—
Which never shall be found—you did suspect
She had disposed with Cæsar, and that your rage
Would not be purged, she sent you word she was dead;
But, fearing since how it might work, hath sent
Me to proclaim the truth; and I am come,
I dread, too late.
Ant. Too late, good Diomed: call my guard, I prithee.
Dio. What, ho, the emperor's guard! The guard, what, ho!
Come, your lord calls.

Enter four or five of the Guard of Antony.

Ant. Bear me, good friends, where Cleopatra bides;
'Tis the last service that I shall command you.
First Guard. Woe, woe are we, sir, you may not live to wear
All your true followers out.
All. Most heavy day!
Ant. Nay, good my fellows, do not please sharp fate
To grace it with your sorrows: bid that welcome
Which comes to punish us, and we punish it
Seeming to bear it lightly. Take me up:
I have led you oft: carry me now, good friends,
And have my thanks for all. [*Exeunt, bearing Antony.*

Scene XV

The same. A monument.

Enter Cleopatra, and her maids aloft, with Charmian, and Iras.

Cleo. O Charmian, I will never go from hence.
Char. Be comforted, dear madam.
Cleo. No, I will not:
All strange and terrible events are welcome,
But comforts we despise; our size of sorrow,
Proportion'd to our cause, must be as great
As that which makes it.

Enter, below, Diomedes.

How now! is he dead?

Dio. His death 's upon him, but not dead.
Look out o' the other side your monument;
His guard have brought him thither.

Enter, below, Antony, borne by the Guard.

Cleo. O sun,
Burn the great sphere thou movest in! darkling stand
The varying shore o' the world. O Antony,
Antony, Antony! Help, Charmian, help, Iras, help;
Help, friends below; let 's draw him hither.

Ant. Peace!
Not Cæsar's valour hath o'erthrown Antony,
But Antony's hath triumph'd on itself.

Cleo. So it should be, that none but Antony
Should conquer Antony; but woe 'tis so!

Ant. I am dying, Egypt, dying; only
I here importune death awhile, until
Of many thousand kisses the poor last
I lay upon thy lips.

Cleo. I dare not, dear,
Dear my lord, pardon, I dare not,
Lest I be taken: not the imperious show
Of the full-fortuned Cæsar ever shall
Be brooch'd with me; if knife, drugs, serpents, have
Edge, sting, or operation, I am safe:
Your wife Octavia, with her modest eyes
And still conclusion, shall acquire no honour
Demuring upon me. But come, come, Antony,—
Help me, my women,—we must draw thee up;
Assist, good friends.

Ant. O, quick, or I am gone.

Cleo. Here 's sport indeed! How heavy weighs my lord!
Our strength is all gone into heaviness;
That makes the weight. Had I great Juno's power,
The strong-wing'd Mercury should fetch thee up
And set thee by Jove's side. Yet come a little—
Wishers were ever fools—O, come, come, come;

[*They heave Antony aloft to Cleopatra.*

And welcome, welcome! die where thou hast lived:
Quicken with kissing: had my lips that power,
Thus would I wear them out.

All. A heavy sight!

Ant. I am dying, Egypt, dying:
Give me some wine, and let me speak a little.

Cleo. No, let me speak, and let me rail so high,
That the false housewife Fortune break her wheel,
Provoked by my offence.
Ant. One word, sweet queen:
Of Cæsar seek your honour, with your safety. O!
Cleo. They do not go together.
Ant. Gentle, hear me:
None about Cæsar trust but Proculeius.
Cleo. My resolution and my hands I'll trust;
None about Cæsar.
Ant. The miserable change now at my end
Lament nor sorrow at, but please your thoughts
In feeding them with those my former fortunes
Wherein I lived, the greatest prince o' the world,
The noblest, and do now not basely die,
Not cowardly put off my helmet to
My countryman, a Roman by a Roman
Valiantly vanquish'd. Now my spirit is going;
I can no more.
Cleo. Noblest of men, woo't die?
Hast thou no care of me? shall I abide
In this dull world, which in thy absence is
No better than a sty? O, see, my women, [*Antony dies.*
The crown o' the earth doth melt. My lord!
O, wither'd is the garland of the war,
The soldier's pole is fall'n: young boys and girls
Are level now with men; the odds is gone,
And there is nothing left remarkable
Beneath the visiting moon. [*Faints.*
Char. O, quietness, lady!
Iras. She's dead too, our sovereign.
Char. Lady!
Iras. Madam!
Char. O madam, madam, madam!
Iras. Royal Egypt,
Empress!
Char. Peace, peace, Iras!
Cleo. No more, but e'en a woman, and commanded
By such poor passion as the maid that milks
And does the meanest chares. It were for me
To throw my sceptre at the injurious gods,
To tell them that this world did equal theirs
Till they had stol'n our jewel. All 's but naught;
Patience is sottish, and impatience does
Become a dog that 's mad: then is it sin

To rush into the secret house of death,
Ere death dare come to us? How do you, women?
What, what! good cheer! Why, how now, Charmian!
My noble girls! Ah, women, women, look,
Our lamp is spent, it 's out! Good sirs, take heart:
We 'll bury him; and then, what 's brave, what 's noble,
Let 's do it after the high Roman fashion,
And make death proud to take us. Come, away:
This case of that huge spirit now is cold:
Ah, women, women! Come; we have no friend
But resolution and the briefest end.
[*Exeunt: those above bearing off Antony's body.*

ACT V—Scene I

Alexandria. Cæsar's camp.

Enter Cæsar, Agrippa, Dolabella, Mæcenas, Gallus, Proculeius, and others, his council of war.

Cæs. Go to him, Dolabella, bid him yield;
Being so frustrate, tell him he mocks
The pauses that he makes.
Dol. Cæsar, I shall. [*Exit.*

Enter Dercetas, with the sword of Antony.

Cæs. Wherefore is that? and what art thou that darest
Appear thus to us?
Der. I am call'd Dercetas;
Mark Antony I served, who best was worthy
Best to be served: whilst he stood up and spoke,
He was my master, and I wore my life
To spend upon his haters. If thou please
To take me to thee, as I was to him
I 'll be to Cæsar; if thou pleasest not,
I yield thee up my life.
Cæs. What is 't thou say'st?
Der. I say, O Cæsar, Antony is dead.
Cæs. The breaking of so great a thing should make
A greater crack: the round world
Should have shook lions into civil streets,
And citizens to their dens. The death of Antony
Is not a single doom; in the name lay
A moiety of the world.
Der. He is dead, Cæsar;
Not by a public minister of justice,
Nor by a hired knife; but that self hand,
Which writ his honour in the acts it did,

Hath, with the courage which the heart did lend it,
Splitted the heart. This is his sword;
I robb'd his wound of it; behold it stain'd
With his most noble blood.

Cæs. Look you sad, friends?
The gods rebuke me, but it is tidings
To wash the eyes of kings.

Agr. And strange it is
That nature must compel us to lament
Our most persisted deeds.

Mæc. His taints and honours
Waged equal with him.

Agr. A rarer spirit never
Did steer humanity: but you, gods, will give us
Some faults to make us men. Cæsar is touch'd.

Mæc. When such a spacious mirror 's set before him,
He needs must see himself.

Cæs. O Antony!
I have follow'd thee to this. But we do lance
Diseases in our bodies: I must perforce
Have shown to thee such a declining day,
Or look on thine; we could not stall together
In the whole world: but yet let me lament,
With tears as sovereign as the blood of hearts,
That thou, my brother, my competitor
In top of all design, my mate in empire,
Friend and companion in the front of war,
The arm of mine own body and the heart
Where mine his thoughts did kindle, that our stars
Unreconciliable should divide
Our equalness to this. Hear me, good friends,—

Enter an Egyptian.

But I will tell you at some meeter season:
The business of this man looks out of him;
We 'll hear him what he says. Whence are you?

Egyp. A poor Egyptian yet. The queen my mistress,
Confined in all she has, her monument,
Of thy intents desires instruction,
That she preparedly may frame herself
To the way she 's forced to.

Cæs. Bid her have good heart:
She soon shall know of us, by some of ours,
How honourable and how kindly we
Determine for her; for Cæsar cannot live
To be ungentle.

Egyp. So the gods preserve thee! [*Exit.*
Cæs. Come hither, Proculeius. Go and say,
We purpose her no shame: give her what comforts
The quality of her passion shall require,
Lest in her greatness by some mortal stroke
She do defeat us; for her life in Rome
Would be eternal in our triumph: go,
And with your speediest bring us what she says
And how you find of her.
Pro. Cæsar, I shall. [*Exit.*
Cæs. Gallus, go you along. [*Exit Gallus.*] Where 's Dolabella,
To second Proculeius?
All. Dolabella!
Cæs. Let him alone, for I remember now
How he 's employ'd: he shall in time be ready.
Go with me to my tent; where you shall see
How hardly I was drawn into this war;
How calm and gentle I proceeded still
In all my writings: go with me, and see
What I can show in this. [*Exeunt.*

Scene II

Alexandria. The monument.

Enter Cleopatra, Charmian, and Iras.

Cleo. My desolation does begin to make
A better life. 'Tis paltry to be Cæsar;
Not being Fortune, he 's but Fortune's knave,
A minister of her will: and it is great
To do that thing that ends all other deeds;
Which shackles accidents and bolts up change;
Which sleeps, and never palates more the dug,
The beggar's nurse and Cæsar's.

Enter, to the gates of the monument, Proculeius, Gallus, and Soldiers.

Pro. Cæsar sends greeting to the Queen of Egypt,
And bids thee study on what fair demands
Thou mean 'st to have him grant thee.
Cleo. What 's thy name?
Pro. My name is Proculeius.
Cleo. Antony
Did tell me of you, bade me trust you, but
I do not greatly care to be deceived,
That have no use for trusting. If your master
Would have a queen his beggar, you must tell him,
That majesty, to keep decorum, must

No less beg than a kingdom: if he please
To give me conquer'd Egypt for my son,
He gives me so much of mine own as I
Will kneel to him with thanks.

Pro. Be of good cheer;
You 're fall'n into a princely hand; fear nothing:
Make your full reference freely to my lord,
Who is so full of grace that it flows over
On all that need. Let me report to him
Your sweet dependency, and you shall find
A conqueror that will pray in aid for kindness,
Where he for grace is kneel'd to.

Cleo. Pray you, tell him
I am his fortune's vassal and I send him
The greatness he has got. I hourly learn
A doctrine of obedience, and would gladly
Look him i' the face.

Pro. This I 'll report, dear lady.
Have comfort, for I know your plight is pitied
Of him that caused it.

Gal. You see how easily she may be surprised.
[*Here Proculeius and two of the Guard ascend the monument by a ladder placed against a window, and, having descended, come behind Cleopatra. Some of the Guard unbar and open the gates.*
Guard her till Cæsar come. [*Exit.*

Iras. Royal queen!

Char. O Cleopatra! thou art taken, queen!

Cleo. Quick, quick, good hands. [*Drawing a dagger.*

Pro. Hold, worthy lady, hold:
[*Seizes and disarms her.*
Do not yourself such wrong, who are in this
Relieved, but not betray'd.

Cleo. What, of death too,
That rids our dogs of languish?

Pro. Cleopatra,
Do not abuse my master's bounty by
The undoing of yourself: let the world see
His nobleness well acted, which your death
Will never let come forth.

Cleo. Where art thou, death?
Come hither, come! come, come, and take a queen
Worth many babes and beggars!

Pro. O, temperance, lady!

Cleo. Sir, I will eat no meat, I 'll not drink, sir;

If idle talk will once be necessary,
I 'll not sleep neither: this mortal house I 'll ruin,
Do Cæsar what he can. Know, sir, that I
Will not wait pinion'd at your master's court,
Nor once be chastised with the sober eye
Of dull Octavia. Shall they hoist me up
And show me to the shouting varletry
Of censuring Rome? Rather a ditch in Egypt
Be gentle grave unto me! rather on Nilus' mud
Lay me stark naked, and let the water-flies
Blow me into abhorring! rather make
My country's high pyramides my gibbet,
And hang me up in chains!

Pro. You do extend
These thoughts of horror further than you shall
Find cause in Cæsar.

Enter Dolabella.

Dol. Proculeius,
What thou hast done thy master Cæsar knows,
And he hath sent for thee: for the queen,
I 'll take her to my guard.

Pro. So, Dolabella,
It shall content me best: be gentle to her.
[*To Cleo.*] To Cæsar I will speak what you shall please,
If you 'll employ me to him.

Cleo. Say, I would die.

[*Exeunt Proculeius and Soldiers.*

Dol. Most noble empress, you have heard of me?

Cleo. I cannot tell.

Dol. Assuredly you know me.

Cleo. No matter, sir, what I have heard or known.
You laugh when boys or women tell their dreams;
Is 't not your trick?

Dol. I understand not, madam.

Cleo. I dream'd there was an emperor Antony:
O, such another sleep, that I might see
But such another man!

Dol. If it might please ye,—

Cleo. His face was as the heavens; and therein stuck
A sun and moon, which kept their course, and lighted
The little O, the earth.

Dol. Most sovereign creature,—

Cleo. His legs bestrid the ocean: his rear'd arm
Crested the world: his voice was propertied
As all the tuned spheres, and that to friends;

But when he meant to quail and shake the orb,
He was as rattling thunder. For his bounty,
There was no winter in 't; an autumn 'twas
That grew the more by reaping: his delights
Were dolphin-like; they show'd his back above
The element they lived in: in his livery
Walk'd crowns and crownets; realms and islands were
As plates dropp'd from his pocket.

Dol. Cleopatra,—

Cleo. Think you there was, or might be, such a man
As this I dream'd of?

Dol. Gentle madam, no.

Cleo. You lie, up to the hearing of the gods.
But if there be, or ever were, one such,
It 's past the size of dreaming: nature wants stuff
To vie strange forms with fancy; yet to imagine
An Antony, were nature's piece 'gainst fancy,
Condemning shadows quite.

Dol. Hear me, good madam.
Your loss is as yourself, great; and you bear it
As answering to the weight: would I might never
O'ertake pursued success, but I do feel,
By the rebound of yours, a grief that smites
My very heart at root.

Cleo. I thank you, sir.
Know you what Cæsar means to do with me?

Dol. I am loath to tell you what I would you knew.

Cleo. Nay, pray you, sir,—

Dol. Though he be honourable,—

Cæs. He 'll lead me then in triumph?

Dol. Madam, he will; I know 't.

[*Flourish and shout within:* 'Make way there: Cæsar!'
Enter Cæsar, Gallus, Proculeius, Mæcenas, Seleucus, and others of his Train.

Cæs. Which is the Queen of Egypt?

Dol. It is the emperor, madam. [*Cleopatra kneels.*

Cæs. Arise, you shall not kneel:
I pray you, rise; rise, Egypt.

Cleo. Sir, the gods
Will have it thus; my master and my lord
I must obey.

Cæs. Take to you no hard thoughts:
The record of what injuries you did us,
Though written in our flesh, we shall remember
As things but done by chance.

Cleo. Sole sir o' the world,
I cannot project mine own cause so well
To make it clear: but do confess I have
Been laden with like frailties which before
Have often shamed our sex.
Cæs. Cleopatra, know,
We will extenuate rather than enforce:
If you apply yourself to our intents,
Which towards you are most gentle, you shall find
A benefit in this change; but if you seek
To lay on me a cruelty by taking
Antony's course, you shall bereave yourself
Of my good purposes and put your children
To that destruction which I 'll guard them from
If thereon you rely. I 'll take my leave.
Cleo. And may, through all the world: 'tis yours; and we,
Your scutcheons and your signs of conquest, shall
Hang in what place you please. Here, my good lord.
Cæs. You shall advise me in all for Cleopatra.
Cleo. This is the brief of money, plate and jewels,
I am possess'd of: 'tis exactly valued,
Not petty things admitted. Where 's Seleucus?
Sel. Here, madam.
Cleo. This is my treasurer: let him speak, my lord,
Upon his peril, that I have reserved
To myself nothing. Speak the truth, Seleucus.
Sel. Madam,
I had rather seal my lips than to my peril
Speak that which is not.
Cleo. What have I kept back?
Sel. Enough to purchase what you have made known.
Cæs. Nay, blush not, Cleopatra; I approve
Your wisdom in the deed.
Cleo. See, Cæsar! O, behold,
How pomp is follow'd! mine will now be yours,
And, should we shift estates, yours would be mine.
The ingratitude of this Seleucus does
Even make me wild. O slave, of no more trust
Than love that 's hired! What, goest thou back? thou shalt
Go back, I warrant thee; but I 'll catch thine eyes,
Though they had wings: slave, soulless villain, dog!
O rarely base!
Cæs. Good queen, let us entreat you.
Cleo. O Cæsar, what a wounding shame is this,
That thou vouchsafing here to visit me,

Doing the honour of thy lordliness
To one so meek, that mine own servant should
Parcel the sum of my disgraces by
Addition of his envy! Say, good Cæsar,
That I some lady trifles have reserved,
Immoment toys, things of such dignity
As we greet modern friends withal; and say,
Some nobler token I have kept apart
For Livia and Octavia, to induce
Their mediation; must I be unfolded
With one that I have bred? The gods! it smites me
Beneath the fall I have. [*To Seleucus*] Prithee, go hence;
Or I shall show the cinders of my spirits
Through the ashes of my chance: wert thou a man,
Thou wouldst have mercy on me.

Cæs. Forbear, Seleucus. [*Exit Seleucus.*

Cleo. Be it known, that we, the greatest, are mis-thought
For things that others do, and when we fall,
We answer others' merits in our name,
Are therefore to be pitied.

Cæs. Cleopatra,
Not what you have reserved, nor what acknowledged,
Put we i' the roll of conquest: still be 't yours,
Bestow it at your pleasure, and believe
Cæsar 's no merchant, to make prize with you
Of things that merchants sold. Therefore be cheer'd;
Make not your thoughts your prisons: no, dear queen;
For we intend so to dispose you as
Yourself shall give us counsel. Feed, and sleep:
Our care and pity is so much upon you
That we remain your friend; and so, adieu.

Cleo. My master, and my lord!

Cæs. Not so. Adieu.

[*Flourish. Exeunt Cæsar and his train.*

Cleo. He words me, girls, he words me, that I should not
Be noble to myself: but, hark thee, Charmian.

[*Whispers Charmian.*

Iras. Finish, good lady; the bright day is done,
And we are for the dark.

Cleo. Hie thee again:
I have spoke already, and it is provided;
Go put it to the haste.

Char. Madam, I will.

Re-enter Dolabella.

Dol. Where is the queen?

Char. Behold, sir. [*Exit.*
Cleo. Dolabella!
Dol. Madam, as thereto sworn by your command,
Which my love makes religion to obey,
I tell you this: Cæsar through Syria
Intends his journey, and within three days
You with your children will he send before:
Make your best of this: I have perform'd
Your pleasure and my promise.
Cleo. Dolabella,
I shall remain your debtor.
Dol. I your servant.
Adieu, good queen; I must attend on Cæsar.
Cleo. Farewell, and thanks. [*Exit Dolabella.*
Now, Iras, what think'st thou?
Thou, an Egyptian puppet, shalt be shown
In Rome, as well as I: mechanic slaves
With greasy aprons, rules and hammers, shall
Uplift us to the view: in their thick breaths,
Rank of gross diet, shall we be enclouded
And forced to drink their vapour.
Iras. The gods forbid!
Cleo. Nay, 'tis most certain, Iras: saucy lictors
Will catch at us like strumpets, and scald rhymers
Ballad us out o' tune: the quick comedians
Extemporally will stage us and present
Our Alexandrian revels; Antony
Shall be brought drunken forth, and I shall see
Some squeaking Cleopatra boy my greatness
I' the posture of a whore.
Iras. O the good gods!
Cleo. Nay, that 's certain.
Iras. I 'll never see 't; for I am sure my nails
Are stronger than mine eyes.
Cleo. Why, that 's the way
To fool their preparation, and to conquer
Their most absurd intents.

Re-enter Charmian.

Now, Charmian!
Show me, my women, like a queen: go fetch
My best attires: I am again for Cydnus,
To meet Mark Antony: sirrah Iras, go.
Now, noble Charmian, we 'll dispatch indeed,
And when thou hast done this chare I 'll give thee leave

To play till doomsday. Bring our crown and all.
[*Exit Iras. A noise within.*
Wherefore 's this noise?

Enter a Guardsman.

Guard. Here is a rural fellow
That will not be denied your highness' presence:
He brings you figs.

Cleo. Let him come in. [*Exit Guardsman.*
What poor an instrument
May do a noble deed! he brings me liberty.
My resolution 's placed, and I have nothing
Of woman in me: now from head to foot
I am marble-constant; now the fleeting moon
No planet is of mine.

Re-enter Guardsman, with Clown bringing in a basket.

Guard. This is the man.

Cleo. Avoid, and leave him. [*Exit Guardsman.*
Hast thou the pretty worm of Nilus there,
That kills and pains not?

Clown. Truly, I have him: but I would not be the party that should desire you to touch him, for his biting is immortal; those that do die of it do seldom or never recover.

Cleo. Rememberest thou any that have died on 't?

Clown. Very many, men and women too. I heard of one of them no longer than yesterday: a very honest woman, but something given to lie; as a woman should not do, but in the way of honesty: how she died of the biting of it, what pain she felt: truly, she makes a very good report o' the worm; but he that will believe all that they say, shall never be saved by half that they do: but this is most fallible, the worm 's an odd worm.

Cleo. Get thee hence; farewell.

Clown. I wish you all joy of the worm. [*Setting down his basket.*

Cleo. Farewell.

Clown. You must think this, look you, that the worm will do [his kind.

Cleo. Ay, ay; farewell.

Clown. Look you, the worm is not to be trusted but in the keeping of wise people, for indeed there is no goodness in the worm.

Cleo. Take thou no care; it shall be heeded.

Clown. Very good. Give it nothing, I pray you, for it is not worth the feeding.

Cleo. Will it eat me?

Clown. You must not think I am so simple but I know the devil himself will not eat a woman: I know that a woman is a dish for the gods, if the devil dress her not. But, truly, these same whoreson devils do the gods great harm in their women; for in every ten that they make, the devils mar five.

Cleo. Well, get thee gone; farewell.

Clown. Yes, forsooth: I wish you joy o' the worm. [*Exit.*

Re-enter Iras with a robe, crown, &c.

Cleo. Give me my robe, put on my crown; I have
Immortal longings in me: now no more
The juice of Egypt's grape shall moist this lip:
Yare, yare, good Iras; quick. Methinks I hear
Antony call; I see him rouse himself
To praise my noble act; I hear him mock
The luck of Cæsar, which the gods give men
To excuse their after wrath. Husband, I come:
Now to that name my courage prove my title!
I am fire and air; my other elements
I give to baser life. So; have you done?
Come then and take the last warmth of my lips.
Farewell, kind Charmian; Iras, long farewell.
[*Kisses them. Iras falls and dies.*
Have I the aspic in my lips? Dost fall?
If thou and nature can so gently part,
The stroke of death is as a lover's pinch,
Which hurts, and is desired. Dost thou lie still?
If thus thou vanishest, thou tell'st the world
It is not worth leave-taking.

Char. Dissolve, thick cloud, and rain, that I may say
The gods themselves do weep!

Cleo. This proves me base:
If she first meet the curled Antony,
He'll make demand of her, and spend that kiss
Which is my heaven to have. Come, thou mortal wretch,
[*To an asp, which she applies to her breast.*
With thy sharp teeth this knot intrinsicate
Of life at once untie: poor venomous fool,
Be angry, and dispatch. O, couldst thou speak,
That I might hear thee call great Cæsar ass
Unpolicied!

Char. O eastern star!

Cleo. Peace, peace!
Dost thou not see my baby at my breast,
That sucks the nurse asleep?

Char. O, break! O, break!

Cleo. As sweet as balm, as soft as air, as gentle,—

O Antony!—Nay, I will take thee too:
[*Applying another asp to her arm.*
What should I stay— [*Dies.*
Char. In this vile world? So, fare thee well.
Now boast thee, death, in thy possession lies
A lass unparallel'd. Downy windows, close;
And golden Phœbus never be beheld
Of eyes again so royal! Your crown 's awry;
I 'll mend it, and then play.

Enter the Guard, rushing in.

First Guard. Where is the queen?
Char. Speak softy, wake her not.
First Guard. Cæsar hath sent—
Char. Too slow a messenger. [*Applies an asp.*
O, come apace, dispatch: I partly feel thee.
First Guard. Approach, ho! All 's not well: Cæsar 's beguiled.
Sec. Guard. There 's Dolabella sent from Cæsar; call him.
First Guard. What work is here! Charmian, is this well done?
Char. It is well done, and fitting for a princess
Descended of so many royal kings.
Ah, soldier! [*Dies.*

Re-enter Dolabella.

Dol. How goes it here?
Sec. Guard. All dead.
Dol. Cæsar, thy thoughts
Touch their effects in this: thyself art coming
To see perform'd the dreaded act which thou
So sought'st to hinder.
[*Within.* 'A way there, a way for Cæsar!'

Re-enter Cæsar and his train.

Dol. O sir, you are too sure an augurer;
That you did fear is done.
Cæs. Bravest at the last.
She levell'd at our purposes, and being royal
Took her own way. The manner of their deaths?
I do not see them bleed.
Dol. Who was last with them?
First Guard. A simple countryman, that brought her figs:
This was his basket.
Cæs. Poison'd then.
First Guard. O Cæsar,
This Charmian lived but now; she stood and spake:
I found her trimming up the diadem
On her dead mistress; tremblingly she stood,
And on the sudden dropp'd.

Cæs. O noble weakness!
If they had swallow'd poison, 'twould appear
By external swelling: but she looks like sleep,
As she would catch another Antony
In her strong toil of grace.

Dol. Here, on her breast,
There is a vent of blood, and something blown:
The like is on her arm.

First Guard. This is an aspic's trail: and these fig-leaves
Have slime upon them, such as the aspic leaves
Upon the caves of Nile.

Cæs. Most probable
That so she died; for her physician tells me
She hath pursued conclusions infinite
Of easy ways to die. Take up her bed,
And bear her women from the monument:
She shall be buried by her Antony:
No grave upon the earth shall clip in it
A pair so famous. High events as these
Strike those that make them; and their story is
No less in pity than his glory which
Brought them to be lamented. Our army shall
In solemn show attend this funeral,
And then to Rome. Come, Dolabella, see
High order in this great solemnity. [*Exeunt.*

GLOSSARY

J. = Johnson. D. = Dyce. S. = Schmidt. H.E.D. = A new English Dictionary on Historical Principles (Murray, Bradley).

ABATED, subdued, depressed.
ABHOR, "protest against.'
ABLE, answer for.
ABODE, forebode.
ABRIDGMENT, (?) a means of shortening or whiling away; or, epitome, abstract (H.E.D.).
ABSOLUTE, perfect; decided.
ABUSE, deception; *v.* deceive.
ACCITE, cite, summon.
ACKNOWN, confessedly acquainted with.
ADDITION, title.
ADDRESS, prepare.
ADMITTANCE, fashion (D.); sanction; admissibility (H.E.D.).
ADVANCE, raise to honour.
ADVERTISEMENT, admonition (D.); public notice or announcement (H.E.D.).
ADVERTISING, attentive.
ADVISED, act with deliberation; informed.
AFFECTION, affectation.
AFFEER'D, confirmed.
AFFRONT, encounter.
AFFY, betroth.
AGAZ'D, amazed, aghast.
AGLET, tag.
AGLET-BABY, "image or head cut on a tag."
AGNIZE, acknowledge.
AIM, conjecture.
ALDER-LIEFEST, most beloved, dearest.
ALLOW, approve.
AMES-ACE, both aces, the lowest throw.
ANCHOR, anchorite.
ANCIENT, ensign.
ANGEL, coin.
ANTHROPOPHAGINIAN, cannibal.
ANTRE, cave.
APE, "lead apes in hell," punishment predicted for old maids.
APPELLANT, challenger.
APPLE-JOHN, a variety of apple.
APPREHENSION, anticipation; perception by the senses; sarcasm (D.).
ARCH, chief.
ARGAL, corruption of *ergo*.
ARGUMENT, subject.
ARM-GAUNT, (?) with gaunt limbs (H.E.D.).
AROINT, away! avaunt!
ARROSE, water.
ARTICULATE, set forth in articles, particularize (H.E.D.).
ASCAUNT, across.
ASINEGO, ASINICO, donkey, fool.
ASSAY, assault.
ASSURED, betrothed.
ATTACH, arrest.
AWFUL, filled with awe.

BACCARE, "Go back."
BAFFLE, a punishment inflicted on recreant knights, who were hung up by their heels and beaten.
BALDRICK, belt.
"BALK LOGIC," chop logic; balked (?) heaped up (H.E.D.).
BALLOW, cudgel.
BAN-DOG, dog tied or chained up.
BANQUET, dessert.
BARBED, in horse armour.
BASE, prisoner's base, a game.
BASES, "a kind of embroidered mantle, which hung down from the middle, worn by knights on horseback."
BASILISK, cocatrice, a creature fabled to kill by its look; piece of ordnance.
BASTARD, a sweet wine.
BAT, cudgel.
BATE, strife, dispute; *v.* flutter with the wings.
BATLET, small bat for beating clothes.
BATTEN, fatten.
BAVIN, faggot of brushwood.
BEADSMAN, one hired to pray for another.
BEAR A BRAIN, have remembrance.
BEAR-HERD, BEAR-WARD, bear keeper.
BEAR-IN-HAND, hold in expectation, in false hopes.
BEARING-CLOTH, mantle in which a child was carried to the font.
BEAVER, movable vizor of helmet.
BECK, bow.
BENT, "utmost degree of any passion or mental quality" (J.).
BERGOMASK, a dance imitated from that of the peasants of Bergamasco.
BESONIAN, needy, base fellow.
BESORT, suite, escort.
BETEEM, allow, suffer.
BIAS, "swelled as the bowl on the biassed side" (J.).
BIGGEN, cap, resembling that worn by the *Beguines*.
BILBO, sword, from *Bilboa*, famous for its steel work.
BILBOES, iron bar and fetters for confining refractory sailors.
BILL, kind of pike, halbert.
BIRD-BOLT, blunt-pointed arrow used for killing birds.
BISSON, blind.
BLACK MONDAY, a reference to the Monday after Easter-day 1360, when many men of King Edward III's host, then before Paris, died of cold as they sat on their horses.
BLANK, white in centre of target.
BLOCK, fashion of hat.
BLOOD, "in blood," in good condition.
BLOOD-BOLTERED, matted with blood.
BOB, taunt; *v.* to cheat.
BODGE, "old form of botch" (H.E.D.).
BODKIN, small dagger.
BOGGLE, swerve, shy.
BOLINS, bowlines, ropes for governing the sails of a ship.

BOLLEN, swollen.
BOLTED, sifted.
BOLTER, sieve.
BOLTING-HATCH, receptacle into which meal is sifted.
BOMBARD, large leather drinking vessel.
BOMBAST, cotton, or other material, used for stuffing.
BONA-ROBA, "good, wholesome, plum-cheeked wench;" Courtesan.
BOOT, profit, something over and above; booty.
BOOTS, "give the boots," allusion to an instrument of torture, or "make a laughing-stock of."
BORE, calibre of a gun, capacity of the barrel.
BOSKY, woody.
BOTTLE, truss (of hay).
BOTTOM, low-lying land.
BRABBLE, quarrel.
BRACE, (?) coat of armour (H.E.D.), state of defence.
BRACH, scent-hound; bitch.
BRAID, (?) deceitful (H.E.D.); *v.* upbraid.
BRAKES ("brakes of vice"), thickets; "engines of torture" (D.).
BRAVE, defy; adorn, make fine.
BRAVERY, finery; bravado.
BRAWL, lively dance.
BRAWN, arm.
BREAK UP, carve; used metaphorically for opening a letter.
BREED-BATE, a hatcher of quarrels.
BREESE, BRIZE, gadfly.
BROCK, badger.
BROGUES, shoes.
BRUIT, report.
BUCK, lye in which linen is washed; linen so washed.
BUCKLE, join in fight.
BUCKLERS, "give the bucklers," yield the victory.
BUG, bugbear.
BULLY, term of familiar affection.
BULLY-ROOK, "jolly comrade, boon companion" (H.E.D.).
BUNG, sharper, cut-purse.
BURGONET, particular kind of helmet.
BUTT-SHAFT, a kind of arrow, used for shooting at butts.
BUTTERY, room where provisions are laid up.
BUZZARD, hawk; various insects that fly by night; large moths, cockchafers (H.E.D.).
BY AND BY, immediately.

CADDIS, worsted tape, riband.
CADE, barrel.
CALIVER, light musket, harquebus.
CANARY, a wine; a lively dance.
CANKER, dog-rose; canker-worm.
CANSTICK, candlestick.
CANTLE, piece, portion.
CANVASS, toss.
CAPTIOUS, "capable of receiving" (D.).
CARACK, large trading vessel; galleon.
CARBONADO, meat sliced for broiling.
CARDED, adulterated.
CAREER, space within the lists; race-course; "short turning of a nimble horse," frisk, gambol (H.E.D., "he passes some . . . careires").
CARKANET, necklace.
CARL, CARLOT, churl, boor.
CASTLE, close helmet.
CATAIAN, Chinese (Cataia, Cathay, old name for China).
CATER-COUSIN, cousin of "quatre," fourth degree.
CATES, table delicacies.
CATLING, lute, violin-string.
CAUTEL, craftiness, caution.
CENSURE, opinion, judgment.
CEREMENTS, waxed cloths for enwrapping embalmed bodies.
CESS, measure, "out of all cess."
CHACES, "a chace at tennis is that spot where a ball falls, beyond which the adversary must strike his ball to gain a point or chace" (Douce).
CHAMBER, piece of ordnance; "Camera Regis," old name of London.
CHAMBERLAIN, one in charge of chambers.
CHANNEL, kennel.
CHAPE, metal mounting of scabbard, "particularly that which covers the point," possibly the scabbard itself (H.E.D.).
CHARACT, distinctive mark, character.
CHARACTER, handwriting.
CHARNECO, wine, probably Portuguese.
CHAUDRON, entrails.
CHEATER, escheator.
CHECK, turn from pursuing one prey to follow another (falconry).
CHERRY-PIT, game in which cherry-stones were thrown into a small hole.
CHEVERIL, leather made of kid-skin.
CHEWET, chough, jackdaw.
CHILDING, fruitful.
CHOPINE, a high clog worn by Venetian ladies, etc.
CINQUE-PACE, a dance, the steps of which were regulated by the number five.
CITTERN, musical instrument, similar to guitar.
CLACK-DISH, or CLAP-DISH, carried about by beggars, who clacked the cover to attract attention.
CLAW, flatter.
CLEPE, call.
CLIFF, clef, key in music.
CLING, shrivel.
CLINQUANT, glittering.
CLIP, embrace.
CLOUD IN 'S FACE, signifying that the horse has a dark-coloured spot between the eyes.
CLOUT, "the mark shot at" (H.E.D.), nail or pin in centre of white of target (D.).
CLOUTED, hobnailed "clouted brogues."
CLOY, claw.
COAST, approach; assail, accost.
COASTING, "coasting welcome," an amorous approach (Nares); some eds., "accosting welcome."
COBLOAF, small round-shaped loaf.
COCKATRICE. *See* Basilisk.
COCKLED, within a shell.
COCKREL, a young cock.

COFFIN, raised crust of a pie.
COG, cheat.
COIL, turmoil, confusion.
COLLOP, slice of meat, portion of flesh.
COLOURS, false appearances; "fear no—" fear no enemy.
COLT, fool.
COMMODITY, advantage, profit.
COMPARATIVE, "quick at comparisons" (S.); one ready to make comparisons; or, compeer, rival (H.E.D.).
COMPASSED, bow (window).
COMPETITOR, confederate.
COMPOSURE, combination.
COMPROMISED, having mutually promised.
COMPTIBLE, sensitive.
CONCEIT, conception, fancy; trifle.
CONCENT, accord, harmony.
CONEY-CATCH, swindle.
CONFECT, a sweetmeat.
CONTEMPTIBLE, contemptuous.
CONTINENT, that which envelops, contains; the thing contained.
CONTRIVE, spend, while away.
CONVENT, cite; suit.
CONVINCE, overpower.
COPATAIN HAT, high-crowned hat.
CORANTO, quick dance.
CORINTHIAN, debauchee.
CORKY, withered.
COSTARD, head.
COTE, overtake, pass by.
COT-QUEAN, a meddler in women's affairs.
COUNTER, debtor's prison.
COUNTERFEIT, likeness; false coin.
COUNTERPOINT, counterpane.
COURSER'S HAIR, old idea that a horse's hair came to life in water.
COURT-CUPBOARD, a movable cupboard, sideboard.
COYSTRIL, low fellow, knave.
COZIER, cobbler.
CRAB, wild apple.
CRACK, lively, forward boy.
CRANTS, garland.
CREDIT, accepted report.
CRESCIVE, increasing, growing.
CRESSET, a beacon light, suspended in an iron vessel or basket.
CRISP, curled.
CROSS, coin stamped with a cross.
CROSS-ROW, alphabet.
CROW-KEEPER, scarecrow.
CRUSADO, Portuguese coin.
CRY, pack.
CUCKOO-BUD, buttercup, cowslip, marsh marigold; "orchis, or cuckoo-pint in bud" (H.E.D.).
CUCKOO-FLOWER, name given to various flowers in bloom when cuckoo is heard: lady's smock, ragged robin, etc. (H.E.D.).
CUISSES, armour for the thighs.
CULLION, low fellow, lout.
CUNNING, skill, knowledge; skilful.
CURB, cringe, crouch.
CURIOUS, CURIOSITY, scrupulous; precision.
CURST, ill-tempered, shrewish, vicious.
CURTAIL, CURTAL-DOG, originally a dog with its tail cut to show that his master was unqualified for hunting; later, a dog not meant, or not good, for sport.
CURTLE-AXE, cutlass.
CUT, a docked horse; term of contempt.
CUT AND LONG TAIL, dogs of every kind.
CUTS, lots.
CUTTLE, knife.
CYPRUS, CYPRESS, material similar to crape.

DAFF, doff.
DANSKERS, Danes.
DARE, terrify.
DARNEL, said to be injurious to the eyes if taken in food or drink.
DARRAIGN, set in order of battle.
DAY-WOMAN, dairy-woman.
DEAR, loving; important; "heartfelt" (S.); used to express the extreme of any emotion, pleasurable or otherwise, aroused by the object to which it is applied.
DEARTH, dearness, value.
DEBATE, fighting.
DEBITOR AND CREDITOR, an account book.
DECEIVABLE, deceptive.
DECK (of cards), pack.
DECKED, "deck'd the sea," sprinkled (D.); covered (S.).
DEFEAT, DEFEATURE, disfigure; disfigurement.
DEFEND, forbid.
DEFIANCE, "declaration of aversion or contempt" (H.E.D., "take my defiance").
DEFUSE, DEFUSED, confuse; disordered, "irregular, uncouth" (J.).
DEFY, renounce, disdain.
DELATION, denunciation, information.
DEMERIT, desert, in good or bad sense (S.).
DENAY, denial; *v.* deny.
DENIER, piece of money of lowest value.
DEPART, departure; *v.* part.
DEPRAVE, DEPRAVATION, detract; detraction.
DEROGATE, disparage; *a.* debased, degenerate.
DESCANT, variations.
DESIGN, designate.
DESPERATE, hopeless; reckless (S.)
DESPITE, hatred, malice.
DETERMINATE, bring to an end; *a.* fixed, final.
DICH, corruption of "do it."
DISABLE, disparage.
DISAPPOINTED, not properly equipped, unprepared.
DISASTER, "obnoxious planet."
DISCANDY, melt.
DISCLOSE, hatch.
DISCOURSE, reasoning power.
DISEASE, discomfort; trouble.
DISEDGE, blunt the edge of appetite.
DISLIMN, obliterate.
DISME, tenth.
DISNATURED, unnatural.
DISPARK, convert into common land.
DISPITEOUS, without pity.
DISPOSE, disposition.
DISTAIN, stain, dishonour.
DISTEMPERED, out of humour; deranged.
DISTEMPERATURE, disorder of mind or body.

Distract, divide.
Distraction, detachment.
Divídant, divided, different.
Division, florid passage in music.
Doff, do off, put off.
Dogged, cruel.
Dolphin, dauphin.
Dout, put out.
Dowlas, coarse linen.
Dowle, fibre of down.
Down-gyved, hanging round the ankles.
Draff, refuse.
Draw, track.
Drollery, puppet show.
Drug, drudge.
Drum, "John Drum's entertainment," proverbial expression for ill-treatment.
Drumble, dawdle.
Dudgeon, handle of a dagger.
Dump, melancholy tune.
Dun, "dun's the mouse"; proverb; "frequently a mere quibble on the word 'done.'"
Dun is in the Mire, old game; a log of wood being dragged out of the supposed mire by the company.
Dup, do up, open.
Durance, "robe, suits, of durance," durable (quibble with other meaning of word).

Eager, sharp, keen; sour.
Eaning, when young are brought forth.
Eanling, new-born lamb.
Ear, till.
Eche, eke out.
Ecstacy, madness.
Eft, (?) ready, convenient (H.E.D.).
Egma, enigma.
Eisel (eysell), vinegar.
Elf, mat; elf-locks = hair matted by the elves.
Emballing, carrying the ball at a coronation (D.), "investing with the ball as an emblem of royalty."
Embarquement, embargo.
Emboss, drive a hunted animal to extremity (H.E.D.).
Embossed, swollen; foaming at the mouth.
Embrasure, embrace.
Emulate, emulous, envious.
Engross, fatten; bring together from all quarters.
Engrossment, accumulation.
Enseam, grease.
Entertain, take into, or retain in, service.
Entertainment, service.
Entreat, treat; entertain, "beguile" (H.E.D.).
Entreatment, entertainment, "conversation, interview" (H.E.D.).
Envy, Envious, spite; spiteful, malicious.
Ephesian, jovial companion.
Escoted, paid for.
Espial, spy.
Estridge, ostrich.
Excrement, hair, beard, nails.
Exequies, funeral ceremonies.
Expedient, Expedience, expeditious, expedition.
Exsufflicate, (?) puffed up, inflated (H.E.D.).
Extent, seizure.
Eyas, Eyas-musket, young hawk.
Eye, slight shade of colour.
Eyliad, œillade, ogle.

Facinorous, wicked, infamous.
Factionary, partisan.
Factious, "characterized by party spirit" (H.E.D.); active, urgent (J.).
Fadge, fit in, suit.
Faitor, vagabond.
Fancy, love.
Fangled, "characterized by crotchets and fopperies" (H.E.D.); "given to tinsel finery" (S.).
Fantastical, a thing of phantasy, imagination.
Farce, stuff.
Fardel, burden.
Far-fet, far-fetched.
Fashions, disease of horses.
Favour, countenance, appearance.
Favours, features.
Fay, faith,
Fear, frighten.
Feat, trim, neat, elegant, dexterous.
Feature, person in general, form.
Fedary (fedarary), confederate.
Fee-farm, grant of lands for all time.
Fell, skin, hide; *a.* savage.
Fellowly, sympathetic.
Fere, companion, mate.
Fern-seed, thought to have power of rendering persons invisible.
Festinate, speedy.
Fetch trick, artifice.
Fettle, make ready.
Fights, cloths put up to screen men in action during a sea-fight.
File, list; *v.* defile.
Fill-horse, shaft horse.
Fills, shafts.
Fineless, endless.
Fire-drake, fiery dragon, meteor, firework (D.).
Firk, thrash.
Fit, division in a song.
Fitchew, pole-cat.
Fives, disease in horses.
Flap-dragon, small combustible body floated alight in liquor; to be drunk down, or caught up by the mouth and swallowed.
Flap-jack, pancake.
Flaw, sudden gust of wind; "flake of snow" (H.E.D.).
Flesh, initiate; give the first taste of blood; feed angry or lustful passion.
Fleshment, pride of successful attempt.
Flewed, with hanging chaps.
Flibbertigibbet, name of a demon.
Flight, light arrow.
Flote, sea.
Flouting-stock, laughing-stock.
Fob, cheat.
Foin, a thrust in fencing.
Foison, abundance.
Fond, foolish; "fond and winnowed" = trite, trivial (S.).

Foot-cloth, horse trappings.
Forced, stuffed.
Fordo, undo.
Forefend, forbid.
Forehand, previous.
Forgetive, inventive.
Formal, having right use of senses; in a usual form, customary.
Fox, sword; perhaps on account of the figure of a wolf engraved on some blades being mistaken for a fox (H.E.D.).
Frampold, peevish, vexatious.
Frank, pig-sty.
Fraught, **Frautage**, freight.
Frayed, frightened.
Fret, stop used for regulating the fingering of stringed instrument.
Fret, chequer.
Frippery, old clothes-shop.
Frontier, outwork.
Frush, dash violently to pieces.
Fullam, a kind of false dice.

Gaberdine, loose coarse outer garment.
Gad, spur; "upon the gad" = on the spur of the moment.
Gain-giving, misgiving.
Galliard, sprightly dance.
Gallias, galley of large size.
Gallow, frighten.
Gallowglasses, heavy-armed foot soldiers of Ireland.
Gape, bawl.
Garboil, uproar, commotion.
Gaskins, wide breeches.
Gear, matter, business in general.
Geck, dupe, fool.
Generous, **Generosity**, of high birth; nobility.
Gentle, raise to the rank of gentleman.
Gentry, complaisance.
German (germane), akin.
Gest, resting stage, and time allotted for pause at same.
Gests, deeds.
Gib, old tom-cat.
Gig, top.
Giglet (giglot), wanton.
Gillyvors (gilliflowers), of the same genus (*Dianthus*) as the carnation.
Gimmal, composed of links or rings.
Gimmor (gimmer), contrivance of machinery; (?) a hinge (H.E.D.).
Ging, gang.
Gird, sarcasm.
Girdle, "turn his girdle," turn buckle behind to prepare for wrestling.
Gleek, jeer.
Gloze, flatter; interpret.
Glut, swallow.
God 'ild, God yield.
Gongarian, Hungarian.
Good den, good even.
Gorbellied, corpulent.
Gossip, sponsor.
Gout, drop.
Government, self-control, well-mannered behaviour.
Gratulate, gratifying (S.), worthy of gratulation (D.).
Greaves, leg armour.
Gripe, griffin.
Grise, degree, step.
Groundlings, spectators in a theatre who had pit seats, or *ground-stands*.
Guard, trim.
Guards, facings, trimmings.
Guidon, standard, and standard-bearer.
Gules, heraldic term for red.
Gulf, anything which engulfs or swallows.
Gull, dupe; cheat, imposition; unfledged nestling.
Gunstones, balls of stone.
Gust, taste.

Haggard, untrained hawk.
Halcyon, kingfisher; it was supposed that the body of this bird, if hung up, would always turn its breast to the wind.
Half-faced, with face in profile; "half-faced groats."
Half-kirtle, a *kirtle* consisted of jacket and petticoat.
Hall, "a hall"; an exclamation used to make space in a crowd.
Hand, "at any hand," at all events; "of his hands," of valour, skill (H.E.D.).
Handfast, marriage contract; confinement.
Hanger, part of sword-belt in which the weapon was suspended.
Happily, haply.
Harlock, unidentified (H.E.D.).
Hatched, engraved.
Havoc, to cry "havoc" was a signal for general slaughter.
Hay, dance, "of the nature of a reel" (H.E.D.).
Hebenon, ebony.
Heft, heaving; "tender-hefted" = agitated by tender emotion.
Henchman, page.
Hent, seized.
Herb of Grace, rue.
Hest, command.
Hide Fox and all after, hide and seek.
Hight, named.
Hilding, low, menial wretch.
Hobbididance, name of a demon.
Hobby-horse, personage in the Morris-dance who had the figure of a horse fastened round his waist.
Hob-nob, have or have not.
Holding, burden of a song.
Hoodman-blind, blind man's buff.
Hopdance, name of a demon.
Horn, "thy horn is dry;" the Bedlam beggars had a horn slung round their necks which they wound as they came to a house for alms.
Hose, stockings, breeches, or both in one.
Hox, cut the hamstrings.
Hugger-mugger, "in huggermugger," in secrecy.
Humour, mood, disposition, caprice. The fashionable abuse of this word is satirized by Shakespeare in his character of Nym, and elsewhere.
Humourous, capricious; moody, out of humour (H.E.D.).
Hurly, hurly-burly.
Hurricano, water-spout.

Hurtle, clash together.
Husband, husbandman; *v.* cultivate, manage economically.
Husbandry, cultivation; thrift, household economy.
Huswife, **Housewife**, hussy.

Idle, frivolous, useless, foolish.
Ill-favoured, of an ill-countenance.
Immanity, savagery.
Immoment, not momentous.
Imp, graft, insert new feathers.
Impair, unequal.
Impartial, not taking part with either side; used also for *partial*.
Impartment, something imparted, communication.
Impeachment, hindrance.
Imperseverant (imperceiverant), undiscerning (H.E.D.); giddy-headed, thoughtless (S.).
Impone, lay down as a wager.
Importance, importunity, import.
Important, importunate.
Incense, instigate; perhaps *insense*=inform, school.
Inch, island.
Inch-meal, piece-meal.
Incontinent, immediately.
Incony, pretty, delicate.
Incorpsed, incorporated.
Indent, bargain, make agreement.
Index, prologue; anything which gives brief account of, or is preparatory to, what is coming in story, play, or pageant (in the latter case possibly a painted emblem).
Indifferency, impartiality; moderate size.
Indifferent, impartial; ordinary, "indifferent children," "indifferent knit."
Indigest, without form; chaos (S.), formless mass.
Indirection, opposed to direct and honest practice or means.
Indurance, confinement (D.); endurance (S.).
Informal. *See* Formal.
Ingenious, ingenuous; "ingenious studies"=befitting a well-born person; "liberal" (H.E.D.); "ingenious feeling," "sense"=conscious, heartfelt (S.).
Inhooped—cocks, while fighting, were confined within hoops.
Inkle, tape.
Innocent, idiot.
Insane root, hemlock, or henbane.
Insisture, persistency, constancy (S.); fixedness, stability (D.).
Instance, motive; proof, example.
Intend, pretend.
Intendment, intention.
Intenible, unable to hold.
Intrinse, **Intrinsicate**, intricate.
Intrenchant, which cannot be cut, not divisible.
Investments, dress.
Inward, intimate acquaintance; *a.* intimate.
Irregulous, irregular, disorderly.
Iterance, iteration.

Jack, used in contempt, "Jack priest," etc.; "play the Jack"=play the knave, do a mean trick (H.E.D.); "Jack o' the clock"=figure that strikes the bell on the outside of clocks; Jack-a-Lent=puppet thrown at during Lent; Minute-Jack="fellows who watch the minutes to offer their adulation;" marking every minute, changing with every minute (S.).
Jack=bowl at which the players aim in game of bowls; a quarter or half-pint measure.
Jar, tick.
Jaunce, ride hard.
Jesses, straps round the legs of a hawk to which the leash was attached.
Jet, strut.
Joint-ring, ring made of closely-fitted, separable halves.
Journal, daily.
Jump, exactly, just; *v.* agree; take the risk of.
Jutty, projection, *v.* project.

Kam, crooked.
Kecksy, kex; dry stem of hemlock, and other plants.
Keech, "tallow-keech," fat rolled up in a lump.
Keel, cool.
Keisar, cæsar, emperor.
Kerne, Irish foot-soldier.
Kibe, a sore on the heel from chap or chilblain.
Kid-fox, young fox (? H.E.D.).
Kind, nature, natural disposition; *a.* kindly, natural.
Kindless, unnatural.
Kirtle. *See* Half-kirtle.
Kissing-comfits, perfumed, to sweeten the breath.
Knot, flower-bed; company, band.
Knot-grass, supposed to hinder growth.
Knotty-pated, block-headed (H.E.D.).

Labras, lips (Span.).
Laced mutton, courtesan.
Lady-smock, cuckoo flower (local: convolvulus, H.E.D.).
Lakin, ladykin.
Lammas, August 1st.
Lampass, disease of horses.
Land-raker, foot-pad.
Larum, alarm; alarum.
Latch, catch; "latched the Athenian's eyes"=anointed (S. and D.).
Lated, belated.
Latten, a mixed metal.
Laund, lawn; glade (S.).
Lavolt, **Lavolta**, a dance, consisting in part of high bounds.
Leasing, lying.
Leather-coat, kind of apple.
Leer, complexion.
Leese, lose.
Leet, "manor court, private jurisdiction for petty offences.
Level, aim; guess.
Lewd, vile.
Libbard, leopard.

LIBERAL, licentious, frank.
LIGHTLY, usually.
LIMB-MEAL, limb by limb.
LIMBECK, alembic.
LIMBO, borders of hell; hell.
LINE, draw, paint.
LINE-GROVE, linden, lime.
LIST, boundary; *v.* listen; please.
LISTS, enclosed space where tournaments were held, or the surrounding barricades.
LITHER, soft, pliable.
LIVELIHOOD, liveliness, vigour.
LIVERY, "delivery, or grant of possession."
LOACH, small fish.
LOCKRAM, cheap sort of linen.
LODE-STAR, pole-star.
LODGE, lay flat.
LOFFE, laugh.
LOGGATS, small logs: the game consisted of throwing loggats at a stake fixed in the ground.
LONG STAFF SIXPENNY STRIKERS, "fellows that infest the road with long staffs and knock men down for sixpence" (J.).
LONGLY, longingly.
LOOFED, luffed, brought close to the wind.
LOON, LOWN, a stupid rascal.
LOUTED, flouted, mocked.
LOVE-IN-IDLENESS, pansy.
LUCE, pike.
LUNES, fits of frenzy.
LURCH, lurk, rob.
LUXURIOUS, unchaste.
LYM, sporting-dog.

MACULATE, spotted, stained.
MAGOT-PIE, magpie.
MAINED, maimed.
MAKELESS, mateless.
MALKIN, diminutive of Mary.
MALT-HORSE, heavy dray horse; used as a term of reproach.
MALT-WORM, lover of ale.
MAMMERING, hesitating, muttering.
MAMMET, puppet.
MAMMOCK, rend in pieces.
MANAGE, management, administration; training (horse); career, course.
MANDRAGORA, MANDRAKE, supposed when torn from the ground to utter groans; a powerful narcotic.
MANKIND, masculine, mannish.
MANNER, "taken with the," caught in the act.
MANNINGTREE OX, fairs were held at this place.
MAN-QUELLER, murderer.
MARCH-PANE, sweet biscuits, made of sugar, flour, and almonds.
MARE, RIDE THE WILD, play see-saw.
MARGENT, margin.
MARTLEMAS, Martinmas, November 11th.
MARY-BUDS, marigold.
MATE, confound, stupefy.
MAUGRE, in spite of.
MAZARD, MAZZARD, head.
MEACOCK, tame coward.
MEAL'D, mingled; sprinkled, tainted (S.).
MEAN, tenor, "means and basses."
MEASURE, slow dignified dance.
MEASLES, leprosy.
MEINY, attendants composing the household; retinue.
MELL, meddle.
MEMORY, memorial.
MERE, simple, only; absolute.
MERELY, simply, absolutely, entirely.
MESS, party of four, "lower messes" = those who sat below the salt.
METAL, used frequently for mettle.
METE-YARD, yard measure.
METHEGLIN, a mixture of various ingredients, of which the main was honey.
MEW, keep shut up.
MICHER, truant.
MICHING MALLECHO, concealed mischief (mich = skulk; mallecho, probably from Spanish malhecho = evil action).
MICKLE, much.
MILCH, "draw tears."
MILL SIXPENCES, coined by a mill or machine.
MIND, call to mind.
MINIM, at one time the shortest note in music.
MIRABLE, admirable.
MISER, a miserable wretch.
MISERY, avarice (D.); S. gives ordinary signification.
MISPRISE, underrate; mistake.
MISPRISION, undervaluing; mistake.
MISSIVE, messenger.
MISTHINK, judge wrongly, think wrongly of.
MO, more.
MOBLE, cover up the head.
MODERN, common, trivial, worthless.
MODESTY, moderation (D.).
MOLDWARP, mole.
MOME, blockhead.
MOMENTANY, lasting for a moment.
MOON-CALF, a deformed creature, monster.
MOP, grimace.
MORAL, meaning.
MORALIZE, interpret, expound.
MORISCO, morris-dancer.
MORRIS-PIKE, moorish pike.
MORT O' THE DEER, certain set of notes blown by the huntsmen at the death of the deer.
MORTAL, fatal, deadly.
MORTIFIED, lifeless, inert, insensible; "the mortified man" = ascetic (D.).
MOSE IN THE CHINE, disease of horses.
MOTION, puppet-show, puppet.
MOTIVE, moving agent; cause.
MOTLEY, parti-coloured dress worn by fools.
MOUSE, to tear in pieces, devour (as a cat a mouse) (D.), "mousing the flesh of men."
MOW, grimace.
MOY, piece of money.
MUM-BUDGET, a cant word implying silence.
MURE, wall.
MUSCADEL, a rich wine.
MUSE, wonder.
MUSS, scramble after things that are thrown down.
MUTINES, mutineers.

MYSTERY, art, trade.

NAPKIN, handkerchief.
NAUGHT, naughty, bad; "be naught awhile," a malediction equivalent to our "be hanged."
NAUGHTY, good for nothing, worthless.
NAYWARD, inclining to a negative, to a denial.
NAYWORD, watchword; by-word.
NEAT, horned cattle.
NEB, bill of a bird.
NEEDLY, necessarily.
NEEZE, sneeze.
NEIF, fist or hand.
NETHER-STOCKS, stockings.
NICE, dainty, precise; over-punctilious; foolish, trifling.
NICELY, NICENESS, punctiliously, subtilely (S.); scrupulousness, coyness (S.).
NICK, notch in a tally; "out of all nick" = "out of all reckoning"; cut in notches, fools being "shaved and nicked in a particular manner."
NIGHT-RULE, night revel.
NINE-MEN'S-MORRIS, a game in which nine holes were made in the ground, some of the players having pegs, the others stones.
NOBLE, gold coin worth 6*s.* 8*d.*
NOISE, company.
NONCE, purpose.
NOOK-SHOTTEN, "shooting out into capes, etc."
NOTT-PATED, having the hair cut close; or equivalent to *knotty-pated* (*q. v.*).
NOURISH, nourice, nurse.
NOVUM, a game at dice.
NOWL, head.
NUTHOOK, metaphorically used for a bailiff.

OB, abbreviation of obolus, halfpenny.
OBLIGATION, bond.
OBSEQUIOUS, pertaining to funeral rites; careful of performing all funeral rites.
OBSEQUIOUSLY, as one at a funeral.
OBSERVANCE, observation.
OBSERVANTS, obsequious attendants.
ODDLY, unevenly.
O'ERCOUNT, out-number, perhaps "overreach."
O'ERLOOKED, bewitched.
O'ER-PARTED, having a part assigned to him beyond his powers.
O'ER-RAUGHT, over-reached, overtaken.
OLD, wold; *a.* frequent, abundant, "old swearing," "old abusing of God's patience."
ONCE, at some time or other; once for all.
ONEYERS, "great oneyers," of uncertain meaning; S. suggests, "persons who converse with great ones."
OPINION, credit, reputation; conceit.
OPPOSITE, antagonist; *a.* antagonistic, hostile.
ORB, orbit; fairy-ring.
ORDINANCE, rank; ordnance; fate, or "divine dispensation" (S.).
ORDINANT, ORDINATE, ordaining.
ORDINARY, public dinner where each pays his share.
ORGULOUS, proud.
ORT, scrap.
OSTENT, OSTENTATION, show, appearance.
OTHERGATES, otherways.
OUPH, fairy, sprite.
OUSEL, blackbird.
OVER-PEER, overhang, look down on; rise above (S.).
OVERSCUTCHED, possibly corruption of "overswitched;" whipped at the cart's tail; "worn in the service" (Malone).
OUCH, OWCH, brooch, or other precious ornament.
OWE, own.
OYES (Fr. oyez), hear ye! the word with which the crier begins his proclamation.

PACK, enter into clandestine agreement with, intrigue; arrange or shuffle cards in a cheating way.
PACKING, underhand connivance.
PACTION, pact, compact.
PADDOCK, toad, frog.
PAINTED CLOTH, cloth, or canvas, painted with subjects and devices or mottoes, with which rooms were hung.
PALABRAS, Spanish for words "paucas pallabris" (pocas palabras), few words.
PALE, enclose.
PALL, fail, wane.
PALLIAMENT, robe.
PALTER, shuffle, equivocate.
PANTLER, servant in care of the pantry.
PARAGON, excel, compare; set forth as a model.
PARCEL, part; *v.* "enumerate by items" (S.).
PARCELED, "particular" (S.).
PARISH-TOP, a top kept in villages to keep the peasants in exercise and out of mischief when work was slack.
PARITOR, officer of the Bishop's Court, who delivers summonses.
PARLOUS, perilous.
PARTAKE, communicate.
PARTAKER, confederate.
PARTED, gifted with parts, endowed.
PARTISAN, pike, halberd.
PARTLET, ruff.
PASH, head (H.E.D.); *v.* strike violently.
PASS, care for, regard.
PASSADO, a forward thrust in fencing.
PASSAGE, passing to and fro of people, ("no passage"?); event, circumstance.
PASSIONATE, give expression in words to passion.
PASSIONATE, sorrowful.
PASSY-MEASURE, a slow dance.
PASTRY, pastry-room.
PATCH, fool.
PATCHERY, knavery; "botchery intended to hide faults" (S.).
PATHETICAL, pathetic (H.E.D.), "pleasing or displeasing in a high degree" (S.).
PATINE, plate on which the bread is laid at the Eucharist; or the cover of chalice.
PAVIN, a grave Spanish dance.
PAX, a plate of various material passed round to the people at mass to be kissed.

PEAK, (?) droop in health and spirits, waste away (H.E.D.); mope, sneak.
PEAKING, skulking, mean-spirited (H.E.D.).
PEAT, pet.
PEDASCULE, pedant, preceptor.
PEEVISH, foolish, idle, trifling.
PEISE, weigh down, oppress.
PELT, rage.
PELTING, paltry.
PERDURABLE, lasting.
PEREGRINATE, foreign in ways and manners.
PERFECT, certain.
PERIAPT, amulet.
PERIOD, end.
PERPEND, consider, think over.
PERSPECTIVE, a picture or figure constructed so as to produce some fantastic effect" (H.E.D.).
PERTLY, alertly.
PETAR, PETARD, engine used to blow up gates, etc.
PHEEZE, beat; "any kind of teazing and annoying" (S.).
PHILIP, a familiar appellation for a sparrow.
PICKT-HATCH, noted resort for bad characters.
PIGHT, pitched.
PILCHER, scabbard.
PILL, pillage.
PIN-AND-WEB, disease of the eye.
PINK, small, half-shut, "pink eyne."
PITCH, the height to which a falcon soars.
PLACKET, (?) petticoat, or opening in it, stomacher.
PLAIN-SONG, simple notes without variation, opposed to "prick song."
PLANCHED, planked.
PLANTAGE, plants generally.
PLASH, pool.
PLATE, piece of silver money.
PLATFORM, plan.
PLAUSIVE, pleasing, plausible.
PLEACH, intertwine.
PLEASANCE, pleasure, delight.
POINT, tagged lace.
POINT-DEVISE, nice to excess.
POISE, weight, importance.
POKING-STICK, stick, or iron, for setting the plaits of ruffs.
POLACK, Pole; much controversy as to the meaning of the "sledded Polacks."
POLLED, stripped, shorn, plundered.
POMANDER, ball filled with perfumes.
POMEWATER, kind of apple.
POOR-JOHN, hake.
POPINJAY, parrot.
PORPENTINE, porcupine.
PORT, state; gate; bearing.
PORTABLE, bearable.
PORTAGE, port; port-hole.
PORTANCE, carriage, deportment.
POTABLE, drinkable.
POTCH (POACH), thrust.
POTENT, potentate.
POTTLE, two quarts.
POULTER, poulterer.
POUNCET-BOX, perforated perfume-box.
PRACTICE, treachery, deceit, artifice.
PRACTISANTS, confederates in treachery.
PRACTISE, to use artifice, plot.
PRECEDENT, rough draft.
PRECEPT, warrant.
PREGNANT, ready, apt, quick of perception; artful, designing; full of meaning, conviction, intelligence, information.
PREMISED, sent beforehand.
PRE NOMINATE, foretell; name beforehand.
PRESCRIPT, direction, written order; *a.* prescribed, written; prescriptive, immemorial (? S.).
PRESENTLY, immediately.
PRESS, commission for forcing men into military service; *v.* impress, force into service.
PRESSURE, impression.
PREST, ready.
PRETENCE, intention, design.
PRETEND, intend.
PREVENT, anticipate.
PRICK-SONG, music written down, noted down with pricks or dots.
PRICKET, buck of the second year.
PRIME, eager.
PRIMERO, game at cards.
PRINCOX, pert, forward youth.
PRINT, "in print," with exactness.
PRIZE, privilege.
PRODIGIOUS, portentous, unnatural, horrible.
PRODITOR, traitor.
PROLIXIOUS, prolix, causing delay.
PRONE, prompt, ready.
PROPER, belonging to a particular person, own; private; handsome.
PROPOSE, conversation; *v.* converse.
PUGGING, thievish (S.); "pegging, peg-tooth=canine tooth" (Walter, quoted by S.).
PUKE (stocking), either colour or material, in either case "dark-coloured."
PUN, pound.
PUNTO, thrust, hit in fencing; "punto reverso"=back-handed stroke.
PURCHASE, cant term used by thieves for their plunder.
PURPLES, purple orchis.
PUT ON, instigate.
PUTTOCK, kite.
PUZZEL, drab.

QUAIL, overpower; faint.
QUAINT, neat, elegant, ingenious; "my quaint Ariel"=ingenious, clever (D.); fine, neat, pretty (S.).
QUALITY, profession.
QUARREL, ("that quarrel fortune"); a square dart; or, quarreller (S.).
QUAT, spot on the skin.
QUATCH, square, flat.
QUEAN, slut.
QUEASY, fastidious, delicate; disgusted.
QUELL, kill.
QUERN, hand-mill.
QUEST, inquest.
QUESTANT, candidate, competitor.
QUESTION, conversation.
QUESTIONABLE, "provoking question"; "capable of being conversed with."
QUICK, living.

QUIDDITS, quiddities, legal subtleties.
QUILLETS, sly turn in argument, chicanery.
QUINTAIN, a figure set up for riders to tilt at.
QUIT, requite.
QUITTANCE, acquittance; requital.
QUIVER, nimble.
QUOIF, cap.
QUOTE, note, mark.

R, "for the dog," because of the sound being like a dog's snarl.
RABATO, ruff, band; originally a turned-back collar.
RABBIT-SUCKER, sucking rabbit.
RACE, flavour; natural disposition (S.); breed.
RACE "OF GINGER," root.
RACK, floating vapourous clouds; *v.* move like clouds.
RAMPALLIAN, a term of low abuse.
RANK, row; "rank to market" = some interpret "pace."
RAPTURE, fit.
RASCAL, lean deer, unfit to hunt.
RASH, strike (applied particularly to the stroke of a boar).
RAT, "Irish rat," it was believed in Ireland that rats could be rhymed to death.
RAUGHT, reached.
RAVIN, devour.
RAWNESS, hasty, unprepared manner.
RAYED, defiled, dirtied (S.).
RAZE, race, root; package (? S.).
RAZED, slashed.
READ, REDE, counsel.
REAR (rere) MOUSE, bat.
REBATE, render obtuse, blunt.
REBECK, stringed instrument.
RECEIVING, "ready apprehension."
RECHEAT, notes sounded on the horn to call the dogs off.
RECORDER, a kind of flute, or flageolet.
RED LATTICE, pertaining to the ale-house, formerly distinguished by its coloured lattice.
REDUCE, bring back.
REECHY, smoky, greasy, filthy.
REFELLED, refuted.
REGIMENT, government, sovereign sway.
REMONSTRANCE, manifestation.
REMORSE, pity, compassion.
REMOTION, "act of keeping aloof, non-appearance" (S.).
REMOVED, secluded, remote.
RENEGE, deny.
REPLICATION, reply.
REPORT, "so likely to report," = "so near to speech" (J.).
REPROOF, disproof.
REPROVE, disprove.
REPUGN, resist.
REPURED, purified.
REPUTING, "valuing at a high rate" (S.).
RESOLUTION, assurance, conviction.
RESOLVE, dissolve; convince, satisfy; "make up one's mind fully" (D.).
RESOLVED, convinced.
RESPECT, regard.
RESPECTIVE, worthy of regard; considerate; respectful, formal.
REST, "set up one's rest," to be fully determined; a metaphor borrowed from gaming.
REVERB, reverberate.
RHEUMATIC, choleric.
RIGOL, circle.
RIVAL, associate.
RIVALITY, equality, association.
RIVE, split; used to express the bursting sound of artillery.
ROAD, roadstead.
ROISTING, bullying, defying.
ROMAGE, tumultuous movement.
RONYON, mangy animal.
ROOKED, squatted.
ROPERY, roguery.
ROTE, repeat from memory.
ROTHER, horned cattle (some editions, "brother").
ROUND, plain spoken; *v.* whisper.
ROUSE, carouse.
RUB, an expression borrowed from game of bowls.
RUDDOCK, redbreast.
RUDESBY, a rude, underbred person.
RUFFLE, to be turbulent and boisterous.
RUSH, rush-ring; used for rural marriages, or mock marriages.
RUSH, openly, eagerly evade (S.); "rush'd aside the law."

SACK, a dry Spanish wine.
SACKBUT, kind of trumpet, trombone.
SACKERSON, a famous bear at Paris-garden; name probably that of his master.
SAD, serious.
SADLY, seriously.
SAG, hang down, flag.
SAGITTARY, the Centaur who fought in the armies of the Trojans; building in Venice bearing sign of.
SALLET, helmet, headpiece; salad.
SALT, licentious.
SALTIERS, blunder for satyrs.
SALUTE, touch, affect (S.).
SAND-BLIND, having imperfect sight.
SANDED, sandy.
SAVAGERY, wildness of growth.
SAW, saying.
SAY, a kind of silk, or satin; taste, relish; assay.
SCALD, low, shabby, "scabby."
SCALE, weigh.
SCAMBLE, scramble.
SCAMEL, uncertain meaning; perhaps sea-mell, *i. e.* sea-mew.
SCANTLING, a given portion.
SCAPE, escape; misdemeanour.
SCAR, broken precipice.
SCARFED, hung with flags.
SCATHE, injury.
SCONCE, round fortification; head.
SCOTCH, score, make shallow cuts.
SCRIMER, fencer.
SCRIP, slip of writing, list; a small bag "scrip and scrippage."
SCROYLE, low wretch.
SCULL, shoal.
SCUT, tail.
SEAM, grease, lard.

Season, temper; "seasons him his enemy," "my blessing season this in thee," confirm (D.); mature (S.).
Sect, sex; section, cutting.
Secure, **Securely**, **Security**, rashly confident, etc.
Seel, close the eyes; the eyes of hawks were seeled by passing a fine thread or small feather through the eyelids.
Seen, skilled; "well seen in music."
Seized, possessed (legal term).
Seldom-when, rarely.
Self, same, self-same; "that self hand."
Semblable, likeness.
Semblative, resembling; appearing, seeming (S.).
Sennet, set of notes, or flourish, on the trumpet.
Senseless, without feeling, perception.
Sensible, having feeling, sensation, perception.
Sere, catch in a gunlock; "tickle of the sere," a gun which explodes on the least touch on the sere. (*See* Wright, quoted by S.)
Serpigo, eruption.
Sessa, "probably a cry exciting to swift running" (S.).
Several, private, "inclosed pasture, as opposed to common land."
Sewer, the attendant who set on and removed dishes.
Shale, shell.
Shard, hard wing-case, "shard-borne," "sharded"; fragment of broken pottery.
Sharked, "collected in a banditti-like manner."
Sheer, clear, transparent; nothing but, mere.
Shent, scolded, reproached, disgraced.
Ship-tire, head-dress in some way resembling a ship.
Shive, a small slice.
Shotten, "having cast its spawn" (D.).
Shough, shaggy dog.
Shove-groat, **Shovel-board**, game in which coins were pushed to reach a certain mark.
Shrieve, sheriff.
Shrift, confession.
Shrowd, shelter.
Sib, akin.
Siege, seat; rank.
Sightless, invisible; unsightly.
Silly, simple, rustic, harmless.
Simplicity, foolishness.
Simular, counterfeited.
Sink-a-pace. *See* Cinque-pace.
Sir-reverence, save-reverence.
Sith, **Sithence**, since.
Sizes, portions, allowances.
Skains-mates, sword-mates (S.); skain = "scapegrace" (Staunton); "swaggering-companions" (Nares).
Skill, matter, "it skills not."
Skirr, scour.
Slab, moist and glutinous.
Sleave, soft floss silk used for weaving.
Sleeveless, useless, fruitless.
Sleided, raw, untwisted, "sleided silk."
Slip, counterfeit coin; noose in which greyhounds were held, before they were let loose to start for the game.
Sliver, slip, portion broken off.
Slop, **Slops**, loose trousers, or breeches.
Slubber, to do things in a slovenly way; to obscure "by smearing over."
Smatch, taste, smack.
Smooth, flatter.
Sneak-cup, one who sneaks from his glass.
Sneap, snubbing, rebuke; check, nip.
Sneek-up, "go and be hanged."
Snuff, anger; "take in snuff" = take offence.
Soiled, high fed.
Solidare, small coin.
Sonties, supposed corruption of *saints*, or *sanctity*.
Sooth, truth; sweetness.
Sooth, **Soother**, flatter, smooth over; flatterer.
Sop o' the Moonshine, "old dish of eggs in moonshine: *i. e.* broken and boiled in salad-oil till the yolks become hard, and eaten with slices of onion" (Douce).
Sore, buck of the fourth year.
Sorel, buck of the third year.
Sort, company; *v.* choose; suit, fit; contrive (S.).
Soused, pickled.
Sowl, pull by the ears.
Sowter, cobbler, name of a hound.
Span-counter, a player throws a coin, or counter, to try and hit another, or come within a span of it; sometimes played with marbles.
Spavin, disease of horses.
Speculation, power of vision, "speculators, observers" (S.).
Speculative, visual (D.); "speculative . . . instruments."
Sperr, make fast.
Spill, destroy (D.).
Spilth, spilling.
Spirit of sense, "utmost refinement of sensation"; "sense or sensibility itself" (S.).
Spleen, caprice, humour; impetuous haste; "hate; any uncontrollable impulse, fit; fire, eagerness" (S.).
Spleeny, ill-tempered, peevish (D.); eager, headstrong (S.).
Splinter, put into splints.
Sprag, sprack, alert.
Sprighted, haunted.
Springhalt, a kind of lameness in horses.
Square, quarrel.
Squash, unripe peas pod.
Squiny, squint.
Squire, square, or measure.
Stain, disgrace; "stain to all nymphs" = that sullies by contrast (D.); *v.* taint, dim, disfigure.
Stale, decoy; stalking-horse.
Stalking-horse, a real or artificial horse, behind which the shooter hid himself from the game.
Staniel, an inferior kind of hawk.
Starred, fated by the stars.
Start-up, up-start.
State, chair of state.

STATION, mode of standing; state of rest, as opposed to motion.
STATUTE-CAPS, woollen caps, worn, as decreed by statute, by all but the nobility, after a certain age, on Sundays and holidays.
STELLED, "quenched the stelled fires," starry; fixed (S.).
STERNAGE, steerage.
STICKLER, umpire.
STIGMATIC, one who has been stigmatised, branded; stigmatised with deformity.
STIGMATICAL, marked with a stigma of deformity.
STINT, stop.
STITHY, smithy.
STOCCADO, a thrust in fencing.
STOCK. *See* Stoccado.
STOMACH, arrogance, anger; stubborn courage; inclination; *v.* resent (D.).
STOUT, bold; unbending, obstinate (D.); overbearing (S.).
STRAIGHT-PIGHT, straight-pitched, straight-built, upright (D.).
STRAIN, lineage; disposition.
STRAIT, close-fitted.
STRAITED, puzzled.
STRANGE, foreign; shy.
STRANGELY, wonderfully; distantly, like a stranger.
STRANGENESS, coyness, shyness.
STRAPPADO, a torture which broke and dislocated the arms and joints.
STRATAGEM, calamity, dire event.
STRICTURE, strictness.
STRIKE, blast by secret influence, "then no planets strike."
STROND, strand.
STROSSERS, trossers, trousers.
SUBSCRIBE, yield, submit.
SUBTILTIES, "when a dish appeared unlike what it really was, they called it a subtilty" (Steevens).
SUCCESS, succession; result, consequence.
SUGGEST, prompt, tempt.
SUMPTER, horse or mule to carry baggage.
SUPER-SERVICEABLE, over-officious.
SUPPLIANCE, supply, gratification, pastime (S.); "suppliance of a minute."
SUR-REINED, over-worked.
SWEETING, a kind of apple.
SWINGE-BUCKLER, a roisterer.
SWINGED, whipped.

TABLE, palm of the hand; tablet.
TABLE-BOOK, memorandum-book.
TABOR, a small drum.
TAKE, blast, bewitch.
TAKE IN, conquer.
TAKE UP, borrow; obtain on credit.
TALL, valiant.
TALLOW-KEECH. *See* Keech.
TANLING, one tanned by the sun.
TARRE, set on.
TARTAR, Tartarus.
TASK, tax.
TASSEL-GENTLE, tiercel, male goshawk.
TAXATION, sarcasm, censure, vituperation.
TEEN, grief, misfortune.
TENDER-HEFTED. *See* Heft.
TENT, probe a wound. Tent being a roll of lint, used as a probe.
TERMAGANT, a Saracen god.
TERMLESS, "beyond the power of words" (D.).
TESTER, a coin worth sixpence.
TETCHY, touchy.
THARBOROUGH, corruption of Thirdborough; constable, or constable's assistant.
THRASONICAL, boastful.
THREAD AND THRUM, "the thread is the substance of the warp, the thrum the small tuft beyond, where it is tied."
THREE-MAN BEETLE, implement for pile-driving.
THROSTLE, thrush.
THRUM. *See* Thread.
THRUMMED, made of thrums, or of very coarse cloth.
THUNDER-STONE, thunder-bolt.
TICK-TACK, sort of backgammon (D.).
TICKLE, ticklish, precarious(ly).
TIKE, common sort of dog.
TILTH, tilled land; tillage.
TIMELESS, untimely.
TIRE, head-dress; *v.* pull, tear, seize eagerly, as birds of prey their food.
TOD, twenty-eight pounds of wool.
TOGE, gown.
TOKEN'D, shewing plague tokens, spots.
TOM O' BEDLAM, the Bedlam beggars were men who had recovered sufficiently to be let out of Bedlam, and were licensed to go begging; many impostors were about who had never seen the inside of a madhouse.
TOPLESS, not to be topped, surpassed.
TORTIVE, tortuous.
TOUCH, test by the touchstone.
TOUSE, drag, tear, pluck.
TOYS, "there's toys abroad" = "rumours, idle reports," "tricks, devices," "follies in the world" (S.).
TOZE. *See* Touse.
TRADE, traffic; in the "gap and trade" = "practised method, general course" (J.).
TRAIN, artifice, stratagem.
TRAMMEL, confine, tie up.
TRANECT, probably from Italian traghetto = ferry (S.).
TRASH, "trash for overtopping," lop, crop (S.); Nares decided that it was some kind of strap, or implement to hold back a hound; according to Madden (quoted by S.) "when the hound was running, the long strap, dragged along the ground, handicapped the overtopping hound."
TRAY-DRIP, a game played with cards and dice; success in it depended upon throwing a *trois* (treys).
TREACHER, traitor.
TRENCH, cut, carve.
TRIBULATION, probably name of a puritanical society; or applied to the whole sect of Puritans (S.).
TRICKING, dress, ornament.
TRICKSY, clever, adroit (D.); full of tricks and devices (S.).
TRIGON, astrological term, signifying the meeting of the three upper planets, which were then called the "fiery Trigon."

Trojan, cant term for thief; "a familiar name for any equal or inferior" (Nares).

Troll-my-dames, Troll-madam, Trou-madam, a game known in England as pigeon-holes, small balls being bowled into these from the farther end of the board.

Tropically, figuratively.

Trundle-tail, dog with a curly tail.

Tucket, flourish, certain set of notes on the trumpet.

Tun-dish, funnel.

Turk, "turn Turk," undergo a complete change (S. adds "for the worse").

Turlygood, Turlygod, apparently a name for a "bedlam-beggar."

Twiggen, covered with wicker-work.

Type, symbol.

Unaneled, not having received extreme unction.

Unavoided, unavoidable.

Unbarbed, unbarbered, unshorn.

Unbated, not blunted, as foils are.

Unbolted, unsifted.

Unbraided, not counterfeit, or, blunder for embroidered (? S.).

Uncape, probably "uncouple" (S.); it has been interpreted as "unearth"; "turn fox out of bag."

Unclew, Unclue, unwind.

Uncoined, "not counterfeit"; real, unrefined, unadorned; having received no previous impression; "without the current stamp, *i. e.* insinuating words, etc." (S.).

Unconfirmed, without experience.

Uncouth, unknown, strange.

Underbear, undergo, bear.

Underskinker, undertapster.

Uneared, untilled.

Uneath, hardly, scarcely.

Unexperient, inexperienced.

Unexpressive, inexpressible.

Unhappy, Unhappily, waggish(ly); mischievous(ly), evilly (S.).

Unhappiness, mischief, "dreamed of unhappiness," = wanton or mischievous tricks (S.).

Unhouseled, without receiving the sacrament.

Unimproved, unreproved, unimpeached (D.); not yet used to advantage, turned to account (S.).

Union, pearl of fine quality.

Unkind, unnatural.

Unmanned, untamed (term in falconry).

Unowed, unowned.

Unplausive, unapplauding.

Unpregnant. *See* Pregnant.

Unproper, not the property of one alone.

Unqualitied, deprived of faculties.

Unquestionable, opposed to conversation.

Unrecuring, incurable.

Unrespective, without respect, inconsiderate; "unrespective sieve," unvalued (D.), used at random (S.).

Unsisting, unresting (? S.).

Unsquared, unfitted to the purpose.

Untented, not to be probed, incurable (S.).

Unvalued, invaluable.

Upspring, upstart; or, a wild German dance "Hüpfauf."

Urchin, hedgehog.

Usance, interest on money.

Utis (Fr. huit), eighth day, or space of eight days, after a feast = the octave; festivities during same.

Utterance (Fr. outrance), extremity.

Vade, fade.

Vail, lower, "angels vailing-clouds" = "letting these clouds which obscured their brightness sink from before them" (J.), clouds letting down, bearing down, angels (? S.).

Validity, value.

Vantage, advantage; "to the vantage" = in addition, to boot; "of vantage" = same sense (S.).

Vantbrace, Vambrace, armour for the arm.

Varlet, servant to a knight.

Vary, variation.

Vast (Waste), "the darkness of midnight in which the prospect is not bounded in by distinct objects" (S.).

Vastidity, immensity.

Vasty, vast.

Vaunt, van, beginning.

Vaward, vanward.

Venew, Veney, Venue, thrust, attack, bout in fencing.

Vengeance, harm.

Ventage, hole or stop in a flute.

Verbal, verbose, or plain-spoken.

Vice, a personage in the old moralities, sometimes dressed as a buffoon; armed at times with a wooden dagger, "Vice's dagger."

Vie, wager, contend in rivalry.

Viewless, invisible.

Villiago (Villiaco), villain.

Vinewedst, most mouldy.

Viol-de-Gamboys, a viol held between the legs, bass-viol, violoncello.

Virginalling, playing with the fingers as on a virginal.

Vulgar, common, general, "the vulgar air;" of common report, "most sure and vulgar."

Vulgarly, publicly.

Waft, beckon; turn, "wafting his eyes."

Waftage, passage by water.

Wake, to keep night revel.

Wanion, Wannion, "with a wanion," apparently equivalent to "with a vengeance."

Wappened, worn.

Ward, posture of defence.

Warden, hard pear used for baking, "warden-pie."

Warder, kind of truncheon.

Wassail, festivity, drinking-bout.

Watch, "I'll watch him tame;" hawks were kept awake to tame them.

Water-work, water-colour painting.

Wax, grow, increase.

Weal, welfare; commonwealth.

WEALS-MAN, commonwealth man, statesman.
WEAR, fashion.
WEEDS, dress.
WEEN, suppose, imagine.
WEET, know.
WEIRD, concerned with fate, "subservient to destiny" (S.); "weird sisters" = Fates.
WELKIN, sky.
WELKIN-EYE, blue, "heavenly" (S.).
WELL-FOUND, tried, approved (S.).
WELL-SEEN, accomplished.
WHEEL "how the wheel becomes it," burden of a ballad (this is queried by S.).
WHELK, wheal, protuberance.
WHELKED, with protuberances, or "twisted, convolved."
WHIFFLER, a person who cleared the way for a procession; originally a fifer.
WHILE, until.
WHIPSTOCK, handle of whip.
WHITING-TIME, bleaching-time.
WHITSTER, WHITESTER, bleacher.
WHITTLE, small clasp-knife.
WHOOBUB, hubbub.
WIDE "speak so wide," far from the mark.
WILDERNESS, wildness.
WIMPLED, veiled, hoodwinked.
WINTER-GROUND, protect from winter weather.
WIS, think, suppose (i-wis = certainly, indeed).
WISH, recommend, "desire, invite, bid" (S.).
WISTLY, earnestly, eagerly.
WIT, know.
WITHOUT, beyond.
WONDERED, able to perform wonders.
WOOD, mad.
WOODCOCK, a proverbially foolish bird.
WOOLWARD, dressed in wool only.
WORLD, "go to the world," = marry; "woman of the world," = married.
WORM, serpent.
WORT, cabbages, and similar plants; sweet infusion of malt before it ferments.
WOT, know.
WREAK, revenge.
WREST, tuning key.
WRITHLED, wrinkled.
WROTH, ruth, misfortune.
WRY, go astray.

YARE, quick, ready, active.
YCLEPED, named.
YEARN, grieve.
YELLOWS, jaundice in horses.
YELLOWNESS, jealousy.
YESTY, frothy.

ZANY, fool, buffoon.
ZED, "unnecessary letter," since "its place may be supplied by S."
ZENITH, highest point of fortune.

THE END